The International Wine and Food Society's

GAZETTEER OF WINES

Other Books in the Series

The International Wine and Food Society's

GAZETTEER OF WINES

by André L. Simon

The International Wine and Food Publishing Company

 DAVID & CHARLES

A publication of
The International Wine and Food Publishing Company
Marble Arch House, 44 Edgware Road, London, w2

This book was designed and produced by
Rainbird Reference Books Limited
Marble Arch House, 44 Edgware Road, London, w2

House Editor: William Delligan
Designer: George Sharp
Cartographer: J. Caldwell

ISBN 0 7153 5184 2

Filmset by Cranmer Brown (Filmsetters) Ltd, London
Printed in Great Britain by A. Wheaton & Co, Exeter

The International Wine and Food Society

The International Wine and Food Society was founded in 1933 by André
L. Simon, C.B.E., as a world-wide non-profit-making society.
The first of its various aims has been to bring together and serve all who
believe that a right understanding of wine and food is an essential part of
personal contentment and health; and that an intelligent approach to the
pleasures and problems of the table offers far greater rewards than the mere
satisfaction of appetite.

For information about the Society apply to the Secretary,
Marble Arch House, 44 Edgware Road, London, w2

FOREWORD

When André L. Simon died in 1970 he had written more than seventy books on wine and gastronomy. The *Gazetteer of Wines* was his last work. This book which describes in some detail the major wines, wine-producing countries and vineyards of the world, as well as the lesser-known 'local' growths, was the fruit of a lifetime's study and research.

At the time of his death the *Gazetteer* was completed but needed revising. During the past two years friends of André Simon, both those who knew him personally and those who knew him by reputation only, have been working to update and verify the information contained in this monumental work.

This task is now complete, and the *Gazetteer of Wines* stands not only as a unique index of world viticulture, but as a final tribute to André L. Simon.

GEORGE RAINBIRD

Publisher's Acknowledgments

The publishers would like to thank Ian H. Seppelt, O.B.E., B.Sc., Chairman of the Australian Wine Board, Professor Maynard A. Amerine, University of California College of Agriculture and Nicholas Ludington, former Turkish correspondent of *The Times* for articles specially written for the *Gazetteer*, and the following individuals and institutions for their generous help and suggestions in checking and revising the text left by André Simon:
J. M. Grintner, Cock Russell & Spedding Ltd, London; Messrs Jean and André Hugel, Riquewihr, France; B. L. Teltscher, Teltscher Brothers Ltd, London; Mr. Istenic, Slovenija Vino, Ljubljana, Yugoslavia; J. Alex, Embassy of Luxembourg, London; F. N. Zimmerman, L. Zimmerman & Sons (London) Ltd; J. L. Ward, Merrydown Wine Company Ltd, Sussex, England; Patrick Forbes, Möet et Chandon, London; M. Joseph Dargent, Le Comité Interprofessionnel du Vin de Champagne, Epernay, France; James C. Reavis, M.D., St Helena, California; James Beard, California; B. W. Howkins, Croft & Co. Ltd, London; Timothy Marshall, Côte d'Or, Burgundy, France; John Lockwood, Jerez de la Frontera, Spain; John Burghart, Burghart & Degenhardt, Nottingham, England; A. J. Ludbrook, South Australia; Vsesojuznoje Objedinenije 'Sojuzplodoimport', Moscow, U.S.S.R.; Station Viticole Remiche, Grand-Duché de Luxembourg; Embassy of the Socialist Republic of Romania, London; Embassy of Tunisia, London; Austrian Commercial Delegation, London; South African Wine Farmers Association Ltd, London; Embassy of the Argentine Republic, London; Swiss Wine Growers Association, Lausanne, Switzerland; Canadian High Commissioners Office, London; Wine & Spirit Association of Great Britain, London; Australian Wine Centre, London; Malta Government Tourist Office, London; Capital Wine Agencies Ltd, London; and special thanks to Anthony S. Hogg of Peter Dominic Ltd, London, for his general and invaluable advice on all points regarding the revision of the manuscript.

CONTENTS

INTRODUCTION

The vineyards of the world bring forth millions of dozens of bottles of wine of all sorts year after year. Obviously no statistics, be they official or not, can ever be entirely satisfactory, especially when they deal with agriculture or viticulture, in which climatic conditions may be responsible for great differences of production from season to season. Nevertheless, statistics have their uses; they do give better than anything else a fairly true picture of the relative importance of viticulture in the many vinelands of the world as well as, indirectly, an idea of the part wine plays in the national economy of different countries It is impressive, for instance, to learn that some $25\frac{1}{2}$ million acres of the earth's surface are occupied by vineyards, and that the soil of the majority of such vineyards is so poor, being sand, lime or rock, that it is practically unfit for any other culture.

The vineyards of the world are very unevenly distributed, in both age and size. The majority are in Europe, where fully half of them have flourished over the past 1,000 years. There are those, however, with a longer history; the vineyards of the Greek islands and mainland, for instance, have been in existence for 3,000 years. In America, North and South, it was only after European conquest that viticulture was introduced, and this to a limited scale because of conditions; Australasia followed much the same pattern. The vineyards in Africa, also North and South, were older than those in the New World, but faced many of the same climatic and soil problems.

If we try to trace the tide of wine which flows from the wine presses of the northern hemisphere every September or October, and from those of the southern hemisphere every February, March or April, we do not find it easy to piece together the figures relating to the home consumption, export and import of wine, given in official statistics.

Most of the wines of all the world's vinelands are *ordinaires*; that is to say undistinguished, homely wines without any claim to breed and with very little if any charm. But they are not without merit.

Obviously, there would not have been any sense, even had it been possible, to find a place in the gazetteer for the thousands of individual vineyards, mostly in Europe, owned by peasants as part of their holding. Such vineyards rarely produce more wine than is drunk by the owner, his family and maybe some of his friends.

There are also a number of vineyards, both large and small, which produce very great quantities of wines of not particularly great quality which are used by 'big business' to manufacture colossal quantities of standardized blends of red, white and rosé wines which are then marketed without any vineyard name or vintage date, under the name of well-advertised brands. These 'mass-produced' wines are not to be found in the following pages.

Admittedly incomplete as our gazetteer may be, we claim that the many thousands of vineyards and wines recorded here, with their geographical location and outstanding characteristics, whenever ascertainable, are those of most, but not all the world's known vineyards and wines.

MAJOR VINELANDS
OF THE WORLD

Major Vinelands
of Western Europe

FRANCE

It was only less than 200 years ago, at the time of the French Revolution, that the provinces of France (some, like Burgundy and Brittany, bigger than Wales, others, like Champagne and Touraine, no bigger than some counties) were divided into smaller territorial administrative units called *départements*. At one time there were vineyards and wine was made in all the provinces of France. These provinces, because they were hemmed in by customs tariffs and plagued by antiquated local legislation, were all self-supporting and wine was an important part of their produce.

It is no longer so, but there are still vineyards cultivated and wine made in seventy out of the eighty-nine *départements* of France. As a matter of fact, there are but eleven *départements* where there are no vineyards, and eight in which there are only what might be called 'token' vineyards. In the Seine *département*, for instance, the smallest but by no means the least, with Paris its metropolis, there is still an ancient vine flourishing at Montmartre and a tiny vineyard of Pinot Noir grapes on Mont Valérien at the western end of Paris. This is all that remains of the many vineyards once in the Paris region. At one time their wines were jealously protected by 'import' taxes, or customs tariffs, from the competition of better wines from Bordeaux, Burgundy and Champagne.

Today there are many fewer vineyards in France than there were a hundred years ago, and therefore France no longer has the largest number of acres under cultivation. The shrinkage is due to a number of causes, the earliest of which was the phylloxera (plant lice) invasion in the middle of the nineteenth century which practically wiped out all the French vineyards in a little more than twenty years. Much of the loss has been recovered after vineyards were planted with the old French vines grafted on American *phylloxera*-resisting briars. Many vineyards have fallen, never to rise again, under the relentless tide of brick and mortar. Also, the cost of labour has risen far more steeply than the prices which people are willing to pay for wine; modern equipment does save labour in the cellar, but no machine exists which will pick the grapes at vintage time or give to the vines the constant care they need at all times. Buying and selling land and properties now demands less labour and pays better dividends than trying to grow wine grapes.

It stands to reason that there must be in France a greater quantity of *ordinaires* and *très ordinaires* wines than anywhere else, since there is so much wine made. But, if we were to switch from quantity to quality, we would find that there is not only a greater quantity of fine wines in France than anywhere else but that there is also a proportion of those wines (admittedly small) which possesses a degree of excellence never reached by even the best wines of other lands. This is no vain boast, but a claim supported by the fact that in the Americas, Australia and Africa, the best sparkling wines are called champagne, not asti or sekt; the best red table wines claret or burgundy, not chianti or barolo; the dry white wines chablis and the sweet ones sauternes, an admission that they have no greater ambition than to make wines as good as the wines made in France in Champagne, Burgundy, Bordeaux, Chablis or Sauternes.

All the vineyards and wines of France possessing what the qualified government officials consider a highly satisfactory degree of excellence are given a quality certificate known as *Appellation d'Origine Contrôlée*, or *AC* for short—which frequently appears in this gazetteer.

Bordeaux

Bordeaux is the metropolis of the Gironde *département*; it stands on the left bank of the Garonne, some three miles south-south-east from the Bec d'Ambès, where the Garonne and the Dordogne meet and become the Gironde, the waterway which flows into the Atlantic thirty-seven miles north-north-west further on. It is the river Gironde, the oldest of these rivers, that gave its name to the *département*. No wine is entitled to the name of Bordeaux wine which is not made from grapes grown within the borders of the Gironde *département*, and no vineyards of the other *départements* of France have been graded or classified with as much care as the wines of Bordeaux. There are a great many red and white table wines from Gironde vineyards which are good but plain, or *ordinaires*, and are not entitled to any more distinguished *AC* than plain 'bordeaux' or, if and when just a little better, *bordeaux supérieur*. Other Gironde wines of similarly modest quality may offer themselves to the somewhat impecunious claret lovers—there are many of them—under the name of any of the different regions of the Gironde in which their native vineyard happens to be, either Médoc or Haut-Médoc, to the left of the Gironde river; Bourgeais or Blayais, to the right of the same river; Graves or Sauternes, to the left of the Garonne; *côtes supérieurs de bordeaux* to the right of the same river; St-Emilion or Pomerol to the right of the Dordogne; Entre-deux-Mers, the stretch of vineyards between the Dordogne and Garonne.

Upon the next rung of the quality ladder, there are the *ordinaires*, although they may be and usually are a little better than those mentioned above. They are the wines marketed under the name of the *commune* or parish of their native vineyard, be it St-Julien, Margaux, St-Estèphe and many more in the Haut-Médoc; or Barsac, Loupiac and others on both sides of the Garonne. The next rung up the quality ladder brings us to the less distinguished of the named vineyards in every part of the Gironde *département*; some of them are known as *crus artisans*, the better ones as *premiers artisans*, but most of them are still *ordinaires*, and the best of them never rise above the mention 'fair'. It is only upon the next two rungs of the ladder that we come to the 'fair' and 'fair to fine' quality wines which are known as *bourgeois* and *bourgeois supérieur*; there are many of them. Higher up, there are a few *crus*, or growths, called *crus exceptionnels*, maybe because there are so few of them.

Finally we come to the top rungs of the quality ladder. The best wines of the Médoc, with Château Haut-Brion from the nearby Graves, were classified in 1855. A similar grading was made at the time for the white wines of Sauternes, when Château Yquem was given top place *hors concours* and the next best allotted to two classes, first and second *crus*, or growths. Strange to say, the vineyards and wines of St-Emilion and Pomerol were ignored in 1855, and they had to wait until 1955 to have their own classification. In the St-Emilion Classification, an official one, the *grands premiers crus* are considered the other best wines of St-Emilion, either from the hill vineyards (*côtes*) or the lower slopes of the same hill (*graves*). This distinction, naturally, is also shown in the next best wines classification of *premiers* and *deuxièmes grands crus*. The classification of the vineyards and wines of Pomerol follows that of St-Emilion with *premiers grands crus* considered the best, followed by *premiers crus* and *deuxièmes crus*.

It is generally agreed that the grading of 1855 did give the right place in its five classes to vineyards and their wines which were the best at the time, but it also recognized that it may not be so today. Obviously, a vineyard which has been given the best possible care in the choice of its vines and their cultivation over a hundred years or more should and does produce a better wine now than it did in 1855. All agree, for instance, that Château Mouton-Rothschild deserves to be a *premier cru* or first growth, and not top of the *deuxièmes crus* or second growths. Likewise, Château Pontet-Canet and Château Cantemerle, first and last of the fifth growths, would be more fairly placed among the third and fourth. Unfortunately, there are also vineyards in the Médoc which no longer merit the rank they were given in 1855 and should be reconsidered, although their present owners cannot be expected to welcome being demoted.

It is probable that the 1855 classification will be revised some day, perhaps soon, but in the meantime its gradings had to be and have been adopted in this gazetteer.

Burgundy

Burgundy was perhaps the greatest province of France to be carved into *départements* in 1789, which is why the wines from the vineyards of the *départements* that were once part of Burgundy are known even today as burgundy. They are, as a matter of fact and birthright, the only wines in the world entitled to the name burgundy. Unlike the vineyards of Bordeaux, grouped, so to speak, within the borders of one vast *département*, the vineyards of Burgundy are scattered through a very long stretch of country, in four different *départements*. Furthest north, in the Yonne *département*, there are the vineyards responsible for the charming and popular white wines of Chablis. Next to the Yonne, to the south, is the Côte d'Or *département*, with vineyards responsible for some of the few really great red wines of the world, as well as white wines which are also the peers of the finest in the world. South of the Côte d'Or lies the Saône-et-Loire *département*, and finally the Rhône *département*, which produces considerable quantities of *ordinaires*, mostly red, as well as many very fair, and a limited quantity of fine, white and red wines.

Most of the wines of Burgundy are made from two sorts of grapes; the red wines from either the aristocratic Pinots, whether Pinots Noirs, Pinots Beaunois, Vrais Pinots or other members of that noble family; or the commoner, but no less valuable, Gamay grapes. The white wines, likewise, are made either from noble Chardonnay grapes, a member of the Pinot family; or the Aligoté, a commoner but most useful white grape. All the great red wines and most of the fair and fine red wines of Burgundy are made from Pinot grapes; all the fair, fine and very fine and great white wines are made from Chardonnay grapes. In fairness to the Gamay grape, however, it must be said that there are vineyards, chiefly in the Beaujolais, but also in the Mâconnais and Chalonnais (whose soil must be particularly well suited to the Gamay), whose Gamay-made wines are quite palatable and very much better than the rather ordinary Gamay-made wines of other vineyards.

There are no great estates or *châteaux* in Burgundy comparable with those of Bordeaux. Most of the vineyards of Burgundy are not only small but divided among a number of proprietors, which makes it more difficult to assess the merit of their wine. Hence the quality grading or classification of the Burgundy vineyards has been made in a very different fashion from what happened in the Gironde, in 1855 and 1955: it has been done sectionally in each of the four *départements*, the vineyards of which are responsible for all genuine burgundies, red or white, still or sparkling.

YONNE. There are many vineyards in the Tonnerre and Auxerre areas of the Yonne *département*, but there are not many of them recorded in this book, because most of the wines they produce are too modest to deserve mentioning. The bacchic reputation of this *département* rests entirely upon the white wines of the little town of Chablis and those of a number of vineyards of the Chablis country, the names of which are duly recorded in this book.

The vineyards of Chablis were officially classified in 1938 and their wines were then given four ratings, *chablis grand cru* or *grand chablis*; *chablis premier cru*; *chablis*, without any qualificative, is the name to which the white wines of good quality from the vineyards of some villages or *communes* of the Chablis area are entitled; *petit chablis*, the modest title of white wines of lower alcoholic strength and more homely quality from the vineyards of the same villages of the Chablis area.

CÔTE D'OR. The vineyards of the Côte d'Or *département* are responsible for the finest red and white wines of Burgundy. They are grown upon the lower slopes of two groups of hills running from north to south, west of the *Route Nationale* RN 74, the highway from Dijon to Lyons. They are known as Côte de Nuits and Côte de Beaune.

The vineyards of the Côte d'Or were classified in 1861, and although this classification is not recognized today as a legal or official quality chart, it is generally accepted by *vignerons* and merchants as a useful guide to price.

The classification of the Côte d'Or vineyards is rather peculiar and somewhat unsatisfactory as its four gradings—*tête de cuvée*, the name given to the best of all; *premier, deuxième* and *troisième crus* or *cuvées*, that is first, second and third growths—are given in that order, not to the vineyards of each *commune*. It is obvious that a *tête de cuvée* vineyard of Volnay or Santenay cannot bring forth a wine comparable to the wine of a Chambolle-Musigny or Vosne-Romanée *tête de cuvée*, or, for that matter any of the best Côte de Nuits *communes* or *villages*.

SAÔNE-ET-LOIRE. In the Saône-et-Loire *département*, there are also two groups of hills facing east to the Saône: the first is the Côte Chalonnaise which begins at Chagny not far from Santenay at the end of the Côte de Beaune, and at Tournus becomes the second, the Côte Mâconnaise. This ends, administratively, at Romanèche-Thorins, where Saône-et-Loire ends and both Beaujolais and the Rhône *département* start. Geographically or geologically speaking, however, the Côte Mâconnaise crosses the border and ends at Chénas, in the Rhône *département*. There is no classification of the Chalonnais and Mâconnais vineyards, but the better ones are commonly known locally as *premiers crus* or first growths. All cannot be first, but none wishes to be second or third.

RHÔNE. The pride and much of the wealth of the Rhône *département* is the Beaujolais and its popular red wine. The Beaujolais stretches from the Saône-et-Loire *département* in the north, nearly as far as Lyons in the south. Until recent times, all Beaujolais wines were red, but the demand for white Beaujolais has brought forth a moderate supply. There are some Beaujolais wines which are distinctly better than others, and unfortunately some wines sold under the name to which they have no right whatever—it is the penalty of popularity.

Champagne

Champagne was once the name of a French province which ceased to exist, as did all French provinces, at the time of the French Revolution. However, its name lives still as does the name of Burgundy, in the wines of its vineyards. Wine lovers in all parts of the civilized world know the names of the great Bordeaux and Burgundy wines: Lafite, Latour, Margaux, Mouton, Haut-Brion, Chambertin, Musigny, Richebourg, Nuits-St-Georges, Yquem, Barsac, Meursault and Montrachet. But how many people, besides the people of Champagne themselves, know which are the vineyards responsible for the best wines of Champagne? Very few, indeed, even in the wine trade. It is a long time since champagne was sold under the names of its parishes or villages, as bordeaux and burgundy, hocks and moselles, and other fine wines are offered. Champagne, like port, sherry and madeira, is now known by the names of its shippers. These are the people who are responsible for choosing the right wines from the many Champagne vineyards, blending them happily together, with more or less sugar added, if and when they think that it will make their wine more attractive, and building up great stocks that will make it possible for the wine to be mature when sold, and allow them to meet the worldwide demand for their brand. All the more important champagne shippers sell at least 1,000,000 bottles of champagne bearing their name or brand, every year; one or two sell as much as 2,000,000 bottles each year. This they could not do had they not had the opportunity, which is theirs at every vintage time, to buy grapes or new wine from a number of vineyards, some better and dearer than others.

The vineyards of Champagne have been officially classified but in a way which is different from the rest of France, not to say unique. Every year, when the time of the vintage approaches, Champagne shippers and *vignerons* meet and, usually after a great deal of heated argument, come to an agreement and settle what price will be paid at the *vintage* per kilo of grapes, by no means for all grapes, but for the grapes of fine villages of the *canton* of Verzy, that is in the Montagne de Reims, viz.: Beaumont-sur-Vesle, Mailly, Puisieulx, Sillery and Verzenay; five in the *canton* of Ay on the Marne or Epernay side of the Montagne, viz.: Ambonnay, Ay, Bouzy, Louvois and Tours-sur-Marne; and two in the *canton* of Avize, viz.: Avize and Cramant. They are the twelve villages whose *vignerons* will be paid 100%, or the full agreed price and whose wines fall in the top rank *grand cru*. The *vignerons* of the *première catégorie* or next best vineyards, will all get just a little less, from 90%–99% of the full price. The *vignerons* of the next best villages will receive from 80%–88% of the full price, so that they are not doing too badly. Besides those three categories, there are many other Champagne villages producing a great deal of genuine champagne wine from ordinary to fair quality which will be bought at a rate given to each village, of up to 79% of the full price.

The names of the Champagne vineyards and their ratings are given in this gazetteer, but not the names of the shippers.

B

Loire

The Loire is the longest river in France, over 600 miles from its source in the Cévennes mountains, to where it flows into the Atlantic beyond Nantes by St-Nazaire. There are vineyards practically all along the Loire valley itself and those of its many tributaries: they add up roughly to half a million acres, and on an average they produce ordinary to fair red, rosé and white wines, yielding nearly twice as much white as red and rosé combined; also a comparatively small quantity of fine red and white table wines. Here, again, there are more, as well as better, white wines.

The vineyards of the Loire may be divided into the following:

(1) *Upper Loire*, from its source in the Haute-Loire *département*, through the Loire and Allier *départements*;

(2) *Touraine*, parts of the Loiret and Loir-et-Cher *départements*, and the whole of the Indre-et-Loire *département*;

(3) *Anjou*, the whole of the Maine-et-Loire *département*;

(4) *Lower Loire*, the south-west end of Maine-et-Loire, and most of the Loire Atlantique *département*. Touraine and Anjou were also provinces until 1789.

UPPER LOIRE. With the exception of the vineyards of St Pourçain-sur-Sioule between the little river Sioule and the Loire, none of the Loire vineyards produces any wines of merit before the river reaches Pouilly-sur-Loire. They produce different sorts of table wines: red, white, rosé and *vins gris*. Some of them, more particularly the white, are of very fair quality, even fine quality when of a particularly good vintage.

Pouilly-sur-Loire is in the Nièvre *département*, on the right bank of the Loire, and its better white table wines, which are all made of white Sauvignon grapes, have no less than three *AC* for anybody to choose from: either Pouilly-sur-Loire, Blanc Fumé de Pouilly and Pouilly-Blanc-Fumé. The name is due to the fact that the Sauvignon grape is known locally as the Blanc Fumé (white smoke) grape.

Upon the opposite side of the Loire, two small rivers have given their names to the two *départements* through which they flow before joining the Loire; the Cher and the Indre respectively. The best wines of the Cher are the white wines of the Sancerre area, while the white wines of Quincy are nearly, or very nearly as fine. The wines of Reuilly are considered the best of the Indre *département*, the peers of the white wines of Château Meillant from vineyards on both sides of the border line between the Cher and the Indre *départements*.

TOURAINE. The greater part of the Touraine vineyards are in the Indre-et-Loire *département*, and they are responsible for the best white and red wines of Touraine. The whites are those of Vouvray and Rochecorbon, the reds those of St Nicolas-de-Bourgueil on the right of the river. The red table wines of Chinon are the best on the opposite side of the Loire.

ANJOU. Most of the vineyards and most of the best wines of Anjou are in the Maine-et-Loire *département*. The best wines of Anjou are the white wines, not only those of the Loire river, like Saumur (better known abroad for its sparkling than its still white wines) but those of the Coteaux de la Loire, such as those of Savennières and those of the Coteaux du Layon, of which none are finer than the Quarts de Chaume. The Coteaux de l'Aubance vineyards and those of the valleys of the rivers Loire and Sarthe, also produce some fair to fine white wines.

LOWER LOIRE. Most of the vineyards of the Lower Loire are in the *département* which was once called Loire Inférieure but is now Loire Atlantique. Its vineyards produce a great deal of ordinary wine, both red and white, but rather more and better white wine than red. Only one quarter of the Loire Atlantique wines are entitled to an *AC*: the Muscadets from vineyards on both sides of the Loire, those of Sèvre-et-Maine on the left, those of the Coteaux d'Ancenis on the right, and those of the Coteaux de la Loire on both the right and left banks of the Loire. Some of these are in the Maine-et-Loire *département*, at its south-western end.

Rhône

The Rhône rises not far from the source of the Rhine, in Switzerland, high in the Alps, entering the Lake of Geneva at its eastern end. Just west of Geneva it enters France and flows almost due west, with the vineyards of Savoie and those of the Bugey on its right, until it reaches Lyons, where, after being joined by the Saône, it turns due south and rushes at full speed through the mountainous country known as Côtes du Rhône. In so doing the river divides a number of *départements*: Isère, Drôme and Vaucluse on its left, Loire, Ardèche and Gard on its right, besides the Rhône *département* itself, of which Lyons is the chief city.

RHÔNE. Some 85% of the Rhône *département* vineyards are north of Lyons, in the Beaujolais districts, but the few vineyards below Lyons, at the southern end of the *département*, produce wines of a much higher standard of quality than any of the Beaujolais vineyards. Ampuis is the only little town at the southern end of the Rhône *département*, and its vineyards are the first ones of the Côtes du Rhône reached after leaving Lyons; they produce the remarkable red table wine of Côte Rôtie, and also the very fine white wine of Condrieu.

LOIRE. There is only a very small part of this *département* which reaches the Rhône, but it is here that the grapes producing the white Château Grillet wine grow, the available supply of which has always been far too small for the demand.

ARDECHE. The vineyards of this *département* produce a great quantity of ordinary red table wines and a negligible quantity of white wines, both still and sparkling, which are rather better than the reds. The still white wines are mostly sold as Vins de Tournon, and the sparkling wines are those of St-Perey.

GARD. Only the westernmost area of the Gard *département* is in the Côtes du Rhône region, but its vineyards have the privilege of producing the rosé wines of Tavel, Lirac, Chusclan and Orsan, which are considered to be the best natural table rosé wines of France.

ISÈRE. The vineyards of this *département*, on the left of the Rhône, above and below Lyons, produce only ordinary table wines; mostly red; the white wines are better than the red but neither is deserving of an *AC*.

DROME. This is the *département* immediately south of the Isère *département*, with greater acreage of vineyards but not a comparably greater production of wine. The wine, however, is of much finer quality than that of any of the Isère wines. The wines of the Drôme are mostly red; a fraction of the total production are white wines. The best wines of the Drôme are undoubtedly those of Tain l'Ermitage, the township facing Tournon on the opposite bank of the Rhône, at the foot of the hill whose vineyards produce the best red wines of the Drôme. Approaching the quality of the Coteau de l'Ermitage wines, more or less, there are red table wines from the vineyards of Crozes, Larnage and Mercurol. The white wines of l'Ermitage Hill and Mercurol are fair to fine quality, but they are never available in large quantities. There is one sparkling white wine made in the Drôme, at Die, which is known as Clairette de Die.

VAUCLUSE. The acreage of vineyards of the Vaucluse is as great as, if not greater than, the combined acreage of all the other Côtes du Rhône vineyards. The proportion of quality *AC* wines and *V.D.Q.S.* wines is also greater than the proportion of quality wines in most of the other *départements* of the Côtes du Rhône. This is due to the important quantity and high standard of excellence of the red wines of Châteauneuf-du-Pape. But there are other red table wines, such as those of Gigondas and of the Côtes du Ventoux, which are either very fair or really fine quality. The vineyards of the Côtes du Luberon produce some fair to fine white table wines, and there are also some dessert wines, very popular locally, made mostly at Rasteau and Beaumes-de-Venise.

Dordogne

The vineyards of the Dordogne *département* are expected to produce every year fair and fine wines, approximately half of them red. The coveted *AC* distinction is granted to approximately one-third of them. The vineyards of the Côtes de Bergerac are responsible for the better red and rosé wines of the Dordogne, but those of Monbazillac produce the sweeter and better white wines, and those of Montravel the next best.

From the Dordogne westwards to the Atlantic and south to the Pyrenees, there are many vineyards which each year bring forth vast quantities of mostly undistinguished red, white and rosé table wines. They also produce a small proportion of very fair wines as well as some of fine quality, the best of them as follows: Côtes de Duras, red and white table wines in the Lot-et-Garonne *département*; Gaillac, red (*ordinaire*) and white (fair to fine) from the Tarn *département*; Jurançon, white and tawny wine from the Basses-Pyrénées *département*.

Alsace

Alsace is divided into two *départements*, the Upper and the Lower Rhine, that is the Haut-Rhin and the Bas-Rhin. Ninety-five per cent of the wines are white, of ordinary, fair and fine quality. Most of the wines of Alsace are sold under the name of their grape, with or without the name of the township or village, which will be the name of the shipper of the wine and not necessarily that of the vineyard. Generally speaking, a Sylvaner white Alsace wine, that is a wine made of Sylvaner grapes, will be lighter than a Riesling wine, which will be bigger and better, yet without the richness of the wine made of Traminer or Gewürztraminer grapes from any of the fine vineyards of the Haut-Rhin *département*, where all the best white wines of the Alsace come from.

Jura and Franche Comte

There are many other vineyards in France, producing small quantities of wines of fair to fine quality in the Jura, Bugey, Savoie, Provence, Languedoc, Rousillon and elsewhere. Their names have been duly recorded in this book.

GERMANY

The acreage of vineyards in Germany is very small compared with the acreage in France and in Italy. Yet, the superlative excellence of some of the white wines of Germany is to some extent a compensation for the quantity of wine made in Germany being so much smaller than that of other vinelands of the world.

All the vineyards of Germany of any importance are in western Germany, in what is usually called the Rhineland, which includes the valleys of a number of the Rhine's tributaries, as well as in the main valley of the Rhine itself. Climatic conditions in the Rhineland are quite unpredictable and late spring frosts, at the dangerous time of what they call locally the Ice Saints, can be catastrophic and produce wide differences in the total quantities of wine made in Germany from year to year.

All the great wines of Germany are white wines and are made from the noble Riesling grapes, and most fine white German wines are made either from Riesling or Müller-Thurgau grapes. A large proportion of German white wines are ordinary to fair wines made from the Sylvaner, a white grape cultivated to a greater extent than any other.

Rhinegau

Although the vineyards of the Rhinegau occupy a relatively low place in the list of Rhineland vinelands, they are responsible not only for some of the greatest Hocks but also for a much higher proportion of fine wines than any of the other Rhineland districts.

The Rhinegau's best vineyards are on the right bank of the Rhine, from Hochheim to Rüdesheim, a strip of land about twenty miles in length and from two to five miles in width, with the protecting heights of the Taunus range at the back, facing the Rhine and the vineyards of Rhinehessia upon the other side of the river. This is why the west-by-south and south-by-west location of the Rhinegau vineyards is ideal.

The three outstanding wines of the Rhinegau are those of Schloss Johannisberg, Steinberg and Schloss Vollrads, not only because the soil of their vineyards is just right, their elevation and aspect are equally so, but because those vineyards each have a single owner, an important and all too rare asset.

The first vineyards of the Rhinegau are those of Hochheim, close to the junction of the Main and the Rhine. The vineyards at Hochheim, facing the Main, are about ten miles south-east of the Rhinegau proper, but they are regarded as part of the Rhinegau, first of all because their white wines are excellent, and second because the name hock given to all white Rhine wines in all English-speaking countries is the anglicized from of Hochheim.

The many vineyards that can be seen on the way from Hochheim to Rüdesheim are those of the following villages and townships:

WALLUF. The lower and upper vineyards used to be known until recently as Ober and Nieder-Walluf. Their best vineyards produce some very fair to fine Riesling wines.

ELTVILLE. A small town but the only one of any size of the Rhinegau. Its vineyards produce some fair to fine white wines, but none of outstanding merit.

RAUENTHAL. A mere village tucked away behind Eltville in the folds of the Taunus foothills; its vineyards produce mostly fine to very fine white wines, and even really great wines occasionally.

KIEDRICH. A hamlet between Rauenthal and Hallgarten; it is surrounded by vineyards which produce fair, fine and very fine white wine.

ERBACH. A small town by the Rhine the vineyards of which produce some of the great wines of the Rhinegau. Its best-known vineyard is Marcobrunn, which is divided among a number of owners, one of whom is Prince Friedrich of Prussia; the wine made from his Marcobrunn grapes is marketed as Schloss Rheinhartshausener Erbacher Marcobrunn.

HATTENHEIM. This large and picturesque village includes a portion of the Marcobrunn vineyards and the whole of the Steinberg, a vineyard name much more famous than Hattenheim itself. Steinberg vineyard was originally planted by Cistercian monks in the twelfth century. Today there is still no finer Hock than a Steinberger of a good vintage, and very few of the great Hocks are its peer.
There are other Hattenheim vineyards, of course, and most, if not all of them, produce fair to fine or very fine white wine.

OESTRICH. This is not an important village, between Hattenheim and Winkel, facing the Rhine, but its vineyards produce more wine than any other individual village or town of the Rhinegau; more but by no means better wines. Oestrich white wines are fair enough and some of them may rightly claim to be fine, but not very fine, and certainly not great.

MITTELHEIM. One of the least important villages and vineyards of the Rhinegau.

HALLGARTEN. A small town on high ground well away from the Rhine; its vineyards produce some fair, fine and very fine white wines.

WINKEL. A small but not unimportant town with a number of small vineyards and one large one, the vineyard of Schloss Vollrads, the largest estate of the Rhinegau in the possession of one owner. Schloss Vollrads wines are among the finest of Germany; the estate is the property of the Matuschka-Greiffenklau family.

JOHANNISBERG is the name of a modest village, by the Rhine, at the foot of the hill on the top of which stands the proud Schloss Johannisberg. There is a range of ordinary, fair and fine white wines produced from the vineyards of the Johannisberg parish other than those of the Schloss; there is also a range of Schloss Johannisberg white wines from fine, to very fine and to great occasionally.

GEISENHEIM. This is the most important town of the Rhinegau, not so much for its important vineyards, but because of its school of viticulture and its work on both viticulture and oenology.

RÜDESHEIM. A small town facing Bingen, on the opposite bank of the Rhine at the mouth of the Nahe. The best wines of Rüdesheim are those from the vineyards on the steepest slopes of the Rüdesheim hill or *Berg*. These all have the word *Berg* prefixing their names.

Palatinate (*Rheinpfalz*)

This is the large wine region, west of the Rhine, east of Lorraine, south of the Nahe and north of Alsace. It was known in medieval times as the Cellar of the Holy Roman Empire because of the great quantity of wine it produced. It still produces more wine than any of the other Rhineland areas, *ordinaires* to fair red table wine, white wines, mostly *ordinaires* to fair also, but a very substantial quantity from fine to very fine, even really great wines, in some particularly good vintages.

The Palatinate vineyards are divided into three sections known as the Upper Haardt, the Middle Haardt, and the Lower Haardt. All the best vineyards of the Palatinate are in the Middle Haardt—Forst, Deidesheim, Ruppertsberg and Wachenheim being the core—some of the finest white wines of the Palatinate and of the Rhineland are produced there. Königsbach and Bad Dürkheim vineyards, and a few more, also produce very fine wine from their best *Lagen* or sites.

There are no great estates in the Palatinate under one ownership comparable with Schloss Johannisberg, Schloss Vollrads or Steinberg in the Rhinegau. It is therefore important to know, if at all possible, not only the best sites of the best vineyards of the best localities, but also who are the best of the owners—who has a share in the site, who is known for his skill and integrity and who bottles his wines on the estate. Any Palatinate white wine, for instance, which is estate-bottled by Reichgraf von Buhl, Bassermann-Jordan or Bürklin-Wolf can be relied upon as being a fine wine.

Rhinehessia

Rhinehessia or *Rheinhessen* is the high ground from Worms to Mainz and Bingen. Its production of wine is second in quantity to the Palatinate, consisting mostly of red and white *ordinaires* table wines. There are nevertheless some fine and very fine white Rhinehessia wines, and even some great wines in particularly favourable vintages. On the whole, the vineyards of Rhinehessia are on slightly undulating or even flat ground.

In the majority of parishes or localities of Rhinehessia, Sylvaner grapes are grown exclusively for white wines (and other sorts of red wines). Both Sylvaner and Riesling grapes are grown in others, and Riesling grapes exclusively in the few which are responsible for the fine white wines of Rhinehessia. Of the dozen or so better vineyards of Rhinehessia, the best sites are usually named as follows:

NIERSTEIN, *facile princeps*, both with the greatest yield of wine and with a greater proportion of very fine wines than any other Rhinehessian town or village.

NACKENHEIM, with beautiful vineyards, south of Mainz, overlooks a very fine stretch of the river. Its soil is as red as its best wines, which are very nearly the peers of the best wines of Nierstein.

BODENHEIM, with both Sylvaner and Riesling in its vineyards, produces fine white wines, but not up to the high standard of Nierstein.

OPPENHEIM, immediately south of Nierstein, has vineyards, with about 30% Riesling grapes and 70% Sylvaner and Müller-Thurgau grapes, slope gently from south of the village towards the river, producing some fine white wines but no great ones.

DIENHEIM, south of Oppenheim, is on the border of the Rheinfront, the Rhinehessian escarpment which here falls away to the alluvial plain towards Worms. Their white wines are mostly fine, even if lacking somewhat in breed.

BINGEN is at the junction of the river Nahe, and the Rhine and its vineyards are the last of Rhinehessia, at its western end. The best white wines of Bingen are those marketed under the hyphenated names of Bingen-Büdesheim; it does not mean that the wines of both neighbouring localities are blended, but that the wine is from these vineyards of Bingen in Rhinehessia, next to Büdesheim and not those on the other side of the river Nahe.

Nahe

The river Nahe meets the Rhine at Bingen opposite Rüdesheim. Around Bad Kreuznach, the chief township of the Nahe valley, the steep red sandstone hills are covered with vineyards of both Riesling and Sylvaner grapes, but with a great deal more Riesling than Sylvaner. There are a number of smallish vineyards down the Nahe valley, at or near places such as Bad Münster, Norheim, Roxheim, Winzenheim, and Bretzenheim, the largest of all such vineyards being the state-owned Schloss Böckelheim. Some of the white wines of Schloss Böckelheim are the best of the Nahe wines and the peers of the finer Rhinehessian ones.

Franconia (*Franken*)

The vineyards of Franconia are those of the Main upper valley, which joins the Rhine as it leaves Hochheim. Most Franconian vineyards are both east and west of Würzburg, the chief city and main wine market of the region. The soil of Franconia suits the Sylvaner grape better than most other soils of the Rhineland. The best white wines of Franconia are bottled on the estate in the traditional bottle or flask of the country, called *Bocksbeutel*; they are drier than most other fine Rhine wines and possess a very distinctive charm of their own. Stein, Äussere and Innere Leister, Neuberg Abstleiste, Harfe, Standerbühl, Schalksberg and Steinmantel produce the only Franconian white wines entitled to the name of Steinwein; and these are on the hill behind Würzburg.

There are over one hundred villages and little market towns in Franconia with vineyards producing both red and white table wines, some of the white wines being of a high standard of quality.

Moselle-Saar-Ruwer

This is the official German name of the last reach of the Moselle, from Trier to the Rhine. It includes besides the vineyards and wines of the Moselle, those of its tributaries, the two most important of them being the Saar and the Ruwer which join the Moselle above and below Trier. The vineyards of the Moselle are divided, like those of the Palatinate, into Upper, Middle and Lower, all the best of them being in the Middle Moselle from Longuich to Pünderich. From Pünderich to Koblenz and the Rhine, there are a number of vineyards in what is known as the Lower Moselle; they produce much white wine, most of it of fair quality and some of it of fine quality in good vintages, but rarely if ever up to the standard of excellence of the Middle Moselle wines.

The vineyards of the Saar and of the Ruwer are fewer in number, most of them of small size, but many of them producing as fine white wines as the best wines of the Middle Moselle.

The best white wines of the Saar are those of Wiltingen and Ockfen. The finest vineyard of Wiltingen is the world-famous Scharzhofberg, one of the great white wines of the world, not to be mistaken, however, for its poor relation, Scharzberg, which produces fair enough white wines but by no means great. The vineyard of Scharzhofberg is planted with Riesling grapes, on a very steep slope of crumbling slaty soil.

The Ruwer is smaller than the Saar and the vineyards are planted only with Riesling on the very steep slopes of the narrow valley. There are two villages which are world-famous; their wines, of a good vintage, of course, are great wines. They are the Eitelsbacher Karthäuserhofberg and Maximin-Grünhauser. The vineyards of Eitelsbach are divided among a number of *vignerons*, but fine as all the wine may be, none can challenge the excellence of Karthäuserhofberg, originally the property of Carthusian monks, but for the past hundred and seventy years belonging to the Rautenstrauch family.

Maximim-Grünhaus is the name of a very small village and of a wine with a great reputation. The vineyard has Riesling grapes and different site names or *Lagen*, but the von Schubert family own the greater part of the vineyard.

In the Moselle-Saar-Ruwer country, the name of the owner of the vineyard given on the wine's label is almost as important as the name of the vineyard and of the grape. Estate-bottled wines bearing such names as Reichgraf von Kesselstatt (in Graach), Johann Joseph Prüm and other members of the Prüm dynasty (in Wehlen), von Schorlemer (in Braüneberg and elsewhere) are among the best.

The outstanding difference between the fine German wines and other fine wines is their far greater individuality. Whether it takes one, two or three weeks to pick and press all the grapes of any of the great châteaux of the Médoc or elsewhere, the grapes picked and pressed on the first day of the vintage and those picked and pressed on the last day will all be mixed together to make one wine eventually, bearing the name of its native vineyard and the vintage date. Not so in Germany. In the case of the best wines, the wine of the grapes picked and pressed each day will bear the number of its individual cask and will keep its identity to the end, with the added qualificative to which it may be entitled, such as *Hochfeine Auslese*, *Hochfeinste Auslese* (the same wine but just a little better), *Beerenauslese* and *Trockenbeerenauslese*.

ITALY

Italy and France are the largest wine-producing countries in the world. Between them they are responsible for half the global production of wine. In Italy, as in all other wine-producing countries, wines for the thirst of the common man are produced in much larger quantities than all other kinds of wine, but there are nevertheless quite large quantities of fair wines as well as not inconsiderable quantities of fine wines, both dry table wines and sweet dessert wines, red and white, rosé and tawny. There are also many sparkling wines, most of which are low-strength and sweet. There are also a few dry sparkling white wines of real merit.

As one soon realizes by even a casual look at the map of Italy, there is a very great variety of wines made under the entirely different geographical and climatic conditions of the country, from the Alpine heights of Val d'Aosta and Val d'Adige to the 'heel' of the 'boot' of Italy, and Sicily as well as in Sardinia and the many charming little off-shore islands along Italy's long line of coastal vineyards.

If we are to consider the vineyards of Italy from north to south, those of the Val d'Aosta in Piedmont come first, and, incredible as it may appear, there are vineyards at Morgex in the Alps that are 1,000 feet above Aosta and some 3,000 feet above sea level. The vines somehow can stand the intense cold of long winters, and their grapes give a thin 8° but quite pleasing white wine known as Blanc de Morgex.

Piedmont

As former French provinces have been cut up in *départements*, so the old kingdom of Piedmont was divided about one hundred years ago into the large provinces of Turin, Asti, Cuneo, Novara, Vercelli and Alessándria. Their vineyards produce wines of many different sorts.

The province of Turin produces more white wine than any of the other provinces and its world-wide reputation rests more upon its vermouths than upon its table or sparkling wines. There are, however, some red table wines made in the province of Turin, such as the Carema which is made from the noble Nebbiolo grape. At Cesnola, in the parish of Settimo Vittorio, a red wine which is lighter, but of equally good quality is made. From Caluso comes a golden wine made from Erbaluce grapes, some as a dry table wine, and some as a sweet dessert wine; the alcoholic strength of the first (*secco*) is usually 12°; that of the second (*dolce*) 15°. Baldissero, Chieri, Monaldo and Pavarolo are best known for their Cari wine, a slightly sparkling rosé wine made from the Cari grape, and a very attractive wine to drink on a summer's day with fruit.

The province of Asti is known all over the world for its sparkling wine, called in Italy Asti Spumante, Moscato d'Asti and Moscato Spumante. It is the ideal, true tempered, festive wine, with plenty of sugar and bubbles and as little as 7°–8° of alcohol. There is, however, a sparkling wine of finer quality, made from Cortese instead of Moscato white grapes, which has less sugar and more alcohol (10°–11°); it is called Cortese d'Asti.

There are, of course, many table wines also made in Asti province. These are mostly red wines which are usually marketed under the name of the grape from which each wine was made, such as Freisa d'Asti, Barbera d'Asti, Grignolino d'Asti, Brachetto d'Asti and Bonardo d'Asti.

Cuneo province deserves to be better known than it is outside Italy since its vineyards produce a far greater proportion of fine table wines than any of the other Italian provinces. Many a good judge of wine would add that of all the red table wines of Italy, none is better than a Barolo or a Barbaresco, and few are as good, to name but two of the wines of the Monferrato vineyards in the province of Cuneo. The Colli Monferrato are, in Italy, what the Côte d'Or hills are in France. They are a range or group of fairly steep hills about sixty miles long and forty wide, facing the wide expanse of the Upper Po valley in Piedmont. The name Barolo is the equivalent of the *AC* in France and cannot be given to any red table wine of the Colli Monferrato other than that which has been made from Nebbiolo grapes grown in the vineyards of Barolo itself, or those of five nearby villages. The same applies to Barbaresco, the next best red table wine of Italy, the vineyards of which are, like those of Barolo, in the Alba area of Cuneo province. Other fair to fine red table wines of the same region are mostly sold under the name of their native village coupled with the name of the grape from which they were made, as: Nebbiolo d'Alba, Nebbiolo di Canale, Nebbiolo di Castellinaldo, Dolcetto delle Langhe, Freisa della Langhe, Moscato di Cuneo and so on.

In the province of Novara there are no wines of great merit, but a number of fair table wines, as well as a very few of better quality.

The province of Alessándria produces a huge quantity of wine, both red and white, practically all of little merit and low in cost; hence a local popularity. One of the few wines of the province to have some claim to fine quality is a white wine made of Cortese white grapes and sold as Castel Tagliolo Superiore, the *de luxe* edition of the plain Castel Tagliolo.

In the Vercelli province, there are no outstanding wines, but a number of fair to fine table wines, such as the red wines of Gattinara and Lessona, which are made from Nebbiolo grapes and the alcoholic strength of which is not below 12° and often as much as 14°. At Miesola, in the parish of Brusengo, they make a very fair red table wine from 75% Nebbiolo and 25% Bonarda grapes known as Messolone. At Cavaglia, a lighter red table wine and a rosé of good quality are made, known respectively as Rosso rubino del Viverone, and Chiaretto del Viverone.

Liguria

This is a narrow stretch of coast running from north to south from the Menton-Ventimiglia Franco-Italian frontier to below La Spezia, and separated from Piedmont by a range of steep mountains, with a number of narrow valleys facing the Gulf of Genoa. There are vineyards, mostly small, practically everywhere, providing their peasant owners with no more than the wine needed for home consumption. There is much more white than red wine made in Liguria, which is understandable since fish is the staple food of the people as well as the best food there is to give to the many foreign visitors to the Italian Riviera. There are not only more white than red wines in Liguria, but as there are no cellars in which to keep wine for any length of time, the very young white table wines sold in all the fish restaurants of the Ligurian coast are much more acceptable than young red wines.

North of Genoa, in the province of Imperia, there is a very pleasant white table wine known as Vermentino di Imperia, Vermentino being the name of the white grape from which the wine is made. In the province of Genoa there are different white wines of fair quality, none better than that made from grapes of the vineyards of the upper Petronio valley, at Monasca; its alcoholic strength is like the white Moscatello of Ventimiglia. A similar, somewhat lighter white wine, made from grapes of the Polcevera valley, is very popular locally. The best white wine of Liguria, however, is that which is made from the grapes of Cinqueterre vineyards, below La Spezia: it is the only wine of Liguria that is ever kept and which is well worth keeping; unfortunately, there is very little of it made and matured.

Lombardy

Lombardy, whose principal city is Milan, is today the richest region of Italy, as well as one of four most important wine-producing areas. As elsewhere in Italy, there are vineyards nearly everywhere, but here there are both more and larger vineyards in the following three areas: (1) near Sondrio; (2) Oltrepo Pavese, south of Pavia and the Po river; (3) western and southern shores of Lake Garda.

Sondrio is the wine centre of the province of Valtellina, the vineyards of which produce much fair to fine red table wine, as well as a little white table wine. The more ordinary red table wines of the province are sold as Valtellina rosso, but the better ones are given under the name of one of the other of the villages, east of Sondrio (Sassella, Grumello, Inferno, Grigioni and Fracia), the first three are generally thought of as producing the best red Valtellina wines. All the better of these wines are made from a Nebbiolo red grape which is known locally by the name of Chiavennasca.

The viticultural region of Oltrepo Pavese is a long way from Valtellina. It consists of a small hilly district overlooking the valley of the Po river; its centre is the little town of Casteggio. Here there are Pinot Noir and Pinot Blanc grapes but no Nebbiolo grapes in its vineyards. Some of the red wines of the Casteggio hills have unusual names, such as Frecciarossa di Casteggio, Sangue di Giuda, Buttafuoco and Barbacarlo. Farther south, between Pavia and Broni, the vineyards of Canneto produce a white wine of fair quality known as Canneto Amaro (dry), and Canneto Dolce (sweet).

In the province of Brescia, the vineyards facing the western and southern shores of Lake Garda produce fair table wines, better than those of Casteggio, but not of the same high quality as the better Valtellina wines. Those which are considered the best are the Chiaretto del Garda, also called Moniga del Garda; the Vino della Riviera or Retico; Valtenesi and others, all of them by no means great wines, yet distinctly better than the wines made farther south from the vineyards of the Brescia hills, the Colli Bresciani.

Val d'Adige

This is the name given to the valley of the Adige river, which rises near the Italo-Austrian frontier and flows through the Alto Adige, past Trento and Verona and into the Adriatic. The many vineyards which grace the lower slopes of the mountains of the narrow upper valley of the Adige and the still narrower valleys of the tributaries of the Adige, bring forth table wines from *ordinaires* to fair mostly, but with some fine wines as well, more especially in the Alto Adige districts. None of the Trentino wines may rightly be called fine wines— sound, solid, wholesome and most acceptable as they be. The only Trentino wine of any repute is the Teroldego, a stoutish red table wine which is mostly drunk much too young, for not only can it stand the test of age but if given time and a good cellar it improves beyond all recognition.

In the Alto Adige, there is a greater variety of wines, and their quality is distinctly superior to that of the Trentino wines. This is due to a number of factors, among them the soil of the vineyards and the grapes grown (mostly fine quality grapes such as the Cabernet, Pinot Noir and Merlot for the red wines, Pinot Blanc, Riesling and Traminer for the white and Lagrein for the rosé). It is also possible that the *vignerons* of the Alto Adige, Italian by law but Austrian by birth or descent, are more industrious or possess greater skill. Many of the Alto Adige wines are still given their former German names as well as their present Italian ones. Thus Keltersee or Lago di Caldaro, Santa Maddalena or Sankt Magdalener, Bolzano or Bozen and so on.

Veneto

This is the region of Venice and one of the lowest in order of production of all the viticultural regions of Italy. Although approximately three quarters of its products are wines of too modest a quality to be recorded here, the remainder of such a large production is by no means a negligible figure.

The best and most popular wine of Veneto is Soave, a white table wine which is made of 80% Garganega grapes and 20% Trebbiano or Riesling from the vineyards of the little town of Soave, west of Verona, and also those of Monforte, a village quite near Soave. Although there may not be any red table wines made in the province of Verona which possess the same high quality as the white Soave, some very nice red table wines are made from grapes grown on the last foothills of the Lessini Mountains, such as the Bardolino, Valpolicello and Valpantena. They also make in Verona province and attractive sweet dessert white wine called Recioto bianco.

Much wine is made, but none of real merit, in the provinces of Vicenza and Treviso, whereas there are some quite interesting wines in the far north, in the Friuli, Udine and Gorizia areas. The better wines, however, both table and dessert wines, such as the Cabernet di Friuli, Merlot di Friuli and Malvazia di Friuli, are all from the Friuli vineyards.

Emilia-Romagna

None of the many wines of Emilia-Romagna is really fine wine, but there are quite a number recorded in this book which are of very fair quality and locally enjoy the reputation of being fine wines, such as the Rosso del Bosco of Ferrara, the Lambrusco di Sorbara of Modena, the Lambrusco Grappa rosso and the Sangiovese of Bologna, the Barbera di Langhirano of Parma and the Sangiovese di Romagna of Forli and Predappio. The nicest of the white table wines is the Albana di Romagna, which is available both dry and sweet, from the Forli, Bertinoro and Cesena vineyards.

Tuscany

This is the land of chianti, the red table wine of Italy which is better known throughout the world than any other, even if by name only. In England, chianti is certainly the Italian wine which has been imported and drunk much longer than any other, although it was not known in bygone days as chianti but as Florence wine, at which time it was bottled in flasks more like the Steinwein *Bocksbeutel* than the modern *fiasco*, and was already covered with a protecting straw jacket. Of course, it was a red wine, as all chianti had always been until recent times when the demand for a white chianti has brought the supply.

All the vineyards of the Tuscan hills which produce the genuine chianti have been officially classified and their wines bear the official Italian *AC*, the privilege of a true chianti classico. Other genuine chianti wines are given the name of their native district or hill, such as Chianti Colli Aretini, Chianti Colli Fiorentini, Colline Chianti, Colli Senesi, Chianti Colline Pisane, Chianti Montalbano, etc.

Besides chianti, there are fair to fine table wines from the vineyards of Tuscany, including those of the island of Elba; none of them, however, is ever likely to be as well known as chianti has been for so long.

It is but fair to record that the owner of the Castello di Brolio, Baron Ricasoli, has done much to raise the standard of viticulture and wine-making in Tuscany, and that there is now chianti to be enjoyed which is of distinctly finer quality than the chianti which was sold in England in pre-Mussolini times.

Umbria

There are comparatively few vineyards in Umbria, one of the smallest vinelands of Italy, but these are nonetheless responsible for the white Orvieto, one of the really fine table wines not only of Italy but of the world. Orvieto is a quaint and charming little city, surrounded by vines, and the wine that bears its name also possesses a distinct charm of its own; it is made in two grades, dry and sweet, is of beautiful deep, old-gold colour and has a discreet yet suave bouquet.

The Marches

There are many vineyards in The Marches but there is no really fine wine to claim this region as its birthplace. Quite a few table wines, however, both red and white, are above the *ordinaire* class and quite fair enough to be recorded.

Lazio

Lazio is the Italian name of the old Roman *Latium*. There are vineyards in the Tiber valley and estuary, but their wines are without charm; their only merit is their inexpensiveness. The better wines of the Lazio come from the half-circle south-west of Rome and are called the Vini dei Castelli Romani. The Castelli Romani are not castles in the medieval sense of the word, but elegant villas with charming gardens—the homes, chiefly in the summer, of the people who own the vineyards on the slopes of the hills. As in other vinelands, the better wines of the Castelli Romani are given the name of their native vineyard or village or hill, such as Colli Albani and Colli Lanuvini, Frascati or Velletri, Aleatico di Genzano or Castel San Girgio, a vineyard of Maccarese, where a popular Moscato di Maccarese is made.

One of the wines of the Lazio with a reputation which it may have deserved some three hundred years ago, when it was given its name, is the Est! Est!! Est!!! of Montefiascone, in the province of Viterbo, only a short distance south-west of Orvieto. In the same province, however, they are quite proud of a remarkable white dessert wine, Aleatico di Gradoli, which is as rich but not so heady as the Aleatico di Terracina.

Campania

There are some very fair table wines, both red and white, from the vineyards of the mainland of Campania and certain of the off-shore islands: chiefly Capri, Ischia and Procida. There is a red table wine called Falerno rosso and a white one called Falerno bianco made from the vineyards of the northern seaboard of Campania, near Mondragone, but it is difficult to imagine that either the one or the other bears any resemblance to the Falernian nectar sung by the poets of ancient Rome.

Apuglia

This is the Roman name of the large areas which the Italians call Puglie (and the French, Les Pouilles). Its many vineyards produce more wine than any of the other Italian vinelands, but no wine approaching in quality the better wines of Piedmont, Tuscany or Lombardy There are, however, a number of fair and quite nice wines from Apulian vineyards.

Calabria

This is probably the poorest part of Italy as regards its soil, but many of the best wines of the world are made from grapes grown in poor soil, so that it is not surprising to find wines of fine quality in Calabria, both table and dessert wines, in small quantities only. The Greco di Gerace, the Pollino di Castrovillari, the Giro di Calabria and the sweet Moscato di Cosenza are among the more popular.

Sicily

There are a number of table and dessert wines, from ordinary to fair and fine quality, but there is only one wine of Sicily which is universally known, if only by name: Marsala. It is the best-known (and it may be the best) of Italian fortified wines. Marsala is a white wine to which grape-brandy is added to raise its strength to 17°–19°: it is also sweetened and coloured, much in the same way as sherry, as well as blended, in order to secure worthwhile reserves of wines of constant types and cost, each type being given a name representing its distinct standard, such as (1) Italia, the cheapest sort which must have 17° alcohol and 5% grape sugar; (2) Marsala Superiore, or S.O.M. or L.P. which must not have less than 18° alcohol and 10% grape sugar, if labelled 'sweet' but some may be dry and unsweetened; (3) Marsala Vergine, which is the driest, also 18° alcohol, and sometimes called Solera.

Among the table wines of Sicily, mention should be made of the Mamertino of the Messina province; also the Eloro both red and white and the Corvo rosso from the province of Syracuse.

Sardinia

There are no less than 150,000 acres of vineyards in the island of Sardinia, 90,000 acres being in the southern province of Cagliari, 33,000 acres in the northern province of Sassari and 27,000 acres in the central province of Nuoro. Their average total yield is about 14,500,000 dozen bottles of wine, mostly ordinary table wines, very little of this huge quantity being exported.

Although the majority of Sardinian wine is very ordinary and rarely exported and although there may not be any really fine Sardinian wines, a number are of very fair quality, such as the Giro di Sardegna, Sangiovese sardo, Malvasia di Cagliari, Monica di Sardegna and Moscato di Campidano.

PORTUGAL

Portugal might well be called the most wine-conscious country in the world. Although port to most people outside Portugal is the best, if not the only wine, of Portugal, all the fortified wines of the country amount to only a fraction of the total production, and more than half of this is exported.

The vinous production of Portugal is officially divided into two main classes: utility and quality. Included in the quality class are all the better wines in what may be compared to the *AC* of France, that is wines made from vineyards of one or the other of the officially 'delimited' areas, either Vinhos Verdes, Douro Dão, Bucelas, Colares, Carcavelos or Setúbal.

PORT. The one and only wine which, in Great Britain, has the exclusive right to the name of port, is a wine made from grapes grown in the valley of the Upper Douro, has had its fermentation checked by brandy at the time of the vintage and has been shipped from Oporto, *the* port of Portugal, whatever Lisbon and other ports of the country may have to say about it.

Port, the fortified wine as we know it today, dates from 1756. There were small shipments of wine from Portugal at an earlier date, but the wine was Portuguese wine, not port; a table wine, not a fortified one. Much the greater proportion of port shipped from Oporto to all parts of the civilized world is blended; that is, made up of port wines kept at Oporto or Vila Nova de Gaia, across the Douro opposite Oporto, where most port is kept and matured. The art of the blender is to give to his clients the wine merchants the type of wine which their customers like best, year after year and as nearly as possible unchanged. Tawny port and ruby port are blends which differ in colour and age but are true to the standard of quality of the particular brand or mark under which they are marketed. The same applies to white and other ports.

Vintage port is another wine altogether. It is the wine of one single year, and always a particularly good year. Also, it must be bottled two years—at most three years—from its vintage date; that is, long before it is fit to drink and before the partially fermented wine and the brandy which checked its fermentation have had time to live together, to lose completely their identity. This is why vintage port must be kept and given time.

It may be worth recording here the fact that what is called in the wine trade an off-vintage does not mean a port of indifferent quality, kept too long or badly stored, but the wine of a vintage which was not generally considered good enough to declare as a vintage, although one or more port shippers were lucky enough to achieve wine of the right high standard of quality.

VINHOS VERDES. These are the most popular table wines of Portugal, not green in colour, but in the sense of Shakespeare's 'green youth'. Many, in fact most, *vinhos verdes* come from the vineyards of the Minho province, a great granite bluff, stretching north from Oporto to the Spanish frontier. The *vinhos verdes* are different from any of the *ordinaires* or even quality table wines; they possess a sort of liveliness and charm which grow upon one.

Needless to say, one cannot expect *vinhos verdes* to be offered under the name of their native vineyard any more than under the date of their vintage. What matters is the name of the man, firm or brand on the wine's label.

DÃO. The red, white and rosé table wines of central Portugal have long been popular in Portugal, but greater care and skill in their making, since 1945, has greatly raised the standard of their quality and has been responsible for a steadily rising demand from overseas, particularly Great Britain. The Dão wines are made mostly from the vineyards of the Dão and Mandego valleys. Viseu, about halfway between Lisbon and Oporto, is the chief wine mart of the Dão wines.

The red table wines of the Dão are made from either Tourigo do Dão or Tinta Pinheira black grapes, grafted on American *phylloxera*-resisting stock, while white Dão wines are mostly made from the Arinto white grape. The Dão vineyards are small and many of them are planted in terraces cut in the rock at great cost and danger with explosives, sledgehammers and crowbars between pine-clad steep slopes and huge rock boulders at between 1,500 and 2,000 feet above sea level.

The wines of the Dão are far better wines than the *vinhos verdes*, having greater 'fruit' or vinosity, more body and a better balance due to the expert blending at Viseu. It is said that the blenders of Viseu give red Dão wines a brilliancy and special charm by blending just the right quantity of white Dão to the red, which is why Dão wines are never sold under the name of their native vineyard, but under the name of their shippers or a shipper's registered brand.

SETÚBAL. This is a little land-locked port immediately south of the Tagus estuary, at the foot of a hill covered with vineyards which produce an excellent Moscatel sweet white dessert wine, as well as less distinguished wine, in important quantities.

CARCAVELOS. This is a town near Estoril, at a point where the estuary of the Tagus opens into the Atlantic, close to Lisbon's suburbs. Carcavelos wine is a sweetish white wine, quite different from any other Portuguese wine, equally acceptable as an apéritif or a dessert wine.

COLARES. The vineyards of Colares are planted upon the outlying spurs of the Sintra range, beyond Estoril in fine, deep, dry sand which has but one thing to its credit: that the *phylloxera* cannot or will not live in it. How any vines can live in that sand and bear good grapes, which make what one authority considers the best table wine of Portugal, is little short of miraculous. It is unfortunate that the Colares wine production is quite small, and therefore not readily available in any quantity.

BUCELAS. The Bucelas vineyards are farther inland than those of Colares, between Sintra and the Tagus, sheltered from blasts from the Atlantic, and planted in more normal soil in which the white Arinto grape flourishes. They produce very fair quantities of very fair quality white table wines.

MADEIRA is, like port, one of the great wines of the world. Madeira bears the name of its native island, and its name, like port, has been protected by the English since 1914 although, strange to say, neither port nor madeira has been since then as popular in England as unprotected sherry.

Madeira is made from different grapes, mostly Boal, Sercial, Malvasia,

Verdelho and Terrantez, grown in small, mostly terraced vineyards of the island's uplands, by small peasant-owners. At Funchal, the chief port and city of the island, some Portuguese families long resident on the island, as well as merchants from the Portuguese mainland, Great Britain, and other lands, have the necessary means, cellars, stores and equipment to enable them to buy the grapes of the peasant-owners at the time of the vintage, make the wine, and put it through the many paces it must take before it becomes the remarkable, fortified dessert wine known throughout the world as madeira.

With the exception of Cama dos Lobos, madeira is never sold under the name of any individual vineyard, but under the name of the grape from which it was made, such as Boal, or Bual (semi-dry), Sercial (dry), Malmsey (sweet), etc., and either the name of the shipper and/or their registered brand or mark.

SPAIN

There are vineyards, and there is wine made in all but two of the provinces of Spain; the only two 'dry' provinces are La Coruña in the north-west, and Vizcaya, the tiny province of Bilbao by the Bay of Biscay. There are also vineyards, and wine is therefore made, in the Balearic and Canary Islands. Spanish wines range from the very plain sort for popular consumption to fair, fine, very fine and great wines with a world-wide reputation. Should one wonder why the quantity of wine per acre is smaller than it is in many other vinelands of the world, the reason is that the rainfall in the southern and central areas is not as good as it is elsewhere, hence an exceptional aridity of the soil in many parts of the country.

The vineyards of Spain, and their wines, may be divided into three main groups, those of the Atlantic or north-west, those of the Mediterranean, and those of the central, land-locked provinces, which is much the largest group of the three.

Atlantic Provinces

This group is made up of the three provinces of Galicia (Lugo, Orense and Pontevedra), the two Basque provinces of Vascongadas (Alava and Guipuzcoa), the Oviedo province of Asturias, and Navarre. The best wines are those of the upper Ebro valley region known as La Rioja.

LA RIOJA. This is the name of a great stretch of the upper Ebro valley where Old Castile, Aragon and Navarre met. La Rioja occupies the whole of Logroño province, parts of Navarre, and of Alava and Burgos provinces. It takes its name from a small river, Rio Oja, which flows into the Ebro near Pamplona, in Navarre, and is divided into Alta and Baja Rioja, the Upper and Lower Rioja, with Haro and Logroño, the two most important townships and wine centres of the district on opposite banks of the Ebro.

The vineyards in La Rioja, mostly up the slopes of the clutter of hills along the valley of the Ebro, are one of the most attractive vinelands in the world.

The vineyards of La Rioja produce red and white table wines, and a very fair proportion of the great quantity of wine produced is of a very high standard of quality. Although in La Rioja there are a large number of villages and a few small towns, the wines of La Rioja are rarely sold under the name of their native vineyard or village. They are usually marketed under the name of the person, or the firm, who first purchased the grapes or wines at the time of the vintage, then cared for or nursed the new wine through its teething troubles, and eventually blended it, (if it seemed best to do so) with other wines of the same or nearby vineyards and of either the same or other vintages. Some purchasers will then wait until it is time to bottle it in the best possible manner and offer it for sale bearing on the label either his own name, or that of his firm, brand or cooperative society, as the case may happen to be. It means that if you want to have the best Rioja wines, what matters most is the name of the best people such as Bodega Berberane, Ollauri; Bodega Bilbainas, Haro; Bodega Franco-Espagnola, Logroño; Martinez Lacuesta Hermanos, Haro; Bodega Montecillo, Fuenmayor; Bodegas Marques de Murrieta, Logroño; Bodegas Palacio, Laguardia; Federico Paternino, Haro; Bodega Ramon Bilbao, Haro; La Rioja Alta S.A., Haro; Bodegas Riojanas, Cenicero; Bodega Rioja Santiago, Haro; Vinos de los Herederos del Marques de Riscal, Elciego; Vinicola del Norte de Espana, Haro; and others, of course.

Many of the wines of La Rioja bear a vintage date, but it seldom happens to be the year of the vintage of the wine in the bottle; it is there just by way of dressing up the label. There is no intention to deceive on the part of the wine-shipper who knows that in Spain, hardly anyone attaches any importance to a vintage date.

Mediterranean Provinces

This group is made up of four provinces of Catalonia (Gerona, Lerida, Barcelona and Tarragona), the three Levante provinces (Castellón de la Plana, Valencia and Alicante) and no fewer than eight provinces of Andalusia (Almeria, Cádiz, Córdoba, Granada, Huelva, Jáen, Málaga and Seville). Of course, the vineyards of Jerez and the wine to which they give the name of sherry is far and away the most remarkable and famous wine of this area.

Sherry is a fortified white wine made from high quality white grapes, mostly Palominos, in the vineyards of Andalusia, near the old city of Jerez de la Frontera, roughly halfway between the rivers Guadalquivir and the Guadalete.

There were grapes grown and wines made in many parts of Andalusia long before its conquest by the Moors and again immediately after they were finally chased out of the country. This wine was not sherry as we know it; it did not become a fortified wine until some two hundred years ago. It was only in comparatively recent times, less than one hundred years ago, that the popular anglicized form of the name Jerez, i.e. sherry, became the exclusive right of the fortified white wines of Jerez vineyards. The name also had been used formerly for similar wines made in a similar manner and from the same grapes in other parts of Andalusia, more particularly in the province of Córdoba, from the vineyards of Montilla and Moriles. Had it not been so, the people of Jerez would not have given to one of their own wines the name of Amontillado.

Sherry is Spain's greatest wine. Like champagne and burgundy, port and madeira, hock and moselle, it has suffered from that most objectionable form of flattery called imitation and, as a matter of fact, more than any other wine.

Central Provinces

This group is much larger than the other two. It is made up of the vineyards of Castile, Madrid, Toledo, Ciudad Real, Cuenca and Guadalajara; the three provinces of Aragon (Huesca, Teruel and Zaragoza), and the three provinces of León (León, Salamanca and Zamora). The best and better known wines of the area are the Valdepeñas table wines.

VALDEPEÑAS. This so-called 'vale of stones' is much more like the Aude or Hersault plains than like the all-stone top-soil of Châteauneuf-du-Pape. The vineyards are in the province of Ciudad Real, part of what used once to be New Castile. There is a huge acreage of vineyards on poor land which mostly produce poor wines. All the wines of Valdepeñas, however, are by no means poor. The great asset of the Valdepeñas red wines is that, like beaujolais, they are quite acceptable at a very early age, from six to eighteen months old. They are light, well balanced (despite their lack of acidity) and really nice wines, although they never pretend to be in the same class as the wines of La Rioja. They are, naturally, much cheaper and very good value but unfortunately do not age well. Strange as it may seem, the white wines of Valdepeñas are fuller, fatter and at their best when very young.

There are, of course, a great many more wines made in Spain—some light, dry table wines, many more sweet, dessert wines from Málaga, Alicante and Valencia; others stouter and of a higher alcoholic strength from Tarragona and Priorato; and also sparkling wines, the demand for which, as in many other countries, has grown considerably and has created an adequate supply, mostly from the vineyards of Catalonia.

There are table wines made in the Balearic Islands, chiefly Majorca, but they have not so far attracted the attention of wine lovers outside their native islands. The same may rightly be said of the table and dessert wines which are made in the Canary Islands.

Other Vinelands
of the World

ARGENTINA

The first vine stocks were introduced to Argentina by Spanish settlers in 1556. Since that time new vines representing the best stocks of France, Italy, Germany and Spain have been planted in the numerous vineyards of the country where they have adapted quite easily.

Because of Argentina's geographical structure—the country extends some 2,300 miles from north to south—a variety of different types of soil and climate make themselves available. It is for this reason that certain regions of the country are ideally suited for producing a variety of wines, both table and fine, which are noted for their colour and alcoholic content.

Viticulture is most important in the western region of the country, a long strip of land at the base of the Andes dominated by Mt Aconcagua, the highest mountain on the American continent (22,834 feet above sea level). The most important wine-producing area is the province of Mendoza located in the central part of this area, followed by its neighbour San Juan, then by Neuquen and Rio Negro in the south and La Rioja, Catamarca and Salta in the north.

The vineyards of Argentina cover nearly 750,000 acres, which places it ninth among world producers of grapes. However, the enormous quantity of wine made from this crop places the country third—after Italy and France—of the top wine-producing countries. The variety of vines used to make the red, white and rosé wines is considerable, but the following are the main stocks used: red, Cabernet, Malbeck, Barbera, Lembrusco, Pinot Negro, Merlot; rosé, Criolla (the Mission grape in the United States) grande, Criolla Chica, San Gioveto Groso; white, Pedro Ximenez, Moscatel Blanco de Alejandria, Pinot Bianco, Sauvignon, Riesling.

A great variety of wines are produced in Argentina including fine table wines, liquor wines, vermouth, concentrated must, sherry-types and a base for champagne (the South American variety). All production is under the supervision of the *Instituto Nacional de Vitivinicultura*, a government agency responsible for the technical control as well as the promotion of wine production. The agency supervises all export and presents the purchaser with an 'analytical protocol' which describes the characteristics—physical, chemical and biological—of the wine. It is a guarantee of quality.

Because of its large production of various types of wine, its storage capacity and standing stock, Argentina has become an international supplier of wines. In general, a great deal of quite decent table wine is being sold in bulk and bottled in the purchaser's home country, or being used for blending with home-grown products. A rather unusual industry is the selling of concentrated must to be used as a base for wines in countries with little or no production of their own: Great Britain is a prime example. The production of this must centres in San Juan where the variety of grape grown is particularly suited to its task.

Argentina also produces its own champagne. Following the traditional processes of 'Champenoise' and 'Chaussepied' the country produces this wine in three varieties: Brut, Demi-Sec and Doux. It goes one step further in offering the customer a choice by manufacturing a rosé, or pink champagne. The grapes for these unique wines are grown in cold areas of the country and harvested before full ripeness. Different vintage musts are used and skilfully blended before fermentation in the bottle takes place at a permanent temperature of about 12°C. (54°F.) much like that of the cellars in France.

Argentinian viticulture is one of the fastest growing in the world today. It is able to produce cheaply, and in vast quantities, a variety of products (including table grapes) that are becoming more and more in demand. Although it does produce some very good vintage wines, its reputation and, probably, its future lies with the inexpensive, good quality table wines.

AUSTRALIA

The history of wine growing in Australia dates from the founding of its first European settlement in 1788. The vine is not indigenous to the country and it was a captain in the Royal Navy, Arthur Phillip, who planted the first vines taken from South African stock, near Sydney Harbour. Unfortunately, the area he chose for planting had soil which was too rich and humidity too great; this attempt was unsuccessful. Although Phillip, later Governor of the colony, kept trying to plant vines successfully, it was not until approximately fifty years later that Australian viticulture became firmly established through the efforts of a young Scot named James Busby who took some 20,000 vine cuttings to Australia from the wine-producing countries of Europe.

The wine industry eventually spread from the hinterland of Sydney and the Hunter River valley further north to the states of Victoria and South Australia. Their first vineyards were begun in the newly cleared bushlands of some of the suburbs of the capital cities. However, the industry quickly spread as the more adventurous settlers quickly founded other vine-growing ventures in favoured valleys or plateau lands, up to one hundred miles from the cities of the south.

Today in the fast-growing modern industrial capitals the suburban vineyards have long since gone, except for a few hardy last-ditch or last hillslope survivals in Adelaide. The outlying strongholds of the industry such as the Barossa Valley and Southern Vales (South Australia), Rutherglen, Tahbilk and Great Western (Victoria) and the Swan Valley (Western Australia) are in a flourishing state. The great irrigation settlements of the river Murray, Australia's greatest river, and its tributary the Murrumbidgee, have become big suppliers of dry and sweet sherry-type wines, grape spirit and fine brandies, and through improved techniques are contributing also to table wine supplies.

Australian wine-producing areas have a warmer, drier atmosphere than their European counterparts, which helps to ensure uniform ripening and a minimum of disease. The best table wine—delicate, dry whites and the lighter dry reds—come mostly from the higher, cooler regions. Heavier wines come largely, though by no means exclusively, from the warmest regions. Vintage is from the middle of February to late April, and because of the mild climate the wines mature fairly quickly.

Australian wines may be blended or unblended. There are estate wines made from the grapes of a single vineyard or area; other wines are blended from various sources to form a standard which the makers have found to have a

popular appeal. The large makers draw grapes not only from their own vineyards but from grape-growers both near and far. Moreover, there is a well-
developed system of interchange of wines between districts and over State
borders.

Australian grapes are of the species *Vitis vinifera*. For the dry red wines,
growing nation offers a greater profusion than Australia in the variety of wines
it produces. Instead of each region being limited to one type of wine, as in
Europe, the main *vignerons* make all types. The typical Australian makers'
range includes all types of dessert wines, table wines and sparkling wines, as
well as brandy. The dessert wine range is a wide one and includes sherry-types,
port-types, muscats and others. Table wines include riesling, moselle, hock,
chablis and sauternes among the whites, bordeaux, burgundy and rosé types
among the reds.

Australian grapes are of the species *Vitis Vinifera*. For the dry red wines,
the variety used principally is Shiraz or Hermitage (having a kinship with the
Syrah known elsewhere), and the classic Cabernet Sauvignon either as an
admixture or in some cases on its own as a noble 'straight' unblended wine.
There are also comparatively small acreages of Pinot Noir, Mataro and Malbec
grapes.

The Grenache grape familiar in Spain and the south of France became a very
widely grown variety in Australia because of the earlier great popularity of
sweet red (port-type) wines—a popularity which has since somewhat dimin-
ished, leaving Grenache to be used more for blending or for rosé wines.

For the dry white wines the Riesling and Semillon grapes are used and for
the sherry-types Pedro Ximenez and Palomino. There are smaller acreages of
many other varieties. Pearl wines have had a tremendous vogue in Australia in
the present day and generation. In the past decade there has also been a great
upsurge in popularity of table wines and this has recently led to new interest
in special varieties such as Gewürztraminer, Sylvaner and Gamay-beaujolais.

Wine production is steadily increasing and about half of a year's output is
ultimately marketed as 'beverage' wine and the remainder is made into brandy.
The industry's greatest economic importance is in South Australia, where
seventy per cent of the production is located.

AUSTRIA

The vineyards of Austria are very unevenly distributed, with more than half of
them in Lower Austria. The remainder are divided between Burgenland (with
the majority), Styria and the area near Vienna. In the Austrian Tyrol and
Vorarlberg, there are patches of grapes here and there but no vineyards of
commercial importance.

LOWER AUSTRIA. Here the better red table wines are those of Voslau, and the
better white ones those of Krems and Wachau. At Dürnstein, on the Danube
in the Wachau area, the local Wine-Growers Co-operative Association make
and market some very good wines. There are also some very fair table wines of
Lower Austria made from grapes grown in or near Baden, Donauland,
Langenlois and Weinviertel.

BURGENLAND. The vineyards of Rust and near Lake Neusiedl's south shore
are responsible for the best wines, but there are other important vineyards at

Eisenberg and Sepp Höld St Georgen which produce some very fair and, in good years, fine table wines.

STYRIA. The best vineyards are in the southern part of the land but there are none of great size. In both the eastern and western areas vineyards are few, but some of them produce very fair wines.

VIENNA. In the neighbourhood of this city there are very few vineyards and the wines which they produce, mostly white table wines, are always in great demand by the Viennese as well as visitors to the capital. The more popular are the Gumpoldkirchners and the Grinzingers usually drunk when still very young and inexpensive. There are, of course, better and more expensive table wines such as Gumpoldkirchner Blaustinger and Loibner Burgstaller from Danube-side vineyards which is sold in *Bocksbeutel*.

The grapes mostly grown in Austria are the Veltliner, Welsch Riesling, Rhine Riesling, Müller-Thurgau, Sylvaner, Gewürztraminer and Muscat-Ottonel for the white wines; and Burgunder and Rotgipfler for the reds.

BULGARIA

The climate of Bulgaria and the nature of the soil are so suitable for viticulture that, in the days before World War II, there were small vineyards as part of almost every farm. Today, however, the 'little man' has little control, and the state has laid out large vineyards in suitable locations, which can be worked more economically with modern mechanical equipment. Modern wineries have also been built and equipped so that they can deal efficiently with the grapes gathered at each year's vintage. Different wines are thus made to meet the demand for red and white, dry and sweet, still and sparkling wines, in sufficient quantities and of suitable quality to meet both home and export demand.

CHILE

Parts of nearly two-thirds of Chile's 3,000 mile length are used for the production of wine. Because of this vast expanse, running north to south, the weather is as varied as the many types of wine it helps produce. The north of the country is arid with little or no rain and produces a very poor quality wine from the local grape. The southern part of the country is the opposite extreme and the rainfall keeps the ground wet most of the year; it too produces a very poor wine. However, the middle region, near Santiago, has a moderate and varied climate which suits the demands of viticulture.

The vines are planted and the wines bottled with the same care as those of Bordeaux. The Cabernet, Sauvignon and Semillon vines are treated with the same respect as their French relatives and bottled in the traditional manner: two years in cask, a following five or six in the bottle to produce a fine quality wine. All wines produced tend to have a somewhat higher alcoholic content and more astringency than might be wished, but given the remarkably low prices and the somewhat erratic weather conditions under which they are produced, these are perfectly acceptable and, once got used to, quite delightful.

Chile is establishing itself among the leaders of those smaller countries which produce large quantities of good, sometimes fine, wine that are filling the large demand on the world market for low-priced, high-quality products.

CYPRUS

The vineyards of Cyprus are mostly in the Limassol district and the Paphos area. A small fraction of the vineyards grow table grapes and the rest grapes from which table and dessert wines are made as well as brandy and sterilized grape juice (sold as the basis of British wines and for other purposes) and thousands of tons of dried grapes or raisins of good quality suitable for export.

The wines of Cyprus which are best known overseas are the fortified wines, the port-type known as Commanderia and sherry-type wines for which there is some demand in Great Britain. The making of fortified wines, brandy, vermouth and concentrated grape juice in Cyprus is of recent date, but there were vineyards in Cyprus and wine made before the birth of Christ and even before the birth of the Roman Empire.

CZECHOSLOVAKIA

The vineyards of Czechoslovakia produce mainly white table wines. The vineyards are in various districts and are cultivated by small farmers. At vintage time they deliver the grapes to local co-operative wineries where the wine is made and stored until ready for drinking.

GREECE

Greece is no longer the chief wine-producing land in Europe, as it was once upon a time, but grapes have been cultivated and wine has been made in the islands and the mainland of Greece much longer than anywhere else in Europe. Roughly 60% of the country's wine production is white wine and 40% red or rosé.

The white wines are of four types:

ATTICA, a hot and dry region, the soil of which is very poor, hence well suited to produce quality wines. The Saviatano grape is mostly grown in Attica and gives beautiful golden wines of fairly high alcoholic strength and rather low acidity content. Their bouquet and flavour differ according to the location of different vineyards but they are on the whole rather subdued and attractive.

CHALKIS, an official AC to which no wine is entitled unless made from grapes from the vineyards to the south-east of Chalkis, the chief city of the island of Euboea. Chalkis wine is made from Savatiano and Rhoditi white grapes. Its bouquet is more developed than that of the Attica wines and its flavour is also quite distinct but just as pleasant.

MANTENEIA vineyards are in the centre of the Peloponnisos, at an altitude of nearly 2,000 feet above sea level. Grapes now grow among the ruins of what was once Manteneia; grapes of different varieties of Moschofilero and Asproudes vines, which give well-balanced table wines of fine colour and agreeable flavour as well as a modest bouquet different from the flavour and bouquet of all other Greek wines.

RETSINA is the most typically Greek white wine. Its golden colour pleases the eye, but its curious smell and taste require some time and practice to be appreciated by any wine drinker accustomed to chablis or hock. Retsina is made of Savatiano white grapes with pine resin added.

The red table wines of Greece are made mostly from vineyards of the following areas:

RHODES. The best red wine of the island is called Chevalier; it is a well-balanced wine made of Amorgiano red grapes, and possesses not only fine colour and plenty of body but also breed.

PATRAS. Santa Laura and Castel Danielis are the names of two red table wines of good quality which are made from vineyards along the rugged buttresses of the Panachikon Mountains, near Patras. They are made from Mavroudia grapes and have a highly-scented bouquet as well as a rather big body, and a charm all their own.

CRETE. The best red table wine of this great island is made from Romeikon grapes and called Romeikon of Fissamos, a vineyard of Canea. There are other red table wines of Crete, darker and stouter, the best of which are entitled to the *AC Archanes*.

MOUNT VELIA. The vineyards which grace the lower slopes of Mount Velia, $62\frac{1}{2}$ miles north-west of Salonika, produce a fair to fine red table wine with the *AC Naoussa*; it is made from the Popolka red grape, which is not grown anywhere else.

Some fine dessert wines are made in Greece; the more popular follow:

MAVRODAPHNE. This is the name of a white grape and of the dessert wine made from it, both as Mavrodaphne and Mavrodaphne Imperial. The number of vineyards in which Mavrodaphne grapes can be and are grown with success is limited by the two important factors of soil and climate. Most of the Mavrodaphne grapes are grown south of Patras and they produce fine wines which must be given time to age in bottle, if they are to show how good they can be.

RION MUSCAT. This is an *AC* to which no wine is entitled other than the white dessert wine made from Muscat Blanc grapes of the Rion vineyards north-east of Patras.

SAMOS. For centuries past this island has been famous for the excellence of its sweet white wines which are made from Muscat Blanc grapes, the only white grape grown in Samos. The clay-silica-lime of its soil has much to do with the excellence of the island's famous muscat dessert wines.

HUNGARY

Hungary is one of the more important wine-producing countries of Europe, not only on account of the quantity and quality of the table wines which its vineyards produce, but also because it has given to the world one of the most remarkable of all dessert wines—Tokay (Tokaj).

The wine production in the Tokay area is white wine of which about 4% is Szamorodni, a fine white table wine, which may be as dry as a dry graves or as sweet as a fine sauternes; 50% Tokay Aszu, or Tokay Ausbruch, the very fine white dessert wine made from overripe white grapes like the Trockenbeeren-auslese Hocks; and some 5% of the year's yield Tokay Essenz, one of the great wines of the world. It is a freak wine, made differently from any other wine and endowed with a longer life than all other wines. It is made from the overripe grapes from a few privileged vineyards of the Tokaji Hegyalgya area and only in the best vintage years. The remainder of the Hungarian wines are the white *ordinaires* and a lesser amount of red table wines.

There are many vineyards and a great deal of wine made in many other regions of Hungary, chiefly by Lake Balaton, in the Villany-Pécs area and elsewhere.

LAKE BALATON. These vineyards produce much table wine which is very fair and considered very fine locally; the white wine known as Badacsonyi Keknelu is a dry, well-balanced table wine, while Badacsonyi Szurke-Baratis is a more luscious golden dessert wine. There is also a Badacsonyi Burgunder, a fair enough red table wine made from Burgunder grapes, a cousin of the Pinot Noir.

EGER. The Eger region, about 120 miles north-west of Budapest, produces more and better table wines than any of the other regions of the country. Its most popular red table wine, not only at home but overseas, is Egri Bikaver, which means Bull's Blood, a stout, dark red wine by no means rough or common.

VILLANY-PÉCS. The vineyards at Vollany, in the Pécs county in the extreme south-west corner of Hungary, produce some very pleasant table wines, both red and white. The red is bottled in bordeaux-shaped bottles and the white in green moselle-shaped bottles. Besides these 'best seller' wines, there are many other table, dessert and sparkling wines made in Hungary, and a number of them are exported.

LUXEMBOURG

The vineyards of Luxembourg grace many of the hills along some twenty-five miles of the meandering course of the Moselle from its entry into the country from Lorraine, until it leaves it at Wasserbillig. The better vineyards of Luxembourg lie on the south, east, or south-east face of the hills in terraces, at altitudes between 450 and 750 feet above sea level. All the vineyards of Luxembourg are in the two cantons of Remich and Wormeldingen. The vineyards of Luxembourg are all planted with good quality white grapes.

For quite a number of people in Luxembourg, to grow grapes is either a family tradition or merely a hobby, but by no means a commercial proposition. The production of wine in Luxembourg, however, is steadily increasing, in spite of the perforcedly limited acreage of the vineyards, thanks to better methods of cultivation and to a greater use of fertilizers. The average annual production is white table wines, but the light, dry white wines of the country are particularly well suited for the making of sparkling wines, which is evidenced by the fact that their production has risen rapidly and steadily over the last thirty years. A high proportion of all wines is exported, mostly to Belgium.

NORTH AFRICA

Until 1962 when Algeria gained its independence from France, North Africa was mainly a supplier of rough wine used for blending with the weak wines of some of the provinces of its colonial ruler. What was not exported, the wines of fair to good quality, was consumed mainly by the resident Europeans—the Muslim religion prohibits alcoholic consumption. At the time, as now, Algeria was North Africa's largest wine-producer and there political upheaval meant change for the rest of the wine-growing areas as well.

After 1962, the wines used for blending found new markets away from France; Germany, Russia and several of the emergent African nations were very willing to buy from Algeria. However, rather than flood the market with vast quantities of *vin ordinaire*, much of the viticulture has now been turned over to production of quality wines—wines which can stand the test of world distribution. Although production of the modest wines which still find a wide local market continues, partially through tourism, the scale is diminishing in favour of those wines which may gain an international reputation.

Algeria's vineyards are now centred around the province of Oran where approximately three-quarters of its potent, dark, non-acidic blending wine is produced. Until its independence, there were also twelve hills that carried the French rank *Vin délimités de Qualité Supérieure*.

Tunisian wines were known in antiquity and the first handbook of wine-growing and vine care was written before the fifth century AD by an inhabitant of Carthage. Although the table wines of Tunisia are as good as those of Algeria, the market for them is shrinking and fewer acres each year are being cultivated for wine production.

Moroccan wine-producing history does not begin until after World War II. The main area of vinelands is east of Rabat. This area produces the best wines of Morocco, though they are by no means of any special quality.

RUMANIA

Rumania is one of the more important wine-producing countries of Europe. The vineyards of Rumania occupy a fraction of the agricultural lands in the country, which is mostly rocky or otherwise poor soil unfit for any other culture. Vineyards are found in many parts of the country; on mountain slopes of the Carpathians, in Dobroudja, Banat, Transylvania, Walachia and Moldavia. Some 90% of Rumanian vineyards are the property of the State or of Farmers Co-operative Societies, but there are still many small farmers who have a few vines that they can call their own, and who make a little wine for themselves. This wine never reaches any market.

The total production of the vineyards of Rumania is red and white table wines mostly, as well as some remarkably fine sweet white muscat dessert wines and some sparkling wines. The more ordinary dry white wines are made from the vineyards of Odobesti, Pancio and Husi from indigenous species of white grapes; better white table wines are made from the vineyards of Iassy, Dealul Bujor-Prut, Cotesti and Dealul Mare-Peteasca Alba. The best of all the white table wines, really fine wines, come from the vineyards of Transylvania, Alba Iulia, Tirnave, Aiud and Simleul Silvaniei, from some of the best indigenous white grapes as well as from some Riesling, Sylvaner, Chardonnay, Traminer and other imported species. As regards the red table wines, most of the better ones come from the vineyards of Nicoresti, Halinga, Corcova and Segarcea, in Oltenia; Minis, in the Banat; and Dealul Mare, in the Ploesti area, from Cabernet, Merlot and Pinot Noir grapes, as well as indigenous Rumanian grapes.

The white dessert wines of Rumania are of quite outstanding quality. They are made from a variety of white Muscat known as Muscat Ottavel at Cotnari, in the north of Moldavia; Tirnave, in central Transylvania; Murfatlar, in Dobroudja, near the Black Sea, on soil rich in lime; Pietroasa, Ploesti, Alba Iulia, Iassy and elsewhere. The sparkling wine industry has also made rapid progress in Rumania during the last few years.

SOUTH AFRICA

The vineyards of South Africa are naturally divided into two areas, each with a different climate. The western regions near the Cape are provided with a plentiful annual rainfall and need no irrigation. The regions beyond the mountains, however, receive only a slight amount of rain and must be irrigated. The quality of the wines produced here, in the Little Karroo, is not equal to that of the Cape and are therefore mainly consumed at home.

The best-known area of South African wine production is the Constantia vineyards which, in the nineteenth century, produced a sweet wine that rivalled the classics: Yquem, Tokay and madeira. Unfortunately, there is very little wine produced in this area today, and none of it is sweet. Today the regions of Worcester, Robertson, Malmesbury, Stellenbosch and Paarl are the major producers.

In recent years, demand for South African fortified wines has been so great that it could not be met. The KWV, the official national wine co-operative of South Africa, increased its strict quotas in light of the export demand and allowed more of these types of wine to be produced. Now, as demand continues, the good quality sherry-type wines and others are always available and will be so in the future. The interest in fortified wines is indicated by the fact that South Africa drinks more brandy than any country in the world.

Although South Africans tend to be spirit-drinking people, there need be no fear that the wines of their country will be overlooked. The industry is thriving, and is constantly expanding to meet the ever-increasing demands of other countries, particularly Britain, for their wines.

SWITZERLAND

Grapes are grown and wine is made in twenty of the twenty-nine cantons of Switzerland, but three-quarters of the production of all Swiss vineyards and the best wine comes from the four cantons of Valais, Vaud, Geneva and Neuchâtel, officially known as Suisse Romande. The Tessin or Ticino canton, known as Suisse Italienne, produces comparatively little wine, mostly red, and the remainder of the cantons, officially known as Suisse Orientale, also produce more red wine than white.

The red wines of Switzerland are mostly *ordinaires* table wines, although the best of them rise to the standard of fair quality wines. Not so, however, with the white wines. Most of these are of very fair quality and many are of from fine to very fine quality. They are made from the same species of white grapes which produce the best white wines of France and Germany, but some of them are given other names in Switzerland: thus the white grape known as Chasselas in France, and Gutedal in Germany, is called Fendant Vert in the western cantons and Markgräfler in the eastern cantons of Switzerland.

VAUD or WAADT. Lausanne lies in this canton, which has the finest stretch of vineyards in Switzerland: the Lavaux semi-circle of hills which face the north-east end of Lake Geneva, stretching some 10 miles from Lausanne to Montreux. The vineyards are terraced and are protected behind by the formidable wall of the Bernese Alps. Some of the better and better-known white wines of Lavaux are the wines of Dezaley and the Johannisberg of Cully, Johannisberg meaning the German Riesling grape from which the wine is made.

VALAIS or WALLIS. The Valais is probably the most perpendicular stretch of vineyards anywhere. It rises from Lake Geneva and the Chablais to the Visp valley, practically where the Rhône begins, and where the vineyards are the highest in Europe, at over 3,600 feet above sea level. Valais wines are more characteristically Swiss than those of Lavaux, but no better. The best known Valais wines are those of Sion, the red is known as Dole de Sion and the white as Fendant de Sion.

NEUCHÂTEL. The Neuchâtel vineyards produce a great deal of nice, light, white wines which may not be the peers of the best white wines of Vaud and Valais, though they are fair to fine. There are, however, a few estate wines of Neuchâtel which are of distinctly higher quality than the rest, such as Domaine de Champreveyres's white wine and the red Cortaillod, a Pinot Noir Beaunois red table wine, probably the best Swiss red wine.

GENEVA. The vineyards of Geneva are distributed in two groups, both of them facing Lake Geneva, from Geneva itself almost as far as Lausanne. The first group is called La Petite Côte, from Coppet to Nyon, and the next is known as either La Côte, La Bonne Côte or La Grande Côte, from Bergoins and Luins eastwards almost as far as Ouchy and Lausanne. The vineyards of La Côte produce more and better white table wines than the vineyards nearer Geneva, but they are not up to the standard of the better wines of Vaud, Valais and Neuchâtel. Those wines can and do compete in the markets of the world.

CHABLAIS. This is really part of the Vaud canton, but its vineyards produce a white wine with a distinctive charm; they extend from Villeneuve, at the eastern end of Lake Geneva, up the Rhône valley to the Valais. Its best wine is Yvorne.

TURKEY

Turkey has the distinction of having planted the first vineyards somewhere between 8000 and 6000 BC, although rival claims have been advanced for Transcaucasia, where the wild grape was indigenous and wine could have been made. However, the early Neolithic tribes of the Caucasus were primitive barbarians, and it is highly unlikely that they would be capable of such an accomplishment.

On the other hand, the peoples of Mesopotamia, settled on the plains of the Tigris and Euphrates where the wild vine was not indigenous, were civilized wine-drinkers by 4000 BC. It seems therefore that the art of viticulture must have been learned from some earlier peoples inhabiting a country where the vine did grow wild. Such conditions exist in the Armenian mountains to the north, where these two rivers of the plains have their sources. Here the soil would have been sufficiently fertile for a nomadic tribe to settle. Each year the flood waters in spring would irrigate the land sufficiently for the growing of wheat and other crops of subsistence; the vine, less exacting in its natural needs, would have flourished in the combination of summer heat and winter rain. Since these earliest times Turkey has become the fifth largest country in the world in area of grape cultivation, but due to primitive methods only twenty-fourth in grape production. Only 3% of the grapes are used for wine. The low consumption is due to Koranic strictures against wine-drinking. The Koran declares in no uncertain terms that wine and lots 'are an abomination of Satan. Therefore avoid them that ye may prosper . . .'

The Christians resident in Turkey during the Ottoman Empire were great wine producers, mostly for export. In the nineteenth century production reached 79,200,000 gallons annually; but after the empire collapsed and Kemal Atatürk, the founder of modern Turkey, instituted large-scale population exchanges in the 1920s, the wine industry almost disappeared. In 1927, production was only 440,000 gallons.

Atatürk, however, was not bound by the Koran and re-introduced wine-making as part of his vast campaign to reform and westernize Turkey. Today production in Turkey is about 10,000,000 gallons annually. Most of it is red and white dry wine, but dessert wines, fortified wines and artificially carbonated wines are also produced in small quantities.

While quantity is held down by demand, quality is held down by primitive viticulture, poor production methods and improper storage; yet the quality is potentially very high and in some cases that potential has been reached.

Export is mainly carried on by the State Monopolies, but of the fine private producers some have started exporting bottled wine to England.

Doluca of Istanbul is the only Turkish wine-maker which produces its own grapes. It is said that some of the Doluca wine might be classed with the top wines of the world. Doluca's owner, Nihat Kutman, raises his own grapes on a small hill at Murefte in Thrace. The other wine-makers buy from farmers and thus their coupage varies from batch to batch and year to year.

Other names worth mentioning in Turkish wine are the red Trakya, made by the state; Kazim Akmanlar, an Ankara wine-maker who turns out a delicious dry white wine with the native grapes of central Anatolia and a new red wine with great potential called Bortacina, made with grapes from the Marmara island of Avsa; Lucien Fettu, who turns out a creditable red wine at a low price in Istanbul; and the Atatürk experimental farm in Ankara which makes a fine, full red wine at five Turkish lira a bottle (twenty new pence or forty-eight cents) surely one of the finest wine bargains in the world. In using adjectives I used 'fine' to mean that this wine, in my opinion would stand up with any wine in the world barring the very top château-bottled wines of France and the few other wines of real distinction.

Districts and Wines

Turkish wines are usually named from the places where they are made, the grape is sometimes given as well on the label.

THRACE. In European Turkey. A large percentage of Turkish wine is made here from imported French Semillon and Cinsault grapes and the local Papazkarasi variety, a fuller, grape with more tannin. The State Monopolies make their Trakya wine here, red and white. The Doluca wines are made from grapes grown at Murefte: Semillon (white), Cinsault and Papazkarasi (red) and a Riesling of the Johannisberger variety.

ANKARA. Good local grape varieties Hasandede (white) and Kalecik (red) are threatened by *phylloxera*. Turkey's largest private wine-maker, Zeki Aral, makes a decent red Papazkarasi wine in Ankara. Kazim Akmanlar makes Kulup, a good white and rosé, along with Bortacina, a young fruity red with grapes from Avsa Island in the Marmara Sea. Kavaklidere wines turn out a quality red, Yakut, and white Cankaya, and rosé, Lal, from grapes purchased in east Turkey, Thrace and Izmir.

IZMIR. (Smyrna) A good Muscat grape is grown here and is used for dessert wine.

ELÂZĬG. East Turkey. The State Monopolies produce their best-selling Buzbag wine here, a hefty red made from the local Okusgozu (Ox-eye) grape.

GAZIANTEP. South-east Turkey. Home of another fine local grape variety, Sergikarasi.

TOKAT. East of Ankara. A grape called Narince is grown here and makes a good semi-dry wine. Best wines are the Monopolies' Narbag and Diren's Vadi.

THE UNION OF SOVIET SOCIALIST REPUBLICS

The amount of land under cultivation for wine production has more than doubled in the twenty years since 1950. This astounding increase is an indication of the ever-growing importance of viticulture to the Soviet states.

Wine production centres around the Black Sea; mainly the north, north-eastern and eastern areas extending from Moldavia, once part of Rumania, to the Armenia-Turkey border. Perhaps the most widely known areas are the Crimean peninsular and Georgia, both recognized from antiquity for the quality of their wines; a quality still unmatched by any other area even today.

The Soviet taste leans toward sweet wines and the industry is guided accordingly. There is, therefore, a rather indiscriminate use of the labels sherry, port, madeira and the like, although the wines of the areas would be able to stand up under their own names as modest to fair dessert-type wines. There is a growing production of sparkling wines, notably in the Rostov area, of which the sweet, red types are especially prized.

The types of grape employed in the making of the wine varies according to the area and a full range grape, wine and quality is therefore possible. As one travels the different vinelands one can sample Cabernet, Aligote, Chumai and Trifesti in the north, Muscat, Riesling, Krasnyi and Kamenj in the north-east and Ashtarak, Oshakan and Getashan in the east.

The wines of the Soviet countries, although they are hardly known outside their boundaries, will likely become more popular and attainable in the various countries of the world as their production continues to grow.

THE UNITED STATES

A large number of species of *Vitis* are native to the continental United States: *V. california*, *V. labrusca*, *V. riparia*, *V. rotundifolia*, *V. rupestris*, etc. More species of *Vitis* are native to this country than to any other.

The early colonists found the native grapes to be small, acid, low in sugar, and to have a different taste from the grapes they knew in Europe. Very soon they began importing cuttings and rooted vines of the European grape, *V. vinifera*, from Europe. For various reasons all these early attempts to grow *V. vinifera* varieties in the eastern regions failed.

It was not until late in the eighteenth century that a serious attempt was made to domesticate varieties of the native species. Probably some crossing of native species with introduced *V. vinifera* vines also inadvertently occurred. As a result of domestication and crossing many varieties were widely planted in the eastern United States in the nineteenth century.

The situation was different on the west coast. There a seedling of *V. vinifera* from Mexico was introduced soon after the first settlements were established in California proper in 1769. In the nineteenth century many direct importations of *V. vinifera* varieties were made from Europe into California. In contrast to the situation in the eastern United States these thrived in California. The extreme cold and the diseases and pests which prevented the development of *V. vinifera* in the eastern United States were absent in California.

Eighty-five percent of the vineyards in the U.S.A. are in California. The main vineyard areas outside California are in New York, Pennsylvania, Ohio and Michigan, with small plantings in a number of other states. Most of these eastern vineyards are planted with the Concord variety. A very small acreage (probably less than one thousand acres) of pure *V. vinifera* varieties or of direct producers (hybrids of *V. vinifera* and of some American species) are planted in the eastern United States. On the other hand, virtually all of the California plantings are in *V. vinifera* varieties. One feature of California viticulture is the large production of table grapes and of seedless grapes for raisins. California is one of the most important table grape areas of the world and also produces about 40% of the world's raisins. Because of the very favourable climatic and soil conditions and modern methods of training, production per acre is very high in California.

Eastern United States

In the eastern United States the early colonists tried to produce wines from native grapes. These attempts were not very successful because of the low sugar content of the grapes which resulted in a low alcoholic content causing the wine to spoil easily. Also the flavour of the wines was strange and came to be called 'foxy', although the reason for this is not known. Possibly as a consequence of this flavour much of the wine consumed in this country up to the nineteenth century was imported. Since this was expensive and spoilage during the long ocean voyages was frequent, the American drinker turned to distilled beverages (bourbon whiskey, peach brandy, and rum) or to fortified wines (madeira was the most popular wine in colonial America.) The original consumption of imported wines was also no doubt due to a certain nostalgia of the newly-arrived colonists for wine of their native country. A certain amount of this nostalgia still survives.

D

The eastern wine industry developed mainly as cottage or small home wineries. There were, however, a few large scale experiments. A number of wineries in the Finger Lake district of New York State were producing quantities of wine in the mid-nineteenth century. Nicolas Longworth developed a large sparkling wine business in Ohio (mainly from Catawba) and there was also much interest in wine making in Missouri and several important wineries developed there.

The Prohibition period from 1918 to 1932 had an especially baneful effect on grape growing and wine making in the eastern United States. The small winery disappeared for lack of customers and much of the vineyard area was removed. The millions of Europeans who migrated to the United States in the early part of the century preferred California wine from *V. vinifera*. During Prohibition many made their own wine from grapes shipped from California.

Following repeal of the Vorstead Act the Eastern industry was rapidly revived but flourished in only a few areas: primarily in New York, Ohio, and Michigan. However, many small wineries were developed in Maryland, Illinois, South Carolina, Arkansas, and other states. Today they mainly supply a local demand, with the exception of a few larger wineries.

Most of the wine produced there is table wine. It may be labelled after the variety from which it is made: Niagara, Delaware, etc., or it may carry a generic designation, such as burgundy, chablis, or claret. Nearly all of these wines have the easily recognizable foxy flavour previously mentioned. There is also an appreciable production of American vermouth in the eastern United States.

The most successful Eastern production has been of sparkling wines (about 50% of the total United States production). Precisely why the foxy flavour is not so objectionable in sparkling wine is not known—possibly it is due to the low temperature at which sparkling wines are served and to the blending of some California wine.

Eastern growers have also been very successful in producing very sweet wines by adding sugar—sometimes called kosher-type wines. The addition of sugar must be noted on the label even though United States regulations permit the addition of specified amounts of sugar and water at the time of the original fermentation providing the volume is not increased by more than 35% and the total acidity is not reduced below a certain level, which need not be stated on the label. This does not apply to California where local regulations prohibit the addition of sugar. These wines, too, have a distinct foxy flavour, although many contain an appreciable portion of California wine. Federal regulations require that at least 75% of the wine must be from a geographical area if the area is to be stated on the label.

Western United States

The Californian wine industry developed originally around the Catholic Missions which were established throughout the state between 1769 and 1823. At one Mission (and possibly at others) stills were used and brandy was produced. When the Missions were secularized by the Mexican government in 1834 the vineyards at most of these disappeared very quickly. This period left three legacies: first, they showed that grapes could be grown in many areas in California; second, they introduced the Mission grape (called Criolla in the Spanish-speaking countries) which, unfortunately, ripens very late, has a low acidity and a poor purple-red colour—it continued to dominate the Californian industry until the 1880s, although its origin has never been clearly established; the third and perhaps the most important legacy was the creation of a new type of wine—Angelica—which appears to have been an attempt to prevent spoilage of the Mission wine. The method developed was to add one part of brandy to three parts of grape juice.

Following the secularization of the Missions, private vineyards developed throughout California. At a very early date, certainly by the 1840s, new varieties of grapes were being imported from Europe. The discovery of gold in 1848 and the subsequent great influx of settlers stimulated the demand for many luxuries. This created an immediate and enormous market for grapes for eating and for wine and during this period grape growing expanded very rapidly. The financial rewards were great and the centre of grape growing and wine production shifted from southern to northern California during this time. Unfortunately, the Mission variety continued to dominate the industry with its poor quality wine.

The chief architect of the young industry was a Hungarian, Count (also Colonel) Agoston Haraszthy de Mokesa. He tried grape growing in Wisconsin in 1845, and went west in 1849, settled in San Diego and planted some grapes. In 1851 he imported cuttings from Europe. He moved later to San Francisco and in 1852 planted grapes just south of the city. In 1857 Haraszthy established the Buena Vista vineyard and cellars near Sonoma. This proved to be an excellent area for grape growing and still has vineyards and wineries. By 1858 he had imported 165 varieties from Europe. One of these was probably a Zinfandel. Its origin is unknown but it thrived in California and soon became the most popular red wine grape variety. When properly made it produces fruity wines with a berry-like flavour. Its main defect is its uneven ripening which, when not harvested at the proper time, may yield wines of excessive alcohol. Haraszthy's main contribution was the importation in 1862 of more than 200,000 grape cuttings, representing 1,400 varieties, from Europe. In 1863 he sold his Buena Vista vineyards which by this time were a major, if not the major, source of wines in the state.

Most of the wine-grape growing regions of the state were discovered and partly exploited by 1870 and wineries established in them by 1885. Wineries were established in the Napa Valley, in the Livermore and Santa Clara valleys, the Valley of the Moon and in the region of the Russian River. There was also a large German venture at Anaheim in southern California, which failed in 1888 due to a mysterious disease, later identified as a virus infection called Pierce's disease.

The early problems were the generally very warm climatic conditions, the adaptation of grape varieties to suitable areas, the nominal quality of many wines, over-production, high taxes and foreign competition.

The climate in almost all parts of the state proved to be extraordinarily favourable to the growth of grapes, in fact, too much so. Grapes thus ripen much earlier here than in most European countries. Also, the temperatures during the harvest period are much warmer than in Europe. The first wines made were thus often produced from overripe grapes and fermented under very warm conditions. The state has now been classified into five viticultural areas from I, the coolest, to V, the warmest.

The nomenclature of Californian wines has never been standardized and is still obviously in a state of change. The nomenclature is controlled by Federal and State regulations. These regulations provide for generic, semi-generic, and non-generic types; burgundy, claret, chablis, champagne, port, sherry, etc. are considered to be semi-generic names. Non-generic names of geographical origin include foreign appellations, such as Bordeaux, Médoc, St-Julien, Vouvray, California, New York State, Napa Valley etc. These geographical terms can only be used for wines from the stated region (or in the case of American regions, 75% from the stated area). Many of these terms have been used for many years. For example, the historian Carosso notes that even in the 1850s many Californian wines were sold as imitations of foreign types, i.e. under European appellations.

In the period immediately before Prohibition the American wine industry used many foreign appellations of a very local character: St-Julien, Margaux, and even Château Yquem (not d'Yquem). Use of such foreign specific appellations has now nearly disappeared except for Chablis but larger regional appellations such as burgundy, chianti, and Rhine are common. Just why the name 'chablis' should be so popular here is not known. Recently there has even been the illogical name 'pink chablis'.

The appellations to which the greatest exception is taken by European countries are American (or Californian) champagne, burgundy, chablis, Rhine, port and sherry. There is still a limited use of sauterne (not sauternes), marsala, malaga (for a sweet kosher-type wine), chianti and, rarely, madeira.

Two types of wines have been developed of which no criticism can be made. The most important are those named for the variety of grape: Cabernet Sauvignon, Chardonnay, Grenache, Pinot Noir, Sauvignon Blanc, Semillon, Sylvaner etc. American regulations provide that the varietal labelled wine must be produced from at least 51% of grapes of the variety listed on the label and possess the characteristic flavour of this variety.

Almost all of the finest Californian wines are now sold under their grape names. In fact, the practice has been so popular that an appreciable volume of wines are now being shipped from France with such labels! In some cases these imported wines cannot be found at their source with a varietal label and there is a strong suspicion that some of these have been especially printed for the American market. The other type of wine which is uniquely American are the flavoured wines with proprietary labels. American consumers go much more by the producer than the region or type. The producers can be loosely classified into those producing very large volumes of bottled standard wines and those producing lesser quantities. Large producers include: Acampo, Allied Growers, California Growers, California Wine Association, East-Side Winery, Franzia Brothers, Gallo Wine Company, Italian Swiss Colony, Roma Wine Company, Wine Growers Guild, etc. These may have a bottling plant in one region to which wines from several fermenting cellars are transported. The wines are blended, stabilized and are sold at highly competitive prices. Rarely do they sell wines with a varietal label.

In the middle range of quantity and of price are wineries such as Almadén, Brookside Vineyards, Christian Brothers, Ellena Brothers, Martini & Prati, Paul Masson Vineyards, Parducci Wine Cellars, Pirrone Wine Cellars, S. Sebastiani, etc. They sell both semi-generic and varietal wines.

Then there are a number of smaller wineries who produce wines at a somewhat higher price. Their best wines are their varietal types. Among these are: Beaulieu Vineyards, Beringer Bros., Buena Vista Vineyards, Concannon Vineyards, Ficklin Vineyards, Hallcrest Vineyard, Heitz Wine Cellars, Inglenook Vineyards, Kornell Cellars, Charles Krug, L. M. Martini, Novitiates of Los Gatos, Martin Ray, Stony Hill Vineyard, Weibel, Wente Bros., etc.

One unique feature of almost all Californian wineries is that they produce wine for sale only as bottled wines in sizes ranging from a half bottle to a gallon (U.S.). Only a few of these wines have the vintage stated on the label, although almost all of the finest wines do. There are two reasons for the relatively small use of vintage labels. The most important is that American regulations make it very difficult for a wine to qualify for a vintage label. The wine must not only be produced in a given geographical region but no admixture with wines of other vintages or regions is permitted. This is particularly difficult for the small winery with a limited amount of a vintage from a single geographical region. The other reason why many Californian vintners do not choose to use vintage labels is that there is relatively much less difference in quality from one year to another in California, except for the finest Californian wines, particularly the reds.

But no vintage chart, comparable to that of various European origins is, therefore, possible. The quality of even the low priced wines is surprisingly good. It is almost impossible to find a cloudy or out-of-condition Californian wine on the market. The quality of the higher priced wines is often exceptional, particularly the reds.

YUGOSLAVIA

Although the majority of Yugoslavian wines are little known outside the country, it is the tenth biggest wine producer in the world. The variety of different wines is great: fruity, light white wines which originate in the north, 'black' and very bitter reds from the south.

The names of the wines might not be familiar, but the grape-types tend to be widely known. The Riesling that is grown is Italian, not the German; there exists the Merlot, Tokay (another Italian grape) and the Cabernet; also the common variety of Malavasia, Pinot Blanc and Sauvignon. The strange names on the label, Krk, Grk, often disguise wines made from vines common the world over.

The wine-producing regions are Slovenia and Croatia in the north, which produce the best wines of Yugoslavia; the coastal areas, particularly around Dubrovnik, whose wine quality can never be safely categorized; and the areas of the east and inland plains, whose wines are virtually unknown.

It is because Yugoslavia's methods of production and attitude toward viticulture still belong to the beginning of this century that the majority of its wines will probably continue to be enjoyed locally and never savoured by a large number of people throughout the world, despite the enormous production.

GAZETTEER OF WINES

Notes on the Gazetteer entries

Each geographical entry in the Gazetteer is keyed to one of the maps and either gives an exact location i.e. a name which appears on a map, or a location with reference to a name which appears on a map e.g. north-east of Bordeaux. However, the text not only lists geographical locations, but also in many cases gives the names of wines that are common in any one area or country. Many different wine types and terms will also be found, e.g. *vin cotto*, when they are indigenous to an area and will help to present a fuller picture of the local wine production. It is hoped that these additional entries will complete the detailed survey of world viticulture that the Gazetteer presents.

All mileage given in the entries is approximate and should serve mainly to show relative distances on any one map. Only those distances above fifteen miles from a particular map reference are indicated. The names on the maps give the location of the better-known vineyards and towns which the visitor is likely to encounter while travelling through the various wine-producing areas. In some cases countries like Japan which produce small quantities of wine, or wine that is mostly drunk locally, have no individual map but are to be found on the world map, or a map encompassing a much larger area.

The German entries give only the English name for the wine-producing areas where there is a difference between English and German usage. The German equivalents are as follows: Rhinehessia – *Rheinhesse* or *Rheinhessen*; Rhinegau – *Rheingau*; Middle Rhine – *Mittelrhein*; Moselle – *Mosel*; Palatinate – *Rheinpfalz*; Franconia – *Franken*; Upper, Middle and Lower Haardt – *Überhaardt, Mittelhaardt* and *Unterhaardt*.

The names 'claret' and 'sauternes', although perfectly acceptable alternatives to red and white bordeaux, have not been included in order to link the wines directly to their places of origin.

Aargau. (31) Swiss canton; its vineyards produce only plain beverage wines. Switzerland.

Abanilla. (29) A little-known locality of Murcia; approx. ninety miles south-east of La Roda. Its vineyards produce a very distinctive wine; semi-sweet at first, becoming quite dry and of very fair quality with age. Spain.

Abbayes, Clos des. (31) Vaud canton; one of the best-known vineyards of Dézaley. Dry, white and fine quality wines. Switzerland.

Abbé, Clos l'. (16) Touraine; Savigny-en-Véron vineyard, below Chinon. Ordinary to fair red table wine. France.

Abenheim. (24) Rhinehessia; village north-west of Worms. Red and white table wines of ordinary quality are produced. West Germany.

Abrau-Dursso. (34) South European Russia, Kuban valley, Krasnodar. One of the more important collective wineries. U.S.S.R.

Abrera. (29) One of the ordinary to fair white table wines from vineyards in the Barcelona area. Spain.

Abruzzo e Molise. (27) Mountainous region of central Italy. Table wines, mostly of undistinguished quality. Some better quality red wines than white. Italy.

Abruzzo Montepulciano Rosso. (27) Abruzzi e Molise; central Italy. Ordinary red table wine. Italy.

Abruzzo Trebbiano Bianco. (27) Abruzzi e Molise; central Italy. Fair white table wine. Italy.

Abstatt. (25) Württemberg; village south-east of Heilbronn. Red and white wines from ordinary to fair quality. West Germany.

Abtsberg. (22) Middle Moselle valley; a small Graach vineyard. White table wine of fine quality. West Germany.

Abtsberg. (23) Palatinate; Middle Haardt, one of the better Forst vineyards. Very fine white wine. West Germany.

Abtsberg. (25) Franconia; vineyard of Hörstein, east of Frankfurt-am-Main. Fair to fine white table wine. West Germany.

Abtsleite. (25) Franconia; vineyard near Würzburg. Fine white table wine usually bottled in the distinctive flat-sided Franconian *Bocksbeutel*. West Germany.

Abtsleiter. (25) Franconia; Abtsleite-Randersacker vineyard. White table wine of fine quality bottled in the traditional flat-sided Franconian *Bocksbeutel*. West Germany.

Acampo Winery. (36) California; Upper San Joaquin valley, winery and vineyards. Table and dessert wines from fair to fine quality. U.S.A.

Acebo. (29) Northern Estremadura; town in the province of Cáceres. Its vineyards produce a fair quantity of quite ordinary red table wine. Spain.

Achaea. (34) A north-western department of the Peloponnisos peninsula of southern Greece. Its vineyards, more particularly those around the chief city, Patras, produce considerable quantities of ordinary to fair table wines. Greece.

Achkarren. (25) Baden; village in the Kaiserstuhl, north-west of Freiburg. Ordinary to fair red and white table wines. West Germany.

Achtmorgen. (23) Palatinate; Middle Haardt, small vineyard of Ruppertsberg. Fine white wines. West Germany.

Aconcagua Valley. (35) Central Chile; its vineyards produce some of the best red table wines of Chile.

Adlersberg. (33) Budapest; Budafok vineyard, just south of Budapest. The German name of the red and white wine, from ordinary to fair quality. Hungary.

Adom Atic. (34) Fair to fine red table wine. Israel.

Adrano. (28) Sicily; Catania. Undistinguished red table wines with powerful bouquet and bitter aftertaste. Italy.

Affaltrach. (25) Württemberg; village producing ordinary red and white table wines. West Germany.

Affenberg. (24) Rhinehessia; vineyard of Ockenheim, south-east of Bingen. Ordinary to fair white table wine. West Germany.

Affentaler. (25) A light red, almost rosé, table wine from Affental vineyards on the Black Forest foothills, not far from Baden-Baden. Although the wine is made mostly from Pinot Noir grapes, it never has the full red burgundy colour, and its quality is generally fair. West Germany.

Agios Georgios. (34) A popular table wine, sometimes a little sweet, but never of really fine quality. Greece.

Aglianichello. (28) Campania; Naples region. Full-strength, ruby-red table wine; somewhat rough at first, it improves greatly and quickly with age. Italy.

Aglianico. (28) Campania. Name of red grape; also red table wine made from this grape, varying greatly in quality from ordinary to good according to soil and age. Italy.

Aglianico del Vulture. (28) Campania; Monte Vulture, Potenza district, east of Naples. Red table wine, generally accepted as the best made from Aglianico grapes, and one of the best of southern Italy. The vines are planted in volcanic soil upon slopes of Monte Vulture. Italy.

Aglie, L'. (26) Turin region. Piedmontese name for

a sweetish, light red table wine, varying a good deal in strength and quality. Italy.

Agly, Côtes d'. (13) Hillside vineyards on slopes of the mountains above little town of Agly, Rousillon, approx. thirty miles north-east of Banyuls, close to Spanish frontier by the Mediterranean. White or tawny dessert wine made from Grenache, Muscat, and Malvoisie grapes; unfortified but with never less than 15° alcoholic strength if and when given the *AC Vin Doux Naturel* (*V.D.N.*). France.

Agnani. (27) Lazio; Frosinone. Name of undistinguished red table wine and some very fair quality white table wine. Italy.

Agritiusberg. (22) Saar valley; Oberemmel. One of the best vineyards producing fine to very fine white table wines. West Germany.

Agros. (34) Island of Cyprus approx. 100 miles off the west coast of Syria. The name of one of the best white dessert wines made from Muscat grapes. Cyprus.

Agua, Quinta. (30) *Região demarcada do Douro* (q.v.). Estate in the Alto Douro with a vineyard of 125 acres. At Guiaes north-east of Régua. Portugal.

Aguado. (29) One of the wine-producing territories of the Cariñena district in the west-central part of the province of Zaragoza. Ordinary to fair red, white and *clarete* wines, both dry and rather sweet. Spain.

Aguamurcia. (29) Catalonia; Panadés, between Tarragona and Barcelona. Dry and some semi-sweet white table wines. Spain.

Aguascalientes. (35) Central Mexico. A wine-producing district; its red and white table wines are of homely quality but popular locally. Mexico.

Aguilar de la Frontera. (29) A locality of the Montilla-Moriles region, in the province of Córdoba, north-east of Seville. The vineyards produce high-strength white wines of fine quality. Spain.

Agulha. (30) Vinhos Verdes. The name of slightly sparkling table wines. Portugal.

Agulio. (29) The name of the sparkling white wines made in Catalonia. Spain.

Ahn. (32) Moselle valley; a village between Grevenmacher and Wormeldange. Ordinary to fair white table wines. Luxembourg.

Ahr. (21) A small river of the Middle Rhine region which joins the Rhine a short distance above Koblenz. The hillside vineyards of the Ahr valley grow mostly Pinot Noir grapes and produce the best red table wines of Germany. West Germany.

Ahrbleichert. (21) The name given in the Rhine-

land to a popular, inexpensive, quite ordinary rosé table wine from any of the vineyards of the Ahr valley, west of Linz. West Germany.

Ahrweiler. (21) One of the better red table wines of the Ahr vineyards, west of Linz, near the village of that name. West Germany.

Aidanil. (34) South European Russia; Crimean peninsula. Red and white table wines. U.S.S.R.

Aigle. (31) Vaud canton; small town with vineyards. Fair to fine quality white table wines. Switzerland.

Aigrefeuille. (20) Charente Maritime *département*. White wine which is distilled into cognac of the *bois ordinaires* standard of quality. France.

Aigrots, Les. (8) Beaune vineyard. *Premier cru*. Good quality red burgundy. France.

Aillerie, L'. (16) Touraine. One of the better vineyards of Jasnières north of Vouvray. White table wine of fair quality. France.

Ain-Bessem-Bouira. (40) An Algerian district; south-east of Algiers. The vineyards produce red and white table wines given, under French rule, the *AC Vins Délimités de Qualité Supérieure* (*V.D.Q.S.*) when their alcoholic strength was not below 12°. Algeria.

Ain-Temouchent. (40) An important district of Oran. The vineyards produce red, white and rosé table wines given, under French rule, the *AC Vins Délimités de Qualité Supérieure* (*V.D.Q.S.*) when their alcoholic strength was not below 13°. Algeria.

Aisne. (2) *Département* approx. sixty miles north-east of Paris. Smallest *département* to be included in the official *région délimitée de la Champagne viticole*. 1,904 acres. France.

Akracas Bianco. (28) Sicily; Agrigento area, approx. fifty-five miles south east of Palermo. Good quality heady, dry white table wine, without any bouquet but from as much as 12° to 15° alcoholic content. Italy.

Alagro. (29) New Castile; Ciudad Real north of Valdepeñas. Ordinary red and white table wines. Spain.

Alajeiros. (29) A locality in the province of Valladolid, to the north-west, near Madrid. The vineyards produce red, white and *clarete* table wines of ordinary to fair quality. Spain.

Alameda. (36) One of the more important wine-producing counties of California. San Francisco Bay area, Livermore valley. Fine quality red and white table wines. U.S.A.

Alameda de la Sangre. (29) New Castile; a locality of the Toledo area, approx. forty miles south-west of Madrid. The vineyards produce red, white and *clarete* table wines of ordinary to fair quality. Spain.

Alanjo. (29) South-west central Spain; a locality of the Badajoz area, between Seville and Trujillo. The vineyards produce some white table wines of fair quality. Spain.

Alaro. (29) Majorca and other Balearic Islands; off the coast, east of Valencia. One of the popular but rather common dry red table wines. Spain.

Alba. (26) Piedmont; town between Asti and Cuneo. Considerable quantities of ordinary to fair quality, mostly red table wines. Italy.

Alba. (29) Santander; approx. forty-five miles west of Bilbao. The name of a popular, inexpensive and undistinguished white table wine. Spain.

Albacete. (29) Murcia; approx. twenty-three miles south-east of La Roda. One of the more popular red and white wines of homely quality. Spain.

Alba Flor. (29) Majorca and other Balearic Islands; off the coast, east of Valencia. A semi-sweet white wine of ordinary to fair quality. Spain.

Albaida. (29) Valencia. A dry white table wine from ordinary to fair quality. Spain.

Albana. (26) Name of a white grape much grown in Italy; also a slightly sweet white table wine made from this grape. Better Albana wines are those from the vineyards of the Bologna, Forli and Ravenna (north-east of Forli) areas. Italy.

Albana di Romagna. (26) Area on the road from Forli to Rimini (south-east of Forli); vineyards on hillsides facing the road. Produces one of the better quality, slightly sweet table wines, of the same name, from Albana white grapes. Italy.

Albanello di Siracusa. (28) Sicily; Syracuse. A fair to fine, dry or sweet golden wine. Alcoholic content is high. The dry is best served as an apéritif; the sweet as a dessert wine. Italy.

Albania. (34) A small country between Greece and Yugoslavia with more vineyards than many larger ones; they cover approximately 30,000 acres and their peak production is over 300,000 dozen bottles. Mostly red and white table wines of ordinary to fair quality.

Albarin. (29) Central Asturias province; Oviedo vineyards. A very dark red, almost black, dry, rough wine. It may be used as a table wine diluted with water, but is more valuable for blending purposes. Spain.

Albarina. (29) Southern Galicia; Orense. Ordinary to fair white table wine. Spain.

Albariza. (29) Jerez de la Frontera. The highly chalky soil in which the finest sherry vineyards are planted. Spain.

Albarracin. (29) Aragon. Ordinary to fair red and white table wines. Spain.

Albemarle. (35) Northern Virginia. A wine-producing county. U.S.A.

Alberique. (29) Valencia. A dry white table wine of fair quality. Spain.

Albersweiler. (23) Palatinate; village between Burrweiler and Oberhofen. Its vineyards produce some red table wine of ordinary quality and fair and fine white table wines. West Germany.

Albert Grivault. (7) The name of one of the Hospices de Beaune *cuvées*. Fair to fine white burgundy. France.

Alberts, Château des. (4) Blayais; Mazion vineyard on the right bank of the Gironde. 2,000 dozen bottles of red bordeaux; 3,000 white. France.

Albig. (24) Rhinehessia; village north-east of Bingen. Ordinary to fair red and white table wines. West Germany.

Albillo Blanco. (29) A popular, inexpensive, homely quality white table wine. Spain.

Albinana. (29) Catalonia; Panadés vineyards, between Tarragona and Barcelona. A dry, white table wine. Spain.

Albisheim. (29) Palatinate; village west of Worms. Moderate red and white table wines. West Germany.

Albsheim. (23) Palatinate; village just north of Grünstadt. Moderate quality red and white table wines. West Germany.

Albunol. (29) Andalusia; Granada, between Málaga and Baza. A white wine from ordinary to fair quality. Spain.

Albuquerque. (29) Badajoz area; village between Seville and Trujillo. The vineyards produce a red table wine of ordinary to fair quality. Spain.

Alburno. (28) Campania; Salerno. A moderate quality red table wine. Italy.

Alcala de Chivert. (29) Castellón de la Plana; approx. forty miles north-east of Valencia. An ordinary to fair red table wine. Spain.

Alcala de la Real. (28) Jaén; Málaga, south coast of Spain. A dry, white table wine from ordinary to fair quality. Spain.

Alcamo. (28) Sicily; Trapani. A fair quality white table wine, often used as a base for vermouth locally and on the mainland. Italy.

Alcazar de San Juan. (29) New Castile; Ciudad Real, north of Valdepeñas. An ordinary to fair red or white table wine. Spain.

Alcobaca. (30) Estremadura. Good white and red table wines from coastal vineyards. Portugal.

Alcoriza. (29) South-central Aragon; Teruel vineyards. One of the ordinary table wines, both red and white. Spain.

Aldea Nueva del Camino. (29) North Estremadura; village of the Cáceres area. Fair quality dry red table wine. Spain.

Aldea Nueva del Ebro. (29) Old Castile; Logroño province, La Rioja area of the upper Ebro valley. Fair full-bodied red table wine. Spain.

Aldegund. (22) Lower Moselle valley; village between Eller and Zell. Fair white table wines. West Germany.

Aleatico. The name of a red grape of the Muscat family much grown in Italy. Also the name of a number of red wines made from this grape; often a little sweet with a faint Muscat bouquet. Italy.

Aleatico di Genzano. (27) Lazio; Genzano, north-west of Velletri. A sweet dessert wine made from Aleatico grapes. Italy.

Aleatico di Gradoli. (27) Lazio; Viterbo area. A ruby-red dessert wine of high alcoholic strength made from Aleatico grapes. Italy.

Aleatico di Portoferraio. (27) Island of Elba; west of Grosseto. A dark, sweet, Muscat-flavoured dessert wine from Aleatico grapes. Considered by many wine connoisseurs as the best Aleatico dessert wine. Italy.

Aleatico di Terracina. (28) Lazio; Gaeta-Terracina area, coastal area north-west of Naples. A ruby-red dessert wine of fair quality and moderate alcoholic content made from Aleatico grapes. Italy.

Aleatico di Viterbo. (27) Lazio; Lake Bolsena, north-west of Viterbo. A full, luscious, red dessert wine of fair quality, made from Aleatico grapes. Italy.

Aleatico Secco. (28) Lazio; Gaeta area, coastal area north-west of Naples. Only Aleatico red dessert wine to be quite dry and have high alcoholic content. Made from Aleatico grapes. Italy.

Alella. (29) A village immediately north of Barcelona. Its vineyards produce both red and white wines, but the only one which has made the name of Alella popular in all parts of Catalonia is the white table wine, not really quite dry, but not sweet. Spain.

Alempassa, Quinta. (30) *Região demarcada do Douro* (q.v.). Estate and vineyard in Ervedosa do Douro east of Régua, at a height between 100 to 380 metres above sea level. Portugal.

Alessándria. (26) Piedmont. One of the more important wine-producing provinces. Produces considerable quantities of ordinary to fair quality red and white table wines, a great deal of the latter used in the making of Italian vermouth. Italy.

Aleyor. (29) Majorca and other Balearic Islands; off the coast, east of Valencia. A dark red, dry and coarse table wine. Spain.

Alf. (22) Lower Moselle valley; village between Eller and Zell. Fair white wine. West Germany.

Alfamen. (29) Cariñena; west-central province of Zaragoza. A dry, red table wine of no great merit. Spain.

Alfano. (29) Old Castile; Logroño province, La Rioja area of the upper Ebro valley. Fair quality dry, red table wine. Spain.

Alfoma. (26) Emilia-Romagna; Bologna area. Popular white table wines. Italy.

Alford. (33) One of the popular table wines of Hungary; some are red and others white. Hungary.

Algaida. (29) Andalusia. One of the few red table wines; there is also a white table wine of the same name, both are from ordinary to fair quality. Spain.

Algarinejo. (29) Andalusia; Granada, between Málaga and Baza. An ordinary to fair red or white table wine. Spain.

Algarroba. (29) Málaga. An ordinary to fair red or white table wine. Spain.

Algeria. (40) Within a hundred years of its conquest and colonization by the French, Algeria produced over 250,000,000 dozen bottles of fair wine, as well as coarse dark red and strong dry wines for blending with paler and weaker French wines. They also produced some wines of very fair and even some of fine quality.

Algodonales. (29) Locality of the Cadiz area. The vineyards produce ordinary to fair white wines. Spain.

Alicante. (29) The name of an important wine-producing province on the south-eastern coast south of Valencia, and of its chief city. It is also the name of much wine made from vineyards in the Alicante area; mostly ordinary to fair red table wines, some fair white table wines and some dessert wines from ordinary to fair quality. Spain.

Aligoté. The name of a white grape much grown in the Chalonnais and Yonne (Chablis) and Haute Côte de Beaune and Nuits regions for making the less distinguished white table wines of Burgundy, sold as *AC Bourgogne Aligoté*. These wines are not comparable to the great white wines of Burgundy, made from Pinot Chardonnay white grapes, but they are, nevertheless, of quite good quality. Fresh fruity wines bottled young for early drinking. France.

Aligoté. (34) South-west European Russia; Moldavia. An ordinary to fair dry white table wine. U.S.S.R.

Alizier, L'. (16) Touraine; Beaumont-en-Véron, below Chinon. A dry white table wine of fair quality. France.

Alken. (22) Moselle; small village on the right

bank of the river Moselle just before it joins the Rhine at Koblenz. Its vineyards produce some dry white wine of ordinary to fair quality. West Germany.

Allied Grape Growers. (36) California; winery and vineyards of Madera now owned by Heublein, Inc. Table and dessert wines; also some fair quality sparkling wines. U.S.A.

Allmersbach. (25) Württemberg; village producing ordinary to fair red and white table wines. West Germany.

Allots, Aux. (7) Nuits-St-Georges vineyard. *Deuxième cru.* Very fair red burgundy. France.

All Saints. (38) One of the earlier wineries and vineyards (1864) of the State of Victoria; it is at Wahgunyah on the southern bank of the river Murray. Property of the Sutherland Smith family. Australia.

Almadén Vineyards. (36) West Central California; San Benito County. 4,000 acres. Storage capacity for vast quantities of wine and brandy. One of the oldest wineries in California. Fine quality table wines; also dessert wines, vermouth and brandy. U.S.A.

Almansa. (29) Albacete vineyards; approx. twenty-three miles south-east of La Roda. A very fair quality *clarete* wine. Albacete is one of the four provinces comprising La Mancha. Spain.

Almeirim. (30) Estremadura. Produces red and white table wines. Portugal.

Almendralejo. (29) Estremadura; Badajoz area, between Seville and Trujillo. An ordinary to fair red or white table wine. Spain.

Almonte. (29) Huelva area; west of the Guadalquivir river. An ordinary red or white table wine. Spain.

Almus. (25) Triefeinstein; hillside vineyard near Aschaffenburg, between Frankfurt-am-Main and Würzburg. Fair white dessert wine. West Germany.

Alora. (29) Málaga. Popular but undistinguished table wine, mostly red but there is a white one. Spain.

Aloupka. (34) South European Russia; Crimean peninsula. Strong and sweet white dessert wine. U.S.S.R.

Aloxe-Corton. (8) Côte d'Or, at the northern end of the Côte de Beaune. Finest red and white burgundies. France.

Alpera. (29) Albacete area; approx. twenty-three miles south-east of La Roda. Fair *clarete* table wine. Spain.

Alpes Maritimes. (13) *Département*, on the Mediterranean coast close to Italian border; it includes lower slopes of the French Alps. Ordinary to fair table wines. France.

Alphen. (39) Cape Province; Cape Town district. One of the oldest wineries and vineyards in South Africa.

Alsace. (19) Easternmost former French province, now divided into two *départements*, Haut-Rhin (Colmar), and Bas-Rhin (Strasbourg). The vineyards of Alsace cover over 30,000 acres. Their optimum production is about 13,000,000 dozen bottles of wine, mostly white table wine. According to French law, the white wines of Alsace are entitled to the *Appellation Contrôlée Alsace* and to the *Appellation Contrôlée Alsace Grand Vin*, when their alcoholic content is not below 11°. France.

Alsenz. (23) Palatinate; village approx. eighteen miles north-west of Grünstadt. Ordinary red and fair white table wines. West Germany.

Alsenz-Nahe. (24) Upper Nahe valley; village south of Bad Münster. Ordinary to fair white tables wines. West Germany.

Alser. (23) Palatinate; small vineyard of Forst. Fair white table wine. West Germany.

Alsheim. (24) Rhinehessia. Village producing ordinary to fair red and white table wines. West Germany.

Altenahr. (21) Upper Ahr valley; west of Linz. yard of Ürzig. Fine white table wines. West Germany.

Altärchen. (22) Middle Moselle valley; small vineyard of Trittenheim. Very fair white table wine. West Germany.

Altbaum. (24) Rhinegau; small vineyard of Geisenheim. Fine white table wine. West Germany.

Altdorr. (24) Rhinehessia; small vineyard of Dalsheim, south-west of Oppenheim. Ordinary to fair white table wine. West Germany.

Altenahr. (21) Upper Ahr Valley; west of Linz. Ordinary to fair red table wines from the hillside vineyards. West Germany.

Altenbamberg. (21) Palatinate; village south-west of Bad Kreuznach. Ordinary red and fair white table wine. West Germany.

Altenbamberg. (24) Upper Nahe valley; village south of Bad Münster. Fair white table wine. West Germany.

Altenburg. (23) Palatinate; vineyard site at both Forst and Wachenheim, two of the chief localities of the Middle Haardt. Fair to fine white table wine. West Germany.

Altenwald. (22) Middle Moselle valley; Bernkastel vineyard. Fair to fine white table wine. West Germany.

Altenweg. (23) Palatinate; Hambach vineyard, between Neustadt and Edenkoben. Fair to fine white table wine. West Germany.

Altesse de Frangy. (31) Haute-Savoie *département*; Altesse vineyard of village of Frangy, on Swiss-French border, western slopes of the Alps, south-west of Geneva. Produces one of the best white table wines of the area. France.

Altesses, Vin des. (31) Savoie *département*; Swiss-French border on western slopes of Alps. Popular white table wine, varying a good deal in quality and cost. France.

Alte Valle del Tevere. (27) Perugia; upper valley of Tiber. Red and white table wines of no great merit. Italy.

Alto, Quinta. (30) *Região demarcada do Douro.* Estate and vineyard in São Miguel de Lobrigos north-east of Régua. Portugal.

Alto Adige. (26) Upper valley of river Adige or Italian Tyrol, transferred from Austria to Italy in 1919. Many hillside vineyards produce red and white, ordinary to fair and some fine quality table wines. Usually marketed under either their present Italian names or their former German names. Italy.

Alto Cilento. (28) Campania; Salerno area. A purple-red, rough, strong, dry wine. Italy.

Alto Douro. (30) The genuine port-producing region which begins some sixty miles east of Oporto and continues along the river Douro nearly to Spain. This mountainous region was first demarcated by law around 1757 to protect the naming of port, and as such is the oldest demarcated wine-producing district in the world. The Douro tributaries, the river Corgo, river Pinhao and river Tua also contain excellent terraced vineyards. The main towns are Régua and Pinhao to the east. Portugal.

Altramura. (28) Apulia. An ordinary but locally popular dessert wine. Italy.

Alvarinho. (30) White wine and grape variety. Never less than 12° alcohol by volume. Produced in one of the six subregions of the Vinhos Verdes district. Portugal.

Alveleda. (30) An estate in the Vinhos Verdes district which produces the brand 'Alveleda' among other fine Vinhos Verdes wines.

Alzey. (24) Rhinehessia; village west of Alsheim. Ordinary red and fair white table wines. West Germany.

Amandi. (29) Central Galicia; near Lugo. Dry red table wine of no great merit. Spain.

Amarante. (30) One of the six subregions of the Vinhos Verdes district. Portugal.

Ambares. (5) Entre-deux-Mers; *commune* in Gironde, north-east of Bordeaux. Ordinary to fair red bordeaux. France.

Amboise. (16) Town on river Loire, north-east of Tours. Ordinary to fair red, white and rosé table wines entitled to the *AC Touraine-Amboise* when their strength is between 9° and 10·5°. France.

Ambonnay. (17) Marne *département*; Ay canton. Rated *grand cru*—100% growth. 712 acres. France.

Ambrato di Comiso. (28) Sicily; Ragusa vineyards, approx. thirty miles south-west of Syracuse. A dry, heavy, amber-coloured white wine of fair quality made from white grapes. Italy.

Amery. (37) South Australia; McLaren Vale, twenty-five miles south of Adelaide. Winery and vineyard (180 acres) the property of Kay Bros Pty Ltd. They produce red and white table wines of fine quality. Australia.

Amigny. (15) Cher *département*; Sancerre area. Ordinary to fair quality white table wine. France.

Ammerschwihr. (19) Haut-Rhin *département*. A village producing fair to fine white Alsace wine. France.

Amontillado. (29) Andalusia; Jerez de la Frontera. One of the most popular types of pre-prandial sherries. There are imitations of Amontillado sherry made in California, Australia, South Africa and elsewhere. Spain.

Amorgiano. (34) Island of Rhodes; north-east of Crete. The best dry red table wine of the island. Greece.

Amoroso. (29) Andalusia; Jerez de la Frontera. Popular type of sherry. It is usually a little darker as well as richer than an Amontillado; it may be served as an apéritif or a dessert wine. Spain.

Amorpfad. (22) Middle Moselle valley; small vineyard of Bernkastel. Fair white table wine. West Germany.

Amoureuses, Les. (8) Côte de Nuits; Cambolle-Musigny vineyard. Very fine red burgundy. France.

Ampuis. (12) Côtes du Rhône; village at the northern end a short distance south of Lyons, on the right bank of the river Rhône. It lies at the foot of the Côte Rôtie hill on the slopes of which there are many vineyards producing some of the best Côtes du Rhône red table wines. France.

Amstgarten. (23) Palatinate; small vineyard of Kirrweiler. Fair white table wine. West Germany.

Amusèries, Clos des. (16) Touraine; vineyard of Rochecorbon, north-east of Tours. Some good table wine. France.

Ana. (29) Valencia. The name of a light and inexpensive red table wine. Spain.

Anberg. (24) Rhinehessia; small vineyard of Bingen, close to where the Nahe joins the Rhine. Fair white table wine. West Germany.

Ancona. (27) The Marches; port on the Adriatic. Red and white table wines of no special merit. Italy.

Andalusia. (29) Southern province of Spain with 282,000 acres of vineyards producing mostly ordinary to fair table wines, but there are some very fine dessert wines, the most famous of all being sherry, the wine of the Jerez vineyards. Also a great deal of brandy and sparkling wine. Spain.

Andel. (22) Moselle valley; small village just east of Brauneberg. Ordinary white table wine. West Germany.

Andlau. (19) Bas-Rhin *département*. Ordinary to fair white Alsace wine. France.

Andujar. (29) Jaén; village north-east of Málaga. Fair sweet white wine. Spain.

Angaston. (37) Town and district in the Barossa valley approx. thirty-five miles north-east of Adelaide, the vineyards and wineries of which are among the oldest and best known of South Australia.

Angelica. (36) Southern California. Name given to a sweet white wine made mostly from sweet new white wine blended with high-strength spirit. It is said to have been named after the city of Los Angeles. U.S.A.

Angelus, Château de l'. (5) Côtes de St-Emilion. One of the *grand cru classé côtes*. 13,000 dozen bottles of fine to very fine red bordeaux. France.

Angera. (26) Lombardy; Lake Varese. Fair quality fruity red wine. Italy.

Anghelu Ruju. (28) Sardinia; Alghero, approx. fifty miles south-west of Sassari. Curiously named ruby-red, strong, sweet wine. It falls somewhere between a ruby port and an Aleatico (q.v.) in style. Italy.

Angles, Les. (8) Côte de Beaune; Volnay vineyard. Fine red burgundy. France.

Angle Vale. (37) South Australia; approx. thirty miles north of Adelaide on the Gawler river. Vineyards of A. Norman & Sons and Angle Vale Vineyards Pty Ltd., which began in 1969 with a 120 acre vineyard planted with Shiraz and Cabernet Sauvignon grapes. It provides a winery to take its own produce as well as that of the smaller 10 acre 'home block' owners.

Angludet, Château. (4) Haut-Médoc; *commune* of Cantenac, close to Margaux. *Cru bourgeois supérieur*. 6,000 dozen bottles of fair to fine red bordeaux. France.

Angove. (37) South Australia. River Murray Winery, and distilleries at Renmark north-east of Berri and Tea Tree Gully (outer suburb of Adelaide). Australia.

Anjou. (16) Former French province, now mostly comprising the *département* of Maine-et-Loire, with Angers as its chief city. Mainly white wines, dry and sweet, still and sparkling, of ordinary, fair and fine quality; also some red table wines of little merit and a great deal of very popular rosé table wines. France.

Anjou-Coteau-de-la-Loire. (16) Maine-et-Loire *département*. The *Appellation Contrôlée* of the better white table wines, the alcoholic strength of which must not be below 12°. France.

Anjou Rosé de Cabernet. (16) Maine-et-Loire *département*. The *Appellation Contrôlée* of the best rosé table wine; its alcoholic strength must not be below 11°. France.

Ankara. (34) Middle Anatolia. Good red and white table wines. Turkey.

Annaberg. (23) Middle Haardt; name of a vineyard site in the vineyards of both Kallstadt and Bad Dürkheim in the Palatinate. Fair to fine white table wine. West Germany.

Annecy. (31) Haute-Savoie *département*; chief town approx. twenty miles south of Geneva in the French Alps, on borders of Switzerland and Italy. Ordinary red table wines and much better quality white table wines. France.

Annereaux, Château des. (5) Lalande-de-Pomerol; north of Pomerol. One of the more important vineyards. 15,000 dozen bottles of ordinary to fair red bordeaux. France.

Anniger-Perle. (33) An undistinguished but very popular light, new, white wine, just a little sparkling. Austria.

Anovar de Tajo. (29) New Castile; Toledo area, approx. forty miles south-west of Madrid. A sweet, white Muscat dessert wine of fair quality. Spain.

Anseillan, Château. (3) Haut-Médoc; Pauillac. *Cru bourgeois supérieur*. 5,000 dozen bottles of fair to fine red bordeaux. France.

Ansonica. (27) Coast of Tuscany; Giglio island, south-west of Grosseto. A white grape and a moderately interesting dry, or semi-sweet white wine made from it. Italy.

Anspach. (24) Rhinegau; one of the vineyards of Winkel. Fine white table wine. West Germany.

Antequera. (29) Andalusia; Málaga area. Both red and white table wines of no particular merit, but popular. Spain.

Anthonic, Château. (4) Médoc; Moulis. An important vineyard which ranks as a *cru bourgeois supérieur*. 2,000 dozen bottles of fair to fine red bordeaux. France.

Antika. (34) Peninsula of southern Greece. One of the better dry white table wines from some Peloponnisos vineyards. Greece.

Antoniusbrunne. (22) Saar valley; small vineyard of Saarburg. Very fair white table wine. West Germany.

Apetlon. (33) Burgenland; Eisenstadt district,

south-east Austria, close to the Hungarian border. Fair table wines. Austria.

Apotheke. (22) Moselle valley; small vineyard of Trittenheim. Fair white table wine. West Germany.

Appenheim. (24) Rhinehessia; village south of Mittelheim. Ordinary to fair red and white table wines. West Germany.

Appenhofen. (23) Palatinate; village south-west of Landau. Ordinary red and fair white table wines. West Germany.

Aprilia (Bianco, Rosso and Rosato). (27) Lazio; Anzio-Alban hills, south-east of Rome. Modest dry white wine, fair red and a rather full rosé wine. Italy.

Apulia. (28) The south-eastern province of Italy, Puglie, in Italian, noted for its wines. Italy.

Aragon. (29) Former kingdom of Spain, now an important wine-producing province with 320,000 acres of vineyards producing mostly ordinary to fair red wine. Spain.

Aragona-Canicatti. (28) Sicily. A fortified, dry, full, fairly strong, cherry-red dessert wine never below 13° alcoholic content and sometimes up to 18°. Italy.

Aranda de Duero. (29) North-east León; Burgos area. Ordinary to fair red table wines. Spain.

Arawatta. (37) A dry white table wine of South Australia made from a blend of Rhine Riesling grapes from Great Western (approx. 100 miles north-west of Geelong), Clare and local Rieslings of the Barossa Valley, thirty-five miles north-east of Adelaide. Also a vineyard at Great Western. Australia.

Arbalète, Clos de l'. (31) Vaud canton; Dézaley vineyard locally well-known. Fine white table wine. Switzerland.

Arbanats. (5) Graves de Bordeaux; near Podensac. *Commune* whose vineyards produce mostly ordinary to fair red bordeaux. 500 dozen bottles of red bordeaux; 3,000 ordinary white graves. France.

Arbanats, Château d'. (5) Principal estate of Arbanats (see above). France.

Arbia. (27) Tuscany; Arbia valley, Siena area. Dry white table wine. Because the must is fermented without stalks or skins, the wine is light, delicate, and does not travel well. Italy.

Arbin. (31) Savoie *département*; western slopes of Alps at the Swiss-French border. Ordinary to fair red table wine. France.

Arbuissonas. (11) Beaujolais village. Fair red beaujolais. France.

Arca or Parades de Arca, Quinta. (30) *Região demarcada do Douro*. Estate and vineyard. Portugal.

Archambeau, Château. (5) Gironde; Illats. 2,500 dozen bottles of ordinary white bordeaux. France.

Archanes. (34) Vineyards of Crete. A red table wine of fair quality. Greece.

Archidona. (29) Andalusia; Málaga area. Ordinary to fair red and white table wines. Spain.

Archova. (34) Delphi vineyards; southern Greece. Ordinary to fair white table wine. Greece.

Arcins. (4) Haut-Médoc; approx. twenty miles north of Bordeaux. The vineyards of this *commune* produce mostly ordinary to fair red bordeaux. France.

Arcins, Château d'. (4) Haut-Médoc. The most important vineyard of the *commune* of Arcins. *Cru bourgeois*. 6,000 dozen bottles of red bordeaux. France.

Arcola (Bianco, Rosso). (26) Liguria; between La Spezia and Lerici (south-east of La Spezia); province of Arcola. Undistinguished white and red table wines. Italy.

Arcos de la Frontera. (29) Cádiz; small village. Very fair dry rosé wine. Spain.

Arcs, Les. (14) Côtes de Provence; Argens valley, north-east of Toulon. Fair red and white table wines. France.

Arcugnano (Bianco, Rosso). (26) Friuli-Venezia-Giulia province (encompassing Udine, Gorizia and Trieste); Colli Berici vineyards, Vicenza area. Good quality white and red table wines. Italy.

Ardenas de San Pedro. (29) Avila area. Village whose vineyards produce a rather rough, dry, red table wine. Spain.

Arenas. (29) Málaga area. The name given to plain but rather pleasant light table wines, both red and white. Spain.

Argamansilla de Alba. (29) New Castile; village in the Ciudad Real area, north of Valdepeñas. Fair red table wine. Spain.

Arganda. (29) León; Valdeorra. Ordinary to fair red and white table wines. Spain.

Argentina. (35) One of the world's most important wine-producing countries, quantitatively speaking. Its average production in recent years has reached up to 200,000,000 dozen bottles of wine. The Mendoza province ranks highest with San Juan, Neuquen, Rio Negro, La Rioja, Catamarca and Sarta following.

Argenton. (29) Barcelona area. A light, ordinary but pleasant white table wine. Spain.

Arghilla Rosato. (28) Calabria; Reggio di Calabria. Strong, rich, rough rosé table wine of ordinary quality. Italy.

Argillats, Aux. (7) Côte de Nuits; Nuits-St-Georges. *Premier cru*. Red burgundy. France.

Argillats, Les. (7) Côte de Nuits; Nuits-St-Georges. *Deuxième cru*. France.

Argillières, Les. (7) Côte de Beaune; Pommard. *Premier cru.* Red burgundy. France.

Arillières, Les. (8) Côte de Nuits; Chambolle-Musigny. *Troisième cru.* Red burgundy. France.

Arillières, Clos des. (7) Côte de Nuits; Prémeaux, Nuits-St-Georges. *Premier cru.* Red burgundy. France.

Arles. (13) Bouches-du-Rhône *département*; approx. twenty-five miles east of Lunel. Chief marketing centre for the red and rosé table wines of the Camargue and Crau vineyards. France.

Arlot, Clos. (7) Prémeaux, Nuits-St-Georges. *Premier cru.* Red burgundy. France.

Armajan, Clos d'. (5) Graves de Bordeaux; Budos. 1,100 dozen bottles of white bordeaux. France.

Armajan-Les-Ormes, Château d'. (5) Sauternes; Preignac. *Cru bourgeois.* 1,500 dozen bottles of white bordeaux. France.

Armsheim. (24) Rhinehessia; east of Bad Münster. Fair red and white table wines. West Germany.

Arnaud-Jouan, Château. (3) Premières Côtes de Bordeaux; Cadillac, north-west of Loupiac. 3,000 dozen bottles of red bordeaux; 18,000 white. France.

Arnauld, Château d'. (4) Haut-Médoc; Arcins, north of Bordeaux. *Cru bourgeois.* 3,000 dozen bottles of red bordeaux. France.

Arnauton, Château. (3) Fronsac. 10,000 dozen bottles of red bordeaux. France.

Arrière-Côtes de Beaune. (7) Vineyards on the western slopes of the Côtes de Beaune (now known as Hautes Côtes de Beaune—with separate *AC* and tasting procedures). Ordinary to fair red burgundy. France.

Arrière-Côtes de Nuits. (7) Vineyards on the hillsides behind and to the west of the main Côte d'Or (now known as Hauts Côtes de Nuits). Ordinary to fair red burgundy. France.

Arrosée, Château l'. (5) Côtes de St-Emilion. *Grand cru classé.* 5,000 dozen bottles of red bordeaux. France.

Arroya de la Luz. (29) Northern Estremadura; Cáceres province, in Trujillo area. Ordinary to fair red and white table wines. Spain.

Arsac. (4) Haut-Médoc *commune.* Mostly ordinary red bordeaux; some fine bordeaux. France.

Artajona. (29) Central Navarre province. Ordinary to fair light red and white wines. Spain.

Arthur Girard. (8) Savigny-les-Beaune. A Hospice de Beaune *cuvée* which originally consisted of two separate *cuvées*, Du Bay Peste and Cyrot; their wines were made as a single *cuvée* from 1937–43. The name was then changed to commemorate Arthur Girard, a recent benefactor of the Hospices. Fine red burgundy. France.

Artimino. (27) Another name for Chianti Montalbano Pistoiese (q.v.). Italy.

Arvelets. (8) Fixin *premier cru.* Vineyard adjoining Les Hervelets. France.

Arvelets. (8) Côte de Nuits; Pommard vineyard. *Premier cru.* Red burgundy. France.

Arvier. (26) Piedmont; Val d'Aosta. Ordinary to fair red table wine. Italy.

Arvisio. (34) Island of Chios; south-east of mainland Greece. Ordinary to fair red and white table wines. Greece.

Arzheim. (23) Palatinate; village between Burrweiler and Oberhofen. Ordinary red and fair white table wines. West Germany.

Arzignano. (26) Vicenza province; Gambellara vineyards. Unimportant light, dry red and white table wines, the latter also known as Durello. Italy.

Ashman's Vineyards. (37) New South Wales; Hunter River Valley, north-east of Sydney. Property of Tyrrell's Vineyards Pty Ltd. Australia.

Aspen. (23) Palatinate; Haardt vineyards. Ordinary to fair red and white table wines. West Germany.

Asperg. (25) Württemberg; north of Stuttgart. Red and white table wines. West Germany.

Aspisheim. (24) Rhinehessia; village south of Geisenheim. Ordinary fair and fine white table wine. West Germany.

Asprinio. (28) Apulia; Capo di Leuca vineyards, the bottom of the 'heel' of Italy. Rather curious white, semi-sweet and semi-sparkling table wine. Italy.

Asprino. (28) Campania; Naples region. A white grape; also a sharp, *frizzante* white table wine made from it. Italy.

Asques. (3) Small town in the Gironde *département*; west of Fronsac in the Fronsadais. Its vineyards produce the more ordinary type of red bordeaux. France.

Assmannshausen. (24) Rhinegau; between Rüdesheim and Lorch. One of the best red table wines of West Germany.

Assolveira, Quinta. (30) *Região demarcada do Douro.* Estate and vineyard in Celeiros north-east of Régua. Portugal.

Astheim. (25) Franconia; north-east of Würzburg. Fair to fine white table wine. West Germany.

Asti. (26) Piedmont. Town and province, chiefly famous for the rather sweet, low alcoholic content, white sparkling wine known as Asti Spumante. Italy.

Asturias. (29) Province of Spain with 14,000 acres of vineyards producing mostly table wines of ordinary to fair quality.

Asztali. (33) Budapest; Tokaj (Tokay) vineyards,

E

approx. 110 miles north-east of Budapest. Ordinary to fair table wines. Hungary.

Athies, Les. (8) Côte de Nuits; Chambolle-Musigny. *Troisième cru.* Fair red burgundy. Vineyard of same name and class also found in Nuits-St-Georges. France.

Athiri. (34) Island of Rhodes; north-east of Crete. Ordinary to fair white table wine. Greece.

Attafi Greco. (28) Calabria; Reggio di Calabria. Fair quality rich, sweet, white dessert wine made from Greco grapes. Italy.

Attafi Mantonaco. (28) Calabria; Reggio di Calabria. Fair quality, sweet, golden dessert wine made from Mantonaco white grapes. Italy.

Attafi Rosso. (28) Calabria; Reggio di Calabria. Coarse, heavy, red, ordinary quality table wine made from Alicante and other red grapes. Italy.

Attica. (34) The south-eastern part of the Greek mainland and the oldest and most important region of Greece as regards wine production.

Aube. (6) *Département*, approx. twenty miles north-east of Auxerre. 12,500 acres. 1,275,000 dozen bottles of fair quality white wine. France.

Aubepin, Château l'. (5) Sauternes; Bommes. *Cru bourgeois supérieur.* 1,500 dozen bottles of good white dessert wine. France.

Auberdière, L'. (16) Touraine; Vouvray, east of Tours. Very fair quality white table wine. France.

Aubière. (15) Puy de Dôme *département*; approx. forty miles south of St-Pourçain in the Allier valley. Some fair red table wine. France.

Aubinière, L'. (16) Coteaux de l'Aubance; Brissac, between Angers and Saumur. Fine *rosé de Cabernet* table wine. France.

Auenstein. (25) Württemberg; approx. twenty miles north-east of Stuttgart. Ordinary to fair red and white table wines. West Germany.

Auerbach. (25) Baden, Bergstrasse; Hesse, approx. seventeen miles north-east of Mannheim. Fair white table wine. West Germany.

Auflangen. (24) Rhinehessia; vineyard of Nierstein. Fair to fine white table wine. West Germany.

Augenscheiner. (22) Upper Moselle valley; near Trier. Ordinary to fair white table wine. West Germany.

Augey, Château d'. (5) Sauternes; vineyards of the *commune* of Bommes. 3,500 dozen bottles of white bordeaux. France.

Augiers, Château des. (3) Bourgeais; Comps, north-east of Bourg. 4,000 dozen bottles of fair red bordeaux. France.

Auldana. (37) South Australia; in the Adelaide foothills suburb of Magill. Vineyard and winery established in 1854 by Patrick Auld now a champagne cellar of Penfolds. Australia.

Aulhausen. (24) Rhinegau; small village between Rüdesheim and Lorch. Fair white table wine. West Germany.

Aumerade, Domaine d'. (14) Côtes de Provence; Hyères vineyard, near Carqueiranne. Ordinary to fair red and rosé wines. France.

Auriol, Cru. (3) Ile-St-Georges, one of the islands in the Gironde river. 4,000 dozen bottles of ordinary red bordeaux. France.

Auros, Château d'. (5) Graves de Bordeaux; Auros, south-east of Langon. 2,000 dozen bottles of red bordeaux; 1,000 white. France.

Ausbruch. (33) German name of Tokaji Aszu wine (q.v.). Hungary.

Ausone, Château. (5) Côtes de St-Emilion. The most famous of the châteaux and vineyards of St-Emilion. *Premier grand cru classé.* 2,500 dozen bottles of very fine red bordeaux. France.

Ausserer-Neuberg. (25) Franconia; Würzburg. Fine white table wine. West Germany.

Aussy, Les. (8) Côte de Beaune; small Volnay vineyard. *Premier cru.* Fair red burgundy; not often used commercially. France.

Australia. (37) Most (70%) of the wines of Australia come from the vineyards of South Australia. Then, in order of quantitative importance, from New South Wales, Victoria, Western Australia, and Queensland. Most of the vintners of Australia produce all wine types, table and dessert wines, still and sparkling.

Austria. (33) The vineyards of modern Austria cover 115,843 acres: 62% in Lower Austria (Niederösterreich); 31·7% in the Burgenland; 4·6% in Styria; 1·7% outside Vienna, in the Austrian Tyrol and the Vorarlberg. The total average yield of Austrian vineyards is 50,000,000 gallons of wine, 85% white table wines of fair quality and 15% red and rosés of mostly ordinary quality.

Authental. (24) Rhinehessia; site name of a Guntersblum vineyard, between Alsheim and Dienheim. Fair white table wine. West Germany.

Autol. (29) Old Castile; Logroño province, La Rioja area of the upper Ebro valley. Stout, heady, red table wine. Spain.

Auvernier. (31) Neuchâtel area. Village producing ordinary to fair white table wine; also a locally popular tawny dessert wine. Switzerland.

Auvernier, Château d' (31) Neuchâtel; best vineyard of Auvernier. Fair to fine white table wine. Switzerland.

Auvernier, Cru d'. (31) Neuchâtel; small vineyard of Auvernier. Fair white table wine. Switzerland.

Avernier-Lerins, Cru d'. (31) Neuchâtel; vineyard of Auvernier. Fair white wine. Switzerland.

Auvillars-sur-Saône. (8) Since 1971 the remaining vines produce ordinary wines for local farmers. Red burgundy. France.

Auxerre. (6) Yonne *département*, chief city. Ordinary red table wine. France.

Auxerrois. (6) Auxerre countryside of lower Burgundy. Mostly white table wines from ordinary to fair and fine quality; also some ordinary red table wines e.g. Coulanges, Iranay (Pinot Noir and César). France.

Auxey-Duresses. (8) Côte de Beaune; small but ancient town. 65% red wine grapes and 35% white wine grapes. The alcoholic strength of the red wine must not go below 10·5° and that of the white wine not below 11° to be entitled to the *AC Auxey-Duresses*. France.

Avallon. (6) Yonne *departement*; south-east of Auxerre. Les Clos du Val Reugne. Ordinary red table wine. France.

Avaux, Clos des. (8) Beaune. A Hospice de Beaune *cuvée*. Fine red burgundy. France.

Avaux, Les. (8) Beaune vineyard. *Premier cru.* Fair to fine red burgundy. France.

Aveleira, Quinta. (30) *Região demarcada do Douro*. Estate and large vineyard in Medroes in the Régua area. Portugal.

Avellino. (28) Campania. Fair quality, ruby-red table wine made from Aglianico grapes. Italy.

Avelsbach. (22) Moselle valley; village between the Moselle and the Ruwer, at their confluence. Much fine white table wine, sometimes classed as a Ruwer wine. West Germany.

Avenay. (17) Ay canton, right bank of river Marne. Rated *premier cru*—93% growth. 434 acres. France.

Avensan. (4) Small town in the Haut-Médoc. Its vineyards produce much fair to fine red bordeaux. France.

Avertrana. (28) Another name for Manduria wine (q.v.). Italy.

Avidagos, Quinta. (30) *Região demarcada do Douro*. Estate and vineyard in Alvacoes do Corgo north-east of Régua. Portugal.

Avila. (29) Famous city of central Spain. Ordinary red and white wine. Spain.

Avino. (29) Barcelona area. Ordinary dry white table wine. Spain.

Avize. (17) Marne *département*; Avize canton. Chief town of the Côte des Blancs range of vine-clad hills. Rated *grand cru*—100% growth. White Chardonnay grapes. 552 acres. France.

Avoca. (37) Central Victoria; a 700-acre vineyard mainly for brandy production by Australian licence-holders for Remy Martin. Mostly White Hermitage, Doradillo. The smaller plots produce table wines. Australia.

Avocat, Clos de l'. (5) Graves de Bordeaux; Cérons. 300 dozen bottles of fair to fine white bordeaux. France.

Avocat, Cru de l'. (5) Graves de Bordeaux; Cérons. 1,500 dozen bottles of fair to fine white bordeaux. France.

Ay-Champagne. (17) Marne *département*; Ay canton, north of river Marne, between Avenay and Epernay. Rated *grand cru*—100% growth. 694 acres. France.

Ay-Danic. (34) South European Russia; Crimean peninsula. White dessert wine of Aligoté white grapes. U.S.S.R.

Ayelo de Malferit. (29) Valencia. Ordinary to fair red table wine. Spain.

Ayerbe. (29) Aragon; approx. forty-five miles north of Zaragoza. Ordinary red, white and rose table wines. Spain.

Ayl. (22) Saar Valley. Fair to fine white table wines. West Germany.

Ayse. (31) Savoie *département*; Annecy area, approx. twenty miles south of Geneva. Ordinary to fair white table wine. France.

Azay-le-Rideau. (16) Touraine; between Chinon and Tours. Ordinary to fair white table wine. France.

Aze. (10) Mâconnais. *AC Mâcon*. Ordinary to fair red and white burgundy. France.

🍇

Babillières, Les. (8) Côte de Nuits; Chambolle-Musigny vineyard. *Deuxième* and *troisième cru*. Fair red burgundy. France.

Baby, Château de. (5) Entre-deux-Mers; the chief vineyard of the Ste-Foy-Bordeaux *commune*, north-east of Langon. 18,000 dozen bottles of red bordeaux; 12,000 white. France.

Bacău. (33) Town in east Rumania. Ordinary to fair red table wine. Rumania.

Bacharach. (24) Rhinegau; town on the Rhine, north-west of Bingen. Fair white table wine. West Germany.

Bächel. (23) Middle Haardt; Wachenheim village vineyard. One of the few villages producing the finest white wines of the Palatinate. West Germany.

Bachenau. (25) Württemberg; village between Mosbach and Heilbronn. Ordinary to fair red and white table wines. West Germany.

Bachhell. (24) Rhinegau; Erbach vineyard. Fine to very fine white table wine. West Germany.

Backenacker. (24) Rhinegau; a small Geisenheim vineyard. Fine white table wine. West Germany.

Bäckhaus. (24) Rhinegau; Eibingen vineyard, between Rüdesheim and Lorch. Fair to fine white table wine. West Germany.

Badacsony, Mount. (33) Western Hungary; facing the north shore of Lake Balaton. An extinct volcano; the many vineyards upon its lower slopes, facing south and south-east, produce much wine, red, white and rosé, dry and sweet, mostly of ordinary and fair quality, but some of fine quality. Hungary.

Badacsonyi Auvergnas Gris. (33) Mount Badacsony vineyards (q.v.). Fine golden dessert wine. Hungary.

Badacsonyi Burgunder. (33) Mount Badacsony vineyards (q.v.). A stout red table wine of Pinot Noir grapes. Hungary.

Badacsonyi Keknelu. (33) Mount Badacsony vineyards (q.v.). A fair, dry, red table wine of Cabernet and other fine red grapes. Hungary.

Badacsonyi Muskotaly. (33) Mount Badacsony vineyards (q.v.). A rich Muscat white dessert wine. Hungary.

Badacsonyi Rizling. (33) Mount Badacsony vineyards (q.v.). A fair white table wine made from Riesling grapes. Hungary.

Badacsonyi Szurke-Baratis. (33) Mount Badacsony vineyards (q.v.). One of the best golden dessert wines of Hungary.

Badailh, Commune de. (5) Entre-deux-Mers. 1,000 dozen bottles of red bordeaux; 800 white. France.

Bad Bellingen. (25) Baden; vineyard approx. twenty-two miles south-west of Freiburg. Fair to fine white table wine. West Germany.

Bad Dürkheim. (23) Middle Haardt; small town. The vineyards produce some ordinary red wine, but a great deal more white table wines from fair to fine, and very fine quality, which are marketed as Dürkheim (not Bad) followed by the name of their native vineyard. West Germany.

Baden. (25) The former Grand Duchy of Baden faces Alsace to the west and stretches from the Swiss frontier to Rhinehessia with Württemberg to the north and east—it includes the Lake Constance (Bodensee) area. Its many vineyards produce considerable quantities of table wines, from ordinary to fair red wines, and from fair to fine white wines. West Germany.

Baden. (31) Aargau canton. Village with 240 acres of vineyards. Ordinary to fair red table wine. Switzerland.

Baden. (33) Village in Lower Austria. The vineyards produce some fair white table wine. Austria.

Badenheim. (24) Rhinehessia; village south of Rüdesheim. Ordinary red and fair white table wine. West Germany.

Badenweiler. (25) Baden; village approx. seventeen miles south-west of Freiburg. Fair white table wine. West Germany.

Badette, Château. (5) St-Emilion; St Christophe-des-Bardes, south-west of Parsac. An unclassified *cru*. 4,500 dozen bottles of red bordeaux. France.

Bad Kreuznach. (24) The historical and commercial centre of the Nahe valley. The vineyards produce white table wines, ordinary to fair, fine and even very fine quality. West Germany.

Bad Krozingen. (25) Baden; village south-west of Freiburg. Ordinary to fair white table wine. West Germany.

Bad Mergentheim. (25) Württemberg; small vineyards approx. twenty-three miles south-west of Stuttgart. Fair white table wine. West Germany.

Bad Münster am Stein. (24) Nahe valley; village west of Linz. Ordinary red and white table wines. West Germany.

Badon, Clos. (5) Côtes de St-Emilion. An unclassified *cru*. 1,500 dozen red bordeaux. France.

Badstube. (22) Middle Moselle valley; one of the better Bernkastel vineyards. Fine white table wine. West Germany.

Baena. (29) Andalusia; vineyards of Montilla-Montiles, Córdoba, approx. seventy-five miles north-east of Seville. Fair quality, dry white wine. Spain.

Baeza. (29) Andalusia; Jaén vineyards, east of Montilla-Montiles, Córdoba, approx. seventy-five miles north-east of Seville. Ordinary to fair red table wine. Spain.

Bagneux. (16) Anjou; Saumur area. Ordinary to fair red and rosé table wines. France.

Baguera. (29) Zaragoza; Teruel area. Ordinary to fair red and white table wine. Spain.

Bahezre de Lanlay, De. (8) A Hospices de Beaune vineyard. The *cuvée* has the *AC Mersault-Charmes*. White burgundy. France.

Baiken. (24) Rhinegau; one of the very best Rauenthal vineyards. Very fine white table wine. West Germany.

Bairrada. (30) One of the biggest wine-producing areas in Portugal, south of the river Douro and north-west of the Dão district. It produces many full-bodied red table wines, but also clean white wines and good sparkling wines. Situated between the Porcaco and Caramulo mountains and the Atlantic ocean. Portugal.

Bairro, Quinta. (30) *Região demarcada do Douro*. Estate and vineyard in Sanhoane in the Régua area. Portugal.

Baja California. (35) Northernmost territory of Mexico which produces ordinary table wines. Mexico.

Balaton, Lake. (33) The largest lake in Europe, approx. fifty miles south-west of Budapest, with many vineyards on its shores. Hungary.

Balbaina. (29) A district of the Jerez vineyards between Jerez de la Frontera and Sanlucar de Barrameda. Its vineyards produce mostly Fino sherries. Spain.

Balbino. (28) Calabria; Cosenza province, approx. thirty-five miles north-west of Cantanzaro. A white grape; also a strong white wine made from it. It can be both sweet or dry, although the sweet is more frequent and better known. Italy.

Balearics. (29) The group of Mediterranean islands off the coast of Spain, east of Valencia. Their vineyards produce only the more ordinary kinds of table wines, mostly red. Spain.

Baleau, Château. (5) Côtes de St-Emilion. *Grand cru classé*. 8,000 dozen red bordeaux. France.

Balestard, Domaine de. (5) Entre-deux-Mers; St Quentin-de-Baron, south-west of St Sulpice-de-Faleyrens. 2,000 dozen bottles of red bordeaux; 500 white. France.

Balestard-la-Tonnelle, Château. (5) Côtes de St-Emilion. *Grand cru classé*. 6,000 dozen bottles of red bordeaux. France.

Balestey, Château. (5) Graves de Bordeaux; Cérons. 4,000 dozen bottles of white bordeaux. France.

Baleyrac, Château de. (5) Entre-deux-Mers; Tizac-de-Curton, south-west of St Sulpice-de-Faleyrens. 1,000 dozen bottles of red bordeaux; 5,500 white. France.

Ballan. (16) Joué vineyard, just south-west of Tours. Ordinary to fair red table wine. France.

Ballrechten. (25) Baden; village approx. twenty-three miles south-west of Freiburg. Fair white table wine. West Germany.

Bamlach. (25) Baden; village approx. twenty-three miles south-west of Freiburg. Fair white table wine. West Germany.

Bandeirinha, Quinta. (30) Estate and vineyard in Poiares, north-east of Régua consisting of 55 acres. Portugal.

Bandol. (14) Côtes de Provence. Small provincial port with many vineyards on the hills of the surrounding country. Fair red, white and rosé table wines. France.

Bandonnier, Clos. (16) Touraine; Vouvray, east of Tours. Fair white table wine. France.

Baneza, La. (29) León. Dry red table wine of ordinary quality. Spain.

Bannay. (15) Sancerre area. Ordinary to fair quality white table wines. France.

Banos de Ebro. (29) Old Castile; Logroño province, La Rioja area of the upper Ebro valley. Fair to fine red table wine. Spain.

Banos de Fitero. (29) Navarre. Big, rough, dry, red table wine. Spain.

Banos de Montemayor. (29) Estremadura; Cáceres vineyards, in the Trujillo area. Fair, dry, red table wine. Spain.

Barabacque, Château. (3) Fronsadais; Côtes-Canon Fronsac. 4,000 dozen bottles of red bordeaux. France.

Barakan, Domaine de. (5) Premières Côtes de Bordeaux area; Tabanac, north-east of Portets. 500 dozen bottles of red bordeaux; 3,000 white. France.

Barande, La. (9) Mâconnais; Givry vineyard. *Premier cru*. Ordinary to fair red burgundy. France.

Barano. (28) Island of Ischia; bay of Naples. Ordinary to fair white table wine. Italy.

Barbacarlo. (26) Lombardy; Broni vineyard, Pavia province. Dry, deep-red table wine; sometimes semi-sweet and semi-sparkling. Italy.

Barbarano (Bianco, Rosso). (26) Colli Berici vineyards, south of Vicenza. Quite popular good quality, fair strength, white and red table wines. Italy.

Barbaresco. (26) East of Alba; between Asti and Cuneo. Good quality red wine made from the Nebbiolo grape. A full-bodied, fragrant wine very similar to, although maturing faster than, Barolo (q.v.). Italy.

Barbarossa. (26) Liguria; Savona. Fair quality rosé wines, some sweet and some dry. Italy.

Barbastro. (29) Aragon; Huesca area, north of Zaragoza. Ordinary to fair red and white table wines. Spain.

Barbe, Château de. (3) Côtes de Bourg; Villeneuve, south-east of Blaye. One of the principal vineyards of the area. 20,000 dozen bottles of red bordeaux. France.

Barbe-Blanche, Château. (5) St-Emilion; Lussac. 3,000 dozen bottles of red bordeaux. France.

Barbe-Morin, Château. (5) Premières Côtes de Bordeaux; Loupiac. 1,300 dozen bottles of red bordeaux; 2,000 white. France.

Barbera. (26) Piedmont (especially). A black grape; also a fair to fine quality red table wine made from it. Italy.

Barbera d'Alessándria. (26) Piedmont; Alessándria province. Fair quality red table wine. Italy.

Barbera d'Asti. (26) Piedmont; Asti province. Fair quality red table wine. Italy.

Barbera di Agnani. (27) Lazio; Agnani vineyards, eastern end of Castelli Romani hills, north of Frosinone. Fair quality, generous, full-bodied red table wine. Italy.

Barbera di Langhirano. (26) Emilia-Romagna;

Parma province. Ordinary to fair red table wine. Italy.

Barbera Leccese. (28) Apulia; Lecce vineyards. Ordinary, strong red table wine, which is drunk young and cooled. Italy.

Barbera Sarda. (28) Sardinia; Cagliari vineyards. Rather coarse, ordinary to fair red table wine. Italy.

Barberati. (26) Piedmont; Le Langhe vineyards, Cuneo province. Ordinary to fair red table wines. Italy.

Barberone. (36) California. The name of an ordinary, rather rough, red table wine. U.S.A.

Barberousse, Cru de. (5) Premières Côtes de Bordeaux; Loupiac. 500 dozen bottles of red bordeaux; 1,200 white. France.

Barbier, Château. (5) Fargues; a *commune* in the Sauternes area. *Cru bourgeois supérieur.* 1,500 dozen bottles of white bordeaux. France.

Barca, Quinta. (30) *Região demarcada do Douro.* Estate and vineyard in Vila Marim in the Régua area. Portugal.

Barde, Château La. (5) St-Emilion; St Laurent-des-Combes, west of St Etienne-de-Lisse. An unclassified *cru.* 2,000 dozen bottles of red bordeaux. France.

Barde, Château La. (3) Bourgeais. 7,000 dozen bottles of red bordeaux; 1,500 white. France.

Barde, Clos La. (5) St-Emilion; St Laurent-des-Combes, west of St Etienne-de-Lisse. An unclassified *cru.* 2,500 dozen bottles of red bordeaux. France.

Barde-Haut, Château. (5) St-Emilion; St Christophe-des-Bardes, south-west of Parsac. An unclassified *cru.* 10,000 dozen red bordeaux. France.

Bardes, Château Les. (5) Montagne de St-Emilion. An unclassified *cru.* 4,000 dozen bottles of red bordeaux. France.

Bardolino. (26) Lake Garda vineyards, Verona area. Fair quality ruby-red table wine, locally drunk young (when it is slightly *frizzante*) and cool. Italy.

Barengo. (26) Piedmont; Novara province. Ordinary to fair straw-coloured dry table wine. Italy.

Baresmes, Clos des. (16) Touraine; Ingrandes, Bourgeuil area. Ordinary to fair red table wine. France.

Baret, Château. (5) Graves de Bordeaux; Villeneuve-d'Ornon. 1,800 dozen bottles of red bordeaux; 2,000 white. France.

Bargetto's. (36) Santa Cruz county; winery and vineyard of Soquel, south of San Francisco and west of Santa Clara. Quality table wines. U.S.A.

Barguins, Les. (16) Touraine; Vouvray, east of Tours. Fair white table wine. France.

Bari. (28) Province of Apulia. Ordinary quality table wines. Italy.

Barletta. (28) Apulia; Trani vineyards, approx. thirty miles north-west of Bari. Fair to fine golden Moscato dessert wine. Italy.

Barolo. (26) Near Alba; commune of Barolo, between Asti and Cuneo. One of the great Italian red wines. Made from the Nebbiolo grape, it spends at least three years in the cask before bottling. Italy.

Barossa Co-operative Winery. (37) South Australia; Winery in the Barossa Valley, approx. thirty-five miles north-east of Adelaide. These wines are mostly marketed under the name of Kaiser Stuhl. Australia.

Barossa Valley. (37) The valley of the river Para from thirty-five miles above Adelaide to Angaston, about twenty miles in length and five miles in width. Its many vineyards produce much wine of fair to excellent quality, including table wines, dessert wines (superb port-type), sparkling, pearl wines, and brandy. Australia.

Barottes, Les. (8) Small Chambolle-Musigny vineyard. *Deuxième cru.* Ordinary to fair red burgundy. France.

Barr. (19) Bas-Rhin *département.* Fair white Alsace wine. France.

Barracos. (30) Fair red and white table wines from vineyards in the Lisbon area. Portugal.

Barras. (35) Northern Mexico; Cohahuila vineyards. Ordinary table wines. Mexico.

Barraults, Les. (9) Chalonnais; Mercurey. Ordinary to fair red burgundy. France.

Barre, Clos La. (16) Touraine; Vouvray vineyard, east of Tours. Ordinary to fair white table wine. France.

Barre, La. (8) Volnay vineyard. *Premier cru.* Fair red burgundy. France.

Barre, Clos de la. (16) Touraine; Montlouis. Ordinary to fair white table wine. France.

Barre, Cru de la. (3) Blayais. 2,500 dozen bottles of red bordeaux. France.

Barreaux, Les. (8) Vosne-Romanée vineyard. *Premier cru.* Fine red burgundy. France.

Barreiro, Quinta. (30) *Região demarcada do Douro* (q.v.). Estate and vineyard in the Vilarinho dos Freires area to the north-east of Régua. Portugal.

Barreyre, Château. (4) Haut-Médoc; Arsac. *Cru bourgeois.* 2,000 dozen bottles of red bordeaux. France.

Barreyre, Château. (5) Premières Côtes de Bordeaux; Langoiran, north-east of Portets. 1,000 dozen bottles of red bordeaux; 4,000 white. France.

Barreyre, Domaine de. (5) Haut-Médoc; Arcins,

north of Bordeaux. *Cru bourgeois*. 4,000 dozen bottles of red bordeaux. France.

Barrières, Aux. (8) Nuits-St-Georges vineyard. Fair to fine red burgundy. France.

Barroqueiro, Quinta. (30) *Região demarcada do Douro*. Estate and vineyard in Provesende north-east of Régua. Portugal.

Barthet, Château. (5) Graves de Bordeaux; Cérons. An unclassified *cru*. 1,000 dozen bottles of white bordeaux. France.

Barthez, Château. (4) Haut-Médoc; Le Pian, south-west of Ludon. *Cru bourgeois supérieur*. 1,500 dozen bottles of red bordeaux. France.

Bas-de-Combe. (8) Nuits-St-Georges vineyard. *Deuxième cru*. Fair red burgundy. France.

Bas-des-Duresses. (8) Auxey-Duresses vineyard. *Premier cru*. Fair red burgundy. France.

Bas-des-Saussilles. (8) Pommard vineyard. *Deuxième cru*. Fine red burgundy. France.

Bas-des-Teurons. (8) Beaune vineyard. *Premier cru*. Fine red burgundy. France.

Bas-Doix. (8) Chambolle-Musigny vineyard. *Deuxième cru*. Red burgundy. France.

Bas-Médoc. (3) Formerly the name of the northernmost part of the Médoc from St Seurin-de-Cadourne, the last *commune* of the Haut-Médoc, to Soulac, where the Gironde flows into the Bay of Biscay. It is now simply called Médoc. Its many vineyards produce much wine, both red and white, of ordinary or fair quality. France.

Basque. (29) Province of north-western Spain. Vineyards: 14,000 acres, producing mostly ordinary table wines. Spain.

Basque, Château du. (5) Castillon; St Pey-d' Armens. An unclassified *cru*. 4,000 dozen bottles of red bordeaux. France.

Basque, Château Le. (5) St-Emilion; Puisseguin. An unclassified *cru*. 7,500 dozen bottles of red bordeaux. France.

Bas-Rhin. (19) *Département*. Northern half of the former province of Alsace. Vineyards: 13,575 acres. Wine production: 5,456,000 dozen mostly white table wine, and wines of fair quality. France.

Basse-Bourgogne. (6) 'Lower Burgundy' is the northernmost part of the former province of Burgundy. Vineyards: 7,500 acres. Wine: 2,000,000 dozen bottles of ordinary to fair table wine; also some fine white table wines including those of Chablis. France.

Basses-Alpes. (12) *Département*. Vineyards: 7,100 acres. Wine: 1,752,000 dozen bottles. Ordinary to fair table wines. France.

Basses-Maizières, Les. (8) Vosne-Romanée vineyard. Red burgundy. France.

Basses-Vergelesses. (8) Pernand-Vergelesses

vineyard. *Premier cru*. Fair to fine red burgundy. France.

Bassets, Les. (9) Chalonnais village and vineyards in the Mercurey area. Ordinary red burgundy. France.

Basso-Cilesto. (28) Salerno vineyards. Ordinary to fair stout red table wine. Italy.

Basso-Scle. (28) Salerno vineyards. Fair red table wine. Italy.

Bastia. (27) Umbria; village approx. two miles from Assisi, south-east of Perugia. Red and white wines of unremarkable quality. Italy.

Bastide Verte, Clos de la. (14) Côtes de Provence; La Garde vineyard on the Côtes des Maures east of Toulon. Ordinary to fair red and white table wines. France.

Bastienne, Château La. (5) St-Emilion; Montagne. An unclassified *cru*. 8,000 dozen bottles of red bordeaux. France.

Basto. (30) One of the six subregions of the Vinhos Verdes district. Portugal.

Bataillère, Clos. (16) Coteaux de la Loire; Brain-sur-l'Authion vineyard, north-west of Bourgueil. Fair white table wine. France.

Batailley, Château. (4) Haut-Médoc; Pauillac. *Cinquième cru classé*. 7,000 dozen bottles of red bordeaux. France.

Bâtard-Montrachet. (8) Côte de Beaune. The name of a number of vineyards which produce some of the finest white burgundy in the *commune* of Chassagne-Montrachet and in the adjoining *commune* of Puligny-Montrachet. *Grand cru*. France.

Bate, Clos de la. (16) Anjou; St Cyr-en-Bourg vineyard, Coteaux de Saumur. Fair red and rosé table wines. France.

Bateira, Quinta. (30) *Região demarcada do Douro*. Estate in Casais do Douro in the Régua area. Portugal.

Batista. (29) Balearic Islands, off the coast east of Valencia. Rough, dry, dark red wine. Spain.

Batonnières, Clos des. (16) Touraine; Roche-corbon vineyard, north-east of Tours. Fair to fine white table wine. France.

Batsalles, Clos. (5) Sauternes; Fargues. *Cru bourgeois*. 3,000 dozen bottles of white bordeaux. France.

Battenberg. (23) Palatinate; village just south of Grünstadt. Ordinary red and fair white table wines. West Germany.

Batteraux. (16) Cravant-les-Coteaux, below Angers. Ordinary to fair red table wine. France.

Baudes, Les. (8) Chambolle-Musigny vineyard. *Premier cru*. Fine red burgundy. France.

Baudoin, Clos. (16) Touraine, Vouvray vineyard, east of Tours. Fair white table wine. France.

Baudot. (8) Hospices de Beaune. White burgundy *cuvée* named after the donor of the vineyard to the Hospices. France.

Baulet, Clos. (8) Côte de Nuits; Morey-St-Denis vineyard. *Deuxième cru*. Red burgundy. France.

Baumberg. (22) Moselle Valley; Aldegund vineyard, between Eller and Zell. Ordinary to fair white table wine. West Germany.

Bazau. (33) Town in south-east central Rumania; Wallachian vineyards. Fair, dry red table wine. Rumania.

Baziliques, Château Les. (5) St-Emilion; St Christophe-des-Bardes, south-west of Barsac. An unclassified *cru*. 1,200 dozen bottles of red bordeaux. France.

Beard, Château. (5) St-Emilion; St Laurent-des-Combes, west of St Etienne-de-Lisse. An unclassified *cru*. 2,500 dozen bottles of red bordeaux. France.

Béarn. (29) Part of Basses Pyrénées *département*; bordering the Navarre and Basque provinces of Spain. *V.D.Q.S.* table wines. France.

Beatas, Quinta. (30) *Região demarcada do Douro* (q.v.). Estate in Gouvaes in the Régua area. Produces a limited quantity of wine. Portugal.

Beau-Cherie, Château de. (5) Graves de Bordeaux; Beautiran. An unclassified *cru*. 1,500 dozen bottles of red bordeaux; 200 white. France.

Beaujeu. (11) Beaujolais. Small town from which the name Beaujolais is derived. Some of the better vineyards of Beaujeu are the property of the municipal hospital and their wines are sold by auction each year in the same way as are the wines of the Hospices de Beaune (q.v.). France.

Beaujolais. (11) The southernmost part of the chain of vineyards running from south of Dijon to the north of Lyons. There are three *Appellations Controlées* corresponding to three grades of quality of the red wines of Beaujolais: *Beaujolais supérieur*, *Beaujolais* and *Beaujolais villages*. France.

Beaulac, Château. (5) Graves de Bordeaux; close to Barsac. 600 dozen bottles of white bordeaux. France.

Beaulieu. (1) Hampshire; south-central England. A thousand-year-old Cistercian Abbey vineyard of 5½ acres replanted after World War II with conspicuous success. England.

Beaulieu. (36) California; Rutherford county, Napa Valley. One of the more famous wineries and vineyards of California. It was recently acquired by Heublein Inc. from the founder's family and produces an excellent Cabernet Sauvignon and Pinot Chardonnay. It is known for its fine table wines; also dessert and sparkling wines. U.S.A.

Beaulieu, Château. (3) Bourgeais; Samonac, north of Bourg. 4,500 dozen bottles of red bordeaux. France.

Beaulieu, Château. (5) Graves de Bordeaux; Cérons. 1,000 dozen bottles of white bordeaux. France.

Beaumont, Château. (4) Haut-Médoc; Cussac. *Cru bourgeois supérieur*. 10,000 dozen bottles of red bordeaux. France.

Beaumes du Ventoux. (12) Côtes du Rhône; Ventoux vineyards, north-east of Avignon. Ordinary to fair red and rosé table wines. France.

Beaumes, Les. (12) Côtes du Rhône; Tain l'Hermitage vineyard. *Deuxième cru*. Ordinary to fair red table wine. France.

Beaumont-en-Véron. (16) Touraine; Côtes de Chinon, below Chinon. Fair red table wine. France.

Beaumont-sur-Vesle. (17) Verzy canton, by river Vesle before it reaches Rheims. Rated *grand cru*—100% growth. 62 acres. France.

Beaune. (8) Côte de Beaune, chief town. Fair, fine and some very fine burgundy, mostly red. Best vineyards: Clos des Mouches, Clos du Roi, Champs-Pimonts, Les Perrières, Les Toussaints, Les Cent-Vignes, Clos de la Mousse aux Cras, Les Boucherottes, Les Vignes Franches, Pertuisots, Les Aigrots, Les Sisies, Les Avaux, Les Reversées, Le Bas-des-Teurons, Les Epenottes, La Mignotte, Montée Rouge. France.

Beaupuy. (16) Touraine; Bourgueil. Fair red table wine. France.

Beauregard. (16) Anjou; Coteaux du Layon, Bonnézeaux, south of the Loire, between Saumur and Angers. Fair to fine white and rosé table wines. France.

Beauregard. (7) Santenay vineyard. *Deuxième cru*. Red burgundy. France.

Beauregard, Château. (5) Pomerol. *Grand cru*. 6,500 dozen bottles of red bordeaux. France.

Beauregard, Clos. (5) Pomerol. 5,000 dozen bottles of red bordeaux. France.

Beaurepaire. (7) Santenay vineyard. *Deuxième cru*. Red burgundy. France.

Beaury. (6) Chablis vineyard. *Premier cru*. White burgundy. France.

Beauséjour, Château. (4) Haut-Médoc; St Estèphe. *Cru bourgeois supérieur*. 6,000 dozen bottles of red bordeaux. France.

Beauséjour, Château. (5) St-Emilion; Puisseguin. An unclassified *cru*. 8,000 dozen bottles of red bordeaux. France.

Beauséjour, Château. (5) St-Emilion; Montagne. An unclassified *cru*. 6,000 dozen bottles of red bordeaux. France.

Beauséjour-Fagouet, Château. (5) St-Emilion;

Côtes de St-Emilion. *Premier grand cru classé.* 4,000 dozen bottles of red bordeaux. France.

Beau-Site, Château. (4) Haut-Médoc; St-Estèphe. *Cru bourgeois supérieur.* 13,000 dozen bottles of red bordeaux. France.

Beau-Site-Haut-Vignoble, Château. (4) Haut-Médoc; St-Estèphe. *Cru bourgeois.* 6,000 dozen bottles of red bordeaux. France.

Beausset, Le. (14) Var *département*; Bandol vineyard. Ordinary to fair red, white and rosé table wines. France.

Beaux-Bruns, Aux. (8) Côte de Nuits; Chambolle-Musigny vineyard. *Premier cru.* Fair red burgundy. France.

Beaux-Monts, Les. (8) Côte de Nuits; Vosne-Romanée vineyard. *Premier cru.* Fine red burgundy. France.

Beaux-Monts-Bas, Les. (8) Côte de Nuits; Flagey-Echézeaux vineyard. *Premier cru.* Fine red burgundy. France.

Beaux-Monts-Hauts, Les. (8) Côte de Nuits; Flagey-Echézeaux vineyard. *Deuxième cru.* Fair red burgundy. France.

Beblenheim. (19) Haut-Rhin *département*; south-east of Riquewihr. Ordinary to fair white Alsace wine. France.

Becas. (29) Catalonia; Panadés area, between Tarragona and Barcelona. Ordinary to fair red and white table wines. Spain.

Bechenheim. (24) Rhinehessia; vineyard east of Bad Kreuznach. Ordinary to fair white table wine. West Germany.

Becherelle. (16) Touraine; small Savennières vineyard, near Angers. Fair to fine white table wine. France.

Bech-Kleinmacher. (32) Moselle valley; a village approx. eleven miles south-east of Luxembourg city. Ordinary to fair white table wine. Luxembourg.

Bechtcim. (24) Rhinehessia; small town just south of Alsheim. Ordinary, fair and some fine white table wines. West Germany.

Bechtolsheim. (24) Rhinehessia; village in the Oppenheim district, just south of Alsheim. Ordinary to fair red and white table wines. West Germany.

Beckstein. (25) Franconia; village in the Main valley, approx. twenty miles south-west of Würzburg. Fair to fine white table wine. West Germany.

Bédat, Château. (5) Graves de Bordeaux; Podensac. 1,000 dozen bottles of white bordeaux. France.

Bégadan. (3) Médoc; small town north-west of St Seurin-de-Cadourne. Ordinary to fair bordeaux wines. France.

Béhuard. (16) Anjou; Coteaux de la Loire, St Georges-sur-Loire below Angers. Ordinary to fair white table wine. France.

Beilstein-Untermosel. (22) Lower Moselle valley; village between Eller and Bruttig. Ordinary to fair white table wine. West Germany.

Beilstein-Württemberg. (25) Württemberg; village east of Heilbronn. Ordinary to fair red table wine. West Germany.

Bekond. (22) Moselle valley; village west of Klüsserath. Ordinary to fair white table wine. West Germany.

Bel-Air. (16) Anjou; Cravant-les-Coteaux vineyard, below Angers. Fair red table wine. France.

Bel-Air. (11) Beaujolais; Chiroubles vineyard. Fair red beaujolais. France.

Belair, Château. (5) St-Emilion. *Premier grand cru classé.* 4,000 dozen bottles of red bordeaux. France.

Bel-Air, Château. (5) Pomerol. 6,000 dozen bottles of red bordeaux. France.

Bel-Air, Château. (5) St-Emilion; Puisseguin. An unclassified *cru.* 5,000 dozen bottles of red bordeaux. France.

Bel-Air, Château-Chevrol. (5) Néac; bordering on Pomerol. 4,500 dozen bottles of red bordeaux. France.

Bel-Air, Château de. (5) Lalande-de-Pomerol; north of Pomerol. 5,000 dozen bottles of red bordeaux. France.

Bel-Air, Clos. (16) Vouvray, east of Tours. Fair white table wine. France.

Bel-Air, Domaine de. (3) Bourgeais; Gauriac, north-west of Bourg. 1,000 dozen bottles of red bordeaux. France.

Bel-Air-Mareil, Cru. (3) Médoc; Ordonnac-et-Potensac, north-west of St Seurin-de-Cadourne. *Cru bourgeois.* 1,500 dozen bottles of red bordeaux. France.

Bel-Air Marquis d'Aligre, Château. (4) Haut-Médoc; Soussans. *Cru exceptionnel.* 5,000 dozen bottles of red bordeaux. France.

Bela Vista, Quinta. (30) *Região demarcada do Douro.* Pocinho, near Vila Nova de Fozcoa in the Régua area. Portugal.

Belchite. (29) Aragon. Ordinary to fair red and white table wines. Spain.

Belfontaine, Château. (5) St Pierre-de-Mons. 500 dozen bottles of red bordeaux; 800 white. France.

Bellagio. (26) Lombardy; Lake Como, holiday resort. Good quality light red wines. Italy.

Bellagio Spumante. (26) Lombardy; Lake Como vineyards. Popular sparkling wine, low in alcoholic content, but high in sugar content. Italy.

Bellay, Château de. (16) Anjou; Allones vineyard,

north-east of Saumur. Ordinary to fair red wine. France.

Belle-Croix. (8) Nuits-St-Georges vineyard. *Deuxième* and *troisième cru*. Fair red burgundy. France.

Bellefont-Belcier, Château. (5) St-Emilion; St Laurent-des-Combes, west of St Etienne-de-Lisse. An unclassified *cru*. 7,000 dozen bottles of red bordeaux. France.

Bellegarde, Château. (3) Fronsadais. 1,500 dozen bottles of red bordeaux; 1,000 white. France.

Bellegrave, Château. (4) Haut-Médoc; Listrac. *Cru bourgeois*. 3,000 dozen bottles of red bordeaux. France.

Bellegrave, Château. (4) Haut-Médoc; Pauillac. *Cru bourgeois*. 2,000 dozen bottles of red bordeaux. France.

Belles-Graves, Château. (5) St-Emilion; Vignonet, south-west of St-Pey-d'Armens. An unclassified *cru*. 3,000 dozen bottles of red bordeaux. France.

Bellevue, Château. (4) Côtes de Blaye. 8,000 dozen bottles of red bordeaux. France.

Bellevue, Château. (5) Côtes de St-Emilion. *Grand cru classé*. 3,000 dozen bottles of red bordeaux. France.

Bellevue, Château. (5) St-Emilion; Lussac. An unclassified *cru*. 9,000 dozen bottles of red bordeaux. France.

Bellevue, Clos de. (16) Rochecorbon, north-east of Tours. Fair white table wine. France.

Bellevue-Gazin, Cru. (4) Blayais; Plassac, south-east of Blaye. 3,000 dozen bottles of red bordeaux. France.

Bellevue Winery. (37) New South Wales. Winery and vineyard in the Hunter River valley, north-east of Sydney. Mostly fair to fine table wines. Australia.

Bellheim. (23) Palatinate; south-east of Landau. Fair white table wines. West Germany.

Bellingham. (39) Little Karroo area; Groot Drakenstein vineyard and winery, inland and to north-east of Cape Town. Mostly fair to fine table wines. South Africa.

Belloy, Château. (3) Côtes Canon-Fronsac; Fronsadais. 2,000 dozen bottles of red bordeaux. France.

Belmonte. (29) La Mancha vineyards; north of Valdepeñas. Fair white table wine. Spain.

Belmonte de Calatayud. (29) Zaragoza. Very dark and strong red table wine. Spain.

Bel-Orme-Tronquoy-de-Lalande, Château. (4) Haut-Médoc; St Seurin-de-Cadourne. *Cru bourgeois*. 12,000 dozen bottles of red bordeaux. France.

Bels. (24) Nahe valley; Bad Kreuznach vineyard. Fine white table wine. West Germany.

Belvedère, Le. (16) Anjou; Coteaux de la Loire, Chalonne-sur-Loire vineyard. Fair white table wine. France.

Benabarba. (29) Aragon; Huesca area, north of Zaragoza. A red table wine. Spain.

Benais. (16) Touraine; village and vineyards near Bourgueil. Fair to fine red table wine. France.

Benavente. (29) Central Léon; Zamora area. Ordinary to fair red table wine, also a *clarete* of fair quality. Spain.

Bende. (24) Rhinehessia; small Bechtheim vineyard, just south of Alsheim. Fair to fine white table wine. West Germany.

Bender. (23) Palatinate; Königsbach vineyard. Fine white table wine. West Germany.

Ben Ean. (37) New South Wales; Hunter valley north-east of Sydney. One of the oldest wineries and vineyards of the Hunter River area. Australia.

Benejama. (29) South-east Spain; Alicante area, approx. forty miles south-east of Valencia. Ordinary to fair table wines. Spain.

Beney, Cru. (3) Blayais; Mazion, north-east of Blaye. 2,500 dozen bottles of red bordeaux. France.

Benicarlo. (29) Valencia area. Ordinary to fair red table wine. Spain.

Benicasim. (29) Castellón de la Plana area; approx. forty miles north-east of Valencia. Ordinary, stout red table wine. Spain.

Beniganim. (29) Valencia area. Ordinary to fair light white table wine. Spain.

Beniquet. (16) Coteaux de Saumur; Parnay vineyard. Fair white table wine. France.

Benisa. (29) Alicante area; 40 miles south of Valencia. Ordinary to fair table wine. South-east Spain.

Benisalem. (29) Balearic Islands; off the coast, east of Valencia. Ordinary to fair Majorcan table wines. Spain.

Benn. (23) Palatinate; Kallstadt vineyard. Fine white table wine. West Germany.

Benningen. (25) Württemberg; village north-east of Stuttgart. Ordinary red table wine. West Germany.

Berdellos. (29) Southern Galicia; Pontevedra vineyards, in the Orense region. Ordinary to fair white table wine. Spain.

Berg. German for hill or mountain; it is the name of many sites of vineyards in a great number of the vinelands of the Rhineland. West Germany.

Bergat, Château. (5) Côtes de St-Emilion. *Grand cru classé*. 1,500 dozen bottles of red bordeaux. France.

Bergères-les-Vertus. (17) Côte des Blancs *dé-*

partement; Avize canton, south of Vertus. Rated *premier cru*—black 90% growth; white 93%. 432 acres. France.

Bergeron, Château. (5) Sauternes; Bommes. *Cru bourgeois supérieur.* 1,200 dozen bottles of white bordeaux. France.

Bergheim. (19) Haut-Rhin *département.* Ordinary to fair white Alsace wine. France.

Bergkloster. (24) Rhinehessia; Westhofen vineyard, south-west of Alsheim. Fair white table wine. West Germany.

Bergstrasse. (21) A wine-producing territory in the south-western region of the Rhineland, partly in Hesse and partly in Baden. West Germany.

Bergweiler. (22) Middle Moselle; west of Zeltingen, Wehlen, Graach and other Moselle villages. Fine white wine. West Germany.

Bergzabern. (23) Palatinate. Ordinary red and fair white table wines. West Germany.

Beringer Brothers. (36) California; winery and vineyard of St Helena, Napa Valley recently acquired by Premium Wines Inc. Quality table and dessert wines; also sparkling wine and brandy. U.S.A.

Berkane. (40) Town in north-easternmost part of Morocco. Fair red wine and rosé table wines; also some Muscat dessert wines. Morocco.

Berlango de Duero. (29) Soria area; approx. eighty-five miles west of Zaragoza. Ordinary red table wine. Spain.

Berliquet, Château. (5) Côtes de St-Emilion. An unclassified *cru.* 3,500 dozen bottles of red bordeaux. France.

Bermatingen. (25) Lake Constance (Bodensee); village south-west of Ulm. Fair white table wine. West Germany.

Bermersheim. (24) Rhinehessia; village south-east of Bad Kreuznach. Ordinary to fair red and white table wines. West Germany.

Bermersheim-Worms. (24) Rhinehessia; village north-west of Worms. Ordinary red and fair white table wines. West Germany.

Bern. (31) Canton of Switzerland; its only vineyards of any importance are those by Lake Biel (Bienne). Fair white table wine. Switzerland.

Bernachot, Château. (5) St-Emilion; St Sulpice-de-Faleyrens. An unclassified *cru.* 4,000 dozen bottles of red bordeaux. France.

Bernadats, Les. (15) Village near Pouilly-sur-Loire. Fair to fine white table wine. France.

Berne. *See* **Bern.**

Berney. (31) Geneva canton; village. Ordinary to fair white table wine. Switzerland.

Bernkasteler Doktor. (22) Moselle; best Bernkastel vineyard and the most famous one of the Moselle vineyards. Very fine white wine. West Germany.

Bernkastel-Kues. (22) Twin towns facing each other across the river Moselle; Bernkastel on the right and Kues (formerly Cues) on the left bank. Fair, fine and some very fine white table wines— among the most highly regarded of German wines. West Germany.

Berri Co-Operative Winery & Distillery. (37) South Australia; on the Murray River, in the Renmark area north-east of Berri. One of the largest wineries and distilleries in South Australia.

Bertelo, Quinta. (30) *Região demarcada do Douro* (q.v.). Estate in Cumeira in the Régua area. Portugal.

Bertelots. (10) Mâconnais; Solutré vineyard. *Premier Cru. AC Pouilly-Fuissé.* Fine white burgundy. France.

Berthou, Château. (3) Bourgeais; Comps, north west of Bourg. 1,500 dozen bottles of red bordeaux. France.

Bertins. (8) Côte de Beaune; Pommard vineyard. *Premier cru.* Red burgundy. France.

Beru. (6) Chablis village. Ordinary to fair white burgundy. France.

Berweg. (23) Palatinate; Bissersheim vineyard, between Grünstadt and Dackenheim. Ordinary to fair white table wine. West Germany.

Berzé-la-Ville. (10) Mâconnais village. Ordinary to fair red burgundy. France.

Besigheim. (25) Württemberg; village south-west of Heilbronn. Ordinary to fair red and white table wines. West Germany.

Bessards, Les. (12) Côtes du Rhône; Tain l'Hermitage vineyard. *Premier cru.* Red table wine. France.

Bessarots, Les. (12) Côtes du Rhône; Tain l'Hermitage vineyard. Fair red table wine. France.

Bessay. (11) Beaujolais; Juliénas. Red burgundy. France.

Betault. (8) Hospices de Beaune *cuvée,* named after the donor of the vineyard to the Hospices, with *AC Beaune.* Fair red burgundy. France.

Bettelmann. (24) Rhinegau; Hochheim vineyard. Fair to fine white table wine. West Germany.

Bettenberg. (25) Franconia; Iphofen vineyard in the Main valley, approx. seventeen miles south-east of Würzburg. Fine white table wine. West Germany.

Beugnons. (6) Chablis vineyard. *Premier cru.* Fine white burgundy. France.

Beutelsbach. (21) Württemberg; vineyard north-east of Stuttgart. Ordinary to fair red and white table wines. West Germany.

Beuvais. (31) Neuchâtel canton. Fair to fine white table wine. Switzerland.

Bex. (31) Vaud canton; Chablais. Fair to fine white table wines. Switzerland.

Beyaz. (34) A medium-sweet white Turkish table wine. Turkey.

Beychevelle, Château. (4) Haut-Médoc; St-Julien. *Quatrième cru classé.* 15,000 dozen bottles of red bordeaux. France.

Beycheville, Domaine de. (4) Cubzaguais; St Andre-de-Cubzac, east of Macau. 8,500 dozen bottles of red bordeaux. France.

Bézé, Clos de. (8) Côte de Nuits; Gevrey-Chambertin vineyard. *Grand cru.* Red burgundy. France.

Bezigon. (16) Anjou; Beaulieu-sur-Layon vineyard, below Angers. Fair to fine white table wine. France.

Biac, Château du. (5) Premières Côtes de Bordeaux; Langoiran, north-east of Portets. 1,000 dozen bottles of red bordeaux; 5,000 white. France.

Biancale di Rimini. (26) Name given in Romagna to the white Trebbiano grape and the sound white table wine made from it. Italy.

Biancavilla Rosso. (28) Sicily; foothills of Mount Etna, south of Catania. Stout, red table wine. Italy.

Bianchello Pesarese. (27) The Marches; Pesaro area, approx. thirty-six miles north-west of Ancona. Fair, popular, rather light, dry white wine. Italy.

Bianchi Carta. (28) Sicily; Castellamare del Golfo vineyards, approx. thirty miles south-west of Palermo. A strong, dry white wine used for blending; a similar, though lighter, wine drunk locally as table wine is known as Bianco Castellamare. Italy.

Biancho di Locorotondo. (28) Apulia; Bari vineyards. Ordinary white table wine, a great deal of which is used as a base for vermouth. Italy.

Bianco Brusco de Teolo. (26) Friuli-Venezia Giulia; Colli Euganei vineyards, Gorizia-Trieste area. Fair white table wine. Italy.

Bianco Castellamare. (28) Sicily; Castellamare del Golfo vineyards. Ordinary, light, dry white table wine, similar to Bianchi Carta (q.v.). Italy.

Bianco Cinqueterre. (26) Liguria; La Spezia area. Fine, full-flavoured dry white wine. A rich, golden dessert wine is also rarely produced. Italy.

Bianco dei Colli Albani. (27) Lazio; Alban hills, Roman part. Fair, light white wine. Italy.

Bianco dei Colli Berici. (26) Berici hills; area south of Vicenza. Fair, slightly sweet, white wine. Italy.

Bianco dei Colli di Asola-Maser. (26) Treviso area. Fair, white wine, best drunk young. Italy.

Bianco dei Colli di Conegliano. (26) Conegliano hills; north of Treviso, Gorizia-Trieste area. Fair, white wine, at its best when young. Italy.

Bianco dei Colli Euganei. (26) Friuli-Venezia Giulia; Gorizia-Trieste area. Ordinary to fair dry, or semi-sweet, still and semi-sparkling white wines. Italy.

Bianco dei Colli Lanuri (Lanurio). (27) Lazio; area north-west of Velletri. Ordinary to fair dry, semi-sweet and sweet white table wines. Italy.

Bianco del Collio. (26) Friuli-Venezia Giulia; Gorizia area, Colli Goriziano. Fair, white table wine that is drunk young. Italy.

Bianco della Riviera. (26) Italian Riviera; Santa Margherita, between Genoa and La Spezia. Ordinary and popular white table wine. Italy.

Bianco della Val d'Elsa. (27) Tuscany. Fair white table wine usually made from Trebbiano grapes. Italy.

Bianco del Littorale Livornese. (27) Another name for the white wine usually called Ugolino Bianco (q.v.). Italy.

Bianco di Martina Franca. (28) Apulia; Taranto vineyards. Fair, white table wine, similar to Bianco di Locorotondo (q.v.). Italy.

Bianco di Montalbuccio. (27) Tuscany. One of the favourite white table wines, and very similar to Arbia (q.v.). Italy.

Bianco di Ronciglione. (27) Lazio; Colli Cimini vineyards, south-east of Viterbo. Fair, white wine. Italy.

Bianco di Santa Margherita. (27) Tuscany; Siena area. Ordinary to fair white table wine, the must of which is fermented without stalks or skins and is therefore light and delicate. Italy.

Bianco di Velletri. (27) Lazio; Rome area. Ordinary to fair white table wine that is so light in flavour, scent and colour that it sometimes seems insipid. Italy.

Biancolella. (28) Island of Ischia; bay of Naples. A white grape, and the light pleasant white table wine made from it. Italy.

Bianco Misto di Caneva. (26) Friuli-Venezia Giulia; Udine vineyards. Ordinary, dry white table wine to be drunk very young. Italy.

Bianco Piceno. (27) The Marches; Ascoli Piceno vineyards, south-east of Perugia. Fair, white table wine. Italy.

Biar. (29) Alicante area; approx. forty miles south-east of Valencia. An ordinary, dry table wine. Spain.

Biaume, La. (11) Beaujolais, Fleurie vineyard. Red beaujolais. France.

Bibaudières, Les. (16) Vouvray vineyard, east of Tours. Fair, white, semi-sweet table wine. France.

Bichon, Cru. (5) Graves de Bordeaux; Arbanats, north-west of Podensac. An unclassified *cru.* 600 dozen bottles of red bordeaux; 2,500 white. France.

Bickensohl. (25) Baden; village north-west of Freiburg. Ordinary to fair red and white table wines. West Germany.

Bickert. (22) Middle Moselle valley; Zeltingen vineyard. Fair to fine white table wine. West Germany.

Biebelhausen. (22) Saar valley; village. Fair white table wine. West Germany.

Biebelnheim. (24) Rhinehessia; village north-west of Alsheim. Fair to fine white table wine. West Germany.

Biebelsheim. (24) Rhinehessia; village north-east of Bad Kreuznach. Fair to fine white table wine. West Germany.

Biegels. (24) Rhinegau; Hallgarten vineyard. Fine white table wine. West Germany.

Biel (Bienne), Lake. (31) Bern canton. Its vineyards on north shore, facing south, produce some fair to fine white table wine. Best vineyards are those of Erlach, Neuville and Twann. Switzerland.

Bienboire, Clos de la. (16) Anjou; Coteaux de Saumur, Souzay-Champigny vineyard. Fair to fine white table wine. France.

Bienenberg. (22) Moselle valley; Treis vineyard, between Kobern and Valwig. Fair white table wine. West Germany.

Bienengarten. (22) Moselle valley; Senheim vineyard, between Bruttig and Eller. Fair white table wine. West Germany.

Bienengarten. (23) Palatinate; Gimmeldingen vineyard. Fair white table wine. West Germany.

Bienengarten. (24) Rhinegau; Rüdesheim and Winkel vineyards. Fair to fine white table wine. West Germany.

Bienengarten. (24) Rhinehessia; Bingen vineyard. Ordinary to fair white table wine. West Germany.

Bienenlay. (22) Moselle valley; Eller vineyard. Fair white table wine. West Germany.

Bienvenue-Bâtard-Montrachet. (8) Côte de Beaune; the northern end of the Bâtard-Montrachet vineyard. Very fine white burgundy. France.

Bieringen. (25) Württemberg; village approx. seventeen miles east of Mosbach. Ordinary to fair red and white table wines. West Germany.

Bietigheim. (25) Württemberg; village north of Stuttgart. Ordinary to fair red and white table wines. West Germany.

Bigotière, La. (16) Coteaux de l'Aubance; Mozé-sur-Loire vineyard, between Angers and Saumur. Fair white table wine. France.

Bikaver. (33) Eger valley; approx. sixty-five miles north-east of Budapest. Stout, dark red, dry red wine. Hungary.

Bildchen. (22) Middle Moselle valley; Piesport vineyard. Fine white table wine. West Germany.

Bildhausel. (23) Palatinate; Diedesfeld vineyard, between Neustadt and Edenkoben. Fair to fine white table wine. West Germany.

Bildstock. (24) Rhinehessia; Nierstein vineyard. Fair white table wine. West Germany.

Biljanski Grici. (33) West Yugoslavia, bordering Italy; Nova Gorica. Range of fine terraced vineyards. Fine red wines such as Barbera. Yugoslavia.

Billardet. (8) Hospices de Beaune *cuvée*, named after the donor of the vineyard to the Hospices. Fair red burgundy. France.

Billigheim. (23) Palatinate; village north-east of Bergzabern. Ordinary red and fine white table wines. West Germany.

Bilyara Vineyards. (37) South Australia; Nariootpa, Barossa Valley, approx. thirty-five miles north-east of Adelaide. Also gold-medal-winning Cabernet Sauvignon and Cabernet-Malbec wines from grapes of Langhorne Creek, thirty-five miles south-east of Adelaide.

Bingen. (24) Rhinehessia; town on the river Nahe where it joins the Rhine. Ordinary, fair and some fine white table wines. West Germany.

Bingen-Büdesheim. (24) The part of Bingen which stands on the left bank of the river Nahe where it joins the Rhine, facing Bingen in Rhinehessia. Ordinary and fair white table wine. West Germany.

Bingen-Kempten. (24) On the right bank of the river Nahe, in the Rhinehessia territory of Bingen. Ordinary, fair and fine white table wines. West Germany.

Bingerbrück. (24) Nahe; on the left bank of the river, above Bingen. Fair white table wine. West Germany.

Birgweg. (24) Rhinegau; Rüdesheim vineyard. Fine white table wine. West Germany.

Birkenberg. (24) Nahe valley; Roxheim vineyard, north-west of Bad Kreuznach. Fair to fine white table wine. West Germany.

Birkweiler. (23) Palatinate village. Ordinary, fair and some fine white table wines. West Germany.

Bisamberg. (33) Village in the Vienna area. Ordinary to fair red and white table wines. Austria.

Bisbal del Panadés. (29) Tarragona region. Ordinary red table wine. Spain.

Bischheim. (23) Palatinate; village north-west of Grünstadt. Ordinary to fair red and white table wines. West Germany.

Bischoffingen. (25) Baden; village north of Freiburg. Ordinary to fair red and white table wines. West Germany.

Bischofsberg. (24) Rhinegau; Rüdesheim vineyard. Very fine white table wine. West Germany.

Bischofshub. (24) Middle Rhine; Oberdiebach vineyard, between Bingen and Lorch. Ordinary white table wine. West Germany.

Bischofsweg. (23) Palatinate; Mussbach vineyard. Fair to fine white table wine. West Germany.

Bissen. (33) A popular white dessert wine of Bulgaria.

Bissersheim. (23) Palatinate; village between Grünstadt and Dackenheim. Ordinary red and fair white table wines. West Germany.

Bisseuil. (17) Marne *département*; Ay canton, north-east of Epernay. Rated *premier cru*—93% growth. 291 acres. France.

Bistum. (22) Middle Moselle; Graach vineyard. Fine white table wine. West Germany.

Bitsch. (22) Moselle valley; Mühlheim and Veldenz vineyards, between Bernkastel and Wintrich. Fair white table wines are produced. West Germany.

Bizay. (16) Anjou; Coteaux de Saumur. Fair white and rosé table wines. France.

Bizeaudun, Cru de. (4) Haut-Médoc; Ludon. *Cru bourgeois.* 1,000 dozen bottles of red bordeaux. France.

Bizeljsko. (33) North-west Yugoslavia, bordering Italy and Austria; Slovenia. Fine red, white and rosé table wines. Yugoslavia.

Bizolière, Château de la. (16) Coteaux de la Loire; La Bizolière vineyard, below Angers. Fine white table wine. France.

Blagny, Château de. (8) Puligny-Montrachet vineyard. *Premier cru.* Very fine white burgundy. France.

Blanc, Clos. (8) Côte de Beaune; Pommard vineyard. *Premier cru.* Red burgundy. France.

Blanc de Blancs. Name given to a champagne made exclusively from the white juice of white grapes, without any of the white juice of black grapes traditionally used in the making of champagne. It is appreciated for its fragrance and delicacy. France.

Blanc de Morgex. (26) Val d'Aosta. One of the highest vineyards in Europe. Light, pleasant, faintly herb-scented and flavoured white wine. Italy.

Blanc de Noirs. Champagne made exclusively from the white juice of black grapes, without any of the white juice of white grapes traditionally used in the making of champagne. It is appreciated for its vivacity and body. France.

Blanc de Vougeot, Clos. (8) Côte de Nuits; Vougeot. Fine white burgundy. France.

Blanc-Fumé. (15) The name given in the Upper Loire area, Sancerre-Pouilly-sur-Loire, to the white Sauvignon grape. Also the name of the quality white table wine made from it. France.

Blanchards, Les. (8) Côte de Nuits; Morey-St Denis vineyard. *Deuxième* and *troisième cru.* Fair red burgundy. France.

Blanches-Fleurs, Les. (8) Beaune vineyard. *Premier cru.* Fine red burgundy. France.

Blanchots. (6) Chablis. *Grand cru.* Very fine white burgundy. France.

Blanderies, Les. (16) Maine-et-Loire *département*; Coteaux du Layon vineyard, south of Angers. Fair white and rosé wines. France.

Blanquefort. (4) Village in the Bordeaux area where the Haut-Médoc area begins. The little stream which runs through Blanquefort's pastures and vineyards divides the Haut-Médoc and the Graves de Bordeaux area. France.

Blanquette de Limoux. (13) Aude *département*; Limoux. A light white sparkling wine which has been for a great many years a speciality of Limoux. France.

Blansingen. (25) Baden; village approx. twenty-five miles south-west of Freiburg. Fair white table wine. West Germany.

Blatina. (33) West-central Yugoslavia; Hercegovina. One of the popular dark red wines. Yugoslavia.

Blattenberg. (22) Moselle valley; Mehring vineyard, between Detzen and Klüsserath. Fair white table wine. West Germany.

Blayais. (4) The stretch of undulating country on the right bank of the Gironde, facing the Haut-Médoc on the opposite bank. Its many vineyards produce a great deal of ordinary to fair red and white bordeaux wines. France.

Blaye, Côtes de. (4) The higher grounds of the Blayais where all the better vineyards of the Blayais are sited. France.

Blaye, Premières Côtes de. (4) Best of the high ground vineyards of the Blayais. France.

Bleasdale Vineyard. (37) South Australia; Langhorne Creek, by the Bremer River, thirty-five miles south-east of Adelaide. Table and dessert wines. Australia.

Blissa, Château de. (3) Bourgeais. 4,000 dozen bottles of red bordeaux. France.

Blondeau. (8) Hospices de Beaune vineyard. The *cuvée* has the *AC Volnay.* Fair to fine red burgundy. France.

Blotters, Les. (16) Anjou; Ingrandes vineyard, south-west of Angers. Ordinary to fair red wine. France.

Boal. *See* **Bual.**

Boavista, Quinta. (30) *Região demarcada do Douro* (q.v.). Estate and vineyard in Fontelo south-east of Régua. Portugal.

Boavista, Quinta. (30) *Região demarcada do Douro* (q.v.). Estate and vineyard in Vilarinho dos Freires, north-east of Régua. Portugal.

Bobal. (29) Northern Murcia, Valencia and Albacete. Rough, very dark red table wine. Spain.

Bobenheim. (23) Palatinate; village west of Dackenheim. Ordinary red and fair white table wines. West Germany.

Böbingen. (23) Palatinate; village east of Edenkoben. Fair white table wine. West Germany.

Boca d'Asti. (26) Piedmont; Asti area. Ordinary to fair dry, ruby-red wine. Italy.

Böchingen. (25) Württemberg; village approx. thirty-four miles south-east of Baden-Baden. Ordinary to fair red and white table wines. West Germany.

Bock. (24) Rhinehessia; Bodenheim vineyard. Fair to fine white table wine. West Germany.

Böckelheim, Schloss. (24) Nahe; village and vineyard west of Bad Münster. Fine to very fine white table wine. West Germany.

Bockenau. (24) Nahe valley; village west of Bad Kreuznach. Fair to fine white table wine. West Germany.

Bocksberg. (32) Moselle valley; near German frontier at Wasserbillig, north-east of Grevenmacher. Ordinary to fair white table wine. Luxembourg.

Bockstein. (22) Saar valley; one of the best Ockfen vineyards. Very fine white table wine. West Germany.

Bodendorf. (21) Ahr valley; village just west of Linz. Fair white table wine. West Germany.

Bodenheim. (24) Rhinehessia. Ordinary red and fair to fine white table wines. West Germany.

Bodenthal. (24) Rhinegau; Lorch vineyard. Fair white table wine. West Germany.

Bodet, Château. (3) Côtes Canon-Fronsac. 5,000 dozen bottles of red bordeaux. France.

Boeufs, Les. (8) Côte de Beaune; Pommard vineyard. *Premier cru*. Fine red burgundy. France.

Böhl. (23) Palatinate; Neustadt-an-der-Haardt vineyard. Fair to fine white table wine. West Germany.

Böhlig. (23) Palatinate; Wachenheim vineyard. Fine white table wine. West Germany.

Bohlingen. (25) Lake Constance (Bodensee); village on the north shore. Fair white table wine. West Germany.

Boillot. (8) Hospices de Beaune *cuvée. AC Auxey-Duresses.* France.

Bois-Chevaux. (9) Chalonnais; Givry vineyard. Fair red burgundy. France.

Bois Duchesne. (16) Anjou; Coteaux de Saumur, Brézé. Fair to fine white table wine. France.

Boisrideau. (16) Indre-et-Loire *département*; Vouvray vineyard, east of Tours. Fair white table wine. France.

Boisset, Château. (4) Blayais; Berson, south-east of Blaye. 3,000 dozen bottles of red bordeaux; 1,000 white. France.

Bois-Tiffray, Domaine de. (5) St-Emilion; Lussac. An unclassified *cru*. 2,000 dozen bottles of white bordeaux. France.

Bois-Turmaux. (16) Indre-et-Loire *département*; Vouvray, east of Tours. Fair white wine. France.

Boivins, Les. (6) Auxerre area vineyard. Ordinary to fair red burgundy. France.

Bol. (33) Central Adriatic coast; small town on island of Brac, Dalmatia. Good red wines. Yugoslavia.

Bolanden. (23) Palatinate; village north-west of Grünstadt. Fair white table wine. West Germany.

Bole. (31) Neuchâtel vineyard. 49 acres. Fair white table wine. Switzerland.

Bolea. (29) Aragon; Huesca. Ordinary red table wine. Spain.

Bolivia. (35) Minor wine-producing country of South America. Some of the vineyards of Bolivia are the highest in the world. More or less ordinary table wines. South America.

Bollschweil. (25) Baden; village south-west of Freiburg. Fair white table wine. West Germany.

Bolullos del Condado. (29) Huelva area. Quite ordinary but popular dry white wine. Spain.

Bolzano. (26) Val d'Adige (Upper Adige valley), chief town. Fair and fine quality red and white table wines. Italy.

Bombach. (25) Baden; village north of Freiburg. Ordinary to fair red and white table wines. West Germany.

Bommes. (5) One of the five *communes* whose white wines are entitled to the *Appellation Contrôlée Sauternes*, the best of the sweet white wines of France.

Bom Retiro, Quinta. (30) *Região demarcada do Douro* (q.v.). Estate and vineyard in Valenca do Douro east of Régua. Produces fine port wine. Portugal.

Bonarda. (26) Piedmont and Lombardy. A red grape; also a red table wine made from it in many parts of northern Italy.

Bonares. (29) Huelva area. Ordinary to fair red table wine. Spain.

Bon-Blanc. (12) Seyssel. Popular white sparkling wine. France.

Bonete. (29) Albacete area of northern Murcia. Fair dry *clarete* wine. Spain.

Bonfim, Quinta. (30) *Região demarcada do Douro* (q.v.). Estate and vineyard owned by Silva and Cosens in Pinhao east of Régua. Portugal.

Bonneau-Livran, Château. (4) Haut-Médoc; St Seurin-de-Cadourne. *Cru bourgeois.* 1,500 dozen bottles of red bordeaux. France.

Bonne Gagné. (16) Anjou; Coteaux de l'Aubance, Juigné-sur-Loire vineyard, in the Saumur area a tributary of the Loire. Fair white table wine. France.

Bonnes Blanches, Les. (16) Anjou; Coteaux du Layon, St Lambert-du-Lattay vineyard, Saumur area. Fair to fine white table wine. France.

Bonnes Mares. (8) Famous Côte de Nuits vineyard. *Grand cru.* Mostly in the *commune* of Chambolle-Musigny, but partly in Morey-St-Denis. Red burgundy. France.

Bonnézeaux. (16) Anjou; town in the Coteaux du Layon, a tributary of the Loire, Saumur area. Fair to fine white table wine with *Appellation Contrôlée* when the alcoholic strength is not under 13·5°. France.

Bönnigheim. (25) Württemberg; village north-east of Heilbronn. Ordinary to fair red and white table wines. West Germany.

Bons Feuvres, Les. (8) Beaune vineyard. *Deuxième* and *troisième cru.* Red burgundy. France.

Boordy. (35) Maryland; Philip Wagner's vineyard at Riderwood, which has done much to improve the quality of East Coast wines through careful and dedicated experimentation using French hybrids. The wines, both red and white, fully deserve their solid reputation as being of the highest quality. U.S.A.

Boos. (24) Nahe valley; village south-west of Bad Münster. Fair white table wine. West Germany.

Boppard. (21) Middle Rhine; town south of Koblenz. Ordinary to fair white table wine. West Germany.

Borba. (29) Badajoz area; between Seville and Trujillo. An ordinary white table wine. Spain.

Bordeaux. (3, 4, 5) Seaport and city on the Garonne. There is an *Appellation Contrôlée Bordeaux* and another *Bordeaux Supérieur*; the first is given to both red and white table wines of the Gironde *département* without blemish or any particular merit; the second to the same type of wine, when just a little better. Its vineyards produce more than a million gallons of wine a year. All the better wines of Bordeaux bear the name of their native village, such as St-Julien, St-Estephe, Barsac or Pomcrol, and all the best wines bear the name of their native châteaux—that is, the particular vineyard of their birth, maybe a *clos*, a *cru*, a *domaine* if not actually a *château.* France.

Bordes, Enclos des. (5) Pomerol. 3,000 dozen bottles of red bordeaux. France.

Borgogna Bianco. (26) Trentino; upper Adige valley and Gorizia area. Ordinary to good white wine, made from Pinot Bianco (Chardonnay) grapes, also used as a base for a fair sparkling wine. Italy.

Borgogna Grigio. (26) Alto Adige, mainly the north. Dry, fair to fine white table wine from Pinot Grigio (Gris) grapes, often *frizzante.* Italy.

Borgogna Rosso. (26) Alto Adige and Gorizia area. Ordinary red table wine from Pinot Nero (Noir) grapes. Italy.

Borja. (29) Zaragoza area. Fine, sweet, white Muscat dessert wine. Spain.

Borne, Clos de la. (31) Vaud canton; Dézaley vineyard. Fair to fine white table wine. Switzerland.

Borngraben. (24) Nahe valley; Langenlonsheim vineyard, south of Bingen. Fair white table wine. West Germany.

Bornheim. (23) Palatinate; village north-east of Landau. Fair white and ordinary red table wines. West Germany.

Bornheim. (24) Rhinehessia; village south-east of Bad Kreuznach. Fair to fine white table wine. West Germany.

Bornich. (21) Middle Rhine; village north-west of Bingen. Ordinary to fair white table wine. West Germany.

Borniques. (8) Côte de Nuits; Chambolle-Musigny vineyard. *Deuxième cru.* Fair red burgundy. France.

Bornova. (34) Fair, sweet, white Muscat Turkish dessert wine. Turkey.

Boroy. (6) Chablis area; Poinchy vineyard. *Premier cru.* Fair white burgundy. France.

Borraccio. (28) Apulia; Capo di Leuca area, Lecce province, the bottom of the 'heel' of Italy. Ordinary to fair rosé wine. Italy.

Borralheira, Quinta. (30) *Região demarcada do Douro* (q.v.). Estate and vineyard in Favaios seventeen miles north-east of Régua. Portugal.

Borriol. (29) Castellón de la Plana; approx. forty miles north-east of Valencia. Stout, dark red, ordinary table wine. Spain.

Bosco Eliceo. (26) Emilia-Romagna; Adriatic coast. Dry, stout, deep-red table wine. Italy.

Boscq, Château Le. (4) Haut-Médoc; St-Estèphe vineyard. *Cru bourgeois.* 7,000 dozen bottles of red bordeaux. France.

Boseberg. (24) Rhinehessia; Pfaffen-Schwaben-heim vineyard, east of Bad Kreuznach. Ordinary to fair white table wine. West Germany.

Bosquets, Les. (12) Côtes du Rhône; Gigondas vineyard. Fair to fine red table wine. France.

Bossières. (8) Côte de Nuits; Vosne-Romanée vineyard. Fine red burgundy. France.

Botticino. (26) Lombardy; Lake Garda area, west of Verona. Bright red, sweetish light wine. Italy.

Bouca, Quinta. (30) *Região demarcada do Douro*. Estate in Cambres, south-west of Régua. Portugal.

Bouca, Quinta. (30) Estate in Valdigem south-west of Régua. Portugal.

Bouchères, Les. (8) Côte de Beaune; Meursault vineyard. *Premier cru*. Fine white burgundy. France.

Boucherottes, Les. (8) Beaune vineyard. *Premier cru*. Fine red burgundy. France.

Bouchet, Clos du. (16) Touraine; Vouvray vineyard, east of Tours. Fair to fine white table wine. France.

Boucou, Le. (12) Côtes du Rhône; Châteauneuf-du-Pape vineyard. Fair to fine red table wine. France.

Boudots, Aux. (8) Nuits-St-Georges vineyard. *Premier cru*. Fine red burgundy. France.

Boudriotte, La. (8) Chassagne-Montrachet vineyard. *Premier cru*. Fine red and white burgundy. France.

Boudry. (31) Neuchâtel canton; village with 213 acres of vineyards. Ordinary red, and fair to fine white table wines. Switzerland.

Bougros. (6) Chablis. One of the few *grands crus* vineyards. Very fine white burgundy. France.

Bouilde, Château. (3) Fronsac. 2,000 dozen bottles of red burgundy. France.

Bouilh, Château du. (3) St André-de-Cubzac, south-east of Blaye. 22,500 dozen bottles of red bordeaux; 4,000 white. France.

Boulay, Le. (16) Touraine; St Martin-le-Beau vineyard, east of Tours. Fair to fine white table wine. France.

Boulotte, La. (8) Côte de Beaune; Aloxe-Corton vineyard. *Deuxième cru*. Fair to fine red burgundy. France.

Bouqueyran, Château. (4) Haut-Médoc; Moulis, west of Soussans. *Cru bourgeois*. 4,000 dozen bottles of red bordeaux. France.

Bourdac, Domaine du. (5) Graves de Bordeaux; Illats. 3,500 dozen bottles of white bordeaux. France.

Bourdieu, Château. (4) Blayais; Berson, south-east of Blaye. 5,000 dozen bottles of red bordeaux; 5,000 white. France.

Bourdieu, Château Le. (4) Haut-Médoc; Vertheuil. *Cru bourgeois*. 15,000 dozen bottles of red bordeaux. France.

Bourdieu, Cru Le. (5) Graves de Bordeaux; Podensac. An unclassified *cru*. 500 dozen bottles of red bordeaux; 800 white. France.

Bourdieu, Cru Le. (5) Premières Côtes de Bordeaux; Gabarnac, south-east of Loupiac. 1,000 dozen bottles of red bordeaux; 2,000 white. France.

Bourdieu-la-Valade, Château. (3) Fronsadais; Fronsac. 3,000 dozen bottles of red bordeaux. France.

Bourdieu-Panet, Cru. (3) Fronsadais; Côtes Canon-Fronsac. 1,000 dozen bottles of red bordeaux. France.

Bourelles, Clos des. (16) Touraine; Brain-sur-l'Authion vineyard, west of Bourgueil. Fair to fine white table wine. France.

Bourg. (3) Chief town in the Bourgeais; small river port on the river Dordogne, and chief wine market for the wines of the Bourgeais and Blayais. France.

Bourg, Château du. (3) Bordeaux; Néac, east of Pomerol. 4,000 dozen bottles of red bordeaux. France.

Bourg, Château du. (3) Fronsadais. 10,000 dozen bottles of white bordeaux. France.

Bourg, Château du. (5) Graves de Bordeaux; Virelade, north-west of Podensac. 800 dozen bottles of red bordeaux; 200 white. France.

Bourg, Clos du. (16) Touraine; Vouvray vineyard, east of Tours. Fair white table wine. France.

Bourgeais. (3) Stretch of undulating land, with many vineyards, on the right bank of the river Dordogne just before it joins the Garonne, when the two rivers become the Gironde. France.

Bourgelat, Clos. (5) Graves de Bordeaux; Cérons vineyard. An unclassified *cru*. 3,000 dozen bottles of white bordeaux. France.

Bourgneuf-Val-d'Or. (9) Chalonnais; village in the centre of the Mercurey vineyards. Fair to fine red burgundy. France.

Bourgneuf-Vayron, Château. (5) Pomerol. 5,000 dozen bottles of red bordeaux. France.

Bourgogne (La). (8) The French name of the former province of Burgundy; also the French name for the wines of vineyards within the limits of the *départements* of the Yonne, Côte d'Or, Saône-et-Loire and part of the Rhône *département*. 'Le Bourgogne' when speaking of the wine. France.

Bourgogne Aligoté. (11) Mostly Saône-et-Loire *département*. The French *Appellation Contrôlée* of a fair white table wine made from the white Aligoté grape. France.

Bourgogne Grand Ordinaire. *Appellation Contrôlée* given in France to red burgundy, mostly made from Gamay grapes, of modest quality but sound and honest. Also some white wines. France.

Bourgogne Passé Tout Grain. *Appellation Contrôlée* given to red burgundy of modest quality made from various grapes. Must contain one-

F

third Pinot and two-thirds Gamay fermented together. France.

Bourgueil. (16) Touraine; town on right bank of the Loire, west of Tours. An important wine centre. Fair to fine quality red wine. France.

Bournais, Les. (16) Anjou; Coteaux de Saumur, Souzay-Champigny vineyard. Fair white table wine. France.

Bourrais, Clos. (4) St-Emilion; St Laurent-des-Combes. *Deuxième* and *premier cru*. 2,500 dozen bottles red bordeaux. France.

Bourrasque, La. (14) Côtes de Provence; St Cyr-sur-Mer vineyard, Bandol area. Fair red table wine. France.

Bourseau, Château. (5) Lalande-de-Pomerol; north of Pomerol. 2,500 dozen bottles of red bordeaux. France.

Bouscaut, Château. (5) Graves de Bordeaux; Cadaujac. *Cru classé de Graves (rouge et blanc)*. 10,000 dozen bottles of red bordeaux; 2,000 white. France.

Bousse d'Or. (8) Côte de Beaune; Volnay vineyard. *Premier cru*. Fair to fine red burgundy. For many years it has been written 'Pousse d'Or'. France.

Bousselots, Aux. (8) Nuits-St-Georges vineyard. *Deuxième cru*. Fair red burgundy. France.

Boutières, Les. (10) Mâconnais; Pouilly vineyard. *Premier cru*. Fair to fine white burgundy. France.

Boutisse, Château de. (5) St-Emilion; St Christophe-des-Bardes, south-west of Parsac. An unclassified *cru*. 6,000 dozen bottles of red bordeaux. France.

Boutza. (34) Island of Crete. Ordinary to fair red table wine. Greece.

Bouygue, Château La. (5) St-Emilion; St Laurent-des-Combes, west of St Etienne-de-Lisse. An unclassified *cru*. 2,500 dozen bottles of red bordeaux. France.

Bouzeron. (9) Côte Chalonnaise village. Ordinary to fair red burgundy, and good Aligoté. France.

Bouzy. (17) Marne *département*; Ay canton. Rated *grand cru*—100% growth. 823 acres. France.

Boxberg. (24) Rhinegau; Hattenheim vineyard, south-east of Hallgarten. Fine white table wine. West Germany.

Boyd-Cantenac, Château. (4) Haut-Médoc; Margaux. *Troisième cru classé*. 2,000 dozen bottles of red bordeaux. France.

Boyrein, Château La Tour-de-. (5) Graves de Bordeaux; Roaillan, south of Fargues. An unclassified *cru*. 2,000 dozen bottles of white bordeaux. France.

Bozen. (26) Alto Adige. The former German name of Bolzano (q.v.). Italy.

Brachetto. (26) Piedmont and Liguria. A black grape; also a red table wine made from it, usually in two types; *secco* and *amabile*, dry and sweet. Italy.

Brachetto d'Asti. (26) Piedmont; Asti province. Good quality light, sweet, sparkling red wine. Italy.

Brackenheim. (25) Württemberg; village south-west of Heilbronn. Ordinary to fair red and white table wines. West Germany.

Bragard, Château. (5) Côtes de St-Emilion. An unclassified *cru*. 4,000 dozen bottles of red bordeaux. France.

Braines, Les. (10) Mâconnais; Romanèche-Thorins vineyard. Fair to fine red burgundy. France.

Brain-sur-l'Authion. (16) Anjou; Coteaux de la Loire, below Angers. Fair to fine white table wine. France.

Branaire-Ducru, Château. (4) Haut-Médoc; St-Julien. *Quatrième cru classé*. 15,000 dozen bottles of fine red bordeaux. France.

Branca, Quinta. (30) Estate in Valdigem, south-west of Régua. Portugal.

Brandenberg. (22) Moselle valley; Bruttig vineyard. Fair white table wine. West Germany.

Brane-Cantenac, Château. (4) Haut-Médoc; Cantenac. *Deuxième cru classé*. 2,000 dozen bottles of fine red bordeaux. France.

Braquetty, Les. (14) Provence; Le Catelet vineyard, Bandol area. Fair red, white and rosé table wines. France.

Brassens-Guiteronde, Château. (5) Sauternes; Barsac. *Cru bourgeois*. 2,500 dozen bottles of white bordeaux. France.

Bratenhöfchen. (22) Moselle valley; Bernkastel vineyard. Fair white table wine. West Germany.

Braubach. (21) Middle Rhine; village south-east of Koblenz. Fair white table wine. West Germany.

Brauenberg. (22) Middle Moselle valley; village whose vineyards produce some of the finest Moselle wines. West Germany.

Brauenfels. (22) Saar valley; Wiltingen vineyard. Fine white table wine. West Germany.

Brauneberg. (21) Middle Rhine village. Fair white table wine. West Germany.

Braune Kupp. (22) Saar valley; Wiltingen vineyard. Fine white table wine. West Germany.

Braunen. (24) Nahe valley; Winzenheim vineyard, south-west of Bingen. Fair white table wine. West Germany.

Braunfels. (22) Saar valley; Wiltingen vineyard. Fine white table wine. West Germany.

Braungarten. (23) Palatinate; St Martin vineyard, south of Neustadt. Fair white table wine. West Germany.

Braunhals. (22) Saar valley; Wiltingen vineyard. Fine white table wine. West Germany.

Braunloch. (24) Rhinehessia; Bodenheim vineyard. Fair to fine white table wine. West Germany.

Braunweiler. (24) Nahe valley; north-west of Bad Kreuznach. Fair to fine white table wine. West Germany.

Brazil. (35) One of the three important wine-producing countries of South America, producing nearly 37,000,000 gallons of mostly quite ordinary table wines. South America.

Brechtal. (24) Rhinehessia; Alsheim vineyard. Fair white table wine. France.

Bregançon. (13) Côtes de Provence; village on the Côte des Maures, in the Marseille area. Fair red, white and rosé table wines. France.

Breganze (Bianco, Rosso). (26) Veneto; plain between Lake Garda and river Piave, west of Verona. Ordinary to fair red and white table wines. Italy.

Breisach. (25) Baden; village west of Freiburg. Ordinary to fair red and white table wines. West Germany.

Breisgau. (25) Baden; a stretch of about thirty miles along the foothills of the Black Forest with many vineyards producing mostly white table wine of fair quality. West Germany.

Breitheck. (23) Palatinate; Asselheim vineyard, north of Grünstadt. Ordinary red and fair white table wines. West Germany.

Breitscheid. (21) Middle Rhine; village north-west of Bingen. Ordinary to fair white table wine. West Germany.

Brelot, Clos. (9) Mâconnais; St Mard-de-Vaux. *Deuxième cru.* Ordinary red burgundy. France.

Bremm. (22) Lower Moselle valley; village between Eller and Zell. West Germany.

Brendola (Bianco, Rosso). (26) Veneto; Colli Berici vineyards, hills just south of Vicenza. Ordinary to fair white and red table wines. Italy.

Bressandes, Les. (8) Beaune vineyard. *Premier cru.* Fine red burgundy. France.

Bressandes, Les. (8) Côte de Beaune; Aloxe-Corton vineyard. *Premier cru.* Fine red burgundy. France.

Bretonnières, Les. (16) Anjou; Côtes de Saumur, Parnay vineyard. Fair white table wine. France.

Bretzenheim. (24) Nahe valley; town south of Bingen. Ordinary, fair, and some fine white table wine. West Germany.

Breuil, Château du. (16) Anjou; Rochefort-sur-Layon, below Angers. Fine white table wine. France.

Breuil, Château du. (4) Haut-Médoc; Cissac. *Cru bourgeois.* 10,000 dozen bottles of red bordeaux. France.

Brey. (21) Middle Rhine; village south of Koblenz. Ordinary to fair red and white table wines. West Germany.

Brézé, Château de. (16) Anjou; Coteaux de Saumur, Brézé. Fair to fine white table wine. France.

Briançon-sur-Sables. (16) Touraine; village on the Côte de Chinon. Fair red table wine. France.

Briedel. (22) Lower Moselle valley; village between Zell and Enkirch. Fair to fine white wine. West Germany.

Bries-Caillou, Château. (4) Médoc; St Germain-d'Esteuil, west of St Seurin-de-Cadourne. *Cru bourgeois.* 8,000 dozen bottles of red bordeaux. France.

Brigne. (16) Anjou; Coteaux du Layon, a tributary of the Loire running south of the Angers area. Fair white table wine. France.

Brinas. (29) Alava; La Rioja area of the upper Ebro valley. Ordinary light, semi-sweet red table wine. Spain.

Brindisi. (28) Apulia; town and port. Homely table wines. Italy.

Brisgau. *See* **Breisgau.**

Brissac. (16) Anjou; Coteaux de l'Aubance, a tributary of the Loire in the Saumur area. Fair, red, white and rosé table wines. France.

Bristol Cream. (1) Bristol; west-central England. Mature, rich dessert sherry. England.

Bristol Milk. (1) Bristol; west-central England. A good quality dessert sherry. England.

Britzingen. (25) Baden; village south-west of Freiburg. White table wines of fair quality. West Germany.

Brochon. (8) Côte de Nuits; Gevry-Chambertin vineyard. *Deuxième* and *troisième crus. Appellation Contrôlée.* Some vineyards classed Gevry-Chambertin—others Côte de Nuits Village.

Brodenbach. (22) Moselle valley; village between Valwig and Kobern. Fair white table wine. West Germany.

Brolas, Quinta. (30) Estate in Valdigem, south-west of Régua, producing table wines. Portugal.

Brolio Riserva. (27) Tuscany; Brolio estate, near Siena. Finest red chianti. Italy.

Brondeau, Château de. (5) Entre-deux-Mers; Graves de Vayres. 3,000 dozen bottles of red bordeaux. France.

Brondes, Clos des. (16) Anjou; Dampierre-sur-Loire *commune* on the Saumur hillsides. Fair to fine white table wine. France.

Broni. (26) Lombardy; Oltrepo Pavese town, south of Pavia across the Po. Ordinary to fair red table wine. Italy.

Bronnen. (24) Rhinegau; Rüdesheim vineyard. Fine white table wine. West Germany.

Brosses, Les. (16) Anjou; Vauchrétien vineyard, Coteaux de l'Aubance, a·tributary of the Loire in the Saumur area. Fair red table wine. France.

Brosses, Les. (10) Mâconnais; St-Amour vineyard. Fair to fine red burgundy. France.

Brouillards, Les. (8) Côte de Beaune; Volnay vineyard. *Premier* and *deuxième cru*. Fair red burgundy. France.

Brouilly. (11) Beaujolais; parts of Odenas, St-Lager, Quincie, Cercie and Charentay vineyards. Fair red burgundy. France.

Broustet, Château. (5) Sauternes; Barsac. *Deuxième cru classé*. 3,000 dozen bottles of white bordeaux. France.

Brozas. (29) Northern Estremadura; Cáceres province, in Trujillo area. Ordinary to fair white table wine. Spain.

Bruchsal. (25) Baden; village north-east of Karlsruhe. Ordinary to fair red and white table wines. West Germany.

Brück. (24) Rhinegau; Kiedrich vineyard. Fair to fine white table wine. West Germany.

Brückes. (24) Nahe valley; Bad Kreuznach vineyard. Fair white table wine. West Germany.

Bruderschaft. (22) Moselle valley; Klüsserath vineyard. Fair white table wine. West Germany.

Brugg. (31) Aargau canton; village with 300 acres of vineyards. Ordinary to fair red table wine. Switzerland.

Brühl. (23) Palatinate; Deidesheim vineyard. Fair white table wine. West Germany.

Brühl. (24) Rhinegau; Erbach vineyard. Fine white table wine. West Germany.

Brühl. (24) Rhinehessia; Bischofsheim vineyard, south-east of Mainz. Fair white table wine. West Germany.

Brulées, Aux. (8) Vosne-Romanée vineyard. *Premier cru*. Red burgundy. France.

Brulées, Les. (10) Mâconnais; Fuissé vineyard. *Premier cru*. White burgundy. France.

Brulées, Les. (8) Nuits-St-Georges vineyard. *Deuxième cru*. Red burgundy. France.

Brûle-Fer. (31) Valais canton; Sion vineyard. Fine white table wine. Switzerland.

Brun, Château. (5) St-Emilion; St Christophe-des-Bardes. 3,000 dozen bottles of red bordeaux. France.

Bruneau, Les. (16) Touraine, Chinon vineyard. Fair red table wine. France.

Brunello di Montalcino. (27) Tuscany; south of Siena. One of the great red wines of Italy. It is aged in the cask for five or six years, and for a further two in the bottle. Made from the Brunello grape, it has been compared to the best of the burgundies. Italy.

Brunet. (8) One of the Hospices de Beaune

cuvées, with the *AC Beaune*. Red burgundy. France.

Brunettes, Les. (16) Anjou; Coteaux du Layon, Bonnézeaux vineyard, below Angers. Fine white table wine. France.

Brunettes, Les. (8) Côte de Beaune; Aloxe-Corton vineyard. *Deuxième cru*. Red burgundy. France.

Brunettes, Les. (16) Touraine; Côte de Montlouis, St Martin-le-Beau vineyard east of Tours. Fair white table wine. France.

Brünnchen. (24) Rhinehessia; Dalsheim vineyard, west of Worms. Fair white table wine. West Germany.

Brunnen. (24) Rhinegau; Rüdesheim vineyard. Fine white table wine. West Germany.

Brunnenhäuschen. (24) Rhinehessia; Westhofen vineyard, north-west of Worms. Fair white table wine. Germany.

Brureaux, Les. (11) Beaujolais; Chénas vineyard. Red beaujolais. France.

Bruttig. (22) Moselle valley; village in the Krampen area (q.v.). Fair to fine white table wine. West Germany.

Bual. (30) Name of grape variety and fine quality sweet madeira dessert wine made from it. Portugal.

Bubenheim. (24) Rhinehessia; village south of Erbach. Fair white table wine. West Germany.

Bubenstück. (24) Rhinehessia; Rüdesheim vineyard. Fair white table wine. West Germany.

Bucelas. (30) Demarcated district producing dry light white table wine north of Lisbon. Near Loures. Portugal.

Buchbrunn. (25) Franconia; village south-east of Würzburg. Fair to fine white table wine. West Germany.

Bucherats. (11) Beaujolais; Juliénas vineyard. Red beaujolais. France.

Bucherdurger. (31) St Gallen canton; village and vineyards. Ordinary red wine. Switzerland.

Budai Zold. (33) West-central Hungary; Somló vineyards. Fair white table wine. Hungary.

Budenheim. (24) Rhinehessia village. Fair white table wine. West Germany.

Budesheim. (24) Rhinehessia; village south of Bingen between Bingen and Bad Kreuznach. Ordinary, fair, and some fine white table wines. West Germany.

Bué. (15) Village in Sancerre area, Upper Loire. Ordinary to fair red and white table wines. France.

Buena Vista Vineyard. (36) California; Sonoma County. Founded by Agorton Hararzthy *c*. 1858. Produces a fine 'Green Hungarian' wine plus table and dessert wines. U.S.A.

Bugey. (18) Ain *département*. Fair red, white and rosé wines with *Appellation Contrôlée V.D.Q.S.* France.

Bühlertal. (25) Baden; village south-east of Baden-Baden. Ordinary to fair red and white table wines. West Germany.

Bulants, Les. (10) Mâconnais; Solutré vineyard. *Premier cru*. White burgundy. France.

Bulgaria. (33) A small eastern European country which produces over 50,000,000 dozen bottles of mostly ordinary to fair table wine.

Bulgarische Sonne. (33) Popular white table wine. Bulgaria.

Bullas. (29) Murcia. Ordinary red table wine. Spain.

Bullay. (22) Moselle valley; town between Eller and Zell. Fair white table wine is produced. West Germany.

Bullenheim. (25) Franconia; village approx. seventeen miles south-east of Würzburg. Ordinary, fair and some fine white table wine. West Germany.

Bundarra. (37) North-east Victoria. Red and white table and dessert wines. Australia.

Bunken. (24) Rhinegau; Eltville vineyard. Fine white table wine. West Germany.

Buñol. (29) Cheste vineyards; Valencia area. Light, dry, white table wine. Spain.

Buonopane. (28) Island of Ischia; bay of Naples. Fair white table wine. Italy.

Burbaguena. (29) South-central Aragon; Teruel. Ordinary to fair red table wine. Spain.

Burg. (22) Moselle valley; village between Zell and Enkirch. Ordinary to fair white table wine. West Germany.

Burgberg. (22) Moselle valley; Klotten vineyard, between Valwig and Kobern. Fair white table wine. West Germany.

Burgberg. (24) Nahe valley; Dorsheim vineyard, south-west of Bingen. Fair white table wine. West Germany.

Burgberg. (22) Ruwer valley; Eitelsbach, Berg vineyard. Fine white table wine. West Germany.

Burgele. (25) Baden; Kirchhofen vineyard, Freiburg. Fair white table wine. West Germany.

Burgen. (22) Moselle valley; village between Valwig and Kobern. Fair white table wine. West Germany.

Burgen-Bernkastel. (22) Moselle valley; village near Bernkastel. Fair white table wine. West Germany.

Burgenland. (33) The eastern province of Austria, close to the Hungarian frontier, responsible for approx. 30% of the total wine production of Austria. Its two best areas for quality table wines are Rust and Eisenberg. Austria.

Burgen-St-Goar. (21) Middle Rhine; village and vineyards near St-Goar approx. sixteen miles north-west of Bingen. Ordinary to fair white table wine. West Germany.

Burgergarten. (23) Palatinate; Haardt vineyard. Fair white table wine. West Germany.

Burgersberg. (33) Budapest; Budafok, Adlersberg vineyard. Fair white table wine. Hungary.

Burgerslay. (22) Moselle valley; Brauneberg vineyard. Fair to fine white table wine. West Germany.

Burggarten. (24) Rhinehessia; Ober-Ingelheim vineyard, east of Bingen. Ordinary to fair red table wine. West Germany.

Burggraben. (24) Rhinegau; Rauenthal vineyard. Fine white table wine. West Germany.

Burggrafen. (21) Rhinegau; Rauenthal vineyard. Fine white table wine. West Germany.

Burglay. (22) Moselle Valley; Zell vineyard. Fair to fine white table wine. West Germany.

Burgsponheim. (24) Nahe Valley; village west of Bad Kreuznach. Fair to fine white table wine. West Germany.

Burgundy. The English name for both the former province of Bourgogne, and the red and white table and sparkling wines made from its vineyards. In Great Britain the name of burgundy (wines) is not protected by law in the same manner as port, madeira and champagne, and red table wines are marketed as burgundies with the name of their country of origin, as, for example, Australian burgundy. France.

Burgweg. (25) Franconia; Iphofen vineyard, approx. sixteen miles south-east of Würzburg. Fair to fine white table wine. West Germany.

Burgweg. (24) Rhinehessia; Bodenheim vineyard. Fair white table wine. West Germany.

Burgy. (10) Mâconnais village. Ordinary red and fair white burgundy. France.

Burignon. (31) Vaud canton; vineyard which is the property of the city of Lausanne. Fair white table wine. Switzerland.

Burkheim. (25) Baden; village north-west of Freiburg. Ordinary to fair red and white table wines. West Germany.

Burrweiler. (23) Palatinate town. Ordinary red, fair and some fine white table wines. West Germany.

Bursa. (34) Between Turkey and Bulgaria; vineyards by the Sea of Marmara. Ordinary to fair red table wine. Turkey.

Buschweg. (23) Palatinate; Deidesheim vineyard. Fair to fine white table wine. West Germany.

Busetto. (26) Liguria; Finale Ligure vineyards, between Savona and Imperia. Ordinary, white table wine, usually drunk young. Italy.

Bussière, Clos de la. (8) Morey-St-Denis vineyard. *Deuxième cru*. Red burgundy. France.

Bussière du Haut. (9) Chalonnais; Mercurey vineyard. Red burgundy. France.

Bussières, Les. (11) Beaujolais; Brouilly vineyard. Red beaujolais. France.

Bussières, Les. (8) Chambolle-Musigny vineyard. *Deuxième cru*. Red burgundy. France.

Busslei. (22) Moselle valley; Erden vineyard. Fair white table wine. West Germany.

Buttafuoco. (26) Lombardy; Pavia vineyards. Mild, fruity red wine, dry, frothy and semi-sparkling. Italy.

Butteaux, Les. (6) Chablis vineyard. *Premier cru*. White burgundy. France.

Butte-de-Saumonssay. (16) Anjou; St Cyr-en-Bourg vineyard, Saumur area. Fair white table wine. France.

Buxy. (9) Chalonnais village. Ordinary to fair white and red table wine. France.

Buzbag. (34) Ordinary red Turkish table wine. Turkey.

Byots, Les. (9) Chalonnais; Mercurey vineyard. Red burgundy. France.

Bzenec. (33) A town in central Czechoslovakia which produces ordinary to fair red and white table wines. Czechoslovakia.

☙

Cabañas, Quinta. (30) *Região demarcada do Douro* (q.v.). Estate in Sanhoane, in the Régua area. Portugal.

Cabanne, Château La. (4) Blayais; St Martin, north-east of Blaye. 1,500 dozen bottles of red bordeaux. France.

Cabanne, Château La. (5) Pomerol. 6,000 dozen bottles of red bordeaux. France.

Cabanne, Clos. (3) Graves de Bordeaux; St Pierre-de-Mons, Langon area. An unclassified *cru*. 400 dozen bottles of red bordeaux; 1,500 white. France.

Cabannes, Les. (12) Côtes du Rhône; Châteauneuf-du-Pape vineyard. Fair to fine red table wine. France.

Cabannieux, Château. (5) Graves de Bordeaux; Portets. An unclassified *cru*. 1,500 dozen bottles of red bordeaux; 1,500 white. Francc.

Cabella. (26) Lombardy; Pavia-Piacenza area. Ordinary to fair red table wine. Italy.

Cabernet di Friuli. (26) Friuli-Venezia-Giulia; encompassing Udine, Gorizia and Trieste. Fair red table wine from Cabernet grapes. Italy.

Cabernet Rosé d'Anjou. (16) The *Appellation Contrôlée* of the best rosé table wine of the lower Loire valley. France.

Cabernet Rosé de Saumur. (16) Name of Cabernet Rosé d'Anjou (above) from the vineyards in the Saumur area. France.

Cabezas. (29) Valladolid area; approx. seventy miles north of Avila. Ordinary to fair red table wine. Spain.

Cabezas, Las. (29) Seville area. Fair sweet white wines. Spain.

Cabezuela del Valle. (29) Estremadura; Cáceres province, in Trujillo area. Ordinary to fair red table wine. Spain.

Cabo, Quinta. (30) *Região demarcada do Douro* (q.v.). Estate in Ceves, in the Régua area. Portugal.

Cabouco, Quinta. (30) *Região demarcada do Douro* (q.v.). Estate in Cambres, south-west of Régua, produces table wines. Portugal.

Cabrera. (29) Barcelona; Panadés vineyards, between Tarragona and Barcelona. Ordinary to fair red table wine. Spain.

Cabrières, *V.D.Q.S.* (13) Rosé table wine from the Herault vineyards. France.

Cabrières, Domaine de. (12) Côtes du Rhône; Châteauneuf-du-Pape. Fair red table wine. France.

Cacabelos. (29) South-western León; Valdeorras area. Ordinary to fair red table wine. Spain.

Cachao, Quinta. (30) *Região demarcada do Douro* (q.v.). Estate and vineyard in Vale de Figueira twenty-two miles south-west of Régua, comprising 228 acres. Portugal.

Cadaques. (29) Gerona province vineyards; north-east of Barcelona. Ordinary to fair sweet white wine. Spain.

Cadaujac. (5) Graves de Bordeaux; town seven miles south-south-east of Bordeaux. France.

Cadenasso Winery. (36) California; Fairfield. 200 acres. 150,000 dozen bottles storage capacity. A new winery plant in the process of construction. Mostly quality table wines; a Johannisberg Riesling is their outstanding wine. U.S.A.

Cadet, Château. (3) Côtes de Castillon; St-Gènes, north-east of Castillon. 9,500 dozen bottles of red bordeaux. France.

Cadet-Bon, Château. (5) Côtes de St-Emilion. *Grand cru classé*. 2,500 dozen bottles of red bordeaux. France.

Cadet-Peychaey, Château. (5) Côtes de St-Emilion. An unclassified *cru*. 500 dozen bottles of red bordeaux. France.

Cadet-Piola, Château. (5) Côtes de St-Emilion. *Grand cru classé*. 2,000 dozen bottles of red bordeaux. France.

Cadière, La. (14) Var *département*; Bandol vineyard. Fair red, white and rosé table wines. France.

Cadillac. (3) Premières côtes de Bordeaux; town approx. twenty-four miles south-east of Bordeaux. Fair red and white bordeaux wines. France.

Cadillon, Cru. (4) Haut-Médoc; Lamarque. *Cru bourgeois.* 2,000 dozen bottles of red bordeaux. France.

Cafaro. (28) Apulia; Gulf of Gioia vineyards, the northern tip of the 'boot'. Ordinary red, dry or semi-sweet, table wine. Italy.

Cagliari. (28) Sardinia; chief town. Ordinary to fair red and white table wines; also some fair to fine white dessert wines. Italy.

Cagnina. (26) Emilia-Romagna; Forli area. Ordinary to fair dry rosé wine. Italy.

Cahors. (13) Lot *département*; town north-west of the Tarn *département*. Unusual, almost legendary red wine made principally from the Malbec grapes. It is perhaps the deepest red wine of France, being almost black in colour. It is a *V.D.Q.S.* classification. France.

Caillavet, Château de. (5) Entre-deux-Mers; Capian, north-west of Loupiac. 8,000 dozen bottles of red bordeaux; 3,500 white. France.

Cailleret, Le. (8) Puligny-Montrachet vineyard. *Premier cru.* Red burgundy. France.

Caillerets-Dessus, Les. (8) Volnay vineyard. *Premier cru.* Red burgundy. France.

Cailles, Les. (8) Nuits-St-Georges vineyard. *Premier cru.* Red burgundy. France.

Caillettes, Les. (8) Aloxe-Corton vineyard. *Troisième cru.* Red burgundy. France.

Caillou, Château Le. (5) Pomerol. 5,000 dozen bottles of red bordeaux. France.

Caino. (29) Pontevedra; Orense. Very dark red, rather rough table wine. North-west Spain.

Cairannes. (12) Village of the Vaucluse *département*; côtes du Rhône. Fair red, white and rosé table wines. France.

Calagrano. (29) Old Castile; Logroño province, La Rioja area of the upper Ebro valley. Ordinary to fair white table wine. Spain.

Calahorra. (29) Old Castile; Logroño province, La Rioja area of the upper Ebro valley. Fair red table wine. Spain.

Calanda 'Malvasia'. (29) South-central Aragon; Teruel. Fair white dessert wine. Spain.

Calaayud. (29) Zaragoza area. Stout, rather coarse, red table wine. Spain.

Caldaro Appiano. (26) Alto Adige; vineyards facing the Lago di Caldaro (Kalterersee). One of the better red wines. Italy.

Caldaro, Lago di. (26) Alto Adige; Bolzano area. One of the better red wines. Italy.

Caldas de Mombuy. (29) Barcelona area. Ordinary to fair white table wine. Spain.

Caldetas. (29) West-central Galicia; Pontevedra area. Ordinary to fair red table wine. North-west Spain.

Caledon. (39) Cape Province. Chief city and wine market of this important wine producing territory. South Africa.

California. (36) The largest wine-producing State of the U.S.A. It is responsible for about 85% of the total American production. U.S.A.

Calon-Ségur, Château. (4) Haut-Médoc; St-Estèphe. *Troisième cru classé.* 20,000 dozen bottles of red bordeaux. France.

Calouère. (8) Côte de Nuits; Morey-St-Denis vineyard. *Premier cru.* Red burgundy. France.

Caluso. (26) Piedmont; Turin province. White table wine made in two grades, *secco* and *dolce*—dry and sweet. Dry Caluso is usually served as an apéritif. Italy.

Calvaire, Domaine du. (5) St-Emilion; St Etienne-de-Lisse. An unclassified *cru.* 6,000 dozen bottles of red bordeaux. France.

Camara de Lobos. (40) An important wine-producing locality in Madeira, an island situated 400 miles off the coast of Morocco. Portugal.

Camarino. (26) Piedmont; Novara province. Rare red wine credited with aphrodisiac qualities. Italy.

Cambados. (29) West-central Galicia; Pontevedra area. Sharp, rough white table wine. North-west Spain.

Camensac, Château. (4) Haut-Médoc; St-Laurent. *Cinquième cru classé.* 10,000 dozen bottles of red bordeaux. France.

Camp. (22) Ruwer; Waldrach vineyard. Fair to fine white table wine. West Germany.

Campañas, Las. (29) Navarre. Light rosé table wine. Spain.

Campanha, Quinta. (30) *Região demarcada do Douro.* (q.v.). Near Régua. Portugal.

Campidano di Cagliari. (28) Sardinia; plain stretching north-west of Cagliari. Ordinary red and white table wines, drunk young. Italy.

Campi Flegrei (Bianco, Rosso and Rosato). (28) Campania. Ordinary dry white and sweetish red and rosé table wines. Italy.

Campiglione. (26) Piedmont, Turin area. Ordinary red table wine. Italy.

Campillos. (29) Málaga area. Sweet high-strength dessert wine. Spain.

Campochiesa (Bianco, Rosso) (26) Liguria; Savona province. Fair, dry white and ordinary red wines. Italy.

Camporrobles. (29) West-central Valencia; Utiel area. Ordinary to fair red table wine. Spain.

Canada. (35) There are vineyards on the Niagra peninsula (near New York state) which produce still and sparkling table wines with this name.

Although demand is increasing slightly, production is still limited to approx. 9·5 million gallons a year.

Canaiolo. (27) Lake Bolsena, south of Rome. A black grape and also a sweet red dessert wine of no great merit made from it. Italy.

Canamaro. (29) Estremadura; Cáceres province in the Trujillo area. Ordinary to fair red and white table wines. Spain.

Canary Islands. (40) The vineyards of this island group off the north-west African coast are mainly on the island of Tenerife but they are also to be found in Gran Canaria and Lanzarote. Production is mostly of ordinary white and red wines. Spain.

Canavesano. (26) Piedmont; Pavia area. Ordinary red table wine. Italy.

Candaigua. (35) New York State; westernmost lake of the Finger Lakes. Ordinary to fair red and white table wines, from the Labrusca grape. U.S.A.

Candano. (29) Central Asturias; Oviedo area. Ordinary red table wine. Spain.

Candia (Bianco, Rosso). (27) Tuscany; Carrara mountain vineyards in the extreme north-west. Fair sweetish to sweet white and ordinary red wines. Italy.

Canéja. (5) Graves de Bordeaux; village approx. seven miles south-west of Bordeaux. France.

Caneva. (26) Friuli-Venezia Giulia; Udine vineyards. Simple white wine meant to be drunk very young. Italy.

Cange. (16) Touraine; Côte de Montlouis; St Martin-le-Beau vineyard, east of Tours. Fair to fine white table wine. France.

Canillas Moscatel. (29) Madrid area. Golden Muscat dessert wine. Spain.

Canina. (26) Emilia-Romagna; Ravenna area, north-east of Forli. Ordinary garnet-red table wine. Italy.

Canizo. (29) Central León; Zamora area. Ordinary to fair red, white and *clarete* table wines. Spain.

Cannellino. (27) Lazio; Frascati vineyards, south of Rome. Fine, sweet white wine. Italy.

Canneto Amare. (26) Lombardy; Oltrepo Pavese area, south of Pavia across the Po. Fair, 'bitter', frothy, dry red wine. Italy.

Canneto Dolce. (26) Lombardy; Oltrepo Pavese area, south of Pavia across the Po. Fair, sweet, frothy red dessert wine. Italy.

Canneto Gran Spumante. (26) Lombardy; Oltrepo Pavese vineyards, south of Pavia across the Po. Sweet, red, sparkling wine. Italy.

Cannonau. (28) Sardinia. A grape; also dry, sweet and semi-sweet red and rosé wines made from it.

Dry wine is fairly commonplace, sweet wines make pleasant dessert wines. Italy.

Cannonau Bianco di Jerzu. (28) Sardinia; Nuoro area. Ordinary to fair rosé dessert wine made in two grades, one sweeter than the other, from the Cannonau grape. Italy.

Canon, Château. (3) Côtes Canon-Fronsac; Fronsac. 2,500 dozen bottles of red bordeaux. France.

Canon, Château. (3) Côtes Canon-Fronsac; St Michel-de-Fronsac. 5,000 dozen bottles of red bordeaux. France.

Canon, Château. (5) Côtes de St-Emilion; *Premier grand cru classé.* 7,500 dozen bottles of red bordeaux. France.

Canon-Chaigneau, Château. (5) Néac; east of Pomerol. 3,000 dozen bottles of red bordeaux. France.

Canon-la-Gaffelière, Château. (5) Côtes de St-Emilion. *Grand cru classé.* 10,000 dozen bottles of red bordeaux. France.

Canon-Lange, Château. (3) Côtes Canon-Fronsac. 800 dozen bottles of red bordeaux. France.

Cantalapiedra. (29) Southern León; Salamanca area. Dry, fair quality white wine. Spain.

Cantalot, Clos. (5) Graves de Bordeaux; St Pierre-de-Mons, Langon area. 3,500 dozen bottles of white bordeaux. France.

Cantalpino. (29) Southern León; Salamanca area. Fair white dry wine. Spain.

Cantalupe in Sabina. (27) Lazio; Tiber valley vineyards, north of Rome. Ordinary white table wine. Italy.

Cantebau-Couhins, Château. (5) Graves de Bordeaux; Villenave-d'Ornon. *Cru classé de Graves (en blanc).* 1,000 dozen bottles of white bordeaux. France.

Cantegril, Château. (5) Sauternes; Barsac. *Cru bourgeois.* 4,500 dozen bottles of white bordeaux. France.

Canteloup, Château. (4) Haut-Médoc; St-Estèphe. *Cru bourgeois supérieur.* 8,000 dozen bottles of red bordeaux. France.

Cantemerle, Château. (3) Blayais; St Genès-de-Blaye, north east of Castillon, Gironde. 2,000 dozen bottles of red bordeaux. France.

Cantemerle, Château. (4) Haut-Médoc; Macau. *Cinquième cru classé.* 7,500 dozen bottles of red bordeaux. France.

Cantenac, Château. (5) Côtes de St-Emilion. An unclassified *cru.* 4,500 dozen bottles of red bordeaux. France.

Cantenac, Clos de. (3) Bourgeais; Lansac, north-east of Bourg. 800 dozen bottles of red bordeaux; 1,000 white. France.

Cantenac-Brown, Château. (4) Haut-Médoc; Cantenac. *Troisième cru classé.* 7,000 dozen bottles of red bordeaux. France.

Canterane, Château. (5) St-Emilion; St Etienne-de-Lisse. An unclassified *cru.* 3,000 dozen bottles of red bordeaux. France.

Cantereau, Château. (5) Pomerol. An unclassified *cru.* 2,500 dozen bottles of red bordeaux. France.

Canzem. *See* **Kanzem.**

Capbern, Château. (4) Haut-Médoc; St-Estèphe. *Cru bourgeois supérieur.* 10,000 dozen bottles of red bordeaux. France.

Cap Bon. (40) The north-east cape of Tunisia. Much sound table wine is made from the vineyards of its peninsula, one example being the red Cap Bon. Tunisia.

Cap-de-Haut, Château. (4) Médoc; Arcins, north of Bordeaux. *Cru bourgeois supérieur.* 1,500 dozen bottles of red bordeaux. France.

Cap-de-Mourlin, Château. (5) Côtes de St-Emilion. *Grand cru classé.* 7,500 dozen bottles of red bordeaux. France.

Capelle, Château La. (5) St-Emilion. 1,200 dozen bottles of red bordeaux. France.

Capena (Bianco, Rosso). (27) Lazio; Tiber valley vineyards, north of Rome. Ordinary red and white wines. Italy.

Capet-Begaud, Château. (3) Côtes Canon-Fronsac. 1,000 dozen bottles of red bordeaux. France.

Capet-Guillier, Château. (5) St-Emilion; St-Hippolyte. An unclassified *cru.* 5,000 dozen bottles of red bordeaux. France.

Capezzano Bianco. (27) Tuscany; Florence area. Fair, semi-sweet white wine. Italy.

Capitans, Les. (11) Beaujolais; Juliénas vineyard. Red beaujolais. France.

Capitans, Les. (10) Mâconnais; St-Amour vineyard. Fair red burgundy. France.

Capo (Bianco, Rosso). (28) Sicily; Strait of Messina vineyards. Ordinary to fair red and white wines. Italy.

Capo di Leuca. (28) Apulia; Lecce province, at the 'heel' of Italy. Ordinary red, dry, *frizzante* wine, and semi-sweet, *frizzante* white table wines. Italy.

Capo Ferrato. (28) Sardinia; Cape Ferrato vineyards on the coast approx. thirty miles north-east of Cagliari. Stout, strong red wine. Italy.

Capri Bianco. (28) Capri island off the coast at Naples. Most popular white table wine; also a red and rosé table wine, but in a limited quantity. Italy.

Capsanas. (29) Tarragona area. Stout, rather sweet red table wine. Spain.

Caradeux, En. (8) Côte de Beaune; Pernand-Vergelesses vineyard. *Premier cru.* France.

Caravaca. (29) Murcia area. Very dark red, semi-sweet table wine. Spain.

Carballino. (29) Southern Galicia; Ribero area, Orense province, north of the Portuguese border. Ordinary to fair white table wines. Spain.

Carbonnieux, Château. (5) Graves de Bordeaux; Léognan. *Cru classé de Graves (en blanc et en rouge).* 8,000 dozen bottles of red bordeaux; 8,000 white. France.

Carcavelos. (30) Small wine-producing area near Estoril, west of Lisbon. Formerly produced full wines, but now of little interest. Portugal.

Cardinal-Villemaurine. Château. (5) St-Emilion. An unclassified *cru.* 4,000 dozen bottles of red bordeaux. France.

Cardonne, Château La. (5) Médoc; Blaignan, north-west of St Seurin-de-Cadourne. *Cru bourgeois.* 20,000 dozen bottles of red bordeaux. France.

Carelles-Dessus. (8) Côte de Beaune; Volnay vineyard. *Premier cru.* Red burgundy. France.

Carelle-sous-la-Chapelle. (8) Côte de Beaune; Volnay vineyard. *Premier cru.* Red burgundy. France.

Carema. (26) Piedmont; Turin province. Fair red table wine. Italy.

Cari. (26) Piedmont; Turin province. Pleasant, light, semi-sweet rosé dessert wine. Italy.

Carignagne. (13) The name of the white grape and the sweet white wine which is made from it. The vineyards are mainly on the foothills of the eastern Pyrenees near the Mediterranean, Roussillon. France.

Carillon, Château Le. (5) Pomerol. 1,000 dozen bottles of red bordeaux. France.

Cariñena. (29) Zaragoza area. Ordinary to fair red and white table wines. Also dessert wines. Spain.

Carles, Château de. (3) Fronsadais; Saillans, north of Fronsac. 8,000 dozen bottles of red bordeaux. France.

Carles, Château de. (5) Sauternes; Barsac. *Cru bourgeois supérieur.* 3,000 dozen bottles of white bordeaux. France.

Carlon. (29) Valencia area. Ordinary dry and sweet red wines. Spain.

Carlsberg. (22) Moselle valley; Veldenz vineyard, just east of Brauneberg. Fair white table wine. West Germany.

Carmeilh, Château de. (3) Ile du Nord at the mouth of the river Gironde. 10,000 dozen bottles of red bordeaux. France.

Carmel. (34) The registered name of various Israeli wines. Israel.

Carmes, Clos de. (16) Anjou; Brézé vineyard south of Saumur. Fair to fine white table wine. France.

Carmes-Haut-Brion, Château Les. (5) Graves de Bordeaux; Pessac. An unclassified *cru*. 1,500 dozen bottles of red bordeaux. France.

Carmignano. (27) Tuscany; Florence area. Popular red chianti. Italy.

Carmignano Bianco. (27) Tuscany; Carmignano vineyards, Florence area. Dry white chianti. Italy.

Carougeot. (8) Gevrey-Chambertin vineyard. *Deuxième cru*. Red burgundy. France.

Carquelin, Le. (10) Mâconnais; Romanèche-Thorins vineyard. *Premier cru*. Red burgundy. France.

Carrascal. (29) A district in the north-east of the Jerez vineyards. It produces some of the finest sherries, principally Olorosos. Spain.

Carrascal, Quinta. (30) *Região demarcada do Douro* (q.v.). Large estate situated in Vale da Vilarica in the Régua area. Portugal.

Carrasquin. (29) Central Asturias; Oviedo area. Very dark, stout, red table wine. Spain.

Carreau. (6) Chablis; Poinchy vineyard. White burgundy. France.

Carrières, Cru des. (5) Premières Côtes de Bordeaux; Ste Croix-du-Mont. 1,000 dozen bottles of red bordeaux; 1,500 white. France.

Carruades, Grand Cru des. (4) Haut-Médoc; Pauillac. Vineyard adjoining the Château Lafite vineyard and part of the same property. Its red bordeaux ranks as the second best wine of the Château Lafite. France.

Cartaxo. (30) Area north of Lisbon producing fair red table wines. Portugal.

Carte et Le Châtelet, Château La. (5) Côtes de St-Emilion. *Grand cru classé*. 3,500 dozen bottles of red bordeaux. France.

Cartillon, Château du. (4) Haut-Médoc; Lamarque. *Cru bourgeois*. 900 dozen bottles of red bordeaux. France.

Cartizze. (26) Veneto; Valdobbiane vineyards, Treviso province. Fair, semi-sparkling white dessert wine from Prosecco grapes. Italy.

Cartuja de Porta Celi. (29) Valencia area. Ordinary to fair sweet white wine. Spain.

Cartuja de Scala Dei. (29) Tarragona province. Fair to fine white dessert wine. Spain.

Carvalhal, Quinta. (30) *Região demarcada do Douro* (q.v.). Estate in Pegarinhos in the Régua area. Portugal.

Carvalhal, Quinta. (30) *Região demarcada do Douro* (q.v.). Estate in Casais do Douro, in the Régua area. Portugal.

Casa da Campo. (30) Brand of *vinho verde* (q.v.). Portugal.

Casal Garcia. (30) Brand of *vinho verde* (q.v.). Portugal.

Casamicciola. (28) Ischia island in the bay of Naples. Ordinary to fair, popular white table wine. Italy.

Casa Nova, Quinta. (30) *Região demarcada do Douro* (q.v.). Estate and vineyard in Gouvaes in the Régua area. Portugal.

Casarino. (28) Apulia; Salento area encompassing the 'heel' of the 'boot'. Ordinary red and white table wines. Italy.

Casas de Benito. (29) Eastern New Castile; Cuenca area. Ordinary to fair red table wine. Spain.

Casas de Haro. (29) Eastern New Castile; Cuenca area. Ordinary to fair red table wine. Spain.

Casas Ibanez. (29) Murcia; Albacete area, approx. twenty-three miles south-east of La Roda. Ordinary to fair red table wine. Spain.

Cascalheira, Quinta. (30) *Região demarcada do Douro* (q.v.). Estate in Sarzedinho, east of Régua. Portugal.

Cascante. (29) Navarre; western Pyrenees. Ordinary red table wine. Spain.

Casel. *See* **Kasel.**

Casinos. (29) Valencia area. Ordinary white table wine. Spain.

Cassevert, Château. (5) Côtes de St-Emilion. An unclassified *cru*. 2,000 dozen bottles of red bordeaux. France.

Cassis. (14) Provence; town in the Bouches du Rhône *département*. Fair red, white and rosé table wines. France.

Cassoret, Château. (5) St-Emilionnais; St-Cibard, Lussac. 1,500 dozen bottles of red bordeaux. France.

Castagnon, Domaine de. (5) Premières Côtes de Bordeaux; Quinsac-Village, east of Cadaujac. 2,000 dozen bottles of red bordeaux. France.

Castaing, Clos. (5) Graves de Bordeaux; Langon. 2,000 dozen bottles of red bordeaux; 4,000 white. France.

Castalla. (29) Alicante area; approx. forty miles south of Valencia. Ordinary to fair red table wine. Spain.

Castegens, Château. (3) Dordogne; Castillon, Belvès-de-Castillon. 5,000 dozen bottles of red bordeaux; 2,000 white. France.

Casteggio. (26) Lombardy; Oltrope Pavese vineyards, south of Pavia across the Po. Ordinary, but locally popular, light yellow, white table wine. Italy.

Castel Asquaro. (28) Apulia; Salento area encompassing the 'heel' of the 'boot'. Ordinary table wines. Italy.

Castelbracciano. (27) Lazio; Lake Bracciano vineyards, between Rome and Viterbo. Sweet golden dessert wine from white grapes. Italy.

Castel Danielis. (34) Peloponnisos peninsula of southern Greece; Patras area. Ordinary to fair red table wine. Greece.

Castel del Monte (Bianco, Rosso and Rosato). (28) Apulia; Bari area. Fair white and ordinary to fair red and rosé table wines. Italy.

Castel del Remy. (29) Catalonia; Lerida, approx. fifty miles north-west of Tarragona. Fine red and white table wines. Spain.

Casteldoria. (26) Another name for Dolceacqua (q.v.). Italy.

Castelfranco. (26) Emilia-Romagna; Modena area. Ordinary to fair dry white table wine. Italy.

Castelinho, Quinta. (30) *Região demarcada do Douro* (q.v.). Estate and vineyard in São João de Pesqueira nineteen miles east of Régua. Portugal.

Castell. (25) Franconia; village approx. twenty miles south-east of Würzburg. Ordinary to fair red and white table wines. France.

Castellabate. (28) Campania; Salento area encompassing the 'heel' of the 'boot'. Ordinary red and rosé table wine. Italy.

Castellana. (28) Apulia; Bari area. Ordinary white, red and rosé table wines to be drunk young. Italy.

Castel la Volta. (26) Piedmont; Santa Vittoria-Monticello area, between Cuneo and Alessándria. Fair, dry, semi-sparkling white table wine. Italy.

Casteller Gran Rubino. (26) Adige valley; Trento area. Light, full, rosé wine. Italy.

Castellet, Le. (14) Côtes de Provence; Bandol vineyard. Fair red and white wines. France.

Castelli do Calepio. (26) Lombardy. Ordinary light red and white table wines. Italy.

Castelli Mezzocorona. (26) Adige valley; Mezzocorona area, south of Trento. Ordinary to fair fruity red wine. Italy.

Castelli Romani. (27) Alban Hills, south-east of Rome. Ordinary, fair and some fine white table wine. Frascati (q.v.) is the most popular. Italy.

Castello di Sommariva. (26) Piedmont; Monferrato Hills, in the Alessándria province. Fair dry white table wine. Italy.

Castellote. (29) South-central Aragon; Teruel. Fair rosé table wine. Spain.

Castelo Borges, Quinta. (30) Estate in Vila Seca twenty-five miles north of Oporto, producing table wines. Portugal.

Castelo, Quinta. (30) *Região demarcada do Douro.* (q.v.); Sanhoane, in the Régua area. Portugal.

Castelot, Château Le. (5) St-Emilion; St Sulpice-de-Faleyrens. An unclassified *cru*. 2,000 dozen bottles of red bordeaux. France.

Castel Rametz Bianco. (26) Alto Adige; Bolzano area. Fair to fine white table wine. Italy.

Castel Rametz Rosso. (26) Alto Adige; Merano area, north-west of Bolzano. Fair to fine popular red table wine, from Pinot Nero (Noir) grapes. Italy.

Castelro. (31) Ticino canton; village near Lugano. Fair white table wine. Switzerland.

Castel Roubine. (14) Côtes de Provence; Lorgues vineyards, north-west of Tradeau. Ordinary to fair red table wine. France.

Castel San Giorgio (Bianco, Rosso). (27) Vineyards west of Rome. Fair to good dry red and white table wines. Italy.

Castelsardo. (28) Sardinia; north of Sassari. Ordinary red table wine. Italy.

Castel Schwanburg (Bianco, Rosso). (26) Alto Adige; Nalles vineyards, Bolzano province. Fair red and white table wines. Italy.

Castel Tagliolo. (26) Piedmont; Alessándria province. Fair quality, dry, fragrant white table wine from Cortese white grapes. Italy.

Castel Tagliolo Superiore. (26) Piedmont; Monferrato area, Alessándria province. Fair to fine white table wine from Riesling grapes. Italy.

Castelvi de la Marca. (29) Catalonia; Panadés area, between Tarragona and Barcelona. Ordinary to fair red and white table wines. Spain.

Castera, Château du. (5) Médoc; St Germaine-d'Esteuil, west of St Seurin-de-Cadourne. *Cru bourgeois.* 15,000 dozen bottles of red bordeaux. France.

Castidum Gran Riserva. (26) Lombardy; Oltrope Pavese area, south of Pavia across the Po. Fair, golden dessert wine from Pinot Noir grapes. Italy.

Castiglione Teverina. (27) Umbria; upper Tiber valley. Fair quality, white wine made in two grades, dry and sweet. Similar but inferior to the white wines of Orvieto (q.v.). Italy.

Castillo de Locubin. (29) Jaén area; north-east of Seville. Ordinary to fair white table wine. Spain.

Castillo de Peralada. (29) Gerona area; approx. twenty-five miles north-east of Barcelona. Ordinary to fair red, white and rosé table wines. Spain.

Castillon. (3) Town, south-east of Libourne on the right bank of the river Dordogne. Ordinary to fair red and white bordeaux wines. France.

Castrelo del Mino. (29) South Galicia; Ribera area, Orense province. Ordinary red table wines. Spain.

Castrense (Bianco, Rosso). (27) Lazio; Grotto di Castro vineyards, Lake Bolsena. Ordinary to fair red and white table wines. Italy.

Castro del Rio. (29) Andalusia; Montilla area,

Córdoba province, north-east of Seville. Fair white table wines. Spain.

Castro Urdiales 'Chacoli'. (29) Asturias; Santander area, approx. forty-five miles west of Bilbao. Ordinary, rather sharp red and white table wines. Spain.

Catalonia. (29) Vineyards: 500,000 acres, producing many kinds of table, dessert and sparkling wines. Spain.

Catamarca. (35) Northwest Argentina. One of the smallest wine-producing regions.

Catheyre, Domaine de. (3) Fronsadais. 500 dozen bottles of red bordeaux; 3,000 white. France.

Caub. *See* **Kaub.**

Caudete. (29) Northern Murcia; Albacete area. Ordinary to fair red, white and *clarete* wines. Spain.

Caudete de las Fuentes. (29) West-central Valencia; Utiel area. Ordinary to fair table wines. Spain.

Cauze, Château Le. (5) St-Emilion; St Christophe-des-Bardes, south-west of Parsac. An unclassified *cru*. 15,000 dozen bottles of red bordeaux. France.

Caversham. (37) Western Australia; vineyard district in the Swan River valley area. Mostly table wines. Five wineries. Australia.

Caves, Les. (11) Beaujolais; Chénas vineyard. Red beaujolais. France.

Cavidena. (29) Estremadura; Badajoz area, between Trujillo and Seville. Ordinary red table wine. Spain.

Cayetana. (29) Estremadura; Cáceres province in Trujillo area. Ordinary to fair white table wine. Spain.

Cazalla de la Sierra. (29) Seville area. Ordinary to fair white sweet wines. Spain.

Cazeaux, Château. (4) Blayais. 15,000 dozen bottles of red bordeaux; 5,000 white. France.

Cazétiers, Les. (8) Gevrey-Chambertin vineyard. *Premier cru.* Red burgundy. France.

Cebreros. (29) Avila area. Ordinary to fair red and white table wines. Spain.

Ceclavin. (29) Estremadura; Cáceres province in Trujillo area. Ordinary to fair red, white and *clarete* wines. Spain.

Cecubo. (28) Lazio; Gulf of Gaeta, north-west of Naples. Ordinary to fair garnet-red table wine. Italy.

Cedovim, Quinta. (30) *Região demarcada do Douro* (q.v.). Estate in Sarzedinho east of Régua. Portugal.

Cèdres, Domaine des. (31) Neuchâtel canton; Cortaillon vineyard. Fair red and white table wines. Switzerland.

Cellatica. (26) Lombardy; Colli Bresciani, hills north of Brescia. Ordinary to fair, semi-sweet, red table wine. Italy.

Cellier-aux-Moines, Le. (9) Mâconnais; Givry vineyard. *Premier cru.* Red burgundy. France.

Celliers, Les. (16) Anjou; Coteaux de Layon, Rablay-sur-Layon vineyard, a tributary of the Loire in the Saumur area. Fair to fine white table wine. France.

Cencibel. (29) La Mancha area of Valdepeñas. Ordinary, very dark red table wine. Spain.

Cendres, Les. (16) Anjou; Savennières vineyard, below Angers. Fair white table wine. France.

Cenicero. (29) Old Castile; Logroño province, La Rioja area of the upper Ebro valley. Fine red table wine. Spain.

Cent Vignes, Les. (8) Beaune vineyard. *Premier cru.* Red burgundy. France.

Cepeda. (29) South León; Salamanca area. Ordinary red table wine. Spain.

Cephalonia. (34) Ordinary to fair red table wine of Greece.

Cerasuolo. (27) Abruzzi; Chieti, L'Aquila and Pescare (north-west of Chieti) regions. Ordinary to fair light red and rosé table wines. Italy.

Cerasuolo delle Murge. (28) Apulia; Bari area. Ordinary cherry-red table wine. Italy.

Cerasuolo di Scilla. (28) Calabria; Messina Straits. Fair cherry-red table wine. Italy.

Cerasuolo di Vittoria. (28) Sicily; Ragusa area, approx. thirty miles south-west of Syracuse. Strong red wine served as an apéritif. Italy.

Cerca de Santa Cruz, Quinta. (30) *Região demarcada do Douro* (q.v.). Estate and large vineyard in the Régua area. Portugal.

Cercié. (11) Beaujolais; north of St-Léger. Red beaujolais. France.

Cerdeirinha, Quinta. (30) *Região demarcada do Douro* (q.v.). Fundo de Agrelos; in Sanfins do Douro in the Régua area. Portugal.

Cerdon. (18) Village in the Ain *département.* Ordinary to fair red, white and rosé table wines. France.

Ceres. (39) Cape Province. Township in an important wine producing area. Ordinary to fair table and dessert wines. South Africa.

Cérons. (5) Graves de Bordeaux area; small town south-east of Bordeaux. Fair and some fine dry and semi-sweet white bordeaux. France.

Cérons et de Calvimont, Château. (5) Graves de Bordeaux; Cérons. An unclassified *cru.* 6,500 dozen bottles of fine white bordeaux. France.

Certan, Château. (5) Pomerol. *Premier cru.* 1,000 dozen bottles of red bordeaux. France.

Certan, Vieux Château. (5) Pomerol. 5,000 dozen bottles of red bordeaux. France.

Certan-de-May, Château. (5) Pomerol. 1,800 dozen bottles of red bordeaux. France.

Certan-Gezaud, Château. (5) Pomerol. *Grand cru.* 2,000 dozen bottles of red bordeaux. France.

Certan-Marzelle, Château. (5) Pomerol. 2,000 dozen bottles of red bordeaux. France.

Cervera del Rio Albama. (29) Old Castile; Logroño province, La Rioja area of the upper Ebro valley. Ordinary to fair red table wine. Spain.

Cerveteri (Bianco, Rosso and Rosato). (27) Lazio; Civita Vecchia area, north-west of Rome. Ordinary red, white and rosé table wines. Italy.

Cervicione. (27) Lazio; Nettuno, south of Rome. Name sometimes locally given to the better quality wines of this area. Italy.

Cesanese d'Affile. (27) Lazio. Ordinary to fair, dry and sweet, often *frizzante* red wine. Italy.

Cesanese del Castelli Romani. (27) Alban hills, south-east of Rome. Ordinary to fair, dry and sweet, often *frizzante*, red wine. Italy.

Cesanese del Piglio. (27) Lazio. Ordinary to fair, dry and sweet, often *frizzante*, red wine. Italy.

Cesnola. (26) Piedmont; Turin province. Ordinary light red table wine, drunk fairly young. Italy.

Cestas. (5) Graves de Bordeaux; small town approx. thirty miles south-west of Bordeaux. France.

Chabiots, Les. (8) Côte de Nuits; Morey-St-Denis vineyard. *Premier cru.* France.

Chabiots, Les. (8) Côte de Nuits; Chambolle-Musigny vineyard. *Deuxième cru.* Red burgundy. France.

Chablais. (31) District of Vaud canton. Some fair to fine white wines. Switzerland.

Chablis. (6) Yonne *département.* Small market town. The vineyards, as well as those of eighteen nearby villages, produce the only white table wines legally entitled in France, and morally entitled anywhere else, to the name of Chablis. In France, the *AC (Appellation Contrôlée) grand Chablis* or *Chablis grand cru* is given to the best wines of Chablis, that is, the wines of the best Chablis vineyards; the *AC Chablis premier cru* is given to the next best Chablis wines; the next grades after these are *Chablis* and *petit Chablis.* France.

Chaboeufs, Les. (8) Côte d'Or; Nuits-St-Georges vineyard. *Premier cru.* Red burgundy. France.

Chacé. (16) Anjou; Coteaux de Saumur. Mostly ordinary red and rosé table wines; some fair to fine white table wines. France.

Chacoli. (29) Navarre; western Pyrenees. Ordinary red table wine. Also some sharp white wine which is best used for distilling. Spain.

Chaffots, Les. (8) Côte de Nuits. Morey-St-Denis vineyard. *Premier cru.* Red burgundy. France.

Chagny. (9) Côte d'Or area. Chalonnais village; vineyards that include among others Le Domaine de la Folie. Fair to fine white burgundy. France.

Chaigneau, Château. (5) Néac; east of Pomerol. 2,000 dozen bottles of red bordeaux. France.

Chaignots, Les. (8) Côte d'Or; Nuits-St-Georges vineyard. *Premier cru.* Red burgundy. France.

Chaillots, Les. (8) Côte d'Or; Aloxe-Corton vineyard. *Deuxième cru.* Red burgundy. France.

Chailots, Les. (8) Côte d'Or; Nuits-St-Georges vineyard. Ordinary red burgundy. France.

Chaines-Carteau, Les. (8) Côte d'Or; Nuits-St-Georges vineyard *Deuxième cru* Red burgundy. France.

Chaintre. (10) Mâconnais village; north-east of St-Amour. The best vineyards are entitled to the *AC Pouilly-Fuissé.* France.

Chaise. (11) Beaujolais; Brouilly vineyard. Red burgundy. France.

Chalambar. (37) Victoria; A burgundy-type dry red Australian table wine named after a hill in the area of Great Western approx. 100 miles north-east of Geelong. Australia.

Chalandins, Les. (8) Côte de Nuits; Flagey-Echézeaux vineyard. *Deuxième cru.* Red burgundy. France.

Chalkis. (34) Island of Eubea off south-eastern coast of Greece. Ordinary to fair red and white table wines. Greece.

Chalonnais. (9) Saône-et-Loire *département*; southern continuation of the Côte d'Or. Red and white burgundy. France.

Chalonnes-sur-Loire. (16) Anjou; Coteaux de la Loire, village and vineyards south-west of Angers. Fair white and rosé table wines. France.

Chalybon. (34) The best-known red table wine of Syria.

Chambave. (26) Val d'Aosta. Fair strong white dessert wine. Italy.

Chambertin, Le. (8) Côte de Nuits; Gevrey-Chambertin vineyard. *Grand cru.* Fine red burgundy. France.

Chambery. (31) Savoie *département*; town in the foothills of the Alps approx. forty-five miles south-west of Geneva noted for its very dry vermouth: its vineyards also produce fair white table wines. France.

Chambolle-Musigny. (8) Côte de Nuits; Côte d'Or. Fair, fine and some great red burgundy. France.

Chambon. (12) Côtes du Rhône; Cornas vineyards. Ordinary to fair red table wine. France.

Chamboureau, Château de. (16) Anjou; vineyard of the *commune* of Savennières, just south-west of Angers. Fair white table wine. France.

Chambraste. (15) Cher *département*; village in the Sancerre region. Fair white table wine. France.

Chambray. (16) Touraine; Joué vineyard, just south-west of Tours. Fair red table wine. France.

Cham-Chardon. (16) Anjou; Coteaux de Saumur, Souzay-Champigny vineyard. Fair to fine white table wine. France.

Chameaux, Les. (18) Arbois region; vineyard of Salins-les-Bains, Jura. Ordinary to fair red table wine. France.

Chamery. (17) Marne *département*; Verzy canton, north-west of Ludes. Rated—88% growth. 362 acres. France.

Chamine, Quinta. (30) *Região demarcada do Douro* (q.v.). Estate and vineyard in Cambres south-west of Régua. Portugal.

Champagne. (17) The name of one of the former provinces of France, as well as of the best, and best known, sparkling wine in the world. To be entitled to the name 'champagne'—legally in France and Great Britain, and morally anywhere else—the wine must be made from grapes grown in this area alone, most of which is now incorporated in the Marne *département*. Unlike other systems of classification, the vineyards of Champagne are judged according to a complicated percentage scale based on 100% as the top-rated (*grand cru*) growth. France.

Champagne, La. (8) Côte d'Or; Savigny-les-Beaune. *AC Savigny*. Red burgundy. France.

Champans, Les. (8) Côte de Beaune; Volnay vineyard. *Premier cru*. Red burgundy. France.

Champ-Canet. (8) Côte d'Or; Puligny-Montrachet vineyard. *Premier cru*. White burgundy. France.

Champeaux. (8) Côte de Nuits; Gevrey-Chambertin vineyard. *Premier cru*. Red burgundy. France.

Champ-Fougres. (16) Anjou; St Cyr-en-Bourg vineyard, just south of Saumur. Ordinary to fair red table wine. France.

Champ Grillé. (10) Mâconnais; St-Amour vineyard. Red beaujolais. France.

Champigny-le-Sec. (16) Anjou, in the Saumur area. Ordinary to fair red table wine. France.

Champillon. (17) Marne *département*; Ay canton, north-west of Ay. Rated *premier cru*—93% growth. 162 acres. France.

Champlain. (6) Chablis vineyard; Les Lys. *Premier cru*. White burgundy. France.

Champ Picard. (16) Anjou; Coteaux de Saumur, Brézé vineyard, just south of Saumur. Fair white table wines. France.

Champreveyres, Cru de. (31) Neuchâtel. Fair to fine white table wine. Switzerland.

Champs-de-Perdrix. (8) Côte de Nuits; Vosne-Romanée vineyard. *Premier cru*. Red burgundy. France.

Champs Fous, Les. (16) Anjou; Dampierre-sur-Loire vineyard south of Saumur. Ordinary to fair red table wine. France.

Champs Fulliots, Les. (8) Côte de Beaune; Monthélie vineyard. *Premier cru*. Red burgundy. France.

Champs-Gain. (8) Côte d'Or; Chassagne-Montrachet vineyard. *Premier cru*. Red burgundy. France.

Champs Gondins. (8) Côte de Nuits; Vosne-Romanée vineyard. *Troisième cru*. Red burgundy. France.

Champs-Martins, Les. (9) Chalonnais; Mercurey vineyard. *Premier cru*. Red burgundy. France.

Champs Mitans. (6) Chablis; Milly. *Deuxième cru*. *AC Chablis*. White burgundy. France.

Champs-Perdrix. (8) Côte de Nuits; Nuits-St-Georges vineyard. *Premier cru*. Red burgundy. France.

Champs Perrier. (8) Côte d'Or; Brochon vineyard. *Troisième cru*. Red burgundy. France.

Champs-Pimont, Les. (8) Beaune vineyard. *Premier cru*. Red burgundy. France.

Champs Traversins. (8) Côte de Nuits; Flagey-Echézeaux vineyard. *Premier cru*. Red burgundy. France.

Champtoce. (16) Anjou; Coteaux de la Loire village, south-west of Angers. Fair white table wine. France.

Cham-sur-Layon. (16) Anjou; Coteaux du Layon village, south of Angers. Fair to fine white table wine. France.

Chanevarie. (9) Chalonnais; Givry vineyard. *Premier cru*. Red burgundy. France.

Chanière, La. (8) Pommard vineyard. *Premier cru*. Red burgundy. France.

Chanlin. (8) Côte de Beaune; Volnay vineyard. *Premier cru*. Red burgundy. France.

Chanlins Bas, Les. (8) Côte de Beaune; Pommard vineyard. *Premier cru*. Red burgundy. France.

Chanoriers, Aux. (11) Beaujolais; Jullie vineyard. Red burgundy. France.

Chantagne. (31) Savoie *département*; village at the north end of Lake Bourget, near Chambery, approx. forty-five miles south-west of Geneva. Fair white table wine. France.

Chante-Alouette. (12) Côtes du Rhône; Tain l'Hermitage vineyard. Ordinary red and fine white table wines. France.

Chantelard, Domaine du. (31) Vaud canton; Montreaux. Fair white table wine. Switzerland.

Chantelle. (15) Puy-de-Dome *département*; Massif Central, Auvergne, province extending from below St-Pourçain south. Best red table wine. France.

Chante-l'Oiseau. (5) Premières Côtes de Bordeaux; St Maixant, south-east of St Croix-de-Mont. 4,500 dozen bottles of white bordeaux. France.

Chante Loiseau, Château. (5) Graves de Bordeaux; Langon. An unclassified *cru*. 2,000 dozen bottles of red bordeaux; 1,500 white. France.

Chanturgne. (15) Puy-de-Dome *département*; Massif Central, Auvergne, the province extending from below St-Pourçain to the south. One of the better red table wines. France.

Chanze. (16) Faye d'Anjou; Coteaux du Layon, a tributary of the Loire running south of Angers. Fine white table wine. France.

Chapelle. (16) Anjou; Coteaux de l'Aubance, Denée vineyard, between Angers and Saumur. Fair to fine white table wine. France.

Chapelle. (12) Côtes du Rhône; Tain l'Hermitage. *Deuxième cru*. Fair red wine. France.

Chapelle, Domaine de la. (5) St-Emilion; St Etiènne-de-Lisse. An unclassified *cru*. 1,000 dozen bottles of red bordeaux. France.

Chapelle-Chambertin. (8) Côte de Nuits; Gevrey-Chambertin. *Grand cru*. Red burgundy. France.

Chapelle-de-la-Trinité, Château. (5) St-Emilion. An unclassified *cru*. 500 dozen bottles of red bordeaux. France.

Chapelle-du-Bois. (11) Beaujolais; Fleurie vineyard. Red beaujolais. France.

Chapelle-Lariveaux, Château La. (3) St Michel-de-Fronsac; north-west of Fronsac. 1,800 dozen bottles of red bordeaux. France.

Chapelle-Lescours, Château La. (5) St-Emilion; St Sulpice-de-Faleyrens. An unclassified *cru*. 1,500 dozen bottles of red bordeaux. France.

Chapelle-Madelaine. (5) Côtes de St-Emilion. *Grand cru classé*. 3,000 dozen bottles of red bordeaux. France.

Chapelle-Monrepos, Domaine de la. (3) Dordogne; Castillon. 3,000 dozen bottles of red bordeaux. France.

Chapelle-Vaupelteigne. (6) Chablis region. Ordinary to fair white burgundy. France.

Chapelots, Les. (6) Chablis; Fyé vineyard. *Premier cru*. Fine white burgundy. France.

Chapineria. (29) Madrid area. Ordinary to fair light *clarete* table wine. Spain.

Chapitre, Clos du. (8) Côte de Nuits; Fixin vineyard. *Premier cru*. Red burgundy is produced. France.

Chaponnières, Les. (8) Côte de Beaune; Pommard vineyard. *Premier cru*. Red burgundy. France.

Charbonnières, Les. (8) Côte d'Or; Prémeaux vineyard. *Deuxième cru*. Red burgundy. France.

Charbottières, Les. (16) Anjou; Coteaux de l'Aubance, Brissac vineyard, south-east of Angers. Fine Cabernet rosé table wine. France.

Chardannes, Les. (8) Chambolle-Musigny vineyard. *Troisième cru*. Red burgundy. France.

Chardon d'Argent. (31) Vaud canton; Chardonne vineyard. Fine white table wine. Switzerland.

Chardonne. (31) Vaud canton; Lavaux village. Fair to fine white table wine. Switzerland.

Chardonnets, Les. (10) Mâconnais; Fuissé vineyard. *Premier cru*. Fine white table burgundy. France.

Charlemagne, En. (8) Côte d'Or; Aloxe Corton. *Grand, premier, deuxième* and *troisième crus*. Very fine white burgundy. For some years now no declaration of annual output has been made under this name, only as Corton Charlemagne. France.

Charlemagne, En. (8) Côte d'Or; Pernand-Vergelesses vineyard. *Premier, deuxième* and *troisième crus*. France.

Charlevaux. (6) Chablis; Milly vineyard. *Deuxième cru*. White burgundy. France.

Charlevaux, Les. (6) Chablis. *Premier cru*. Fine white burgundy. France.

Charlotte Dumay. (8) Hospices de Beaune *cuvée* with the *AC Aloxe-Corton*. Red burgundy. France.

Charmes, Aux. (8) Côte d'Or; Morey-St Denis vineyard. *Premier cru*. Red burgundy. France.

Charmes, Les. (8) Chambolle-Musigny vineyard. *Premier cru* and *deuxième cru*. Red burgundy. France.

Charmes-Chambertin, Les. (8) Côte de Nuits; Gevrey-Chambertin vineyard. *Premier cru*. Red burgundy. France.

Charmes-Dessous, Les. (8) Côte d'Or; Meursault vineyard. *Premier cru*. White burgundy. France.

Charmes-Dessus, Les. (8) Côte d'Or; Meursault vineyard. *Premier cru*. White burgundy. France.

Charmois, Les. (8) Côte d'Or; Nuits-St-Georges vineyard. *Deuxième cru*. Red burgundy. France.

Charmots. (8) Côte de Beaune; Pommard vineyard. *Premier cru*. Red burgundy. France.

Charnay-les-Mâcon. (10) Mâconnais. Ordinary to fair red burgundy. France.

Charnières, Les. (8) Côte de Beaune; Savigny-les-Beaune vineyard. *Premier cru*. Red burgundy. France.

Charrières, Les. (8) Côte de Beaune; Morey-St-Denis vineyard. *Premier cru*. Red burgundy. France.

Charron, Château. (3) Blayais; St Martin-Lacaussade, north-east of Blaye. 8,000 dozen bottles of red bordeaux; 2,000 white. France.

Charrons, Les. (8) Côte d'Or; Meursault vineyard. *Deuxième cru.* White burgundy. France.

Chartrons, Clos des. (4) Haut-Médoc; St Julien. The name under which the second best red bordeaux from Château Lagrange (St Julien) is marketed. France.

Chassagne-Montrachet. (8) Côte d'Or; Côte de Beaune village. Very fine white burgundy, including some Montrachet; also some very fine red burgundy. France.

Chasseignes, Les. (15) Cher *département*; Chavignol vineyard, Sancerre area. Fair to fine white wine. France.

Chasse-Spleen, Château. (4) Haut-Médoc; Moulis. *Cru exceptionnel.* 18,000 dozen bottles of red bordeaux. France.

Chassière, La. (9) Chalonnais; St Martin-sous-Montaigu. *Premier cru.* Red burgundy. France.

Chatain, Château. (3) Néac; bordering on Pomerol. 3,000 dozen bottles of red bordeaux. France.

Chatain, Domaine du. (3) Néac; bordering on Pomerol. 2,500 dozen bottles of red bordeaux. France.

Chatains. (6) Chablis vineyard. *Premier cru.* White burgundy. France.

Château, Clos du. (16) Côtes de Saumur; Montsoreau vineyard. Fair white table wine. France.

Château-Bégadan-Médoc. (3) The registered name of the red bordeaux made and marketed by the Cave Cooperative de Bégadan, north-west of St Seurin-de-Cadourne. France.

Château Chalon. (18) Jura *département*. Fair to fine *vin jaune* (q.v.) and *vin de paille* (q.v.). France.

Château d'Epire. (16) Coteaux de la Loire; vineyard of the Savennières *commune*, just southwest of Angers. Fair, popular, white table wine. France.

Château Gris. (8) Name used for a *premier cru* Nuits St-Georges vineyard, 'Les Crots'. France.

Château-Neuf. (5) Graves de Bordeaux; Léognan. An unclassified *cru.* 2,000 dozen bottles of red bordeaux; 2,000 white. France.

Château-Noire. (16) Touraine; Chinon vineyard. Fair red table wine. France.

Château-Renard. (13) Arles-en-Provence, between Lunel and Costières. Ordinary to fair red table wine. France.

Chatelet, Domaine du. (5) St-Emilion. An unclassified *cru.* 1,000 dozen bottles of red bordeaux. France.

Chatelguyon. (15) Puy-de-Dome *département;*

Massif Central. Ordinary to fair red table wine. France.

Chatelières, Les. (16) Anjou; Coteaux de l'Aubance, Müre-Erigne vineyard, between Angers and Saumur. Fair white table wine. France.

Chatillon-sur-Seine. Northernmost point of the former province of Burgundy. Ordinary to fair red and white table wines. Now little wine made. France.

Chatterie, La. (16) Touraine; Vouvray vineyard, east of Tours. Fair white table wine. France.

Chaudefonds. (16) Anjou; Coteaux du Layon, a tributary of the Loire running south of Angers. Fair to fine white table wine. France.

Chaulet, Domaine de. (5) Premières Côtes de Bordeaux; Rions, north of Podensac. 300 dozen bottles of red bordeaux; 6,000 white. France.

Chaume. (16) Anjou; Coteaux du Layon village, below Angers. It has given its name to the famous Quarts de Chaume vineyard nearby, whose luscious white wine is one of the finest Anjou white wines. France.

Chaume, La. (9) Chalonnais; Rully vineyard. *Premier cru.* White burgundy. France.

Chaumées, Les. (8) Côte de Beaune; Chassagne-Montrachet vineyard. *Premier cru.* Red burgundy. France.

Chaume-Gaufriot. (8) Beaune vineyard. *Premier cru.* Red burgundy. France.

Chaumes, Les. (8) Côte de Nuits; Vosne-Romanée vineyard. *Premier cru.* Red burgundy. France.

Chaumes, Les. (8) Côte de Beaune; Aloxe-Corton vineyard. *Premier cru.* Red burgundy. France.

Chaumes, Les. (15) Pouilly-sur-Loire vineyard. Fair to fine white table wines. France.

Chaumes, Château Les. (4) Blayais; Fours. 4,000 dozen bottles of red bordeaux; 2,000 white. France.

Chaumes, Château Les. (5) Néac; east of Pomerol. 3,500 dozen bottles of red bordeaux. France.

Chaumes-de-Voirosse. (8) Côte de Beaune; Aloxe-Corton vineyard. *Premier cru.* Red burgundy. France.

Chaumiennes, Les. (15) Pouilly-sur-Loire vineyard. Fair to fine white table wine. France.

Chautauqua. (35) Partly in the Eastern states of New York and Pennsylvania; narrow strip of vineyards along the northern shore of Lake Erie. U.S.A.

Chauvin, Château. (5) St-Emilion. *Grand cru classé.* 6,000 dozen bottles of red bordeaux. France.

Chauvin, Château. (5) St-Emilion. *Premier cru graves de St-Emilion.* 5,500 dozen bottles of red bordeaux. France.

Chavagnes. (16) Anjou; Coteaux du Layon, below Angers. Fair to fine white and rosé table wines. France.

Chavignol. (15) Cher *département;* hamlet near Sancerre. Ordinary red and fair to fine white table wines. France.

Chavot-Courcourt. (17) Marne *département;* Avize canton, south of Epernay. Rated—87% growth for black; white 88%. 263 acres. France.

Chay, Château Le. (4) Berson; south-east of Blaye. 2,000 dozen bottles of red bordeaux; 4,000 white. France.

Cheille. (16) Touraine; Loire valley, north-east of Chinon. Ordinary to fair red table wine. France.

Cheilly-les-Maranges. (7) Côte d'Or village, near Santenay. *AC Côte de Beaune.* Red burgundy. France.

Cheilly-sur-Serein. (6) Yonne *département;* Chablis region. White burgundy. France.

Chénas. (11) Village on the border of Mâconnais and Beaujolais. Its best, and best-known vineyard is Moulin-à-Vent. Red burgundy. France.

Chène. (9) Chalonnais; Rully vineyard. Fair to fine white burgundy. France.

Chène-Liège, Château. (5) Pomerol. 1,000 dozen bottles of red bordeaux. France.

Chènes, Clos des. (8) Côte de Beaune; Volnay vineyard. *Premier cru.* Red burgundy. France.

Chènes, Les. (15) Pouilly-sur-Loire vineyard. Fair to fine white table wine. France.

Chène-Vieux, Château. (5) St-Emilion; Puisseguin. An unclassified *cru.* 4,000 dozen bottles of bordeaux. France.

Chènove. (8) Côte de Nuits (Côte d'Or). Former Côte Dijonnaise, but now major part of vineyard is replaced by houses and roads. Fair red burgundy. France.

Cher. (15) *Département* of France, of which Bourges is the main city. Vineyards: 10,979 acres. Wine: 2,000,000 dozen bottles. Mostly white table wines. France.

Chesaux, Aux. (8) Morey-St-Denis vineyard. *Premier cru.* Red burgundy. France.

Chesnaye-Sainte-Gemme, Château La. (4) Haut-Médoc; Cussac. *Cru bourgeois supérieur.* 5,000 dozen bottles of red bordeaux. France.

Cheusots, Aux. (8) Côte de Nuits; Fixin vineyard. *Premier cru.* Red burgundy. France.

Chevalerie, La. (16) Touraine; Bourgueil. Fair to fine red table wine. France.

Chevalerie, La. (16) Touraine; Restigné vineyard of the *commune* in the Bourgueil area. Fair red table wine. France.

Chevalier, Domaine de. (5) Graves de Bordeaux; Léognan. *Cru classé de Graves (en blanc et en rouge).* 3,000 dozen bottles of red bordeaux; 1,500 white. France.

Cheval Blanc, Château. (5) St-Emilion. *Premier grand cru classé.* 15,000 dozen bottles of red bordeaux. France.

Chevalier. (34) Island of Rhodes; north-east of Crete. A fair red table wine. Greece.

Chevalier-Montrachet. (8) Puligny-Montrachet vineyard. *Premier cru.* Fine white burgundy. France.

Cheval Noir, Château. (5) Côtes de St-Emilion. An unclassified *cru.* 1,600 dozen bottles of red bordeaux. France.

Chevelière, La. (8) Côte de Beaune; Meursault vineyard. *Deuxième cru.* White burgundy. France.

Chevenottes, Les. (8) Côte de Beaune; Chassagne-Montrachet vineyard. *Deuxième cru.* Red burgundy. France.

Chevret, En. (8) Côte de Beaune; Volnay vineyard. *Premier cru.* Red burgundy. France.

Chevrier, Château. (16) Touraine; Rochecorbon, Chinon. Fair to fine white table wine. France.

Chianti. (27) Tuscany; Siena area. Best known of the red table wines of Italy. Originally known in England as 'Florence wine'. Most chianti is bottled in the traditional Tuscan straw-coloured *fiaschi*, but the best are mostly bottled in the bordeaux-type bottle. Italy.

Chianti Classico. (27) Tuscany; vineyards between Siena and Florence. Classification given to red chianti from this area. All bottles bear the *Marco Gallo*, or black cockerel, trade mark. Italy.

Chianti Di Montalbano. *See* **Carmignano.**

Chianti Montalbano Pistoiese. (27) Tuscany; Montalbano district, between Florence and Pistoia. Ordinary to fair red Chianti. Italy.

Chianti Putto. (27) Fair quality chianti from grapes outside the *chianti classico* privileged area. It bears the seal of the grower's association, somewhat like a Della Robbia angel. Italy.

Chiaretto del Faro. (26) Liguria; Cinqueterre area, north-west of La Spezia. Ordinary to fair pink table wine. Italy.

Chiaretto del Garda. (26) Lake Garda, west of Verona. Ordinary to fair rosé table wine. Italy.

Chiaretto del Lago d'Iselo. (26) Lombardy; Lake Iselo area, north-west of Brescia. Fair rosé table wine. Italy.

Chiaretto del Viverone. (26) Piedmont; Vercelli province. Ordinary to fair very light red, slightly frizzante wine. Italy.

Chiaretto di Cavaglia. (26) Piedmont; Vercelli province. Sweetish, rosé table wine of no great distinction. Italy.

G

Chiaretto di Cellatica. (26) Lombardy; Colli Bresciani, hills north of Brescia. Ordinary to fair rather sweet pink wine. Italy.

Chiaretto di Liguria. (26) Liguria; Imperia valley and Andora hills, north-east of Imperia. Ordinary to fair rosé table wine. Italy.

Chichée. (6) Village in the Chablis area, with the AC Chablis. France.

Chiclana. (29) Andalusia; Jerez-Cadiz region. Ordinary to fair dry white wine. Spain.

Chihuahua. (35) Northern Mexico. Ordinary to fair red table wine. Mexico.

Chile. (35) One of the largest wine producing countries of South America, with an average production of over 80,000,000 dozen, mostly ordinary to fair table wines, as well as some fair and fine table wines which are among the best of all South American wines.

Chilènes, Les. (8) Beaune vineyard. Premier cru. Red burgundy. France.

Chilleau, Clos. (16) Anjou; Coteaux de la Loire, La Possonnière vineyard, south-west of Angers. Fair white table wine. France.

Chinchon. (29) Madrid area. Strong, dry, red table wine. Spain.

Chinon. (16) Touraine. Ordinary to fair red table wine. France.

Chiomonte. (26) Piedmont; Doria Riparia vineyard, Turin province. Ordinary red table wine. Italy.

Chios. (34) Greek island off western coast of Turkey which has been reputed for its table and dessert wines since classical times. Greece.

Chipiona. (29) Jerez-Cadiz region. Ordinary to fair white wines. Spain.

Chiroubles. (11) Beaujolais. Fair red beaujolais. France.

Chiva. (29) Valencia area. Ordinary red table wine. Spain.

Chorey-les-Beaune. (8) Côte de Beaune village. AC Chorey-les-Beaune. Ordinary to fair red burgundy. France.

Chouilly. (17) Marne département; Epernay canton. Rated premier cru—black, 90% growth; white 93%. 1,060 acres. France.

Chourcheux, Les. (8) Beaune vineyard. Premier cru. Red burgundy. France.

Christian Brothers. (36) California; Mount La Salle vineyards, Napa Valley. Cellars in St Helena, Napa County. 1,000,000 dozen bottles. Table, dessert and sparkling wines, also brandy and vermouth. Production and storage now being doubled. U.S.A.

Chypre, Les. (31) Neuchâtel area; Le Landeron vineyard. Fair to fine white table wine. Switzerland.

Ciclopi (Bianco, Rosso and Rosato). (28) Sicily; Catania area vineyards. Ordinary white, rosé and red table wines. Italy.

Cico Casas. (29) New Castile; Ciudad Real, an area north of Valdepeñas. Ordinary to fair table wines. Spain.

Cidro, Quinta. (30) Região demarcada do Douro. (q.v.). Estate and vineyard in São Joao de Pasqueira, nineteen miles east of Régua. Portugal.

Cieza. (29) Murcia; Jumilla area, approx. seventy miles south-east of La Roda. Ordinary to fair table wines. Spain.

Cigales. (29) Valladolid area; approx. seventy miles north of Avila. Ordinary to fair white table wine. Spain.

Cilleres. (29) Estremadura; Cáceres province, in the Trujillo area. Ordinary to fair red table wine. Spain.

Cima Corgo. (30) The district east of the River Corgo, a tributary of the River Douro north of Régua, producing quality port. Portugal.

Cinco Villas, Las. (29) Aragon; Zaragoza area. Ordinary to fair table wines. Spain.

Cinq Mars. (16) Touraine; village west of Tours. Ordinary to fair red table wine. France.

Cinqueterre. (26) Liguria; five villages between Capo Mezzo and Capo Cave, north of La Spezia. Mostly ordinary white table wines; also a rather superior white dessert wine known as Sciacchetra. Italy.

Cintryenigo. (29) Navarre; western Pyrenees. Dark, dry red table wine. Spain.

Cirò. (28) Calabria; vineyards approx. thirty miles north-east of Crotone. Ordinary to fair red table wine; also a rosé and sweet red wine, and a white wine. Italy.

Cissac, Château. (4) Haut-Médoc village and commune. Ordinary to fair red bordeaux. France.

Citernes, Les. (8) Aloxe-Corton vineyard. Troisième cru. Red burgundy. France.

Citran, Château. (4) Haut-Médoc; Avensan. Cru bourgeois supérieur. 10,000 dozen bottles of red bordeaux. France.

Citta di Sant Angelo. (27) Abruzzi: Pescara area, north-east of Chieti. Ordinary red and white table wines. Italy.

Citta Lavinia. (27) Lazio. Ordinary to fair white table wine. Italy.

Clairette de Bellegarde. (13) Languedoc. Ordinary to fair white table wine. France.

Clairette de Die. (12) Drome département; Côtes du Rhône. Fair semi-sparkling white wine. France.

Clairette du Languedoc. (13) Languedoc; fair white table wine. France.

Clape, La. (13) Village in the Narbonne area

south-west of Béziers. Fair table wines, red, white and rosé. France.

Clapeyranne, La. (12) Côte Rôtie; Ampuis. *Premier cru.* Fine red table wine. France.

Clapière, Domaine de la. (14) Côtes de Provence; Hyères vineyard west of Toulon. Ordinary to fair red, white and rosé table wines. France.

Claret. The traditional name for red bordeaux wine in Great Britain and Ireland. The wine became a British favourite as early as the 13th century, at which time it was called *clairet* by the French who made it.

Clarete. (29) The name given in Spain to light red table wines. Spain.

Clare-Watervale. (37) South Australia; eighty miles north of Adelaide. One of the leading wine regions of the State. It produces dry white and red wines as well as brandy and sherries. It is the site of one co-operative winery and four others. In 1969 a southerly extension was made into the Auburn district. Australia.

Clariana. (29) Lerida; approx. fifty miles north-west of Tarrogona. Ordinary white wine. Spain.

Clary, Château de. (12) Côtes du Rhône; Roquemaure, Tavel. *AC Tavel.* Fair to fine rosé table wine. France.

Clastidio (Bianco, Rosso and **Rosato).** (26) Lombardy; Casteggio vineyards, Oltropo Pavese area south of Pavia across the Po. Fair to fine white wine, and ordinary rosé and red table wines. Italy.

Clastidium Gran Riserva. (26) Lombardy; Casteggio vineyards, Oltropo Pavese area, south of Pavia across the Po. Fine sweet golden dessert wine. Italy.

Clauzet, Château. (4) Haut-Médoc; St-Estèphe. *Cru bourgeois.* 1,000 dozen bottles of red bordeaux. France.

Clavoillon. (8) Côte de Beaune; Puligny-Montrachet vineyard. *Premier cru.* Red burgundy. France.

Clement, Clos. (15) Touraine; Chinon vineyard. Ordinary to fair red table wine. France.

Clerc-Milon-Mondon, Château. (4) Haut-Médoc; Pauillac. *Cinquième cru classé.* 5,000 dozen bottles of red bordeaux. France.

Clessé. (10) Mâconnais. One of the better to fair red and white table wines. France.

Cleyrac, Château. (3) Fronsadais; Tarnes, north-west of Fronsac. 3,000 dozen bottles of red bordeaux; 3,000 white. France.

Climens, Château. (5) Sauternes; Barsac. *Premier cru classé.* 4,500 dozen bottles of white bordeaux. France.

Clinet, Château. (5) Pomerol. 3,000 dozen bottles of red bordeaux. France.

Clinet, Château. (5) Premières Côtes de Bordeaux; St Caprais de Bordeaux, north-west of Podensac. 700 dozen bottles of red bordeaux; 700 white. France.

Clocher, Clos du. (5) Pomerol. 2,000 dozen bottles of red bordeaux. France.

Cloître, Clos du. (31) Vaud canton, Aigle vineyard. Fair to fine white table wine. Switzerland.

Clos, Au. (10) Mâconnais; Pouilly vineyard. *Grand cru.* Fine white burgundy. France.

Clos, Le. (10) Mâconnais; Fuissé vineyard. *Grand cru.* Fine white burgundy. France.

Clos, Les. (6) Chablis. One of the few *grand Chablis* vineyards. Fine white burgundy. France.

Closeaux, Les. (16) Touraine; Chinon vineyard. Fair red table wine. France.

Closerie-Grand Poujeaux, Château La. (4) Haut-Médoc; Moulis. *Cru bourgeois supérieur.* 3,800 dozen bottles of red bordeaux. France.

Clotte, Château La. (5) Côtes de St-Emilion. *Grand cru classé.* 1,600 dozen bottles of red bordeaux. France.

Clotte, Domaine de la. (5) St-Emilion; St-Hippolyte. An unclassified *cru.* 2,000 dozen bottles of red bordeaux. France.

Clotte-Blanche, Domaine de. (3) Bourgeais; Bourg. 2,000 dozen bottles of red bordeaux; 1,500 white. France.

Clotte-Grande-Côte, Château La. (5) Côtes de St-Emilion. An unclassified *cru.* 2,000 dozen bottles of red bordeaux. France.

Cluzière, Château La. (5) Côtes de St-Emilion. *Grand cru classé.* 1,500 dozen bottles of red bordeaux. France.

Coahuila. (35) Northern Mexico. Ordinary to fair table wines. Mexico.

Cochem. *See* **Kochem.**

Colares. (30) A demarcated wine-producing district north-west of Lisbon, on the coast. Mainly red wines, although some white wines are produced. Both from the Ramisco grape, they have a particular style of their own, which is dry, light, yet stringent, owing to the fact that the vineyards are among sand dunes. The only European ocean wine. Portugal.

Colatamburo. (28) Apulia; Bari area. Ordinary to fair dry white table wine. Italy.

Colbert, Château. (3) Bourgeais; Comps, north-west of Bourg. 5,000 dozen bottles of red bordeaux; 2,000 white. France.

Colgenstein-Heidesheim. (23) Palatinate; village north-east of Grünstadt. Ordinary to fair quite popular, red and white table wines. West Germany.

Collet. (29) Balearic Islands; off the coast east of Valencia. A very dark red, dry table wine. Spain.

Colli Albani, Bianco dei. (27) Lazio; Alban hills, south-east of Rome. Dry white table wines; also unimportant red and sweet white wine. Italy.

Colli Berici. (26) Vicenza hills, south of the city. Pleasant, full, slightly sweet white wines and good red table wine. Italy.

Colli Cimini. (27) Lazio; Cimini hills, south-east of Vicerbo. Mostly ordinary semi-sweet and dry wines. Italy.

Colli dei Frati. (26) Lombardy; Frati hills, Bergamo area. Light, dry red table wines usually drunk young. Italy.

Colli del Sannio (Bianco, Rosso and **Rosato)**. (28) Campania; Benevento hills, north of Avellino. Mostly ordinary red, white and rosé wines. Italy.

Colli di Asolo-Maser. (26) Veneto; Piave valley hills, north-west of Treviso. Fair light white table wines. Italy.

Colli di Congeliano. (26) Veneto; Piave river valley, north of Treviso. Mostly fair, light, dry white table wines. Italy.

Colli di Valdobbiadene. (26) Vittoria Veneto area; Piave valley hills, approx. twenty-five miles north of Treviso. Two types of white wine: a still dry and a sweetish *frizzante* (sometimes *spumante*). Italy.

Colli Etruschi. (27) Lazio; Etruscan hills, near Viterbo. Table wines similar to Castrense wines (q.v.). Italy.

Colli Euganei. (26) Friuli-Venezia Giulia and Veneto; Euganei hills, approx. twenty miles south-east of Vicenza. Ordinary to fair table wines. Italy.

Colli Friulani. (26) Friuli-Venezia Giulia and Veneto; Friuli hills, north-west of Venice. Mostly fair white table wines from white Pinot grapes. Italy.

Colli Lanuvi. (27) Lazio; Lanuvio hills, south of Lake Nemi, south of Frascati. Mostly fair, dry semi-sweet and sweet, white table wines. Italy.

Colline Bolzano. (26) Alto Adige; Bolzano area. Name given to the more common red table wines of varying quality. Italy.

Colline della Lunigiuana Bianco. (27) Tuscany; Massa-Carrara region. Ordinary, dry, semi-sweet and sweet white table wines. Italy.

Colline del Trasimeno (Bianco, Rosso). (26) Umbria; Lake Trasimeno, west of Perugia. Ordinary to fair red and white table wines. Italy.

Colline di Merano. (26) Alto Adige; Merano hills, above Bolzano. Ordinary to fair red and white table wines. Italy.

Colline Lucchesi. (27) Tuscany; between Lucca and the sea. Ordinary to fair dry red and white table wines. Italy.

Colline Rocciose. (26) Lombardy; Lake Garda, west of Verona. Ordinary to fair, brilliantly red rather sweet table wine. Italy.

Colline Sanminiatesi. (27) Tuscany; Empoli area, south-west of Florence. Ordinary to fair red table wine of the chianti type. Italy.

Colline Trevigiane. (26) Veneto; lower reaches of the Piave river, north-east of Venice. Ordinary white table wine. Italy.

Colline Val di Nievole. (27) Tuscany; Montecatini area, north-east of Lucca. Ordinary to fair dry white table wines, often semi-sparkling. Italy.

Colli Veronesi. (26) Name given to a wide range of wines grown north and north-west of Verona, including such well-known growths as Bardolino (q.v.) and Valpolicella (q.v.). Italy.

Colli Perugino, (Bianco, Rosso). (26) Umbria; hills by Lake Trasimeno, west of Perugia. Ordinary table wines. Italy.

Colli Piceni. (27) Hillside of the Ancona-Ascoli range, near Ancona. Mostly ordinary dry and sweet, red and white table wines, but some sparkling wines. Italy.

Colli Salveti. (27) Tuscany; Livorno hills area, south-west of Siena. Fair red, chianti type table wines. Italy.

Colli Sorrentini. (28) Sorrentine peninsula hills, near Naples. Ordinary to fair red and white table wines. Some of the reds are semi-sweet. Italy.

Colli Vicentini Centrale. (26) Vineyards of Vicenza hills. Same type of wines as Colli Berici (q.v.) and Valpolicella (q.v.). Italy.

Cölln. (24) Nahe; village south-west of Bad Kreuznach. Fair white table wines. West Germany.

Colmeal, Quinta. (30) *Região demarcada do Douro* (q.v.). Estate in Guiaes in the Régua area. Portugal.

Colmenar. (29) Málaga area. Ordinary to fair red table wines. Spain.

Colmenar de Oreja. (29) Madrid region. Very strong dark red table wine. Spain.

Colognola. (26) Veneto; Soave area, east of Verona. Ordinary to fair red and pink table wine. Italy.

Colombier. (31) Neuchâtel region; village producing fair to fine white table wine; also a rosé table wine. Switzerland.

Colombière, La. (8) Côte de Nuits; Vosne-Romanée vineyard. *Deuxième cru*. Red burgundy. France.

Colonna. (27) Palestrina-Colonna vineyards, north-eastern end of the Castelli Romani area of the Alban hills, south-east of Rome. Fair, golden table wine. Italy.

Combe-aux-Moines, La. (8) Côte de Nuits; Gevrey-Chambertin vineyard. *Premier cru*. Red burgundy. France.

Combe-Brulée, La. (8) Côte de Nuits; Vosne-Romanée vineyard. *Deuxième cru*. Red burgundy. France.

Combe-Dessus. (8) Côte de Beaune; Pommard vineyard. *Premier cru*. France.

Combe d'Orveau. (8) Côte de Nuits; Chambolle-Musigny vineyard. *Premier cru*. Red burgundy. France.

Combe-du-Dessus. (8) Côte de Nuits; Gevrey-Chambertin vineyard. *Troisième cru*. Red burgundy. France.

Combes, Les. (8) Côte de Beaune; Aloxe-Corton vineyard. *Deuxième cru*. Red burgundy. France.

Combettes, Les. (8) Côte de Beaune; Puligny-Montrachet vineyard. *Premier cru*. White burgundy. France.

Combotte, La. (8) Côte de Beaune; Pommard vineyard. *Deuxième cru*. Red burgundy. France.

Combottes, Aux. (8) Côte de Nuits; Chambolle-Musigny. *Deuxième cru*. Fair red burgundy. France.

Combottes, Les. (8) Côte de Nuits; Gevrey-Chambertin. *Premier cru*. Red burgundy. France.

Comiso. (28) Sicily; Ragusa area, approx. thirty miles south-west of Syracuse. Fair, amber dessert wine. Italy.

Commanderia. (34) Island of Cyprus approx. 100 miles off the west coast of Syria. The finest dessert wine from the island. Cyprus.

Commanderie, Château de la. (5) Lalande-de-Pomerol; north of Pomerol. 5,000 dozen bottles of red bordeaux. France.

Commanderie, Château La. (5) Pomerol. 2,000 dozen bottles of red bordeaux. France.

Commandeur, Clos du. (5) Pomerol. 1,000 dozen bottles of red bordeaux. France.

Commaraine, Clos de la. (8) Côte de Beaune; Pommard vineyard. *Premier cru*. Red burgundy. France.

Comme, La. (7) Côte de Beaune; Santenay vineyard. *Premier cru*, *deuxième* and *troisième crus*. Red burgundy. France.

Commet-Magey, Château. (5) Graves de Bordeaux; Preignac. An unclassified *cru*. 1,000 dozen bottles of white bordeaux. France.

Communes, Les. (8) Côte de Nuits; Romanée vineyard. *Troisième cru*. Red burgundy. France.

Como. (34) Island of Syra (Syros) off the south-east coast of Greece. Red dessert wine. Greece.

Competa. (29) Málaga area. Sweet dessert wine. Spain.

Completer. (31) Graubünden (Grisons) canton. Ordinary red table wine. Switzerland.

Comte, Château. (3) Fronsac. 1,000 dozen bottles of red bordeaux. France.

Comtesse, Clos de la. (15) Sancerre; Chavignol vineyard. Fair white table wine. France.

Comtesses, Cru des. (15) Sancerre; Chavignol vineyard. Fair to fine white table wine. France.

Condorcet. (12) Côtes du Rhône; Châteauneuf-du-Pape. Fair to fine red table wine. France.

Condrieu. (12) Côtes du Rhône; town on the Rhône, south of Lyons. Château Grillet is its finest vineyard. France.

Conegliano. (26) Veneto. Ordinary to fair red and white table wines. Italy.

Cone-Neveu, Château Le. (4) Blayais. 2,000 dozen bottles of red bordeaux; 2,000 white. France.

Concro Rosso. (27) The Marches; Ancona area. Rather ordinary fruity red table wine. Italy.

Cone-Sebillon, Château Le. (4) Blayais. 4,000 dozen bottles of red bordeaux. France.

Cone-Taillasson-Saubourin, Château Le. (4) Blayais. 2,500 dozen bottles of red bordeaux. France.

Conflans, Domaine de. (12) Côtes de Rhône; Croze-Hermitage area vineyard. Fair white table wine. France.

Conil de la Frontera. (29) Cadiz area. Fair white, dry wine. Spain.

Conilh-Haute-Libarde, Château. (3) Bourgeais. 2,500 dozen bottles of red bordeaux. France.

Conseillante, Château La. (5) Pomerol. *Grand cru*. 4,000 dozen bottles of red bordeaux. France.

Constantia. (39) Cape Peninsula; below Cape Town. The oldest and most famous winery and vineyard. South Africa.

Constantina. (29) Seville area. Ordinary semi-sweet white wine. Spain.

Consueda. (29) La Mancha; Toledo area, approx. forty miles south-west of Madrid. Ordinary to fair red and white table wines. South-central Spain.

Consumo. (30) The Portuguese equivalent of 'vin ordinaire' or plain red, white or rosé table wine not produced in a demarcated area. Portugal.

Conterie, La. (16) Anjou; Coteaux de la Loire, a vineyard of the Savennières *commune* just south-west of Angers. France.

Conthey. (31) Valais canton; village. Very fair white table wines. Switzerland.

Contra Costa. (36) California; San Francisco area. One of the minor wine-producing regions of California. U.S.A.

Contrie, La. (16) Touraine; Bourgueil vineyard. Fair red table wine. France.

Conversano (Rosato, Rosso). (28) Apulia; Conversano and Castellana Grotte vineyards, approx. twenty-five miles south-east of Bari. Ordinary white, rosé and red table wines, the red probably being the best of the three. Italy.

Coonawarra. (37) South Australia; near Mount Gambier. Famous vineyard district. Quality red table wine. Australia.

Copertina. (28) Apulia; Salento area, encompassing the 'heel' of the 'boot'. Ordinary to fair red and white table wines. Italy.

Coqueries, Les. (16) Anjou; Coteaux du Layon, Bonnézeaux vineyard, south of Angers. Fair to fine white and rosé table wines. France.

Corbara. (28) Campania; Sorrentine hills, near Naples. Fair garnet-red table wine; also some whites and semi-sweet reds. Italy.

Corbières, Les. (13) Aude *département;* Languedoc. Fair red, white and rosé table wines. France.

Corbières du Roussillon. (13) Pyrenées Orientales *département*; Roussillon. Fair, red, white and rosé table wines. France.

Corbières Supérieures. (13) Aude *département*; Languedoc. Fair to fine red, white and rosé table wines. France.

Corbières Supérieures du Roussillon. (13) Pyrenées Orientales *département*; Roussillon. Fair to fine red, white and rosé table wines. France.

Corbin, Château. (5) Côtes de St-Emilion. *Grand cru classé.* 10,000 dozen bottles of red bordeaux. France.

Corbin, Château. (5) St-Emilion; Montagne. An unclassified *cru*. 10,000 dozen bottles of red bordeaux. France.

Corbin-Fortin, Cru. (5) St-Emilion. 2,000 dozen bottles of red bordeaux. France.

Corbin-Michotte, Château. (5) St-Emilion. *Grand cru classé.* 5,000 dozen bottles of red bordeaux. France.

Corbins, Les. (8) Côte de Beaune; Meursault vineyard. *Deuxième cru.* White burgundy. France.

Corcelles-Dormondrèche. (31) Neuchâtel region; district with 126 acres of vineyards. Mostly fair white table wines. Switzerland.

Corconac, Château. (4) Haut-Médoc; St-Laurent. *Cru bourgeois.* 1,500 dozen bottles of red bordeaux. France.

Corde, La. (16) Touraine; Dampierre-sur-Loire, a *commune* on the Saumur hillsides. Fair white table wine. France.

Cordeira, Quinta. (30) *Região demarcada do Douro* (q.v.). Estate in Poiares north-east of Régua, producing many red table wines. Portugal.

Cordeliers, Clos des. (16) Anjou; vineyard of Champigny-le-Sec in the Saumur area. Fair red table wine. France.

Cordella. (29) Navarre; western Pyrenées. Strong, dark red, dry table wine. Spain.

Córdoba. (29) A region north-east of Seville producing one of the better quality high-strength white wines. Spain.

Córdoba. (35) North-central Argentina; one of the minor wine-producing regions.

Cordovin. (29) Old Castile; Logroño province, La Rioja area of the upper Ebro valley. Fair, red and rosé table wine. Spain.

Corent. (15) Puy-de-Dôme *département*; Massif Central area south of St-Pourçain. Ordinary to fair red table wine. France.

Corfu. (34) Island off the west coast of Greece in the Ionian Sea. Mostly ordinary table wines, some fair Muscat dessert wine. Greece.

Corgo. (30) One of the main northern tributaries of the River Douro which joins the latter at Régua. Portugal.

Corgoloin. (8) Côte de Nuits; last village. *AC Côte de Nuits village.* Red burgundy. France.

Cori. (27) Lazio; Lepini hills, approx. thirty miles south-east of Rome. Ordinary to fair dry red and white table wines. Italy.

Cormey-Figeac, Château. (5) Côtes de St-Emilion. An unclassified *cru*. 500 dozen bottles of red bordeaux. France.

Cormiers, Les. (16) Anjou; Côtes de Saumur, Parnay vineyard, Loire valley. Fair white table wine. France.

Cornas. (12) Ardèche *département*; Côtes du Rhône. Fair to fine red table wine. France.

Cornaux. (31) Neuchâtel area; village with 46 acres of vineyards. Mostly fair white table wine. Switzerland.

Cornets, Les. (15) Pouilly-sur-Loire vineyard. Fair to fine white table wine. France.

Cornudella. (29) Tarragona area; Piorato vineyards. Ordinary to fair red table wine. Spain.

Cornuelles, Les. (16) Touraine; vineyard of Cravant-les-Coteaux, south-east of Chinon. Ordinary to fair red and white table wines. France.

Coronata. (26) Liguria; Genoa area. Ordinary to fair dry white table wine with a slight lemon taste. Italy.

Corrales. (29) Central León; Zamora area. Ordinary dark red table wine and some fair *clarete* table wine. Spain.

Corrona. (27) Tuscany; Lake Trasimeno, west of Perugia. Ordinary to fair white table wine. Italy.

Cortaillod. (31) Neuchâtel district; town. About 77% fair to fine, white table wines, and 23% ordinary to fair, red and white table wines. Switzerland.

Corte, Quinta. (30) *Região demarcada do Douro*

(q.v.). Estate and vineyard in Valenca do Douro east of Régua. Portugal.

Cortese. The name of a white grape and of a white wine made from it in various parts of Italy.

Cortese d'Asti. (26) Piedmont; Asti province. Fair white table wine. Italy.

Cortese dell'Alto Monferrato. (26) Piedmont; upper Monferrato vineyards, Alessándria province. Fair to fine dry white table wine. Italy.

Cortese di Liguria. (26) Genoa coastal area. Most popular white table wine, strong and rather coarse. Italy.

Corton, Le. (8) Côte de Beaune; Aloxe-Corton and Pernand-Vergelesses vineyards. *Grand cru.* Fine red burgundy. France.

Cortona. (27) Tuscany; Arezzo province, south-east of Florence. Fair dry white table wine. Italy.

Corton-Charlemagne. (8) Côte de Beaune; Aloxe-Corton and Pernand-Vergelesses vineyards. *Grand cru.* Fine white burgundy. France.

Corval, Quinta. (30) *Região demarcada do Douro* (q.v.). Estate in Pinhao east of Régua. Portugal.

Corvées, Clos des. (8) Côte de Nuits; Prémeaux vineyard. *Premier cru.* Red burgundy. France.

Corvées-Paget, Les. (8) Côte de Nuits; Prémeaux vineyard. *Premier cru.* Red burgundy. France.

Corvo di Casteldaccia (Bianco, Rosso). (28) Sicily; Casteldaccia vineyards, Palermo province. Ordinary white and good to fine red wines. The red is one of the best of the island. Italy.

Corvo di Colomba Platina. (28) Sicily; Palermo province. Fair to fine white table wine. Italy.

Corvos, Quinta. (30) *Região demarcada do Douro* (q.v.). Estate in Sabrosa. Portugal.

Cos d'Estournel, Château. (4) Haut-Médoc; St-Estèphe. *Deuxième cru classé.* 20,000 dozen bottles of red bordeaux. France.

Cos Labory, Château. (4) Haut-Médoc; St-Estèphe. *Cinquième cru classé.* 4,000 dozen bottles of red bordeaux. France.

Cosson, Clos de. (16) Touraine; Vouvray vineyard, east of Tours. Fair to fine white table wines. France.

Cosson, Les. (16) Touraine; Vernou-sur-Brenne vineyard, north-east of Tours. Fair white table wine. France.

Costa da Cima, Quinta. (30) *Região demarcada do Douro* (q.v.). Estate and vineyard in Gouvinhas in the Régua area. Portugal.

Costières du Gard. (13) Gard *département.* *V.D.Q.S.* Red, white and rosé table wines. France.

Costoza. (26) Veneto; Colli Berici, just south of Vicenza. Ordinary to fair red and white table wines. Italy.

Cosuenda. (29) Cariñena; in the west-central part of the province of Zaragoza. Ordinary to fair, dry and semi-sweet, red table wines. Spain.

Côte, La. (31) Between Geneva and Lausanne. Range of vine-clad hills running down to the Lake. Ordinary to fair white wine. Switzerland.

Coteau, Clos du. (16) Anjou; Coteaux de la Loire, La Possonnière vineyard, south-west of Angers. Fair white table wine. France.

Coteau, Cru Le. (4) Haut-Médoc; Arsac. *Cru bourgeois.* 500 dozen bottles of red bordeaux. France.

Coteau des Nouelles. (16) Anjou; Coteaux de l'Aubance, between Angers and Saumur. Fair to fine white table wine. France.

Coteaux, Les. (16) Anjou; Coteaux de la Loire, Ingrandes vineyard, south-west of Angers. Fair to fine white table wine. France.

Coteaux d'Aix. (13) Bouches-du-Rhône *département*; Aix-en-Provence area, north-east of Marseilles. Fair red, white and rosé table wines. France.

Coteaux d'Ancenis. (16) Loire Atlantique *département*; the vine-clad slopes on the right bank of the river Loire above Nantes. Ordinary to fair white table wine. France.

Coteaux de Beaupoits. (16) Touraine; the vineyards on high ground near Bourgueil. Fair to fine red table wine. France.

Coteaux de la Loire. (16) The vine-clad hills of the lower Loire valley, mostly in Anjou. Ordinary, fair and fine white table wines. Also some very fine white table wines. France.

Coteaux de la Trevaresse. (13) Bouches-du-Rhône *département*; Aix-en-Provence area, north-east of Marseilles. Ordinary to fair red, white and rosé table wines. France.

Coteaux de l'Aubance. (16) The vine-clad hills of the Aubance, a small tributary of the Loire. Fair to fine white and rosé table wines. France.

Coteaux de Mejanelle. (13) Roussillon; Hérault. Ordinary to fair red and white table wines. France.

Coteaux de Saint Christol. (13) Montpellier area. Fair red and rosé table wines. *V.D.Q.S.* France.

Coteaux de Sainte Victoire. (13) Bouches-du-Rhône *département;* Aix-en-Provence area, north-east of Marseilles. Ordinary to fair red, white and rosé table wines. France.

Coteaux de Saint Louans. (16) Touraine; high vine-clad ground near Chinon. Ordinary to fair red table wine. France.

Coteaux de Sonnay. (16) Touraine; vine-clad hillsides in the centre of which is the village of Cravant-les-Coteau, south-east of Chinon. Ordinary to fair red table wine. France.

Coteaux de Verargues. (13) Montpellier. Vine-clad high ground. Fair red and rosé table wines. *V.D.Q.S.* France.

Coteaux du Layon. (16) The vine-clad hills of the Layon river, a tributary of the Loire. This area produces mostly fine, and very fine white table wines. France.

Côte Blonde, La. (12) Côte Rôtie; one side of the hill above Ampuis, the vineyards of which produce some very fine red table wine. France.

Côte Brune. (12) Côte Rôtie; part of the hillside above Ampuis which produces very fine red table wine. France.

Côte Chalonnaise. (9) The range of low hills between the Côte d'Or and the Côte Mâconnais in the Saône-et-Loire *département*. Towns with *AC*—Givry, Mercurey, Buxy, Montagny, etc. France.

Côte d'Agly. (13) Roussillon. The vine-clad hillsides between Rivesaltes and Maury to the west. Fair dessert wines from Muscat, Grenache and Malvoisie grapes. France.

Côte de Beaune. (8) The southern half of the vine-clad slopes of the Côte d'Or; Pernand-Vergelesses to Cheilly-les-Maranges in the south. It is responsible for many of the greater burgundies, the white being equally as famous as the red. France.

Côte de Beaune Villages. The *Appellation Contrôlée* of red burgundy wines of good quality from some of the Côte de Beaune vineyards. France.

Côte de Bourgueil. (16) The high ground on the right bank of the river Loire of which Bourgueil, near Tours, is the centre. Its vineyards produce the best red table wines of Touraine. France.

Côte de Brouilly. (11) Beaujolais; the higher ground of the Brouilly area. Fair to fine red beaujolais. France.

Côte de Brouilly. (11) Beaujolais; parts of Odenas, St-Léger, Cercie, Quincie vineyards. *Premier cru*. Fair red burgundy. France.

Côte de Chinon. (16) The vine-clad hillsides between Chinon and Beaumont-en-Véron south of Chinon, Touraine. Ordinary to fair red table wine. France.

Côte de Fontenay. (6) Yonne *département*; the best vineyard of Poinchy. Chablis *premier cru*. White burgundy. France.

Côte de Lechct. (6) Yonne *département*; Milly vineyard. Chablis *premier cru*. White burgundy. France.

Côte de Maures. (14) One of the groups of vine-clad hills of the Côtes de Provence, in the Var *département*, along the Mediterranean coast. France.

Côte de Montlouis. (16) The vine-clad hillsides on the left bank of the river Loire, opposite Vouvray, east of Tours, Touraine. Fair white table wine. France.

Côte de Nuits. (8) The northern half of the narrow vine-clad hillside belt running from near Dijon to Corgoloin, facing south-east over the flat Saône valley. Most of the great burgundies are grown here. France.

Côte de Nues. (15) Vineyard of Pouilly-sur-Loire. Fine white table wine of Sauvignon grapes, known locally as *fumé*, hence Pouilly Fumé (q.v.). France.

Côte des Blancs. (17) The group of vine-clad hills on the river Marne, between the area south of Epernay and Chalons-sur-Marne, approx. twenty miles south-east of Epernay. Here Chardonnay grapes are exclusively grown and the white wine made from these white grapes is known as *blanc de blancs* (q.v.). France.

Côte de Troesme. (6) Yonne *département*; Beine. *Premier cru* chablis. White burgundy. France.

Côte de Vouvray. (16) The vine-clad high ground to the east of Tours, on the right bank of the river Loire. The home of the best white Loire wines, made only from Chenin Blanc grapes. France.

Côte d'Or. (7) *Département*. It takes its name from the celebrated 'golden' clad hillside on which most of the great burgundies are grown. See Côte de Beaune and Côte de Nuits. France.

Côte Rôtie. (12) The vine-clad hill above Ampuis, Côtes du Rhône. Red burgundy. France.

Côte Rôtie. (8) Côte de Nuits; smallest vineyard of Morey-St-Denis. Fine red burgundy. France.

Côtes-Canon-Fronsac. (3) The vine-clad higher ground of the Fronsadais region. Ordinary to fair red bordeaux. France.

Côtes d'Auvergne. (15) Puy-de-Dôme *département*; south of St-Pourçain. Ordinary to fair red, white and rosé table wines. *V.D.Q.S.* France.

Côtes de Gien. (15) Gien is on the Loire, approx. forty miles east of Orléans, and due south of Paris. Rosé table wines and also ordinary to fair red and white. France.

Côtes de Provence. (14) Bouches-du-Rhône, Var and Alpes Maritimes *département*. Ordinary to fair red and rosé table wines, also white. *V.D.Q.S.* France.

Côtes de Rol-Valentin. (5) Côtes de St-Emilion. An unclassified *cru*. 1,500 dozen bottles of red bordeaux. France.

Côtes du Haut-Roussillon. (13) Hillside vineyards between Perpignan, south of Rivesaltes, and the Franco-Spanish frontier. Ordinary red, white and rosé table wines; also some fair *V.D.Q.S.* Muscat dessert wine. France.

Côtes du Jura. (18) Jura; Arbois. Fair red, white and rosé table wines, also *vin jaune* (q.v.) and *vin de paille* (q.v.) sparkling wine. France.

Côtes du Luberon. (12) Vaucluse *département*. The hillside vineyards of about thirty villages in the Durance valley. Ordinary to fair red, white and rosé table wines. *V.D.Q.S.* France.

Côtes du Rhône. (12) The vinelands on both sides of the river Rhône from Vienne below Lyons to Avignon, some 120 miles south. Fair and some fine red and rosé wines and ordinary, but quite popular, fair and fine white wines. France.

Côtes du Ventoux. (12) Côtes du Rhône. Some sixty villages of the Mont Ventoux area, south-west of Ouvèze, producing ordinary to fair red, white and rosé table wines. France.

Côtes Neuves, Les. (6) Chablis; Fleys vineyard. *Premier cru* chablis. White burgundy. France.

Cotière, La. (16) Touraine; Bourgueil vineyard. Fair to fine red table wine. France.

Cotnari. (33) Moldavia; village in north-east Rumania. Fair to fine white dessert wine. Rumania.

Coucherais, Aux. (8) Beaune vineyard. *Premier cru*. Red burgundy. France.

Couchey. (7) Côte d'Or vineyard, Dijon area. Ordinary red burgundy made from Gamay and Pinot grapes. France.

Coucy, Château. (5) St-Emilion; Montagne. An unclassified *cru*. 4,000 dozen bottles of red bordeaux. France.

Coudert, Château. (5) St-Emilion; St Christophe-des-Bardes, south-west of Parsac. An unclassified *cru*. 1,000 dozen bottles of red bordeaux. France.

Coudert-Pelletan, Château. (5) St-Emilion; St Christophe-des-Bardes, south-west of Parsac. An unclassified *cru*. 4,000 dozen bottles of red bordeaux. France.

Coufran, Château. (4) Haut-Médoc; St Seurin-de-Cadourne. *Cru bourgeois supérieur*. 15,000 dozen bottles of red bordeaux. France.

Couhins, Château. (5) Graves de Bordeaux; Villenave-d'Ornon. *Cru classé de Graves (en blanc)*. 1,500 dozen bottles of red bordeaux; 3,000 white. France.

Coulaines. (16) Anjou; Coteaux de la Loire, Savennières vineyard, below Angers. Fair to fine white table wines. France.

Coulange-la-Vineuse. (6) Auxerre region. Ordinary to fair red table wine from Pinot and Gamay grapes. France.

Coulée de Sarrant. (16) Anjou; Coteaux de la Loire, Savennières vineyard, below Angers. Very fine white table wine. France.

Coulées, Les. (15) Anjou; Coteaux de la Loire, Chalonne-sur-Loire vineyard, south-west of Angers. Fair white table wine. France.

Coulommes-la-Montagne. (17) Marne *département*; Ville-en-Tardenois canton, south-west of Rheims. Rated—89% growth. 139 acres. France.

Cour-Cheverny. (16) Blois; village in the Loire valley. Fair white table wine. France.

Courgis. (6) Village in the Chablis district. Fair white burgundy. France.

Courlat, Domaine du. (5) St-Emilion; Lussac. An unclassified *cru*. 3,500 dozen bottles of red bordeaux. France.

Couronne, Château La. (3) Haut-Médoc; Pauillac. *Cru exceptionnel*. 1,500 dozen bottles of red bordeaux. France.

Courreau, Château de. (5) Premières Côtes de Bordeaux; Haux, north of Podensac. 1,000 dozen bottles of red bordeaux; 8,000 white. France.

Courthézon. (12) Vaucluse *département*; Côtes du Rhône. *AC Châteauneuf-du-Pape*. Fair red table wine. France.

Couspaude, Château La. (5) Côtes de St-Emilion. *Grand cru classé*. 3,000 dozen bottles of red bordeaux. France.

Coutelin-Merville, Cru. (4) Haut-Médoc; St-Estèphe. *Cru bourgeois*. 6,000 dozen bottles of red bordeaux. France.

Coutet, Château. (5) Barsac. *Premier cru classé*. 6,000 dozen bottles of white bordeaux. France.

Coutet, Château. (5) Côtes de St-Emilion. *Grand cru classé*. 5,000 dozen bottles of red bordeaux. France.

Coutures, Les. (16) Touraine; Cravant-les-Coteau vineyard, south-east of Chinon. Fair red table wine. France.

Couvent, Château Le. (5) Côtes de St-Emilion. *Grand cru classé*. 500 dozen bottles of red bordeaux. France.

Couvent des Jacobins. (5) Côtes de St-Emilion. An unclassified *cru*. 1,000 dozen bottles of red bordeaux. France.

Covelo, Quinta. (30) *Região demarcada do Douro*. Estate in Cumieira in the Régua area. Portugal.

Covelo, Quinta. (30) *Região demarcada do Douro*. Estate in Poiares north-east of Régua. Portugal.

Crabitey, Château. (5) Graves de Bordeaux; Portets. An unclassified *cru*. 2,000 dozen bottles of red bordeaux; 1,000 white. France.

Craiova. (33) City in south Rumania; Oltenia vineyards. Fair to fine red table wine made from Pinot Noir grapes. Rumania.

Cramant. (17) Marne *département*; Côte des Blancs, Avize canton. Rated *grand cru*—100% growth. 765 acres. France.

Cras, Aux. (8) Côte de Nuits; Nuits-St-Georges vineyard. *Premier cru.* Red burgundy. France.

Cras, Les. (8) Côte de Nuits; Chambolle-Musigny vineyard. *Premier cru.* Red burgundy. France.

Cras, Les. (8) Côte de Beaune; Pommard vineyard. *Deuxième cru.* Red burgundy. France.

Crais, Les. (8) Côte de Beaune; Aloxe-Corton vineyard. *Troisième cru.* Red burgundy. France.

Cras, Les. (8) Beaune vineyard. *Premier cru.* Red burgundy. France.

Cras-Poussuets, Les. (8) Côte de Beaune; Aloxe-Corton. *Troisième cru.* Red burgundy. France.

Cravant. (6) Yonne *département*; Auxerre area. Red burgundy. France.

Creata. (33) A variety of Riesling grown in Rumania; also the name of the white wine made from it. Rumania.

Crebillon. (8) Côte d'Or; Brochon vineyard, Gevrey-Chambertin. *Deuxième cru.* Ordinary to fair red burgundy. The better one is entitled to the Gevrey-Chambertin name. France.

Creixell. (29) Lower Panadés vineyards; Tarragona area. Ordinary to fair red table wine. Spain.

Créole. (8) Côte de Nuits; Brochon vineyard, Gevrey-Chambertin. *Troisième cru.* Fair red burgundy. *See* **Crebillon.** France.

Créot, Le. (8) Côte de Nuits; Brochon vineyard, Gevrey-Chambertin. *Troisième cru.* Ordinary to fair red burgundy. *See* **Crebillon.** France.

Cressier. (31) Neuchâtel area; village with 150 acres of vineyards. Ordinary, fair and some fine white table wines. Switzerland.

Cresta Blanca. (36) California; winery and vineyard in the Livermore area, owned by Schenley Distilling Co. Quality table wines; also dessert and sparkling wines. U.S.A.

Cret, Le. (9) Chalonnais; Mercurey vineyard. *Premier cru.* Red burgundy. France.

Cretas. (29) South-central Aragon; Teruel. Ordinary to fair red and white table wines. Spain.

Crets, Les. (8) Côte de Beaune; Chassagne-Montrachet vineyard. *Deuxième cru.* Red burgundy. France.

Creux-Baissants. (8) Côte de Nuits; Chambolle-Musigny vineyard. *Troisième cru.* Red burgundy. France.

Creux-de-la-Net. (8) Côte de Beaune; Pernand-Vergelesses vineyard. *Premier cru.* Red burgundy. France.

Crezancy. (15) Cher *département*; Sancerre. Ordinary to fair red and white table wines. France.

Crimea. (34) Peninsula of south European Russia and one of the oldest and still important wine producing areas of Russia. Chiefly noted for its sweet white and red dessert wines; also table and sparkling wines. U.S.S.R.

Criots, Les. (8) Côte de Beaune; Meursault vineyard. *Deuxième cru.* Red burgundy. France.

Cripa. (29) Alava; La Rioja area of the upper Ebro valley. Fair red table wine. Spain.

Cristal, Clos. (16) Anjou; vineyard of Château de Parnay, Saumur area. Fair to fine white table wine. France.

Croatia. (33) One of the six Federal republics of Yugoslavia, in the north-west of the country. The grape grows almost everywhere, namely in Dalmatia, on the central Adriatic coast and in inland areas named Slavonia. The most famous are Grasevina (Riesling), Traminer, Sylvaner and Mali Plavac. Yugoslavia.

Croattina. (26) Lombardy; Oltrepo Pavese, south of Pavia across the Po. Name of a black grape and the ordinary red table wine made from it. Italy.

Croix, Aux. (8) Côte de Nuits; Chambolle-Musigny vineyard. *Deuxième cru.* Red burgundy. France.

Croix, Château La. (3) Fronsadais; Fronsac. 6,000 dozen bottles of red bordeaux. France.

Croix, Château La. (3) Néac; east of Pomerol. 3,000 dozen bottles of red bordeaux. France.

Croix, Château La. (5) Pomerol. *Grand cru.* 5,000 dozen bottles of red bordeaux are produced. France.

Croix, Château La. (3) Premières Côtes de Bordeaux. 1,000 dozen bottles of red bordeaux; 1,000 white. France.

Croix, Clos de la. (16) Coteaux de Saumur; vineyard of the Souzay-Champigny *commune* on the Saumur hillsides. Fair white table wine. France.

Croix-Blanche, La. (8) Côte de Nuits; Vosne-Romanée. *Troisième cru.* Red burgundy. France.

Croix-Chantecaille, Château La. (5) St-Emilion. An unclassified *cru.* 2,500 dozen bottles of red bordeaux. France.

Croix-de-Gay, Château La. (5) Pomerol. 2,000 dozen bottles of red bordeaux. France.

Croix-de-Justice, Château. (5) St-Emilion; Puisseguin. An unclassified *cru.* 2,500 dozen bottles of red bordeaux. France.

Croix-de-Merlet, Domaine de la. (4) Blayais. 6,000 dozen bottles of red bordeaux; 500 white. France.

Croix-de-Mission, Domaine. (5) St-Emilion; Montagne. An unclassified *cru.* 4,000 dozen bottles of red bordeaux. France.

Croix-Gandineau, Château La. (3) Fronsac; Fronsadais. 2,500 dozen bottles of red bordeaux. France.

Croix-Miliorit, Château de la. (3) Bourgeais. 10,000 dozen bottles of red bordeaux; 1,000 white. France.

Croix-Saint-Georges. (5) Pomerol. 2,000 dozen bottles of red bordeaux. France.

Croix-Violette, La. (8) Côte de Nuits; Brochon, Gevrey-Chambertin. *Troisième cru.* Red burgundy. *See* **Crebillon.** France.

Croizet-Bages, Château. (4) Haut-Médoc; Pauillac. *Cinquième cru classé.* 6,000 dozen bottles of red bordeaux. France.

Cromin, Le. (8) Meursault. *Deuxième cru.* White burgundy. France.

Croque-Michotte, Château. (5) St-Emilion. *Grand cru classé.* 6,000 dozen bottles of red bordeaux. France.

Cröv. *See* **Kröv.**

Cruots, Les. (8) Côte de Nuits; Flagey-Echézeaux vineyard. *Premier cru.* Fine red burgundy. France.

Croute-Camponac, Château. (3) Bourgeais. 4,000 dozen bottles of ordinary red bordeaux. France.

Croute-Charlus, Château. (3) Bourgeais. 4,000 dozen bottles of red bordeaux. France.

Crozes-Hermitage. (12) Côtes du Rhône. Left bank of the Rhône, near Tain-l'Hermitage. The better quality red table wines of Crozes and of the ten nearby villages are entitled to be marketed as Crozes-Hermitage. France.

Cruscaut, Château. (4) Haut-Médoc; St-Laurent. *Cru bourgeois.* 800 dozen bottles of red bordeaux. France.

Crusquet de Lagarcie, Château. (4) Blayais; Cars, east of Blaye. 6,500 dozen bottles of red bordeaux; 1,000 white. France.

Cruzeau, Château. (5) Sables de St-Emilion. 3,500 dozen bottles of red bordeaux. France.

Cruzelles, Château des. (3) Néac; *commune* east of Pomerol. 3,500 dozen bottles of red bordeaux. France.

Csopaki Furmint. (33) Lake Balaton area; approx. fifty miles south-west of Budapest. Fair to fine white table wine. Hungary.

Cuarte. (29) Valencia area. Light, semi-sweet red table wine. Spain.

Cubnik. (34) Ankara region. Ordinary to fair red and white table wines. Turkey.

Cues. *See* **Kues.**

Cuevas de San Marco. (29) Málaga area. Ordinary to fair red table wine and dessert wine. Spain.

Cuis. (17) Marne *département*; Avize canton, between Cramaut and Pierry. Rated *premier cru—* black 90% growth; white 93%. 340 acres. France.

Cul de Beaujeu. (15) Sancerre; Chavignol vineyard. Fair to fine white table wine. France.

Cully. (31) Vaud canton; Lavaux. Fine white table wine. Switzerland.

Cumières. (17) Marne *département*; Ay canton. Rated *premier cru—*90% growth. 342 acres. France.

Cure, Château La. (4) Blayais. 2,300 dozen bottles of red bordeaux; 1,000 white. France.

Curé-bon-la-Madelaine, Château. (5) Côtes de St-Emilion. *Grand cru classé.* 2,500 dozen bottles of red bordeaux. France.

Cure d'Attalens. (31) Vaud canton; Vevey. Fair to fine white table wine. Switzerland.

Curiel. (29) Valladolid; approx. seventy miles north of Avila. Ordinary to fair red wine. Spain.

Currais, Quinta. (30) *Região demarcada do Douro* (q.v.). Estate of eighty acres in Poiares north-east of Régua. Portugal.

Cuzcurrita. (29) Old Castile; Logroño province, La Rioja area of the upper Ebro valley. Fair to fine red table wine. Spain.

Cyprus. (34) The most important of the Mediterranean wine-producing islands, located approx. 100 miles off the west coast of Syria. Mostly red and white table wines for home consumption as well as important quantities of a sherry-type wine for export.

Cyrot. (8) Savigny-les-Beaune. One of the minor Hospices de Beaune *cuvées*, with *AC Savigny*, Fouquerand, Forneret, Arthur Girard. No longer extant. Fair red burgundy. France.

Czechoslovakia. (33) There are more than 35,000 acres of vineyards with an approx. production of 18,000,000 dozen bottles of table and dessert wines of ordinary, fair and some fine quality.

Czopak. (33) Lake Balaton; town and vineyards facing the north shore, approx. fifty miles south-west of Budapest. Ordinary to fair red and white table wines. Hungary.

❦

Dabhaus. (24) Rhinehessia; Oppenheim vineyard. Fair white table wine. West Germany.

Dachsberg. (24) Rhinehessia; Hahnheim vineyard, south-west of Bodenheim. Ordinary to fair white table wine. West Germany.

Dachsberg. (24) Rhinegau; Winkel vineyard. Fine white table wine. West Germany.

Dackenheim. (23) Lower Haardt; Palatinate, between Grünstadt and Neustadt. Ordinary red, and fair and fine white table wine. West Germany.

D'Agostini Winery. (36) California; Plymouth, Amador County; Sierra foothills, the 'Mother Lode' country. Quality table wines. U.S.A.

Dahnfeld. (25) Württemberg; north-east of Heilbronn. Ordinary to fair red and white table wine. West Germany.

Dalberg. (24) Nahe; north-west of Bad Kreuznach. Fair white table wine. West Germany.

Dalem, Cru. (3) Fronsadais; Saillans, north of Fronsac. 4,500 dozen bottles of red bordeaux. France.

Dalheim. (24) Rhinehessia; south-west of Oppenheim. Ordinary to fair red and white table wines. West Germany.

Dalsheim. (24) Rhinehessia; north-west of Worms. Ordinary red and fair white table wines. West Germany.

Dalwood. (37) New South Wales; Hunter River area, north-east of Sydney. One of the oldest wineries and vineyards. The Penfolds have transferred their operations from Dalwood to the new Dalwood Estate at Wybong, in the Upper Hunter valley. Australia.

Dambach. (19) Bas-Rhin *département*. Quite popular ordinary to fair white Alsace table wine. France.

Dame-Blanche, Château La. (4) Haut-Médoc; Le Taillan. 5,000 dozen bottles of white bordeaux. France.

Dames de la Charité. (8) Côte de Beaune; Pommard vineyard. One of the Hospices de Beaune *cuvées*. *AC Beaune.* Fair red burgundy. France.

Dames Hospitalières. (8) One of the Hospices de Beaune *cuvées*. *AC Beaune.* Fair red burgundy. France.

Damiel. (29) New Castile; Ciudad Real, north of Valdepeñas. Ordinary to fair red table wine. South-central Spain.

Dammemoine. (6) Yonne *département*; Tonnerre area. Ordinary to fair red and white table wines. France.

Dammheim. (23) Palatinate; just north of Landau. Ordinary red and fair white table wines. West Germany.

Damodes, Aux. (8) Côte de Nuits; Nuits-St-Georges vineyard. *Deuxième cru.* Red burgundy. France.

Damos. (29) Tarragona. Ordinary to fair dark red, sweet, dessert wine. Spain.

Dampierre-sur-Loire. (16) Anjou; Saumur area. Mostly fair red, white and rosé table wines. France.

Damscheid. (21) Middle Rhine; approx. twenty miles south-east of Koblenz. Ordinary to fair white table wine. West Germany.

Danguerins, Les. (8) Côte de Nuits; Chambolle-Musigny vineyard. *Troisième cru.* Red burgundy. France.

Dankental. (23) Rhinehessia; Wachenheim vineyard. Fair white table wine. West Germany.

Danzay, Château de. (16) Touraine; Beaumont-en-Véron, Chinon. Ordinary to fair red table wine. France.

Dão. (30) A demarcated wine-producing district in the centre of Portugal around Viseu. The area produces well-balanced red and white table wines of consistently high quality. Portugal.

D'Arche, Château. (4) Haut-Médoc; Ludon. *Cru bourgeois.* 2,000 dozen bottles of red bordeaux. France.

D'Arche, Château. (5) Sauternes. *Deuxième cru classé.* 2,500 dozen white bordeaux. France.

D'Arche-Lafaurie, Château. (5) Sauternes. *Deuxième cru classé.* 3,500 dozen bottles of white bordeaux. France.

D'Arche-Prugneau. (5) Sauternes; Preignac. *Cru bourgeois.* 2,500 dozen bottles of white bordeaux. France.

D'Arche-Vimeney, Château. (5) Sauternes. *Cru bourgeois.* 1,200 dozen bottles of white bordeaux. France.

D'Arenberg. (37) South Australia; McLaren Vale, approx. twenty-five miles south of Adelaide. Vineyards and winery which produce full-flavoured wines of the claret and burgundy type; also a white burgundy-type wine made from Palomino grapes. Australia.

Daroca. (29) Aragon; Zaragoza. Ordinary red table wine. Spain.

Dartus, Château. (5) St-Emilion; Vignonet, south-west of St Pey-d'Armens. An unclassified *cru.* 3,000 dozen bottles of red bordeaux. France.

Dattenberg. (21) Middle Rhine; outside and to the south of Linz. Ordinary to fair red and white table wines. West Germany.

Daubhaus. (24) Rhinegau; site name of Winkel and Hochheim vineyards. West Germany.

Daubhaus. (24) Rhinehessia; Oppenheim vineyard. Fair to fine white table wine. West Germany.

Dauphine, Château La. (3) Fronsadais. 8,000 dozen bottles of red bordeaux. France.

Dautenheim. (24) Rhinehessia; south-east of Bad Kreuznach. Ordinary red and fair white table wines. West Germany.

Dautenpflänzer. (24) Nahe; Bad Münster vineyard. Fair white table wine. West Germany.

Dauvellerie. (16) Touraine; Champigny-le-Sec vineyard, south of Chinon. Ordinary to fair red table wine. France.

Dauzac, Château. (4) Médoc; Labarde. *Cinquième cru classé.* 10,000 dozen bottles of red bordeaux. France.

Davaye. (10) Mâconnais village; north of Pouilly. Ordinary to fair red and white table wines. France.

Dealul-Bujor-Prut. (33) Ordinary to fair red table wine. Rumania.

Dealul-Mare. (33) Ordinary to fair white table wine; also some fair to fine Muscat dessert wine. Rumania.

Debroi Harslevelu. (33) Eger area; approx. sixty-five miles north-east of Budapest. Fair to fine white table wine of Harslevelu white grapes. Hungary.

Decker. (24) Rhinegau; site name of Rüdesheim and Geisenheim vineyards. Fair to fine white table wine. West Germany.

Deez. (24) Rhinegau; site name of Oestrich and Hallgarten vineyards. Fine white table wine. West Germany.

D'Egmont, Château. (4) Haut-Médoc; Ludon. *Cru bourgeois.* 500 dozen bottles of red bordeaux. France.

De Haux, Château. (5) Premières Côtes de Bordeaux; Haux, north of Podensac. 1,000 dozen bottles of red bordeaux; 4,000 white. France.

De Hilde, Château. (5) Graves de Bordeaux; Bègles. An unclassified *cru.* 7,000 dozen bottles of red bordeaux. France.

Deidesheim. (23) Middle Haardt; Palatinate. Fine to very fine white table wine. 'Paradiesgarten' is the generic name for all Deidesheim wines. West Germany.

Deitelsberg. (24) Rhinegau; Hattenheim vineyard, between Erbach and Mittelheim. Fine white wine. West Germany.

Delaware. (35) Small state east of Maryland. Ordinary still and sparkling white wines from the white Eastern American Delaware grape. U.S.A.

Delichen. (24) Nahe; Norheim vineyard, between Bad Münster and Bad Kreuznach. Fair to fine white table wine. West Germany.

Dellhofen. (21) Middle Rhine; north-west of Bingen. Fair white table wine. West Germany.

Demestica. (34) Peloponnisian peninsula of southern Greece. Fair, dry red and white wine. Greece.

Denée. (16) Anjou; Coteaux de l'Aubance between Angers and Saumur. Fair white wine. France.

Dernau. (21) Ahr valley; west of Linz. Ordinary to fair red table wine. West Germany.

Derrière-la-Grange. (8) Côte de Nuits; Chambolle-Musigny vineyard. *Premier cru.* Red burgundy. France.

Derrière-le-Four. (8) Côte de Nuits; Chambolle-Musigny vineyard. *Deuxième cru.* Red burgundy. France.

Derrière-Saint-Jean. (8) Côte de Beaune; Pommard vineyard. *Premier cru.* Red burgundy. France.

De Selle, Château. (14) Provence; Taradeau. Fair red, white and rosé table wines. France.

Desert, Château Le. (5) Graves de Bordeaux; Léognan. An unclassified *cru.* 3,000 dozen bottles of red bordeaux; 1,000 white. France.

Desloch. (24) Nahe; south-west of Bad Kreuznach. Fair white table wine. West Germany.

Desmirail, Château. (4) Haut-Médoc; Margaux. *Troisième cru classé.* 3,000 dozen bottles of red bordeaux. France.

Des Moines, Château. (4) St-Emilion; Montagne. An unclassified *cru.* 5,000 dozen bottles of red bordeaux. France.

Despagne, Cru. (5) Graves de Bordeaux; St Pierre-de-Mons. 2,000 dozen bottles of red bordeaux. France.

Dessus-du-Chateau. (16) Touraine; Chinon vineyard. Fair red table wine. France.

Destieu, Château. (5) St-Emilion; Vignonet, south-west of St Pey-d'Armens. An unclassified *cru.* 2,000 dozen bottles of red bordeaux. France.

Dettelbach. (25) Franconia; east of Würzburg. Fair white table wine. West Germany.

Dettingen. (25) Württemberg; approx. nineteen miles south-east of Stuttgart. Ordinary to fair white table wine. West Germany.

Detzem. (22) Moselle valley. Fair to fine white table wine. West Germany.

Deubach. (25) Württemberg; approx seventeen miles south-west of Würzburg. Ordinary to fair white table wine. West Germany.

Deutelsberg. (24) Rhinegau; Hallgarten vineyard. Fine white table wine. West Germany.

Devant, Clos. (8) Côte de Beaune; Chassagne-Montrachet vineyard. *Deuxième cru.* Red burgundy. France.

Devant-le-Jeu. (16) Anjou; Coteaux de la Loire, La Possonnière vineyard, below Angers. Fair white table wine. France.

Deves, Quinta. (30) *Região demarcada do Douro* (q.v.). Estate and vineyard of 120 acres in Poiares north-east of Régua. Portugal.

Devins, Domaine des. (31) Neuchâtel area; Cressier vineyard. Fair to fine white table wine. Switzerland.

Dexheim. (24) Rhinehessia; south-west of Oppenheim. Ordinary red and fair to fine white table wines. West Germany.

Dézaley. (31) Vaud canton. Fair, fine and some very fine white table wines. Switzerland.

Dezize-les-Maranges. (8) Côte de Beaune *commune. AC Côte de Beaune villages.* Red burgundy. France.

Dhron. (22) Moselle valley; between Neumagen and Wintrich. Fair, fine and very fine white table wines. West Germany.

Dickerstein. (24) Rhinegau; Rüdesheim vineyard. Fine white table wine. West Germany.

Didiers, Les. (8) Côte de Nuits; Prémeaux vineyard. *Premier cru. AC Nuits-St Georges.* Red burgundy. France.

Diebach. (25) Franconia; approx. twenty miles east of Mosbach. Fair white table wine. West Germany.

Dieblich. (22) Moselle valley; between Kobern and Winningen. Ordinary to fair white table wine. West Germany.

Diedel. (23) Palatinate; Ruppertsberg vineyard. Fine white table wine. West Germany.

Diedesfeld. (23) Palatinate; between Kirrweiler and Neustadt. Ordinary red and fine white table wines. West Germany.

Diedesheim. (25) Neckar. Ordinary to fair red and white table wines. West Germany.

Diefenbach. (25) Württemberg; approx. twenty miles north-west of Stuttgart. Ordinary to fair red and white table wines. West Germany.

Dieffert. (32) Moselle valley; Stradtbredimus vineyard. Ordinary to fair white table wine. Luxembourg.

Dielkirchen. (24) Nahe; south of Bad Münster. Ordinary to fair white table wine. West Germany.

Diemart. (23) Palatinate; Ungstein vineyard. Fair white table wine. West Germany.

Dienheim. (24) Rhinehessia. Ordinary red and fair white table wines. West Germany.

Dierbach. (23) Palatinate; south of Landau. Ordinary red and fair white table wines. West Germany.

Diersburg. (25) Baden; south-west of Strasbourg. Ordinary to fair red and white table wines. West Germany.

Dieterkapp. (24) Rhinehessia; Nackenheim vineyard. Fair, but popular, white table wine. West Germany.

Dictershcim. (24) Rhinehessia; just south of Bingen. Ordinary red and fair white table wines. West Germany.

Dietlingen. (25) Baden; south-east of Karlsruhe. Ordinary to fair red and white table wines. West Germany.

Dijon. (7) Côte d'Or *département;* in medieval times, the capital of the Dukes of Burgundy and now the principal city of Burgundy. It is less important to the wine trade than Beaune or Nuits-St Georges. Its nearest vineyards are those of Dijon-Larrey, not however the best ones of the Côte d'Or. France.

Dikmen. (34) Very popular fair red table wine. Turkey.

Dillmetz. (24) Rhinegau; Hattenheim vineyard, between Erbach and Mittelheim. Fine white table wine. West Germany.

Dillon, Château. (4) Haut-Médoc; Blanquefort.

Cru bourgeois. 7,000 dozen bottles of red bordeaux. Château Dillon itself is used as the Bordeaux School of Viticulture. France.

Dimiat. (33) The name of a golden-green grape and also of the fair to fine white table wine made from this grape, chiefly from the vineyards of Tronvo, on the hills facing the Black Sea. Bulgaria.

Dingac. (33) Central Adriatic coast; Peljesac peninsula, Dalmatia. Dark red, strong, full, *sec* to *demi sec* wine. The grape used is a Mali Plavac. Yugoslavia.

Dintesheim. (24) Rhinehessia; south-west of Alsheim. Ordinary to fair white table wine. West Germany.

Diognières, Les. (12) Côtes du Rhône; Tain l'Hermitage vineyard. Fair red table wine. France.

Dirmstein. (23) Palatinate; between Mannheim and Grünstadt. Ordinary red and fair to fine white table wines. West Germany.

D'Issan, Château. (4) Haut-Médoc; Cantenac. *Deuxième cru classé.* 8,000 dozen bottles of red bordeaux. France.

Dittelsheim. (24) Rhinehessia; south-west of Oppenheim. Ordinary red and fair to fine white table wines. West Germany.

Dittwar. (25) Franconia; approx. eighteen miles south-west of Würzburg. Fair white table wine. West Germany.

Division, La. (16) Anjou; Coteaux de l'Aubance, between Angers and Saumur, Brissac vineyard. Fair to fine rosé de Cabernet table wine. France.

Dizay. (16) Anjou; Coteaux de Saumur. Fair to fine white table wine. France.

Dizy. (17) Marne *département;* Ay canton. Rated *premier cru*—95% growth. 410 acres. France.

Dohr. (22) Saar valley; Wiltingen vineyard. Fine white table wine. West Germany.

Doisy-Daene, Château. (5) Barsac. *Deuxième cru classé.* 2,000 dozen bottles of white bordeaux. France.

Doisy-Vedrines, Château. (5) Barsac. *Deuxième cru classé.* 8,000 dozen bottles of white bordeaux. France.

Doktor. (22) Moselle valley. The most famous of all Bernkastel vineyards, if not of all Moselle vineyards. West Germany.

Doktor. (24) Rhinehessia; Dexheim vineyard, south-west of Oppenheim. Fair white table wine. West Germany.

Doktor und Graben. (22) Graben is the vineyard next to the original Doktor vineyard, Bernkastel. The wine is sold as Doktor und Graben. Fine white table wine. West Germany.

Dolceacqua. (26) Liguria; Ventimiglia or Rossea

di Val di Nervia area, east of Genoa, approx. twenty miles south-west of Imperia. Fair ruby red table wine. Italy.

Dolcetto. (26) Piedmont and Liguria. Free-bearing red grape for the more ordinary types of red table wines which usually bear the grape name. Italy.

Dolcetto d'Alba. (26) Piedmont; Alba province, south-west of Asti. The best dry red table wine made from the Dolcetto grape. Italy.

Dolcetto delle Langhe. (26) Piedmont; Langhe vineyards, between Asti and Savona. Ordinary to fair dry red table wines. Italy.

Dolcetto Ligure. (26) Liguria; hillside vineyards above Bordighera, approx. twenty miles south-west of Imperia. Ordinary to fair red table wine. Italy.

Dôle de Sion. (31) Valais canton; Sion. Fair to fine red table wines made from Pinot Noir known as Dôle in the Valais; poor quality so-called Dôle de Sion is made from Gamay grapes. Switzerland.

Dolgesheim. (24) Rhinehessia; south-west of Dienheim. Ordinary red and fair to fine white table wines. West Germany.

Dom-Avelbach. (22) Moselle; Avelbach vineyard, the property of Trier (Trèves) Cathedral. Fair to fine white table wine. West Germany.

Domdechaney. (24) Rhinegau; Hochheim's best-known vineyard. Fine white table wine. The name is the original ecclesiastical one, the vineyard having been the property of the Deanery of Mainz Cathedral from 1273 to 1830. See also Kirchenstück. West Germany.

Dom-Herrenberg. (22) Moselle valley; Avelbach vineyard, the property of Trier (Trèves) Cathedral. Fine white table wine. West Germany.

Dominikanberg. (22) Ruwer valley; Kasel vineyard. Fine white table wine. West Germany.

Dominique, Château La. (5) Graves de St-Emilion. *Grand cru classé.* 6,000 dozen bottles of red bordeaux. France.

Domprobst. (22) Moselle valley; Graach vineyard. Fine white table wine. West Germany.

Domscharzhofberger. (22) The name under which wine from that part of the Schwarzhof vineyard, Wiltingen, belonging to Trier (Trèves) Cathedral is sold. Very fine white table wine. West Germany.

Domtal. (24) Rhinehessia; Nierstein vineyard. Fine to very fine white table wine. West Germany.

Domtal. (24) Rhinehessia; site of Schwabsburg vineyard west of Oppenheim. Fair white table wine. West Germany.

Donauland. (33) Ordinary to fair red and white table wines from some of the Lower Austria vineyards. Austria.

Dona Mercia. (29) North-central Andalusia; Montilla, Córdoba province. Fair white table wine. Spain.

Donna Camilla. (28) Calabria; Cioia-Tauro area, approx. twenty-five miles north-east of Reggio. Sharp, rough, red table wine; also a rosé. Italy.

Donnaz. (26) Val d'Aosta; highest Alpine vineyards. Ordinary to fair red table wine. Italy.

Doosberg. (24) Rhinegau; Oestrich vineyard, between Mittelheim and Erbach. Fine white table wine. West Germany.

Dopp. (23) Palatinate; Deidesheim vineyard. Fair to fine white table wine. 'Paradiesgarten' is the generic name for all Deidesheim wines. West Germany.

Doppo Secco. (28) Apulia; Squinzano area, north-west of Lecce. Dark red and strong table wines. Italy.

Dorato di Sorso. (28) Sardinia. Reddish-tawny rather sweet wine served as an apéritif or dessert wine. Italy.

Dorgali (Rosso, Rosato). (28) Sardinia; east coast. Ordinary red and rosé table wines. Italy.

Dorn-Dürkheim. (24) Rhinehessia; west of Alsheim. Ordinary red and white table wines. West Germany.

Dörrenbach. (23) Palatinate; between Bergzabern and Rechtenbach. Ordinary red and fair white table wines. West Germany.

Dörscheid. (21) Middle Rhine; approx. nineteen miles south-east of Koblenz. Ordinary to fair red and white table wines. West Germany.

Dorsheim. (24) Nahe valley; south-west of Bingen. Fair to fine white wine. West Germany.

Dörzbach. (25) Württemberg; approx. twenty-five miles east of Mosbach. Ordinary red and white table wines. West Germany.

Dos d'Ane, En. (8) Côte de Beaune; Meursault vineyard. *Premier cru.* White burgundy. France.

Dos d'Ane, Sous le. (8) Côte de beaune; Meursault vineyard. *Premier cru.* White burgundy. France.

Dossenheim. (25) Baden; south-east of Mannheim. Ordinary to fair red and white table wines. West Germany.

Douby. (11) Beaujolais; Morgon vineyard. Red beaujolais. France.

Doumayne, Château. (5) St-Emilion area. 1,500 dozen bottles of red bordeaux. France.

Douro. (29, 30) The famous river which flows from Spain westwards across northern Portugal at Oporto. The river Douro flows through mountainous country flanked by terraces of schistose rock on which the vines thrive.

Drachenfels. (21) Königswinter, south-east of Bonn. The most northerly Rhineland vineyard. Light, ordinary red table wine, locally acceptable and known as *Drachenblut* (Dragon's Blood). West Germany.

Dragasani. (33) South-west Rumania. The best vineyard area of this district, particularly famous for its fair rosé table wine and its fine sweet Muscat dessert wines. Rumania.

Drakenstein. (39) Western Cape Province. One of the important wine-producing areas. South Africa.

Drayton's Bellevue. (37) New South Wales; Hunter River area, north-east of Sydney. Winery and vineyard. Australia.

Drazey, Les. (8) Côte de Beaune; Chambolle-Musigny. *Deuxième cru.* Red burgundy. France.

Dreimorgen. (24) Rhinehessia; Elsheim vineyard, south of Niederwalluf. Ordinary to fair white table wine. West Germany.

Dromersheim. (24) Rhinehessia; south-east of Bingen. Ordinary to fair white table wine. West Germany.

Drumborg. (37) Victoria; south-west corner of state near Portland. Most southerly commercial vineyard in mainland Australia. Planted for supplementary sparkling wine material for Seppelt's Great Western cellars, 100 miles north-west of Geelong. Australia.

Du Bay Peste. (8) Savigny-les-Beaune vineyard. One of the *cuvées* of the Hospices de Beaune. Its wines were made as a single *cuvée* with those from Cyrot from 1937–43. Since then the name has been changed to Arthur Girard. Fair red burgundy. France.

Dube, La. (16) Anjou; Coteaux de l'Aubance, between Angers and Saumur, Mozé-sur-Loire vineyard. Fair white table wine. France.

Dubois, Clos. (16) Touraine; Vouvray vineyard, east of Tours. Fair to fine white table wine. France.

Du Breuil, Château. (16) Anjou; Coteaux de Layon, Beaulieu-du-Layon, east of Tours. Fine white table wine. France.

Duchroth. (24) Palatinate; south-west of Bad Münster. Ordinary to fair white table wine. West Germany.

Ducru-Beaucaillou, Château. (4) Haut-Médoc; St-Julien. *Deuxième cru classé.* 20,000 dozen bottles of red bordeaux. France.

Ducs, Clos des. (8) Côte de Beaune; Volnay vineyard. *Premier cru.* Red burgundy. Monopole d'Angerville. France.

Dudenhofen. (23) Palatinate; east of Landau. Ordinary to fair white table wine is produced. West Germany.

Dudon, Château. (5) Barsac. *Cru bourgeois.* 2,500 dozen bottles of white bordeaux. France.

Duenas. (29) Valencia. Ordinary red table wine and fair *clarete* table wine. Spain.

Duhart-Milon, Château. (4) Haut-Médoc; Pauillac. *Quatrième cru classé.* 14,000 dozen bottles of red bordeaux. France.

Dupeyrat, Château. (4) Blayais; Mazion, north-east of Blaye. 2,500 dozen bottles of red bordeaux; 500 white. France.

Duplessis-Hauchecorne, Château. (4) Haut-Médoc; Moulis. *Cru bourgeois supérieur.* 13,000 dozen bottles of red bordeaux. France.

Durand-Moureau, Château. (5) St-Emilion; Puisseguin. An unclassified *cru.* 5,000 dozen bottles of red bordeaux. France.

Durango. (35) Northern Mexico vineyard area. Ordinary to fair table wines. Mexico.

Durbach. (25) Baden; approx. twenty miles south-west of Baden-Baden. Ordinary to fair red and white table wines. West Germany.

Durello. (26) Veneto; Vicenza area. Ordinary dry white table wine. Italy. *See* **Arzignano.**

Duresses, Les. (8) Côte de Beaune; Auxey-Duresses. Red burgundy. France.

Durfort-Vivens, Château. (4) Haut-Médoc; Margaux. *Deuxième cru classé.* 8,000 dozen bottles of red bordeaux. France.

Durnstdier. (33) Danube valley. Fair white table wine. Austria.

Dürrenzimmern. (25) Württemberg; just west of Heilbronn. Ordinary to fair red and white table wines. West Germany.

Dutruch-Grand-Poujeaux, Château. (4) Haut-Médoc; Moulis. *Cru bourgeois supérieur.* 5,000 dozen bottles of red bordeaux. France.

Duttweiler. (23) Palatinate; south-east of Neustadt. Ordinary red and fair to fine white table wines. West Germany.

♀

East Side Winery. (36) California; Lodi. Table and dessert wines, brandy and vermouth. U.S.A.

Ebenbreit. (24) Rhinehessia; Oppenheim vineyard. Also one of the Dienheim vineyards. Fair white table wine. West Germany.

Ebernburg. (24) Nahe; just south-west of Bad Münster. Ordinary to fair white table wine. West Germany.

Eberniger. (25) Baden; Freiburg area. Ordinary to fair red and white table wines. West Germany.

Ebersberg. (24) Rhinehessia; Bodenheim and Schwabsburg vineyards. Fair white table wine. West Germany.

Ebersheim. (24) Rhinehessia; west of Nackenheim. Ordinary red and fair white table wines. West Germany.

Eberstadt. (25) Württemberg; north-east of Mosbach. Ordinary to fair red and white table wines. West Germany.

Ebringen. (25) Baden; south-west of Freiberg. Ordinary to fair red and white table wines. West Germany.

Ecarts, Domaine des. (4) St-Sauveur. *Cru bourgeois.* 500 dozen bottles of red bordeaux. France.

Echanges, Aux. (8) Côte de Beaune; Chambolle-Musigny vineyard. *Deuxième cru.* Red burgundy. France.

Echeshaux, Aux. (8) Côte de Nuits; Gevrey-Chambertin vineyard. *Troisième cru.* Red burgundy. France.

Echeshaux, Les. (8) Côte de Beaune; Chambolle-Musigny vineyard. *Premier cru.* Red burgundy. France.

Echézeaux-du-Dessus, Les. (8) Côte de Nuits; Flagey-Echézeaux vineyard. *Grand cru, AC Echézeaux.* Red burgundy. France.

Echo, Clos de l'. (16) Touraine; Chinon vineyard. Fair red table wine. France.

Ecija. (29) Seville. Ordinary to fair white wine. Spain.

Eckeberg. (24) Rhinegau; Winkel vineyard. Fine white table wine. West Germany.

Eckelsheim. (24) Rhinehessia; south-east of Bad Münster. Ordinary to fair white table wine. West Germany.

Eckenroth. (24) Nahe valley; north-west of Bad Kreuznach. Fair to fine white table wine. West Germany.

Ecluse, Domaine de l'. (5) Entre-deux-Mers. 1,200 dozen bottles of red bordeaux. France.

Ecu, A l'. (8) Beaune vineyard. *Premier cru.* Red burgundy. France.

Ecueil. (17) Marne *département*; Ville-en-Tardenois canton, south-west of Rheims. Rated *premier cru*—90% growth. 279 acres. France.

Edelmann. (24) Rhinegau; Mittelheim vineyard. Fair to fine white table wine. West Germany.

Edelmann. (24) Rhinehessia; Laubenheim vineyard. Fair to fine white table wine. West Germany.

Edelzwicker. (19) Haut-Rhin *département*. White table wine from Alsace, made of a blend of white grapes of medium quality and price. France.

Edenkoben. (23) Palatinate. Ordinary, fair, and some fine white table wine. West Germany.

Eden Valley. (37) South Australia, south-east of Barossa Valley. An area greatly admired for its white wines. Higher altitude than the Barossa. Australia.

Ediger. (22) Moselle valley; Krampen (q.v.) area, just east of Eller. Fair to fine white table wine. West Germany.

Efringen-Kirchen. (25) Baden; approx. twenty-six miles south-west of Freiburg. Ordinary to fair white table wine. West Germany.

Eger. (33) Town and vineyards, approx. sixty-five miles north-east of Budapest. Ordinary, fair and some fine table and dessert wines. Hungary.

Egersberg. (24) Rhinegau; Hallgarten vineyard. Fine white table wine. West Germany.

Eglise, Château de l'. (5) Lalande-de-Pomerol. *Cru bourgeois.* 2,000 dozen bottles of red bordeaux. France.

Eglise, Clos de l'. (5) St-Emilion; Puisseguin. *Cru bourgeois.* 2,500 dozen bottles of red bordeaux. France.

Eglise, Clos l'. (5) Pomerol. 2,500 dozen bottles of red bordeaux. France.

Eglise-Clinet, Clos l'. (5) Pomerol. *Grand cru* 2,000 dozen bottles of red bordeaux. France.

Egmont, Château d'. (4) Haut-Médoc; Ludon. *Cru bourgeois supérieur.* 500 dozen bottles of red bordeaux. France.

Egri Bikaver. (33) Eger area; approx. sixty-five miles north-east of Budapest. Dark red, dry, good quality table wine. Hungary.

Egri Kadarka. (33) Eger area; approx. sixty-five miles north-east of Budapest. Lighter and finer red table wine that the Egri Bikaver (above), made from Kadarka grapes. Hungary.

Eguisheim. (19) Haut-Rhin *département*. Fair white Alsace table wine. France.

Ehr. (24) Rhinegau; Rauenthal vineyard. Fine white table wine. West Germany.

Ehrenberg. (22) Ruwer valley; Waldrach vineyard. Fine white table wine. West Germany.

Ehrenbreitstein. (21) Middle Rhine; near Koblenz. Ordinary to fair white table wine. West Germany.

Ehrenstetten. (25) Baden; south-west of Freiburg. Fair red and white table wines. West Germany.

Eibelstadt. (25) Franconia; south-east of Würzburg. Ordinary to fair red and white table wines. West Germany.

Eibensbach. (25) Württemberg; south-west of Heilbronn. Ordinary to fair red and white table wines. West Germany.

Eibingen. (25) Rhinegau; just north of Rüdesheim. Ordinary to fair red table wine. West Germany.

Eichstetten. (25) Baden; north-east of Freiburg. Ordinary to fair red and white table wines. West Germany.

Eimeldingen. (25) Baden; approx. twenty-six miles south-west of Freiburg. Fair white table wine. West Germany.

H

Eimsheim. (24) Rhinehessia; north-west of Alsheim. Ordinary to fair red and white table wines. West Germany.

Einselthum. (23) Palatinate; north-west of Grünstadt. Ordinary to fair red and white table wines. West Germany.

Eiravelha, Quinta. (30) *Região demarcada do Douro* (q.v.). Estate in Gouvaes in the Régua area which existed in 1512. Portugal.

Eisel. (24) Rhinehessia; Bingen vineyard. Fair white table wine. West Germany.

Eisenberg. (33) Burgenland; south-east Austria, close to the Hungarian border. Ordinary to fair white table wine. Austria.

Eisenberg. (21) Middle Rhine; Boppard vineyard, south of Koblenz. Fair white table wine. West Germany.

Eisenberg. (24) Rhinegau; Oestrich vineyard. Fine white table wine. West Germany.

Eisental. (25) Baden; south-west of Baden-Baden. Ordinary to fair red and white table wines. West Germany.

Eiserberg. (24) Rhinegau; Oestrich vineyard. Fair to fine white table wine. West Germany.

Eiserne. (24) Rhinehessia; Guntersblum vineyard. West Germany.

Eiserweg. (24) Rhinegau; Oestrich vineyard. Fine white table wine. West Germany.

Eisingen. (25) Baden; south-east of Karlsruhe. Ordinary to fair red and white table wines. West Germany.

Eisweg. (24) Rhinegau; Rauenthal vineyard. Fine white table wine. West Germany.

Eiswein. 'Ice-wine', the fine white wine made from late-gathered, over-ripe Riesling grapes after the first frosts of autumn in the Rhineland, West Germany.

Eitelsbach. (22) Ruwer valley. Fine and very fine white table wine. West Germany.

Elâziğ. (34) East central Turkey. One of the better wine-producing areas. Turkey.

Elche. (29) Alicante; approx. forty miles south-east of Valencia. Ordinary to fair table wines. Spain.

El Ciego. (29) Alava; La Rioja area of the upper Ebro valley. Fair to fine red table wine. Spain.

Elda. (29) Alicante; approx. forty miles south of Valencia. Ordinary red table wine. South-east Spain.

Elero (Bianco, Rosso and Rosato). (28) Sicily; Syracuse area, Tellaro, formerly called Elovo. Rather coarse, white, red and rosé table wines. Italy.

Elisenberg. (22) Moselle valley; Mühlheim vineyard, between Bernkastel and Wintrich. Fair white table wine. West Germany.

Ellenz-Poltersdorf. (22) Moselle valley; Krampen area (q.v.), south-west of Bruttig. Fair to fine white table wine. West Germany.

Eller. (22) Moselle valley. Fair white table wine. West Germany.

Ellerstadt. (23) Palatinate; north-east of Neustadt. Ordinary red and fair white table wines. West Germany.

Ellhofen. (25) Württemberg; east of Heilbronn. Ordinary to fair red and white table wines. West Germany.

Elliot's Oakvale. (37) New South Wales; Hunter River valley, north-east of Sydney. Winery and vineyard. Australia.

Ellmendingen. (25) Baden; south-east of Karlsruhe. Ordinary to fair red and white table wines. West Germany.

Elsheim. (24) Rhinehessia; south of Niederwalluf. Ordinary to fair red and white table wines. West Germany.

Elslay. (22) Moselle valley; Treis vineyard, between Valwig and Kobern. Fair white table wine. West Germany.

Elster. (23) Palatinate; Forst vineyard. Fine white table wine. West Germany.

Elterberg. (32) Moselle valley; Wormeldange vineyard. Ordinary to fair white table wine. Luxembourg.

Eltville. (24) Rhinegau. Fair, fine and some very fine white table wines. West Germany.

Eltzerberg. (22) Saar valley; Oberemmel vineyard. Fine white table wine. West Germany.

Elzosberg. (22) Saar valley; Ediger vineyard. Tributary, near Wiltingen. Fair white table wine. West Germany.

Emigré, Château de l'. (5) Graves de Bordeaux; Cérons. An unclassified *cru*. 1,000 dozen bottles of white bordeaux. France.

Emilia-Romagna. (26) The wine-producing region of Central Italy of which Bologna and Modena are the two chief cities. Italy.

Emu Wines. (37) South Australia; Morpeth Vales south of Adelaide. Shippers for Co-operative Wines (Australia) Ltd., a joint exporting organization of South Australia's seven wine co-operatives. Emu Wine Co., former large wine exporter on its own account, does not now make wine in South Australia but has several important producing properties in Western Australia.

Encinacorra. (29) Cariñena; west-central Zaragoza province. Ordinary to fair red and white table wines. Spain.

Enclos, Château L'. (5) Pomerol. 4,000 dozen bottles of red bordeaux. France.

Enclos, Domaine de l'. (12) Côtes du Rhône;

Châteauneuf-du-Pape. Fair to fine red table wine. France.

Endersbach. (25) Württemberg; Remsthal, just west of Stuttgart. Ordinary to fair red and white table wines. West Germany.

Enfant-Jesus, L'. (8) Beaune; Les Grèves vineyard. Red burgundy. France.

Enfer. (26) Val d'Aosta. Common red table wine made from Petit Rouge grapes. Italy.

Engäss. (22) Moselle valley; Thörnich vineyard, between Klüsserath and Detzem. Fair white table wine. West Germany.

Engelmannsberg. (24) Rhinegau; Hattenheim vineyard, between Erbach and Mittelheim. Fine white table wine. West Germany.

Engelsberg. (25) Franconia; Sommerach vineyard, west of Würzburg. Fair white table wine. West Germany.

Engelsberg. (22) Moselle valley; Zeltingen vineyard. Fair white table wine. West Germany.

Engelsberg. (24) Rhinehessia; Nackenheim vineyard. Fair to fine white table wine. West Germany.

Engelsburg. (22) Moselle valley; Kröv vineyard, between Zell and Enkirch. Fair white table wine. West Germany.

Engelsberg. (22) Moselle valley; Kröv vineyard, vineyard. Fair white table wine. West Germany.

Engelstadt. (24) Rhinehessia; south of Erbach. Ordinary table wines. West Germany.

Engerweg. (24) Rhinegau; Rüdesheim vineyard. Fine white table wine. West Germany.

Enkirch. (22) Moselle valley. Fair, fine and some very fine white table wine. West Germany.

Ensch. (22) Saar valley; south-west of Klüsserath. Fair white table wine. West Germany.

Ensheim. (24) Rhinehessia; west of Bad Kreuznach. Ordinary to fair white table wines. West Germany.

Ensing. (24) Rhinegau; Winkel vineyard. Fine white table wine. West Germany.

Entre-Deux-Mers. (5) The undulating vine-clad stretch of land between the rivers Garonne and Dordogne. France.

Entre-Deux-Velles. (8) Côte de Nuits; Fixin vineyard. Deuxième cru. Red burgundy. France.

Enxodreiro, Quinta. (30) Região demarcada do Douro (q.v.). Estate in Poiares north-east of Régua. Portugal.

Enzberg. (25) Württemberg; south-east of Karlsruhe. Ordinary to fair red and white table wines. West Germany.

Epaisse, Clos de l'. (16) Touraine; Bourgueil vineyard. Fair to fine red table wine. France.

Epeneaux, Clos des. (8) Pommard; walled vineyard within the larger area of Epenots 'climat'. France.

Epenots, Les. (8) Côte de Beaune; Pommard vineyard. Premier cru. Red burgundy. France.

Epenottes, Les. (8) Beaune vineyard. Premier cru. Red burgundy. France.

Epernay. (17) Marne département. Rated—88% growth. 396 acres. France.

Epesses. (31) Vaud canton. Fair to fine white table wine. Switzerland.

Epila. (29) Aragon; Zaragoza. Ordinary to fair red and white table wines. Spain.

Epinay, L'. (16) Touraine; Vouvray vineyard, east of Tours. Fair white table wine. France.

Epinay, L'. (16) Anjou; Coteaux de l'Aubance, between Angers and Saumur, Müre-Erigne vineyard. Fair white table wine. France.

Epinettes, Clos des. (31) Vaud canton; Bonvillers vineyard. Fair to fine white wine. Switzerland

Epineuil. (6) Yonne département; Tonnerre area. Ordinary to fair red and white table wines. France.

Epinola. (29) New Castile; Toledo, approx. forty miles south-west of Madrid. Ordinary to fair red and white table wines. South-central Spain.

Epinottes, Les. (6) Chablis. Sechet, south-west of Chablis. Premier cru. White burgundy. France.

Epire, Château d'. (16) Anjou; Coteaux de la Loire, below Angers, Savennières vineyard. Fair to fine white table wine. France.

Eppan. (33) South Tyrol area of western Austria bordering Germany. Ordinary to fair red and white table wines. Austria.

Eppelsheim. (23) Rhinehessia; north of Grünstadt. Ordinary red and fair to fine white table wines. West Germany.

Erbach. (24) Rhinegau. Fair, fine and some very fine white table wines. West Germany.

Erbaluce. (26) Piedmont. Name of a white grape; also a dry white wine of no great merit made from it. Italy.

Erbes-Büdesheim. (24) Rhinehessia; south-east of Bad Münster. Fair to fine white table wine. West Germany.

Erden. (22) Middle Moselle valley. Fair to fine, some very fine white table wine. West Germany.

Erlabrunn. (25) Franconia; north-west of Würzburg. Fair to fine white table wine. West Germany.

Erlach. (31) Bern canton; Thunersee (Lake Thun) area. Ordinary to fair red and white table wines. Switzerland.

Erlenbach. (25) Franconia; north-west of Karlsruhe. Fair red and white table wines. West Germany.

Erlenbach. (25) Württemberg; west of Würzburg. Ordinary to fair red and white table wines. West Germany.

Ermitage. *See* **Hermitage.**

Ermitage, Château L'. (4) Haut-Médoc; Listrac, north-west of Moulis. 1,800 dozen bottles of red bordeaux. France.

Ermite, L'. (12) Côtes du Rhône; Tain L'Hermitage vineyard. Fair red table wine. France.

Ernsbach. (25) Württemberg; approx. twenty-one miles north of Mosbach. Ordinary to fair red and white table wines. West Germany.

Ernst. (22) Moselle valley; opposite Bruttig. Mostly ordinary, but popular, white table wine. West Germany.

Erntebringer. (24) Rhinegau; Johannisberg vineyard. Fair white table wine. West Germany.

Erntebringer. (24) Rhinegau; Winkel vineyard. Fine white table wine. West Germany.

Erpel. (21) Middle Rhine; north-west of Linz. Ordinary red and white table wines. West Germany.

Erpolzheim. (23) Palatinate; west of Kallstadt. Ordinary to fair red and white table wines. West Germany.

Ersingen. (25) Baden; south-east of Karlsruhe. Fair to fine white table wine. West Germany.

Erzgrube. (24) Nahe valley; Ebernburg vineyard, just south-west of Bad Münster. Fair white table wine. West Germany.

Escalona. (24) New Castile; Toledo, approx. forty miles south-west of Madrid. Ordinary to fair red table wine. South-central Spain.

Eschelbach. (21) Württemberg; south-east of Heidelberg. Ordinary to fair red and white table wine. West Germany.

Escherndorf. (25) Franconia; north-east of Würzburg. Fair to fine white table wine. West Germany.

Espartina. (29) Seville. Ordinary to fair white wine. Spain.

Esperance, Château de l'. (5) Graves de Bordeaux; Labrède, between Podensac and Martillac. 500 dozen bottles of red bordeaux; 2,500 white. France.

Espinglet, Château de l'. (5) Premières Côtes de Bordeaux; Rions, north of Podensac. 1,000 dozen bottles of red bordeaux; 7,000 white. France.

Espirito Santo da Lameira, Quinta. (30) *Região demarcada do Douro* (q.v.). Estate of sixty acres in Poiares north-east of Régua. Portugal.

Espolla. (29) Gerona; approx. twenty-five miles north-east of Barcelona. Ordinary strong and sweet red table wine. Spain.

Esquivias. (29) New Castile; Toledo, approx. forty miles south-west of Madrid. Ordinary to fair red table wine. South-central Spain.

Esselborn. (24) Rhinehessia; south-west of Alsheim. Fair white table wine. West Germany.

Essenheim. (24) Rhinehessia; south of Niederwalluf. Ordinary to fair red and white table wines. West Germany.

Essingen. (23) Palatinate; north-east of Landau. Ordinary to fair white table wine. West Germany.

Esslingen. (25) Württemberg; approx. thirty-nine miles east of Freiburg. Ordinary to fair red and white table wines. West Germany.

Estella. (29) Navarre. Ordinary red table wine and fair to fine *clarete*. Spain.

Estepa. (29) Seville. Ordinary red table wine. Spain.

Estepona. (29) Málaga. Ordinary red and white table wines. Spain.

Est! Est!! Est!!! (27) Lazio; Montefiascone, north-west of Viterbo. Fair white table wine, either dry or semi-sweet and sometimes slightly *frizzante*. Italy.

Esteveira, Quinta. (30) *Região demarcada do Douro* (q.v.). Estate of 125 acres in Ervedosa do Douro east of Régua. Portugal.

Estienne. (8) One of the Hospices de Beaune *cuvées*. *AC Beaune*. Discontinued and grouped with other *cuvées*. Red burgundy. France.

Estremadura. (29) Province of central Spain. Vineyards: 194,000 acres. Wine: 13,486 dozen bottles. Spain.

Etna (Bianco, Rosso). Sicily; Catania. Ordinary to fair white and red table wines. Italy.

Etoile, L'. (18) Jura *département*; Arbois area. White table wines, *vin jaune* (q.v.), *vin de paille* (q.v.). France.

Etournelles, Les. (8) Côte de Nuits; Gevrey-Chambertin vineyard. *Premier cru*. Red burgundy. France.

Ettenheim. (25) Baden; Offenburg area, Breisgau. Fair white table wine. West Germany.

Euchariusberg. (22) Saar valley; Niedermennig and Krettnach vineyards, north-east of Wiltingen. Ordinary to fair white table wine. West Germany.

Eulenberg. (22) Moselle valley; Kinheim vineyard. Ordinary to fair white table wine. West Germany.

Eulengrube. (25) Franconia; Eschendorf vineyard, north-east of Würzburg. Fair white table wine. West Germany.

Eulenlay. (22) Moselle; Kinheim vineyard. Fair white table wine. West Germany.

Eussenheim. (25) Franconia; north-west of Würzburg. Fair to fine white table wine. West Germany.

Evangile, Château L'. (5) Pomerol. *Grand cru*. 4,500 dozen bottles of red bordeaux. France.

Evêque, Le Clos l'. (9) Chalonnais; Mercurey vineyard. *Premier cru*. Red burgundy. France.

Evois. (16) Anjou; Ingrandes vineyard, south-west of Angers. Fair red table wine. France.

Ewell. (37) South Australia; Warradaell near Adelaide. *See* **Hamilton's Ewell.** Australia.

Eyquem, Château. (3) Bourgeais; Bayon, north-east of Bourg. 10,000 dozen bottles of red bordeaux; 1,500 white. France.

Ezcola. (29) Navarre. Ordinary red and fair white table wines. Spain.

Ezerjó. (33) Mör, near Budapest. Fair to fine white table wine. Hungary.

❦

Fachbach. (21) Middle Rhine; east of Koblenz. Fair white table wine. West Germany.

Façonnières, Les. (8) Côte de Nuits; Morey-St-Denis vineyard. *Premier cru.* France.

Fahr. (22) Moselle; best side of the Burg vineyard of Zell. Fine white table wine. West Germany.

Fahrberg. (22) Moselle; Kobern vineyard. Fair to fine white table wine. West Germany.

Fahrfels. (22) Moselle; Trittenheim vineyard. Fair white table wine. West Germany.

Fahrlay. (22) Moselle; Karden vineyard. Fair white table wine. West Germany.

Faisca, Quinta. (30) *Região demarcada do Douro* (q.v.). Estate of ninety-six acres in Favaios north-east of Régua. Portugal.

Falbert. (23) Palatinate; Middle Haardt, Königsbach vineyard. Fine white table wine. West Germany.

Falerno (Bianco, Rosso). (28) Campania; Caserta, approx. seventeen miles north-east of Naples. Ordinary to fair dry red and white table wines; also a sweet red wine. Italy.

Falernum. (28) Lazio; Gulf of Gaeta, north-west of Naples. Ordinary dry white table wine with a bitter after-taste. Italy.

Falfas, Château. (3) Bourgeais; Bayon, north-east of Bourg. 7,000 dozen bottles of red bordeaux. France.

Falkenberg. There are vineyards of this name in Bernkastel and Trittenheim, Moselle (22); also in Dienheim and Oppenheim, Rhinehessia (24). Ordinary to fair white table wine. West Germany.

Falkenstein. (22) Saar valley; Konz vineyard north of Saarburg, only vineyard of any importance. Fair white table wine. West Germany.

Falklay. (22) Moselle valley; Reil vineyard. Fair white table wine. West Germany.

Falset. (29) Tarragona. Ordinary, dark, strong, sweet red wine. Spain.

Famines, Les. (8) Côte de Beaune; Volnay vineyard. *Troisième cru.* Red burgundy. France.

Fankel. (22) Moselle; just south of Bruttig. Ordinary to fair white table wine. West Germany.

Fara-in-Sabina. (27) Lazio; Tiber valley vineyards. Ordinary to fair white table wine. Italy.

Fara-Vicentino. (26) Veneto; between Lake Garda and river Piave, west of Verona. Ordinary to fair red table wine. Italy.

Fargues. (5) One of the four *communes* in the Barsac area whose white wines are entitled to the *AC Sauternes*, the very fine sweet dessert or table wine. France.

Fargues, Château de. (5) Barsac; Fargues. 3,500 dozen bottles of fine white bordeaux. France.

Farlay. (22) Moselle; Pünderich vineyard, north-west of Zell. Fair white table wine. West Germany.

Farlet. (29) Aragon; Zaragoza. Ordinary red table wine. Spain.

Faro. (28) Sicily; Messina. One of the island's better red table wines. Italy.

Fasanengarten. (23) Palatinate; Bad Dürkheim vineyard. Fine white table wine. West Germany.

Fastrau. (22) Saar; north-east of Trier. Ordinary to fair white table wine. West Germany.

Faubernet, Château. (5) Premières Côtes de Bordeaux; Langoiran, north-east of Portets. 10,000 dozen bottles of white bordeaux. France.

Faurie, Château. (5) Néac; *commune* east of Pomerol. 3,000 dozen bottles of red bordeaux. France.

Fautenbohl. (23) Palatinate; Meckenheim vineyard, north-east of Neustadt. Fair white table wine. West Germany.

Favagreca. (28) Calabria; Messina Strait. Ordinary cherry-red table wine. Italy.

Faverges. (31) Vaud canton; Lavaux vineyard. Fair to fine white table wine. Switzerland.

Favettes, Les. (16) Anjou; Dampierre-sur-Loire vineyard, Saumur. Ordinary to fair red table wine. France.

Fayal. (30) Azores. Ordinary to fair table and dessert wines. Portugal.

Fayau, Château. (5) Premières Côtes de Bordeaux; Cadillac, north-west of Loupiac. 2,000 dozen bottles of red bordeaux; 10,000 white. France.

Faye d'Anjou. (16) Anjou; Coteaux du Layon, south of Angers. Fine white table wine. France.

Federberg. (24) Rhinehessia; Schwabsburg vineyard, south-east of Würzburg. Ordinary to fair white table wine. West Germany.

Fefinanes. (29) West-central Galicia; Pontèvedra. Fair, light, dry, white table wine. Spain.

Feilbingert. (24) Nahe; south-west of Bad Münster. Fair to fine white table wine. West Germany.

Feinter. (22) Moselle; Wehlen vineyard. Fine white table wine. West Germany.

Felanit. (29) Majorca; Balearic Islands, off the coast east of Valencia. Ordinary red and white semi-sweet table wines. Spain.

Feldberg. (25) Baden; approx. eighteen miles south-west of Freiburg. Fair white table wine. West Germany.

Fell. (22) Saar; east of Trier. Ordinary to fair white table wine. West Germany.

Fellbach. (25) Württemberg; just east of Stuttgart. Ordinary to fair red and white table wines. West Germany.

Fellerich. (22) Saar; north-west of Saarburg. Ordinary to fair white table wine. West Germany.

Felletin, Château. (4) Haut-Médoc; Lamarque. *Cru bourgeois.* 1,200 dozen bottles of red bordeaux. France.

Fellonneau-Labrie, Château. (4) Haut-Médoc; Macau. *Cru bourgeois supérieur.* 500 dozen bottles of red bordeaux. France.

Fels. (32) Moselle; Grevenmacher. Fair white table wine. Luxembourg.

Fels. (24) Nahe; Niederhausen vineyard, west of Bad Münster. Fair to fine white table wine. West Germany.

Fels. (22) Saar; Könen vineyard, north of Saarburg. Fair white table wine. West Germany.

Felsberg. (32) Moselle; Wintrange vineyard. Fair white table wine. Luxembourg.

Felsenberg. (24) Nahe; Schloss Böckelheim vineyard, west of Bad Münster. Fine white table wine. West Germany.

Felseneck. (24) Nahe; Bad Münster vineyard. Fair white table wine. West Germany.

Feltu. (34) Ordinary to fair red table wine. Turkey.

Fenchelberg. (24) Rhinehessia; Nackenheim vineyard. Fair white table wine. West Germany.

Fendant de Sion. (31) Valais canton; Sion vineyards, Rhône valley. Best white table wine made from Chasselas grapes, known as *Fendant.* Switzerland.

Fermoselle. (29) Central León; Zamora. Ordinary dark red table wine and fair *clarete.* Northwest Spain.

Ferradosa, Quinta. (30) *Região demarcada do Douro* (q.v.). Estate in Linhares in the Régua area comprising 300 acres. Portugal.

Ferran, Château. (5) Graves de Bordeaux; Martillac. An unclassified *cru.* 1,000 dozen bottles of red bordeaux; 1,000 white. France.

Ferrand, Château. (5) Pomerol. 7,500 dozen bottles of red bordeaux. France.

Ferrande, Château. (5) Graves de Bordeaux; Castres, west of Portets. An unclassified *cru.* 3,000 dozen bottles of red bordeaux; 5,000 white. France.

Ferrière, Château. (4) Haut-Médoc; Margaux. *Troisième cru classé.* 2,000 dozen bottles of red bordeaux. France.

Ferronnières, Les. (16) Anjou; Dampierre-sur-Loire vineyard, Saumur. Fair to fine white table wine. France.

Fesle, Château de. (16) Anjou; Coteaux du Layon, Bonnézeaux vineyard, south of Angers. Fair to fine white table wine. France.

Fessenbach. (25) Baden; east of Strasbourg. Ordinary to fair red and white table wine. West Germany.

Fetiaska. (34) South-west European Russia; Moldavia. Fair red and white table wines. U.S.S.R.

Feuer. (23) Palatinate; Hambach vineyard, between Neustadt and Edenkoben. Fair white table wine. West Germany.

Feuerberg. (22) Moselle; Ediger vineyard, just east of Eller. Fair white table wine. West Germany.

Feuerberg. (23) Palatinate; Bad Dürkheim vineyard. Fine white table wine. West Germany.

Feuerberg. (24) Rhinehessia; Mettenheim vineyard, south of Alsheim. Fair white table wine. West Germany.

Feuerthal. (25) Franconia; approx. fifty-three miles east of Frankfurt. Fair white table wine. West Germany.

Feuille d'Or. (16) Anjou; Coteaux de la Loire, Chalonnes-sur-Loire vineyard, south-west of Angers. Fair white table wine. France.

Fèves, Les. (8) Beaune vineyard. *Premier cru.* Red burgundy. France.

Feytit-Clinet, Château. (5) Pomerol. 2,500 dozen bottles of red bordeaux. France.

Fiano. (28) Campania; Avellino vineyards. Ordinary to fair white wine, frequently *frizzante*, from Fiano white grapes. Also a sweet dessert wine and a Fiano *spumante.* Italy.

Ficklin Vineyard. (36) California; Madera County. Remarkably fine port-type dessert wine, Tinto Madeira Port and Emerald Riesling. U.S.A.

Fieuzal, Château. (5) Graves de Bordeaux; Léognan. An unclassified *cru.* 3,000 dozen bottles of red bordeaux; 1,500 white. France.

Figeac, Château. (5) St-Emilion. *Premier grand cru classé.* 10,000 dozen bottles of red bordeaux. France.

Filh, Domaine du. (5) Premières Côtes de Bordeaux; Donzac, east of Podensac. 2,500 dozen bottles of red bordeaux; 5,000 white. France.

Filhot, Château. (5) Sauternes. *Deuxième cru classé.* 5,000 dozen bottles of white bordeaux. France.

Filtrato de Lancellotta. (26) Emilia-Romagna.

Ordinary to fair red semi-sweet, semi-sparkling wine. Italy.

Filtrato di Lancellotta. *See* **Lancellotta.**

Filzen. (22) Moselle valley; between Brauneberg and Wintrich. Vineyards: Klostergarten, Nonnenberg. White wine. West Germany.

Filzen. (22) Saar; just north-west of Kanzem. Fair white table wine. West Germany.

Findling. (24) Rhinehessia; site name of Spiegelberg vineyard, Nierstein. Fair to fine white wine. West Germany.

Finger Lakes. (35) New York State. A series of long, narrow lakes not unlike the fingers of a giant's open hand. A great deal of wine, red and white, still and sparkling. U.S.A.

Fino. (29) Jerez de la Frontera region. The best preprandial or apéritif type of sherry; never dark, never sweet, with much charm and breed if from a first-class shipper. Spain.

Fiorano Bianco. (27) Lazio; Roman Appian Way, *Via Appia*, approx. ten miles from Rome. Fair to fine white table wine from Malvasia di Candia grapes. Italy.

Fiorano Rosso. (27) Vineyards within approx. ten miles south-west of Rome. Fair to fine red table wine from Cabernet and Merlot grapes. Italy.

Fior di Romangia. (28) Sardinia. Popular, although quite undistinguished, rosé table wine. Italy.

Fischerpfad. (24) Rhinehessia; Alsheim vineyard, Worms area. Fair white table wine. West Germany.

Fitaro. (29) Navarre. Dark red, strong, dry table wine. Spain.

Fixin. (8) Côte de Nuits; village. *Appellation Contrôlée.* Fair red burgundy. France.

Flachenthal. (24) Rhinehessia; Nierstein vineyard. Fair white table wine. West Germany.

Flagey-Echézeaux. (8) Côte de Nuits. Fair, fine and some very fine red burgundy. France.

Flecht. (24) Rhinegau; Rüdesheim vineyard. Fine white table wine. West Germany.

Fleckinger. (23) Palatinate; Forst vineyard. Fine white table wine. West Germany.

Fleur, Château La. (5) Côtes de St-Emilion. An unclassified *cru.* 4,000 dozen bottles of red bordeaux. France.

Fleur, Château La. (5) Néac *commune*; east of Pomerol. 2,000 dozen bottles of red bordeaux. France.

Fleur-du-Gazin, Château La. (5) Pomerol. 1,200 dozen bottles of red bordeaux. France.

Fleurie. (11) Beaujolais; one of the nine named Beaujolais villages called locally 'Crus Beaujolais'. Fair and very popular red beaujolais. France.

Fleurières, Aux. (8) Côte de Nuits; Nuits-St-Georges vineyard. *Deuxième et troisième cru.* Red burgundy. France.

Fleur-Petrus, Château La. (5) Pomerol. *Grand cru.* 3,500 dozen bottles of red bordeaux. France.

Fleur-Pourret, Château La. (5) Côtes de St-Emilion. An unclassified *cru.* 1,500 dozen bottles of red bordeaux. France.

Fleur-Saint-Laurent, Château La. (4) Haut-Médoc; St Laurent. *Cru bourgeois.* 600 dozen bottles of red bordeaux. France.

Fleys. (6) Yonne *département*. Its best wines are entitled to the *AC Chablis*. White burgundy. France.

Flörsheim. (24) Rhinegau; east of Hochheim. Fair white table wine. West Germany.

Flür. (21) Middle Rhine; Steeg vineyard, north-west of Bingen. Fair white table wine. West Germany.

Fockenberg. (24) Rhinehessia; Nierstein vineyard. Fair white table wine. West Germany.

Fogarina. (26) Emilia-Romagna; Parma area. Ordinary frothy, red table wine. Italy.

Fojo, Quinta. (30) *Região demarcada do Douro* (q.v.). Estate in Cambres south-west of Régua. Portugal.

Folatières, Les. (8) Côte de Beaune; Puligny-Montrachet vineyard. *Premier cru.* Fine white burgundy. France.

Folie, La. (16) Anjou; Coteaux de la Loire, Dampierre-sur-Loire vineyard, below Angers. Fair red table wine. France.

Folie, Clos de la. (16) Anjou; Coteaux de Saumur, Parnay vineyard. Fair white table wine. France.

Folie, Domaine de la. Côte Chalonnais; important property at Chagny/Rully. France.

Fombauge, Château. (5) St-Emilion; St Christophe-des-Bardes, south-west of Parsac. An unclassified *cru.* 2,000 dozen bottles of red bordeaux. France.

Fonbadet, Château. (4) Haut-Médoc; Pauillac. *Cru bourgeois supérieur.* 10,000 dozen bottles of red bordeaux. France.

Fond-du-Pape, Château de la. (12) Côtes du Rhône; Châteauneuf-du-Pape. Fair red table wine. France.

Fondis, Le. (16) Touraine; Bourgueil vineyard. Fair to fine red table wine. France.

Fonpetite, Château. (4) Haut-Médoc; St-Estèphe. *Cru bourgeois supérieur.* 13,000 dozen bottles of red bordeaux. France.

Fonpiqueyre, Château. (4) Haut-Médoc; St-Sauveur. *Cru bourgeois.* 6,000 dozen bottles of red bordeaux. France.

Fonplégade, Château. (5) Côtes de-St-Emilion.

Grand cru classé. 5,000 dozen bottles of red bordeaux. France.

Fonrazade, Château. (5) Côtes de St-Emilion. An unclassified *cru.* 3,000 dozen bottles of red bordeaux. France.

Fonréaud, Château. (4) Haut-Médoc; Listrac. *Cru bourgeois supérieur.* 15,000 dozen bottles of red bordeaux. France.

Fonroque, Château. (5) Côtes de St-Emilion. *Grand cru classé.* 8,000 dozen bottles of red bordeaux. France.

Fontaine, Château La. (3) Fronsadais; Fronsac. 4,000 dozen bottles of red bordeaux. France.

Fontanafredda. (26) Piedmont; Alba area, province of Cuneo. Model winery and school of viticulture. Italy.

Fontana-Serrara. (28) Campania; Ischia island, bay of Naples. Fair to good white wine, one of the *bianchi superiori.* Italy.

Fontana Winery Inc. (36) California; Fontana. Dessert and table wines. U.S.A.

Fontanet, Château. (4) Haut-Médoc; Le Taillan. *Cru bourgeois.* 4,000 dozen bottles of red bordeaux. France.

Fontebride, Château. (5) Barsac. *Cru bourgeois supérieur.* 1,000 dozen bottles of white bordeaux. France.

Fonte do Peso de Cima, Quinta. (30) *Região demarcada do Douro* (q.v.). Estate of Canelas, in Poiares north-east of Régua. Portugal.

Fontenay. (6) Yonne *département.* Its best wines are entitled to the *AC Chablis.* White burgundy. France.

Fontesegale. (27) Lazio; Tiber valley, north of Rome. Ordinary red and white semi-sweet table wines. Italy.

Fontesteau, Château. (4) Haut-Médoc; St-Sauveur. *Cru bourgeois.* 5,000 dozen bottles of red bordeaux. France.

Fontillon. (29) Alicante; approx. forty miles south of Valencia. Dark, strong table wine. South-east Spain.

Fontmurée, Château. (5) St-Emilion; Montagne. *Cru bourgeois.* 4,000 dozen bottles of red bordeaux. France.

Fontrubi. (29) Upper Panadés; between Tarragona and Barcelona. Fair red wines. Spain.

Foppiano Wine Company. (36) California; Healdsburg, Sonoma County. Table and dessert wines. U.S.A.

Forcadière, Domaine de la. (12) Côtes du Rhône; Tavel. Fair to fine rosé wine. France.

Forcine, La. (16) Touraine; Bourgueil vineyard. Fair to fine red table wine. France.

Forêts. (6) Chablis; Yonne *département. Premier cru.* White burgundy. France.

Forêts, Clos des. (8) Côte de Nuits; Prémeaux vineyard. *Premier cru. AC Nuits-St-Georges.* Red burgundy. France.

Formiga, Quinta. (30) *Região demarcada do Douro* (q.v.). Estate and vineyard. Portugal.

Forneret. (8) Savigny-les-Beaune vineyard; one of the Hospices de Beaune *cuvées.* 900 dozen bottles of red burgundy. France.

Forst. (23) Palatinate; Middle Haardt. Popular, fair, fine and very fine white table wines. West Germany.

Forsterlay. (22) Moselle; Lösnich vineyard, just east of Erden. Fair white table wine. West Germany.

Fortanella. (26) Emilia-Romagna; San Seconda Parmense vineyard, north-west of Parma. Ordinary ruby-red table wine. Italy.

Fort-Médoc, Cru. (4) Haut-Médoc; Cussac. *Cru bourgeois.* 8,000 dozen bottles of red bordeaux. France.

Fortuna. (29) Murcia. High-strength semi-sweet red wine. Spain.

Forzato di Valtellina. (26) Lombardy; Sondrio, chief town of the Valtellina region. Strong, sweet, red dessert wine of fair quality. Italy.

Fosse, La. (9) Chalonnais; Rully vineyard. *Premier cru.* White burgundy. France.

Fouchères, Les. (8) Côte de Nuits; Chambolle-Musigny vineyard. *Troisième cru.* Red burgundy. France.

Fougeailles, Château. (5) Néac *commune;* bordering on Pomerol. 1,000 dozen bottles of red bordeaux. France.

Fougeray, Clos du. (16) Touraine; Vérnon-sur-Brenne vineyard, north-east of Tours. Fair white wine. France.

Fougères, Château des. (5) Graves de Bordeaux; Labrède, between Podensac and Martillac. 1,000 dozen bottles of red bordeaux; 1,500 white. France.

Fougeyrat, Château. (5) Côtes de St-Emilion. An unclassified *cru.* 2,500 dozen bottles of red bordeaux. France.

Fouquerand. (8) Savigny-les-Beaune vineyard. One of the Hospices de Beaune *cuvées.* 525 dozen bottles of red burgundy. France.

Fouquet, Château. (16) Anjou; Côte de Saumur, Brézé vineyard. Fair to fine white wine. France.

Fourcas-Dupré, Château. (4) Haut-Médoc; Listrac. *Cru bourgeois supérieur.* 5,000 dozen bottles of red bordeaux. France.

Fourcas-Hostein, Château. (4) Haut-Médoc; Listrac. *Cru bourgeois supérieur.* 7,000 dozen bottles of red bordeaux. France.

Fourchaume. (6) Yonne *département;* Poinchy. *Premier cru* Chablis. White burgundy. France.

Fourche, Domaine de la. (5) St-Emilion; Vignonet, south-west of St Pey-d'Armens. *Cru bourgeois*. 2,500 dozen bottles of red bordeaux. France.

Fourneau-Saint-Jacques, Le. (16) Touraine; Coteaux de la Loire, Ingrandes vineyard, below Tours. Fair white table wine. France.

Fourneaux, Les. (6) Chablis; Fleys vineyard. White burgundy. France.

Fourneaux, Les. (9) Chalonnais; St-Martin-sous-Montaigu vineyard. Red burgundy. France.

Fourneaux, Les. (16) Touraine; Coteaux de la Loire, Montjean vineyard, below Tours. Fair white wine. France.

Fourney, Château. (5) St-Emilion; St-Pey-d'Armens. An unclassified *cru*. 5,000 dozen bottles of red bordeaux. France.

Fourtet, Clos. (5) Côtes de St-Emilion. *Premier grand cru classé*. 6,000 dozen bottles of red bordeaux. France.

Foussach. (32) Moselle; Bech-Kleinmacher, south-east of Luxembourg city. Ordinary to fair white table wine. Luxembourg.

Fousselottes, Les. (8) Côte de Nuits; Chambolle-Musigny vineyard. *Premier cru*. Red burgundy. France.

Foz, Quinta. (30) *Região demarcada do Douro* (q.v.). Estate and vineyard in Gonvaes in the Régua area. Fine property. Portugal.

Frada-Gorda, Quinta. (30) *Região demarcada do Douro* (q.v.). Estate and vineyard in Ervedosa do Douro east of Régua which is 400–500 metres above the River Torto. Portugal.

Frades, Quinta. (30) *Região demarcada do Douro* (q.v.). Estate and vineyard in Folgosa, east of Régua. Portugal.

Frairie. (10) Mâconnais; Solutré vineyard. *Premier cru. AC Pouilly-Fuissé*. White burgundy. France.

Framersheim. (24) Rhinehessia; west of Alsheim. Fair white and ordinary red wines. West Germany.

France, Château de. (5) Graves de Bordeaux; Léognan. An unclassified *cru*. 9,000 dozen bottles of red bordeaux. France.

Franciacorta. (26) Lombardy; Lake Iseo, east of Bergamo. Ordinary to fair light red table wine. Italy.

Franc-Laporte, Château. (5) St-Emilion; St Christophe-des-Bardes, south-west of Parsac. An unclassified *cru*. 3,000 dozen bottles of red bordeaux. France.

Franc-Maillet, Château. (5) Pomerol. 3,000 dozen bottles of red bordeaux. France.

Franc-Mayne, Château. (5) Côtes de St-Emilion. *Grand cru classé*. 3,000 dozen bottles of red bordeaux. France.

Franc-Mazerat, Château. (5) St-Emilion. *Deuxième cru*. 1,000 dozen bottles of red bordeaux. France.

Francofonte. (28) Sicily; approx. twenty-five miles north-west of Syracuse. Ordinary, dark red, dry table wine. Italy.

Franconia. (25) A large area producing mostly white table wines of fair, fine and some very fine quality: they are chiefly in the valleys of the river Main and its tributaries. West Germany.

Franc-Patarabet, Château. (5) Côtes de St-Emilion. An unclassified *cru*. 2,000 dozen bottles of red bordeaux. France.

Franc-Pourret, Château. (5) Côtes de St-Emilion. An unclassified *cru*. 3,500 dozen bottles of red bordeaux. France.

Franken. *See* **Franconia.**

Frankweiler. (23) Palatinate; north-west of Landau. Ordinary red and fair white table wines. West Germany.

Franschhoek. *See* **French Hook.**

Franzenheim. (22) Saar; south of Trier. Fair white table wine. West Germany.

Frappato di Vittoria. (28) Sicily. Popular, ordinary to fair, full-bodied, cherry-red table wine. Italy.

Frascati. (27) Lazio; Castelli Romani town and vineyards outside Rome. Mostly fair to good, dry, semi-sweet and sweet white wines. The popular sweet wine is known as Cannellino. Italy.

Frascati Rosso. (27) Lazio; Frascati vineyards and near them, Castelli Romani. Ordinary red table wine. Italy.

Frauenzimmern. (25) Württemberg; south-west of Heilbronn. Ordinary to fair red and white table wines. West Germany.

Frecciarossa Ambrato. (26) Lombardy; Casteggio area, Pavia province. Fair, semi-sec white wine. Italy.

Frecciarossa Bianco. (26) Lombardy; Casteggio area, Pavia province. Fair, dry white wine. Italy.

Frecciarossa Rosato. (26) Lombardy; Casteggio area, Pavia province. Fair rosé table wine. Italy.

Frecciarossa Rosso. (26) Lombardy; Casteggio area, Pavia province. One of the country's best red wines. Italy.

Freckenfeld. (23) Palatinate; south of Landau. Fair white and ordinary red table wines. West Germany.

Freemarkabbey Winery. (36) St Helena, Napa Valley. An old winery inactive for ten years, recently re-established. Good quality red and white table wines are now being sold. U.S.A.

Frégate, Domaine de la. (14) Côtes de Provence; St Cyr-de-St Maur vineyard, near Bandol. Fair red, white and rosé table wines. France.

Fregenal de la Sierra. (29) Estremadura; Badajoz, between Seville and Trujillo. Fair to fine *clarete* wines. Spain.

Freiburg-Breisgau. (25) Baden; just east of Freiburg. Ordinary, fair and some fine white wines. West Germany.

Freienborn. (24) Rhingau; Eltville vineyard. Fine white table wine. West Germany.

Frei-Laubersheim. (24) Rhinehessia; just east of Bad Münster. Ordinary to fair white table wine. West Germany.

Freinsheim. (23) Palatinate. Fair to fine white table wines. West Germany.

Freisa. (26) Piedmont. Name of a black grape; also a red wine made from it in two grades, dry and sweet. Italy.

Freisa delle Langhe. (26) Piedmont. Better quality red table wine from Freisa grapes. Italy.

Freisa di Chieri. (26) Piedmont; Turin province. Ordinary to fair garnet-red table wine; also a sweet, sparkling version. Italy.

Frelonnerie, Clos de la. (16) Touraine; Montlouis vineyard. Fair white table wine. France.

Fremières, Les. (8) Côte de Beaune; Morey-St-Denis vineyard. *Premier cru.* Red burgundy. France.

Fremières, Les. (8) Côte de Nuits; Chambolle-Musigny vineyard. *Deuxième cru.* Red burgundy. France.

Fremiers, Les. (8) Côte de Beaune; Pommard vineyard. *Premier cru.* Red burgundy. France.

Fremiets, Les. (8) Côte de Beaune; Volnay vineyard. *Premier cru.* Red burgundy. France.

Fremine, La. (16) Anjou; Coteaux de la Loire, La Possonnière vineyard, south-west of Angers. Fair white table wine. France.

French Hook. (39) Cape Province; east of Stellenbosch. One of the oldest wine-producing districts. South Africa.

Fresnay, Château. (16) Anjou; Coteaux du Layon, St Aubin-de-Luigné, south of Angers. Fair white table wine. France.

Fresne, Le. (16) Anjou; Coteaux de la Loire, St Georges-sur-Loire, below Angers. Fair white table wine. France.

Fresno. (36) An area of California heavily planted with the Thompson seedless grape. There are some dessert wines produced but no really decent wines can be produced from this grape. U.S.A.

Fressens. (31) Neuchâtel vineyard. Ordinary to fair red and white table wines. Switzerland.

Frettenheim. (24) Rhinehessia; west of Alsheim. Ordinary to fair red and white table wines. West Germany.

Freudenstein. (25) Württemberg; east of Karls-

ruhe. Ordinary to fair red and white table wines. West Germany.

Freundstück. (23) Palatinate; Forst vineyard. Fair white table wine. West Germany.

Fricambault. (15) Cher *département*; Sancerre vineyard. Fair white table wine. France.

Frickenhausen. (25) Franconia; south-east of Würzburg. Fair white and ordinary red table wines. West Germany.

Friedelsheim. (23) Palatinate; east of Wachenheim. Ordinary red and fair, fine and some very fine white table wines. West Germany.

Friedrichsberg. (24) Rhinehessia; Alsheim vineyard, Worms area. Fair white table wine. West Germany.

Friesenheim. (25) Baden; south-east of Strasbourg. Fair white table wine. West Germany.

Friesenheim. (24) Rhinehessia; west of Dienheim. Ordinary to fair red and white wines. West Germany.

Fritzenhölle. (24) Rhinehessia; Nackenheim vineyard. Fair white table wine. West Germany.

Friularo. (26) Veneto; Parma area. Ordinary to fair sharp-tasting red table wine. Italy.

Fröhngewann. (24) Rhinehessia; Gau-Bickelheim vineyard, east of Bad Kreuznach. Fair white table wine. West Germany.

Fröhnholz. (24) Nahe valley; Niederhausen, west of Bad Münster. Fair white table wine. West Germany.

Fröhnwelt. (22) Middle Moselle valley; Graach vineyard. Fair to fine white table wine. West Germany.

Froichots, Les. (8) Côte de Nuits; Morey-St-Denis vineyard. *Premier cru.* Red burgundy. France.

Fronsadais. (3) Important stretch of vineyards of the Gironde *département*, centred on Fronsac, a town north of Libourne and west of St-Emilion. Mostly red bordeaux from the *AC 'bordeaux'* and *'bordeaux supérieur'*—undistinguished wines —to the *AC 'côtes de Fronsac'* and *'côtes de Canon-Fronsac'*, of quite fair quality. France.

Frontignan. (13) Languedoc. Fine tawny Muscat dessert wine. France.

Frühenberg. (24) Rhingau; Hallgarten vineyard. Fair to fine white table wine. West Germany.

Fuchs. (22) Saar; Niederleuken vineyard, just north of Saarburg. Fair white table wine. West Germany.

Fuchsberg. (24) Rhingau; Geisenheim vineyard. Fair to fine white table wine. West Germany.

Fuchsloch. (24) Rhinehessia; Mettenheim vineyard, south of Alsheim. Fair white table wine. West Germany.

Fuchsmantel. (23) Palatinate; Bad Dürkheim and

Wachenheim vineyards. Fair to fine white table wines. West Germany.

Fuées, Les. (8) Côte de Nuits; Chambolle-Musigny vineyard. *Premier cru.* Red burgundy. France.

Fuencarral. (29) Madrid. Ordinary to fair golden dessert wine. Spain.

Fuenmayor. (29) Old Castile; Logroño province, La Rioja area of the upper Ebro valley. Fine red table wine. Spain.

Fuente del Maestro. (29) Estremadura; Badajoz, between Seville and Trujillo. Ordinary white table wine. Spain.

Fuenteobejuna. (29) North-central Andalusia; Montilla, Córdoba area, north-east of Seville. Fair dry white wine. Spain.

Fuenterrobles. (29) West-central Valencia; Utiel. Ordinary to fair red and white table wines. Spain.

Fuentesauco. (29) Central León; Zamora. Ordinary dark red table wine and fair to fine *clarete.* North-west Spain.

Fuentes del Ebro. (29) Aragon; Zaragoza. Ordinary red table wine. Spain.

Fuentes del Jiloca. (29) Aragon; Zaragoza. Ordinary to fair red and white table wines. Spain.

Fullkopf. (24) Rhinehessia; Ockenheim vineyard, south-east of Bingen. Fair white table wine. West Germany.

Fünfkirchen. (33) Southern Hungary; Baranya Komitat. Fair table and dessert white wines. Hungary.

Funkelshölle. (22) Moselle; Reil vineyard, east of Zell. Fair white table wine. West Germany.

Furminti. (33) West-central Hungary; Somló. Fair white table wines made from Furmint grapes. Hungary.

Furnari. (28) Sicily; coastal region west of Messina. Ordinary red and white table wines. Italy.

Furore Divina Costiera. (28) Campania; Amalfi, south-west of Salerno. Ordinary to fair red and white table wines. Italy.

Fürstenberg. (25) Franconia; Escherndorf, north-east of Würzburg. Fine white table wine. West Germany.

Fürstenberg. (21) Middle Rhine; Oberdiebach vineyard, north-west of Bingen. Fair white table wine. West Germany.

Fuzerta. (30) Area in the Algarve, the southernmost territory, which used to produce table wines. Portugal.

Gabsheim. (24) Rhinehessia; west of Dienheim. Ordinary to fair red and white table wines. West Germany.

Gaby, Château. (3) Fronsadais; Fronsac. 5,000 dozen bottles of red bordeaux. France.

Gachet, Château. (5) Néac, *commune* east of Pomerol. 2,400 dozen bottles of red bordeaux. France.

Gaffelière, Château La. (5) Côtes de St-Emilion. St-Emilion *grand cru classé.* 10,000 dozen bottles of red bordeaux. France.

Gagneries, Les. (16) Anjou; Coteaux du Layon, Bonnézeaux vineyard, south of Angers. Fair to fine white table wine. France.

Gaienhofen. (25) Lake Constance (Bodensee); west of Konstanz. Fair red and white table wines. West Germany.

Gaiersberg. (24) Rhinehessia; Dittelsheim vineyard, south-west of Oppenheim. Fair white table wine. West Germany.

Gaiersbühl. (23) Palatinate; Bad Dürkheim vineyard. Fair white table wine. West Germany.

Gaillac. (13) Tarn *département,* approx. seventy-five miles north-west of Béziers. Fair still and sparkling white wines. France.

Gaillac Premières Côtes. (13) Tarn *département*; the better white table wine of Gaillac, a town approx. seventy-five miles north-west of Béziers. France.

Gaillard, Château. (16) Anjou; Côtes de Saumur, St Cyr-en-Bourg vineyard. Fair white table wine. France.

Gaillard, Château. (16) Anjou; Côtes de Saumur, Turquant vineyard. Fair white and rosé table wines. France.

Gaillard, Château. (11) Beaujolais; Lancié vineyard. Fair red beaujolais. France.

Gaillardière, La. (16) Touraine; Rochecorbon vineyard, Vouvray, just above Tours. Fair white table wine. France.

Gaimont, Le. (16) Touraine; Vouvray vineyard, just above Tours. Fair white table wine. France.

Gaiole. (27) Tuscany; north-east of Siena. Ordinary to fair red and white table wines. Italy.

Gaisbach. (25) Baden; approx. sixteen miles south-west of Baden-Baden. Ordinary to fair red and white table wines are produced. West Germany.

Gaisböhl. (23) Palatinate; Ruppertsberg vineyard. Fine white table wine. West Germany.

Galamus. (13) Roussillon. Fair, tawny, dessert wine. France.

Galgenberg. (24) Nahe; Bad Kreuznach vineyard. Fair to fine white table wine. West Germany.

Galgenberg. (24) Rhinehessia; Nierstein and Bodenheim vineyards. Fair white table wine. West Germany.

Galgenhohe. (23) Palatinate; Edenkoben vineyard. Fair white table wine. West Germany.

Galicia. (29) Important wine-producing region of Spain. Ribadavia is the chief wine centre. Vineyards: 84,000 acres; producing mainly sharp, light white wines. Spain.

Gallegos, Vinos. (29) 'Wines of Galicia'; mostly quite ordinary white table wines. Spain.

Gallo Winery (E. & J.). (36) California; Modesto. The largest wine producer in California. Some of their table wines are made from coastal valley grapes. A very innovative firm which makes blended and fruit wines as well as table, dessert and sparkling wines in enormous quantities. U.S.A.

Galluches, Les. (16) Touraine; Cravant-les-Coteaux vineyard, south-east of Chinon. Ordinary to fair red table wine. France.

Galluches, Les. (16) Touraine; Savigny-en-Véron vineyard, below Chinon. Ordinary to fair red table wine. France.

Gallura. (28) Sardinia; Sassari area. Ordinary, light, dry red table wine. Italy.

Galoupet, Domaine du. (14) St-Tropez vineyard; west of Grimaud on coast. Fair red, white and rosé table wines. France.

Galuches, Les. (16) Touraine; Bourgueil vineyard. Fair red table wine. France.

Gamaires, Les. (8) Chambolle-Musigny. *Troisième cru*. Red burgundy. France.

Gambellara Rosso. (26) Veneto; Vicenza area. Ordinary red table wine. Italy.

Gamza. (33) Parelikeni area of north Bulgaria. Ordinary to fair red table wine. Bulgaria.

Gandesa. (29) Tarragona. Ordinary red table wine. Spain.

Gansberg. (24) Rhinehessia; Dalsheim vineyard; south-west of Oppenheim. Ordinary to fair white table wine. West Germany.

Garanche. (11) Beaujolais; Brouilly vineyard. Red beaujolais. France.

Garant, Au. (11) Beaujolais; Fleurie vineyard. One of the top-grade *communes* and villages. Red burgundy. France.

Garants, Les. (11) Beaujolais; Fleurie vineyard. One of the top-grade *communes* and villages. Red burgundy. France.

Garda, Lake. (26) West of Verona. There are many vineyards facing both the south shore (Lugano) and the north shore (Trentino) of Lake Garda. They produce much wine, mostly table wines of ordinary to fair quality. Italy.

Garda Trentino. (26) Trentino; Lake Garda. Ordinary to fair dry to semi-sweet white wine, and dry red and rosé wines. Italy.

Garde, Château La. (5) Graves de Bordeaux;

Martillac. An unclassified *cru*. 10,000 dozen bottles of red bordeaux; 1,000 white. France.

Garderose, Château. (5) Sables de St-Emilion. An unclassified *cru*. 2,500 dozen bottles of red bordeaux. France.

Gardine, Château La. (12) Côtes du Rhône; Châteauneuf-du-Pape. Fair to fine red table wine. France.

Garganega di Gambellara. (26) Veneto; Vicenza area. Ordinary to fair white table wine from Garganega grapes. Italy.

Garganta de la Olla. (29) Estremadura; Cáceres, province in Trujillo area. Ordinary red table wine. Spain.

Garnacha Blanca. (29) Tarragona. Ordinary white table wine. Spain.

Garnacha Tinta. (29) Tarragona. Ordinary but very popular red table wine. Spain.

Garosse, Domaine de la. (4) St André-de-Cubzac, east of Blaye. 2,500 dozen bottles of red bordeaux; 3,000 white. France.

Garraud, Château. (5) Néac, *commune* east of Pomerol. 4,000 dozen bottles of red bordeaux. France.

Garrido Fino. (29) Cadiz. Ordinary to fair white table wine. Spain.

Garten. (24) Rhinehessia; Oppenheim vineyard. Fair white table wine. West Germany.

Gatal. (29) Upper Estremadura; Cáceres. Ordinary to fair red table wine. Spain.

Gattinara. (26) Piedmont; Vercelli province. Garnet-red, moderately strong, elegant red wine considered by some the greatest of the Italian red wines. Like Barolo (q.v.) it is made from the Nebbiolo grape. It needs a minimum of three years in the bottle before it can be appreciated. Italy.

Gau-Algesheim. (24) Rhinehessia; south of Mittelheim. Fair white table wine. West Germany.

Gaubert, Château. (5) St Christophe-des-Bardes, south-west of Parsac. An unclassified *cru* of St-Emilion. 4,500 dozen bottles of red bordeaux. France.

Gau-Bickelheim. (24) Rhinehessia; east of Bad Kreuznach. Fair white table wine. West Germany.

Gau-Bischofsheim. (24) Rhinehessia; west of Nachenheim. Fair white table wine. West Germany.

Gaucherie, La. (16) Touraine; Restigné vineyard, below Tours. Fair red table wine. France.

Gaucin. (29) Andalusia; Málaga. Ordinary red table wine. Spain.

Gaude, La. (14) Côtes de Provence; west of Toulon. Ordinary to fair red table wine. France.

Gaudet-Saint-Julien, Château. (5) Côtes de

St-Emilion. *Grand cru classé côtes*. 1,000 dozen bottles of red bordeaux. France.

Gaudichots, Les. (8) Côte de Nuits; Vosne-Romanée vineyard. *Premier cru*. Red burgundy. France.

Gau-Grehweiler. (23) Palatinate; south of Bad Münster. Fair white table wine. West Germany.

Gau-Heppenheim. (24) Rhinehessia; west of Alsheim. Fair white table wine. West Germany.

Gaulsheim-Bingen. (24) Rhinehessia; just east of Bingen. Fair white table wine. West Germany.

Gau-Nieder-Weinheim. (24) Rhinehessia; near Gau Bickelheim east of Bad Kreuznach. Fair white table wine. West Germany.

Gau-Odernheim. (24) Rhinehessia; west of Alsheim. Ordinary to fair red and white table wines. West Germany.

Gauthey, Le Clos. (8) Côte de Beaune; Monthelie. *Premier cru*. Red burgundy. France.

Gauvain. (8) Hospice de Beaune *cuvée*. *AC Volnay-Santenots*. Red burgundy. France.

Gauvin, Château. (4) Blayais; Cars, east of Blaye. 1,500 dozen bottles of red bordeaux; 600 white. France.

Gavi. (26) Piedmont; Monferrati hills, Alessándria province. Ordinary to fair semi-sweet white table wine from Cortese white grapes. Italy.

Gay, Château Le. (5) Pomerol. 2,500 dozen bottles of red bordeaux. France.

Gazin, Château. (5) Graves de Bordeaux; Léognan. An unclassified *cru*. 1,200 dozen bottles of white bordeaux. France.

Gazin, Château. (5) Pomerol. *Grand cru*. 8,000 dozen bottles of red bordeaux. France.

Gazin-Montaigu, Château. (3) Blayais; Plassac, south of Blaye. 1,000 dozen bottles of red bordeaux. France.

Geddelsbach. (25) Württemberg; south-east of Heilbronn. Ordinary to fair red and white table wines. West Germany.

Gehaneweg. (24) Rhinehessia; Ockenheim vineyard, south-east of Bingen. Fair white table wine. West Germany.

Gehen. (23) Palatinate; Deidesheim vineyard. Fine white table wine. West Germany.

Gehitz. (24) Rhinegau; Hochheim vineyard. Fair white table wine. West Germany.

Gehren. (23) Palatinate; Deidesheim vineyard. Fair to fine white table wine. West Germany.

Gehren. (24) Rhinegau; Rauenthal vineyard. Fine white table wine. West Germany.

Geiersberg. (24) Rhinehessia; Worms and Bechtheim vineyards, north-west of Worms. Fair white table wines. West Germany.

Geierscheid. (24) Rhinehessia; Dienheim vineyard. Ordinary to fair white table wine. West Germany.

Geierskopf. (22) Moselle; Wintrich vineyard. Fair white table wine. West Germany.

Geierslay. (22) Moselle; Wintrich vineyard. Fair white table wine. West Germany.

Geierstein. (21) Rhinegau; Rauenthal vineyard. Fine white table wine. West Germany.

Geig. (24) Rhinehessia; Aspisheim vineyard, south-east of Bingen. Ordinary to fair white table wine. West Germany.

Geisberg. (22) Moselle; Trier vineyard. Ordinary to fair white table wine. West Germany.

Geisberg. (22) Saar; Ockfen vineyard. Fair to fine white table wine. West Germany.

Geisberg. (24) Rhinegau; Martinsthal vineyard. Fair white table wine. West Germany.

Geisenheim. (24) Rhinegau. Fair, fine and some very fine white table wines. West Germany.

Gellmersbach. (25) Württemberg; north-east of Heilbronn. Ordinary to fair red and white table wines. West Germany.

Gemark. (24) Rhinegau; Erbach vineyard. Fine white table wine. West Germany.

Gemarkgasse. (24) Rhinehessia; Nierstein vineyard. Fair to fine white table wine. West Germany.

Gemeaux. (8) Côte de Nuits; Gevrey-Chambertin vineyard. *Premier cru*. Red burgundy. France.

Gemmrigheim. (25) Württemberg; south-west of Heilbronn. Ordinary to fair red and white table wine. West Germany.

Geneau, Château de. (4) Cubzaguais, east of Blaye. 2,000 dozen bottles of red bordeaux; 1,000 white. France.

General Muteau. (8) Côte de Beaune; Volnay vineyard. One of the Hospices de Beaune *cuvées*. Red burgundy. France.

Genestière, Domaine de la. (12) Côtes du Rhône; Tavel. Fair to fine rosé table wine. France.

Genet, En. (8) Beaune. *Premier cru*. Red burgundy. France.

Geneva. (31) City and canton. 2,250 acres of vineyards. Mostly ordinary to fair table wines. Switzerland.

Genevrières, Les. (8) Côte de Beaune; Aloxe-Corton vineyard. *Deuxième cru*. Red burgundy. France.

Genevrières, Les. (8) Côte de Beaune; Meursault vineyard. *Premier cru*. White burgundy. France.

Gengenbach. (25) Baden. Ordinary to fair red and white table wine. West Germany.

Genheim. (24) Nahe; south-west of Bingerbrück. Fair white table wine. West Germany.

Gensingen. (24) Rhinehessia; between Bingen and Bad Kreuznach. Ordinary to fair red and white table wines. West Germany.

Gerbach. (23) Palatinate; south of Bad Münster.

Ordinary to fair red and white table wines. West Germany.

Gerbeaux, Les. (10) Mâconnais; Solutré vineyard. Entitled to the *AC Pouilly-Fuissé*. White burgundy. France.

Gerlachsheim. (25) Baden; south-west of Würzburg. Fair white table wine. West Germany.

Gerlingen. (25) Württemberg; west of Stuttgart. Ordinary to fair red table wine. West Germany.

Germany, Clos de. (31) Geneva canton; La Côte-Mont vineyard. Fair white table wine. Switzerland.

Gerolsheim. (23) Palatinate; south-west of Worms. Fair white table wine. West Germany.

Gerolzhofen. (25) Franconia; approx. twenty miles north-west of Würzburg. Fair white table wine. West Germany.

Gers. (2) *Département* of south-west France, north of the Pyrénées. France.

Gertwiller. (19) Bas-Rhin *département*; east of Barr. Ordinary to fair white Alsace wine. France.

Gerumpel. (23) Palatinate; Wachenheim vineyard. Fair white table wine. West Germany.

Geslets, Les. (16) Touraine; Bourgueil vineyard. Fair red table wine. France.

Getafe. (29) Madrid. Ordinary red table wine. Spain.

Gevrey-Chambertin. (8) Côte de Nuits. Fair, fine and some great red burgundy. France.

Geyersberg. (24) Rhinegau; Hallgarten vineyard. Fine white table wine. West Germany.

Geyerscheid. (24) Rhinehessia; Ludwigshöhe vineyard, between Oppenheim and Alsheim. Fair white table wine. West Germany.

Ghemme. (26) Piedmont; Novara province. Fair to good red wine, similar to Gattinara (q.v.), but not as fine. A locally consumed sweetish white wine is called Greco di Ghemme. Italy.

Gibson Wine Company. (36) California; Elk Grove. Table, dessert and sparkling wines; mostly berry and fruit wines but some grape wines also. U.S.A.

Gien, Côte de. (15) Upper Loire; above Orléans. Ordinary to fair white and rosé table wines. France.

Gigault, Château. (4) Blayais; Mazion, north-east of Blaye. 4,000 dozen bottles of red bordeaux; 500 white. France.

Gigondas. (12) Vaucluse *département*; Côtes du Rhône. Ordinary to fair red and rosé table wines. France.

Gigotte, La. (8) Volnay. *Premier cru*. Red burgundy. France.

Gilette, Château. (5) Sauternes; Preignac. *Cru bourgeois*. 4,000 dozen bottles of white bordeaux. France.

Gimbsheim. (24) Rhinehessia; east of Alsheim. Ordinary to fair red and white table wines. West Germany.

Giovi Rosso. (28) Campania; Salerno area. One of the better red table wines of the district. Italy.

Gippel. (22) Moselle; Nittel vineyard, north-west of Saarburg. Ordinary to fair white table wine. West Germany.

Girlaner Hugel. (26) Alto Adige; Merano area, north-west of Bolzano. Ordinary to fair mild and dry red table wine. Italy.

Girò. (28) Sardinia; Campidano di Cagliari, Cagliari area. Fair light dessert wine made from Girò grapes. Italy.

Giron, Domaine du. (5) Premières Côtes de Bordeaux; Haux, west of Podensac. 1,500 dozen bottles of white bordeaux. France.

Gironde. (3) The most important wine-producing *département*, of which Bordeaux is the chief city and centre. The Gironde is the tidal estuary formed by the junction of the Garonne and Dordogne rivers. France.

Girouette, Domaine de la. (4) Blayais; Fours, north-east of Blaye. 2,500 dozen bottles of red bordeaux; 2,500 white. France.

Girrardières, Les. (16) Touraine; Vouvray vineyard, just above Tours. Fair white table wine. France.

Giscours, Château. (4) Haut-Médoc; Labarde. *Troisième cru classé*. 20,000 dozen bottles of red bordeaux. France.

Giulianova (Bianco, Rosso). (27) Abruzzi. Ordinary white and very light, almost rosé, red table wines. Italy.

Giuramento. (26) Lombardy; Bergamo area. Fair, light, red table wine meant to be drunk young. Italy.

Glacier. (31) Valais canton; highest vineyards. White table wine. Switzerland.

Glana, Château du. (4) Haut-Médoc; St-Julien. *Cru bourgeois supérieur*. 20,000 dozen bottles of red bordeaux. France.

Gleisweiler. (23) Palatinate; Upper Haardt, north-west of Landau. Ordinary to fair red and white table wines. West Germany.

Glenloth. (37) Vineyard and winemaking business owned in turn by two pioneer families, then by Seager Evans, now by Allied Breweries (U.K.) and affiliated Australian interests. Australia.

Glenrowan. (37) North-east Victoria. Mostly quality red table wine. Australia.

Glenvale. (38) Bay Road, Hawke's Bay. Quality table wines. New Zealand.

Glock. (24) Rhinehessia; Nierstein vineyard. Fair white table wine. West Germany.

Glockenberg. (24) Rhinehessia; Gau-Bishofsheim

vineyard, west of Nackenheim. Fair white table wine. West Germany.

Glockenstrang. (24) Rhinehessia; Zornheim vineyard, north-west of Nierstein. Ordinary to fair white table wine. West Germany.

Glockenzeit. (23) Palatinate; Mussbach. Ordinary to fair white table wine. West Germany.

Gloria, Château. (4) Haut-Médoc; St-Julien. *Cru bourgeois*. 12,000 dozen bottles of red bordeaux. France.

Göcklingen. (23) Palatinate; south-west of Landau. Ordinary to fair red and white table wines. West Germany.

Godeau, Château. (5) St-Emilion; St Laurent-des-Combes, west of St Etienne-de-Lisse. An unclassified *cru* of St-Emilion. 1,500 dozen bottles of red bordeaux. France.

Godeaux, Les Petits. (8) Savigny-les-Beaune vineyard. *Premier cru*. Red burgundy. France.

Godramstein. (23) Palatinate; just north of Landau. Ordinary to fair red and white table wine. West Germany.

Gold. (33) Burgenland; south-east Austria, close to the Hungarian frontier. Ordinary to fair white table wine. Austria.

Goldbächel. (23) Palatinate; Wachenheim vineyard. Fair white table wine. West Germany.

Goldbrümchen. (22) Moselle; Ellenz-Poltersdorf vineyard. Fair white table wine. West Germany.

Goldgrübchen. (22) Moselle; Mesenich vineyard, west of Trier. Ordinary to fair white table wine. West Germany.

Goldgrube. (22) Moselle; Wolf vineyard, north-east of Graach. Ordinary to fair white table wine. West Germany.

Goldgrube. (24) Rhinehessia; Friesenheim vineyard, west of Dienheim. Ordinary to fair white table wine. West Germany.

Goldkupp. (22) Moselle; Mehring vineyard, south-west of Klüsscrath. Fair white table wine. West Germany.

Goldlay. (22) Moselle; Reil vineyard, east of Zell. Fair to fine white table wine. West Germany.

Goldloch. (24) Nahe; Dorsheim vineyard, south-west of Bingen. Fair white table wine. West Germany.

Goldmorgen. (23) Palatinate; Diedesfeld vineyard, between Kirrweiler and Neustadt. Fair white table wine. West Germany.

Goldschmidt. (23) Palatinate; Ruppertsberg vineyard. Fine white table wine. West Germany.

Goldtröpfchen. (22) Moselle; Piesport vineyard. Fine white table wine. West Germany.

Goldwingert. (22) Moselle; Graach vineyard. Fine white table wine. West Germany.

Gollebour. (32) Moselle; Machtum vineyards, just south of Grevenmacher. Ordinary to fair white table wine. Luxembourg.

Gombaude-Guillet, Château. (5) Pomerol. 2,500 dozen bottles of red bordeaux. France.

Gommersheim. (23) Palatinate; north-east of Landau. Ordinary to fair red and white table wines. West Germany.

Gontier, Château. (4) Blayais; Blaye. 12,500 dozen bottles of red bordeaux. France.

Goorjuani. (34) Western Georgia; bordering on Turkey and Black Sea. Ordinary to fair white table wine. U.S.S.R.

Gorgier-Chez-le-Bart. (31) Neuchâtel. Mostly fair white table wine. Switzerland.

Gossmannsdorf. (25) Franconia; south-east of Würzburg. Ordinary to fair red and white table wines. West Germany.

Gottenheim. (25) Baden; north-west of Freiburg. Ordinary to fair red and white table wines. West Germany.

Gottesacker. (23) Palatinate; Freinsheim vineyard. Ordinary to fair red and white table wines. West Germany.

Gottesacker. (24) Rhinegau; Niederwalluf vineyard. Fair white table wine. West Germany.

Gottesfüss. (22) Saar; Wiltingen vineyard. Fine white table wine. West Germany.

Gottesgarten. (24) Rhinehessia; Selzen vineyard west of Oppenheim. Ordinary to fair white table wine. West Germany.

Gotteshäuschen. (22) Moselle; Poltersdorf vineyard, near Achen. Ordinary to fair white table wine. West Germany.

Gotteshilfe. (24) Rhinehessia; Worms and Bechtheim vineyards, north-west of Worms. Ordinary white table wine. West Germany.

Gottestal. (24) Rhinegau; Oestrich vineyard. Fine white table wine. West Germany.

Gotzenfels. (24) Nahe; Norheim vineyard, just south-west of Bad Münster. Fair white table wine. West Germany.

Goureau. (8) Côte de Beaune; Meursault. Hospices de Beaune *cuvée*. White burgundy. France.

Goutte d'Or. (16) Anjou; Savennières vineyard, below Angers. Fair, popular white table wine. France.

Goutte d'Or. (8) Côte de Beaune; Meursault vineyard. *Premier cru*. White burgundy. France.

Goyener Riesling. (26) Alto Adige; Merano area, north-west of Bolzano. Fair white table wine. Italy.

Graach. (22) Middle Moselle. Fair, fine and some very fine white table wines. West Germany.

Graben. (22) Moselle; Bernkastel vineyard. Fine white table wine. West Germany.

Grâce-Dieu, Cru. (5) Côtes de St-Emilion. An unclassified *cru*. 1,500 dozen bottles of red bordeaux. France.

Graciano. (29) Navarre province. Very dark red, dry ordinary table wine. Spain.

Grafels. (22) Moselle; Kiedrich vineyard. Fair white table wine. West Germany.

Grafenberg. (22) Moselle; Piesport vineyard. Fair to fine white table wine. West Germany.

Grafenhausen. (23) Palatinate; north-west of Landau. Ordinary to fair red and white table wine. West Germany.

Gräfenhausen. (25) Württemberg; south-east of Karlsruhe. Ordinary to fair red and white table wine. West Germany.

Gragnano. (28) Campania; bay of Naples. Ordinary dry red and white wines. Italy.

Grain. (23) Palatinate; vineyard in Deidesheim, Neustadt-an-der-Haardt, and Hambach, between Neustadt and Edenkoben. Fair to fine white table wine. West Germany.

Grainhubel. (23) Palatinate; Deidesheim vineyard. Fine white table wine. West Germany.

Grand-Arnaud. (4) Premières Côtes de Bordeaux; Carignan, east of Bordeaux. 2,000 dozen bottles of red bordeaux; 200 white. France.

Grand-Barrail-Lamarzelle-Figeac, Château. (5) Côtes de St-Emilion. *Grand cru classé*. 12,000 dozen bottles of red bordeaux. France.

Grand Brulé. (31) Vaud canton; Riddes vineyard. Fair white table wine. Switzerland.

Grand Chablis. Another *Appellation Contrôlée* for *Chablis grand cru* given to the wines from the finest sites of Chablis. Actually totally unused, if not obsolete. France.

Grand-Clapaud-Olivier, Château. (4) Haut-Médoc; Blanquefort. *Cru bourgeois*. 2,500 dozen bottles of red bordeaux. France.

Grand-Clos. (16) Touraine; Bourgueil vineyard. Fair red table wine. France.

Grand-Duroc-Milon, Château. (4) Haut-Médoc; Pauillac. *Cru bourgeois*. 1,500 dozen bottles of red bordeaux. France.

Grande Champagne. (20) Charente *département*; vineyards on the left bank of the river Charente, near Cognac. The white wines, when distilled, produce the finest Cognac. France.

Grande Côte, La. (15) Cher *département*; Amigny vineyard, Sancerre district. Fair white table wine. France.

Grand Enclos du Chateau de Cérons. (5) Graves de Bordeaux; Cérons. An unclassified *cru*. 13,000 dozen bottles of white bordeaux. France.

Grande Plantée. (12) Côte Rôtie; Ampuis. Fine red table wine. France.

Grande Roche. (16) Anjou; Coteaux de la Loire; Savennières vineyard, Angers. Fair to fine white table wine. France.

Grande Rue. (8) Côte de Nuits; Vosne-Romanée. *Premier cru*. Red burgundy. France.

Grandes Côtes de Chavignol. (15) Cher *département*; Chavignol, Sancerre area. Fair to fine white table wine. France.

Grandes-Murailles, Château. (5) Côtes de St-Emilion. *Grand cru classé côtes.* 1,000 dozen bottles of red bordeaux. France.

Grandes Versaines. (5) Néac, *commune* east of Pomerol. 2,000 dozen bottles of red bordeaux. France.

Grandes Vignes, Clos des. (8) Côte de Nuits; Prémeaux vineyard. *Premier cru*. Red burgundy. France.

Grandes-Vignes, Clos des. (5) Preignac. *Cru bourgeois*. 800 dozen bottles of red bordeaux. France.

Grandes Vignes, Les. (8) Côte de Beaune; Auxey-Duresses vineyard. White burgundy. France.

Grandes Vignes, Les. (8) Côte de Nuits; Prémeaux vineyard. *Deuxième cru*. Red burgundy. France.

Grandes Vignes, Les. (9) Touchés; Bourgneuf Val d'Or. Red burgundy. France.

Grand Vigne. (12) Côte Rôtie; Ampuis. Fine red table wine. France.

Grand-Faurie, Château le. (5) Côtes de St-Emilion. An unclassified *cru*. 1,500 dozen bottles of red bordeaux. France.

Grand-Faurie, Domaine du. (5) Côtes de St-Emilion. An unclassified *cru*. 2,000 dozen bottles of red bordeaux. France.

Grand-Gibet, Le. (16) Touraine; Bourgueil vineyard. Fair red table wine. France.

Grand-Gonteil, Château. (5) Côtes de St-Emilion. An unclassified *cru*. 600 dozen bottles of red bordeaux. France.

Grand-Goulet, Château du. (12) Côtes du Rhône; Châteauneuf-du-Pape. Fair to fine red table wine. France.

Grandjo. (30) Brand of a fine sweet white table wine first sold in 1909. Portugal.

Grand-Jour, Château. (3) Bourgeais. 12,500 dozen bottles of red bordeaux; 1,500 white. France.

Grandmaison, Domaine de. (5) Graves de Bordeaux; Léognan. An unclassified *cru*. 500 dozen bottles of red bordeaux; 500 white are produced. France.

Grand-Mayne, Château. (5) Côtes de St-Emilion. St-Emilion *grand cru classé*. 6,000 dozen bottles of red bordeaux. France.

Grand-Mirande, Château. (5) Côtes de St-Emilion. An unclassified *cru*. 4,000 dozen bottles of red bordeaux. France.

Grandmont. (16) Touraine; Benais vineyard, Bourgueil. Fair red table wine. France.

Grand-Moueys, Château du. (5) Premières Côtes de Bordeaux; Capian, north-west of Loupiac. 10,000 dozen bottles of red bordeaux; 10,000 white. France.

Grand-Ormeau, Château. (5) Lalande de Pomerol; north of Pomerol. 2,500 dozen bottles of red bordeaux. France.

Grand-Ormeau, Cru. (5) Lalande de Pomerol; north of Pomerol. 1,000 dozen bottles of red bordeaux. France.

Grand-Ormeau, Domaine du. (5) Lalande de Pomerol; north of Pomerol. 3,000 dozen bottles of red bordeaux. France.

Grand-Pey-Lescours, Château. (5) St-Emilion; St Sulpice-de-Faleyrens. An unclassified *cru*. 12,500 dozen bottles of red bordeaux. France.

Grand-Peyrot, Château du. (5) Ste Croix-du-Mont, Entre-deux-Mers. 400 dozen bottles of red bordeaux; 2,000 white. France.

Grand Pin, Le. (14) Côtes de Provence; Cassis vineyard. Fair red and rosé table wines. France.

Grand-Pirouet. (16) Anjou; Chalonne-sur-Loire, south-west of Angers. Fair white table wine. France.

Grand-Pontet, Château. (5) Côtes de St-Emilion. St-Emilion *grand cru classé*. 5,000 dozen bottles of red bordeaux. France.

Grand-Porto, Domaine de. (4) Cubzaguais, east of Blayé. 2,500 dozen bottles of red bordeaux; 2,500 white. France.

Grand-Puy-Ducasse, Château. (4) Haut-Médoc; Pauillac. *Cinquième cru classé*. 4,000 dozen bottles of red bordeaux. France.

Grand-Puy-Ducasse, Château. (4) Haut-Médoc; (4) Haut-Médoc; Pauillac. *Cinquième cru classé*. 10,000 dozen bottles of red bordeaux. France.

Grand Roussillon. (13) *AC* of the better Roussillon dessert wines. France.

Grand-Saint-Julien, Château. (4) St-Julien. *Cru bourgeois supérieur*. 2,000 dozen bottles of red bordeaux. France.

Grands-Champs. (16) Touraine; Restigné vineyard, below Tours. Fair red table wine. France.

Grands-Champs, Les. (8) Côte de Beaune; Auxey-Duresses vineyard. *Premier cru*. Red burgundy. France.

Grands-Champs. (8) Côte de Beaune; Puligny-Montrachet vineyard. *Deuxième cru*. Good white burgundy. France.

Grands-Champs. (8) Côte de Beaune; Volnay vineyard. *Premier cru*. Red burgundy. France.

Grands-Echézeaux, Les. (8) Côte de Nuits; Flagey-Echézeaux vineyard. *Grand cru*. Red burgundy. France.

Grands-Murs, Les. (8) Côte de Nuits; Chambolle-Musigny vineyard. *Deuxième cru*. Red burgundy. France.

Grands-Picotins. (8) Côte de Beaune; Savigny-les-Beaune vineyard. *Deuxième et troisième cru*. Red burgundy. France.

Grands-Poisots. (8) Côte de Beaune; Volnay vineyard. *Deuxième et troisième cru*. Red burgundy. France.

Grands-Voyens. (9) Chalonnais; Mercurey vineyard. *Premier cru*. Red burgundy. France.

Grand-Village-Capbern, Château. (4) Haut-Médoc; St-Estèphe. *Cru bourgeois*. 10,000 dozen bottles of red bordeaux. France.

Gran Canaria. (40) Canary Islands; Las Palmas, off the north-west coast of Africa. Ordinary sweet white wine. Spain.

Gran Furor Divina Costiera Bianco. (28) Campania; Furore vineyard, Salerno area. Ordinary to fair white table wine, a little sweet. Italy.

Gran Furor Divina Costiera Rosso. (28) Campania; Salerno area. Ordinary to fair red table wine. Italy.

Grange-Marquis-de-Lupe, Château La. (4) Blayais; Blayé. 2,500 dozen bottles of red bordeaux. France.

Granich. (23) Palatinate; Forst vineyard. Fine white table wine. West Germany.

Granja, Quinta. (30) *Região demarcada do Douro* (q.v.). An interesting estate and vineyard of 40 acres in Cambres south-west of Régua. Portugal.

Gran Moscato. (26) Lombardy; Santa Maria della Versa, Pavia province. Fair golden dessert wine. Italy.

Gran Spumante di Canneto. (26) Lombardy. Ordinary white sparkling wine which is marketed as *secco*, *semi-secco* and *abbocato*, i.e. dry, medium-dry and sweet. Italy.

Gran Spumante la Versa. (26) Lombardy. Another name for a white sparkling wine like the Gran Spumante di Canneto (q.v.). Italy.

Grantschen. (25) Württemberg; east of Heilbronn. Ordinary to fair red and white table wine. West Germany.

Grao, El. (29) Valencia. Ordinary red table wine. Spain.

Gratallops. (29) Tarragona; Priorato. Ordinary red table wine. Spain.

Grauberg. (22) Moselle; Ürzig, west of Kinheim, south-east of Piesport, vineyards. Fair white table wine. West Germany.

Grauves. (17) Marne *département*; Avize canton,

I

west of Avize. Rated *premier cru*—black 90% growth, white 93%. 386 acres. France.

Grava, Château du. (5) Premières Côtes de Bordeaux; Haux, north of Podensac. 1,000 dozen bottles of red bordeaux; 5,000 white. France.

Gravains, Aux. (8) Côte de Beaune; Savigny-les-Beaunes vineyard. *Premier cru*. Red burgundy. France.

Grave, Château La. (3) Fronsac, Fronsadais. 2,000 dozen bottles of red bordeaux. France.

Graves, Vin de. (3, 5) Usually means an ordinary or fair white table wine from the Graves de Bordeaux area vineyards. France.

Graves-de-Bordeaux. (3, 5) Vineyards south of Blanquefort, along the left bank of the river Garonne as far as and beyond the Sauternes district. It is the only part of Bordeaux where both the red and white wines are equally well-known. White graves is one of the most popular basic white wines. France.

Graves-de-Saint-Emilion. (5) Gironde *département*. The vineyards on the strip of land on the lower gravelly slopes of the hill upon which stands the town of St-Emilion. France.

Graves-de-Vayres. (3, 5) The district across the river Dordogne opposite the southern end of the Côtes de Fronsac. Also the *AC* given to the better red wines of the district so called because of its gravelly soil. France.

Graves-Geyrosse. (5) Sables de St-Emilion. An unclassified *cru*. 1,200 dozen bottles of red bordeaux. France.

Gravières, Les. (8) Côte de Beaune; Santenay vineyard. *Premier cru*. Red burgundy. France.

Gray. (16) Touraine; Côte de Montlouis; Lussault vineyard. Fair white table wine. France.

Great Western. (37) Victoria; approx. 100 miles north-west of Geelong. Small township chiefly famous for the sparkling wine bearing its name. Australia.

Greco di Gerace. (28) Reggio di Calabria area. Distinguished amber dessert wine, from Greco di Gerace grapes. Italy.

Greco di Tufo. (28) Campania; Avellino province. Ordinary, dry and semi-sweet white wine, often *frizzante* from Greco del Vesuvio grapes. Italy.

Greco Rizziconi. A popular brand of Greco di Gerace (q.v.). Italy.

Greco Rosso di Pontegrande. (28) Calabria; Cantanzaro. Ordinary to fair cherry-red table wine. Italy.

Greece. (34) One of the most ancient wine-growing countries of Europe, with over 500,000 acres. Today its table grapes and sultanas are perhaps better known abroad than its wines, although

more than 50% of the total acreage produces wine.

Greffieux, Les. (12) Côtes du Rhône; Tain l'Hermitage vineyard. Fair red table wine. France.

Greismund. (22) Moselle; Pommern vineyard, north-east of Valwig. Fair white table wine. West Germany.

Greiveldange. (32) Moselle; east of Luxembourg city. Ordinary to fair white table wine. Luxembourg.

Grelots, Clos des. (31) Vaud canton; Blonay-sur-Vevey vineyard. Fair white table wine. Switzerland.

Grenache. (13) The name of a grape grown chiefly in Roussillon and also the name of the tawny, unfortified dessert wine made from it. France.

Grenouilles. (6) North-east of Chablis. One of the few vineyards of the *commune* of Chablis with the *AC grand cru*, other *grand crus* lying in neighbouring *communes*. Fine white burgundy. France.

Grenzach. (25) Baden; south-west of Freiburg. Fair white table wine. West Germany.

Gresigny. (9) Chalonnais; Rully. *Premier cru*. White burgundy. France.

Gresille, La. (16) Touraine; Cravant-les-Coteaux, south-east of Chinon. Fair red table wine. France.

Gresilles, Les. (16) Touraine; Beaumont-en-Véron vineyard, below Chinon. Fair red table wine. France.

Grèves, Les. (8) Beaune vineyard. *Premier cru*. Red burgundy. France.

Grèves, Les. (8) Côte de Beaune; Aloxe-Corton vineyard. *Premier cru*. Red burgundy. France.

Grewenich. (22) Moselle; west of Trier. Ordinary to fair white table wine. West Germany.

Grézolle, Domaine de la. (5) St-Emilion; St Sulpice-de-Faleyrens. An unclassified *cru*. 2,500 dozen bottles of red bordeaux. France.

Griffith. (37) New South Wales; approx. 175 miles north-east of Swan Hill in the Murrumbridge Irrigation Area. Important region of wineries and vineyards. Australia.

Grigionasco. (26) Piedmont; Novara province. Ordinary red table wine. Italy.

Grigioni. (26) Lombardy; Sondrio, chief town of the Vallentina region. Ordinary red table wine. Italy.

Grignolino. (26) Piedmont. A grape much grown in this area. Also a fair to good red table wine from it known as Grignolino d'Asti. Italy.

Grille, Château de la. (16) Touraine; Chinon vineyard. Fair red table wine. France.

Grillet, Château. (12) Côtes du Rhône; Condrieu. Fine white table wine. France.

Grillette, La. (31) Neuchâtel, Cressier vineyard. Fair white table wine. Switzerland.

Grimmen. (24) Rhinegau; Eltville vineyard. Fine white table wine. West Germany.

Grinatino. (26) Lombardy; Bellagio, on Lake Como north-east of Como. Fair red table wine. Italy.

Grinzing. (33) Vienna district; north-west of city centre. Ordinary white table wine mostly drunk within the first weeks and months after being made each year. Austria.

Griotte-Chambertin. (8) Côte de Nuits; Gevrey-Chambertin vineyard. *Grand cru*. Red burgundy. France.

Grk. (33) Central Dalmatian coast. Dry, white, very full table wine. Yugoslavia.

Groerd. (32) Moselle; Grevenmacher vineyard. Ordinary to fair white table wine. Luxembourg.

Grolet, Château La. (3) St Ciers-de-Cannesse, north-west of Bourg. 8,000 dozen bottles of red bordeaux; 2,000 white. France.

Grolet, Château la. (4) St Ciers-de-Canesse, north-west of Bourg. 8,000 dozen bottles of red bordeaux; 2,000 white. France.

Grolsheim. (24) Rhinehessia; south of Bingen. Ordinary to fair red and white table wines. West Germany.

Grombalia. (40) North-east part of the country. Chief wine-producing area. Tunisia.

Gronau. (25) Württemberg; south-east of Heilbronn. Ordinary to fair red and white table wines. West Germany.

Gros-Caillou, Château. (5) St-Emilion; St Sulpice-de-Faleyrens. An unclassified *cru*. 4,000 dozen bottles of red bordeaux. France.

Gros Plant. (16) Loire-Atlantique *département*. Ordinary to fair *V.D.Q.S.* white table wines from the last vineyards on the right bank of the Loire before the river reaches the Atlantic. France.

Grossbockenheim. (23) Palatinate; north of Grünstadt. Ordinary to fair red and white table wines. West Germany.

Grossbottwar. (25) Württemberg, south-east of Heilbronn. Ordinary to fair red and white table wines. West Germany.

Grosser Herrgott. (22) Moselle; Wintrich vineyard. Fair white table wine. West Germany.

Grosse Roche, La. (12) Côtes du Rhône; Ampuis. Fair to fine red wine. France.

Grossfischlingen. (23) Palatinate; south-east of Edenkoben. Ordinary to fair red and white table wines. West Germany.

Grossgartach. (25) Württemberg; east of Heilbronn. Ordinary to fair red and white table wines. West Germany.

Grossheppach. (25) Württemberg; east of Stuttgart. Ordinary to fair red and white table wines. West Germany.

Grossheubach. (25) Franconia; south-east of Darmstadt. Ordinary to fair red and white table wines. West Germany.

Grosskarlbach. (23) Palatinate; Lower Haardt, south-east of Grünstadt. Ordinary red and white table wines. West Germany.

Grosslangheim. (25) Franconia; approx. twenty-five miles north of Mosbach. Fair white table wine. West Germany.

Grosslay. (22) Moselle; Müden vineyard, north-east of Valwig. Fair white table wine. West Germany.

Grossniedesheim. (23) Palatinate; south-west of Worms. Ordinary to fair red and white table wines. West Germany.

Grossostheim. (25) Franconia; approx. forty miles north of Mosbach. Ordinary to fair red and white table wines. West Germany.

Gross-Sachsen. (21) Baden; Bergstrasse; north of Heidelberg. Ordinary to fair red and white table wines. West Germany.

Gross-Umstadt. (21) Baden, Bergstrasse; Hesse, east of Darmstadt. Fair white table wine. West Germany.

Grosswallstadt. (21) Franconia; approx. twenty-two miles east of Darmstadt. Ordinary to fair red and white table wines. West Germany.

Gross-Winternheim. (24) Rhinehessia; south of Erbach. Ordinary to fair red and white table wines. West Germany.

Grottaferrata. (27) Lazio; vineyard adjoining the Frascati vineyards outside Rome. Ordinary to fair white table wine. Italy.

Grottaglie. (28) Apulia; Taranto area. Strong, coarse, red wines used mainly for blending. Italy.

Gruenchers, Les. (8) Côte de Nuits; Chambolle-Musigny. *Premier cru*. Red burgundy. France.

Grumello. (26) Lombardy; Sondrio vineyard, chief town of the Veltellina province. Very good red wine, said to be its best after four years in the bottle. Italy.

Grünberg. (24) Nahe. Fair to fine white table wine. West Germany.

Grünstadt. (23) Palatinate. Ordinary to fair red and white table wines. West Germany.

Guadalajara 'Pardillo'. (29) Guadalajara; north-east of Madrid. Ordinary to fair white table wine. Spain.

Guadalcazar. (29) North-central Andalusia; Córdoba, north-east of Seville. Fair white table wine. Spain.

Guadix. (29) Andalusia; Granada, between Málaga and Baza. Ordinary red table wine. Spain.

Guanajuato. (35) Central Mexico. Ordinary to fair table wines. Mexico.

Guarena. (29) Estremadura; Badajoz, between Seville and Trujillo. Ordinary red and white table wines. Spain.

Guckingsland. (23) Palatinate; Neustadt vineyard. Fair white table wine. West Germany.

Gueberschwihr. (19) Haut-Rhin *département*; north-west of Pfaffenheim. Ordinary to fair white Alsace wine. France.

Guebwiller. (19) Haut-Rhin *département*. Fair to fine white Alsace wine. France.

Gué d'Amant, Le. (16) Touraine; Vouvray vineyard, just above Tours. Fair to fine white wine. France.

Guerets, Les. (8) Côte de Beaune; Aloxe-Corton vineyard. *Premier cru*. Fine red burgundy. France.

Guettes, Aux. (8) Côte de Beaune; Savigny-les-Beaune vineyard. *Premier cru*. Red burgundy. France.

Guerry, Château. (3) Tauriac, north-east of Bourg. 4,000 dozen bottles of red bordeaux; 500 white. France.

Güglingen. (25) Württemberg; south-west of Heilbronn. Ordinary to fair red and white table wines. West Germany.

Guibeau, Château. (5) St-Emilion; Puisseguin. An unclassified *cru*. 18,000 dozen bottles of red bordeaux. France.

Guibeau-La Fourvieille, Château. (5) St-Emilion; Puisseguin. An unclassified *cru*. 10,000 dozen bottles of red bordeaux. France.

Guidonnière, La. (16) Touraine; Jasnières vineyard, below Angers. Fair white table wine. France.

Guiet, Clos du. (16) Touraine; Bourgueil vineyard. Fair red table wine. France.

Guild Wine Company. (36) (Wine Growers Guild.) California; Lodi. Table, dessert and sparkling wines, brandy and vermouth are produced. U.S.A.

Guillons, Les. (10) Beaujolais; St-Amour vineyard. One of the top-grade red beaujolais. France.

Guillons, Les. (11) Beaujolais; Juliénas vineyard. One of the top-grade beaujolais. France.

Guillou, Château. (5) St-Emilion; St-Georges. An unclassified *cru*. 2,000 dozen bottles of red bordeaux. France.

Guimonières, Les. (16) Anjou; Coteaux du Layon, Chaume vineyard, south of Angers. Fine white table wine. France.

Guinot, Château. (5) St-Emilion; St Etienne-de-Lisse. An unclassified *cru*. 1,500 dozen bottles of red bordeaux. France.

Guiraud, Château. (5) Sauternes. *Premier cru classé*. 8,000 dozen bottles of white bordeaux. France.

Guitara. (29) Guipuzcoa; north-east Basque Provinces. Ordinary, sharp, low-strength red and white table wines. Spain.

Guiteronde, Château. (5) Barsac; Sauternes area. *Cru bourgeois*. 1,000 dozen bottles of white bordeaux. France.

Guldenmorgen. (24) Rhinehessia; Dienheim and Zornheim vineyards, north-west of Nierstein. Fair white table wine. West Germany.

Gumben. (24) Rhinehessia; Dienheim vineyard. Ordinary to fair white table wine. West Germany.

Gumbsheim. (24) Rhinehessia; east of Bad Münster. Ordinary to fair white table wine. West Germany.

Gumpoldskirchen. (33) Town south of Vienna. Popular, fair to fine white table wine. Austria.

Guncina (Guntschna). (26) Alto Adige, Bolzano area. Fair soft red table wine which improves with bottle age. Italy.

Gündelbach. (25) Württemberg; approx. sixteen miles north-west of Stuttgart. Ordinary to fair red and white table wines. West Germany.

Gundelfingen. (25) Baden; north of Freiburg. Fair white table wine. West Germany.

Gundelsheim. (25) Württemberg; north-west of Heilbronn. Ordinary to fair table wines. West Germany.

Gundheim. (24) Rhinehessia; north-west of Worms. Ordinary to fair red and white table wines. West Germany.

Guntersblum. (24) Rhinehessia; between Alsheim and Dienheim. Ordinary to fair, and some fine red and white table wines. West Germany.

Güntersleben. (25) Franconia; north of Würzburg. Fair red and white table wines. West Germany.

Guntherslay. (22) Moselle; Piesport and Niederemmel, opposite Piesport, vineyards. Fair white table wine. West Germany.

Gurgue, Château La. (4) Haut-Médoc; Margaux. *Cru bourgeois supérieur*. 3,000 dozen bottles of red bordeaux. France.

Gussago. (26) Lombardy; Colli Bresciani, hills north of Brescia. Ordinary to fair, sweetish, brilliantly red table wine to be drunk young. Italy.

Gutenberg. (24) Nahe; north-west of Bad Kreuznach. Fair white table wine. West Germany.

Gutenberg. (24) Rhinegau; Winkel vineyard. Fine white table wine. West Germany.

Gutturnio. (26) Emilia-Romagna; Piacenza area. Clear, dryish bright red table wine intended to be drunk young and usually served cool. Italy.

Gyöngyös. (33) Approx. forty-five miles north-east of Budapest. Ordinary to fair red and white table wines; also some sparkling wine. Hungary.

♣

Haardt. (23) Palatinate. Fair to fine white table wine. West Germany.

Haardtberg. (21) Ahr; Dernau vineyard, west of Linz. Fair red table wine. West Germany.

Haberschlacht. (25) Württemberg; south-east of Heilbronn. Ordinary to fair red and white table wines. West Germany.

Hackenheim. (24) Rhinehessia; just south-east of Bad Kreuznach. Ordinary to fair red and white table wines. West Germany.

Hackgraben. (25) Württemberg; Gundesheim vineyard, north-west of Worms. Ordinary to fair white table wine. West Germany.

Hafenberg. (24) Rhinehessia; Worms and Becht-heim vineyards, north-west of Worms. Fair white wine. West Germany.

Häfnerhaslach. (25) Württemberg; south-west of Heilbronn. Ordinary to fair red and white table wines. West Germany.

Hagnau. (25) Lake Constance (Bodensee); east of Konstanz. Ordinary to fair red and white table wines. West Germany.

Hahl. (24) Rhinehessia; Alsheim. Fair white table wine. West Germany.

Hahlkreuz. (24) Rhinehessia; Nackenheim vine-yard. Fair white table wine. West Germany.

Hahn. (21) Middle Rhine; Bacharach vineyard, north-west of Bingen. Ordinary to fair white table wine. West Germany.

Hahn. (22) Moselle; Beilstein vineyard, south of Bruttig. Fair white table wine. West Germany.

Hahnen. (22) Moselle; Ürzig vineyard, west of Kinheim. Fine white table wine. West Germany.

Hahnenkampf. (24) Nahe; Bretzenheim vine-yard, north-east of Bad Kreuznach. Fair white table wine. West Germany.

Haie-Longue, La. (16) Anjou; Coteaux du Layon, St Aubin-de-Luigné vineyard, south of Angers. Fair white table wine. France.

Haie-Longue, La. (16) Anjou; Coteaux du Layon, Chaudefonds vineyard, south of Angers. Fair white table wine. France.

Haie-Martel. (16) Touraine; Cravant-les-Coteaux, south-east of Chinon. Ordinary to fair red table wine. France.

Hakutsuru. (1) One of the best and largest pro-ducers of the rice wine, Sake (q.v.). The name means 'White Crane', which is a symbol of good luck. Japan.

Halbrot. Light red, or rosé, dry table wine from black and white grapes pressed together; ordi-nary but refreshing wine, similar to the German *Schillerwein* (q.v.). Switzerland.

Halinga. (33) South-west Rumania; Oltenia. Fair, dry, red table wine made from Pinot Noir grapes. Rumania.

Hallauer. (31) Schaffhausen canton. Ordinary to fair red table wine. Switzerland.

Hallet, Château. (3) Barsac. *Cru bourgeois.* 3,000 dozen bottles white bordeaux. France.

Halletière, Clos de la. (16) Touraine; Ste-Radegonde vineyard, just above Tours. Fair white table wine. France.

Hallgarten. (24) Rhinegau. Fair fine and some very fine white table wine. West Germany.

Halmheim. (24) Rhinehessia; Oppenheim vine-yard. Fair white table wine. West Germany.

Halsbach. (22) Moselle; Kröv vineyard, east of Kinheim. Fair white table wine. West Germany.

Halsberg. (22) Moselle; Trarbach vineyard. Fair white table wine. West Germany.

Haltingen. (25) Baden; approx. twenty-eight miles south-west of Freiburg. Fair white table wine. West Germany.

Hambach. (24) Baden, Bergstrasse; Hesse, north-east of Mannheim. Fair white table wine. West Germany.

Hambach. (23) Palatinate; Upper Haardt. Ordi-nary, fair and some fine table wine. West Germany.

Hambledon. (1) Hampshire; south-central England. 4½ acres. Ordinary to fair white table wine. England.

Hameau de la Milletière. (16) Touraine; Mont-louis. Fair white table wine. France.

Hameau du Cormier. (16) Touraine; Montlouis. Fair white table wine. France.

Hamilton's Ewell Vineyard. (37) South Australia; Warradale, outer Adelaide suburb. One of the two earliest vineyards and wineries of the Adelaide area. Land was purchased in 1837 by ancestor of present owner-family. Produces all types of wine, also whiskey. Australia.

Hamm. (21) Middle Rhine; Boppard vineyard, south of Koblenz. Ordinary to fair white table wine. West Germany.

Hamm. (22) Moselle; Winningen vineyard. Fair white table wine. West Germany.

Hammelburg. (25) Franconia; approx. fifty miles east of Frankfurt-am-Main. Fair white table wine. West Germany.

Hammerstein. (21) Middle Rhine; north-west of Koblenz. Ordinary to fair red and white table wine. West Germany.

Hammerstein. (22) Moselle; Avelsbach vineyard, at juncture of Moselle and Ruwer. Ordinary to fair white table wine. West Germany.

Hammondsport. (35) Northern New York State; Lake Keuka. Principal wine centre of the Finger Lakes vineyards. U.S.A.

Hanach. (24) Rhinegau; Eltville vineyard. Fair to fine white table wine. West Germany.

Hand. (24) Rhinehessia; Guntersblum vineyard, between Alsheim and Dienheim. Fair white table wine. West Germany.

Handelberg. (24) Rhinegau; Hallgarten vineyard. Fair to fine white table wine. West Germany.

Hangen-Weisheim. (24) Rhinehessia; southwest of Alsheim. Ordinary to fair red and white table wines. West Germany.

Hannetot, Château Le. (5) Graves de Bordeaux; Léognan. An unclassified *cru*. 1,000 dozen bottles of red bordeaux; 500 white. France.

Hannteillan, Château. (4) Haut-Médoc; Cissac. *Cru bourgeois*. 15,000 dozen bottles of red bordeaux. France.

Hansenberg. (24) Rhinegau; Johannisberg vineyard. Fair to fine white table wine. West Germany.

Hanweiler. (25) Württemberg; north-east of Stuttgart. Ordinary to fair red and white table wines. West Germany.

Hanzell Vineyard. (36) California; Sonoma County. Quality table wines from Pinot Noir and Chardonnay grapes. U.S.A.

Hardy's Tintara Winery. (37) South Australia; main winery at McLaren Vale, approx. twenty-five miles south of Adelaide. Head office in Adelaide. Thomas Hardy planted his first vineyard in the Adelaide suburb in 1853 and bought Tintara, McLaren Vale in 1873. Branch wineries in Barossa Valley, thirty-five miles north-east of Adelaide and at Waikerie (River Murray).

Harff. (25) Franconia; Würzburg. Site of the Stein vineyard. Fine white table wine. West Germany.

Hargesheim. (24) Nahe; north-east of Bad Kreuznach. Fair to fine white table wine. West Germany.

Hargue, La. (4) Plassac; south of Blayé. 4,000 dozen bottles of red bordeaux. France.

Haro. (29) Capital of the province of Logroño in Old Castile and centre of the La Rioja area where the finest Spanish red, and many white, table wines are produced. Spain.

Hartenberg. (24) Rhinehessia; Harxheim vineyard, west of Nackenheim. Fair white table wine. West Germany.

Harxheim. (23) Palatinate; Lower Haardt, north-west of Grünstadt. Ordinary to fair white table wines. West Germany.

Harxheim. (24) Rhinehessia; west of Nackenheim.

Ordinary, fair and fine white table wine. West Germany.

Hasandede. (34) Ankara. Ordinary to fair red and white table wines. Turkey.

Haschen. (22) Moselle; Dhron, between Neumagen and Wintrich, and Kröv, east of Kinheim vineyards. Fair white table wine. West Germany.

Hasenbiss. (24) Rhinehessia; Osthofen vineyard, between Worms and Alsheim. Fair white table wine. West Germany.

Hasenlauf. (23) Palatinate; Kallstadt vineyard. Fair to fine white table wine. West Germany.

Hasenlauf. (24) Rhinehessia; Dromersheim vineyard, south-east of Bingen. Fair white table wine. West Germany.

Hasenlaufer. (22) Moselle; Brauneberg vineyard. Fair to fine white table wine. West Germany.

Hasensprung. (22) Moselle; Ediger just east of Eller. Fair white table wine. West Germany.

Hasensprung. (24) Rhinegau; Winkel vineyard. Fine white table wine. West Germany.

Hasensprung. (24) Rhinehessia; Gau-Algesheim vineyard, south of Mittelheim. Fair white table wine. West Germany.

Hassel. (24) Rhinegau; Hattenheim vineyard, south-west of Erbach. Fair to fine white table wine. West Germany.

Hates, Les. (9) Chalonnais; St-Martin-sous-Montaigu. *Premier cru*. Red burgundy. France.

Hattenheim. (24) Rhinegau; Hattenheim vineyard, south-west of Erbach. Fair, fine and very fine white table wines. West Germany.

Hattstatt. (19) Haut-Rhin *département*; north-east of Pfaffenheim. Ordinary to medium white Alsace wine. France.

Hatzenport. (22) Moselle; south of Kobern. Ordinary to fair white table wine. West Germany.

Hauben. (24) Rhinehessia; Nieder Saulheim vineyard, west of Nierstein. Fair white table wine. West Germany.

Haura. Château. (5) Illats. 600 dozen bottles of red bordeaux; 5,000 white. France.

Häuschen. (24) Rhinehessia; Laubenheim vineyard. Fair white table wine. West Germany.

Hauserweg. (24) Rhinegau; Rüdesheim vineyard. Fair to fine white table wine. West Germany.

Haut-Bailly, Château. (5) Graves de Bordeaux; Léognan. *Cru classé de Graves en rouge.* 6,000 dozen bottles of red bordeaux. France.

Haut-Barsac. (3) A non-official name given to those white wines of Barsac, in the official Sauternes area, which are somewhat better than plain 'Barsac'. France.

Haut-Batailley, Château. (4) Haut-Médoc; Pauillac. *Cinquième cru classé.* 7,000 dozen bottles of red bordeaux. France.

Haut-Bergeron, Château. (5) Graves de Bordeaux; Preignac. *Cru bourgeois*. 1,500 dozen bottles of white bordeaux. France.

Haut-Bommes, Château. (5) Bommes, Sauternes area. *Cru bourgeois*. 1,500 dozen bottles of white bordeaux. France.

Haut-Brion, Château. (5) Graves de Bordeaux; Pessac. *Premier cru classé* and *cru classé de France en rouge*. The only red bordeaux from outside the Haut-Médoc to have been classified as a 1st growth in the 1855 classification. 15,000 dozen bottles of red Graves de Bordeaux. France.

Haut-Cadet, Château. (5) Côtes de St-Emilion. An unclassified *cru*. 2,500 dozen bottles of red bordeaux. France.

Haut-Camensac. (4) Haut-Médoc; St-Laurent. The registered name of the white bordeaux wine of Château Camensac. France.

Hauts-Champs, Les. (16) Touraine; Restigné vineyard, below Tours. Fair red table wine. France.

Haut-Dahara. (40) The mountainous region near Algiers. Fair red table wine, accorded under French rule the *V.D.Q.S.* appellation if alcoholic strength reached 12°. Algeria.

Haute-Perche. (16) Anjou; Coteaux de l'Aubance, Vauchrêtien vineyard, between Angers and Saumur. Fair white table wine. France.

Hauterive. (31) Neuchâtel vineyard. Fair to fine white table wine. Switzerland.

Haute-Rouchonne, Château La. (5) St-Emilion; Vignonet, south-west of St Pey-d'Armens. An unclassified *cru*. 2,000 dozen bottles of red bordeaux. France.

Hautes-Graves, Domaine des. (5) Entre-deux-Mers; Rions, north of Podensac. 500 dozen bottles of red bordeaux; 3,000 white. France.

Hautes-Rouzes, Château des. (5) Pomerol. 500 dozen bottles of red bordeaux are produced. France.

Haut-Grand-Faurie, Château. (5) Côtes de St-Emilion. An unclassified *cru*. 2,500 dozen bottles of red bordeaux. France.

Haut-La Grace-Dieu, Château. (5) Côtes de St-Emilion. An unclassified *cru*. 800 dozen bottles of red bordeaux. France.

Haut-Langlade, Château. (5) St-Emilion; Parsac. An unclassified *cru*. 800 dozen bottles of red bordeaux. France.

Haut-La Rose, Château. (5) Côtes de St-Emilion. An unclassified *cru*. 3,000 dozen bottles of red bordeaux. France.

Haut-Lavallade, Château. (5) St-Emilion; St Christophe-des-Bardes, south-west of Parsac. An unclassified *cru*. 3,000 dozen bottles of red bordeaux. France.

Haut-Libarde, Château de. (4) Bourgeais. 5,500 dozen bottles of red bordeaux. France.

Haut-Maillet, Château. (5) Pomerol. 1,700 dozen bottles of red bordeaux. France.

Haut-Mayne, Château. (5) Graves de Bordeaux; Cérons. An unclassified *cru*. 2,500 dozen bottles of white bordeaux. France.

Haut-Médoc. (3) The classic great red bordeaux wines of the Médoc come from this region in the area between Blanquefort, almost in Brittany, to St Seurin-de-Cadourne in the north. The names of the principal communes are world famous and include Cantenore, Pauillac, Margaux.

Haut-Myles, Château. (3) Médoc; Blaignan, north-west of St Seurin-de-Cadourne. *Cru bourgeois*. 1,500 dozen bottles of red bordeaux. France.

Haut-Nouchet. (5) Graves de Bordeaux; Martillac. 1,000 dozen bottles of red bordeaux; 1,000 white. France.

Haut-Patarabet, Château de. (5) Côtes de St-Emilion. An unclassified *cru*. 1,000 dozen bottles of red bordeaux. France.

Haut-Peyraguey, Château. (5) Sauternes; Bommes. *Premier cru classé*. 1,500 dozen bottles of white bordeaux. France.

Haut-Pignon, Château de. (5) Pomerol. 1,000 dozen bottles of red bordeaux. France.

Haut-Pirouete, Le. (16) Anjou; Coteaux de la Loire, Montjean vineyard, below Angers. Fair white table wine. France.

Haut-Plaisance, Château. (5) St-Emilion; Montagne. An unclassified *cru*. 1,500 dozen bottles of red bordeaux. France.

Haut-Pontet, Château. (5) Côtes de St-Emilion. An unclassified *cru*. 2,500 dozen bottles of red bordeaux. France.

Haut-Pourret, Château. (5) St-Emilion. An unclassified *cru*. 2,500 dozen bottles of red bordeaux. France.

Haut-Renondeau, Château. (16) Touraine; Ingrandes vineyard, south-west of Tours. Fair white table wine. France.

Haut-Rhin, *Département*. (19) Alsace. Vineyards: 15,884 acres. Wine: 6,610,000 dozen. Mostly white table wines of ordinary, fair and some fine quality. France.

Haut-Rocher, Château. (5) St-Emilion; St Etienne-de-Lisse. An unclassified *cru*. 4,000 dozen bottles of red bordeaux. France.

Haut-Saint-Georges, Château. (5) St-Emilion; St-Georges. An unclassified *cru*. 4,000 dozen bottles of red bordeaux. France.

Haut-Sarpe, Château. (5) St-Emilion; St Christophe-des-Bardes, south-west of Parsac. An unclassified *cru*. 10,000 dozen bottles of red bordeaux. France.

Hauts-Beaux-Monts, Les. (8) Côte de Nuits; Vosne-Romanée vineyard. *Deuxième cru*. Red burgundy. France.

Hauts-Doix, Les. (8) Côte de Nuits; Chambolle-Musigny vineyard, neighbour of Les Amoureuses. *Premier cru*. Fine red burgundy. France.

Haut-Simard, Château. (5) Côtes de St-Emilion. An unclassified *cru*. 3,000 dozen bottles of red bordeaux. France.

Hauts-Maizières, Les. (8) Côte de Beaune; Vosne-Romanée vineyard. *Deuxième cru*. Red burgundy. France.

Hauts-Pruliers, Les. (8) Côte de Nuits; Nuits-St-Georges vineyard. *Deuxième cru*, part classed *premier cru*. Red burgundy. France.

Haut-Trimoulet, Château. (5) Côtes de St-Emilion. An unclassified *cru*. 1,000 dozen bottles of red bordeaux. France.

Haut-Tropchaud, Domaine de. (5) Pomerol. 600 dozen bottles of red bordeaux. France.

Hautvillers. (17) Marne *département*; Ay canton. Rated *premier cru*—90% growth. 586 acres. France.

Havarduere, La. (16) Anjou; Brissac, between Angers and Saumur. Fair to fine Rosé de Cabernet. France.

Haye, Château la. (4) Haut-Médoc; St-Estèphe. *Cru bourgeois supérieur*. 2,000 dozen bottles of red bordeaux. France.

Hayerweg. (24) Rhinehessia; Dittelsheim vineyard, south-west of Oppenheim. Fair white table wine. West Germany.

Haye-Martel, La. (16) Touraine; Cravant-les-Coteaux vineyard, below Angers. Fair red table wine. France.

Hechtsheim. (24) Rhinehessia; west of Laubenheim. Ordinary to fair red and white table wines. West Germany.

Hecklingen. (25) Baden; north-west of Freiburg. Ordinary to fair white table wine. West Germany.

Heddesheim. (24) Nahe; north-west of Bad Kreuznach. Ordinary to fair white table wine. West Germany.

Hegronnière, La. (16) Touraine; Ligré, north-west of Chinon. Fair red table wine. France.

Heidelberg-Handschuhsheim. (25) Baden. Ordinary to fair red and white table wines. West Germany.

Heidelberg-Rohrbach. (25) Baden. Ordinary to fair red and white table wines. West Germany.

Heidelsheim. (25) Baden; north-east of Karlsruhe. Fair white table wine is produced. West Germany.

Heidenkupp. (22) Moselle; Mehring vineyard, south-west of Klüsserath. Fair white table wine. West Germany.

Heidenwein. (31) Valais canton; Visp valley. Fair white table wine made from Traminer grapes locally called Heiden. Switzerland.

Heidesheim. (24) Rhinehessia; south of Erbach. Ordinary to fair red and white table wines. West Germany.

Heilbronn. (25) Württemberg; Neckar valley. Mostly ordinary to fair red table wine. West Germany.

Heilig. (23) Palatinate; Edenkoben vineyard. Fair white table wine. West Germany.

Heiligenbaum. (24) Rhinehessia; Nierstein vineyard. Fair to fine white table wine. West Germany.

Heiligenberg. (23) Palatinate; Maikammer vineyard, between Edenkoben and Neustadt. Fair white table wine. West Germany.

Heiligen Stadt. (33) Vienna area. Ordinary to fair white table wine. Austria.

Heiligenstein. (23) Palatinate; north-east of Landau. Ordinary to fair white table wine. West Germany.

Heiligenstock. (24) Rhinegau; Kiedrich vineyard, north of Erbach. Fair white table wine. West Germany.

Heiligenwann. (24) Rhinehessia; Gau-Bickelheim vineyard, east of Bad Kreuznach. Fair white table wine. West Germany.

Heiligenzell. (25) Baden; approx. sixteen miles south-east of Strasbourg. Fair white table wine. West Germany.

Heimbach. (25) Baden; north of Freiburg. Fair white table wine. West Germany.

Heimberg. (24) Nahe; Schloss Böckelheim vineyard, west of Bad Münster. Fair to fine white table wine. West Germany.

Heinsheim. (25) Baden; north-west of Heilbronn. Ordinary to fair white table wine. West Germany.

Heislay. (22) Moselle; Kröv vineyard east of Kinheim. Fair white table wine. West Germany.

Heissenstein. (22) Moselle; Reil vineyard, east of Zell. Fair white table wine. West Germany.

Heitz Wine Cellars. (36) California; St Helena. Table, dessert and sparkling wines. U.S.A.

Helbig. (23) Palatinate; Ruppertsberg vineyard. Fair to fine white table wine. West Germany.

Held. (22) Moselle; Bernkastel vineyard. Fair white table wine. West Germany.

Hellborn. (24) Rhinehessia; Mettenheim vineyard, south of Alsheim. Ordinary to fair white table wine. West Germany.

Hell Holz. (23) Palatinate; Wachenheim vineyard. Fair white table wine. West Germany.

Hellin. (29) Albacete; approx. twenty-three miles south-east of La Roda. Ordinary, semi-sweet, red table wine. Spain.

Hellpfad. (24) Rhinegau; Rüdesheim vineyard.

Fair and fine white table wines. West Germany.

Hemsbach. (25) Baden, Bergstrasse. Ordinary to fair red and white table wines. West Germany.

Hengelberg. (22) Moselle; Neumagen and Dhron, between Neumagen and Wintrich, vineyards. Fair white table wine. West Germany.

Hengstberg. (25) Franconia; Eschendorf vineyard, north-east of Würzburg. Fine white table wine. West Germany.

Henri Gelicot. (7) Beaune; Monthelie. Hospices de Beaune *cuvée*, named Lebelin, discontinued now. Red burgundy. France.

Henschke Winery. (37) South Australia; Keyneton, approx. thirty-five miles north-east of Adelaide. Quality table wines. Australia.

Heppel. (24) Rhinehessia; Gau-Algesheim vineyard, south of Mittelheim. Fair white table wine. West Germany.

Heppenheim. (25) Baden, Bergstrasse; Hesse, east of Worms. Ordinary to fair white table wine. West Germany.

Heppenstein. (22) Saar valley; Ockfen vineyard, just north-east of Saarburg. Fair to fine white wine. West Germany.

Heraklion. (34) Crete. Fair red table wine. Greece.

Herbolzheim. (25) Baden, south-east of Mosbach. Ordinary to fair red and white table wines. West Germany.

Herbues, Les. (8) Côte de Nuits; Chambolle-Musigny vineyard. *Deuxième cru*. Red burgundy. France.

Hère, Château Le. (5) Sauternes; Bommes. *Cru bourgeois*. 3,000 dozen bottles of white bordeaux. France.

Hergenfeld. (24) Nahe; north-west of Bad Kreuznach. Fair to fine white table wine. West Germany.

Hergolshausen. (25) Franconia; north-east of Würzburg. Fine white table wine. West Germany.

Herl. (22) Moselle; Bremm, west of Eller. Ordinary to fair white table wine. West Germany.

Hermannhohle. (24) Nahe; Niederhausen vineyard, west of Bad Münster. Fair to fine white table wine. West Germany.

Hermannsberg. (24) Nahe; Niederhausen vineyard, west of Bad Münster. Fair white table wine. West Germany.

Hermitage. (12) Côtes du Rhône; Tain. Ordinary, fair, and some fine red table wine; also a little fair to fine white table wine. France.

Hermitage, Château L'. (3) Médoc; Couquèques, north-west of St Seurin-de-Cadourn. *Cru bourgeois*. 4,000 dozen bottles of red bordeaux. France.

Hermitage, L'. (16) Anjou; Coteaux de l'Aubance, Müre-Erigné vineyard, between Angers and Saumur. Fair white table wine. France.

Herradilla. (29) Santander; approx. forty-five miles west of Bilbao. Very dark, dry, red table wine. Spain.

Herrenberg. (32) Moselle; Greiveldange vineyard, east of Luxembourg city. Luxembourg.

Herrengarten. (23) Palatinate; Haardt vineyard. Fair white table wine. West Germany.

Herrenweiler. (24) Rhinehessia; Oppenheim vineyard. Fair to fine white table wine is produced. West Germany.

Herrgottsacker. (23) Palatinate; Deidesheim vineyard. Fine white table wine. 'Paradiesgarten' is the generic name for all Deidesheim wines. West Germany.

Herrnbaumgarten. (33) Niederösterreich (Lower Austria); to the north of Vienna. Ordinary white table wine. Austria.

Herrnberg. (24) Rhinehessia; Gau-Bischofheim vineyard, west of Nackenheim. Fair to fine white table wine. West Germany.

Herten. (25) Baden; approx. thirty miles south-west of Freiburg. Fair red and white table wines. West Germany.

Hertingen. (25) Baden; approx. twenty-two miles south-west of Freiburg. Fair white table wine. West Germany.

Hertmannsweiler. (25) Württemberg; north-east of Stuttgart. Ordinary to fair red and white table wines. West Germany.

Hervas. (29) Cáceres province; approx. twenty miles west of Trujillo. Ordinary to fair red table wine. Spain.

Hervelets, Les. (8) Côte de Nuits; Fixin vineyard. *Premier cru*. The part of this vineyard situated in the hamlet of Fixey is spelt Arvelets. Red burgundy. France.

Herxheim. (23) Palatinate. Ordinary to fair and fine white table wines. West Germany.

Herzchel. (22) Moselle; Briedel vineyard, north-east of Enkirch. Fair white table wine. West Germany.

Herzlay. (22) Moselle; Erden and Zeltingen vineyards. Fair to fine white table wine. West Germany.

Herzog. (23) Palatinate; Haardt vineyard. Fair white table wine. West Germany.

Hessensprung. (24) Rhinehessia; Framersheim vineyard, west of Alsheim. Fair white table wine. West Germany.

Hessheim. (23) Palatinate; Lower Haardt, east of Grünstadt. Fair to fine white table wine. West Germany.

Hessigheim. (25) Württemberg; south of Heilbronn. Ordinary to fair red and white table wines. West Germany.

Hessloch. (24) Rhinehessia; south-west of Alsheim.

Ordinary to fair red and white table wines. West Germany.

Heuchelheim. (23) Palatinate; Lower Haardt, south-west of Landau. Ordinary to fair red and white table wines. West Germany.

Heuchelheim-Frankenthal. (23) Palatinate; east of Grünstadt. Fair white table wine. West Germany.

Heurige. (33) The 'new' wine served during and soon after the vintage in Vienna and Grinzing (q.v.) inns and taverns. Austria.

Heuweiler. (25) Baden; north-east of Freiburg. Ordinary to fair red and white table wines. West Germany.

Heyl. (24) Rhinehessia; Laubenheim vineyard. Fair white table wine. West Germany.

Hierro. (40) Santa Cruz de Tenerife; Canary Islands off the north-west coast of Africa. Ordinary white dessert wine. Spain.

High Tor. (35) South-east New York State; Rockland County, Hudson Valley. Ordinary to fair white and rosé table wines. U.S.A.

Hijon. (29) South-central Aragon; Teruel. Ordinary to fair white table wine. Spain.

Hilbitz. (24) Rhinegau; Rauenthal vineyard. Fine white table wine. West Germany.

Hilde, Château de. (5) Graves de Bordeaux; Bègles. 7,000 dozen bottles of red bordeaux. France.

Himmelreich. (22) Moselle; Graach vineyard. Fine white table wine. West Germany.

Himmelreich. (23) Palatinate; Herxheim vineyard. Fine white table wine. West Germany.

Himmelseiten. (22) Moselle; Mülheim vineyard, between Bernkastel-Kues and Brauneberg. Fair white table wine. West Germany.

Himmelstadt. (25) Franconia; north-west of Würzburg. Fair white table wine. West Germany.

Himmelthal. (23) Rhinehessia; Guntersblum vineyard, between Alsheim and Dienheim. Fair white table wine. West Germany.

Hindelberg. (24) Rhinegau; Hallgarten vineyard. Fair to fine white table wine. West Germany.

Hindenburglay. (22) Saar; Serrig vineyard. Fair white table wine. West Germany.

Hinkelstein. (24) Nahe; Bad Kreuznach vineyard. Fair to fine white table wine. West Germany.

Hinkelstein. (24) Rhinehessia; Nierstein vineyard. Fair to fine white table wine. West Germany.

Hinojos. (29) Huelva. Ordinary white table wines. Spain.

Hinterberg. (22) Moselle; Enkirch vineyard. Fair to fine white table wine. West Germany.

Hinterberg. (24) Nahe; Langenlonsheim vineyard, between Bad Kreuznach and Bingen. Fair white table wine. West Germany.

Hinter der Kirche. (24) Rhinehessia; Hochheim vineyard. Fair to fine white table wine. West Germany.

Hintere. (24) Rhinehessia; Bingen vineyard. Fair white table wine. West Germany.

Hinterfels. (24) Nahe; Norheim vineyard, west of Bad Münster. Fair to fine white table wine. West Germany.

Hinterhaus. (24) Rhinegau; Rüdesheim vineyard. Fair to fine white table wine. West Germany.

Hinterhaus. (24) Rhinehessia; Gau-Bischofsheim vineyard, west of Nackenheim. Fair to fine white table wine. West Germany.

Hinterhäuser. (24) Rhinehessia; Kempten vineyard, east of Bingen. Fair white table wine. West Germany.

Hintersaal. (24) Rhinehessia; Nierstein vineyard. Fair to fine white table wine. West Germany.

Hintersaune. (24) Rhinegau; Hallgarten vineyard. Fair to fine white table wine. West Germany.

Hinterslay. (22) Moselle; Niederemmel vineyard, just south of Piesport. Fair white table wine. West Germany.

Hipping. (24) Rhinehessia; Nierstein vineyard. Fair white table wine. West Germany.

Hirzenach. (21) Middle Rhine; south-east of Koblenz. Fair white table wine. West Germany.

Hitz. (24) Rhinegau; Hallgarten vineyard. Fair to fine white table wine. West Germany.

Hitz. (24) Rhinehessia; Laubenheim vineyard. Fair white table wine. West Germany.

Hitzlay. (22) Ruwer valley; Kasel vineyard. Fine white table wine. West Germany.

Hoch. (24) Rhinehessia; Bodenheim vineyard. Fair white table wine. West Germany.

Hochbenn. (23) Palatinate; Bad Dürkheim vineyard. Fair white table wine. West Germany.

Hochheim. (24) Rhinegau. Fair, fine and some very fine white table wines. West Germany.

Hochmess. (23) Palatinate; Bad Dürkheim vineyard. Fine white table wine. West Germany.

Hochstätten. (24) Nahe; south-west of Bad Münster. Fair to fine white table wine. West Germany.

Hockbruck. (24) Rhinehessia; Oppenheim vineyard. Fair white table wine. West Germany.

Hockenmuhle. (24) Rhinehessia; Ockenheim vineyard, south-east of Bingen. Fair white table wine. West Germany.

Hockweiler. (22) Moselle; south-east of Trier. Ordinary to fair white table wine. West Germany.

Hofberg. (22) Moselle; Dhron, between Neumagen and Wintrich, and Osann, north of Wintrich, vineyards. Ordinary to fair white table wine. West Germany.

Hoffmann's. (37) South Australia; Tanunda,

Barossa Valley, approx. thirty-five miles north-east of Adelaide. Dessert and table wines. Australia.

Hofstück. (23) Palatinate; Ruppertsberg, Deidesheim, Haardt and Gimmeldingen vineyards. Fair to fine white table wine. West Germany.

Hof-unter-Lembach. (25) Württemberg. Ordinary to fair red and white table wines. West Germany.

Hohburg. (25) Franconia; Randersacker vineyard, south-east of Würzburg. Fine white table wine. West Germany.

Hohe. (23) Palatinate; Wachenheim vineyard. Fair to fine white table wine. West Germany.

Hoheburg. (23) Palatinate; Ruppertsberg vineyard. Fine white table wine. West Germany.

Hoheim. (25) Franconia, south-east of Würzburg. Fair white table wine. West Germany.

Hohenfeld. (25) Franconia; south-east of Würzburg. Fair white table wine. West Germany.

Hohenhaslach. (25) Württemberg; approx. sixteen miles south-west of Heilbronn. Ordinary to fair red and white table wines. West Germany.

Hohenmorgen. (23) Palatinate; Deidesheim vineyard. Fine white table wine. 'Paradiesgarten' is the generic name of all Deidesheim wines. West Germany.

Hohenrain. (24) Rhinegau; Erbach vineyard. Fine white table wine. West Germany.

Hohenstein. (25) Württemberg; south-west of Heilbronn. Ordinary to fair red and white table wines. West Germany.

Hohen-Sülzen. (24) Rhinehessia; west of Worms. Ordinary to fair red and white table wines. West Germany.

Hohenwarther Veltliner. (33) Ordinary to fair white table wines. Austria.

Hoher Dekker. (24) Rhinegau; Geisenheim vineyard. Fair to fine white table wine. West Germany.

Hohl. (23) Palatinate; Asselheim vineyard, just north of Grünstadt. Ordinary to fair white table wine. West Germany.

Hohlweid. (22) Moselle; Niederemmel vineyard, just south of Piesport. Fair white table wine. West Germany.

Hohweg. (23) Palatinate; Duttweiler, east of Kirrweiler. Fair white table wine. West Germany.

Hollbacker. (25) Baden; Kirchhofen, south-west of Freiburg. Fair white table wine. West Germany.

Hollenberg. (24) Rhinehessia; Asselheim vineyard, just north of Grünstadt. Fair white table wine. West Germany.

Hollenpfad. (24) Nahe; Roxheim vineyard, north-west of Bad Kreuznach. Ordinary to fair white table wine. West Germany.

Hollerbach. (25) Baden; north-east of Mosbach. Ordinary to fair white table wine. West Germany.

Homburg. (25) Franconia; west of Würzburg. Ordinary to fair white table wines. West Germany.

Hommelsberg. (32) Moselle; Wintrange vineyard. Ordinary to fair white table wine. Luxembourg.

Hondon de los Frailes. (29) Alicante; approx. forty miles south of Valencia. Ordinary table wines. Spain.

Honigberg. (24) Nahe; Dorsheim, south of Bingen and Heddesheim, south-west of Bingen, vineyards. Fair white table wine is produced. West Germany.

Honigberg. (24) Rhinegau; Erbach, Lorch, Mittelheim and Winkel vineyards. Fair to fine white table wine. West Germany.

Honigberg. (24) Rhinehessia; Bodenheim and Dromersheim vineyards, south-east of Bingen. Fair white table wine. West Germany.

Honigsack. (22) Moselle; Mehring vineyard, south-west of Klüsserath. Ordinary white table wine. West Germany.

Honigsberg. (24) Rhinegau; Erbach vineyard. Fine white table wine. West Germany.

Honnef, Bad. (21) Middle Rhine; north-west of Linz. Ordinary to fair white table wine. West Germany.

Hönningen. (21) Middle Rhine; south-west of Linz. Ordinary to fair red and white table wines. West Germany.

Hopertsbourg. (32) Moselle; Remich vineyard. Fair white table wine. Luxembourg.

Höpfigheim. (25) Württemberg; north-east of Stuttgart. Ordinary to fair red and white table wines. West Germany.

Hôpital de Pourtalès. (31) Neuchâtel canton; Neuville. Fair golden table wine. Switzerland.

Hôpital de Sion. (31) Valais canton; Rhône valley. Fair to fine white table wine. Switzerland.

Horcajo de Santiago. (29) Eastern New Castile; Cuenca. Ordinary red table wine. Spain.

Horeker. (22) Saar; Kanzem vineyard. Fair to fine white table wine. West Germany.

Horkheim. (25) Württemberg; south-west of Heilbronn. Ordinary to fair red and white table wines. West Germany.

Horn. (31) Lake Constance (Bodensee); north-west of Konstanz. Ordinary red and white table wines. West Germany.

Horn. (23) Palatinate; Kallstadt vineyard. Fair to fine white table wine. West Germany.

Horrheim. (25) Württemberg; north-west of Stuttgart. Ordinary to fair red and white table wines. West Germany.

Horrweiler. (24) Rhinehessia; north-east

of Bad Kreuznach. Ordinary to fair red and white table wines. West Germany.

Horst. (23) Palatinate; Hambach, just south of Neustadt. Fair white table wine. West Germany.

Hospices, Clos des. (16) Anjou; Champigny-le-Sec vineyard in the Saumur area. Fair white table wine. France.

Hospices Cantonnaux. (31) Vaud canton; vineyards of Aigle and Villeneuve, the property of the Hospices. Fair to fine white table wines marketed for the upkeep of this charitable institution. Switzerland.

Hospices de Beaujeu. (11) Beaujolais vineyards owned by the Beaujeu Hospices, charitable institutions. *AC Beaujolais* villages. The wines are sold by auction each year for the upkeep of the hospital. France.

Hospices de Beaune. (7) 127 acres of vineyards owned by this charitable institution the first of which were bequeathed by Chancelier Rolin, their founder, in the fifteenth century, and his widow, Guigone de Salins, and many benefactors ever since. Their wines are sold by auction separately under the names of the *cuvées* every year in November for the upkeep of this charitable institution. The majority are red wines, but there are also some whites. They are of superior quality. France.

Hospices de Nuits. (7) Côte de Nuits; Nuits-St-Georges. All are of the *AC Nuits-St-Georges*. Fair to fine red burgundy from the vineyards bequeathed to the Hospice for its upkeep. Many are of high quality. France.

Hotlay. (22) Moselle; Aldegund vineyard, between Eller and Zell. Fair white table wine. West Germany.

Hotlei. (22) Moselle; Erden vineyard. Fair to fine white table wine. West Germany.

Houghton. (37) Western Australia. One of the oldest wineries and vineyards of the Perth region. It produces a famous white burgundy-style wine. Australia.

Houissant, Château. (4) Haut-Médoc; St-Estèphe. *Cru bourgeois supérieur.* 8,000 dozen bottles of red bordeaux. France.

Hoyos. (29) Cáceres province; Cáceres, approx. twenty miles west of Trujillo. Ordinary to fair red and white table wines. Spain.

Hrad. (33) Bzenec; central Czechoslovakia, which produces ordinary to fair red table wine. Czechoslovakia.

Hub. (21) Middle Rhine; Oberdiebach vineyard, north-west of Bingen. Fair white table wine. West Germany.

Hubbaum. (23) Palatinate; Kallstadt vineyard. Fair to fine white table wine. West Germany.

Hubertusberg. (22) Saar Valley; Irsch vineyard, east of Saarburg. Ordinary white table wine. West Germany.

Hubertushofberg. (22) Moselle; Kinheim vineyard. Fair white table wine. West Germany.

Hubertuslay. (22) Moselle; Kinheim vineyard. Fair to fine white table wine. West Germany.

Huelva. (29) Province producing ordinary white table wines, mostly rather high-strength. Spain.

Huercanos. (29) Old Castile; Logroño province, La Rioja area of the upper Ebro valley. Fair to fine red table wine. Spain.

Huerta. (29) Toledo; approx. forty miles south-west of Madrid. Ordinary red and white table wines. Spain.

Huette. (32) Moselle; Greiveldange vineyard, east of Luxembourg city. Ordinary to fair white table wine. Luxembourg.

Hüffelsheim. (24) Nahe; west of Bad Münster. Fair white table wine. West Germany.

Hügelsheim. (25) Baden; north-west of Baden-Baden. Ordinary to fair white table wine. West Germany.

Hugsweier. (25) Baden; south-east of Strasbourg. Ordinary to fair red and white table wines. West Germany.

Huguenot. (39) Western Cape Province. One of the oldest vineyard settlements where the vine still flourishes. South Africa.

Hühneracker. (23) Palatinate; Kallstadt vineyard. Fine white table wine. West Germany.

Hühnerberg. (22) Moselle; Traben-Trarbach vineyard. Fair white table wine. West Germany.

Hühnerberg. (24) Rhinegau; Rauenthal vineyard. Fine white table wine. West Germany.

Humprechtsau. (25) Franconia; approx. twenty-five miles south-east of Würzburg. Fair white table wine. West Germany.

Hunawihr. (19) Haut-Rhin *département*; north-west of Riquewihr. Fair to fine and very fine white Alsace wine. France.

Hundertmorgen. (23) Palatinate; Maikammer vineyard, between Neustadt and Edenkoben. Fair white table wine. West Germany.

Hungary. (33) Approximate annual wine production is 120,000,000 dozen red and white wines; table and dessert, ordinary, fair and some fine quality. The most famous are the sweet strong Tokaji (Tokay) wines (q.v.).

Hungerford Hill Vineyards. (37) New South Wales; Pokolbin, Hunter Valley, north-east of Sydney. Established 1968 by a group of cotton-growing, petroleum and other interests, which bought an 850-acre property. It has been planted with 90% Shiraz vines plus some Cabernet Sauvignon and Semillon. Australia.

Hunter River Valley. (37) In spite of the unpredictable moods of the Hunter river north-east of Sydney, there are many vineyards in its valley and some of them produce the best table wines of New South Wales. There were vast developments in the decade from 1961, and in November 1971 the total acreage was 7,327 acres—a rise of 2,409 over the previous year. Australia.

Hupperath. (22) Moselle; west of Erden. Ordinary white table wine. West Germany.

Husi. (33) Town in east Rumania. Ordinary to fair white table wine. Rumania.

Hutte. (24) Rhinehessia; Dromersheim vineyard, south-east of Bingen. Fair white table wine. West Germany.

Hutte. (22) Saar; Oberemmel vineyard. Fair white table wine. West Germany.

Hutte, La. (16) Anjou; Coteaux de la Loire, La Possonnière vineyard, south-west of Angers. Fair white table wine. France.

Hüttenberg. (22) Moselle; Karden vineyard, north-east of Valwig. Fair white table wine. West Germany.

Hüttenberg. (24) Nahe; Roxheim vineyard, north-west of Bad Kreuznach. Fair to fine white table wine. West Germany.

Hüttenheim. (25) Franconia; approx. sixteen miles south-east of Würzburg. Fair white table wine. West Germany.

Huxlay. (22) Moselle; Mehring vineyard, south-west of Klüsserath. Fair white table wine. West Germany.

Hymettus. (34) East-central Greece; Attica mountain vineyard. Ordinary to fair table wines are produced. Greece.

☙

Iassy. (33) Ordinary to fair table wines; also some fair to fine Muscat dessert wine. Rumania.

Ibersheim. (24) Rhinehessia; south-east of Oppenheim. Ordinary to fair white table wines. West Germany

Idig. (23) Palatinate; Königsbach vineyard. Fine white table wine. West Germany.

Ieracare. (28) Calabria; Scilla, north-east of Reggio. Ordinary, rather sweet, fairly light cherry-red table wine. Italy.

Iffigheim. (25) Franconia; south-east of Würzburg. Fair white table wine. West Germany.

Igel. (22) Moselle; south-west of Trier. Fair white wine. West Germany.

Igreja, Quinta. (30) *Região demarcada do Douro* (q.v.). Estate in Penajoia in the Régua area. Portugal.

Igreja, Quinta. (30) *Região demarcada do Douro* (q.v.). Estate and vineyard in Sedielos in the Régua area. This Quinta dates back to 1543. Portugal.

Iguanada. (29) Catalonia; Barcelona. Ordinary red and white table wines. Spain.

Ihringen. (25) Baden; Kaiserstuhl's largest vineyard, north-west of Freiburg. Ordinary to fair white table wine. West Germany.

Ilbesheim. (23) Palatinate; north-west of Grünstadt. Ordinary to fair red and white table wines. West Germany.

Ile Margaux. (3) Island in the Gironde off Margaux. 10,000 dozen bottles of red bordeaux. France.

Illana. (29) Central Spain; Guadalajara province of New Castile. Ordinary to fair red and white table wines.

Illats. (5) Graves de Bordeaux. Ordinary to fair red and white bordeaux. France.

Illingen. (25) Württemberg; south-west of Karlsruhe. Ordinary to fair red and white table wines. West Germany.

Illinois. (35) One of the less important States, south-west of Michigan, as regards its acreage of vineyards. U.S.A.

Impfingen. (25) Franconia; south-west of Würzburg. Fair white table wine. West Germany.

Impflingen. (23) Palatinate; south of Landau. Ordinary to fair red and white table wines. West Germany.

Inca. (29) Majorca; Balearic Islands, off the coast east of Valencia. Ordinary sweet red table wine. Spain.

Indre-et-Loire. (16) *Département*; a part of what was formerly called Touraine. France.

Inferno. (26) Lombardy; Valtelline. Very good red wine made principally from the Nebbiolo grape. Italy.

Ingelfingen. (25) Württemberg; approx. twenty-three miles south-east of Mosbach. Ordinary to fair red and white table wines. West Germany.

Ingelheim. (24) Rhinehessia; east of Bingen. Fair, fine and some very fine white table wine. West Germany.

Inglenook Vineyards (Operating Division of United Vintners). (36) California; Rutherford. 175,000 dozen bottles storage capacity. Outstanding red wines and also an unusual red wine from Pinot St George grapes called Red Pinot. Its wines are among the best of California. U.S.A.

Ingersheim. (19) Haut-Rhin *département*; just north-west of Colmar. Ordinary to medium white Alsace wine. France.

Iniesta. (29) Eastern New Castile; Cuenca. Ordinary to fair red table wine. Spain.

Inkermann. (34) South European Russia; district of Crimean peninsula. Red and white table wines from ordinary to fair quality. U.S.S.R.

Insheim. (23) Palatinate. Ordinary to fair, and some fine red and white table wines. West Germany.

Iphofen. (25) Franconia; south-east of Würzburg. Fair to fine and some very fine white table wine. West Germany.

Ipiani. (28) Sardinia; Alghero vineyard, Sassari area. Ordinary red table wine. Italy.

Ippenheim. (24) Rhinehessia; north-east of Bad Kreuznach. Ordinary to fair white table wine. West Germany.

Ippesheim. (25) Franconia; approx. eighteen miles south-east of Würzburg. Fair white table wine. West Germany.

Iran (Persia). (34) A country once famous for the quality of its wines, but now with few vineyards. Its wine production has fallen at times as low as 20,000 dozen bottles per year.

Irno (Bianco, Rosso). (28) Campania; vineyards in the Irno Valley, Salerno area. Ordinary red and white table wines. Italy.

Irsch-Saarburg. (22) Saar; east of Saarburg. Ordinary to fair white table wine. West Germany.

Irsch-Trier. (22) Moselle; south-east of Trier. Ordinary to fair white table wine. West Germany.

Ischia. (28) Campania; island in the Bay of Naples. Ordinary to fair red and white table wines. Also some fair white table and dessert wines which are usually marketed as Capri wines are produced. Italy.

Ischia Bianco Superiore. (28) Campania; island of Ischia, Bay of Naples. The name of one of the better white table wines. Italy.

Isera. (26) Trentino; vineyards above Lake Garda west of Verona. Red, white and rosé table wines. Italy.

Iskra. (33) Ordinary to fair sparkling red wine. Bulgaria.

Isle-Saint-Georges. (5) Graves de Bordeaux. Ordinary to fair red and white bordeaux. France.

Israel. (34) Ordinary table, sparkling, Port and Sherry type, and dessert wines, the best of which are those from the Sharon and Samaria hills vineyards of Israel.

Issan, Château d'. (4) Haut-Médoc; Cantenac. *Troisième cru classé.* 8,000 dozen bottles of red bordeaux. France.

Istein. (25) Baden; approx. twenty-four miles south-west of Freiburg. Fair white table wine. West Germany.

Italian-Swiss Colony. (36) (Operating Division of United Vintners). California; Asti. Table,

dessert and sparkling wines; also brandy and vermouth of interesting quality. U.S.A.

🍇

Jacobins, Clos des. (5) Côtes de St-Emilion. *Grand cru classé.* 4,000 dozen bottles of red bordeaux. France.

Jacquerie. (16) Anjou; Coteaux de la Loire, Ingrandes vineyard, south-west of Angers. Fair white table wine. France.

Jacques, Château des. (11) Beaujolais; Grand Carquelin vineyard, Moulin-à-Vent, south-east of Chénas. Red beaujolais. France.

Jacquines, Les. (7) Côte de Nuits; Vosne-Romanée vineyard. *Troisième cru.* Red burgundy. France.

Jaén Blanco. (29) Jaén province, north-east of Seville. An ordinary white table wine. Spain.

Jaén Doradillo. (29) Jaén province, north-east of Seville. Fair golden dessert wine. Spain.

Jaén Tinto. (29) Jaén province, north-east of Seville. Ordinary, very dark, red table wine. Spain.

Jalisco. (35) Central Mexico vineyard area. Ordinary to fair table wines. Mexico.

Jana, La. (29) Castellón de la Plana; approx. forty miles north-east of Valencia. Ordinary to fair high-strength red table wine. Spain.

Jarandilla. (29) Cáceres province; Cáceres, approx. twenty miles west of Trujillo. Ordinary to fair red table wine. Spain.

Jarollières, Les. (8) Côte de Beaune; Pommard vineyard. *Premier cru.* Red burgundy. France.

Jarretière, La. (16) Anjou; Coteaux de l'Aubance, Denée vineyard, between Angers and Saumur. Fair white table wine. France.

Jarrons, Les. (8) Côte de Beaune; Savigny-les-Beaune vineyard. *Premier cru.* Red burgundy. France.

Jasnières. (16) Anjou; Coteaux de la Loire, below Angers. Fair to fine white table wine. France.

Jatiel. (29) South-central Aragon; Teruel. Ordinary to fair table wines. Spain.

Játiva. (29) Valencia. Ordinary to fair white table wine. Spain.

Jaubertes, Château des. (5) St Pierre-de-Mons, Langon area. 5,000 dozen bottles of red bordeaux; 4,000 white. France.

Jean, Clos. (5) Loupiac. Entre-deux-Mers. 2,000 dozen bottles of red bordeaux; 6,000 white. France.

Jean-Faure, Château. (5) Graves de St-Emilion. *Grand cru classé.* 8,000 dozen bottles of red bordeaux. France.

Jean Humblot. (7) Côte de Beaune; Hospices de Beaune *cuvée* vineyard, Meursault. France.

Jechtingen. (25) Baden; north-west of Freiburg. Ordinary to fair red and white table wines. West Germany.

Jeckenbach. (24) Nahe; south-west of Bad Kreuznach. Fair to fine white table wine. West Germany.

Jehan de Massol. (8) Côte de Beaune; Hospices de Beaune *cuvée*. *AC Volnay-Santernots*. Red burgundy. France.

Jennelotte, La. (7) Côte de Beaune; Meursault vineyard. *Premier cru.* White burgundy. France.

Jerez de la Frontera. (29) The hub of the sherry trade, on the main road from Seville to Cadiz, in Andalusia, and surrounded by the vineyards which are responsible for the finest sherries of Spain.

Jesuitengarten. (23) Palatinate; one of the finest Forst vineyards. Very fine white table wine. West Germany.

Jesuitengarten. (23) Palatinate; one of the finest Fine white table wine. West Germany.

Jesuitengarten. (22) Ruwer; Waldrach vineyard. Fair to fine white table wine. West Germany.

Jimenez, Pedro. *See* **Ximenez, Pedro.**

Johannisberg. (22) Moselle; Brüttig and Mülheim vineyards, between Bernkastel-Kues and Brauneberg. Fair white table wine. West Germany.

Johannisberg. (22) Moselle; Mertesdorf vineyard, north-east of Trier. Fine white table wine. West Germany.

Johannisberg. (24) Rhinegau. Fair, fine and very fine white table wines. West Germany.

Johannisberg, Schloss. (24) Rhinegau. The most spectacular castle and vineyard of the Rhinegau; its wines are carefully graded from those of the least to those of the most remarkable quality. West Germany.

Johannisberg de Dézaley. (31) Vaud canton; Dézaley vineyard. Fine white table wine. Switzerland.

Johanniskirchel. (23) Palatinate; Diedesfeld, between Kirrweiler and Neustadt. Fair to fine white table wine. West Germany.

Johannislay. (22) Saar; Wiltingen vineyard. Fair to fine white table wine. West Germany.

Joly, Château. (5) St-Emilion; Vignonet, south-west of St Pey-d'Armens. An unclassified *cru*. 2,000 dozen bottles of red bordeaux. France.

Jongerberg. (32) Moselle; Remerschen vineyard, south-east of Luxembourg city. Fair white table wine. Luxembourg.

Jonka, Château. (5) Preignac, Langon area. *Cru bourgeois.* 1,000 dozen bottles of white bordeaux. France.

Jordan. (34) There are many vineyards in this country south-west of Syria. Most of them grow table grapes, producing a quite ordinary table wine.

Jordão, Quinta. *See* **Sibio.**

Josephshofer. (22) Moselle; Graach vineyard. Fine white table wine. West Germany.

Jouets, Les. (16) Anjou; Coteaux du Layon, Faye d'Anjou vineyard, south of Angers. Fair to fine white table wine. France.

Jourdan, Château. (5) Premières Côtes de Bordeaux; Rions, north of Podensac. 8,000 dozen bottles of red bordeaux; 12,000 white. France.

Juffer. (22) Moselle; Brauneberg vineyard. Fine white table wine. West Germany.

Juge, Château du. (4) Premières Côtes de Bordeaux; Cadillac, north-west of Loupiac. 18,000 dozen bottles of white bordeaux. France.

Jugenheim. (24) Rhinehessia; north-east of Bad Kreuznach. Ordinary to fair red and white table wines. West Germany.

Juhfarku. (33) West-central Hungary; Somló. Fair to fine white table wine. Hungary.

Juigne-sur-Loire. (16) Anjou; Coteaux de l'Aubance, between Angers and Saumur. Fair to fine white table wine. France.

Jujuy. (35) Extreme north-west of the country of Argentina; one of the more important wine-producing provinces.

Juliénas. (11) Beaujolais. One of the top-grade beaujolais. France.

Julius-Echter-Berg. (25) Franconia; Iphofen vineyard, south-east Würzburg. Fair white table wine. West Germany.

Juliusspital. (25) Franconia; Würzburg vineyard. The Würzburg Hospital vineyards produce some of the finest Franconian white wines which are sold for the upkeep of the Hospital. West Germany.

Jumilla. (29) Murcia. Ordinary to fair red and rosé tables wines. Spain.

Junay. (6) Yonne *département*; Tonnerre area. Ordinary to fair white burgundy. France.

Junayme, Château. (3) Fronsac. 7,000 dozen bottles of red bordeaux. France.

Junco, Quinta. (30) *Região demarcada do Douro* (q.v.). Estate and vineyard in São Cristóvão e Provezende north-east of Régua. 195 acres. Portugal.

Jungfer. (24) Rhinegau; Hallgarten vineyard. Fair to fine white table wine. West Germany.

Jungfrau. (26) Alto Adige. Very light, fair, dry white table wine. Italy.

Junkerberg. (22) Saar valley; Oberemmel vineyard. Fair to fine white table wine. West Germany.

Jura-Plaisance, Château. (5) St-Emilion; Montagne. An unclassified *cru*. 6,000 dozen bottles of red bordeaux. France.

Jussy. (6) Yonne *département*; Auxerre area. Fair red burgundy. France.

Justices, Château les. (5) Sauternes; Preignac. *Cru bourgeois*. 1,000 dozen bottles of white bordeaux. France.

⚘

Kaberne. (34) Ordinary to fair red table wine made from Cabernet grapes. U.S.S.R.

Kafels. (24) Nahe; Norheim vineyard, just southwest of Bad Münster. Fine white table wine. West Germany.

Kafferkopf. (19) Haut-Rhin *département*; Ammerschwihr vineyard. Fine white Alsace table wine. France.

Kaft. (23) Palatinate; Ruppertsberg vineyard. Fine white table wine. West Germany.

Kahlenberg. (22) Moselle; Kröv vineyard, east of Kinheim. Fair white table wine. West Germany.

Kahlenberg. (24) Nahe; Bad Kreuznach vineyard. Fine white table wine. West Germany.

Kahlenberg. (24) Rhinehessia; Bodenheim and Nackenheim vineyards. Fair white table wine. West Germany.

Kaimt. (22) Moselle. Ordinary to fair white table wine. West Germany.

Kaiserstuhl. (25) Baden; volcanic ledge in Breisgau on which there are many villages. Mostly white table wines of fair quality. West Germany.

Kaiser Stuhl. (37) South Australia; Barossa Valley, approx. thirty-five miles north-east of Adclaide. Brand name of wines of Barossa Co-operative Winery, Nuriootpa. Notable dry reds and whites. Australia.

Kalavryta. (34) Northern Peloponnisos peninsula of southern Greece; Achaea province. Ordinary to fair red table wine. Greece.

Kalb. (25) Franconia; Iphofen vineyard, southeast of Würzburg. Fair white table wine. West Germany.

Kälbchen. (24) Rhinehessia; Alsheim vineyard. Fair white table wine. West Germany.

Kalbpflicht. (24) Rhinegau; Eltville vineyard. Fair to fine white table wine. West Germany.

Kalbrech. (22) Middle Moselle; Kues vineyard. Fair white table wine. West Germany.

Kalebag. (34) Ordinary to fair red and white table wines. Turkey.

Kalecik. (34) Ankara region. Ordinary to fair red table wine. Turkey.

Kalkberg. (23) Palatinate; Duttweiler vineyard, south-west of Neustadt. Fair white table wine. West Germany.

Kalkgrübe. (23) Palatinate; Haardt vineyard. Fair white table wine. West Germany.

Kalkofen. (24) Nahe; south of Bad Münster. Fair white table wine. West Germany.

Kalkofen. (23) Palatinate; Deidesheim and Leistadt vineyards, just west of Kallstadt. Fair to fine white table wine. West Germany.

Kalkofen. (24) Rhinehessia; Laubenheim vineyard. Fair white table wine. West Germany.

Kallmuth. (25) Franconia; Homburg, west of Würzburg. Fine white table wine. West Germany.

Kallstadt. (23) Middle Haardt, Palatinate. Fair, fine and some very fine white table wines. West Germany.

Kalmond. (22) Moselle; Eller and Bremm, west of Eller. Fair white table wine. West Germany.

Kalterer. (26) Alto Adige; Bolzano area. One of the better red wines from the vineyards close to the (Kalterersee) Lake Caldero. Italy.

Kalterersee. *See* **Caldaro, Lago Di.**

Kammer. (22) Moselle; Brauneberg and Erden vineyards. Fair white table wine. West Germany.

Kamp. (21) Middle Rhine; south-east of Koblenz. Ordinary to fair red and white table wines. West Germany.

Kamp. (22) Moselle; Briedel vineyard, west of Zell. Fair white table wine. West Germany.

Kamptal. (33) Southern Austria; vineyards of the Kampouren hillsides. Ordinary to fair white table wine. Lower Austria.

Kandel. (22) Moselle; Dhron vineyard, between Neumagen and Wintrich. Fair to fine white table wine. West Germany.

Kandelberg. (24) Rhinegau; Mittelheim vineyard. Fair white table wine. West Germany.

Kandelweg. (24) Rhinehessia; Dienheim vineyard. Fair white table wine. West Germany.

Kansel. (23) Palatinate; Herxheim vineyard. Fair to fine white table wine. West Germany.

Kanzelberg. (19) Haut-Rhin *département*. Bergheim's best vineyard. Fair to fine white Alsace wine. France.

Kanzem. (22) Saar valley. Fair to fine and some very fine white table wines. West Germany.

Kapelle. (24) Rhinehessia; Gau-Bickelheim and Nackenheim vineyards, east of Bad Kreuznach. Fair white table wine. West Germany.

Kapelle. (24) Rhinehessia; Lorch vineyard. Fair white table wine. West Germany.

Kapellenberg. (22) Moselle; Alf, Klotten (north of Valwig), Pommern and Treis (both northeast of Valwig) vineyards. Ordinary to fair white table wines. West Germany.

Kapellenberg. (24) Nahe; Bad Münster vineyard. Fair to fine white table wine. West Germany.

Kapellengarten. (23) Palatinate; Deidesheim vineyard. Fair to fine white table wine. 'Paradiesgarten' is the generic name for all Deidesheim vineyards. West Germany.

Kapellengarten. (24) Rhinegau; Geisenheim vineyard. Fair to fine white table wine. West Germany.

Kappelrodeck. (25) Baden; south-west of Baden-Baden. Ordinary to fair red and white table wines. West Germany.

Kappishäusern. (25) Württemberg; approx. eighteen miles south-east of Stuttgart. Ordinary to fair white table wine. West Germany.

Kapplay. (22) Moselle; Eller vineyard. Fair white table wine. West Germany.

Kapsweyer. (23) Palatinate; south-west of Landau. Ordinary to fair red and white table wines. West Germany.

Kararka-Silles. (33) Eger area; approx. sixty-five miles north-east of Budapest. Ordinary to fair red table wine. Hungary.

Karlstadt. (25) Franconia; north-west of Würzburg. Fair to fine white table wine. West Germany.

Karstweg. (24) Rhinehessia; Alsheim vineyard. Fair white table wine. West Germany.

Karthäuser. (31) Thurgau canton. Ordinary red table wine. Switzerland.

Karthäuserhofberg. (22) Ruwer valley; Eitelsbach's best vineyard, north-east of Trier. Fine to very fine white table wine is produced. West Germany.

Karweiler. (21) Ahr valley; west of Linz. Ordinary to fair red and white table wines. West Germany.

Kasbach. (21) Middle Rhine; north of Linz. Ordinary red and white table wines. West Germany.

Kasel. (22) Ruwer valley. Ordinary, fair fine and some very fine white table wines. West Germany.

Katharinenberg. (22) Ruwer valley; Kasel vineyard. Fine white table wine. West Germany.

Katharinenbild. (23) Middle Haardt, Palatinate; Deidesheim vineyard. Fair to fine white table wine. 'Paradiesgarten' is the generic name for all Deidesheim wines. West Germany.

Kattenes. (22) Moselle; south-west of Kobern. Ordinary to fair white table wine. West Germany.

Katzenkopf. (25) Franconia; Sommerach vineyard, north-east of Würzburg. Fair white table wine. West Germany.

Katzenloch. (24) Rhinegau; Geisenheim vineyard. Fair to fine white table wine. West Germany.

Katzenthal. (19) Haut-Rhin *département*; village south-east of Ommerschwir. Ordinary to fair white Alsace table wine. France.

Kaub. (21) Middle Rhine; north-west of Bingen. Ordinary to fair white table wine. West Germany.

Kaufmannsberg. (22) Moselle; Erden vineyard. Fair white table wine. West Germany.

Kaulgen. (22) Ruwer valley; Kasel vineyard. Fair white table wine. West Germany.

Kauzenberg, Schloss. (24) Nahe; Bad Kreuznach vineyard. Fair to fine white table wine. West Germany.

Kavklidere. (34) Ordinary to fair red table wine. Turkey.

Kayserberg. (19) Bas-Rhin *département*. Ordinary to fair white Alsace wine. France.

Kea. (34) Ionian island off south-eastern coast of Greece. Ordinary to fair red table wine. Greece.

Kecskemet. (33) Approx. fifty miles south-east of Budapest. Fair to fine white table wine. Hungary.

Kehl. (24) Rhinehessia; Guntersblum vineyard. Fair white table wine. West Germany.

Kehr. (24) Rhinehessia; Nierstein vineyard. Fine white table wine. West Germany.

Kehrenberg. (24) Nahe; Bad Kreuznach vineyard. Fair to fine white table wine. West Germany.

Kehrnagel. (22) Ruwer; Kasel vineyard. Fair to fine white table wine. West Germany.

Kellerberg. (24) Rhinegau; Oestrich vineyard. Fair to fine white table wine. West Germany.

Kellerberg. (24) Rhinehessia; Gau-Bischofsheim, west of Nackenheim. Fair to fine white table wine. West Germany.

Kellerstein. (24) Rhinehessia; Westhofen vineyard, south-west of Alsheim. Fair white table wines. West Germany.

Kelterberg. (22) Saar valley; Kanzem vineyard. Fair white table wine. West Germany.

Kelterweg. (24) Rhinehessia; Oppenheim and Ludwigshöhe vineyards, between Alsheim and Dienheim. Fair white table wine. West Germany.

Kenn. (22) Moselle; north-east of Trier. Ordinary to fair white table wine. West Germany.

Kenzenheim. (23) Palatinate; approx. twenty-two miles south-west of Stuttgart. Fair white table wine. West Germany.

Kenzingen. (25) Baden; north-west of Freiburg. Ordinary to fair white table wine. West Germany.

Keopp. (32) Moselle; Wormeldange vineyard. Ordinary to fair white table wine. Luxembourg.

Keos. *See* KEA.

Kephesia. (34) East-central Greece; Attica. Ordinary to fair, and some fine red and white table wines. Greece.

Keppoch. (37) South Australia; north of Coonawarra. A new wine-growing region; first planted by Seppelts in 1964. Recently several other companies have also followed suit, all producing mainly dry red wine. Australia.

Kerbersberg. (24) Rhinegau; Oestrich vineyard. Fair to fine white table wine. West Germany.

Kern. (36) California County at southern end of San Joaquin Valley. Mostly grows Thompsen seedless grapes, and produces no fine table wines. U.S.A.

Kerz. (24) Nahe; Niederhausen-Schloss Böckelheim vineyard, west of Bad Münster. Fine white table wine. West Germany.

Kerzenstück. (24) Rhinegau; Johannisberg vineyard. Fine white table wine. West Germany.

Kesselring. (24) Rhinegau; Rauenthal vineyard. Fine white table wine. West Germany.

Kesten. (22) Middle Moselle valley; north of Wintrich. Best vineyards: Herrenberg, Niederberg, Paulinshofberg. Fair to fine white table wine. West Germany.

Kestert. (21) Middle Rhine; south-east of Koblenz. Ordinary white table wine. West Germany.

Kette. (24) Rhinehessia; Oppenheim vineyard. Fair white table wine. West Germany.

Kettenheim. (24) Rhinehessia; south-west of Alsheim. Fair white table wine. West Germany.

Keuka, Lake. (35) Northern New York State; one of the Finger Lakes. Ordinary to fair still and sparkling wines. U.S.A.

Khios. *See* CHIOS.

Khullar. (34) South-central Iran; Shiraz. Ordinary to fair red and white wines. Iran.

Kiechlinsbergen. (25) Baden; north-west of Freiburg. Ordinary to fair red and white table wines. West Germany.

Kiedrich. (24) Rhinegau. Fair to fine and some very fine white table wines. West Germany.

Kientzheim. (19) Haut-Rhin *département*. Fair to fine white Alsace wine. France.

Kies. (23) Palatinate; Neustadt vineyard. Fair white table wine. West Germany.

Kiesel. (24) Rhinegau; Rüdesheim vineyard. Fair to fine white table wine. West Germany.

Kieselberg. (23) Palatinate; Deidesheim and Gimmeldingen vineyards. Fair to fine white table wine. West Germany.

Kieselberg. (24) Rhinehessia; Budenheim vineyard. Fair white table wine. West Germany.

Kilb. (24) Nahe; Heddesheim vineyard, south-west of Bingen. Fair white table wine. West Germany.

Kilb. (24) Rhinegau; Hattenheim vineyard, west of Erbach. Fair to fine white table wine. West Germany.

Kindenheim. (24) Palatinate; north of Grünstadt.

Ordinary to fair red and white table wines. West Germany.

Kings County. (36) Central California; Great Central Valley vineyards. Mostly ordinary dessert and table wines. U.S.A.

Kinheim. (22) Middle Moselle. Fair to fine white table wines. West Germany.

Kintzheim. (19) Bas-Rhin *département*. Ordinary to fair white Alsace wine. France.

Kippenhausen. (25) Lake Constance (Bodensee); east of Konstanz. Fair white table wine. West Germany.

Kippenheim. (25) Baden; approx. twenty miles south-east of Strasbourg. Ordinary to fair white table wine. West Germany.

Kippenheimweiler. (25) Baden; approx. eighteen miles south-east of Strasbourg. Ordinary to fair white table wines. West Germany.

Kirchberg-an-der-Murr. (25) Württemberg; north-east of Stuttgart. Ordinary to fair red and white table wines. West Germany.

Kirche. (22) Moselle; Burg vineyard, between Zell and Enkirch. Ordinary to fair white table wine. West Germany.

Kircheck. (24) Rhinehessia; Gau-Bischofsheim vineyard, west of Nackenheim. Fair white table wine. West Germany.

Kirchenacker. (24) Rhinegau; Hallgarten vineyard. Fair to fine white table wine. West Germany.

Kirchenberg. (23) Palatinate; Hambach vineyard, just south of Neustadt. Fair to fine white table wine. West Germany.

Kirchenpfad. (22) Moselle; Zeltingen vineyard. Fair to fine white table wine. West Germany.

Kirchenrain. (22) Moselle; Senheim vineyard, south-east of Eller. Fair white table wine. West Germany.

Kirchenrech. (22) Moselle; Senheim vineyard, south-east of Eller. Fair white table wine. West Germany.

Kirchenstück. (23) Palatinate; Forst vineyard. Fine white table wine. West Germany.

Kirchenstück. (24) Rhinegau; Hochheim vineyard. Fine white table wine. West Germany.

Kirchgarten. (23) Palatinate; Herxheim vineyard. Fair white table wine. West Germany.

Kirchheim-am-Neckar. (25) Württemberg. Ordinary red and white table wine. West Germany.

Kirchheim-an-der-Eck. (23) Palatinate; Unterhaardt vineyard, just south of Grünstadt. Ordinary to fair white table wine. West Germany.

Kirchheim-an-der-Weinstrasse. *See* **Kirchheim-an-der-Eck.**

Kirchheimbolanden. (23) Palatinate; Unterhaardt vineyard, north-west of Grünstadt. Ordinary to fair red and white table wines. West Germany.

Kirchhofen. (25) Baden; Freiburg-Breisgau. Ordinary to fair red and white table wines. West Germany.

Kirchlay. (22) Moselle; Graach and Zeltingen vineyards. Fair white table wine. West Germany.

Kirchpfad. (23) Palatinate; Haardt vineyard. Fair white table wine. West Germany.

Kirchspiel. (24) Rhinehessia; Westhofen vineyard, south-west of Alsheim. Fair white table wine. West Germany.

Kirchtal. (23) Palatinate; Herxheim vineyard. Fair white table wine. West Germany.

Kirchweiler. (23) Palatinate. Ordinary to fair and some fine white table wine. West Germany.

Kirkton. (37) Oldest named vineyard in New South Wales planted by James Busby in 1830. The vineyard exists no longer but the name has been given to one of the best red table wines marketed by Lindeman. Australia.

Kirschheck. (24) Nahe; Bad Münster vineyard. Fair white table wine. West Germany.

Kirschley. (22) Moselle; Osann vineyard, north of Wintrich. Ordinary to fair white table wine. West Germany.

Kirschplatt. (24) Rhinehessia; Schwabsburg vineyard, just south-west of Nierstein. Ordinary to fair white table wine. West Germany.

Kirschroth. (24) Nahe; south-west of Bad Münster. Fair white table wine. West Germany.

Kirwan, Château. (4) Haut-Médoc; Cantenac. *Troisième cru classé.* 6,000 dozen bottles of red bordeaux. France.

Kissamos. (34) Island of Cyprus, approx. 100 miles off the west coast of Syria. Ordinary to fair red table wine. Cyprus.

Kissel. (23) Palatinate; Wachenheim vineyard. Fair white table wine. West Germany.

Kissling. (24) Rhinegau; Erbach vineyard. Fine white table wine. West Germany.

Kitzingen. (25) Franconia; south-west of Bad Münster. Fair to fine white table wine. West Germany.

Klamm. (24) Nahe; Niederhausen-Schloss Böckelheim vineyard, west of Bad Münster. Fine white table wine. West Germany.

Klausenberg. (24) Rhinehessia; Westhofen vineyard, south-west of Alsheim. Fair to fine white table wine. West Germany.

Klauser Berg. (24) Rhinegau; Johannisberg vineyard. Fair white table wine. West Germany.

Klauserweg. (24) Rhinegau; Geisenheim vineyard. Fair to fine white table wine. West Germany.

Kleinbockenheim. (23) Palatinate; north of Grünstadt. Ordinary to fair white table wine. West Germany.

Kleinbottwar. (25) Württemberg; south-east of Heilbronn. Ordinary to fair red and white table wine. West Germany.

Kleingartach. (25) Württemberg; east of Darmstadt. Ordinary to fair red and white table wine. West Germany.

Kleinheppach. (25) Württemberg; north-east of Stuttgart. Ordinary red and white table wine. West Germany.

Kleinkarlbach. (23) Palatinate; just south of Grünstadt. Ordinary to fair red and white table wines. West Germany.

Kleinkems. (25) Baden; approx. twenty-five miles south west of Freiburg. Fair white table wine. West Germany.

Kleinniedesheim. (23) Palatinate; south-west of Worms. Ordinary to fair red and white table wines. West Germany.

Kleinochsenfurt. (25) Franconia; south-east of Würzburg. Fair to fine white table wine. West Germany.

Klein-Winternheim. (24) Rhinehessia; west of Bodenheim. Fair white table wine. West Germany.

Klepsau. (25) Baden; approx. twenty-three miles east of Mosbach. Ordinary to fair white table wine. West Germany.

Klingen. (23) Palatinate; south-west of Landau. Fair red and white table wines. West Germany.

Klingenberg. (25) Württemberg; just south-west of Heilbronn. Ordinary to fair red and white table wines. West Germany.

Klingenberg-am-Main. (21) Franconia; approx. twenty-three miles south-east of Darmstadt. Ordinary to fair red and white table wines. West Germany.

Klingenmünster. (23) Palatinate; south-west of Landau. Ordinary to fair red and white table wines. West Germany.

Kloch. (33) Steiermark (Styria); south-east Austria. Fair to fine white table wine. Austria.

Kloppberg. (24) Rhinehessia; Dittelsheim vineyard, south-west of Alsheim. Fair white table wine. West Germany.

Kloster. (22) Moselle; Mühlheim vineyard, between Bernkastel Kues and Brauneberg. Ordinary to fair white table wine. West Germany.

Kloster Erbach. (24) Rhinegau. The former home of the Cistercian monks who planted the first Steinberg vineyard nearby in the 12th century. It is now a wine museum. West Germany.

Kloster Fürstensthal. (21) Middle Rhine; Bacharach vineyard, north-west of Bingen. Fair white table wine. West Germany.

Klosterkammer. (22) Moselle; Aldegund vine-yard, between Eller and Zell. Ordinary to fair white table wine. West Germany.

Klosterkiesel. (24) Rhinegau; Rüdesheim vine-yard. Fair to fine white table wine. West Germany.

Klosterlay. (22) Moselle; Wehlen vineyard. Fine white table wine. West Germany.

Klosterneck. (24) Rhinehessia; Laubenheim vine-yard. Fair white table wine. West Germany.

Klosterneuberg. (33) Fair red and white table wines from the Austrian School of Viticulture. Austria.

Klotten. (22) Moselle valley; north of Valwig. Ordinary to fair white table wines. West Germany.

Klümbchen. (24) Rhinegau; Eltville vineyard. Fair to fine white table wine. West Germany.

Klüsserath. (22) Middle Moselle valley. Fair to fine white table wine. West Germany.

Knittelsheim. (23) Palatinate; east of Landau. Ordinary to fair red and white table wines. West Germany.

Knittlingen. (25) Württemberg; approx. sixteen miles east of Karlsruhe. Ordinary to fair red and white table wine. West Germany.

Kobern. (22) Lower Moselle. Ordinary, fair and some fine white table wines. West Germany.

Koblenz. (21) Middle Rhine. Ordinary white table wine. West Germany.

Kobnert. (23) Palatinate; Kallstadt and Üngstein vineyards, just north of Bad Dürkheim. Fair white table wine. West Germany.

Kochem. (22) Moselle; west of Valwig. Fair white table wine. West Germany.

Kohlenberg. (22) Ruwer valley; Kasel vineyard. Fair to fine white table wine. West Germany.

Kohlkaut. (24) Rhinegau; Hochheim vineyard. Fair to fine white table wine. West Germany.

Kohm. (24) Rhinehessia; Osthofen vineyard, north of Worms. Fair white table wine. West Germany.

Kokkineli. (34) Island of Cyprus, approx. 100 miles off the west coast of Syria. Ordinary to fair, slightly sweet red and rosé table wines. Cyprus.

Kolbern. (24) Rhinehessia; Dromersheim vine-yard, south-east of Bingen. Fair white table wine. West Germany.

Köllig. (22) Moselle; south-west of Kobern. Fair white table wines. West Germany.

Kommlingen. (22) Moselle; north of Wiltingen. Ordinary to fair white table wine is produced. West Germany.

Köndringen. (25) Baden; north-west of Freiburg. Ordinary to fair white table wine. West Germany.

Könen. (22) Baden, Saar valley; north-west of Filzen. Ordinary to fair white table wine. West Germany.

Köngernheim. (24) Rhinehessia; west of Oppen-heim. Ordinary to fair white table wine. West Germany.

Königheim. (25) Franconia. Fair white table wine. West Germany.

König Johannberg. (22) Saar valley; Stadt vine-yard, south of Saarburg. Ordinary to fair white table wine. West Germany.

Königsbach. (23) Palatinate; Middle Haardt vine-yard. Fair to fine and some very fine white table wines. West Germany.

Königsberg. (22) Middle Moselle; Detzem and Klüsserath vineyards. Fair white table wine. West Germany.

Königsberg. (24) Nahe; Schloss Böckelheim vine-yard, east of Bad Münster. Fine white table wine. West Germany.

Königschaffhausen. (24) Baden; north-west of Freiburg. Fair white wine. West Germany.

Königsfels. (24) Nahe; Waldböckelheim vine-yard, west of Bad Münster. Fair to fine white table wine. West Germany.

Königshofen. (25) Baden; approx. eighteen miles south-west of Würzburg. Fair white table wine. West Germany.

Königshofen. (25) Franconia; approx. nineteen miles south-west of Würzburg. Fair white table wine. West Germany.

Königslay. (22) Moselle; Merl and Traben vine-yards, north of Zell. Fair white table wine. West Germany.

Königsstuhl. (22) Moselle; Bernkastel vineyard. Fair to fine white table wine. West Germany.

Königswingert. (23) Palatinate; Wachenheim vineyard. Fair white table wine. West Germany.

Konstanz. (25) Lake Constance (Bodensee). Ordi-nary white table wine. West Germany.

Konz. (22) Saar valley; north of Filzen. Fair white table wine. Most of its wines are sold as *Ober-emmeler* and some as *Falkenstein*. West Germany.

Korbel & Brothers Inc. (36) California; Guerne-ville, Sonoma County. Table, sparkling and dessert wines; brandy and a fine natural-process American champagne. U.S.A.

Korb-Steinreinach. (25) Württemberg; north-east of Stuttgart. Ordinary to fair red and white table wines. West Germany.

Kornell, Hanns, Champagne Cellars. (36) California; St Helena. Noted for natural-process American champagne, 'blancs de blancs' also table, dessert and sparkling wines and vermouth. U.S.A.

Kosakenberg. (24) Rhinegau; Geisenheim vine-yard. Fair to fine white table wine. West Germany.

Kosovo. (33) South-central Yugoslavia; autonomous

province south of Serbia. Produces fruit raisins and wines. Best known of the latter are Cabernet, Gamay and Pinot Noir red wines. Yugoslavia.

Kourschels. (22) Moselle; Wellesstein vineyard. Ordinary white table wine. West Germany.

Krajina. (33) East-central Yugoslavia; eastern part of Serbia. Table wines and quality red wines. Yugoslavia.

Krampen. (22) Moselle. The local name of the hairpin bend of the Moselle between Eller and Kochem. West Germany.

Kranich. (23) Palatinate; Forst vineyard. Fine white table wine. West Germany.

Kranklay. (22) Moselle; Erden and Ürzig vineyards. Fair white table wines. West Germany.

Kranklay (24) Rhinegau; Oestrich vineyard. Fine white table wine. West Germany.

Kränzchen. (24) Rhinegau; Erbach vineyard. Fair to fine white table wine. West Germany.

Kranzler. (23) Palatinate; Deidesheim vineyard. Fair to fine white table wine. 'Paradiesgarten' is the generic name for all Deidesheim wines. West Germany.

Krassolzheim. (25) Franconia; approx. twenty-two miles south-east of Würzburg. Fair white table wine. West Germany.

Krauterhaus. (22) Moselle; Traben vineyard. Fair white table wine. West Germany.

Krautsostheim. (25) Franconia; approx. twenty-five miles south-east of Würzburg. Fair white table wine. West Germany.

Krebsweiler. (24) Nahe; approx. sixteen miles south-west of Bad Münster. Fair white table wine. West Germany.

Kreidekeller. (23) Palatinate; Kallstadt vineyard. Fair to fine white table wine. West Germany.

Kreitzberg. (32) Moselle; Remerschen vineyard, south-east of Luxembourg city. Fair white wine. Luxembourg.

Krems. (33) Lower Austria; on the Danube to the west of Vienna. Ordinary to fair red and white table wines. Austria.

Kressbronn. (25) Lake Constance (Bodensee); approx. twenty miles south-east of Konstanz. Fair red and white table wines. West Germany.

Krettnach. (22) Saar valley; north-east of Wiltingen. Ordinary to fair white table wine. West Germany.

Kreuzberg. (21) Ahr valley; west of Linz. Ordinary red table wine. West Germany.

Kreuzberg. (24) Rhinegau; Hallgarten and Winkel vineyards. Fair to fine white table wine. West Germany.

Kreuzberg. (22) Saar valley; Niederleuken vineyard, at Saarburg. Fair white table wine. West Germany.

Kreuzmorgen. (23) Palatinate; Ungstein vineyard, between Bad Dürkheim and Kallstadt. Fair white table wine. West Germany.

Kreuzweiler. (22) Moselle; south-west of Saarburg. Ordinary white table wine. West Germany.

Kreuzwertheim. (25) Franconia; approx. eighteen miles west of Würzburg. Fair white table wine. West Germany.

Kreuzwingert. (22) Moselle; Ürzig vineyard. Fair to fine white table wine. West Germany.

Kreuzwingert. (24) Rhinehessia; Gau-Bischofsheim vineyard, west of Nackenheim. Fair white table wine. West Germany.

Krk. (33) Eastern Adriatic island. Ordinary red table wines. Yugoslavia.

Krone. (24) Rhinegau; Lorch vineyard. Ordinary white table wine. West Germany.

Krone. (22) Ruwer valley; Waldrach vineyard. Fair white wine. West Germany.

Kronzberg. (25) Franconia; Iphofen vineyard, south-east of Würzburg. Fair to fine white table wine. West Germany.

Krotenberg. (24) Rhinehessia; Oppenheim vineyard. Fair to fine white table wine. West Germany.

Krotenbrunnen. (24) Rhinehessia; Dienheim and Oppenheim vineyards. Fair white table wine. West Germany.

Krotenpfühl. (24) Nahe; Bad Kreuznach vineyard. Fine white table wine. West Germany.

Kröv. (22) Moselle; west of Enkirch. Fair to fine white table wines. West Germany.

Kruck. (25) Rhinehessia; Heppenheim vineyard, south-west of Worms. Fair white table wine. West Germany.

Krug, Charles, Winery. (36) California; St Helena. Vineyards owned by C. Mondavi & Sons. One of the sons, Robert Mondavi, has his own winery (q.v.). The other, Peter, has remained in charge of the Charles Krug Winery since Cesare Mondavi died in 1959. Quality table and dessert wines. U.S.A.

Krutweiler. (22) Moselle; just south of Saarburg. Fair white table wine. West Germany.

Küchelberger. (26) Alto Adige; Merano vineyard, north-west of Bolzano. Fair white table wine. Italy.

Kuckucksberg. (22) Moselle; Bruttig vineyard. Fair white table wine. West Germany.

Kuckuckslay. (22) Moselle; Mehrig vineyard, south-west of Klüsserath. Fair white table wine. West Germany.

Kues. (22) Moselle; town linked to Bernkastel on the left bank of the Moselle. Fair and fine white wines. West Germany.

Kugel. (24) Rhinehessia; Oppenheim vineyard. Fair white table wine. West Germany.

Kunk. (22) Moselle; Wittlich vineyard, west of Ürzig. Fair white table wine. West Germany.

Künzelsau. (25) Württemberg; approx. eighteen miles north-east of Heilbronn. Ordinary red and white table wines. West Germany.

Kupfergrube. (24) Nahe; Schloss Böckelheim vineyard, west of Bad Münster. Fair to fine white table wine. West Germany.

Kupp. (22) Saar valley; Wiltingen vineyard. Fine to very fine white table wine. Also Niederleuken vineyard—fair white table wine. West Germany.

Kuppel. (24) Rhinehessia; Nackenheim vineyard. Fair white table wine. West Germany.

Kurtatscherleiten. (26) Alto Adige; Cortazzio vineyard, Lake Caldaro area south-west of Bolzano. Fair red table wine. Italy.

Kymi. (34) Island of Eubea off south-east coast of Greece. Ordinary to fair red table wine. Greece.

Kytaera. (34) Greek Island in the Aegean off southern coast of Greece. Fair red and white table wines. Greece.

❧

Labatut, Château. (5) Premières Côtes de Bordeaux; St-Maxiant, south-east of St Croix-du-Mont. 1,500 dozen bottles of red bordeaux; 3,500 white. France.

Labatut, Domaine. (5) St-Emilion; Montagne. An unclassified *cru*. 2,000 dozen bottles of red bordeaux. France.

Labégorce. (4) Haut-Médoc; Margaux. *Cru bourgeois supèrieur*. 10,000 dozen bottles of red bordeaux. France.

Labégorce-Zédé, Château. (4) Haut-Médoc; Soussans. *Cru bourgeois supèrieur*. 6,000 dozen bottles of red bordeaux. France.

Laberstahl. (24) Rhinehessia; Dromersheim vineyard (south-east of Bingen) and Ockenheim vineyard (south of Geisenheim). Ordinary to fair white table wine. West Germany.

Laborde, Château. (5) Lalande de Pomerol; north of Pomerol. 4,000 dozen bottles of red bordeaux. France.

Laborie, Château. (5) Ste Croix-du-Mont; Côte de Bordeaux area. 5,000 dozen bottles of white bordeaux. France.

La Brède (Labrède). (5) Graves de Bordeaux; south of Martillac. Mostly fair white bordeaux. France.

La Brède, Château. (5) Graves de Bordeaux; Arbanats, north-west of Podensac. 500 dozen bottles of red bordeaux; 1,600 white are produced. France.

Labrousse, Château La. (4) Blayais; St-Martin, north of Blaye. 2,500 dozen bottles of red bordeaux. France.

Lacanau, Domaine de. (3) Entre-deux-Mers; Ambarès, east of Blanquefort. 2,000 dozen bottles of red bordeaux. France.

Lacassière, Clos de la. (16) Touraine; Vouvray vineyard, just above Tours. Fair to fine white table wine. France.

Lacco Ameno. (28) Campania; island of Ischia, in the Bay of Naples. Italy.

Lach. (24) Rhinegau; Lorchhausen vineyard, just north-west of Lorch. Ordinary white table wine. West Germany.

Lachassagne. (11) Beaujolais; Villefranche area. *AC Beaujolais*. Fair red burgundy. France.

Lachen-Speyerdorf. (23) Palatinate; south-east of Neustadt. Ordinary to fair red and white table wines. West Germany.

Lacrima Christi. (28) Vineyards on the seaward slopes of Mount Vesuvius, south-east of Naples. Fair to good sweetish white wine. Italy.

Lacrima d'Aretusa. (27) Tuscany; Arbia valley in the area south-east of Siena. Ordinary to fair light dry white table wine. Italy.

Lacrima di Corato. (28) Apulia; Bari. Ordinary to fair dry rosé table wine. Italy.

Lacrima di Gallipoli. (28) Apulia; Gallipoli Peninsula, Salento, the area encompassing the 'heel' of the 'boot'. Ordinary to fair dry rosé table wine. Italy.

Lacrima Vitis. (26) Lombardy; Santa Maria della Versa vineyards, Oltrepo Pavese, south of Pavia across the Po. Fair to fine golden dessert wine made from Moscato Fior d'Arancio grapes. Italy.

Ladoix-Serrigny. (8) Côtc de Beaune; village and vineyards close to Aloxe-Corton. The best red wines have the right to the *AC Corton*. The remainder have *AC Aloxe-Corton* or *Côte de Beaune* village. Red burgundy. France.

Lafaurie-Peyraguey, Château. (5) Sauternes; Bommes. *Premier cru classé*. 6,000 dozen bottles of white bordeaux. France.

Laffite-Carcasset, Château. (4) St-Estèphe. *Cru bourgeois supèrieur*. 6,000 dozen bottles of red bordeaux. France.

Lafite or **Lafite-Rothschild, Château.** (4) Haut-Médoc; Pauillac. *Premier cru classé*. 20,000 dozen bottles of red bordeaux. France.

Lafite-Canteloup, Château. (4) Haut-Médoc; Ludon area. *Cru bourgeois supèrieur*. 2,000 dozen bottles of red bordeaux. France.

Lafleur, Château. (5) Pomerol. *Grand cru*. 1,600 dozen bottles of red bordeaux. France.

Lafon, Château. (4) Haut-Médoc; Listrac. *Cru*

bourgeois supérieur. 3,000 dozen bottles of red bordeaux. France.

Lafon, Château. (5) Sauternes. *Cru bourgeois*. 600 dozen bottles of white bordeaux. France.

Lafran-Veyrolles. (14) Côtes de Provence; La Cadière vineyard, north-west of Toulon. Ordinary to fair table wines, *AC Bandol*. France.

Lafue, Château. (5) Ste Croix-du-Mont, Côtes de Bordeaux. 300 dozen bottles of red bordeaux; 6,000 white. France.

Lagarina Rosato. (26) Alto Adige; Bolzano area. Very popular ordinary rosé table wine of Lagrina red grapes. Italy.

Lagoa. (30) Algarve. Ordinary red and white table wines. Portugal.

Lago di Caldaro. (26) Alto Adige; Lake Caldaro, south-east of Bolzano. Fair red table wine. Italy.

Lagosta. (28) Sardinia; Alghero, approx. eighteen miles south-west of Sassari. Ordinary dry, even tart, white table wine. Italy.

Lagrange, Château. (4) Bourgeais. 6,000 dozen bottles of red bordeaux. France.

Lagrange, Château. (4) Haut-Médoc; St-Julien. *Troisième cru classé*. 20,000 dozen bottles of red bordeaux. France.

Lagrange, Château. (5) Pomerol. *Grand cru*. 2,000 dozen bottles of red bordeaux. France.

Lagrange, Domaine de. (5) Premières Côtes de Bordeaux; Monprimblanc, east of Loupiac. 2,000 dozen bottles of red bordeaux; 8,000 white. France.

Lagrein (Lagarina). (26) Alto Adige; Bolzano area. Fair red and pleasing rosé table wines made from Lagrein grapes. Italy.

Lagrima. (29) Málaga. Fair to fine dessert wine. Spain.

Laguardia. (29) Old Castile; Logroño province, La Rioja area of the upper Ebro valley. Ordinary to fair red table wine. Spain.

Lague, Château. (3) Fronsac. 2,500 dozen bottles of red bordeaux. France.

Lagueloup, Château. (5) Graves de Bordeaux; Portets. An unclassified *cru*. 2,000 dozen bottles of red bordeaux; 2,000 white. France.

Lagune, Château la. (4) Haut-Médoc; Ludon area. *Troisième cru classé*. 20,000 dozen bottles of red bordeaux. France.

Lagune, Domaine de la. (3) Médoc; Bégadan, north-west of St Seurin-de-Cadourne. 1,500 dozen bottles of red bordeaux. France.

Lahr. (25) Baden; approx. twenty-seven miles north of Freiburg. Ordinary to fair red and white table wines. West Germany.

Laibach. (25) Württemberg; approx. twenty-four miles east of Mosbach. Ordinary to fair white table wine. West Germany.

Lairen. (29) Málaga and Córdoba. Ordinary to fair white table wine. Spain.

Lake's Folly. (37) New South Wales; Hunter River area, north-east of Sydney. Small vineyard mainly Cabernet planted in 1963. Property of Sydney surgeon, winemaker and author of books on wine, Dr Max Lake. Australia.

Lalande, Château. (4) Haut-Médoc; Listrac. *Cru bourgeois*. 2,500 dozen bottles of red bordeaux. France.

La Lande. (16) Touraine; Bourgueil. Fair red table wine. France.

Lalunez. (29) Aragón; Huesca area, north of Zaragoza. Ordinary red table wine. Spain.

Lama do Lagar, Quinta. (30) *Região demarcada do Douro* (q.v.). Estate and vineyard in Castedo north-east of Régua. Portugal.

Lamarque, Château. (5) Ste Croix-du-Mont; Côtes de Bordeaux area. 2,500 dozen bottles of red bordeaux; 5,000 white. France.

Lamarque, Château de. (4) Haut-Médoc; Lamarque. *Cru bourgeois supérieur*. 10,000 dozen bottles of red bordeaux. France.

Lambrays, Clos des. (8) Côte de Nuits; Morey-St-Denis vineyard. *Premier cru*. Red burgundy. France.

Lambrusco. (26) Alto Adige; Trentino. Good, dry red wine with an evanescent sparkle. Italy.

Lambsheim. (23) Palatinate; north-east of Bad Dürkheim. Ordinary to fair white table wine. West Germany.

Lamego, Quinta. (30) *Região demarcada do Douro* (q.v.). Santa Comba. Estate and vineyard in São Miguel de Lobrigos north-east of Régua. Portugal.

Lametino. (28) Calabria. Ordinary but somewhat heady white table wine, tasting rather of Madeira. Italy.

Lammerberg. (25) Franconia; Randersacker vineyard, south-east of Würzburg. Fair to fine white table wine. West Germany.

Lamothe, Château. (4) Bourgeais; Lansac, north-east of Bourg. 7,000 dozen bottles of red bordeaux. France.

Lamothe, Château. (4) St André-de-Cubzac, east of Blaye. 3,000 dozen bottles of red bordeaux. France.

Lamothe, Domaine de. (5) Entre-deux-Mers; Montignac, north of Langon. 300 dozen bottles of red bordeaux; 5,500 white. France.

Lamothe-Bergey, Château. (5) Sauternes. *Deuxième cru classé*. 2,000 dozen bottles of white bordeaux. France.

Lamothe-Bouscaut, Cru. (5) Graves de Bordeaux; Cadaujac. An unclassified *cru*. 1,500 dozen bottles of red bordeaux. France.

Lamothe-de-Bergeron, Château. (4) Haut-Médoc; Cussac. *Cru bourgeois supérieur.* 6,000 dozen bottles of red bordeaux. France.

La Motte, Clos de. (16) Coteaux de Saumur; Souzay-Champigny vineyard, on the Saumur hillsides. Fair white table wine. France.

Lamoureyre, Cru. (5) Ste Croix-du-Mont, Côtes de Bordeaux area. 1,000 dozen bottles of white bordeaux. France.

Lamouroux, Château. (4) Haut-Médoc; Margaux. *Cru bourgeois supérieur.* 2,000 dozen bottles of red bordeaux. France.

Lancellotta (Filtrato di Lancellotta). (26) Emilia-Romagna; Reggio-Emilia province. Ordinary to fair, sweet, clear red table wine. Italy.

Lancie. (11) Beaujolais village. *AC Beaujolais village.* Ordinary to fair red burgundy. France.

Landau. (23) Palatinate; south of Edenkoben. Ordinary to fair red and white table wines. West Germany.

Lande-de-Gravet, Château. (5) St-Emilion; St Sulpice-de-Faleyrens. An unclassified *cru.* 2,000 dozen bottles of red bordeaux. France.

Landeron, Le. (31) Neuchâtel; Combes vineyard. Fair white and ordinary red table wines. Switzerland.

Landon, Château. (3) Médoc; Bégadan, north of St Seurin-de-Cadourne. *Cru bourgeois.* 4,000 dozen bottles of red bordeaux. France.

Landshausen. (25) Baden; approx. eighteen miles west of Heilbronn. Ordinary to fair white table wine. West Germany.

Lanessan, Château. (4) Haut-Médoc, Cussac. *Cru bourgeois supérieur.* 10,000 dozen bottles of red bordeaux. France.

Langalerie, Château. (5) Ste Foy-de-Bordeaux; north-east of Langon. 5,000 dozen bottles of red bordeaux; 10,000 white. France.

Lange, Château. (5) Sauternes; Bommes. 3,000 dozen bottles of white bordeaux. France.

Langenacker. (23) Palatinate; Forst vineyard. Fine white table wine. West Germany.

Langenbächel. (23) Palatinate; Wachenheim vineyard. Fine white table wine. West Germany.

Langenberg. (22) Moselle; Kochem vineyard, west of Valwig. Fair white table wine. West Germany.

Langenberg. (24) Nahe; Bad Münster and Niederhausen vineyards, west of Bad Münster. Fair to fine white table wine. West Germany.

Langenberg. (24) Rhinegau; Kiedrich and Martinsthal vineyards. Fair to fine white table wine. West Germany.

Langenbohl. (23) Palatinate; Forst and Deidesheim vineyards. Fair to fine white table wines. West Germany.

Langenbrücken. (21) Baden; south of Heidelberg. Ordinary to fair red and white table wine. West Germany.

Langenlois. (33) Lower Austria. Ordinary to fair white table wine. Austria.

Langenlonsheim. (24) Nahe; south of Bingen. Ordinary, fair, fine and some very fine white table wines. West Germany.

Langenmorgen. (23) Palatinate; Forst and Deidesheim vineyards. Fair to fine white table wine. West Germany.

Langenstück. (23) Palatinate; Deidesheim vineyard. Fair to fine white table wine is produced. West Germany.

Langenstück. (24) Rhingau; Eltville and Rauenthal vineyards. Fair to fine white table wine. West Germany.

Langen Tag. (24) Rhinehessia; Nackenheim vineyard. Fair white table wine. West Germany.

Langenweg. (24) Rhinehessia; Dienheim vineyard. Fair white table wine. West Germany.

Langhe, Le. (26) Piedmont; the area of the Monferrato Hills, Alessándria province, whose vineyards produce not only the best Barolo (q.v.) red wines, but the only one entitled to the name by law. Italy.

Langkammer. (23) Palatinate; Forst vineyard. Fair to fine white table wine. West Germany.

Langlade, Château. (5) St-Emilion; Parsac. An unclassified *cru.* 800 dozen bottles of red bordeaux. France.

Langoa, Château. (4) Haut-Médoc; St-Julien. *Troisième cru classé.* 10,000 dozen bottles of red bordeaux. France.

Langoiran. (5) Premières Côtes de Bordeaux; north-east of Portets. Ordinary to fair red and white bordeaux. France.

Langon, Cru du. (16) Touraine; Beaumont-en-Véron vineyard, below Chinon. Fair red table wine. France.

Languettes, Les. (8) Côte de Beaune; Aloxe-Corton vineyard. *Premier cru. AC Corton Languettes.* Red burgundy. France.

Langscheid. (21) Middle Rhine; approx. twenty-five miles south-east of Koblenz. Ordinary to fair white table wine. West Germany.

Langsur. (22) Moselle; north-west of Kanzem. Ordinary to fair white table wine. West Germany.

Languedoc. (13) Former province, now covering part of the Gard, Hérault and Aude *départements.* France.

Langweg. (24) Rhinehessia; Dienheim vineyard. Fair white table wine. West Germany.

Laniote, Château. (5) St-Emilion. An unclassified *cru.* 3,000 dozen bottles of red bordeaux. France.

Lantigne. (11) Beaujolais. One of the best *Beaujolais Villages* just short of *cru* status. Ordinary to fair red burgundy. France.

Lanzarote. (40) Canary Islands off the north-west coast of Africa. Ordinary dry and sweet white wines. Spain.

Lapelletrie, Château. (5) St-Emilion; St Christophe-des-Bardcs, south-west of Parsac. An unclassified *cru*. 1,000 dozen bottles of red bordeaux. France.

Lapeyre, Château. (5) St-Emilion; St Etienne-de-Lisse. An unclassified *cru*. 4,000 dozen bottles of red bordeaux. France.

Larchevesque, Château. (3) Fronsac. 1,000 dozen bottles of red bordeaux; 500 white. France.

Larcis-Ducasse, Château. (4) St-Emilion; St Laurent-des-Combes. *Grand cru classé*. 4,000 dozen bottles of red bordeaux. France.

Larcis-Sirey, Château. (5) St-Emilion; St-Hippolyte. An unclassified *cru*. 1,000 dozen bottles of red bordeaux. France.

Laribotte, Château. (5) Sauternes; Preignac. *Cru bourgeois*. 1,500 dozen bottles of white bordeaux. France.

Larmande, Château. (5) St-Emilion. An unclassified *cru*. 4,500 dozen bottles of red bordeaux. France.

Larmande, Domaine de. (5) Côtes de St-Emilion. An unclassified *cru*. 4,500 dozen bottles of red bordeaux. France.

Laroche, Domaine de. (3) Entre-deux-Mers; Tresses, east of Bordeaux. 1,500 dozen bottles of red bordeaux; 800 white. France.

La Rosa, Quinta. (30) *Região demarcada do Douro*. Estate and vineyard below Pinhao east of Régua. Portugal.

Laroze, Château. (5) Côtes de St-Emilion. An unclassified *cru*. 10,000 dozen bottles of red bordeaux. France.

Larrivaux, Château. (4) Haut-Médoc; Cissac. *Cru bourgeois*. 4,000 dozen bottles of red bordeaux. France.

Larrivet-Haut-Brion, Château. (5) Graves de Bordeaux; Léognan. *Cru classé en rouge*. 2,000 dozen bottles of red bordeaux. France.

Larrouquey, Château. (5) Graves de Bordeaux; Cérons. 2,500 dozen bottles of white. France.

Lartigue, Château. (3) Médoc; Valeyrad, north-west of St Seurin-de-Cadourne. *Cru bourgeois*. 1,000 dozen bottles of red bordeaux. France.

Lascombes, Château. (4) Haut-Médoc; Margaux. *Deuxième cru classé*. 20,000 dozen bottles of red bordeaux. France.

La Seca. (29) Western Old Castile; Valladolid north of the Valdepeñas area. Ordinary to fair white table wine. Spain.

Lasenberg. (22) Moselle; Neumagen vineyard. Fair white table wine. West Germany.

Lassalle, Cru. (3) Médoc; Ordonnac-et-Potensac, north-west of St Seurin-de-Cadourne. *Cru bourgeois*. 3,000 dozen bottles of red bordeaux. France.

Lassègue, Château. (5) St-Emilion; St-Hippolyte. An unclassified *cru*. 8,000 dozen bottles of red bordeaux. France.

Latour, Château. (4) Haut-Médoc. Pauillac. *Premier cru classé*. 25,000 dozen bottles of red bordeaux. France.

Latour-Maudan, Château. (5) Premières Côtes de Bordeaux; Langoiran, north-east of Portets. 500 dozen bottles of red bordeaux; 2,500 white. France.

Latour-Pomerol, Château. (5) Pomerol. *Grand cru*. 4,000 dozen bottles of red bordeaux. France.

Latricières-Chambertin. (8) Côte de Nuits; Gevrey-Chambertin vineyard. *Grand cru*. Red burgundy. France.

Laubenheim. (24) Rhinehessia. Fair to fine white table wines. West Germany.

Lauberterie, Cru. (4) Cubzaguais, east of Blaye. 15,000 dozen bottles of white bordeaux. France.

Laubu, Domaine de. (5) Entre-deux-Mers; St-Macaire. 1,000 dozen bottles of red bordeaux; 500 white. France.

Lauda. (25) Franconia; approx. twenty-four miles south-west of Würzburg. Fair white table wine. West Germany.

Laudamus Berg. (22) Moselle; Neumagen vineyard. Fair white table wine. West Germany.

Laudenbach. (25) Baden, Bergstrasse; approx. seventeen miles north-east of Mannheim. Fair white table wine. West Germany.

Laudenbach. (21) Franconia; approx. twenty-five miles south-east of Darmstadt. Fair white table wine. West Germany.

Laudun. (12) Côtes du Rhône. Red and white table wines. France.

Lauerbaum. (21) Middle Rhine; Oberwesel vineyard, approx. eighteen miles north-west of Bingen. Fair white table wine is produced. West Germany.

Lauf. (25) Baden; south-west of Baden-Baden. Fair white table wine. West Germany.

Laufen. (25) Baden; approx. twenty miles south of Freiburg. Fair white table wine. West Germany.

Laufenberg. (31) Aargau canton. 75 acres. Ordinary to fair red table wine. Switzerland.

Lauffen. (25) Württemberg; south-west of Heilbronn. Ordinary red and white table wines. West Germany.

Laujac, Château. (3) Médoc; Bégadan, north-west of St Seurin-de-Cadourne. *Cru bourgeois.* 5,000 dozen bottles of red bordeaux. France.

Laumersheim. (23) Palatinate; just east of Grünstadt. Ordinary red, fair and some fine white table wines. West Germany.

Launay, Château. (4) Bourgeais. 1,000 dozen bottles of red bordeaux; 2,000 white. France.

Laurensanne, Château. (4) Bourgeais; St Seurin-de-Bourg, north-west of Bourg. 10,000 dozen bottles of red bordeaux. France.

Laurentiusberg. (24) Rhinegau; Rauenthal vineyard. Fine white table wine. West Germany.

Laurentiusberg. (22) Ruwer valley; Mertesdorf vineyard, east of Trier. Fair to fine white table wine. West Germany.

Laurentiuslay. (22) Moselle; Trittenheim vineyard. Fair to fine white table wine. West Germany.

Laurets, Château des. (5) St-Emilion; Puisseguin. An unclassified *cru.* 20,000 dozen bottles of red bordeaux. France.

Laurette, Château. (5) Ste Croix-du-Mont; Côtes de Bordeaux area. 1,000 dozen bottles of red bordeaux; 7,000 white. France.

Lausserie. (15) Pouilly-sur-Loire vineyard. Fair to fine white table wine. France.

Lautenbach. (25) Baden; approx. seventeen miles south-west of Baden-Baden. Fair white table wine. West Germany.

Lauterberg. (22) Saar valley; Oberemmel vineyard. Fair to fine white table wine. West Germany.

Lavalade, Château. (5) St-Emilion; St Christophe-des-Bardes, south-west of Parsac. An unclassified *cru.* 2,000 dozen bottles of red bordeaux. France.

Lavaux. (31) Vaud canton; the half-circle of terraced vineyards from Lausanne to Vevey. Ordinary, fair, fine and some very fine white table wines. Switzerland.

Lavaux, Combe de. (8) Côte de Nuits; Gevrey-Chambertin vineyard. *Deuxième cru.* Red burgundy. France.

Lavières, Aux. (8) Côte de Nuits; Nuits-St-Georges vineyard. *Deuxième cru.* Red burgundy. France.

Lavières, Les. (8) Côte de Beaune; Pommard vineyard. *Deuxième cru.* Red burgundy. France.

Lavières, Les. (8) Côte de Beaune; Savigny-les-Beaune. *Premier cru.* Red burgundy. France.

La Ville, Cru de. (31) Neuchâtel vineyard. Fair white table wine. Switzerland.

Laville-Haut-Brion, Château. (5) Graves de Bordeaux; Talence. *Cru classé de Graves en blanc.* 2,200 dozen bottles of white bordeaux. France.

Lavrottes, Les. (8) Côte de Nuits; Chambolle-Musigny vineyard. *Premier cru.* Red burgundy. France.

Layen. (22) Moselle; Kröv, west of Enkirch and Neumagen vineyards. Fair white table wine. West Germany.

Layenweg. (24) Nahe; Heddesheim vineyard, north-west of Bad Kreuznach. Fair to fine white table wine. West Germany.

Layon. (16) Small river which flows into the Loire, south of Angers, Anjou. The hillside vineyards of its valley produce some very nice white wines, a little sweet, which are known as wines of the Coteaux du Layon. France.

Lazio. (27) The province, including Rome itself, whose vineyards produce mostly ordinary to fair table wines. Italy.

Lebelin. (8) Côte de Beaune; Monthélie vineyard. Hospices de Beaune *cuvée* named after the donor. 375 dozen bottles of red burgundy. France.

Lebena Tostadillo. (29) Northern Spanish coast, Santander, 45 miles west of Bilbao. Ordinary dry red and fair to fine white sweet wine is produced. Spain.

Lechinta. (33) One of the best white dessert wines. Rumania.

Leckerberg. (24) Rhinehessia; Dittelsheim vineyard, south-west of Dienheim. Fair white table wine. West Germany.

Le Crock, Château. (4) Haut-Médoc; St-Estèphe. *Cru bourgeois supérieur.* 15,000 dozen bottles of red bordeaux. France.

Lehmen. (22) Moselle; south of Kobern. Fair white table wine. West Germany.

Lehrensteinsfeld. (25) Württemberg; east of Heilbronn. Ordinary to fair red and white table wines. West Germany.

Leidhecke. (24) Rhinehessia; Bodenheim vineyard. Fair to fine white table wine. West Germany.

Leimen. (25) Baden, Bergstrasse; south of Heidelberg. Ordinary to fair red and white table wines. West Germany.

Leimen. (24) Rhinehessia; Bodenheim vineyard. Fair to fine white table wine. West Germany.

Leinhöhle. (23) Palatinate; Deidesheim vineyard. Fair to fine white table wine is produced. West Germany.

Leinsweiler. (23) Palatinate; south-west of Landau. Ordinary to fair, and some fine white table wines. West Germany.

Leiro. (29) South Galicia; Orense, Ribero. Ordinary white table wine. Spain.

Leiselheim. (25) Baden; north-west of Freiburg. Fair white table wine. West Germany.

Leistadt. (23) Palatinate; south of Grünstadt. Ordinary to fair red and white wines and some fine white table wines. West Germany.

Leisten. (25) Franconia; Würzburg area. Fine white table wine. West Germany.

Leistenberg. (24) Rhinehessia; Bodenheim vineyard. Fair to fine white table wine. West Germany.

Leitacher. (26) Alto Adige; Bolzano area. One of the finest wines of the region. Dry, moderately light red wine. Italy.

Leitwein. (26) Another name for the Colline Bolzano (q.v.) wines.

Leiwen. (22) Moselle; between Neumagen and Detzen. Ordinary, fair and some fine white table wines. West Germany.

Le Mesnil-sur-Oger. (17) Marne *département*; Avize canton. Rated *premier cru*—99% growth. 432 acres. France.

Lemnos. (34) Aegean Sea island off north-west coast of Turkey. Ordinary dry red and fair sweet white wines. Greece.

Lemoine-Lafont-Rochet, Château. (1) Médoc; Ludon area. *Cru bourgeois*. 1,500 dozen bottles of red bordeaux. France.

Lenchen. (24) Rhinegau; Oestrich vineyard. Fine white table wine. West Germany.

Lende. (24) Rhinehessia; Hessloch vineyard, south-west of Alsheim. Fair white table wine. West Germany.

Lengfurt. (25) Franconia; west of Würzburg. Ordinary to fair red and white table wines. West Germany.

Lenzburg. (31) Aargau canton. 30 acres. Ordinary red table wine. Switzerland.

Leognan. (5) Graves de Bordeaux. Fair, fine and some very fine red bordeaux. France.

Leonay, Château. (37) South Australia; Tanunda, south of Adelaide. Winery and vineyard. Superb dry white wines. Australia.

Leonbronn. (25) Württemberg; south-west of Heilbronn. Ordinary to fair red and white table wine. West Germany.

Leonforte (Bianco, Rosso). (28) Sicily; Mount Etna area approx. forty miles north-west of Catania. Ordinary dry white, and rather coarse red table wines. Italy.

Léoville-Barton, Château. (4) Haut-Médoc; St-Julien. *Deuxième cru classé*. 10,000 dozen bottles of red bordeaux. France.

Léoville-Las-Cases, Château. (4) Haut-Médoc; St-Julien. *Deuxième cru classé*. 20,000 dozen bottles of red bordeaux. France.

Léoville-Poyferré, Château. (4) Haut-Médoc; St-Julien. *Deuxième cru classé*. 17,000 dozen bottles of red bordeaux. France.

Le Pis. (11) Beaujolais; Morgon vineyard producing most characteristic wine of this *AC Le Pis*. One of the top-grade beaujolais, red burgundy. France.

Lercherberg. (23) Palatinate; Kirrweiler vineyard. Fair to fine white table wine. West Germany.

Lesbos. (34) Aegean island off north-west coast of Turkey whose wines have been praised since Homeric days. Greece.

L'Escadre, Château. (4) Blayais; Cars, east of Blaye. 13,000 dozen bottles of red bordeaux; 2,000 white. France.

Lescours, Château. (5) St-Emilion; St Sulpice-de-Faleyrens. An unclassified *cru*. 7,000 dozen bottles of red bordeaux. France.

Lespaut, Château. (5) Graves de Bordeaux; Martillac. An unclassified *cru*. 1,000 dozen bottles of red bordeaux; 500 white. France.

Lessona. (26) Piedmont; Vercelli province. Fine red wine similar to, although not quite so fine as, Gattinara (q.v.). Italy.

Lestage, Château. (4) Haut-Médoc; Listrac. *Cru bourgeois supérieur*. 18,000 dozen bottles of red bordeaux. France.

Lestage-Darquier-Grand-Poujeaux, Château. (4) Haut-Médoc; Moulis. *Cru bourgeois supérieur*. 3,000 dozen bottles of red bordeaux. France.

Letschenberg. (32) Moselle; Schwebsingen vineyard, north of Wintrange. Fair white wine. Luxembourg.

Lett. (24) Rhinegau; Winkel vineyard. Fair to fine white table wine. West Germany.

Letten. (23) Palatinate; Dürkheim, Hambach and Maikammer vineyards (latter two both just south of Neustadt). Fair to fine white table wine. West Germany.

Letten. (24) Rhinehessia; Friedelsheim vineyard, south-east of Bad Dürkheim. Fair white table wine. West Germany.

Lettere. (28) Campania; Sorrentine peninsula, approx. twenty miles south-east of Naples. Ordinary red and white table wines. Some of the reds are semi-sweet. Italy.

Lettweiler. (23) Palatinate; south-west of Bad Münster. Fair white table wine. West Germany.

Leurey. *See* **Leurrées, Au.**

Leurrées, Au. (8) Côte de Nuits; Prémaux-Prissey vineyard. *Deuxième cru. AC Côte de Nuits*. Red burgundy. France.

Leutershausen. (25) Baden, Bergstrasse; approx. forty-five miles south-east of Würzburg. Ordinary to fair red and white table wines. West Germany.

Leutesdorf. (21) Middle Rhine; approx. fifteen miles north-west of Koblenz. Ordinary to fair red and white table wines. West Germany.

Levante. (29) Coastal area of eastern Spain embracing the vineyards of the provinces of Murcia, Valencia and Alicante, south of Valencia. The 810,000 acres of vineyards produce ordinary to fair white, rosé and red wines. Spain.

Leyenkaut. (22) Saar valley; Saarburg area. Fair white table wine. West Germany.

Leyer. (24) Rhinehessia; Ockenheim vineyard, south of Geisenheim. Fair white table wine. West Germany.

Leza. (29) Alava region; La Rioja area of the upper Ebro valley. Ordinary red table wine. Spain.

Liards, Les. (16) Touraine; Côte de Montlouis, St Martin-le-Beau vineyard, east of Tours. Fair white table wine. France.

Libertins, Les. (9) Chalonnais; St Martin-sous-Montaigu vineyard. *Deuxième cru.* Red burgundy. France.

Lickerstein. (24) Rhinegau; Geisenheim vineyard. Fair to fine white table wine. West Germany.

Liebfrauenberg. (24) Rhinehessia; Westhofen vineyard, south-west of Alsheim. Fair white table wine. West Germany.

Liebfrauenstift. (24) Rhinehessia; Worms Cathedral vineyard. Very fine white table wine. West Germany.

Liebfrauental. (24) Rhinehessia; Mettenheim vineyard south of Alsheim. Fair white table wine. West Germany.

Liechtenstein. (31) Very small Principality on Swiss-Austrian border: its vineyards produce a light, fair red wine.

Liel. (25) Baden; approx. twenty miles south-west of Freiburg. Fair white table wine. West Germany.

Lies. (24) Rhinehessia; Kempten vineyard, just east of Bingen. Fair white table wine. West Germany.

Lieser. (22) Middle Moselle. Fair to fine and some very fine white table wine. West Germany.

Lieth. (24) Rhinehessia; Harxheim vineyard, west of Nackenheim. Fair white table wine. West Germany.

Lignes, Les. (16) Touraine; Savigny-en-Véron below Chinon. Fair red table wine. France.

Ligny-le-Château. (6) Chablis; Yonne *département*. Fair white burgundy. France.

Ligorelles. (6) Chablis; Yonne *département*. Fair white burgundy. France.

Ligré. (16) Touraine; Côte de Chinon. Fair red table wine. France.

Liguria. (26) The mountainous coastal territory from the Franco-Italian frontier in the north to La Spezia in the south. Most of its vineyards are on mountain slopes and produce chiefly dry white table wines. Italy.

Lillo. (29) West New Castile; Toledo; approx. forty miles south-west of Madrid. Ordinary red table wine. Spain.

Liloy, Domaine de. (5) Premières Côtes de Bordeaux; Verdelais, north of Langon. 1,000 dozen bottles of red bordeaux; 3,000 white. France.

Lilydale. (37) Victoria; in Yarra Valley, approx. thirty miles east of Melbourne. The Lilydale region includes nearby Yering, where Victoria's first vines were planted in 1838. Region fell into disuse viticulturally but since 1969 some planting activity has been revived. Australia.

Limassina. (26) Liguria; Finale Liguria between Sorona and Imperia. Very popular ordinary white table wine. Italy.

Limassol. (34) Island of Cyprus, approx. 100 miles off the west coast of Syria. Town on south coast with an important vineyard area. Cyprus.

Limbadi Rosso. (28) Calabria; Catanzaro. Ordinary dry or semi-sweet red table wine. Italy.

Limbourg, Château. (5) Graves de Bordeaux; Villenave-d'Ornon. An unclassified *cru*. 1,500 dozen bottles of white bordeaux. France.

Limnos. *See* **Lemnos.**

Limoux. (13) Aude *département*. Chiefly noted for its gently sparkling white wine, known as *Blanquette de Limoux*. France.

Limpias. (29) North coast of Spain; Santander, 45 miles west of Bilbao, close to the French frontier. Fair *clarete* table wine. Spain.

Lindeman's Ben Ean. (37) New South Wales; Hunter Valley, north-east of Sydney. Important, long-established winery and vineyard, now owned by the Philip Morris tobacco company. Australia.

Lindenbusch. (23) Palatinate; Ruppertsberg vineyard. Fine white table wine. West Germany.

Linsenstein. (23) Palatinate, Forst vineyard. Fine white table wine. West Germany.

Linz. (21) Middle Rhine. Fair white wine. West Germany.

Lionner, Cru. (4) Haut-Médoc; Listrac. *Cru bourgeois.* 1,500 dozen bottles of red bordeaux. France.

Lions, Les. (16) Anjou; Coteaux de la Loire, Montjean vineyard, below Angers. Fair white wine. France.

Liot, Château. (5) Barsac. *Cru bourgeois.* 6,000 dozen bottles of white bordeaux are produced. France.

Lipari. (28) Island off the north-east coast of Sicily. Fair golden dessert wine. Italy.

Lippoldsweiler. (25) Württemberg; approx. twenty miles north-east of Stuttgart. Ordinary to fair red and white table wines. West Germany.

Lirac. (12) Gard *département;* Côtes du Rhône. Red, white and rosé table wines. France.

Lisse, Château de. (5) St-Emilion; St Etienne-de-Lisse. An unclassified *cru*. 8,000 dozen bottles of red bordeaux. France.

Listrac. (4) Haut-Médoc. Fair and some fine red bordeaux. France.

Livermore. (36) California; a valley in Alameda County. Quality table and dessert wines. Most famous for white wines which are among the best of California whites. U.S.A.

Liversan, Château. (4) Haut-Médoc; St-Sauveur. *Cru bourgeois supérieur.* 7,000 dozen bottles of red bordeaux. France.

Livran, Château. (3) Médoc; St Germain-d'Esteuil, west of St Seurin-de-Cadourne. *Cru bourgeois.* 15,000 dozen bottles of red bordeaux; 5,000 white. France.

Ljutomer. *See* **Lutomer.**

Llacuna, La. (29) Upper Panadés; Barcelona, between Tarragona and Barcelona. Ordinary to fair table wines. Spain.

Llansa. (29) Gerona; approx. twenty-five miles north-east of Barcelona. Ordinary to fair red and white dessert wines. Spain.

Lledoner. (29) Gerona; approx. twenty-five miles north-east of Barcelona. Very dark, dry red table wine. Spain.

Lloa. (29) Tarragona. Ordinary red table wine. Spain.

Lluchmayor. (29) Majorca; Balearic Islands, off the coast of Spain, east of Valencia. Ordinary to fair red sweet wine. Spain.

Loachausses. (8) Côte de Nuits; Flagey-Echézeaux vineyard. *Premier cru.* Red burgundy. France.

Loarre. (29) Aragón; Huesca area, north of Zaragoza. Ordinary table wines. Spain.

Lobata, Quinta. (30) *Região demarcada do Douro* (q.v.). Estate and vineyard in Adorigo east of Régua. Portugal.

Lobazim, Quinta (30) *Região demarcada do Douro* (q.v.). Large estate and vineyard in Vilarinho de Castanheira in the Régua area of 505 acres. Portugal.

Loche. (10) Mâconnais; close by Pouilly Fuissé, Solutré-Vinzelles vineyards. Fair to fine white burgundy. France.

Löchgau. (25) Württemberg; north of Stuttgart. Ordinary to fair red and white table wines. West Germany.

Locorotondo, Bianco Di. (28) Apulia; Bari area. Popular, ordinary, light, almost colourless white table wine, enormous quantities of which are used as a neutral base for vermouth. Italy.

Lodeiro, Quinta. (30) *Região demarcada do Douro* (q.v.). Estate and vineyard in São João da Pesqueira nineteen miles east of Régua. Portugal.

Loewenberg. (22) Moselle; Kinheim vineyard. Fair to fine white table wine. West Germany.

Longue Toque, Domaine de. (12) Côtes du Rhône; Gigondas vineyard. Fair red table wine. France.

Lopera. (29) Jaén; north-east of Seville. Ordinary to fair white table wine. Spain.

Loureiro, Quinta. (30) *Região demarcada do Douro* (q.v.). Fine estate and vineyard in Loureiro north-west of Régua. Portugal.

Löf. (22) Moselle; south of Kobern. Ordinary to fair white table wine. West Germany.

Logroño. (29) La Rioja Alta area of the upper Ebro valley. Fair to fine mostly red table wines. Spain.

Lomassina. *See* **Limassina.**

Lombardy. (26) The most important part of northern Italy, quantitatively, as regards its vineyard acreage and wine production. The best wines of Lombardy are those of the Valtelline, Lake Garda and Brescia areas. Italy.

Longen. (22) Moselle; south-west of Klüsserath. Ordinary to fair table wine is produced. West Germany.

Long Poil. (10) Mâconnais; Fuissé vineyard. *Premier cru.* White burgundy. France.

Longuich. (22) Middle Moselle; east of Trier. Fair to fine white wine. West Germany.

Longuich-Kirch. (22) Moselle; north-east of Trier. Ordinary to fair white table wine. West Germany.

Lonsheim. (24) Rhinehessia. Ordinary to fair red and white table wines. West Germany.

Loppin. (8) Côte de Beaune; Hospices de Beaune *cuvée,* Meursault. White burgundy. France.

Lorch. (24) Rhinegau. Ordinary, fair and some fine white table wines. West Germany.

Lorchhausen. (24) Rhinegau; just north of Lorch. Ordinary to fair red and white table wines. West Germany.

Lorenzberg. (22) Ruwer; Kasel vineyard. Fine white table wine. West Germany.

Lorenzberg (Mertesdorf). *See* **Laurentiusberg.**

Loro Piceno. (27) The Marches; a village near Macerata approx. twenty miles south of Ancona which produces a particularly fine Verdicchio wine (q.v.). It also produces a very strong, sweet *vin cotto* or 'cooked wine'. Italy.

Lorraine. (32) Former province of eastern France south-west of Luxembourg now mostly in the Meurthe-et-Moselle *département;* the hillside vineyards in the Moselle valley and other Lorraine vineyards produce much ordinary to fair table wines, red, white and *gris.* France.

Lörzweiler. (24) Rhinehessia; south-west of Nackenheim. Ordinary to fair red and white table wines. West Germany.

Los Gatos, Novitiate of. (36) California; Santa Clara Valley. Quality table and dessert wines. U.S.A.

Lösnich. (22) Middle Moselle; between Erden and

Traben-Trabach. Fair to fine white table wines. West Germany.

Loubens, Château. (5) Ste Croix-du-Mont; Côte de Bordeaux. 600 dozen bottles of red bordeaux; 6,000 white. France.

Loudenne, Château. (3) Médoc; St-Yzans, north-west of St Seurin-de-Cadourne. *Cru bourgeois.* 12,500 dozen bottles of red bordeaux. France.

Loué-sur-Lourt. (16) Coteaux de l'Aubance, between Angers and Saumur. Fair white and rosé table wines. France.

Louis Max, Domaine. (8) Beaune vineyards. Red burgundy. France.

Louloumet, Clos. (5) Graves de Bordeaux; Toulenne. 800 dozen bottles of red bordeaux; 3,000 white. France.

Loumède, Domaine de. (4) Blayais. 500 dozen bottles of red bordeaux; 700 white. France.

Loupiac. (5) Graves de Bordeaux. Ordinary to fair red and white bordeaux. France.

Loupiac-Gaudiet, Château. (5) Entre-deux-Mers; Loupiac. 1,000 dozen bottles of red bordeaux; 9,000 white. France.

Lousteaneuf-Doumayne, Domaine de. (5) Sables de St-Emilion. 2,500 dozen bottles of red bordeaux. France.

Louvière, Château La. (5) Graves de Bordeaux; Léognan. An unclassified *cru*. 8,500 dozen bottles of red bordeaux. France.

Louvois. (17) Marne *département;* Ay canton, south-west of Trépail. Rated *grand cru*—100% growth. 70 acres. France.

Louzada, Quinta. *See* Viana.

Löwenberg. (22) Moselle; Kinheim vineyard. Fair white table wine. West Germany.

Löwenberg. (24) Rhinehessia; Bechtheim vineyard, south-west of Alsheim. Fair white table wine. West Germany.

Löwenstein mit Reizach und Rittelhof. (25) Württemberg; south-east of Heilbronn. Ordinary to fair red and white table wines. West Germany.

Loxton. (37) South Australia; in the Berri area. 7,000 acres of irrigated vineyards by the River Murray. The Loxton Co-operative Winery and Distillery is one of the largest wine and brandy producers of Australia.

Loyse, Château de. (11) Beaujolais. Fair white burgundy. France.

Lubat, Château de. (5) Graves de Bordeaux; St Pierre-de-Mons. An unclassified *cru*. 2,000 dozen bottles of white bordeaux. France.

Lucas, Château. (3) St-Emilion; Lussac. An unclassified *cru*. 8,000 dozen bottles of red bordeaux; 2,000 white. France.

Lucena. (29) Córdoba area; north-east of Seville and Montilla, approx. seventy-five miles north-east of Seville and Moriles. Fair to fine white table wine. Spain.

Ludes. (17) Marne *département;* Verzy canton. Rated *premier cru* for black grapes—94% growth; white 88%. 717 acres. France.

Ludon. (4) Haut-Médoc; north of Bordeaux. Fair and fine red bordeaux; also some quite ordinary 'Palus' Bordeaux. France.

Ludon-Pomies-Agassac, Château. (4) Haut-Médoc; Ludon. *Cru bourgeois supérieur*. 1,000 dozen bottles of red bordeaux. France.

Ludwigsberg. (25) Württemberg; north of Stuttgart. Ordinary to fair red and white table wines. West Germany.

Ludwigshöhe. (24) Rhinehessia; between Alsheim and Dienheim. Ordinary to fair white table wines. West Germany.

Lugana. (26) Lombardy; Lake Garda vineyards, west of Verona. The best wine of the Garda district, and one of the best of Lombardy. It is aged in the cask for as much as four years and acquires a pale, golden colour. Italy.

Luginsland. (23) Palatinate; Wachenheim vineyard. Fair white table wine. West Germany.

Luke Lunievich's Golden Vineyard. (38) North Island; Kaitaia, approx. 150 miles north-west of Auckland. New Zealand.

Lumbien. (29) Navarre. Ordinary, low-strength dry red wine. Spain.

Lump. (25) Franconia; Escherndorf vineyard, north-east of Würzburg. Fine to very fine white table wine. West Germany.

Lumpiaque. (29) Aragon; Zaragoza. Ordinary red table wine. Spain.

Lunel. (13) Roussillon. One of the best of French dessert unfortified wines made of Muscat de Frontignan grapes. France.

Lurets, Les. (8) Volnay. *Premier cru.* Red burgundy. France.

Lussac. (5) North-east of St-Emilion. Ordinary to fair red bordeaux. France.

Lussac, Château de. (5) St-Emilion; Lussac. An unclassified *cru*. 17,500 dozen bottles of red bordeaux. France.

Lutomer. (33) Slovenia; North-western Yugoslavia. Town with 1000 years of wine-growing tradition. Highest quality of all Yugoslav white table wines. These wines include Riesling, Sylvaner, Traminer, Sauvignon, Sipon and Pinot Blanc. Yugoslavia.

Lutomer Sipon. (33) A very dry white wine of characteristic bouquet and also named Furmint or Mosler, from the same name of grape. Yugoslavia.

Lützelsachen. (21) Baden, Bergstrasse; north of

Heidelberg. Ordinary to fair red and white table wines. West Germany.

Luxembourg. (32) The vineyards upon the lower hillsides of the Moselle valley produce much ordinary to fair white table wines; also some white sparkling wines.

Lyndoch. (37) South Australia; southern part of the Barossa Valley, approx. thirty-five miles north-east of Adelaide. Large vineyard area. Australia.

Lyonnat, Château du. (5) St-Emilion; Lussac. An unclassified *cru*. 25,000 dozen bottles of red bordeaux. France.

Lys, Les. (6) Chablis. *Premier cru*. White burgundy. France.

🍇

Maasborn. (24) Rhinegau; Rauenthal vineyard. Fine white table wine. West Germany.

Macabeo. (29) A kind of grape widely used in Catalonia for producing ordinary to fair white wines. Spain.

Macau. (4) Haut-Médoc. Ordinary to fair, and some fine red bordeaux. France.

Maccadam, Vin de. (5) The local name of an ordinary but popular white table wine from Montravel, Dordogne. France.

Maccarella. (28) Sicily; Syracuse. Fair golden dessert wine. Italy.

Maccarese (Bianco, Rosso and Rosato). (27) Lazio; vineyards planted on the drained marshes between Rome Airport and the sea. Ordinary white and rosé table wines. There is also a sweet dessert Moscato di Maccarese. Italy.

MacCarthy, Château. (4) Haut-Médoc; St-Estèphe. *Cru bourgeois supérieur*. 2,000 dozen bottles of red bordeaux. France.

Macedonia. (33) Extreme south of Yugoslavia, bordering on Greece, Albania and Bulgaria; one of the republics. Biggest producer of table raisins. Also white table wines and red wines such as Merlot, Vranac, Plavac and others.

Macedos, Quinta. (30) *Região demarcada do Douro* (q.v.). Estate and vineyard in Sarzedinho east of Régua. Portugal.

Macharnudo. (29) The major district of the sherry vineyards, lying to the north of Jerez de la Frontera. It produces mainly Finos and Amontillados of the highest quality. Spain.

Machtilshausen. (25) Franconia; approx. twenty-two miles north of Würzburg. Fair to fine white table wine. West Germany.

McLaren Vale. (37) South Australian valley; approx. twenty-five miles south of Adelaide. Long famous for its vineyards and wineries. Table wines, port type and brandy. Australia.

Mâcon. (10) Chief town in the Mâconnais area on the Saône. Much ordinary to fair white table wine of the Mâconnais is marketed under the name 'Mâcon Blanc' and 'Mâcon Supérieur'. France.

Mâconnais. (10) The hills and plains of the Saône-et-Loire *département* between Chalonnais and Beaujolais. Approx. 2,073,600 dozen bottles of ordinary to fair red, white and rosé table wines; also some fair to fine wines. France.

McWilliams Mount Pleasant Winery and Vineyard. (37) New South Wales; Hunter Valley, north-east of Sydney. Formerly managed by late Maurice O'Shea, one of Australia's most famous winemakers. A premier wine estate.

Madeira. (40) Island, twenty miles by eight miles, belonging to Portugal and situated 500 miles off the coast of Morocco. Fortified wines of the same name are made from four grape varieties: Bual, Malmsey, Verdelho and Sercial in descending order of sweetness. Madeira wines never really recovered their popularity after oidium and phylloxera attacks of late 19th century.

Madelaine, Clos la. (5) Côtes de St-Emilion. An unclassified *cru*. 1,000 dozen bottles of red bordeaux. France.

Madeleine, La. (16) Anjou; Coteaux de la Loire, Faye d'Anjou vineyard, below Angers. Fair to fine white table and dessert wines. France.

Madeleine-Bouhou, Château La. (4) Blayais; Cars, east of Blaye. 4,000 dozen bottles of red bordeaux; 1,000 white. France.

Madera. (36) California county. All ordinary white wines, mostly dessert. U.S.A.

Madère, Château. (5) Graves de Bordeaux; Podensac. 500 dozen bottles of red bordeaux; 2,000 white. France.

Madères, Les. (16) Touraine; Vernon-sur-Brenne, above Tours. Ordinary to fair red wine. France.

Madiran. (2) Hautes-Pyrénées *département*, south-west France near Spanish border. Ordinary to fair stout, red table wine. France.

Madrac, Château. (5) Premières Côtes de Bordeaux; Tabanac, north-east of Portets. 1,500 dozen bottles of red bordeaux; 5,000 white. France.

Madridanos. (29) Central León; Zamora. Mostly ordinary stout, red table wines, some fair to fine *clarete* table wine. Spain.

Madridejos. (29) West New Castile; in the Toledo area, approx. forty miles south-west of Madrid. Ordinary to fair table wines. Spain.

Madrigueras. (29) Albacete; Murcia; approx. twenty-three miles south-east of La Roda. Fair *clarete* wine. Spain.

Madrolanes. (29) Andalusia; Jerez de la Frontera. Fine white moscatel wine. Spain.

Maella. (29) Aragon; Zaragoza. Ordinary red table wine. Spain.

Magdalenenacker. (24) Rhinegau; Mittelheim vineyard. Fair to fine white table wine. West Germany.

Magdalenengarten. (24) Rhinegau; Oestrich vineyard. Fine white table wine. West Germany.

Magdelaine, Château. (5) Côtes de St-Emilion. *Premier grand cru classé*. 2,000 dozen bottles of red bordeaux. France.

Magdeleine, Clos de la. (5) Côtes de St-Emilion. An unclassified *cru*. 600 dozen bottles of red bordeaux. France.

Magil. (37) South Australia; Adelaide. First home and vineyard (1844) of Dr Penfold, founder of the present Penfolds Wine Pty Ltd. Australia.

Magliocco (di Calabria). (28) Calabria; Cantanzaro. Coarse, dark, red table wine with a high alcoholic content (14°) which is often used for blending. Italy.

Magnan, Château. (5) Côtes de St-Emilion. An unclassified *cru*. 2,000 dozen bottles of red bordeaux. France.

Magnan-La Gaffelière, Château. (5) Côtes de St-Emilion. An unclassified *cru*. 3,000 dozen bottles of red bordeaux. France.

Magnenaz, Clos de la. (31) Vaud canton; Yvorne vineyard. Fair white table wine. Switzerland.

Mahlberg. (25) Baden; approx. twenty miles south-east of Strasbourg. Ordinary to fair red and white table wines. West Germany.

Mahlstein. (23) Palatinate; Herxheim vineyard. Fair to fine white table wine. West Germany.

Mahon. (29) Minorca; Balearic Islands, off the coast east of Valencia. Ordinary red and white table wines. Spain.

Maikammer-Alsterweiler. (23) Palatinate; between Neustadt and Edenkoben. Ordinary to fair and some fine red and white table wines. West Germany.

Maillaud. (16) Anjou; Dampierre-sur-Loire, Saumur. Ordinary to fair white table wine. France.

Maille, Château. (5) Premières Côtes de Bordeaux; Corignon, east of Bègles. 1,500 dozen bottles of red bordeaux; 1,000 white are produced. France.

Mailles, Château des. (5) Côtes de Bordeaux; Ste Croix-du-Mont. 4,000 dozen bottles of white bordeaux. France.

Mailly Champagne. (17) Marne *département*; Verzy canton. Rated *grand cru* for black—100% growth; white 86%. 608 acres. France.

Mainberg. (25) Franconia; approx. twenty-five miles north-east of Würzburg. Fair white table wine. West Germany.

Maine-et-Loire. (16) *Département*. Capital Angers, part of the old province of Anjou. Vineyards: 68,841 acres. Wine: 17,411,500 dozen bottles. France.

Mainstockheim. (25) Franconia; east of Würzburg. Fair white table wine. West Germany.

Mainz. (24) Rhinehessia. Ordinary white table wine. West Germany.

Mainz-Kostheim. (24) Rhinehessia; opposite Mainz. Ordinary to fair red and white table wines. West Germany.

Mainz-Weisenau. (24) Rhinehessia; between Laubenheim and Mainz. Ordinary to fair red and white table wines. West Germany.

Maison Blanche, Château. (5) St-Emilion; Montagne. An unclassified *cru*. 13,000 dozen bottles of red bordeaux. France.

Maison-Brulée. (8) Côte de Nuits; Morey-St-Denis vineyard. *Premier cru*. Red burgundy. France.

Maison-Neuve. (10) Beaujolais; Romanèche vineyard. Red burgundy. France.

Maisonneuve, Château. (5) St-Emilion; Montagne. An unclassified *cru*. 2,000 dozen bottles of red bordeaux. France.

Maizières-Basses. (8) Côte de Nuits; Flagey-Echézeaux vineyard. *Troisième cru*. Red burgundy. France.

Maizières-Hautes, Les. (8) Côte de Nuits; Flagey-Echézeaux vineyard. *Deuxième cru*. Red burgundy. France.

Malabe. (16) Anjou; Coteaux du Layon, Bonnézeaux vineyard, south of Angers. Fair to fine white table wine. France.

Maladière, La. (8) Côte de Nuits; Nuits-St-Georges vineyard. *Deuxième cru*. Red burgundy. France.

Maladière, La. (8) Côte de Beaune; Santenay vineyard. *Deuxième cru*. Red burgundy. France.

Maladière, Les. (8) Côte de Nuits; Chambolle-Musigny vineyard. *Troisième cru*. Red burgundy. France.

Málaga. (29) City and vineyards in the south-east chiefly noted for its dessert wines. Spain.

Malangin, Château. (5) St-Emilion; Parsac. An unclassified *cru*. 5,000 dozen bottles of red bordeaux. France.

Malartic-Lagravière, Château. (5) Graves de Bordeaux; Léognan. *Cru classè de Graves (en blanc et en rouge)*. 5,000 dozen bottles of red bordeaux; 1,000 white. France.

Malbec, Château. (3) Entre-deux-Mers; Ste-Eulalie, east of Blanquefort. 6,000 dozen bottles of red bordeaux; 2,000 white. France.

Mal-Carrées, Les. (8) Côte de Nuits; Chambolle-Musigny vineyard. *Deuxième cru.* Red burgundy. France.

Malconsorts, Aux. (8) Côte de Nuits; Vosne-Romanée. *Premier cru.* Red burgundy. France.

Malescasse, Château. (4) Haut-Médoc; Lamarque. *Cru bourgeois.* 3,000 dozen bottles of red bordeaux. France.

Malescot-Saint-Exupéry, Château. (4) Haut-Médoc; Margaux. *Troisième cru classé.* 8,000 dozen bottles of red bordeaux. France.

Malgarni-et-Coutreau, Château de. (3) Côtes de Fronsac; Saillans, north of Fronsac. 4,000 dozen bottles of red bordeaux. France.

Maligne, Cru de. (16) Anjou; Coteaux du Layon, Martigné-Briand vineyard, below Angers. Fair to fine white table wine. France.

Malijay, Domaine du. (12) Côtes du Rhône, Gigondas vineyard. Fair to fine red and white table wines. France.

Malineau, Château. (5) Côtes de St-Emilion. An unclassified *cru.* 2,000 dozen bottles of red bordeaux. France.

Malle, Château de. (5) Sauternes; Preignac. *Deuxième cru classé.* 4,000 dozen bottles of white bordeaux. France.

Mallen. (29) Aragon; Zaragoza. Ordinary red table wine. Spain.

Malleprat, Château. (5) Graves de Bordeaux; Martillac. 1,500 dozen bottles of red bordeaux; 1,500 white. France.

Malleret, Château. (4) Haut-Médoc; Le Pian. *Cru bourgeois supérieur.* 1,000 dozen bottles of red bordeaux. France.

Malliauge, Vigne de la. (9) Chalonnais; Bourgneuf-Val d'Or vineyard. *Premier cru.* Red burgundy. France.

Malmesbury. (39) Western Cape Province. Township and vineyards. Chiefly noted for fortified wines. South Africa.

Malmsey. (40) Fine sweet dessert wine from Madeira, an island 500 miles west of Morocco. Produced from the Malvasia grape. Portugal.

Malsch. (21) Baden, Bergstrasse; south of Heidelberg. Ordinary to fair red and white table wines. West Germany.

Malschenberg. (25) Baden; south of Heidelberg. Ordinary to fair red and white table wines. West Germany.

Malta. (58) There are over 2,500 acres of vineyards on the island of Malta, which lies approx. sixty miles south of Sicily. Although the majority produce table grapes, there is a production of ordinary red, white and rosé table wines.

Malterdingen. (25) Baden; north-west of Freiburg. Fair white table wine. West Germany.

Maltroie, La. (8) Côte de Beaune; Chassagne-Montrachet vineyard. *Premier cru.* Red and white burgundy. France.

Malvasia. (30) A grape variety producing both red and white wines mainly in the Douro district. Also found in Spain and Italy.

Malvasia Bianca/Friulana. (26) Venezia-Giulia province; the Gorzia-Trieste area, near Friuli. Fair to fine white dessert wine from vineyards on the hillsides. Italy.

Malvasia de Collio. (26) Venezia-Giulia province; the Gorizia-Trieste area near Gorizia. Fair to fine golden dessert wine from vineyards on the hillsides. Italy.

Malvasia di Bosa. (28) Sardinia; Nuoro province. Ordinary to fair white dessert wine. Italy.

Malvasia di Cagliari. (28) Sardinia; Cagliari. Ordinary to fair white wine made in two grades of sweetness, one to be served as an apéritif and the sweeter as a dessert wine. Italy.

Malvasia di Brindisi. (28) Apulia; Brindisi area. Ordinary to fair white dessert wine; it is made in three grades of sweetness: sweet, sweeter and sweetest. Italy.

Malvasia di Cantanzaro. (28) Calabria. Ordinary to fair strong white dessert wine. Italy.

Malvasia di Lipari. (28) Islands of Lipari, Stromboli and Salina; off the north-east coast of Sicily. One of the best of the Malvasia white dessert wines of Italy.

Malvasia di Malatico. (26) Emilia-Romagna; Parma area. Ordinary white dessert wines. Italy.

Malvasia di Milazzo. (28) Sicily; Messina area. Fine white dessert wine. Italy.

Malvasia di Nanto. (26) Veneto; Vicenza area. Ordinary to fair light white dessert wine. Italy.

Malvasia di Nus. (26) Piedmont; Val D'Aosta. Highly esteemed, but rare white dessert wine produced by one grower. Italy.

Malvasia di Pietro Ligure. (26) Liguria. Ordinary white dessert wine very popular in all the seaside resorts from Bordighera approx. twenty miles south-west of Anperia to La Spezia. Italy.

Malvasia di Puglia. (28) Another name for Malvasia di Brindisi (q.v.). Italy.

Malvasia di Ronchi. (26) Ordinary to fair deep yellow wine from the vineyards between Gorizia and the Adriatic. Italy.

Malvasia di Vulture. (28) Apulia; Rapolla area approx. fifty miles east of Avellino near Melfi in the Basilicata region. Ordinary to fair, golden semi-sparkling dessert wine from the slopes of the extinct volcano. Italy.

Malvasia, Toscana. (27) Tuscany. Fair to fine, very sweet golden dessert wine made from semi-dried Malvasia grapes. Italy.

L

Malvedos, Quinta. (30) *Região demarcada do Douro* (q.v.). Estate and well-situated vineyard in São Mamede de Riba Tua in the Régua area. 92 acres. Produces popular good quality port. Portugal.

Malvoisie. The obsolete name of Malmsey wine in France as well as in England in olden times.

Mamertino. (28) Sicily; Messina area. Ordinary to fair very sweet white dessert wine. Also a semi-sweet and dryish variety. Italy.

Mancha, La. (29) Important wine-producing territory of south-central Spain.

Mandel. (24) Nahe; west of Bad Kreuznach. Ordinary, fair and some fine white table wines. West Germany.

Mandelacker. (23) Palatinate; Ruppertsberg vineyard. Fine white table wine. West Germany.

Mandelberg. (23) Palatinate; Ruppertsberg vineyard. Fine white table wine. West Germany.

Mandelgarten. (22) Moselle; Brauneberg vineyard. Fair white table wine. West Germany.

Mandelgarten. (23) Palatinate; Bad Dürkheim and Wachenheim vineyards. Fine white table wine. West Germany.

Mandement, Cave du. (31) Geneva canton. Ordinary to fair white table wine. Switzerland.

Mandrolisai. (28) Sardinia; Nuoro province. Good table wine, dry and brilliantly red. Italy.

Manduria. (28) Apulia; Taranto area. Ordinary frothy, sweet purple-red table wine. Italy.

Manera. *See* **Chiaretto del Garda.**

Maneru. ((29) Ordinary light red table wine. Spain.

Mangot, Château. (5) St-Emilion; St Etienne-de-Lisse. An unclassified *cru.* 6,000 dozen bottles of red bordeaux. France.

Manik. (24) Nahe; Winzenheim vineyard, just north of Bad Kreuznach. Fair white table wine. West Germany.

Manissy, Domaine de. (12) Côtes du Rhône, Tavel. Fair to fine rosé table wines. France.

Mannberg. (24) Rhinegau; Hattenheim vineyard, south-west of Erbach. Fair to fine white table wine. West Germany.

Mannweiler. (24) Nahe; south of Bad Münster. Fair white table wine. West Germany.

Manteneia. (34) Southern Greece; Peloponnisian peninsula. Fair white table wine. Greece.

Manto Negro. (29) Majorca; Balearic Islands, off coast east of Valencia. Dark red, ordinary table wine. Spain.

Manubach. (21) Middle Rhine; north-west of Bingen. Fair white table wine. West Germany.

Manzanares. (29) New Castile; Ciudad Real, in the Valdepeñas area. Ordinary, stout, red table wine. South-central Spain.

Manzanilla. (29) Andalusia; village near Seville. Fair white wines. Spain.

Manzanilla. (29) Andalusia; town of Sanlucar de Barrameda, near Jerez de la Frontera. Straw-coloured and very dry sherry. Spain.

Maran, Château. (5) Premières Côtes de Bordeaux; Cambes, south-east of Cadaujac. 1,000 dozen bottles of red bordeaux; 2,000 white. France.

Marausan, Château de. (13) Gard *département;* Côtes du Rhône (q.v.). Ordinary to fair red and rosé table wines. France.

Marbach. (25) Württemberg; approx. eighteen miles south-west of Würzburg. Ordinary red and white table wines. West Germany.

Marbuzet, Château de. (4) Haut-Médoc; St-Estèphe. *Cru bourgeois supérieur.* 5,000 dozen bottles of red bordeaux. France.

Marchans. (24) Rhinehessia; Elsheim vineyard, south of Niederwalluf. Ordinary to fair white table wine. West Germany.

Marche-Canon, La. (4) Fronsac. 14,000 dozen bottles of red bordeaux. France.

Marcobrunnen. (24) Rhinegau; Erbach's most famous vineyard. Very fine white table wine. West Germany.

Marconnets, Les. (8) Côte de Beaune; Beaune vineyard. *Premier cru.* Red burgundy. France.

Mardeuil. (17) Marne *département;* Epernay canton, north-west of Epernay. Rated—82% growth. 319 acres. France.

Maréchale, Clos de la. (8) Côte de Nuits; Prémeaux vineyard. *Premier cru. AC Nuits-St-Georges.* Red burgundy. France.

Maréchaudes, Les. (8) Côte de Beaune; Aloxe-Corton vineyard. *Premier cru.* Part classed as an *AC Corton,* remainder *AC Aloxe-Corton.* Red burgundy. France.

Maremma. (27) Vineyards on the mainland opposite the island of Elba, west of Grosetto. Ordinary to fair red and white table wines, both rather sweet. Italy.

Mareuil-sur-Ay. (17) Marne *département;* Ay canton, south-east of Ay. Rated *premier cru—*98% growth. 634 acres. France.

Margaux. (4) Town and vineyard of the Haut-Médoc, approx. sixteen miles from Bordeaux. Mostly fair and fine red bordeaux, and also some very fine to great red wines or claret. Also a very small quantity of fair quality white wine. France.

Margaux, Château. (4) Haut-Médoc; Margaux. *Premier cru classé.* 18,000 dozen bottles of red bordeaux. Also some white wine marketed under the name of *Pavillon Blanc* (q.v.). France.

Margottey. (9) Chalonnais; Rully. White burgundy. France.

Marialva, Quinta. (30) *Região demarcada do Douro* (q.v.). Estate and vineyard in Alvacoes do Corgo north-east of Régua. Portugal.

Maribor. (33) Slovenia; north-west Yugoslavia. Cultural and economic centre of north-eastern Slovenia, on River Drava, with centuries old wine-growing tradition. Yugoslavia.

Marienberg. (22) Moselle; Pünderich vineyard, west of Zell. Fair white table wine. West Germany.

Marienholz. (22) Ruwer; Eitelsbach vineyard, north-east of Trier. Fine white table wine. West Germany.

Marienlay, Schloss. (22) Ruwer; Waldrach vineyard. Fair white table wine is produced. West Germany.

Marignan. (31) Haute-Savoie *département;* Sciez vineyard, north-east of Geneva. Ordinary to fair white table wine. France.

Marigny. (16) Touraine; Vouvray vineyard, east of Tours. Fair to fine white table wine. France.

Marin, Château. (5) St-Emilion; St Christophe-des-Bardes, south-west of Parsac. An unclassified *cru.* 3,500 dozen bottles of red bordeaux. France.

Marinasco. (26) Liguria; La Spezia area. Fair, dry and semi-sweet table and dessert wine, made from Trebbiano grapes. Italy.

Marin-Epagier. (31) Neuchâtel vineyard. 2·74 acres. Fair to fine white table wine. Switzerland.

Maring. (22) Middle Moselle; west of Bernkastel. Ordinary, fair and some fine white table wines. The full name of this village is Maring-Noviand-an-der-Lieser. West Germany.

Marino. (27) Lazio; vineyards on the northern shore of Lake Albano south-east of Rome. Ordinary to fair red, white and rosé table wines. The white is dry while the others are rather sweet and some are semi-sparkling. Italy.

Marisson. (9) Chalonnais; Rully vineyard. *Premier cru.* Red burgundy. France.

Maritza. (33) Ordinary to fair red and white table wines. Bulgaria.

Markdorf. (25) Lake Constance (Bodensee); north-east of Konstanz. Fair white table wine. West Germany.

Markelsheim. (25) Württemberg; approx. twenty-two miles south-west of Würzburg. Fair white table wine. West Germany.

Markgrafler. (25) Baden; Freiburg vineyard. Fair white table wine. West Germany.

Markgröningen. (25) Württemberg; north-west of Stuttgart. Ordinary to fair red and white table wines. West Germany.

Markovich's. (38) North Island; Kerikeri winery and vineyard in Bay of Islands, approx. 120 miles north-west of Auckland. New Zealand.

Marktsteft. (25) Franconia; south-east of Würzburg. Ordinary to fair white table wine. West Germany.

Marktbreit. (25) Franconia; south-east of Würzburg. Fair to fine white table wine. West Germany.

Marlenheim. (19) Bas-Rhin *département;* north of Masheim. Medium to fair white Alsace wine. France.

Marmilla. (28) Sardinia; vineyards on the Campidano plain stretching north-west from Cagliari. Ordinary red and white table wines. Italy.

Marnoz. (18) Jura; Arbois area. Ordinary to fair red, white and rosé table wines. France.

Marolles, Les. (9) Chalonnais; Givry vineyard. *Premier cru.* Red burgundy. France.

Marques de Murietta. (29) Old Castile; Ygay, near Logroño, La Rioja area of the upper Ebro valley. Fine red table wine. Spain.

Marques de Riscal. (29) Elciego; near Haro, La Rioja area of the upper Ebro valley. Fine red table wine. Spain.

Marquis d'Alesme-Becker, Château. (4) Haut-Médoc; Margaux. *Troisième cru classé.* 4,000 dozen bottles of red bordeaux. France.

Marquis-de-Terme, Château. (4) Haut-Médoc; Margaux. *Quatrième cru classé.* 15,000 dozen bottles of red bordeaux. France.

Marsala. (28) Sicily; vineyards between Palermo and Messina. Fair to fine rich fortified dessert wine. Although not now generally popular, at one time it rivalled Madeira in consumption. It is Sicily's most famous wine. Italy.

Marsala Vergine. (28) Sicily. Unfortified Marsala wine which must be at least five years old and reach 18° alcohol. Italy.   ◯

Marsannay-la-Côte. (7) Côte d'Or; village and vineyard, south of Dijon. Ordinary red burgundy. Also produces fine rosé, *AC Rosé de Marsannay* from Pinot grapes. France.

Marsberg. (25) Franconia; Randersacker vineyard, just south-east of Würzburg. Fine white table wine. West Germany.

Marsens. (31) Vaud canton; Dézaley vineyard. Fair to fine white table wine is produced. Switzerland.

Marsicano (Rosso, Rosato). (27) Abruzzi. Ordinary red and pink table wines usually drunk young. Italy.

Marsillac, Château. (4) Bourgeais; Bourg. 7,000 dozen bottles of red bordeaux. France.

Martelière, La. (16) Touraine; Bourgueil vineyard. Fair red table wine. France.

Martenweg. (23) Palatinate; Deidesheim vineyard. Fair to fine white table wine. West Germany.

Martigneau. (16) Anjou; Juigné-sur-Loire, between Angers and Saumur. Fair to fine white table wine. France.

Martigne-Briand. (16) Anjou; Coteaux du Layon (q.v.), south of Angers. Fair to fine white and rosé table wines. France.

Martigny. (31) Vaud canton. Fair to fine white table wine. Switzerland.

Martillac. (5) Graves de Bordeaux. Red and white bordeaux. France.

Martin, Clos. (16) Touraine; Rochecorbon vineyard, north-east of Tours. Fair white table wine. France.

Martina Franca. (28) Apulia; Bari area. Ordinary and popular white table wine much of which is used as a neutral base for vermouth in factories of the north. Italy.

Martinens, Château. (4) Haut-Médoc; Cantenac. *Cru bourgeois supérieur.* 5,000 dozen bottles of red bordeaux. France.

Martinet, Château. (5) Sables de St-Emilion. An unclassified *cru*. 10,000 dozen bottles of red bordeaux. France.

Martinet, Le. (16) Touraine; Beaumont-en-Véron vineyard, below Chinon. Fair red table wine. France.

Martini, Louis M. (36) California; St Helena. One of the few family-owned wineries in the Napa Valley and a producer of some of the best red wines, Cabernet Sauvignon, Pinot Noir, Zinfandel. Notable for an excellent Barbera capable of great development with ageing. U.S.A.

Martini and Prati Wines Inc. (36) California; Santa Rosa, Vine-Hill winery. Table, dessert and sparkling wines; also Vermouth. Uses the old Fountaingrove label as well as 'Martini and Prati'. U.S.A.

Martinière, La. (16) Anjou; Coteaux de Saumur, Turquant vineyard. Fair white table wine. France.

Martino. (29) Northern Spanish coast; Santander, 45 miles west of Bilbao. Fair white table wine. Spain.

Martins, Les. (16) Coteaux de l'Aubance, Juigné-sur-Loire vineyard between Angers and Saumur. Fair white table wine. France.

Martinstein. (24) Nahe; west of Bad Münster. Fair to fine white table wine. West Germany.

Martinsthal. (24) Rhinegau. Fair to fine white table wine. West Germany.

Martorell. (29) Barcelona. Ordinary to fair white table wine. Spain.

Marzemino. (26) Trentino; Alto Adige area. Ordinary to fair red table wine from Marzemino grapes. There is also a rosé. Italy.

Marzemino Trevigiano. (26) Veneto; Trevigiano

hills in the lower reaches of the Piane river north-east of Venice. Ordinary unimportant light red table wine. It is usually semi-sweet to sweet. Italy.

Mascale. (28) Sicily; vineyard in the Etna foot-hills north of Catania. Ordinary red and white table wines. The whites, which are more plentiful, are dry and a little *frizzante*. The reds tend to be coarse and exported for use in making brandies and vermouths. Italy.

Mas Calen. (14) Côtes de Provence; Cassis vineyard. Fair red, white and rosé table wines. France.

Mascara, Coteaux de Mascara. (40) Oran. Mountain vineyards (1,800 ft.). Red, white and rosé table wines, accorded under French rule the *V.D.Q.S.* appellation if alcoholic strength reached 13°. Algeria.

Maslas. (33) Tokaj (Tokay); approx. 110 miles north-east of Budapest. Fair white dessert wine. Hungary.

Masnou. (29) Barcelona; Alella. Fair white table wine. Spain.

Masquefa. (29) Upper Panadés; Barcelona, between Tarragóna and Barcelona. Ordinary to fair table wines. Spain.

Mas Saint-Louis. (12) Côtes du Rhône, Châteauneuf-du-Pape. Fair to fine red table wine. France.

Massandra. (34) South European Russia; Yalta area, Crimean peninsula. Ordinary to fair dessert and table wines. U.S.S.R.

Massarda. (26) Liguria; Finale Ligure between Savona and Imperia. Ordinary and popular white table wine. Italy.

Massas, Quinta. (30) Molaes. *Região demarcada do Douro* (q.v.). Estate and vineyard in Penajoia in the Régua area. Already in existence in 1747. Portugal.

Massenheim. (24) Rhinegau; north-east of Hochheim. Ordinary to fair white table wine. West Germany.

Masserano. (26) Piedmont; Vercelli province. Fine red table wines made from Niebbolo grapes. Similar to Gattinara (q.v.). Italy.

Massereau-Lapachère, Château. (5) Sauternes; Barsac. *Cru bourgeois.* 2,000 dozen bottles of white bordeaux. France.

Masson, Paul Vineyards. (36) California; Saratoga and Gilroy, Santa Clara County. Mostly table wines and large bulk process American champagne cellar in Saratoga. New vineyards are producing in Gilroy, southern Alameda County. U.S.A.

Mata de Baizo, Quinta. (30) *Região demarcada do Douro* (q.v.). Estate and vineyard in Parada do Bispo south-east of Régua. Portugal.

Mata do Porto de Bois, Quinta. (30) Estate and vineyard in Valdigem south-west of Régua comprising thirty-five acres. Portugal.

Mathalin, Château. (5) Sauternes; Barsac. *Cru bourgeois*. 5,000 dozen bottles of white bordeaux. France.

Matheisbildchen. (22) Moselle; Bernkastel vineyard. Fair to fine white table wine. West Germany.

Matras, Château. (5) Côtes de St-Emilion. An unclassified *cru*. 3,500 dozen bottles of red bordeaux. France.

Mattaosso. (26) Liguria; Finale Ligure between Savona and Imperia. Popular ordinary white table wine. Italy.

Mauchen. (25) Baden; approx. twenty miles south-west of Freiburg. Ordinary to fair red and white table wines. West Germany.

Mauchenheim. (23) Palatinate; west of Alsheim. Ordinary red and fair to fine white table wines. West Germany.

Maucoil, Château. (12) Côtes du Rhône, Châteauneuf-du-Pape. Fair to fine red table wine. France.

Mauer. (23) Palatinate; Deidesheim vineyard. Fine white table wine. West Germany.

Mäuerchen. (24) Rhinegau; Geisenheim vineyard. Fair to fine white table wine. West Germany.

Maulbronn. (25) Württemberg; approx. eighteen miles east of Karlsruhe. Ordinary to fair red and white table wines. West Germany.

Maurac, Château. (4) Haut-Médoc; St Seurin-de-Cadourne. *Cru bourgeois*. 1,500 dozen bottles of red bordeaux. France.

Mauras, Château. (5) Sauternes; Bommes. *Cru bourgeois*. 3,500 dozen bottles of white bordeaux. France.

Maurens, Château. (5) St-Emilion; St-Hippolyte. An unclassified *cru*. 3,000 dozen bottles of red bordeaux. France.

Maury. (13) Roussillon. Unfortified, sweet white dessert wine. France.

Mausbrunnen. (24) Rhinehessia; Alsheim vineyard. Fair white table wine. West Germany.

Mauserberg. (22) Moselle; Reil vineyard, east of Zell. Fair white table wines. West Germany.

Maushöhle. (23) Palatinate; Deidesheim vineyard. Fair to fine white table wine. West Germany.

Mauvanne, Domaine de. (14) Côtes de Provence; Salins d'Hyères, Côtes de Maures east of Toulon. Ordinary to fair red and white wines. France.

Mauves, Château de. (5) Graves de Bordeaux; Podensac. An unclassified *cru*. 3,500 dozen bottles of white bordeaux. France.

Mauvezin, Château. (5) Côtes de St-Emilion. *Grand cru classé*. 2,000 dozen bottles of red bordeaux. France.

Mavraud. (33) Assenovgard; Maritza valley south-east of Sofia. Fair red table wine is produced. Bulgaria.

Mavrodaphne. (34) One of the best and best-known sweet red dessert wines from Greece.

Maxberg. (22) Moselle; Ürzig vineyard. Fair to fine white table wine. West Germany.

Maximiner-Grünhauser. (22) Ruwer valley; Mertesdorf vineyard, north-east of Trier. Very fine white table wine. West Germany.

Maximiner-Herrenberg. (22) Moselle; Longuich vineyard, north-east of Trier. Fair white table wine. West Germany.

Maximiner-Klosterlay. (22) Moselle; Detzen vineyard. Fair to fine white table wine. West Germany.

Maximiner-Staadter. (22) Saar valley; Staadt vineyard, by Kastel. Fair to fine white table wine. West Germany.

Mayacamas Vineyards. (36) California; Napa Valley. Recently sold to Robert Travers Quality table wines. U.S.A.

Mayence, Château. (4) Blayais; Mazion, north-east of Blaye. 1,000 dozen bottles of red bordeaux; 700 white. France.

Mayne-Bert, Château. (5) Sauternes; Barsac. *Cru bourgeois*. 1,000 dozen bottles of white bordeaux. France.

Mayne-Boyer, Château. (4) Blayais; Cars, east of Blaye. 600 dozen bottles of red bordeaux; 500 white. France.

Mayne-Gazin, Château Le. (4) Blayais; Massac, south of Blaye. 1,200 dozen bottles of red bordeaux. France.

Mayne-Vieil, Château. (3) Fronsadais; Galgon. 15,000 dozen bottles of red bordeaux; 2,500 white. France.

Mayschoss. (21) Ahr; west of Linz. Ordinary red and white table wines. West Germany.

Mazarin, Château. (5) Entre-deux-Mers; Loupiac. 2,500 dozen bottles of red bordeaux; 8,000 white. France.

Mazeran, Château. (5) St-Emilion; St Christophe-des-Bardes, south-west of Parsac. An unclassified *cru*. 1,500 dozen bottles of red bordeaux. France.

Mazeyres, Clos. Pomerol. 5,000 dozen bottles of red bordeaux. France.

Mazoyères-Chambertin. (8) Côte de Nuits; Gevrey-Chambertin vineyard. *Grand cru*. Red burgundy. France.

Mazoyères-Charmes. *See* **Mazoyères-Chambertin.**

Mazuelo. (29) Alva and Logroño; La Rioja area of the upper Ebro valley. Stout, dark red table wine. Spain.

Mazures, Les. (8) Côte de Beaune; Chassagne-Montrachet vineyard. *Deuxième cru.* Red or white burgundy. France.

Mazys-Chambertin. (8) Côte de Nuits; Gevrey-Chambertin vineyard. *Grand cru.* Red burgundy. France.

Méal, Le. (12) Côtes du Rhône, Tain-l'Hermitage vineyard. Produces fair to fine red table wine. France.

Mechtersheim. (23) Palatinate; north-east of Landau. Fair white table wine. West Germany.

Meddersheim. (24) Nahe; west of Bad Münster. Ordinary to fair red and white table wines. West Germany.

Medea. (40) Algiers. Red and white table wines accorded *V.D.Q.S.* appellation under French rule if strength reached 12°. Algeria.

Medina del Campo. (29) West Old Castile; Valladolid, approx. seventy miles north of Avila. Ordinary to fair red table wines. Spain.

Mediona. (29) Barcelona; upper Panadés, between Tarragona and Barcelona. Ordinary table wines. Spain.

Médoc. (3) The undulating stretch of woodland, vineyards, grasslands and villages between the Gironde and the Bay of Biscay. Its soil is light, sandy and poor, yet its vineyards produce more and finer red table wines than all the other vineyards of France put together. It has now been divided into Bas and Haut-Médoc. Haut-Médoc stretches from Blanquefort to St Seurin-de-Cadourne. Here are all the finest growths or *crus.* Bas-Médoc, now known simply as Médoc, stretches from Haut-Médoc to where the Gironde flows into the sea. France.

Médoc, Château. (4) Haut-Médoc; St Julien. *Cru bourgeois supérieur.* 2,000 dozen bottles of red bordeaux. France.

Meersburg. (25) Lake Constance (Bodensee); north-east of Konstanz. Fair white table wine. West Germany.

Meerspinne. (23) Palatinate; Gimmeldingen vineyard. Fair to fine white table wine. West Germany.

Megaspileon. (34) Southern Greece; Peloponnisos peninsula of Kalavryta. Ordinary to fair red table wine. Greece.

Mehrhölzchen. (24) Rhinegau; Hallgarten vineyard. Fair to fine white table wine. West Germany.

Mehring. (22) Middle Moselle; south-west of Klüsserath. Fair to fine white table wines. West Germany.

Meigne. (16) Anjou; Brézé vineyard, just south of Saumur. Fair to fine white table wine. France.

Meira. (29) West-central Galicia; Albarina, Pontevedra. Fair to fine white table wine. North-west Spain.

Meisenberg. (22) Ruwer valley; Waldrach vineyard. Fair to fine white table wine. West Germany.

Meisenheim. (24) Nahe; south-west of Bad Münster. Fine white table wine. West Germany.

Meissenheim. (25) Württemberg; south-east of Strasbourg. Ordinary red and white table wines. West Germany.

Meix, Les, (8) Côte de Beaune; Aloxe-Corton vineyard. *Premier cru.* Red burgundy. France.

Meix-Bas. (8) Côte de Nuits; Fixin vineyard. *Premier cru.* Red burgundy. France.

Meix-des-Ouches, Clos des. (8) Côte de Nuits; Gevrey-Chambertin vineyard. *AC Gevrey-Chambertin.* Fair white wine. France.

Meix-Lallement, Les. (8) Côte de Beaune; Aloxe-Corton vineyard. *Premier cru.* Red burgundy. France.

Meix-Rentier, Le. (8) Morey-St-Denis. *Premier cru.* Red burgundy. France.

Melinots, Les. (6) Chablis; Yonne *département.* *Premier cru.* White burgundy. France.

Melisano. (28) Apulia; Lecce province. Very ordinary purple-red table wine made from Malvasia grapes, much of which is exported and used as fortifiers. Italy.

Melnik. (33) A town in north-central Czechoslovakia which produces ordinary fair, and some fine red and white table wines. Also some sweet sparkling wine. Czechoslovakia.

Membrilla. (29) New Castile; Ciudad Real, in the Valdepeñas area. Ordinary to fair table wines. Spain.

Menais, Les. (16) Anjou; St Cyr-en-Bourg vineyard, just south of Saumur. Fair red table wine. France.

Menauchon, Domaine de. (5) Graves de Bordeaux; St Pierre-de-Mons, Langon area. 1,000 dozen bottles of red bordeaux; 1,000 white. France.

Mendoce, Château. (4) Bourgeais. 5,000 dozen bottles of red bordeaux. France.

Mendocino County. (36) California; Mostly red and white table wines. *See* **Martini, Louis M.** U.S.A.

Mendogorria. (29) Navarre. Ordinary light red table wine. Spain.

Mendoza. (35) The most important of the Argentine wine-producing provinces. Approx. 50% red table wines, 30% white and rosé table wines. 20% dessert and sparkling wines. Argentina.

Meneau, Château. (4) Blayais; Villeneuve, south-east of Blaye. 2,000 dozen bottles of red bordeaux; 3,000 white. France.

Menestrières, Les. (10) Mâconnais; Fuissé vineyard. Entitled to the *AC Pouilly-Fuissé*. White burgundy. France.

Ménétru-le-Vignoble. (18) Jura; Arbois area. Ordinary to fair red table wine. France.

Ménétu-Salon. (15) Cher *département*; near Bourges. 4,000 dozen bottles. Fair red and rosé table wines. France.

Meneux, Les. (17) Marne *département;* Ville-en-Tardenois canton, south-west of Rheims. 17 acres. *Deuxième cru*, champagne. France.

Menicia. (29) South Galicia; Orense. Very dark, rather rough table wine. Spain.

Mentrida. (29) West New Castile; Toledo, approx. forty miles south-west of Madrid. Ordinary to fair table wines. Spain.

Meranese di Collina. (26) Alto Adige; Merana vineyards, Bolzano province. Fair red table wines. Italy.

Merced. (36) California; wine-producing county, Central Valley. Dessert wines. U.S.A.

Mercier, Château. (5) Sauternes; Barsac. *Cru bourgeois.* 1,500 dozen bottles of white bordeaux. France.

Mercurey. (9) Chalonnais. Fair to fine red burgundy; also a little white burgundy. France.

Mercurol. (12) Drôme *département;* Côtes du Rhône. Fair red table wine. France.

Merdingen. (25) Baden; west of Freiburg. Ordinary to fair red and white table wines. West Germany.

Mergerei-Ketterschauberg. (22) Moselle; Briedel vineyard, west of Zell. Ordinary to fair white table wine. West Germany.

Merida. (29) Estremadura; Badajoz, between Seville and Trujillo. Ordinary to fair white table wine. Spain.

Merl. (22) Lower Moselle; north-west of Zell. Ordinary to fair white table wine. West Germany.

Merle-Saint-Emilion, Domaine de. (5) St-Emilion; St-Hippolyte. An unclassified *cru*. 2,000 dozen bottles of red bordeaux. France.

Merlot. (26) Alto Adige and Veneto. The name given to any red wine made from Merlot grapes. Italy.

Mersch. (24) Rhinehessia; Nierstein vineyard. Fair to fine white table wine. West Germany.

Merta. (34) Chios; island off western Turkish coast. Ordinary to fair red and white table wines. Greece.

Mertesdorf-Grünhaus. (22) Ruwer; north-east of Trier. Fair to fine and some very fine white table wines. West Germany.

Mertesheim. (23) Palatinate; just west of Grünstadt. Ordinary to fair white table wine. West Germany.

Merxheim. (24) Nahe; west of Bad Münster. Fair white table wine. West Germany.

Merzhausen. (25) Baden; south-west of Freiburg. Ordinary to fair white table wine. West Germany.

Mesagne. (28) Apulia; Salento, the area encompassing the 'heel' of the 'boot'. Very ordinary red and white tables wines, much of which is exported as fortifiers. Italy.

Mesas, Las. (29) East New Castile; Cuenca. Ordinary red table wine. Spain.

Mesenich. (22) Lower Moselle; south-west of Bruttig. Ordinary to fair white table wine. West Germany.

Mesiand. (16) Touraine. Ordinary red, white and rosé table wines. France.

Mesneux, Les. (17) Marne *département;* Ville-en-Tardenois canton, south-west of Rheims. Rated *premier cru*—90% growth. 23 acres. France.

Mesolone. (26) Piedmont; Meisola vineyard, Vercelli province. Ordinary to fair, full-bodied red table wine. Italy.

Mentana. (27) Lazio; Tiber valley, north of Rome. Ordinary, usually sweetish, red and white table wines from the hillsides. Italy.

Mettenheim. (24) Rhinehessia; south of Alsheim. Fair to fine white table wine. West Germany.

Metzdorf. (22) Moselle; west of Trier. Ordinary to fair white table wine. West Germany.

Metzler. (24) Nahe; Winzenheim vineyard, just north of Bad Kreuznach. Fair white table wine. West Germany.

Meung-sur-Loire. (15) Orléans region. Ordinary red table wine. France.

Meursault. (8) Côte de Beaune; Côte d'Or. Fair to fine red burgundy; fine white. France.

Mexico. (35) There has been wine produced in Mexico ever since the sixteenth century when the early Spanish missionaries planted the first vineyards. Today Mexico produces approximately 2,500,000 dozen bottles of ordinary to fair quality table wines yearly. Mexico.

Meyney, Château. (4) Haut-Médoc; St-Estèphe. *Cru bourgeois supérieur.* 20,000 dozen bottles of red bordeaux. France.

Meyre-Estèbe, Château. (4) Haut-Médoc; Avensan. *Cru bourgeois.* 500 dozen bottles of red bordeaux. France.

Mezesfehrer. (33) West-central Hungary; Somlo. Fair to fine white table wine. Hungary.

Miajadas. (29) Northern Estremadura; Cáceres, approx. twenty miles west of Trujillo. Ordinary white table wine. Spain.

Mia Mia. (37) Victoria; Rutherglen. Vineyard planted by George Francis Morris in 1859 and in Morris family's hands until 1970, when take-over of this vineyard and winery and a branch winery at Griffith, New South Wales, was effected by Reckitt & Colman. Red and white sweet wines. Australia.

Micaut, Clos. *See* **Micot, Clos.**

Michelfeld. (21) Baden; south-east of Heidelberg. Ordinary to fair red and white table wines. West Germany.

Michelmark. (24) Rhinegau; Erbach vineyard. Fine white table wine. West Germany.

Michelon, Le. (11) Beaujolais; Chénas vineyard. One of the top-grade *cru beaujolais*. Fair to fine red burgundy. France.

Michelons, Les. (11) Chénas vineyard, Beaujolais. Fair to fine red burgundy. One of the top-grade beaujolais. France.

Michelsberg. (22) Moselle; Eller, Piesport and Klüsserath vineyards. Fair table wine. White. West Germany.

Michelsberg. (23) Palatinate; Bad Dürkheim and Ungstein, between Bad Dürkheim and Kallstadt, vineyards. Fair to fine white table wine. West Germany.

Michelsberg. (24) Rhinehessia; Mittelheim vineyard. Fair to fine white table wine. West Germany.

Michelslay. (22) Moselle; Ürzig vineyard. Fair to fine white table wine. West Germany.

Michelsripp. (22) Moselle; Ürzig vineyard. Fair to fine white table wine. West Germany.

Michelton Vineyard. (37) Victoria; Nagambie, approx. seventy-five miles north of Melbourne. On banks of Goulburn River, opposite Château Tahbilk. Planting began in 1969. Australia.

Michet, Clos. (16) Touraine; Côte de Montlouis, St Martin-le-Beau vineyard. Fair to fine white table wine. France.

Michoacan. (35) Central Mexico. Wine-producing territory. Mexico.

Micot, Clos. (8) Côte de Beaune; Pommard vineyard. *Premier cru*. Red burgundy. France.

Middle Haardt. (23) Palatinate. The vineyards between the Upper and Lower Haardt, that is, between Neustadt and Bad Dürkheim; they produce the finest wines of the Palatinate. West Germany.

Midi, Vins du. (13) The name often given to the vast quantity of rough, cheap, red wines of the Aude, Hérault and Gard *départements* of France.

Miglan. (9) Bourgneuf-Val d'Or vineyard, Chalonnais. Fine quality red burgundy. France.

Migraines, Les. (6) Chablis; Auxerre vineyard. *Premier cru*. Red burgundy. France.

Mila, Bianco Di. (28) Sicily. Ordinary, light, rather acid dry white wine. Italy.

Milagre, Quinta. (30) *Região demarcada do Douro* (q.v.). Estate and vineyard in Freixo de Espada a Cintra in the Régua area. Portugal.

Milawa. (37) Victoria; between two rivers, the Ovens and the King, south of Wangaratta, in the north-east of the state in the Rutherglen area. Mostly table wines. Australia.

Milazzo (Bianco, Rosso). (28) Sicily; Messina Straits vineyards. Ordinary white and red table wines. Italy.

Mildura Wines Limited. (37) Victoria; near River Murray, in north-west of State, but draws grapes also from premium districts of other States. Top-class sherries, brandies, dessert and dry red wines. Australia.

Miliana. (40) Ordinary to fair red and white table wines associated with Zaccar (q.v.). Algeria.

Millandes. (8) Côte de Nuits; Morey-St-Denis vineyard. *Premier cru*. Red burgundy. France.

Mille-Secousses, Château. (4) Bourgeais; Bourg. 45,000 dozen bottle of red bordeaux. France.

Millet, Château. (5) Graves de Bordeaux; Portets. *Cru bourgeois*. 3,000 dozen bottles of red bordeaux; 3,000 white. France.

Milly. (6) Chablis; Yonne *département*. Fair, white burgundy. France.

Miltenberg. (25) Franconia; approx. twenty-four miles north-east of Mosbach. Fair white table wine. West Germany.

Mina, Quinta. (30) *Região demarcada do Douro* (q.v.). Estate and vineyard in Freixo de Espada a Cintra in the Régua area. Portugal.

Minas Gerais. (35) Brazil, north of Rio de Janeiro. Minor wine-producing province. Brazil.

Minchinbury. (37) New South Wales; approx. twenty-five miles inland from Sydney. One of the early Australian vineyards, which has since been built over but retains cellars where sparkling wines are made by Penfolds under the estate name.

Minglanilla. (29) Eastern New Castile; Cuenca. Ordinary red table wine. Spain.

Minheim. (22) Moselle; south-west of Wintrich. Ordinary, fair and some fine white table wines. West Germany.

Minis. (33) Village in west Rumania. Fair to fine white and red table wine. Rumania.

Minuty, Domaine de. (14) Côtes de Provence, Gassin vineyard, Côte de Maures east of Toulon. Ordinary to fair red and white table wines are produced. France.

Miranda. (29) South León; Salamanca. Ordinary red table wine. Spain.

Mirassou Vineyards. (36) California; San José.

Superb Zinfandel; especially noteworthy Chenin
Blanc and Pinot Blanc. As the valuable wine lands
of Santa Clara County are encroached upon,
vineyards are being established near King City
in Monterey Co. U.S.A.

Mireille, Clos. (14) Côtes de Prôvence, Côte de
Maures east of Toulon. Ordinary to fair red and
white table wines. France.

Miroir, Le. (16) Anjou; Coteaux du Layon, Faye
d'Anjou vineyard, south of Angers. Fair to fine
white table wine. France.

Mirrhe. (23) Palatinate; Forst vineyard. Fair to
fine white table wine. West Germany.

Misket Karlova. (33) Fair, white dessert wine,
made from Muscat grapes. Bulgaria.

Missianer. (26) Alto Adige; Appiano Hills vineyards, Bolzano province. Fair red table wine.
Italy.

Mission Haut Brion, Château La. (5) Graves
de Bordeaux; Talence. *Cru classé de Graves (en
rouge).* 8,000 dozen bottles of red bordeaux.
France.

Mistelas. (29) Not a true wine, but grape-juice,
the fermentation of which has been checked by
the addition of brandy, for use as sweetening,
principally of fortified wines. Spain.

Mitans, Les. (8) Côte de Beaune; Volnay vineyard. *Premier cru.* Red burgundy. France.

Mittelheim. (24) Rhinegau. Fair, fine and some
very fine white table wines. West Germany.

Mittelholle. (24) Rhinegau; Johannisberg vineyard. Fair to fine white table wine. West
Germany.

Mittelwihr. (19) Haut-Rhin *département;* south-
east of Riquewihr. Fair to fine white Alsace wine.
France.

Mittlere-Reitel. (24) Rhinehessia; Osthofen,
north of Worms. Fair white table wine. West
Germany.

Mochamps. (8) Côte de Nuits; Morey-St-Denis
vineyard. *Premier cru.* Red burgundy. France.

Möckmühl. (25) Württemberg; south-east of
Mosbach. Ordinary to fair red and white table
wines. West Germany.

Modbury. (37) South Australia; approx. eight
miles from Magill, Adelaide suburb. One of
Adelaide's remaining 'Metropolitan' vineyard
districts, noted for its white wines. Australia.

Mogoro (Bianco, Rosso and Rosato). (28)
Sardinia; vineyards on the Campidano plain
stretching north-west from Cagliari. Fair, dry,
even rather acid red, white and rosé table wines.
Italy.

Moguer. (29) Ordinary white wines. Spain.

Moine, Domaine du. (12) Côtes du Rhône,
Gigondas vineyard. Fair red table wine. France.

Moines, Clos des. (31) Vaud canton; Lavaux
vineyard. Fine white table wine. Switzerland.

Moja. (29) Barcelona; Panadés, between Tarragona
and Barcelona. Fair red table wine and sparkling
wines. Spain.

Mollières. (16) Touraine; Jasnières vineyard,
Vouvray area east of Tours. Fair white table wine.
France.

Molsheim. (19) Bas-Rhin *département.* Modest
white Alsace table wine. France.

Molsheim. (24) Rhinehessia; north-west of Worms.
Ordinary, fair and some fine white table wines.
West Germany.

Molvizar. (29) Andalusia; Granada, between
Málaga and Boza. Fair white wine. Spain.

Mombeltran. (29) Avila. Ordinary red table wine.
Spain.

Mommenheim. (24) Rhinehessia; north-west of
Nierstein. Ordinary to fair white table wine.
West Germany.

Monbartier. (13) Tarn-et-Garonne *département;*
near Montauban, south-central France, approx.
one hundred miles north-west of Béziers. Ordinary red table wine. France.

Monbies, Les. (8) Côte de Nuits; Chambolle-
Musigny vineyard. *Deuxième cru.* Red burgundy.
France.

Monbousquet, Château. (5) St-Emilion; St
Sulpice-de-Faleyrens. An unclassified *cru.* 15,000
dozen bottles of red bordeaux. France.

Monbrio. (29) Tarragona. Ordinary to fair white
dessert wine. Spain.

Monbrison, Château. (4) Haut-Médoc;
Margaux. *Cru bourgeois supérieur.* 4,000 dozen
bottles of red bordeaux. France.

Moncao. (30) The most northerly of the six subregions of the Vinhos Verde region. Portugal.

Moncets, Château. (5) Néac *commune;* east of
Pomerol. 8,000 dozen bottles of red bordeaux.
France.

Mönchberg. (24) Rhinehessia; Hahnheim vineyard. Fair white table wine. West Germany.

Mönchberg. (24) Nahe; Bad Kreuznach vineyard,
west of Oppenheim. Fair white table wine. West
Germany.

Mönchhanach. (24) Rhinegau; Eltville vineyard.
Fine white table wine. West Germany.

Mönchlay. (22) Moselle; Merl vineyard, north-
west of Zell. Fair white table wine. West
Germany.

Monchot. (33) Burgenland, south-east Austria,
close to the Hungarian border. Fair white table
wine. Austria.

Monconseil-Gazin, Château. (4) Blayais;
Plassac, south of Blaye. 5,000 dozen bottles of red
bordeaux. France.

Moncontour, Château de. (16) Touraine; Vouvray vineyard just north-east of Tours. Fine white table wine. France.

Moncontour, Clos. (16) Touraine; Vouvray vineyard, east of Tours. Fine white table wine. France.

Mondavi, Robert Winery. (36) California; Oakville. A new winery (1966) established by Robert Mondavi, a son of Cesare Mondavi. Quality table wines. *See* **Krug, Charles, Winery.** U.S.A.

Mondésir, Cru. (5) Sables de St-Emilion. 1,200 dozen bottles of red bordeaux. France.

Mondotte-Belille, Château. (5) St-Emilion; St Laurent-des-Combes, west of St Etienne-de-Lisse. An unclassified *cru*. 2,000 dozen bottles of red bordeaux. France.

Monfalcone (Bianco, Rosso). (26) Trieste. Fair to fine white and ordinary to fair red table wines. Italy.

Monferrato. (26) Piedmont; vine-clad hills south of Pavia facing the plain of the River Po. Italy.

Monforte d'Alba. (26) Piedmont; Le Langhe vineyards in the Alba area between Asti and Arnes. Fine red Barolo table wine. Italy.

Mongat. (29) Barcelona; Alella. Ordinary to fair white table wine. Spain.

Monge, Château de la. (4) Bourgeais; Bourg. 6,000 dozen bottles of red bordeaux. France.

Monge, Cru de la. (4) Bourgeais; Bourg. 1,000 dozen bottles of red bordeaux. France.

Mongrand, Château. (4) Haut-Médoc; Pauillac. *Cru bourgeois.* 1,000 dozen bottles of red bordeaux. France.

Monica di Sardegna. (28) Sardinia; Cagliari and Nuoro areas. Ordinary to fair sweet red dessert wine. Italy.

Monjos. (29) Barcelona; Panadés, between Tarragona and Barcelona. Ordinary to fair table wines. Spain.

Monlabert, Château. (5) St-Emilion; St Christophe-des-Bardes, south-west of Parsac. An unclassified *cru*. 800 dozen bottles of red bordeaux. France.

Monovar. (29) Alicante; approx. forty miles south of Valencia. Ordinary red table wine. South-east Spain.

Monreale. (28) Sicily. Ordinary to fair strong but pale white table wine popular in the Palermo area as an apéritif. Italy.

Monsanto, Quinta. (30) Cruz Alta area seventy miles north-west of Lisbon. Estate and vineyard in Almacave. Portugal.

Monsheim. (24) Rhinehessia; west of Worms. Ordinary to fair and some fine white table wines. West Germany.

Monsul, Quinta. (30) Estate and vineyard of fifty-five acres in Cambres south-west of Régua. Historically interesting since the 15th century. Portugal.

Mont, Château de. (31) Vaud canton; vineyard between Vufflens-le-Château and Béguins. Switzerland.

Mont, Château de. (31) Valais canton; Sion vineyard, Rhône valley. Fair white table wine. Switzerland.

Mont, Château du. (5) Côtes de Bordeaux; Ste Croix-du-Mont. 500 dozen bottles of red bordeaux; 3,600 white. France.

Mont, Clos le. (16) Touraine; Vouvray vineyard, east of Tours. Fine white table wine. France.

Montagne. (5) Village and vineyard near St-Emilion. Its wines have the *AC Montagne-St-Emilion*. Red bordeaux. France.

Montagne, La. (16) Anjou; Coteaux du Layon, Bonnézeaux vineyard, south of Angers. Fair to fine white table wine. France.

Montagne-Saint-Désire. (8) Beaune vineyard. *Deuxième cru.* Red burgundy. France.

Montagnes, Château. (4) Haut-Médoc; Macau. 2,500 dozen bottles of red bordeaux. France.

Montagny. (9) Chalonnais; south-west of Romanèche-Thorins. Fair white burgundy. France.

Montagny, Schloss. (31) Vaud canton. Fair to fine white table wine. Switzerland.

Montagny-les-Buxy. (9) Chalonnais in the Buxy area. Ordinary, fair and some fine white burgundy. France.

Montagu. (39) Western Cape Province. Table and dessert wines. South Africa.

Montaiguillon, Château. (5) St-Emilion; Montagne. An unclassified *cru*. 13,000 dozen bottles of red bordeaux. France.

Montalbano. (27) Tuscany; Monte Albano area west of Florence. Fair red table wine of the Chianti type. Italy.

Montalegré. (31) Geneva canton; Cologny vineyard. Fair white table wine. Switzerland.

Montallier, Château de. (5) Entre-deux-Mers; Loupiac. 300 dozen bottles of red bordeaux; 1,000 white. France.

Montanchez. (29) Northern Estremadura; Cáceres, approx. twenty miles west of Trujillo. Ordinary to fair red, white and *clarete* table wines. Spain.

Montblanch. (29) Tarragona; Conca de Barbara. Ordinary table wines. Spain.

Montbrun, Château. (4) Haut-Médoc; Cantenac. *Cru bourgeois supérieur.* 4,000 dozen bottles of red bordeaux. France.

Montdespic, Château. (3) St-Emilionnais;

Salles-de-Castillon. An unclassified *cru*. 18,000 dozen bottles of red bordeaux; 1,500 white. France.

Monte-Bravo, Quinta. (30) *Região demarcada do Douro* (q.v.). Estate and vineyard in Ervedosa de Douro east of Régua. Portugal.

Montecarlo (Bianco, Rosso). (27) Tuscany; Pistoia vineyard, Lucca province. Fair to good white and red wines. Italy.

Montecastelli (Bianco, Rosso). (27) Umbria; Alte Val del Tenere, upper Tiber valley north of Perugia. Ordinary to fair red and white table wines. Italy.

Monteceresino. (26) Lombardy; Oltrepo Pavese area, south of Pavia across the Po. Modest red, white and rosé table wines. Italy.

Montecompatri. (27) Lazio; Castello Romani area of the Alban hills south-east of Rome. Fair dry golden table wine. Italy.

Montée de Tonnerre. (6) Chablis; Fyé vineyard. *Premier cru*. France.

Montée Rouge. (8) Côte de Beaune; Beaune vineyard. *Premier cru*. Red burgundy. France.

Montefiascone. (27) Lazio; vineyards in the foothills of the Volsini, near Lake Bolsena northwest of Viterbo. Fair white table wine. Italy.

Monte Giove. (28) Lazio; Gaeta coastal area north-west of Naples. Ordinary to fair red table wine. Italy.

Monteguada. (29) Navarre. Stout, dry, red table wine. Spain.

Montelio. (26) Lombardy; Oltrepo area south of Pavia across the Po. Red and white table wines of above average quality. Italy.

Monteluciano del Conero. *See* Conero.

Montelungo. (26) Veneto; vineyards between Padua, south-east of Vicenza, and Vicenza. Ordinary to fair dry light red table wine. Italy.

Montenapoleone. (26) Lombardy; Oltrepo Pavese area south of Pavia across the Po. Ordinary to fair red table wine. Italy.

Montenoires, Les. (16) Touraine; Avoine vineyard. Ordinary to fair red table wine. France.

Montepulciano. (27) Tuscany; Siena area. Ordinary very light wines. Italy.

Montepulciano. (27) Abruzzi; Campobasso Chieti and L'Aquila vineyard. Ordinary to fair red table wine. Italy.

Monteregio. (27) Tuscany; vineyards on the coast, opposite the island of Elba, west of Grosetto. Ordinary to fair red and white table wine. The white tends to be sweet; the red sweetish. Italy.

Monterosso. (27) Emilia-Romagna. Ordinary to fair, somewhat sweet, and sometimes semi-sparkling, white wine. Italy.

Monterre. (29) South Galicia; Orense province. Ordinary to fair red and white table wines. Spain.

Monterubio de la Serena. (29) Estremadura; Badajoz, between Seville and Trujillo. Ordinary to fair white dessert wine. Spain.

Montes, Quinta. (30) *Região demarcada do Douro*. Estate and vineyard in Gouvinhas in the Régua area. One of the oldest Quintas in the Douro valley. Portugal.

Montesanto (Rosso). (27) The Marches; Macerata area, approx. twenty miles south of Ancona. Fair dry red table wine. Italy.

Montevecchio. (26) Lombardy; Como area. Ordinary dry red and fair dry white table wines. Italy.

Montezargues, Domaine de. (12) Côtes du Rhône; Tavel vineyard. Fair to fine rosé table wine. France.

Mont Fleuri. (31) Valais canton; Sion vineyard, Rhône valley. Fair white table wine. Switzerland.

Montfleury. (12) Ardèche *département*; Côtes du Rhône. Ordinary to fair red table wine. France.

Mont Garcin. (10) Mâconnais; Solutré vineyard. *Premier cru*. Entitled to the *AC Pouilly-Fuissé*. White burgundy. France.

Montgenets, Les. (18) L'Etoile vineyard, south-west of Château Chalen, Jura. Ordinary to fair white table wine. France.

Monthallier. (18) Arbois vineyard, Jura. *Deuxième cru*. Ordinary red and rosé table wines. France.

Monthaux. (31) Savoie *département*; Lac du Bourget vineyards, near Chambery approx. forty-five miles south-west of Geneva. Fair white table wine. France.

Monthélie. (8) Côte de Beaune; village and vineyards. Fair and some fine red burgundy. France.

Monthélon. (17) Marne *département*; Avize canton, south of Pierry. Rated—88% growth. 235 acres. France.

Monthénault. (16) Coteaux du Layon, Faye d'Anjou vineyard, south of Saumur. Fair to fine white table wine. France.

Monthil, Cru. (3) Médoc; Bégadan, north-west of St Seurin-de-Cadourne. *Cru bourgeois*. 2,000 dozen bottles of red bordeaux. France.

Montibeux, Clos de. (31) Valais canton; Martigny vineyard. Fine white table wine. Switzerland.

Montignac. (5) Premières Côtes de Bordeaux; Cénac, east of Villenave d'Ornon. 6,000 dozen bottles of red bordeaux; 1,000 white. France.

Montijo. (29) Estremadura; Badajoz, between Seville and Trujillo. Ordinary white table wine. Spain.

Montilla. (29) North-central Andalusia; Córdoba. Fair to fine apéritif and dessert white wines, often fortified. Spain.

Montjean. (16) Anjou; Saumur area. Ordinary to fair red table wine. France.

Mont-Joie, Château. (5) Sauternes; Barsac. *Cru bourgeois*. 2,000 dozen bottles of white bordeaux. France.

Montjon-le-Gravier, Château. (3) Entre-deux-Mers; St-Eulalie, east of Blanquefort. 1,500 dozen bottles of red bordeaux. France.

Montlouis. (16) Touraine; Vouvray area, north-east of Tours. Ordinary to fair red table wine. France.

Montluçon. (15) Allier *département*; approx. forty-five miles south-west of Moulins in the Massif Central. Ordinary to fair red and white table wines. France.

Montmell. (29) Tarragona; Panadés, between Tarragona and Barcelona. Ordinary to fair table wines. Spain.

Montmorins, Les. (18) L'Etoile vineyard, south-west of Château Chalen, Jura. Fair white table wine. France.

Montolivet, Le. (12) Côtes du Rhône, Châteauneuf-du-Pape. Fair to fine red and white table wines. France.

Montopoli-in-Sabina. (27) Lazio; Tiber valley. Ordinary light, white table wine. Italy.

Montouvert. (26) Piedmont; Villeneuve vineyard, Val d'Aosta. Fair white dessert wine and occasionally a German-type *Eiswein* (q.v.). Italy.

Mont Palais. (9) Chalonnais; Rully vineyard. *Premier cru*. White burgundy. France.

Montpeyroux. (13) Hérault *département*; Béziers area. *V.D.Q.S.* Red and rosé table wines. France.

Mont-près-Chambord. (16) Cour-Cheverny vineyard, near the Château de Chambord, east of Blois. Fair white table wine. France.

Montrachet, Le. (8) Côte de Beaune; Chassagne-Montrachet, and Puligny-Montrachet. *Grand cru*. Possibly the greatest white burgundy. France.

Mont-Redon. (12) Côtes du Rhône, Châteauneuf-du-Pape. Fair to fine red table wine, also some sparkling white wine. France.

Montremenots, Les. (8) Beaune vineyard. *Premier cru*. Red burgundy. France.

Montrose, Château. (4) Haut-Médoc; St-Estèphe. *Deuxième cru classé*. 24,000 dozen bottles of red bordeaux. France.

Montreuil-Bellay. (16) Anjou; Saumur area. Ordinary to fair red and white table wines. France.

Monts-Damnes, Les. (15) Cher *département*; Chavignol vineyard, Sancerre district. Fair white table wine. France.

Monts-Luisants, Les. (8) Côte de Nuits; Morey-St-Denis vineyard. *Premier cru*. A large section is planted in white Chardonnay. Red burgundy. France.

Montsoreau. (16) Anjou; Coteaux de Saumur. Fair white table wine. France.

Montu. *See* **Montuni.**

Montuni. (26) Emilia-Romagna; Castelfranco, north-west of Bologna. Fair, rather hard, white table wine. Italy.

Mony, Château. (5) Premières Côtes de Bordeaux; Rions, north of Podensac. 1,500 dozen bottles of red bordeaux; 6,000 white. France.

Monzernheim. (24) Rhinehessia; south-west of Alsheim. Ordinary, fair and some fine white table wine. West Germany.

Monzingen. (24) Nahe; west of Bad Münster. Fair to fine white table wines. West Germany.

Moosberg. (24) Rhinehessia; Hahnheim and Zornheim vineyards, north-west of Nierstein. Fair white table wine. West Germany.

Moquegua. (35) City in the southernmost part of the country. Wine centre of Peru. Peru.

Mór. (33) Town and vineyard approx. fifty miles west of Budapest. Ordinary to fair, and some fine red and white table wines. Hungary.

Mora. (29) West New Castile; Toledo, approx. forty miles south-west of Madrid. Ordinary to fair red table wine. Spain.

Morains. (16) Anjou; Coteaux de Saumur, Dampierre-sur-Loire. Fair white table wine. France.

Morange et la Gravière, Domaine de. (5) Premières Côtes de Bordeaux; Ste Croix-du-Mont. 1,000 dozen bottles of red bordeaux; 6,500 white. France.

Morasca Cinqueterre. (26) Liguria; the Cinqueterre area north-west of La Spezia. Ordinary to fair popular white apéritif and table wine. Italy.

Morastell. (29) Stout, 'black' red table wine which is very popular in many parts of Spain.

Morata del Jalon. (29) Aragon; Zaragoza. Ordinary to fair red and white table wines. Spain.

Moratell. (29) Murcia. Ordinary to fair, rather sweet white table wine which becomes dry if allowed to age in the bottle. Spain.

Morera, La. (29) Tarragona; Priorata. Ordinary to fair red table wine. Spain.

Morère, Château La. (4) Haut-Médoc; Moulis. *Cru bourgeois*. 2,000 dozen bottles of red bordeaux. France.

Morey. (8) Côte de Nuits; Morey-St-Denis vineyard. *Premier cru*. Red burgundy. France.

Morey-Saint-Denis. (8) Côte de Nuits. Fair, fine and some very fine red burgundy. France.

Morgeot, Abbaye de. (8) Côte de Beaune; Chassagne-Montrachet. *Premier cru*. Red burgundy. France.

Morgon. (11) Villié-Morgon vineyard, Beaujolais. *Premier cru.* One of the top-grade beaujolais. Red burgundy. France.

Moriers, Les. (11) Beaujolais; Fleurie vineyard. One of the top-grade *cru beaujolais.* Red burgundy. France.

Móri Ezerjo. (33) Mór vineyards; approx. fifty miles west of Budapest. Fair to fine white table wine from Ezerjo grapes. Hungary.

Moriles. (29) North-central Andalusia; Córdoba. Fair to fine apéritif and dessert white wines, often fortified. Spain.

Morillon, Château. (4) Blayais; Campugnan, north-east of Blaye. 800 dozen bottles of red bordeaux; 3,000 white. France.

Morin, Château. (4) Haut-Médoc; St-Estèphe. *Cru bourgeois supérieur.* 5,000 dozen bottles of red bordeaux. France.

Morlupo (Bianco, Rosso). (27) Lazio; Tiber valley vineyards, north of Rome. Ordinary rather sweetish white and red table wines are produced. Italy.

Moron-Lafitte, Château. (5) Graves de Bordeaux; Arbanats, north-west of Podensac. An unclassified *cru.* 3,000 dozen bottles of red bordeaux; 200 white. France.

Morphett Vale. (37) South Australia; south of Adelaide. Former vineyard district now almost entirely built up with housing but still the Australian H.Q. of the Emu Wine Co., which is shipper for Co-operative Wines (Australia) Ltd. Australia.

Morra, La. (26) Piedmont; Le Langhe district in the area between Arnes and Asti. Fine red Barolo table wine. Italy.

Morris. (37) *See* **Mia Mia.**

Morschberg. (24) Rhinegau; Geisenheim vineyard. Fine white table wine. West Germany.

Mörstadt. (24) Rhinehessia; north-west of Worms. Ordinary to fair red and white table wines. West Germany.

Morteron. (16) Anjou; Coteaux de la Loire, La Possonnière vineyard south-west of Angers. Fair to fine white table wine. France.

Moscadello. (26) Liguria; hillside vineyards near Bordighera approx. twenty miles south-west of Imperia. Ordinary white table wine. Italy.

Moscadello di Montalcino. (27) Tuscany; Montalcino-Siena vineyards. Ordinary, light dessert wine. Italy.

Moscadello Lucuoroso. (27) Tuscany; Siena. Fair, white dessert wine. Italy.

Moscatel. (29) White, sweet dessert wine made from Muscat grapes in most parts of Spain, in many different grades of excellence of homeliness. Spain.

Moscato. The Italian name of a white Muscat grape grown in many parts of Italy; also the name of the sweet dessert wines produced from it and marketed under the name of their native village or province. Italy.

Moscato (Moscato Sardo). Fair white sweet dessert wine, still or sparkling, made from Moscatello grapes. Italy.

Moscato Rosa. (26) Alto Adige. Fair, cherry-red dessert wine. Italy.

Moscato Spumante. Another name for Asti Spumante (q.v.). Italy.

Moscato Spumante di San Marino. (27) San Marino white sparkling wine with more sugar and bubbles than alcohol. From the tiny independent republic of San Marino between Ancona and Bologna, Italy.

Mosel. The German spelling of the river Moselle. West Germany.

Moselkern. (22) Moselle; south-west of Kobern. Ordinary, fair and some fine white table wine. West Germany.

Mosny. (16) Touraine; St Martin-le-Beau vineyard, east of Tours. Fair white table wine. France.

Mostaganem. (40) Oran. Principally red wines, which were entitled under French rule to the *V.D.Q.S.* appellation provided strength reached 12·5°. Algeria.

Mota del Cuervo. (29) East New Castile. Ordinary to fair red and white table wines. Spain.

Motilla del Palancar. (29) East New Castile. Ordinary to fair red table wine. Spain.

Mottalciata. (26) Piedmont; Vercelli province. Fine red wine similar to Gatteriara (q.v.) but generally not thought to be so fine. Italy.

Motte-Pesque, La. (16) Touraine; Borgueil vineyard. Fair red table wine. France.

Mottouse, La. (16) Anjou; Coteaux de l'Aubance, Müre-Erigne vineyard, between Angers and Saumur. Fair white table wine. France.

Mouches, Clos des. (8) Beaune vineyard. *Premier cru.* Red and white burgundy. France.

Mouènes, Les. (9) Rully vineyard, Chalonnais. Fine quality red burgundy. France.

Mouilles, Les. (11) Juliénas vineyard, Beaujolais. One of the top-grade beaujolais; fine quality red burgundy. France.

Mouilles, Les. (11) Beaujolais; Juliénas vineyard. One of the top-grade beaujolais. Red burgundy. France.

Moulenes, Les. (9) Chalonnais; Rully vineyard. *Premier cru.* Red burgundy. France.

Mouleyre, La Château. (5) Côtes de Bordeaux; Ste Croix-du-Mont. 500 dozen bottles of red bordeaux; 3,000 white. France.

Moulières, Domaine des. (14) Côtes de Provence; Côte de Maures, La Valette vineyard, just north-east of Toulon. Fair red, white and rosé table wines. France.

Moulin, Domaine du. (12) Côtes du Rhône; Lirac vineyard. Fair to fine rosé table wine. France.

Moulin, Le. (12) Côtes du Rhône; Cornas vineyard, immediately north of St Péray. Fair red table wine. France.

Moulin, Le. (11) Beaujolais; Chiroubles vineyard. One of the top-grade *cru beaujolais*. Red burgundy. France.

Moulin-à-Vent. (9) Rully vineyard, Chalonnais. *Premier cru*. White burgundy. France.

Moulin-à-Vent. (11) Beaujolais; spread over parts of Chénas, Romanèche and La Chapelle de Guinchey. Fair to fine red burgundy. One of the top-grade *cru beaujolais*. France.

Moulin-à-Vent. (9) Chalonnais; Rully vineyard. *Premier cru*. White burgundy. France.

Moulin-à-Vent. (11) Chénas vineyard, Côte Mâconnais and Beaujolais. Fair to fine red burgundy. A top-grade beaujolais. France.

Moulin-à-Vent, Château. (4) Haut-Médoc; Moulis. *Cru bourgeois supérieur*. 5,000 dozen bottles of red bordeaux. France.

Moulin-à-Vent, Château. (5) Néac *commune*; east of Pomerol. 4,000 dozen bottles of red bordeaux. France.

Moulin-à-Vent, Château du. (5) Graves de Bordeaux; Cérons. 3,000 dozen bottles of white bordeaux. France.

Moulin-à-Vent, Clos du. (5) Langon; St Pierre-de-Mons. 500 dozen bottles of red bordeaux; 3,000 white. France.

Moulin-Bellegrave, Château. (5) St-Emilionnais; Vignonet, south-west of St Pey-d'Armens. An unclassified *cru*. 2,500 dozen bottles of red bordeaux. France.

Moulin-Blanc, Château. (5) Néac *commune*; east of Pomerol. 1,000 dozen bottles of red bordeaux. France.

Moulin-Blanc, Château. (5) St-Emilion; Montagne-St-Emilion. An unclassified *cru*. 5,000 dozen bottles of red bordeaux. France.

Moulin-de-Bachelot. (16) Anjou; Coteaux de la Loire, St Georges-sur-Loire, below Angers. Fair white table wine. France.

Moulin-de-Laborde, Domaine du. (4) Haut-Médoc; Listrac. *Cru bourgeois*. 2,500 dozen bottles of red bordeaux. France.

Moulin-de-la-Roque. (14) Côtes de Provence; La Cadière vineyard, north of Bandol. *AC Bandol*. Fair red, white and rosé table wines. France.

Moulin-de-la-Rose, Château. (4) Haut-Médoc; St-Julien. *Cru bourgeois*. 2,000 dozen bottles of red bordeaux. France.

Moulin-du-Bourg, Domaine de. (4) Haut-Médoc; Listrac. *Cru bourgeois*. 3,500 dozen bottles of red bordeaux. France.

Moulin, Le. (11) Chiroubles vineyard, Beaujolais. *Premier cru*. Red burgundy. One of the top-grade beaujolais. France.

Moulinet, Château. (5) Pomerol. 4,000 dozen bottles of red bordeaux. France.

Moulin-Lanciat. (11) Lancié vineyard, Beaujolais. Red burgundy. France.

Moulin-Meziat. (11) Beaujolais; Lancié vineyard. *AC Beaujolais villages*. Red burgundy. France.

Moulin-Neuf, Cru du. (5) Entre-deux-Mers; Haut-Loupiac. 1,000 dozen bottles of red bordeaux; 1,000 white. France.

Moulin-Pey-Labrie, Domaine du. (4) Fronsac. Produces 8,000 dozen bottles of red bordeaux. France.

Moulin-Saint-Georges-Côte-Pavie, Château. (5) Côtes de St-Emilion. An unclassified *cru*. 5,500 dozen bottles of red bordeaux. France.

Moulins-à-Vent, Château des. (5) Graves de Bordeaux; Cérons. An unclassified *cru*. 3,000 dozen bottles of white bordeaux. France.

Moulis, Château. (4) Haut-Médoc; Moulis. *Cru bourgeois supérieur*. 3,000 dozen bottles of red bordeaux. France.

Mount Dangar. (37) New South Wales; Hunter valley, north-east of Sydney. Site of a venture begun in 1969 as joint enterprise of Hamilton's Ewell Vineyards and Adelaide Steamship Company, both of South Australia.

Mount la Salle. (36) California; Napa Valley. Location of the Christian Brothers novitiate vineyard and winery. Quality table, dessert and sparkling wines. U.S.A.

Mount Pleasant. (37) New South Wales; Hunter valley, north-east of Sydney. Estate and vineyard made famous by the late Maurice O'Shea. Table wines. Australia.

Moura, Quinta. (30) *Região demarcada do Douro* (q.v.). Small estate in Cambres south-west of Régua. Portugal.

Mousse, Clos de la. (8) Côte de Beaune; Beaune vineyard. *Premier cru*. Red burgundy. France.

Moussière, Domaine de la. (15) Sancerre, upper Loire valley. Fair white table wine. France.

Moussy. (17) Marne *département*; Epernay canton, west of Pierry. Rated—88% growth. 267 acres. France.

Mouton-Cadet. The registered name under which the owner of Château Mouton-Rothschild (q.v.) and Mouton-Baron Philippe market a cheaper red bordeaux. France.

Moutonne, La. *See* **Chablis-Moutonne.**

Mouton-Rothschild, Château. (4) Haut-Médoc; Pauillac. *Deuxième cru classé.* 25,000 dozen bottles of red bordeaux. France.

Moyne, Château Le. (4) Entre-deux-Mers; Loupiac. 500 dozen bottles of red bordeaux; 4,500 white. France.

Moyston. (37) Victoria; a tiny village near Great Western 100 miles north-west of Geelong. Also the name of a claret made by Seppelts from Shiraz cabernet and malbec grapes. Australia.

Müchenhaus. (23) Palatinate; Königsbach vineyard. Fine white table wine. West Germany.

Müden. (22) Lower Moselle; south-west of Kobern. Ordinary to fair white table wine. West Germany.

Mühl. (24) Nahe; Waldböckelheim; west of Bad Münster. Fair table wine. West Germany.

Mühl. (24) Rhinehessia; Aspisheim vineyard, south of Rüdesheim. Ordinary to fair white table wine. West Germany.

Mühlacker. (23) Palatinate; Gleisweiler vineyard, north-west of Landau. Ordinary to fair white table wine. West Germany.

Mühlacker. (25) Württemberg; approx. twenty miles south-east of Karlsruhe. Ordinary to fair red and white table wines. West Germany.

Mühlbach. (25) Baden; approx. twenty-six miles north-west of Würzburg. Ordinary to fair red and white table wines. West Germany.

Mühlberg. (21) Middle Rhine; Steeg vineyard, north-west of Bingen. Fair white table wine. West Germany.

Mühlberg. (24) Nahe; Schloss Böckelheim vineyard, west of Bad Münster. Fair white table wine. West Germany.

Mühlberg. (24) Rhinegau; Oestrich vineyard. Fine white table wine. West Germany.

Mühle. (23) Palatinate; Edenkoben and Deidesheim vineyards. Fair to fine white table wine. West Germany.

Mühlenberg. (24) Nahe; Bad Münster and Roxheim vineyards, north-west of Bad Kreuznach. Fair white table wine. West Germany.

Mühlenberg. (24) Nahe; Bad Münster and Roxheim vineyard, north-west of Bad Kreuznach. Fair white table wine. West Germany.

Mühlenberg. (22) Saar; Saarburg vineyard. Fair white table wine. West Germany.

Mühlpieth. (24) Nahe; Bretzenheim vineyard, north-east of Bad Kreuznach. Fair white table wine. West Germany.

Mühlstein. (24) Rhinegau; Rüdesheim vineyard. Fair to fine white table wine. West Germany.

Mühlweg. (23) Palatinate; Königsbach and Ruppertsberg vineyards. Fine white table wine. West Germany.

Mukuzani. (34) Georgia; bordering on Turkey and the Black Sea. Ordinary, stout, dark red table wine. U.S.S.R.

Mula. (29) Murcia. Stout, heavy, sweet, red table wine which becomes dry with age. Spain.

Mulay-Hofberg. (22) Moselle; Reil vineyard, east of Zell. Fair white table wine. West Germany.

Mülheim. (22) Middle Moselle; just east of Brauneberg. Ordinary, fair and some fine white table wines. West Germany.

Mullayhofberg. (22) Moselle; Reil vineyard, east of Zell. Fair white table wine. West Germany.

Mullonières, Les. (16) Coteaux du Layon; Beaumont-sur-Layon, south of Angers. Fair white table wine. France.

Mundelsheim. (25) Württemberg; south of Heilbronn. Ordinary to fair red and white table wines. West Germany.

Mundingen. (25) Baden; north of Freiburg. Ordinary to fair red and white table wines. West Germany.

Münster. (25) Württemberg. Ordinary red and white table wines. West Germany.

Münster-bei-Bingerbrück. (24) Nahe. Ordinary to fair red and white table wines are produced. West Germany.

Münster-Sarmsheim. (24) Nahe; just east of Bingen. Ordinary to fair red and white table wines. West Germany.

Munzlay. (22) Moselle; Graach and Wehlen vineyard. West Germany.

Murailles, Clos des. (31) Vaud canton; Aigle vineyard. Fair to fine white table wine. Switzerland.

Murcas, Quinta. (30) *Região demarcada do Douro* (q.v.). Estate in Covelinhas near Régua. Portugal.

Murcas de Cima, Quinta. (30) *Região demarcada do Douro* (q.v.). Estate and vineyard in Covelinhas in the Régua area. Portugal.

Mure, La. (12) Côtes du Rhône; Cornas. Fair red table wine. France.

Mure, La. (10) Mâconnais; Solutré vineyard. White burgundy. France.

Müre-Erigne. (16) Coteaux de l'Aubance; between Angers and Saumur. Ordinary, fair and some fine white table wines. France.

Murets, Les. (12) Côtes du Rhône; Tain l'Hermitage vineyard. Fair red and white table wines. France.

Murettes, Les. (31) Valais canton; Sion vineyard. Fair to fine white table wine. Switzerland.

Murfatlar. (33) South-east Rumania; vineyards between the Danube and the Black Sea, former name of the Dobrudja area. Fine white dessert wine. Rumania.

Murgers, Aux. (8) Côte de Nuits; Nuits-St-Georges vineyard. *Premier cru.* Red burgundy. France.

Murillo del Rio Lera. (29) Logroño; La Rioja area of the upper Ebro valley. Fair to fine red and white table wines. Spain.

Murinais. (12) Isère *département*. Fair red and white table wines. France.

Murr. (25) Württemberg; north-east of Stuttgart. Ordinary red table wine. West Germany.

Murs, Clos des. (16) Coteaux de Saumur; Parnay vineyard and commune on the Saumur hillsides. Fair white table wine. France.

Muscadet, Château. (5) Premières Côtes de Bordeaux; Bassens, south-east of Blanquefort. 2,000 dozen bottles of red bordeaux; 800 white. France.

Muscat de Frontignan. (13) Hérault *département*; Frontignan: Fair to fine, tawny dessert wine. France.

Muscat de Lunel. (13) Hérault *département;* Lunel. Fair to fine, tawny dessert wine. France.

Muscat de Saint Jean de Minervois. (13) Aude *département*. Fair to fine white dessert wine. France.

Musenhang. (23) Palatinate; Forst vineyard. Fine white table wine. West Germany.

Musigny. (8) Chambolle-Musigny vineyard. *Grand cru.* Considered by some the greatest red burgundy. A fine dry white wine, Musigny Blanc, is from the same vineyard. France.

Muskotaly. (33) Villany; approx. 120 miles south of Budapest. Fair to fine white muscat dessert wine. Hungary.

Müssbach. (23) Palatinate; Middle Haardt. Ordinary to fair red table wines; fair to fine and some very fine white. West Germany.

Musset, Château. (5) Lalande-de-Pomerol; north of Pomerol. 2,000 dozen bottles of red bordeaux. France.

Musset, Château. (5) St-Emilionnais; Parsac. An unclassified *cru.* 3,000 dozen bottles of red bordeaux. France.

Mustoasa. (33) Maderat. Sweet, sparkling dessert wine. Rumania.

Mutigny. (17) Marne *département*. Ay canton, north-east of Ay. Rated *premier cru*—93% growth. 136 acres. France.

Mutonich. (33) Hodonin area of central Czechoslovakia; Zaribnicke vineyard. Ordinary to fair red and white table wines. Czechoslovakia.

Mykonos. (34) Island off south-eastern coast of Greece. Ordinary to fair red and white table wines. Greece.

Myrat, Château. (5) Sauternes; Barsac. *Deuxième cru classé.* 5,000 dozen bottles of white bordeaux. France.

♣

Nack. (24) Rhinehessia; south-east of Bad Münster. Ordinary to fair white table wine. West Germany.

Nackenheim. (24) Rhinehessia. Ordinary red table wine and fair to fine white table wine. West Germany.

Nacktarsch. (22) Moselle; Kröv (Cröv) vineyard. Fair white table wine. West Germany.

Nahe. (24) The river which flows from the Hünsruck to the Rhine, which it joins at Bingen. The many vineyards along its valley produce some ordinary red wine but more and much better white wines. The best wines are those grown on the left bank up to and including Bad Kreuznach. West Germany.

Nairac, Château. (5) Sauternes; Barsac. *Deuxième cru classé.* 2,500 dozen bottles of white bordeaux. France.

Najera. (29) Logroño province; La Rioja area of the upper Ebro valley. Mostly fair to fine red table wine. Spain.

Nallys. (12) Côtes du Rhône; Châteauneuf-du-Pape. Fair to fine red table wine. France.

Napa. (36) California; county north-east of San Francisco. Napa Valley is located totally in Napa County and the upper valley is the site of most of the vineyards and wineries. The district is noted for the excellence of its wines, chiefly table wines. U.S.A.

Napareuli. (34) Georgia; bordering on Turkey and the Black Sea. Ordinary red and white table wines. U.S.S.R.

Napoleon, Clos. (8) Côte de Nuits; Fixin vineyard. This vineyard was formerly called Aux Cheusots. Fine red burgundy. France.

Napoles, Quinta. (30) Estate and vineyard in Vila Seca twenty-five miles north of Oporto. 107 acres. Portugal.

Narbag. (34) Ordinary red table wine. Turkey.

Narbantons, Les. (8) Côte de Beaune; Savigny-les-Beaune vineyard. *Premier cru.* Red burgundy. France.

Narince. (34) North-central Turkey; Toka. Ordinary red and white table wines. Turkey.

Nasco. (28) Sardinia; Cagliari. Fair sweet golden dessert wine with a charming orange blossom bouquet and a faintly bitter undertaste which makes it intriguing. Italy.

Nassau. (22) Lahn; on the Lahn, east of Koblenz.

Ordinary to fair red and white table wines. West Germany.

Nauges, Les. (9) Chalonnais; Mercurey vineyard. *Premier cru.* Red burgundy. France.

Nava del Rey. (29) Western Old Castile; Valladolid, approx. seventy miles north of Avila. Ordinary to fair white table wine. Spain.

Navarrete. (29) Logroño province, La Rioja area of the upper Ebro valley. Mostly fair red table wines. Spain.

Naxos. (34) Island off south-eastern coast of Greece. Fair red and white table wines. Greece.

Nazarcea. (33) South-east Rumania; Dobrudja vineyard. Fair to fine white dessert wine. Rumania.

Nazoires, Les. (8) Côte de Nuits; Chambolle-Musigny vineyard. *Deuxième cru.* Red burgundy. France.

Néac. (5) *Commune* and vineyards north-east of Libourne in the Pomerol area, with the *AC Néac.* Ordinary to fair red bordeaux. France.

Nebbiolo d'Alba. (26) Piedmont; Alba vineyards, Cuneo province. Fair to fine red table wine. Italy.

Nebbiolo di Canale. (26) Piedmont; Alba vineyards, Cuneo province. Fair to fine red table wine. Italy.

Nebbiolo di Castellinaldo. (26) Piedmont; Castellinaldo vineyards, Cuneo province. Fair to fine red table wine. Italy.

Nebbiolo di Retorbido. (26) Lombardy; the Valtelline area. Ordinary to fair red table wine. Italy.

Neckarmühlbach. (25) Baden; north-west of Heilbronn. Ordinary red and white table wines. West Germany.

Neckarsulm. (25) Württemberg; north of Heilbronn. Ordinary to fair red and white table wines. West Germany.

Neckartaler. The name given to all ordinary wines from the Neckar valley. West Germany.

Neckarweihingen. (25) Württemberg; north-west of Stuttgart. Fair white table wine. West Germany.

Neckarzimmern. (25) Baden; south of Mosbach. Ordinary to fair red and white table wines. West Germany.

Nederburg. (39) Western Cape Province; Paarl area. Fair table and dessert wines. South Africa.

Neef. (22) Moselle; Krampen (the local name of the hairpin bend of the Moselle between Eller and Kochem, west of Valwig). Ordinary to fair white table wine. West Germany.

Negra de Almandralejo. (29) Estremadura; Badajoz, between Seville and Trujillo. Very dark and stout red table wine. Spain.

Negrara. (26) Alto Adige. Ordinary to fair dry, full red table wines made from Negrara grapes. Italy.

Negrin. (29) Central Asturias; Oviedo area. Dark red, dry, ordinary table wine. Spain.

Negro Rancio. (29) Central León; Zamora. Ordinary to fair golden dessert wine. Spain.

Neiperg. (25) Württemberg; south-west of Heilbronn. Ordinary to fair red and white table wines. West Germany.

Nemea. (34) Southern Greece; Peloponnisos peninsula, Corinth area. Ordinary to fair white table wine. Greece.

Nenenberg. (24) Rhinehessia; Alsheim vineyard. Fair white table wine. West Germany.

Nenin, Château. (5) Pomerol. *Grand cru.* 10,000 dozen bottles of red bordeaux. France.

Nennig. (??) Moselle; south-west of Saarburg. Ordinary to fair white table wine. West Germany.

Nerja. (29) Málaga. Ordinary red. Spain.

Nero del Brindisino. (28) Apulia. Common, dark red wine chiefly used in blends. Italy.

Nerthe, Château de la. (12) Côtes du Rhône; Châteauneuf-du-Pape. Fair to fine red table wine. France.

Nervo Winery. (36) California; Geyserville, Sonoma County. Quality table wines. U.S.A.

Nerzweiler. (23) Palatinate; approx. nineteen miles south-west of Bad Münster. Fair white table wine. West Germany.

Nesselried. (25) Baden; south-east of Strasbourg. Ordinary to fair red and white table wines. West Germany.

Nettuno Bianco. (28) Lazio; vineyards between Nettuno and Anzio, south of Rome. Fair white table wine. Italy.

Neu-Bamberg. (24) Rhinehessia; south-east of Bad Münster. Fair white table wine. West Germany.

Neuchâtel. (31) Swiss canton with 2,175 acres of vineyards. Mostly fair white table wines. Switzerland.

Neuershausen. (25) Baden; north-west of Freiburg. Ordinary to fair red and white table wines. West Germany.

Neufeld. (24) Rhinegau; Hallgarten vineyard. Fine white table wine. West Germany.

Neuffen. (25) Württemberg; approx. eighteen miles south-east of Stuttgart. Ordinary to fair red and white table wines. West Germany.

Neuleiningen. (23) Palatinate; just south-west of Grünstadt. Ordinary to fair red and white table wines. West Germany.

Neumagen. (22) Middle Moselle. Fair to fine white table wines. West Germany.

Neuquen. (35) One of the smallest wine-producing provinces of Argentina.

M

Neusatz. (25) Baden; south-west of Baden-Baden. Ordinary to fair red and white table wines. West Germany.

Neuses. (25) Franconia; approx. twenty miles south of Würzburg. Fair white table wine. West Germany.

Neusetz. (25) Franconia; north-east of Würzburg. Fair white table wine. West Germany.

Neusiedl, Lake. (33) Burgenland; south-east Austria close to the Hungarian frontier. Ordinary to fair red and white table wines. Austria.

Neustadt. (23) Palatinate, Middle Haardt. Ordinary, fair and some fine red and white table wines. West Germany.

Neuweg. (24) Rhinehessia; Dienheim vineyard. Fair white table wine. West Germany.

Neuweier. (25) Baden; south-west of Baden-Baden. Ordinary to fair red and white table wines. West Germany.

New Jersey. (35) State with a few wine-making vineyards. U.S.A.

New South Wales. (37) The cradle of viticulture in Australia. Although now producing less wine than South Australia, New South Wales has been closing the gap somewhat by vigorous development. Australia.

New York. (35) Second State, after California, in wine production. Wines are mostly made from native grape varieties, other than vitis vinifera. U.S.A.

New Zealand. (38) Viticulture was introduced in New Zealand early in the nineteenth century. Vineyards are now cultivated and wine is now being made on a commercial scale in the North Island, chiefly in the Auckland and Napier regions.

Nexon-Lemoyne, Château. (4) Haut-Médoc; Ludon. *Cru bourgeois supérieur.* 2,000 dozen bottles of red bordeaux. France.

Nicastro Bianco. (28) Calabria; Bay of Eufemia vineyards, west of Cantanzaro. Ordinary semi-sweet fragrant white table wine. Italy.

Nichelini Vineyards. (36) California; St Helena. A small family-owned winery which produces a fine Zinfandel, the wine so distinctively Californian. U.S.A.

Nicolas Rolin. (8) Hospices de Beaune *cuvée*, named after the founder of the Hospices who bequeathed the Beaune vineyard. The wines of the Hospices are auctioned annually for the upkeep of the Hospices. Red burgundy. France.

Nicoresti. (33) Village in East Rumania. Fair white table wines. Rumania.

Niebelsbach. (25) Württemberg; south-east of Karlsruhe. Ordinary to fair red and white table wines. West Germany.

Niebla. (29) Huelva. Ordinary red table wine. Spain.

Niederberg. (21) Middle Rhine; opposite Koblenz. Ordinary to fair red and white table wines. West Germany.

Niedereisenbach. (24) Nahe; approx. nineteen miles south-west of Bad Münster. Ordinary to fair white table wine. West Germany.

Niederfell. (22) Moselle; south-east of Kobern. Ordinary to fair white table wine. West Germany.

Niederhausen-Schloss Böckelheim. (24) Nahe; west of Bad Münster. Fine and very fine white table wine. West Germany.

Niederheimbach. (21) Middle Rhine; north-west of Bingen. Fair white table wine. West Germany.

Nieder-Hilbersheim. (24) Rhinehessia; south-east of Bingen. Fair white table wine. West Germany.

Niederhochstadt. (23) Palatinate; north-east of Landau. Ordinary to fair red and white table wines. West Germany.

Niederhorbach. (23) Palatinate; south-west of Landau. Ordinary to fair red and white table wines. West Germany.

Niederhorsheim. (23) Palatinate. Ordinary to fair red and white table wines. West Germany.

Niederkirchen. (23) Palatinate; Middle Haardt. Fair to fine white table wine. West Germany.

Niedermennig. (22) Saar valley; north-east of Wiltingen. Ordinary to fair white wines. West Germany.

Niedermorschwihr. (19) Haut-Rhin *département;* north of Türckheim. Medium to fair white Alsace wine. France.

Niedermoschel. (23) Palatinate; south of Bad Münster. Fair white wine. West Germany.

Nieder-Olm. (24) Rhinehessia; west of Nackenheim. Ordinary to fair white table wine. West Germany.

Nieder-Österreich. (33) Lower Austria, the Danube valley west of Vienna to the frontier. Its vineyards are responsible for approx. 60% of the total wine production of Austria.

Niederrimbach. (25) Württemberg; approx. twenty-two miles south of Würzburg. Ordinary to fair red and white table wines. West Germany.

Niederrimsingen. (25) Baden; west of Freiburg. Ordinary to fair red and white table wines. West Germany.

Nieder-Saulheim. (24) Rhinehessia; west of Nierstein. Ordinary to fair white table wines. West Germany.

Niederschopfheim. (25) Baden; south-east of Strasbourg. Ordinary to fair red and white table wines. West Germany.

Niederstetten. (25) Württemberg; approx. twenty-seven miles south of Würzburg. Ordinary to fair red and white table wines. West Germany.

Niederwalluf. (24) Rhinegau. Ordinary red and fine white table wines. West Germany.

Nieder-Wiesen. (24) Rhinehessia; approx. sixteen miles west of Alsheim. Ordinary to fair red and white table wines. West Germany.

Niefernheim. (23) Palatinate; Lower Haardt, north-west of Worms. Ordinary to fair red and white table wines. West Germany.

Nierstein. (24) Rhineshessia; the foremost wine town of Rhinehessia. Ordinary, fair, fine and some very fine white table wines; the best made from Riesling grapes. West Germany

Niesgen. (22) Ruwer valley; Kasel vineyard. Fair to fine white table wine. West Germany.

Nikolausberg. (24) Rhinehessia; Pfaffen-Schwabenheim vineyard, east of Bad Kreuznach. Fair white table wine. West Germany.

Nildottle. (37) South Australia; near Swan Reach of the Murray river in the Swan Hill area. Hamilton Ewell vineyards and others. Australia.

Nill. (23) Palatinate; Kallstadt vineyard. Fair white table wine. West Germany.

Ninfeo. (28) Sardinia; La Nurra area, the north-west tip of the island. Fair to fine sweet, strong white dessert wine. Italy.

Nipozzano. (27) Tuscany; Florence area. Fine, full red wine. Italy.

Nittel. (22) Moselle; west of Wiltingen. Fair white table wine. West Germany.

Noblaie, La. (16) Touraine; Ligré vineyard, above Chinon. Fair red table wine. France.

Noble, Domaine du. (5) Entre-deux-Mers; Loupiac. 1,600 dozen bottles of red bordeaux; 4,000 white. France.

Noblejos. (29) West New Castile; Toledo, approx. forty miles south-west of Madrid. Ordinary table wines. Spain.

Nobles, Cru des. (16) Touraine; Joué-les-Tours. Fair red table wine. France.

Nochen. (21) Middle Rhine; south-east of Koblenz. Fair white table wine. West Germany.

Nodeau, Domaine de. (4) Bourgeais; St Ciers-de-Cannasse, north-west of Bourg. 2,000 dozen bottles of red bordeaux. France.

Nöels, Les. (16) Anjou; Coteaux du Layon, Faye d'Anjou vineyard, south of Angers. Fine white table wine. France.

Nogueiras, Quinta. (30) *Região demarcada do Douro* (q.v.). Estate and vineyard in Godim in the Régua area. Portugal.

Nogues, Les. (9) Mercurey vineyard, Chalonnais. Fine quality red burgundy. France.

Noire. (16) Touraine; Chinon vineyard. Fair red table wine. France.

Noirots, Les. (8) Côte de Nuits; Chambolle-Musigny vineyard. *Premier cru.* Red burgundy. France.

Nola's Dargaville Vineyard. (38) North Island; Dargaville, approx. sixty miles north-west of Auckland. 10 acres. New Zealand.

Nonnenberg. (22) Middle Moselle; Wehlen and Filzen vineyards. Fair to very fine white table wine. West Germany.

Nonnenberg. (24) Rhinegau; Rauenthal vineyard. Fine white table wine. West Germany.

Nonnengarten. (23) Palatinate; Bad Dürkheim vineyard. Fine white table wine. West Germany.

Nonnenhorn. (25) Lake Constance (Bodensee); by Lindau. Fair white table wine. West Germany.

Nonnenlay. (22) Moselle; Brauneberg vineyard. Fine white table wine. West Germany.

Nonnenstück. (23) Palatinate; Deidesheim vineyard. 'Paradiesgarten' is the generic name for all Deidesheim wines. Fine white table wine. West Germany.

Nordhausen. (25) Württemberg; south-west of Heilbronn. Ordinary to fair red and white table wines. West Germany.

Nordheim. (25) Franconia; approx. sixty-five miles north-east of Frankfurt-am-Main. Fair to fine white table wine. West Germany.

Nordweil. (25) Baden; north of Freiburg. Fair white table wine. West Germany.

Norheim. (24) Nahe; just south-west of Bad Münster. Fair to fine white table wine. West Germany.

Norion-la-Libarde. (4) Bourgeais; Bourg. 8,500 dozen bottles of red bordeaux. France.

Nosiola. (26) Alto Adige; vineyards of the Trentino. The name of a white grape and of the white table wine made from it. Italy.

Nostrano. (31) Ticino (Tessin) canton. Ordinary to fair red table wine. Switzerland.

Notre Dame d'Alençon. (16) Anjou; Coteaux de l'Aubance between Angers and Saumur. Fair white and rosé table wines. France.

Nouis, Clos de. (16) Touraine; Vouvray vineyard, just north-east of Tours. Fair white table wine. France.

Nouvelle-Église, Château de la. (5) Pomerol. 1,000 dozen bottles of red bordeaux. France.

Nouvelles. (18) Arbois area, Jura. Ordinary to fair red, white and rosé table wines. France.

Nova do Rio Torto, Quinta. (30) *Região demarcada do Douro* (q.v.). Estate and well-situated vineyard in Sarzedinho east of Régua. Portugal.

Noval, Quinta. (30) *Região demarcada do Douro*

(q.v.). Estate and well-known vineyard in Vale de Mendiz, north-east of Régua. Well-terraced vineyards with a few pre-phylloxera vines which provide good quality port. Vintage ports declared as single Quintas. Portugal.

Noyer, Domaine du. (14) Côtes de Provence; Côte des Maures east of Toulon. Ordinary to fair red, white and rosé table wines. France.

Nozet, Château du. (15) Nièvre *département;* Sancerre area. Fair white table wine. France.

Nuenberg. *See* Neuchâtel.

Nuits-Saint-Georges. (8) Côte d'Or. Well-known town on the Côte de Nuits, from which the name is derived. The village of Prémaux (q.v.) is considered part of *AC Nuits-St-Georges.* France.

Nules. (29) Castellón de la Plana; approx. forty miles north-east of Valencia. Strong, dry, fair quality red table wine. Spain.

Nuoro. (28) Sardinia; one of the more important wine-producing areas and the name of very ordinary strong red wine. Italy.

Nuraghe Majore. (28) Sardinia; Sassari, of the Murra area. Ordinary to fair white table wine. Italy.

Nuragus. (28) Sardinia; Campidano, the plains stretching north-west from Cagliari. Ordinary white table wine drunk locally and largely exported for blending. Italy.

Nuriootpa. (37) South Australia; Barossa Valley, approx. thirty-five miles north-east of Adelaide. Important township, wine and brandy centre. Australia.

Nurra (Bianco, Rosso). (28) Sardinia; north-eastern area. Ordinary white wine, and rather coarse nondescript red wine. Italy.

Nussbaum. (32) Moselle; Wormeldingen vineyard. Fair white table wine. Luxembourg.

Nussberg. (22) Moselle; Zell vineyard. Fair white table wine. West Germany.

Nussbien. (23) Palatinate; Ruppertsberg vineyard. Fine white table wine. West Germany.

Nussbrunnen. (24) Rhinegau; Hattenheim vineyard, west of Erbach. Fine white table wine. West Germany.

Nussdorf. (23) Palatinate; north of Landau. Ordinary, fair and fine white table wines. West Germany.

Nyons. (12) Drôme *département;* Haut-Comtat. Ordinary to fair red table wine. France.

❦

Oberachern. (25) Baden; south-west of Baden-Baden. Ordinary to fair red and white table wines. West Germany.

Oberberg. (24) Rhinegau; Winkel, Niederwalluf and Mittelheim vineyards. Fair to fine white table wine. West Germany.

Oberbillig. (22) Moselle; north-west of Filzen. Ordinary to fair white table wine. West Germany.

Oberderdingen. (25) Württemberg; approx. eighteen miles north-east of Karlsruhe. Ordinary to fair red and white table wines. West Germany.

Oberdiebach - mit - Winzberg - und - Rheindiebach. (21) Middle Rhine; north-west of Bingen. Ordinary to fair red and white table wines. West Germany.

Obereggenen. (25) Baden; approx. eighteen miles south-west of Freiburg. Ordinary, fair, and some fine white table wines. West Germany.

Obereisenheim. (25) Franconia; north-east of Würzburg. Fair and some fine white table wines. West Germany.

Oberemmel. (22) Saar. Fair and some fine white table wines. West Germany.

Oberfell. (22) Moselle; south of Kobern. Ordinary to fair white wine. West Germany.

Ober-Flörsheim. (24) Rhinehessia; north-west of Worms. Ordinary to fair red and white table wines. West Germany.

Obergriesheim. (25) Württemberg; north of Heilbronn. Ordinary to fair red and white table wines. West Germany.

Obergrombach. (25) Baden; north-east of Karlsruhe. Ordinary to fair red and white table wines. West Germany.

Oberhausen. (23) Palatinate; approx. twenty-eight miles west of Neustadt. Fair red and white table wines. West Germany.

Oberhochstadt. (23) Palatinate; north-east of Landau. Fair red and white table wines. West Germany.

Ober-Ingelheim. (24) Rhinehessia; east of Bingen. Fair and some fine white table wines. West Germany.

Oberkirch. (25) Baden; approx. seventeen miles south-west of Baden-Baden. Ordinary to fair red and white table wines. West Germany.

Oberlahnstein. (21) Middle Rhine; south-east of Koblenz. Ordinary to fair white table wines. West Germany.

Oberlauda. (25) Franconia; approx. nineteen miles south-west of Würzburg. Fair white table wine. West Germany.

Oberleinach. (25) Franconia; north-west of Würzburg. Fair white table wine. West Germany.

Obernay. (19) Bas-Rhin *département.* Ordinary to fair white Alsace wine. France.

Obernbreit. (25) Franconia; south-east of Würzburg. Fair white table wine. West Germany.

Ober-Olm. (24) Rhinehessia; north-west of

Nackenheim. Ordinary to fair red and white table wines. West Germany.

Oberrödchen. (24) Rhinegau; Martinsthal vineyard. Fair to fine white table wine. West Germany.

Oberrotweil. (25) Baden; north-west of Freiburg. Ordinary to fair red and white table wines. West Germany.

Obersasbach. (25) Baden; south-west of Baden-Baden. Fair red and white table wine. West Germany.

Ober-Saulheim. (24) Rhinehessia; west of Nierstein. Ordinary to fair red and white table wines. West Germany.

Obersberg. (22) Moselle; Brauneberg vineyard. Fair to fine white table wine. West Germany.

Oberschopfheim. (25) Baden; south-east of Strasbourg. Fair white table wine. West Germany.

Oberschupf. (25) Franconia; approx. twenty-two miles south-west of Würzburg. Fair to fine white table wine. West Germany.

Oberschwarzach. (25) Franconia; approx. twenty-two miles west of Würzburg. Fair white table wine. West Germany.

Oberstenfeld-mit-Weingutlichtenberg. (25) Württemberg; southeast of Heilbronn. Ordinary to fair red and white table wines. West Germany.

Oberstetten. (25) Württemberg; approx. thirty miles south-east of Stuttgart. Ordinary red and white table wines. West Germany.

Oberstreit. (24) Nahe; west of Bad Münster. Fair white table wine. West Germany.

Obervolkach. (25) Franconia; north-east of Würzburg. Fair white table wine. West Germany.

Oberwalluf. (24) Rhinegau. Fair to fine white table wine. West Germany.

Oberweiler. (25) Baden; south-west of Baden-Baden. Ordinary to fair white table wine. West Germany.

Oberweiler-im-Tal. (23) Palatinate; approx. twenty miles south-west of Bad Kreuznach. Red and white table wines. West Germany.

Oberwesel. (24) Middle Rhine; north-west of Bingen. Ordinary to fair white table wine. West Germany.

Obrigheim. (23) Palatinate; north-east of Grünstadt. Ordinary to fair red and white table wines. West Germany.

Ocana. (29) West New Castile; Toledo, approx. forty miles south-west of Madrid. Ordinary red and white table wines. Spain.

Ochsenbach. (25) Württemberg; south-west of Heilbronn. Ordinary red and white table wines. West Germany.

Ochsenfurt. (25) Franconia; south-east of Würzburg. Fair to fine white table wine. West Germany.

Ockenfels. (21) Middle Rhine. Ordinary to fair red and white table wines. West Germany.

Ockenheim. (24) Rhinehessia; just north of Linz. Ordinary to fair and some fine white table wines. West Germany.

Ockfén. (22) Saar valley; south of Geisenheim. In good years the Riesling grapes planted here produce very fine white wines indeed. Fair to fine white table wine. West Germany.

Ocucaje. (35) One of the few dry, white wines of Peru.

Odénas. (11) Beaujolais. Part of the production is sold as Côte de Brouilly and Brouilly. Ordinary to fair red burgundy. France.

Odernheim. (24) Nahe; south-west of Bad Münster. Fair white table wine is produced. West Germany.

Odinstal. (23) Palatinate; Wachenheim vineyard. Fair white table wine. West Germany.

Odobesti. (33) Eastern province of Rumania, north-west Galati. Fair to fine red and white dessert wine. Rumania.

Oedheim. (25) Württemberg; north-east of Heilbronn. Ordinary to fair red and white table wines. West Germany.

Oelberg. (24) Rhinehessia; Nierstein vineyard. Fair to fine white table wine. West Germany.

Oestrich. (24) Rhinegau. Ordinary red table wine; fair, fine and some very fine white. West Germany.

Offenbach-am-Glan. (24) Nahe; approx. eighteen miles south-west of Bad Münster. Fair white table wine. West Germany.

Offenbach-am-Queich. (23) Palatinate; just east of Landau. Ordinary to fair red and white table wines. West Germany.

Offenburg. (25) Baden; south-east of Strasbourg. Chief town of the wine-producing region of Ortenau. Ordinary red and white table wines. West Germany.

Offenheim. (24) Rhinehessia; west of Alsheim. Fair red and white table wines. West Germany.

Offstein. (24) Rhinehessia; south-west of Worms. Fair to fine white wine. West Germany.

Oger. (17) Marne *département*; Avize canton. Rated *premier cru*—99% growth. 870 acres. France.

Oggau. (33) Burgenland's chief wine centre in south-east Austria close to the Hungarian border. Austria.

Ogliastra (Bianco, Rosso and Rosato). (28) Sardinia; Nuoro. Fair red, white and rosé sweet and semi-sweet wines. Italy.

Ohligberg. (22) Moselle; Leiwen vineyard, between Neumagen and Detzen. Fair white table wine. West Germany.

Ohligberg. (24) Rhinehessia; Bingen vineyard. Fair to fine white table wine. West Germany.

Ohligsberg. (22) Moselle; Wintrich vineyard. Very fine white table wine. West Germany.

Ohligstück. (24) Rhinehessia; Alsheim vineyard. Fair to fine white table wine. West Germany.

Ohligswingert. (22) Ruwer valley; Waldrach. Fair to fine white table wine. West Germany.

Ohlsbach. (25) Baden; south-east of Strasbourg. Fair to fine red and white table wines. West Germany.

Öhningen. (25) Lake Constance (Bodensee); west of Konstanz. Ordinary to fair red and white table wines. West Germany.

Oiry. (17) Marne *département*; Avize canton, east of Chouilly. Rated *premier cru*—99% growth. 189 acres. France.

Ölberg. (24) Rhinehessia; Nierstein vineyard. Fair white table wine. West Germany.

Ölbronn. (25) Württemberg; approx. sixteen miles east of Karlsruhe. Ordinary to fair red and white table wines. West Germany.

Olesa de Bonesvallo. (29) Barcelona; central Panadés, between Tarragona and Barcelona. Ordinary to fair red and white table wines. Spain.

Oliena. (28) Sardinia. Ordinary to fair full-flavoured, almost bitter, red table wine. Italy.

Olite. (29) Navarre. Ordinary red table wine. Spain.

Olivares. (29) Seville. Fair white dessert wine. Spain.

Olivares de Douro. (29) West Old Castile; Valladolid, approx. seventy miles north of Avila. Ordinary to fair red and white table wines. Spain.

Olive, L' (16) Touraine; Chinon vineyard. Fair red table wine. France.

Olivella. (27) Lazio; Ponte Corvo area, approx. twenty miles south-east of Frosinone. Light, ordinary red table wine. Italy.

Olivier, Château d'. (5) Graves de Bordeaux; Léognan. *Cru classé de Graves (en blanc et en rouge)*. 2,000 dozen bottles of red bordeaux; 10,000 white. France.

Olivier, Clos l'. (16) Touraine; Rochecorbon vineyard north-east of Tours. Fair to fine white table wir.e. France.

Ollauri. (29) Logroño province; La Rioja (q.v.) area of the upper Ebro valley. Fair to fine red table wine. Spain.

Ollioules. (14) Côtes de Provence; Bandol vineyard. Fair red and white table wines. France.

Olmos, Los. (29) South-central Aragon; Teruel. Ordinary red and white table wines. Spain.

Olnhausen. (25) Württemberg; south-east of Mosbach. Ordinary to fair red and white table wines. West Germany.

Oloroso. (29) One of the two basic types of sherry, darker and fuller than a Fino. Spain.

Oltrepo Pavese. (26) The vineyards of the strip of land between the river Po and the hills of Padua south-east of Vicenza. Italy.

Olvera. (29) Cadiz. Fair white table wine. Spain.

Ombra. (28) Sicily; Catania. Cherry-red light ordinary table wine, meant to be drunk young. Italy.

Ongkaf. (32) Moselle; Machtum vineyard, just south of Grevenmacher. Fair white table wine. Luxembourg.

Onnis, Les. (16) Côteaux du Layon; Chaume vineyard, below Angers. Fine white table wine. France.

Onsdorf. (22) Moselle; north-west of Saarburg. Fair white table wine. West Germany.

Onteniente. (29) Valencia. Ordinary red table wine. Spain.

Oppenheim. (24) Rhinehessia. Fair to fine, and some very fine white table wines. West Germany.

Orange. (12) Côtes du Rhone; north of Avignon. *AC Châteauneuf-du-Pape*. France.

Oratoriens, Les. (16) Anjou; Dampierre-sur-Loire vineyard, Saumur. Fair red table wine. France.

Orbaia. (28) Sardinia. Similar to Gallura (q.v.) but rather better. Italy.

Orbel. (24) Rhinehessia; Nierstein vineyard. Fair to fine white table wine. West Germany.

Ordonnac-et-Potensac. (3) Médoc neighbouring villages, north-west of St Seurin-de-Cadourne making a single *commune*. Ordinary to fair red bordeaux or claret. France.

Oregon. (36) One of the minor wine-producing States, north of California. U.S.A.

Orense. (29) South Galicia; Ribero. Ordinary to fair white wine. Spain.

Orgaz. (29) West New Castile; Toledo, approx. forty miles south-west of Madrid. Ordinary table wines. Spain.

Orgiano Bianco, Rosso. (26) Veneto; Colli Berici just south of Vicenza. Ordinary to fair white and red table wines. Italy.

Orihuela de Segura. (29) Alicante; approx. forty miles south of Valencia. Ordinary to fair red dessert wine. Spain.

Orlando. (37) South Australia; Barossa Valley, approx. thirty-five miles north-east of Adelaide. One of the oldest (1847) and most important wineries of the Barossa Valley. The original winery owned by G. Gramp and Sons (Pty) Ltd. was taken over by Reckitt & Colman in late 1970, but the name Gramp has been retained. Australia.

Orlenberg. (24) Palatinate; Bissersheim vineyard, between Grünstadt and Nackenheim. Fair white table wine. West Germany.

Orme, Clos de l'. (8) Côte de Nuits; Chambolle-Musigny vineyard. *Deuxième cru.* Red burgundy. France.

Orme, En l'. (8) Côte de Beaune; Beaune vineyard. *Premier cru.* Red burgundy. France.

Ormeau, En l'. (8) Côte de Beaune; Volnay vineyard. *Premier cru.* Red burgundy. France.

Ormeau-du-Maur. (16) Touraine; Bourgueil vineyard. Fair red table wine. France.

Ormes, Aux. (8) Côte de Nuits; Vosne-Romanée vineyard. *Troisième cru.* Red burgundy. France.

Ormes, Clos des. (8) Côte de Nuits; Morey-St-Denis vineyard. *Premier cru.* Red burgundy. France.

Oro di Lugnano. (27) Emilia-Romagna. Ordinary to fair dry white table wine. Italy.

Oropesa. (29) Castellón de la Plana; approx. forty miles north-east of Valencia. Ordinary red table wine. Spain.

Orotava, La. (40) Canary Islands; Santa Cruz de Tenerife off the north-west coast of Africa. Fair to fine white Malvasia dessert wine. Spain.

Orschwihr. (19) Haut-Rhin *département.* Ordinary to fair white Alsace wine. France.

Ortenau. (25) Baden. Region with the poorest soil, but producing the best wines of Baden. West Germany.

Orthsberg. (22) Ruwer; Eitelsbach vineyard. Fair to fine white table wine. West Germany.

Ortibière, L'. (16) Anjou; Beaujeu-sur-Layon vineyard, south of Angers. Fine white table wine. France.

Ortinière, L'. (16) Anjou; Beaujeu-sur-Layon vineyard, south of Angers. Fair to fine white table wine. France.

Orveaux, En. (8) Côte de Nuits; Flagey-Echézeaux vineyard. *Premier cru.* Red burgundy. France.

Orvieto. (27) Umbria. Cathedral town and its light, fair to fine white wine, dry and more often slightly sweet. Italy.

Osann. (22) Middle Moselle; north-west of Brauneberg. Fair to fine white table wine. West Germany.

Oschelskopf. (23) Palatinate; Freinsheim vineyard. Fair to fine white table wine. West Germany.

Osterberg. (23) Palatinate; Ungstein vineyard, between Bad Dürkheim and Kallstadt. Fair to fine white table wine. West Germany.

Osterlämmchen. (22) Moselle; Ediger vineyard, just east of Eller. Fair white table wine. West Germany.

Ostertal. (24) Rhinehessia; Dexheim vineyard, west of Oppenheim. Ordinary to fair white table wine. West Germany.

Osthofen. (24) Rhinehessia; between Worms and Alsheim. Ordinary, fair and some fine white table wines. West Germany.

Östringen. (21) Baden; south of Heidelberg. Ordinary to fair red and white table wines. West Germany.

Ostuni Bianco. (28) Apulia; Brindisi area. Uninteresting ordinary white table wines. Italy.

Ötisheim. (25) Württemberg; approx. eighteen miles south-east of Karlsruhe. Ordinary red and white table wines. West Germany.

Ottavianella. (28) Apulia; Brindisi area. Ordinary rosé table wine. Italy.

Ottonese. (27) Lazio; Rome area. Ordinary local dry white table wine. Italy.

Outeiro, Quinta. (30) *Região demarcada do Douro* (q.v.). Estate and vineyard in Medroes in the Régua area 340 to 420 metres above sea level. Portugal.

☙

Paarl. (39) Western Cape Province. The most important wine centre of the district. Headquarters of the K.W.V. South Africa.

Pabst. (23) Palatinate; Mussbach vineyard. Fair white table wine. West Germany.

Paceta. (29) La Rioja area of the upper Ebro valley. Fair red table wine. Spain.

Pachère, Clos de la. (5) Sauternes; Barsac. *Cru bourgeois.* 1,000 dozen bottles of white bordeaux. France.

Pachino Rosso. (28) Sicily; Syracuse area. Stout, heady, ordinary red table wine. Italy.

Pachs del Panadés. (29) Barcelona; Panadés, between Tarragóna and Barcelona. Ordinary table wines. Spain.

Paci. (28) Calabria; Scilla vineyard, north-east of Reggio. Ordinary cherry-red table wine. Italy.

Paco, Quinta. (30) *Região demarcada do Douro* (q.v.). Estate and vineyard in Vilamarim in the Régua area. Portugal.

Pageot-Couloumet, Château. (5) Entre-deux-Mers; Loupiac. 300 dozen bottles of red bordeaux; 1,000 white. France.

Pailhas, Château. (5) St-Emilion; St Hippolyte. An unclassified *cru.* 6,000 dozen bottles of red bordeaux. France.

Paillèrie, Château la. (4) Blayais. 1,000 dozen bottles of red bordeaux. France.

Paillet, Château de. (5) Premières Côtes de Bordeaux; Paillet, north of Podensac. 3,000 dozen bottles of red bordeaux; 3,000 white. France.

Pajarete. (29) An extremely dark, sweet wine made in the Jerez area by blending Pedro Ximenez (q.v.) sweet wine and Vino de Color (q.v.). Spain.

Palatinate. (23) The largest of the Rhineland's main regions. Ordinary red table wines; fair, fine and some very fine or great white table and dessert wines. The three main divisions of the Palatinate are the Upper Haardt, from the Franco-Palatinate frontier to Hambach; the Middle Haardt, from Neustadt to Herxheim, where all the best Palatinate wines come from; and the Lower Haardt, the northernmost tip of the Palatinate and the least important for wine. West Germany.

Paleda de Naves. (29) Valencia. Ordinary to fair white table wine. Spain.

Palestrina Bianco. (27) Lazio. Ordinary local white table wine. Italy.

Palhote, Quinta. (30) Fountainhas. *Região demarcada do Douro* (q.v.). Estate and vineyard near Régua. Portugal.

Palis, Clos du. (16) Touraine; Chinon vineyard. Fair red table wine. France.

Palizzi. (28) Calabria; Reggio di Calabria area. Ordinary ruby-red table wine much of which is exported for blending. Italy.

Pallières, Les. (12) Côtes du Rhône; Gigondas vineyard. Fair red table wine. France.

Palma del Condado. (29) Huelva province. Ordinary to fair white wines. Spain.

Palma del Rio. (29) North-central Andalusia; Córdoba area north-east of Seville. Fair to fine white table wine. Spain.

Palmas, Las. (40) Canary Islands off the north-west coast of Africa. Ordinary table wines and fair white dessert wines. Spain.

Palmberg. (32) Moselle; Ahn vineyard, between Grevenmacher and Wormeldange. Ordinary to fair white table wine. Luxembourg.

Palmela. (30) A town and district eighteen miles south-east of Lisbon near the Arrabida hills which produces full-bodied table wines. Mostly white. Portugal.

Palmenberg. (22) Moselle; Aldegund vineyard, between Eller and Zell. Fair white table wine. West Germany.

Palmer, Château. (4) Haut-Médoc; Cantenac. *Troisième cru classé* (but is actually very superior to its classification). 12,000 dozen bottles of red bordeaux. France.

Palomino. (29) The name of the white grape chiefly grown for the making of fine Sherry wines. Spain.

Palos de la Frontera. (29) Huelva province. Ordinary to fair white wines. Spain.

Palu. (16) Anjou; Cravant-les-Coteaux vineyard, below Angers. Fair red table wine. France.

Palzem. (22) Moselle; south-west of Saarburg. Ordinary to fair white table wine. West Germany.

Pamid. (33) The most popular rosé table wine of Bulgaria.

Pamplona. (29) Navarre; approx. sixty-five miles south-east of Bilbao. Ordinary to fair red and white table wines. Spain.

Panadés. (29) Between Tarragóna and Barcelona. Mostly ordinary to fair white wines, dry and sweet, most still, but some sparkling. The best come from Upper and Central Panadés. Spain.

Panciu. (3) Town in east Rumania. Ordinary to fair white table wine. Rumania.

Pandars, Les. (9) Chalonnais; Mercurey area. Fair red burgundy. France.

Pandars, Les. (9) Chalonnais; Montagny vineyard, south-west of Romanèche-Thorin. Fair white burgundy. France.

Panet, Château. (4) Fronsac. 2,500 dozen bottles of red bordeaux. France.

Panet, Château. (5) St-Emilion; St Christophe-des-Bardes, south-west of Podensac. An unclassified *cru*. 10,000 dozen bottles of red bordeaux. France.

Panicale. (27) Umbria; Upper Tiber valley north of Perugia. Ordinary red table wine usually drunk young. Italy.

Panigon, Château. (3) Médoc; Civrac, north-west of St Seurin-de-Cadourne. *Cru bourgeois.* 5,000 dozen bottles of red bordeaux. France.

Paniza. (29) Zaragoza; Cariñena. Mostly rather sweet red table wines. Spain.

Pannarano. (28) Campania; Benevento area, north of Avellino. Stout, very ordinary, very dark red table wine. Italy.

Pantellaria. (28) Small island between Sicily and Malta (south of Sicily). Ordinary to fair table and dessert wines. Italy.

Panzoult. (16) Touraine; Chinon. Fair red table wine. France.

Papazkarsib. (34) Red table wine reputed to be the best made in Turkey.

Pape, Château du. (5) Graves de Bordeaux; Preignac. An unclassified *cru*. 1,200 dozen bottles of white bordeaux. France.

Pape, Château le. (5) Graves de Bordeaux; Léognan. An unclassified *cru*. 1,500 dozen bottles of red bordeaux; 1,000 white. One of the best of the graves. France.

Pape-Clément, Château. (5) Graves de Bordeaux; Pessac. *Cru classé de Graves (en rouge).* 10,000 dozen bottles of red bordeaux. France.

Papeterie, Château La. (5) St-Emilion; Montagne. An unclassified *cru*. 5,000 dozen bottles of red bordeaux. France.

Paphos. (34) Island of Cyprus; approx. 100 miles off the west coast of Syria. Ordinary to fair red table wines. Cyprus.

Papillon, Clos du. (16) Anjou; Savennières vineyard below Angers, Coteaux de la Loire. Fair to fine white table wine. France.

Paracuellos de Jiloca. (29) Aragon; Zaragoza. Ordinary to fair red and white table wines. Spain.

Paradeita, Quinta. (30) *Região demarcada do Douro* (q.v.). Estate and vineyard in Guiaes north-east of Régua. The Quinta was rebuilt in 1853. Portugal.

Parades de Arca, Quinta. *See* **Arca, Quinta.**

Paradies. (22) Moselle; Kröv vineyard, west of Enkirch. Fair white table wine. West Germany.

Paradis, Clos le. (16) Touraine; Vouvray vineyard, just north-east of Tours. Fair white table wine. France.

Paradis, Le. (16) Touraine; Ligré vineyard above Chinon. Fair red table wine. France.

Paradis, Le. (15) Sancerre. Fair to fine white table wine. France.

Paradis, Le. (10) Mâconnais; St Martin-sous-Montaigu vineyard in the St-Amour area. Red burgundy. France.

Paradis, Château. (5) St-Emilion; Montagne. An unclassified *cru*. 7,000 dozen bottles of red bordeaux. France.

Paradis, Château du. (5) St-Emilion; Vignonet, south-west of St Pey-d'Armens. An unclassified *cru*. 5,000 dozen bottles of red bordeaux. France.

Paradis, Clos (9) St Martin-sous-Montaigu vineyard, Mâconnais. Fine quality red burgundy. France.

Parana. (35) Southern Brazil. A minor wine-producing state. Brazil.

Parasani. (28) Apulia; Capo di Leuca, the bottom of the 'heel'. Ordinary to fair, semi-sparkling, dry, pale red wine. Italy.

Pardillo. (29) Eastern New Castile; Cuenca, Madrid and Guadeljaro. Ordinary to fair white table wine. Spain.

Parduca. (29) Northern coast; Santander, approx. forty-five miles west of Bilbao. Stout, 'black' red table wine. Spain.

Parducci Wine Cellars Inc. (36) California; Ukiah, Mendocino County. Quality table wines. U.S.A.

Parempuyre, Château de. (4) Haut-Médoc; Parempuyre. *Cru bourgeois supérieur*. 1,000 dozen bottles of red bordeaux. France.

Parenchère, Château de. (5) Ste Foy-de-Bordeaux; north-east of Langon. 3,000 dozen bottles of red bordeaux; 12,000 white are produced. France.

Pares. (24) Rhinegau; Rüdesheim vineyard. Fine white table wine. West Germany.

Pargues. (6) Chablis; Yonne *département*. *Deuxième cru*. White burgundy. France.

Parnay. (16) Saumur area. Fair to fine white, red and rosé table wines, *AC Saumur*. France.

Parnay, Château de. (16) Parnay, Saumur area. The best vineyard of Parnay (q.v.). One of the homes of modern viticulture in the beginning of this century. Fine white table wine. France.

Paroisse-Saint-Seurin-Haut-Médoc. (4) The registered name under which the *Cave Co-opérative* de St Seurin-de-Cadourne markets the wines of its members. France.

Paros. (34) Island south-east of Greece. Ordinary to fair red and white table wines. Greece.

Parsac. (5) Village and vineyards close to St-Emilion. Ordinary to fair red bordeaux with the *AC Parsac-St-Emilion*. France.

Partarieu, Château. (5) Sauternes; Fargues. *Cru bourgeois*. 6,000 dozen bottles of white bordeaux. France.

Partenheim. (24) Rhinehessia; south of Erbach. Ordinary to fair red and white table wines. West Germany.

Partento. (28) Campania; Benevento area, north of Avellino. Very ordinary stout red wine usually used for mixing. Italy.

Parteollese. (28) Sardinia; Campidano plains stretching north-west from Cagliari. Ordinary red and rosé table wines. Italy.

Partinico Bianco. (28) Sicily. Fair to good white apéritif and table wine. Italy.

Passe-Tout-Grain or **Passe-Tous-Grains.** Red burgundy wine made of both Pinot and Gamay grapes, fermented in vat together, it must contain at least one-third Pinot grapes. France.

Passito. Wine made from grapes, partially dried. Generally a dessert wine, although used in making many dry wines such as Muscats and Malvana. Italy.

Passito de Arco. (26) Trentino; north-western shore vineyards of Lake Garda, west of Verona. Fair to fine sweet white dessert wine. Italy.

Passito della Val d'Aosta. (26) Piedmont; Val d'Aosta. Ordinary to fair white dessert wine. Italy.

Passito di Caluso. (26) Piedmont. Fair golden dessert wine. Italy.

Passito di Misilmiri. (28) Sicily; Misilmiri-Linguaglossa vineyards, south-east of Palermo. Fair sweet golden dessert wine. Italy.

Passito di Moncrivello. (26) Piedmont; Vercelli province. Fair white dessert wine. Italy.

Passito di Novoli. (28) Apulia; Novoli-Leuca vineyards. Ordinary to fair very strong, amber-coloured dessert wines. Italy.

Passito di Trapani. (28) Apulia. Ordinary to fair golden dessert wine. Italy.

Passonne, Château de la. (5) Premières Côtes

de Bordeaux; Cadillac, north-west of Loupiac. 5,000 dozen bottles of white bordeaux. France.

Pasto, Vino da, Vino de. Spanish and Italian for taking with food for 'table wines' even when referring to Sherries. Spain, Italy.

Pastoso. (27) Lazio; Alban Hills south-east of Rome. Ordinary and inexpensive white wine usually drunk within a year or so of its vintage. Italy.

Pastrana. (29) Guadalajara; approx. thirty miles north-east of Madrid. Ordinary red table wine. Spain.

Patache, Château la. (5) Pomerol. 1,500 dozen bottles of red bordeaux. France.

Patache-d'Aux, Château. (3) Médoc; Bégadan, north-west of St Seurin-de-Cadourne. *Cru bourgeois*. 15,000 dozen bottles of red bordeaux. France.

Paterberg. (24) Rhinehessia; Nierstein vineyard. Fair to fine white table wine. West Germany.

Paternel, Domaine du. (14) Côtes de Provence, Cassis vineyard. Fair red and rosé table wines. France.

Patersberg. (21) Middle Rhine; north-west of Bingen. Ordinary to fair red and white table wines. West Germany.

Patiras, Château. (5) Côtes de St-Emilion. An unclassified *cru*. 4,500 dozen bottles of red bordeaux. France.

Pativilca. (35) West-central Peru. Wine centre. Peru.

Patras. (34) South-eastern Greece; Athens region. Ordinary to fair red and white table wines and Muscatel. Greece.

Patriciens, Clos des. (12) Orange area, Rhône valley. *AC Châteauneuf-du-Pape*. Fair red table wine. France.

Pauillac. (4) Haut-Médoc. One of the most famous Haut-Médoc *communes*. Fair, fine, very fine red bordeaux. France.

Pauizzi. (28) Calabria; the tip of the 'toe' of Italy. Dark red, rather rough red table wine. Italy.

Paulands, Les. (8) Côte de Beaune; Aloxe-Corton vineyard. *Deuxième cru*. Red burgundy. France.

Paulinsberg. (22) Ruwer; Kasel vineyard. Fine to very fine white table wine. West Germany.

Paulinshofberg. (22) Moselle; Kesten vineyard, opposite Filzen. Ordinary to fair white table wine. West Germany.

Pave, Le. (11) Beaujolais; Brouilly vineyard. Brouilly is one of the top-grade *Beaujolais cru AC's*. Red burgundy. France.

Pavé, Le. (11) Beaujolais; Brouilly vineyard. Brouilly is one of the top-grade Beaujolais *communes*. Red burgundy. France.

Pavé, Le. (15) Sancerre vineyard. Fair white table wine. France.

Paveil-de-Luze, Château. (4) Haut-Médoc; Soussans. *Cru bourgeois supérieur*. 3,500 dozen bottles of red bordeaux. France.

Pavie, Château. (5) Côtes de St-Emilion. *Premier grand cru classé*. 15,000 dozen bottles of red bordeaux. France.

Pavie-Decesse, Château. (5) Côtes de St-Emilion. *Grand cru classé*. 4,000 dozen bottles of red bordeaux. France.

Pavie-Macquin, Château. (5) Côtes de St-Emilion. *Grand cru classé*. 6,000 dozen bottles of red bordeaux. France.

Pavignolles, Les. (16) Anjou; Dampierre-sur-Loire, a *commune* on the Saumur hillsides. Fair red table wine. France.

Pavillon, Château du. (5) Côtes de Bordeaux; Ste Croix-du-Mont. 5,000 dozen bottles of white bordeaux. France.

Pavillon, Le. (16) Anjou; Coteaux de l'Aubance, Denée vineyard, between Angers and Saumur. Fair white table wine. France.

Pavillon Blanc du Château Margaux. (4) Haut-Médoc; Margaux. White bordeaux, a dry white wine from Château Margaux (q.v.). France.

Pavillon-du-Cadet, Château. (5) Côtes de St-Emilion. *Grand cru classé*. 2,500 dozen bottles of red bordeaux. France.

Pavillon-Figeac. (5) St-Emilion; St Christophe-des-Bardes, south-west of Parsac. An unclassified *cru*. 1,200 dozen bottles of red bordeaux. France.

Pavillon-Haut-Gros-Bonnet, Château du. (4) Fronsadais; Fronsac. 3,000 dozen bottles of red bordeaux. France.

Paxarete. *See* Pajarete.

Payrabon, Château. (4) Haut-Médoc; St-Sauveur. *Cru bourgeois*. 20,000 dozen bottles of red bordeaux. France.

Péage, Clos du. (12) Côtes du Rhône; Gigondas vineyard. Fair red table wine. France.

Pechstein. (23) Palatinate; Forst vineyard. Fair to fine white table wine. West Germany.

Pécs. (33) Near Yugoslav border; approx. 100 miles south-west of Budapest. Fair red and white table wines. Also fine table grapes. Hungary.

Pedare. (37) South Australia. Brand name of wines of Douglas A. Tolley (Pty) Ltd, Hope valley, in Adelaide foothills. Name Pedare is formed from first two letters of Christian names of Peter, David and Reginald Tolley, who run the business. All types of wine, featuring Cabernet-Shiraz, Red Hermitage and dry whites.

Pedesclaux, Château. (4) Haut-Médoc; Pauillac. *Cinquième cru classé*. 6,000 dozen bottles of red bordeaux. France.

Pedra Caldeira, Quinta. (30) *Região demarcada do Douro* (q.v.). Estate and vineyard in Fontelo south-east of Régua. Portugal.

Pedralba. (29) Valencia. Ordinary red and white table wines. Spain.

Pedrecouto, Quinta. (30) *Região demarcada do Douro* (q.v.). Estate and vineyard near Régua. Portugal.

Pedroncelli, John, Winery. (36) California; Geyserville. Privately owned. Excellent Zinfandel and Johannisberg Riesling. U.S.A.

Pedroneras, Las. (29) West New Castile; Cuenca. Ordinary to fair white table wine. Spain.

Pedro Ximenez. (29) Often abbreviated to P.X.; a sweet white grape which is dried in the sun after cutting to produce a sweet and luscious wine of the same name. Córdoba and Jerez. Spain.

Peillon-Claverie, Château. (5) Sauternes; Fargues. *Cru bourgeois*. 4,000 dozen bottles of white bordeaux. France.

Pelayos. (29) South León; Salamanca. Ordinary to fair white table wine. Spain.

Peligno Bianco. (27) Abruzzi; l'Aquila vineyards. Fair to good white table wine. Italy.

Pellagrello (Bianco, Rosso and Rosato). (28) Campania; Caserta, approx. seventeen miles north-east of Naples. Ordinary to fair rather sweetish red, white and rosé table wines. Italy.

Pellaro. (28) Calabria; Reggio di Calabria area. Ordinary, rather heady red table wines from the tip of the toe of Italy, much of which is exported for blending. Italy.

Pellaverga. (26) Piedmont; Cuneo province. Ordinary light and sweet red table wine. Italy.

Pelletan, Château. (5) St-Emilion; St Christophe-des-Bardes, south-west of Parsac. An unclassified *cru*. 2,000 dozen bottles of red bordeaux. France.

Pelletans, Château Les. (5) Ste Foy-de-Bordeaux, north-east of Langon. 3,000 dozen bottles of red bordeaux; 3,000 white. France.

Pellingen. (22) Moselle; east of Wiltingen. Ordinary to fair white table wine is produced. West Germany.

Peloponnisos. (34) The southernmost region of mainland Greece. Its vineyards produce about one-fifth of all Greek table wines and over half of the country's raisins and currants. Greece.

Peloux, Les. (10) Pouilly vineyard, Mâconnais. *Premier cru*. White burgundy entitled with the *AC Pouilly-Fuissé*. France.

Penafiel. (30) One of the six subregions of the Vinhos Verde district. Portugal.

Penafiel. (29) West Old Castile; Valladolid, approx. seventy miles north of Avila. Ordinary to fair red, white and *clarete* wines. Spain.

Peneau, Château. (5) Premières Côtes de Bordeaux; Haux, north of Podensac. 1,000 dozen bottles of red bordeaux; 6,000 white are produced. France.

Penfolds. (37) New South Wales and South Australia. Founded 1844 at Magill, Adelaide, by Dr Rawson Penfold, a great-grandson of whom is chairman of the present public company. All types of wine. Australia.

Penim, Quinta. (30) *Região demarcada do Douro* (q.v.). Estate and vineyard in Penajoia in the Régua region. Portugal.

Peniscola. (29) Castellón de la Plana; approx. forty miles north-east of Valencia. Ordinary to fair red and white table wine. Spain.

Pennyan. (35) New York State; Finger Lakes area. Ordinary to fair still and sparkling wines. U.S.A.

Pentes, Clos des. (16) Touraine; Rochecorbon vineyard north-east of Tours. Fair white table wine. France.

Peralada. (29) Gerona; north-east of Barcelona. Ordinary to fair and some fine table and sparkling wines. Spain.

Peralta. (29) Navarre. Fair to fine golden dessert wine. Spain.

Perapedra. (34) One of the more important wine centres. Turkey.

Perdrix, Les. (8) Côte de Nuits; Prémeaux vineyard. *Premier cru*. Red burgundy. France.

Perena. (29) South León; Salamanca. Ordinary to fair red table wine. Spain.

Perenne, Château. (3) Blayais; St Genès-de-Blaye, north-west of Blaye. 10,000 dozen bottles of red bordeaux; 900 white. France.

Pères, Clos des. (16) Anjou; Montsoreau vineyard, Saumur area. Fair white table wine. France.

Periquita. (30) Wine producing area north of Lisbon producing mainly red table wines. Portugal.

Perl. (22) Saar; south-west of Serrig. Fair white table wine. West Germany.

Perla. (33) Ordinary to fair sparkling white wine. Bulgaria.

Perla del Garda. Another name for Garda Trentino (q.v.). Italy.

Perlant. A French name for a semi-sparkling wine, almost always a natural and temporary phenomenon. France.

Perla Villa. (26) Lombardy; Valtelline. Fair to fine red table wine from the area which produces the best wines in Lombardy. Italy.

Pernand-Vergelesses. (8) Côte de Beaune. Entitled with the *AC Corton* hyphenated with the name. *See* **Aloxe-Corton**. Fair to fine red burgundy. France.

Perray, Clos du. (16) Anjou; Coteaux de la Loire, La Poissonière vineyard below Angers. Fair to fine white table wine. France.

Perre-Souris, Le. (16) Touraine; Beaumont-en-Veron vineyard below Chinon. Fair red table wine. France.

Perreyre, Château. (4) Blayais; St-Martin (north-east of Blaye). 1,700 dozen bottles of red bordeaux. France.

Perrière, La. (8) Côte de Nuits; Nuits-St Georges vineyards. *Premier cru*. Fine white burgundy. France.

Perrière, Château la. (5) St-Emilion; Lussac. An unclassified *cru*. 1,000 dozen bottles of red bordeaux. France.

Perrière, Clos de la. (8) Côte de Nuits; Fixin vineyard. *Premier cru*. Red burgundy. France.

Perrière, Clos des. (16) Coteaux de la Loire; Savonnières vineyard below Angers. Fair to fine white table wine. France.

Perrière-Noblet, En la. (8) Côte de Nuits; Nuits-St-Georges vineyard. *Deuxième cuvée*. Red burgundy. France.

Perrières, Aux. (8) Côte de Beaune; Meursault vineyard. *Premier cru*. Fine white burgundy. France.

Perrières, Les. (8) Côte de Beaune; Beaune vineyard. *Premier cru*. Red burgundy. France.

Perrières, Les. (8) Côte de Beaune; Aloxe-Corton vineyard. *Premier cru*. Red burgundy. France.

Perrières, Les. (8) Pommard vineyard. *Deuxième cru*. Red burgundy. France.

Perrières, Les. (16) Touraine; Bourgueil vineyard. Fair red table wine. France.

Perron, Château. (5) Lalande-de-Pomerol; north of Pomerol. 5,000 dozen bottles of red bordeaux. France.

Perroy, Château de. (31) Vaud canton; Perroy. Fair to fine white table wine. Switzerland.

Perruno Fino. (29) Cádiz. Fine, dry, white wine. Spain.

Perscheid. (21) Middle Rhine; north-west of Bingen. Fair white table wine. West Germany.

Pertuis. (12) Durance valley, Vaucluse. Fair white table wine with the *AC Côte du Luberon*. France.

Pertuisots, Les. (8) Côte de Beaune; Beaune *Premier cru*. Fine red burgundy. France.

Peru. (35) One of the smaller wine-producing countries of South America. Approx. 2,000,000 dozen bottles of wine per annum, mostly ordinary red and white table wines. Peru.

Pescoca, Quinta. (30) *Região demarcada do Douro* (q.v.). Estate and vineyard in Vilarinho north-east of Régua. Portugal.

Péseux. (31) Neuchâtel vineyard. 69 acres. Fair to fine white table wine. Switzerland.

Peso, Quinta. (30) *Região demarcada do Douro* (q.v.). Estate and vineyard near Régua. Portugal.

Peste, Dr. (8) Aloxe-Corton vineyard. Hospices de Beaune *cuvée* named after the donor of the vineyard to the Hospices. *AC Corton*. Red burgundy. France.

Peterberg. (24) Rhinehessia; Gau-Odernheim vineyard, west of Alsheim. Fair white table wine. West Germany.

Petersberg. (22) Moselle; Kröv, Neef, south-west of Eller and Pünderich, east of Zell, vineyards. Fair white table wine. West Germany.

Petersbrunnen. (23) Palatinate; Maikammen vineyard, between Edenkoben and Neustadt. Fair to fine white table wine. West Germany.

Petit-Bois, Domaine du. (5) Néac *commune*; east of Pomerol. 4,500 dozen bottles of red bordeaux. France.

Petit Chablis. The official *AC* given to the outlying vineyards producing white wines in the Chablis area. France.

Petit-Clos-Figeac. (5) St-Emilion. An unclassified *cru*. 1,500 dozen bottles of red bordeaux. France.

Petite Champagne. (20) A strip of vineyards next to those of the Grande Champagne district, in the Charente, nearly as rich in lime. They produce the white wine from which the best Cognac brandy is distilled, other than the Grande Champagne Cognac. France.

Petite-Fontenelle, La. (16) Anjou; Coteaux de l'Aubance, Soulaines vineyard, between Angers and Saumur. Fair white table wine. France.

Petite-Roque, Cru la. (4) Blayais; Plassac, south-east of Blaye. 4,000 dozen bottles of red bordeaux. France.

Petit-Faurie-de-Soutard, Château. (5) Côtes de St-Emilion. *Grand cru classé*. 5,500 dozen bottles of red bordeaux. France.

Petit-Faurie-Troquard, Château. (5) Côtes de St-Emilion. An unclassified *cru*. 2,000 dozen bottles of red bordeaux. France.

Petit-Gravet, Château. (5) Côtes de St-Emilion. An unclassified *cru*. 1,500 dozen bottles of red bordeaux. France.

Petit-Mayne, Château. (5) Barsac. *Cru bourgeois*. 1,000 dozen bottles of white bordeaux. France.

Petit-Mongot, Château. (5) St-Emilion; St Etiènne-de-Lisse. An unclassified *cru*. 3,000 dozen bottles of red bordeaux. France.

Petit-Mont, Le. (16) Touraine; Vouvray vineyard just north-east of Tours. Fair white table wine. France.

Petit Vouvray, Le. (16) Touraine; Vérnon-sur-Brenne vineyard above Tours. Fair white table wine. France.

Petits-Arnauds, Château des. (4) Blayais. 8,000 dozen bottles of red bordeaux; 3,000 white. France.

Petits-Epenots, Les. (8) Côte de Beaune; Pommard vineyard. *Premier cru.* Fine red burgundy. France.

Petits-Monts, Aux. (8) Côte de Nuits; Vosne-Romanée vineyard. *Deuxième cru.* Fine red burgundy. France.

Petits-Noizons, Les. (8) Côte de Beaune; Pommard vineyard. *Deuxième cru.* Red burgundy. France.

Petits-Picottins, Les. (8) Côte de Beaune; Savigny-les-Beaune vineyard. *Troisième cru.* Red burgundy. France.

Petits-Voyens, Les. (9) Chalonnais; Mercurey. *Premier cru.* Red burgundy. France.

Petit-Val, Domaine de. (5) Côtes de St-Emilion. An unclassified *cru.* 2,000 dozen bottles of red bordeaux. France.

Petit-Village, Château. (5) Pomerol. *Grand cru.* 6,000 dozen bottles of red bordeaux. France.

Petrus. (22) Moselle; Graach vineyard. Fair to fine white table wine. West Germany.

Petrusberg. (22) Moselle; Kinheim vineyard. Fair white table wine. West Germany.

Pettental. (24) Rhinehessia; Nierstein vineyard. Very fine white table wine. West Germany.

Petures, Les. (8) Côte de Beaune; Meursault vineyard. *Premier cru.* Fine white burgundy. France.

Peuilles, Les. (16) Touraine; Beaumont-en-Véron vineyard, Chinon. Fair red table wine. France.

Peuillets, Les. (8) Côte de Beaune; Savigny-les-Beaune vineyard. *Premier cru.* Red burgundy. France.

Pewsey Vale. (37) South Australia; between Lyndoch and Eden Valley thirty miles north-east of Adelaide. Vineyard originally planted in 1847. For over a century Penfolds were celebrated for the excellence of their wines until they went out of production. Replanted in 1961. Choice white wine. Australia.

Peybonhomme-les-Tours, Château. (4) Blayais; Cars, east of Blaye. 4,000 dozen bottles of red bordeaux; 700 white. France.

Peychaud, Château. (4) Bourgeais; Teuillac, north of Bourg. 6,000 dozen bottles of red bordeaux; 3,000 white. France.

Pey-la-Brie, Château. (3) Fronsadais; Fronsac. 1,000 dozen bottles of red bordeaux are produced. France.

Pey-Neuf, Domaine le. (14) Côtes de Provence; La Cadire vineyard. *AC Bandol.* Fair red and rosé table wines. France.

Peyraguey-le-Rousset, Château. (5) Sauternes Preignac. *Cru bourgeois.* 1,000 dozen bottles of white bordeaux. France.

Peyrat, Château du. (5) Cérons. 6,000 dozen bottles of white bordeaux. France.

Peyrat, Château du. (5) Entre-deux-Mers; Capian, north-west of Loupiac. 6,000 dozen bottles of red bordeaux; 15,000 white. France.

Peyrat, Château du. (5) Premières Côtes de Bordeaux. 1,000 dozen bottles of red bordeaux; 4,500 white. France.

Peyreau, Château. (5) Côtes de St-Emilion. An unclassified *cru.* 6,000 dozen bottles of red bordeaux. France.

Peyrebrune, Château. (4) Blayais; Plassac, south-east of Blaye. 3,000 dozen bottles of red bordeaux; 500 white. France.

Peyredoulle, Château. (4) Blayais; Bersin, south-east of Blaye. 3,000 dozen bottles of red bordeaux; 500 white. France.

Peyrelongue, Cru. (5) St-Emilion; St Laurent-des-Combes, west of St Etienne-de-Lisse. An unclassified *cru.* 1,200 dozen bottles of red bordeaux. France.

Peyrolan, Château. (4) Bourgeais; St Ciers-de-Canesse, north-west of Bourg. 4,000 dozen bottles of red bordeaux; 1,000 white. France.

Peyron, Château. (5) Fargues; Langon. *Cru bourgeois.* 1,500 dozen bottles of white bordeaux. France.

Peyrou-Grand-Champ, Cru. (5) St-Emilion; St Etienne-de-Lisse. An unclassified *cru.* 3,000 dozen bottles of red bordeaux. France.

Peyroutas (R. Chaineaud), Château. (5) St-Emilion; Vignonet, south-west of St Pey-d'Armens. 2,000 dozen bottles of red bordeaux. France.

Peyruche, Château La. (5) Langoiran; north-east of Portets. 1,500 dozen bottles of red bordeaux; 4,000 white. France.

Pez, Château de. (4) Haut-Médoc; St-Estèphe. *Cru bourgeois supérieur.* 10,000 dozen bottles of red bordeaux. France.

Peza. (34) Crete. Ordinary to fair red and white table wines. Greece.

Pezenok. (33) Ordinary to fair white table wine from Carpathian vineyards of eastern Czechoslovakia.

Pézerolles. (8) Pommard. *Premier cru.* Red burgundy. France.

Pezzalunga. (26) Lombardy; Oltrepo Pavese area south of Pavia across the Po. Fair to good red table wine of Barbera grapes. Italy.

Pfaffenhofen. (25) Württemberg; south-west of Heilbronn. Ordinary to fair red and white table wines. West Germany.

Pfaffenpfad. (24) Rhingau; Oestrich vineyard. Fine white table wine. West Germany.

Pfaffen-Schwabenheim. (24) Rhinehessia; east of Bad Kreuznach. Mostly ordinary and fair, also some fine white table wines. West Germany.

Pfaffensteig. (25) Franconia; Iphofen vineyard, south-east of Würzburg. Fair to fine white table wine. West Germany.

Pfaffenwees. (24) Rhingau; Lorch vineyard. Fair white table wine. West Germany.

Pfaffenweg. (24) Rhinehessia; Gau-Bischofs-heim vineyard, west of Nackenheim. Fair to fine white table wine. West Germany.

Pfaffenweiler. (25) Baden; south-west of Frei-burg. Ordinary to fair white table wine. West Germany.

Pfalz. Short for Rheinpfalz (Palatinate). Germany.

Pfalzgraben. (22) Moselle; Bernkastel and Eiger vineyards. Fair white table wine. West Germany.

Pfalzgraben. (24) Rhingau; Rauenthal vineyard. Fine white table wine. West Germany.

Pfanloch. (24) Rhingau; Hochheim vineyard. Fair to fine white table wine. West Germany.

Pfarrberg. (22) Moselle; Kobern vineyard. Fair white table wine. West Germany.

Pfarrgarten. (24) Rhinehessia; Kempten vine-yard, east of Bingen. Fair white table wine. West Germany.

Pfarrwingert. (24) Nahe; Altenbamberg, Alsenz valley, south-west of Bad Kreuznach. Fair white table wine. West Germany.

Pfeddersheim. (24) Rhinehessia; west of Worms. Ordinary to fair red and white table wines. West Germany.

Pfeiffer. (23) Palatinate; Forst and Edenkoben vineyards. Fair to fine white table wines. West Germany.

Pfingstweider. (24) Nahe; Niederhausen vine-yard, west of Bad Münster. Fair to fine white table wine. West Germany.

Pflanzer. (24) Rhingau; Oestrich and Hattenheim vineyards, west of Erbach. Fine white table wine. West Germany.

Pflanzer. (24) Rhinehessia; Dienheim vineyard. Fair white table wine. West Germany.

Pfuhlweg. (24) Rhinehessia; Nierstein vineyard. Fine white table wine. West Germany.

Pfulben. (25) Franconia; Randersacker vineyard, just south-east of Würzburg. Fine white table wine. West Germany.

Phelan-Ségur, Château. (4) Haut-Médoc; St-Estèphe. *Cru bourgeois supérieur*. 20,000 dozen bottles of red bordeaux. France.

Philosophe. (31) Vaud canton; Dézaley vineyard. Fair to fine white table wine is produced. Switzerland.

Pia, Château du. (4) Bourgeais; Tauriac, north-east of Bourg. 2,500 dozen bottles of red bor-deaux; 500 white. France.

Piada, Château. (5) Barsac. *Cru bourgeois*. 20,000 dozen bottles of white bordeaux. France.

Piana di Catania, Vini Della. (28) Sicily. Dark red, harsh and strong red wine, used for blending. Italy.

Pian-Médoc, Le. (4) Haut-Médoc. Ordinary to fair red bordeaux. France.

Piar, Quinta. *See* **Pilar.**

Piat, Clos du. (4) Bourgeais; Gauriac, north-west of Bourg. 3,000 dozen bottles of red bordeaux. France.

Pibran, Château. (4) Haut-Médoc; Pauillac. *Cru bourgeois*. 3,000 dozen bottles of red bor-deaux. France.

Pic, Château de. (5) Premières Côtes de Bordeaux. 500 dozen bottles of red bordeaux; 4,000 white. France.

Picapoll. (29) Barcelona; Tarragona. Ordinary dark red and white table wines. Spain.

Picard, Château. (4) Haut-Médoc; St-Estèphe. *Cru bourgeois*. 6,000 dozen bottles of red bor-deaux. France.

Picasses, Les. (16) Touraine; Beaumont-en-Véron vineyard, below Chinon. Fair red table wine. France.

Piccolit (Picolit). (26) Veneto; Udine province. Fine golden table wine of Picolit white grapes, sometimes described as the Château d'Yquem (q.v.) of Italy.

Pichelèvre, Château. (3) Côtes de Fronsac. 3,000 dozen bottles of red bordeaux. France.

Pichon, Château. (5) Barsac. *Cru bourgeois*. 5,000 dozen bottles of white bordeaux. France.

Pichon-Longueville (Baron), Château de. (4) Haut-Médoc; Pauillac. *Deuxième cru classé*. 10,000 dozen bottles of red bordeaux. France.

Pichon-Longueville-Comtesse de Lalande, Château. (4) Haut-Médoc; Pauillac. *Deuxième cru classé*. 16,000 dozen bottles of red bordeaux. France.

Pichter. (22) Moselle. There is a vineyard of that name at Dhron, between Neumagen and Wintrich, Longuich, north-east of Trier, Neu-magen and Wittlich. Fair white table wine. West Germany.

Pick, Château du. (5) Sauternes; Preignac. *Cru bourgeois*. 5,000 dozen bottles of white bordeaux. France.

Picot-la-Planteyre, Domaine de. (3) Entre-deux-Mers; Salleboeuf, east of Bordeaux. 1,000 dozen bottles of red bordeaux; 1,000 white. France.

Picourneau, Château. (4) Haut-Médoc; Vertheuil. *Cru bourgeois.* 5,000 dozen bottles of red bordeaux. France.

Picpoul de Pinet. (13) Hérault *département.* *V.D.Q.S.* red table wine. 11·5°. France.

Pièce-sous-le-Bois. (8) Meursault. *Premier cru.* White burgundy. France.

Pied-la-Vigne. (12) Côtes du Rhône; Cornas vineyard. Fair red table wine. France.

Piedmont. (26) The former kingdom of which Turin was the capital. It has now been divided into six provinces: Alessándria, Asti, Cuneo, Novara, Torino and Vercelli, all of them having vineyards which produce chiefly ordinary to fair red table wines, also some fine red wine; as well as most of the sparkling wine of Italy. Turin is the centre of the Vermouth trade. Italy.

Piegon. (12) Drôme *département;* Haut-Comtat. Ordinary to fair red table wine. France.

Piemarore (Bianco, Rosso and **Rosato).** (26) Liguria; vineyards above Bordighera approx. twenty miles south-west of Imperia. Ordinary to fair white, red and rosé table wines. Italy.

Piemonte. Piedmont in Italian. Also the name given to an ordinary white table wine from Ischia in the Bay of Naples. Italy.

Pierelle, La. (12) Côtes du Rhône; Tain l'Hermitage vineyard. Fair red table wine. France.

Pierola. (29) Barcelona. Ordinary to fair red and rosé table wines. Spain.

Pierre, La. (11) Beaujolais, Romanèche-Thorins vineyard. *Premier cru.* Red burgundy. France.

Pierre, La. (10) Beaujolais; Romanèche-Thorins vineyard. *AC Moulin-à-Vent.* Red burgundy. France.

Pierre-Bibian, Château. (4) Haut-Médoc; Listrac. *Cru bourgeois supérieur.* 7,000 dozen bottles of red bordeaux. France.

Pierre Bise. (16) Anjou; Beaulieu-sur-Layon, south of Angers. Fine white table wine. France.

Pierre Blanche. (16) Anjou; Coteaux de Saumur, Parnay vineyard. Fair to fine white table wine. France.

Pierrefeu. (14) Côtes de Provence, east of Toulon. Ordinary to fair white and rosé table wines. France.

Pierre Gauderie. (16) Anjou; Coteaux du Layon, Faye d'Anjou vineyard, south of Angers. Fair to fine white table wine. France.

Pierre-Jean, Clos de. (5) Premières Côtes de Bordeaux. 500 dozen bottles of red bordeaux; 1,000 white. France.

Pierres, Domaine des. (3) Fronsadais. 4,000 dozen bottles of red bordeaux. France.

Pierres Blanches, Les. (16) Anjou; Coteaux de la Loire, Chalonne-sur-Loire below Angers. Fair to fine white table wine. France.

Pierreux, Le. (11) Beaujolais, Brouilly vineyard. Red burgundy. France.

Piesport. (22) Middle Moselle. Fair, fine, and some very fine white table wine. West Germany.

Pietroasa. (33) Town in north Rumania. Ordinary to fair table wines; fair to fine dessert wines. Rumania.

Pignons, Les. (14) Côtes de Provence. East of Toulon. Ordinary to fair red, white and rosé table wines. France.

Pilar, Quinta. (30) *Região demarcada do Douro* (q.v.). Estate and vineyard in Barqueiros in the Régua area. Portugal.

Pilas. (29) Seville. Mostly full-strength, sweet white wines. Spain.

Pilgerborn. (24) Rhinehessia; Westhofen vineyard, south-east of Alsheim. Fair to fine white table wines. West Germany.

Pillot. (9) Chalonnais; Rully vineyard. *Premier cru.* Red burgundy. France.

Pimentiers, Les. (8) Côte de Beaune; Savigny-les-Beaune. *Deuxième cru.* Red burgundy. France.

Pin, Château du. (5) Entre-deux-Mers; St-Vincent-de-Pertignas, north-east of Bordeaux. 4,000 dozen bottles of red bordeaux. France.

Pin, Château du. (5) Premières Côtes de Bordeaux; Cardan, north of Podensac. 500 dozen bottles of red bordeaux; 4,000 white. France.

Pin, Clos du. (16) Touraine; Chinon vineyard. Fair red table wine. France.

Pin, Cru du. (5) Côtes de Bordeaux; Ste Croix-du-Mont. 500 dozen bottles of red bordeaux; 1,000 white. France.

Pin, Domaine du. (5) Premières Côtes de Bordeaux; Beguey, east of Podensac. 1,000 dozen bottles of red bordeaux; 12,000 white. France.

Pineau, Clos. (16) Touraine; Beaumont-en-Véron vineyard below Chinon. Fair red table wine. France.

Pineau, Cru. (5) Graves de Bordeaux; Cérons. 2,000 dozen bottles of white bordeaux. France.

Pinell de Bray. (29) Tarragona. Ordinary to fair red, white and rosé table wines. Spain.

Pinesse, Cru de la. (5) Barsac. *Cru bourgeois.* 600 dozen bottles of white bordeaux. France.

Pinet, Château. (4) Blayais; Berson, south-east of Blaye. 1,200 dozen bottles of red bordeaux; 1,200 white. France.

Pinet-la-Roquette, Château. (4) Blayais; Berson, south-east of Blaye. 1,000 dozen bottles of red bordeaux; 1,000 white. France.

Piney, Clos du. (4) Cubzagais; east of Blaye. 1,500 dozen bottles of red bordeaux; 4,000 white. France.

Pinhel. (30) Area in the Douro valley producing mainly rosé and red table wines. Portugal.

Pinnerkreuzberg. (22) Moselle; Kanzem vineyard. Fair white table wine. West Germany.

Pinoso. (29) Alicante; approx. forty miles south of Valencia. Ordinary red and white table wines. South-east Spain.

Pinot. (29) Madrid. Ordinary to fair red table wine. Spain.

Pinot Bianco. Another name for Borgogna Bianco (q.v.). Italy.

Pinot dell'Oltrepo. (26) Lombardy; Oltrepo Pavese area, south of Pavia across the Po. Good red table wine made of Pinot Noir grapes. Italy.

Pinot Nero. (26) Veneto; Colli Berici vineyard, just south of Vincenza. Fair red table wine of Pinot Noir grapes. Italy.

Pins, Les. (16) Touraine; Bourgueil vineyard. Fair red table wine. France.

Pinte, La. (18) Arbois area. Fair red table wine. France.

Pintray. (16) Touraine; Côte de Montlouis, Lussault east of Montlouis. Fair white table wine. France.

Pipeau, Cru. (5) St-Emilion; St-Hippolyte. An unclassified *cru*. 1,200 dozen bottles of red bordeaux. France.

Pira. (29) Tarragona. Conca de Barbara. Ordinary table wines. Spain.

Pireau, Domaine de. (5) Ste Foy-de-Bordeaux; north-east of Langon. 1,000 dozen bottles of red bordeaux; 2,000 white. France.

Piron, Château. (5) St-Emilion; Parsac. An unclassified *cru*. 3,000 dozen bottles of red bordeaux. France.

Pirramimma. (37) South Australia; McLaren Vale, approx. twenty-five miles south of Adelaide. Winery and vineyards of Johnston family. Red table wine. Australia.

Pirrone Wine Cellars. (36) California; Salida, north-west of Modesto. 120 acres. Table and dessert wines. U.S.A.

Pitigliano. (27) Tuscany. Ordinary dry, soft white table wine, not unlike a dry Orvieto (q.v.). Italy.

Pitillas. (29) Navarre. Ordinary red and fair *clarete* table wines. Spain.

Pitois, Clos. (8) Chassagne-Montrachet vineyard. *Premier cru*. Red burgundy. France.

Pittermännchen. (24) Nahe; Dorsheim vineyard, south-west of Bingen. Fair white table wine. West Germany.

Pittersberg. (24) Nahe; Münster-bei-Binger-brück vineyard. Fair white table wine. West Germany.

Pitures-Dessus, Les. (8) Côte de Beaune; Volnay vineyard. *Deuxième cru*. Red burgundy. France.

Pizay, Château de. (11) Beaujolais, Morgon. Red burgundy. France.

Plainpoint, Château. (3) Fronsadais; St-Aignan, north-west of Fronsac. 8,000 dozen bottles of red bordeaux. France.

Plaisance. (16) Anjou; Coteaux du Layon, St Aubin-de-Luigne vineyard south of Saumur. Fine white table wine. France.

Plaisance. (16) Anjou; Coteaux du Layon, Chaume vineyard south of Angers. Fine white table wine. France.

Plaisance, Château. (5) St-Emilion; Montagne. An unclassified *cru*. 8,000 dozen bottles of red bordeaux. France.

Planchots, Les. (8) Côte de Nuits; Aloxe-Corton vineyard. *Deuxième cru*. Red burgundy. France.

Planig. (24) Rhinehessia; Alzey vineyard, west of Alsheim. Ordinary to fair red and white table wines. West Germany.

Plankener. (24) Rhinegau; Winkel vineyard. Fair white table wine. West Germany.

Planta de Pedralba. (29) Valencia. Ordinary to fair white table wine. Spain.

Planta Nova. (29) North Estremadura; Cáceres, approx. thirty miles west of Trujillo. Ordinary to fair white table wine. Spain.

Plantes, Les. (8) Côte de Beaune; Chambolle-Musigny vineyard. *Premier cru*. Red burgundy. France.

Plantier-Rose, Château. (4) Haut-Médoc; St-Estèphe. *Cru bourgeois*. 3,000 dozen bottles of red bordeaux. France.

Plantonne, Domaine de la. (4) Bourgeais; Bourg. 1,300 dozen bottles of red bordeaux. France.

Plasencia. (29) Central north-west Spain. Ordinary to fair white and *clarete* table wines. Spain.

Plateaux, Les. (8) Côte de Nuits; Nuits-St-Georges vineyard. *Deuxième cru*. Red burgundy. France.

Platerie, Clos de la. (16) Touraine; Restigné vineyard below Tours. Fair red table wine. France.

Platière. (8) Pommard vineyard. *Premier cru*. Red burgundy. France.

Platin, Château. (5) St-Emilion; Vignonet, south-west of St Pey d'Armens. An unclassified *cru*. 1,000 dozen bottles of red bordeaux. France.

Platte. (24) Rhinehessia; Nackenheim, Kempten, just east of Bingen, and Mettenheim, south of Alsheim, vineyards. Fair white table wine. West Germany.

Platten. (22) Moselle; west of Zeltingen. Ordinary to fair white table wine. West Germany.

Platz. (24) Rhinegau; Rüdesheim vineyard. Fair white table wine. West Germany.

Pleisweiler-Oberhofen. (23) Palatinate; south-west of Landau. Ordinary to fair red and white table wines. West Germany.

Plessis, Le. (16) Anjou; Coteaux de la Loire, Juigné-sur-Loire below Angers. Fair to fine white table wine. France.

Pleytegeat, Château. (5) Graves de Bordeaux; Preignac. An unclassified *cru*. 5,000 dozen bottles of white bordeaux. France.

Plince, Château. (5) Pomerol. 4,000 dozen bottles of red bordeaux. France.

Plombeira, Quinta. (30) *Região demarcada do Douro* (q.v.). Estate and vineyard in Casais do Douro in the Régua area. Portugal.

Plovdiv. (33) This southern province of Bulgaria is one of the three main wine-producing regions of the country. Bulgaria.

Pluwig. (22) Moselle; south-east of Trier. Ordinary white table wine. West Germany.

Pobleda. (29) Tarragóna; Priorato. Mostly fair to fine white dessert wine. Spain.

Pocinho, Quinta. (30) *Região demarcada do Douro*. Estate and vineyard in Vila Nova de Fozcoa in the Régua area. Portugal.

Pocos de Cima, Quinta. (30) *Região demarcada do Douro* (q.v.). Estate and vineyard in Valdigem south-west of Régua. Portugal.

Pohardy. (16) Anjou; Coteaux de la Loire, Brain-sur-l'Authion vineyard below Angers. Fair, sweet white wine. France.

Point-du-Jour. (11) Fleurie vineyard, Beaujolais. Red burgundy. France.

Pointe, Château La. (5) Pomerol. *Grand cru*. 7,000 dozen bottles of red bordeaux. France.

Pointes d'Angle. (8) Côte de Beaune; Volnay vineyard. *Premier cru*. Red burgundy. France.

Poirets, Les. *See* **Porrets, Les.**

Poissonnière, La. (16) Anjou; Coteaux de la Loire (q.v.) below Angers. Fair red and white table wines. France.

Poitevin, Château. (5) Graves de Bordeaux; Castres, west of Portets. An unclassified *cru*. 1,000 dozen bottles of red bordeaux; 500 white. France.

Pokolbin. (37) New South Wales; Hunter River area, north-east of Sydney. Township surrounded by important vineyards. Australia.

Polcevera. (26) Liguria; La Spezia area. Ordinary to dry and semi-dry white table wine. Italy.

Poldras, Quinta. (30) *Região demarcada do Douro* (q.v.). Estate and vineyard in Sarzedinho east of Régua. Portugal.

Pölich. (22) Moselle; south of Klüsserath. Ordinary to fair white table wine. West Germany.

Polidoro, Quinta. (30) *Região demarcada do Douro* (q.v.). Estate and vineyard in Cambres south-west of Régua. Portugal.

Poligny. (18) Jura. Ordinary to fair white table wine; also some *vin jaune* and *vin de paille*. France.

Pollens. (29) Majorca; Balearic Islands, off the coast east of Valencia. Ordinary to fair table and dessert wines. Spain.

Pollera. (26) Liguria; La Spezia. Ordinary sweet red dessert wine. Italy.

Pollino. (28) Calabria; Castrovillari approx. seventy miles south-west of Taranto. Ordinary to fair dry ruby-red table wine. Italy.

Poltersdorf. (33) Burgenland; south-east Austria close to the Hungarian border. Fair to fine white table wine. Austria.

Poltersdorf. (22) Moselle; south-west of Bruttig. Fair white table wine. West Germany.

Pommard, Clos. (4) Blayais; St Martin Lacaussade, north-east of Blaye. 3,000 dozen bottles of red bordeaux. France.

Pomerol. (5) Designated Bordeaux district above Libourne and below St-Emilion. Its vineyards produce much fair and fine red bordeaux. France.

Pomet. (16) Coteaux de la Loire; Ingrandes vineyard below Tours. Fair white table wine. France.

Pomeys, Château. (4) Haut-Médoc; St-Estephe. *Cru bourgeois supérieur*. 2,500 dozen bottles of red bordeaux. France.

Pomino (Bianco, Rosso). (27) Tuscany; Rufina, east of Florence. Good white and red wines. Italy.

Pomard. (8) Côte de Beaune; town and vineyards of the Côte d'Or, immediately south of Beaune. Ordinary, fair, fine and some very fine red burgundy. France.

Pommarède, Château de. (5) Graves de Bordeaux; Castres, west of Portets. An unclassified *cru*. 600 dozen bottles of red bordeaux; 2,500 white. France.

Pommarede-de-Haut, Château. (5) Graves de Bordeaux; Castres, west of Portets. An unclassified *cru*. 600 dozen bottles of red bordeaux; 1,500 white. France.

Pommeraye, La. (16) Anjou; Coteaux de la Loire below Angers. Fair white table wine is produced. France.

Pommern. (22) Moselle; north-east of Valwig. Fair to fine white table wines. Best vineyards: Greismund, Kapellenberg, Rosenberg. West Germany.

Pomori. (33) Popular fortified dessert wine. Bulgaria.

N

Pomposa Bianco. (27) Emilia-Romagna. Ordinary to fair dry white table wines. Italy.

Pomys, Château. (4) Haut-Médoc; Moulis. *Cru bourgeois supérieur.* 2,500 dozen bottles of red bordeaux. France.

Poncier, Le. (11) Beaujolais; Fleurie vineyard. Red burgundy. France.

Ponsal. (29) Tarragona and the Balearic Islands, off the coast east of Valencia. Ordinary white table wine. Spain.

Pontac, Château. (5) Entre-deux-Mers; Loupiac. 4,000 dozen bottles of white bordeaux. France.

Pontac-Lynch, Château. (4) Haut-Médoc; Cantenac. *Cru bourgeois supérieur.* 1,500 dozen bottles of red bordeaux. France.

Pontac-Monplaisir, Château. (5) Graves de Bordeaux; Villenave d'Ornon. An unclassified *cru.* 3,500 dozen bottles of red bordeaux; 5,500 white. France.

Pontet, Château du. (5) Côtes de St-Emilion. An unclassified *cru.* 1,500 dozen bottles of red bordeaux. France.

Pontet-Canet, Château. (5) Haut-Médoc; Pauillac. *Cinquième cru classé.* 40,000 dozen bottles of red bordeaux. France.

Pontida. (26) Lombardy; Bergamo, Colli dei Frati. Ordinary to light red table wine usually drunk young. Italy.

Pontoise-Cabarrus-Brochon, Château. (4) Haut-Médoc; St Seurin-de-Cadourne. *Cru bourgeois.* 6,000 dozen bottles of red bordeaux. France.

Pontons. (29) Barcelona; upper Panadés, between Tarragona and Barcelona. Ordinary to fair table wines. Spain.

Pontrique, Château La. (5) Graves de Bordeaux; Cadaujac. An unclassified *cru.* 1,000 dozen bottles of red bordeaux. France.

Ponzano. (29) Aragon; Huesca, area north of Zaragoza. Ordinary to fair table wines. Spain.

Poppenweiler. (25) Württemberg; north-east of Stuttgart. Ordinary red and white table wines. West Germany.

Porrera. (29) Tarragona; Priorato. Ordinary to fair table wines. Spain.

Porrets, Les. (8) Côte de Nuits; Nuits-St-Georges. *Premier cru.* Fine red burgundy. France.

Portail, Le. (16) Vouvray vineyard, just east of Tours. Fair to fine white table wine. France.

Portets. (5) Graves de Bordeaux. Ordinary to fair red and white bordeaux wines. France.

Portnesberg. (22) Moselle; Wintrich vineyard. Fair white table wine. West Germany.

Porto Casteldaccia. (28) Sicily. Ordinary to fair sweet white dessert wine. Italy.

Portofino. (26) Liguria; Santa Margharita Ligure between Genoa and La Spezia. Modest white table wines. Italy.

Porusot Dessus, Le. (8) Côte de Beaune; Meursault vineyard. *Premier cru.* Red burgundy. France.

Posadas. (29) North-central Andalusia; Córdoba. Fair to fine white table wine. Spain.

Posinkovich's. (38) North Island; Herekino, approx. 140 miles north-west of Auckland. Winery and vineyard. New Zealand.

Posten. (21) Middle Rhine; Bacharach vineyard, north-west of Bingen. Fair white table wine. West Germany.

Port or Porto. (30) *Região demarcada do Douro in Portugal* (q.v.). Port, Porto or Vinho do Porto can only be produced in this area. It is always fortified with brandy to 20° alcohol by volume. Port can only be matured in the Douro valley or in the Entreposto of V.N. de Gaia. Red port is made from red grapes: white port from white grapes. Port is either matured in wood as a 'ruby' port and then attains the colour 'tawny' or else is bottled as a ruby port of one year, after two years in wood, as a 'vintage port'. Strict control from the government (Instituto Do Vinho Do Porto) and the shippers' (Gremio dos Exportadores do Vinho do Porto) representatives ensure its authenticity.

Porto de Bois, Quinta (30) *Região demarcada do Douro* (q.v.). Estate and vineyard in Seixas in the Régua area. Portugal.

Portugal. (30) Portugal is currently the fourth largest wine-producing country in the world, split into two distinct categories—table wines, (including vinho verde (q.v.)) and fortified wines (port and madeira). Table wines mainly come from three geographical areas. In the north around Oporto and the Douro Valley, in the centre in the Dao district, and in the south around Lisbon and the river Tagus. Both vinho verde and port and madeira have demarcated areas of origin. For years the U.K. was Portugal's traditional market place, but now France drinks the most port, and there is an ever increasing market in the U.S. for Portuguese table wines.

Poteau, Domaine du. (5) Côtes de St-Emilion. An unclassified *cru.* 1,500 dozen bottles of red bordeaux. France.

Potensac, Château de. (3) Médoc; Potensac-et-Ordonnac, north-west of St Seurin-de-Cadourne. *Cru bourgeois.* 5,000 dozen bottles of red bordeaux. France.

Pouèze. (16) Anjou; Coteaux du Layon, Chaume vineyard south of Angers. Fine white table wine. France.

Pougets, Les. (8) Côte de Nuits; Aloxe-Corton vineyard. *Premier cru*. Red burgundy. France.

Pouilly. (10) Hamlet in the *commune* of Fuissé, Mâconnais. Fine white burgundy with the *AC Pouilly-Fuissé*. France.

Pouilly, Château de. (10) Best Pouilly vineyard, Mâconnais. White burgundy. France.

Pouilly, Vers. (10) Fuissé's best vineyard, Mâconnais. White burgundy. France.

Pouilly-Blanc-Fumé. (15) Another name for Pouilly-Fumé (q.v.). White table wine. France.

Pouilly-Fuissé. (10) Mâconnais. The *AC* given to the fair to fine white table wines made from the Chardonnay grape in the following communes: Fuissé, Solutré, Vergisson and Chaintré. White burgundy. France.

Pouilly-Fumé. (10) Pouilly-sur-Loire. Fine white table wines made from Sauvignon grapes known locally as *blanc-fumé* grapes, literally 'white-smoke'. France.

Pouilly-Loche. (10) Loche vineyard, Mâconnais. Fine white burgundy usually marketed as Pouilly-Fuissé. France.

Pouilly-sur-Loire. (15) Town on right bank of the upper Loire, part of which is planted with Chasselas grapes, giving an ordinary to fair white table wine, and the rest with Sauvignon grapes, locally known as *blanc-fumé*, giving a white table wine of fine quality. France.

Pouilly-Vinzelles. (10) Mâconnais. Village and vineyard immediately south of the Pouilly-Fuissé group. Fair to fine white burgundy. France.

Poulettes, Les. (8) Côte de Nuits; Nuits-St-Georges vineyard. *Premier cru*. Red burgundy. France.

Poullaillières, Les. (8) Côte de Nuits; Flagey-Echézeaux vineyard. *Premier cru*. Red burgundy. France.

Poumey, Château. (5) Graves de Bordeaux; Gradignan. An unclassified *cru*. 2,000 dozen bottles of red bordeaux; 1,000 white. France.

Pousada, Quinta. (30) *Região demarcada do Douro* (q.v.). Estate and vineyard in Penajoia in the Régua area. Portugal.

Poutures, Les. (8) Côte de Beaune; Pommard vineyard. *Premier cru*. Red burgundy. France.

Pouvray, Clos du. (16) Touraine; Vérnon-sur-Brenne, above Tours. Fair to fine white wine. France.

Poyanne, Cru de. (4) Bourgeais; Gauriac, north-west of Bourg. 2,000 dozen bottles of red bordeaux. France.

Poyette, La. (12) Côtes du Rhône; Ampuis, Côte Rôtie. Fine red table wine. France.

Poyeux, Les. (15) Anjou; St Cyr-en-Bourg south of Saumur. Fair red wine. France.

Pozaldes. (29) West Old Castile; Valladolid, approx. seventy miles north of Avila. Ordinary to fair red and white table wines. Spain.

Pradeaux, Château. (14) Côtes de Provence; St Cyr-sur-Mer vineyard. *AC Bandol*. Fair red and rosé table wines. France.

Prälat. (22) Moselle; Pommern, north-east of Valwig, and Erden vineyards. Fair white table wine. West Germany.

Preau. (9) Chalonnais; Rully vineyard. *Premier cru*. Red burgundy. France.

Prée, La. (15) Pouilly-sur-Loire. Fair to fine white table wine. France.

Pregiros. (6) Chablis region. Ordinary white burgundy. France.

Préhy. (6) Chablis region. *AC Chablis*. Ordinary to fair white burgundy. France.

Preignac. (5) Village and vineyards near Sauternes, with fair, fine and some very fine white wines with the *AC Sauternes*. France.

Prémeaux. (8) Côte d'Or village and vineyards. Fair to fine red burgundy with the *AC Nuits-St-Georges* for the best. *AC Côte de Nuits village* for others. France.

Premoureux, Les. (18) Jura; Salins vineyard. Ordinary to fair red table wine. France.

Pres-Hauts, Les. (6) Tonnerre area. Ordinary to fair red and white burgundy. France.

Pressac, Château de. (5) St-Emilion; St Etienne-de-Lisse. An unclassified *cru*. 10,000 dozen bottles of red bordeaux. France.

Pressburg (Bratislava). (33) Pressburg; thirty-five miles south-east of Vienna was the German name for Bratislava until 1918. Ordinary to fair red and white table wines are produced. Czechoslovakia.

Pressoire, Clos du. (16) Anjou; Coteaux de la Loire, La Possonnière vineyard below Angers. Fair white table wine. France.

Preuses, Les. (6) Chablis vineyard. *Grand cru*. Fine white burgundy. France.

Prévoles, Les. (8) Côte de Beaune; Beaune vineyard. *Deuxième cru*. Red burgundy. France.

Priego de Córdoba. (29) North-central Andalusia; Córdoba. Fair to fine white table wine. Spain.

Prieur, Clos du. (5) Premières Côtes de Bordeaux; Loupiac. 1,000 dozen bottles of white bordeaux. France.

Prieure, Château Le. (4) Blayais; St Genes-de-Blaye, north of Blaye. 1,000 dozen bottles of red bordeaux; 200 white. France.

Prieure-Lichine, Château. (4) Haut-Médoc; Cantenac. *Quatrième cru classé*. 7,500 dozen bottles of red bordeaux. France.

Prieuse, Clos de la. (5) Entre-deux-Mers; St

Genès de Lombaud, east of Cadaujac. 1,500 dozen bottles of white bordeaux. France.

Prignac. (4) Haut-Médoc, near Lesparre. Ordinary to fair bordeaux wines. France.

Primativo di Manduria (Primitivo del Tarantino). (28) Apulia; Taranto area. Ordinary to fair red table wine. *Primitivo* here really means *primaticcio*—early. This is the earliest vintage in Europe—in August. It is mostly used for blending wines further north. The second harvest produces a big full-flavoured wine that is worth trying. Italy.

Primitivo di Gioia. (28) Apulia; Bari area vineyards. Very dark and full-flavoured red wine. Italy.

Prince. (16) Anjou; Coteaux de l'Aubance, Vauchrétin vineyard, between Angers and Saumur. Fair white table wine. France.

Princes, Clos des. (5) Barsac. 500 dozen bottles of white bordeaux. France.

Pringuey. (5) Premières Côtes de Bordeaux area; Camplares, north-east of Cadaujac. 1,500 dozen bottles of red bordeaux; 500 white. France.

Priorato. (29) Tarragona. Fair to fine red and 'black' table wine; also fair white dessert wines. Spain.

Prioulette, Château La. (5) Premières Côtes de Bordeaux; St Maixant, south-east of Ste Croix-du-Mont. 1,000 dozen bottles of red bordeaux; 4,000 white. France.

Prisse. (8) Côte de Nuits *commune* and vineyards. *AC Côte de Nuits villages.* Ordinary to fair red burgundy. France.

Prisse. (10) Mâconnais; north-east of Vergisson. *AC Macon villages blanc.* Ordinary to fair red, white and rosé burgundy. France.

Probstberg. (22) Moselle; Longuich vineyard, north-east of Trier. Ordinary to fair white table wine. West Germany.

Procanico. (27) Tuscany; vineyards on the island of Elba, west of Grossetto. Fair white table wine but the best from the island where it is produced. Italy.

Proces, Les. (8) Côte de Nuits; Nuits-St-Georges vineyard. *Premier cru.* Red burgundy. France.

Procida (Bianco, Rosso). (28) Campania; small island of Procida lying between Ischia (in the Bay of Naples) and Naples. Ordinary to fair light dry and rather sharp white table wine and a sometimes sweetish ordinary red wine. Italy.

Proppenstein. (23) Palatinate; Bad Dürkheim vineyard. Fine white table wine. West Germany.

Prokupac. (33) Serbia; east-central Yugoslavia. Indigenous and common vine which gives good red and rosé table wines. Yugoslavia.

Prosecco dell'Oltrepo. (26) Lombardy; Oltrepo

Pavese area, south of Pavia across the Po. Ordinary to fair white semi-sweet semi-sparkling wine. Italy.

Prosecco Spumante. (26) Veneto; Conegliano north of Treviso. Fair to good white sparkling wine. Italy.

Prosecco Triestino. (26) Friuli Venezia-Giulia; the Gorizia-Trieste area. Fair light sweetish white dessert wine usually served with fruit. Italy.

Prosek. (33) Dalmatia; central Adriatic coast. Brown/red unique liqueur/sweet dessert wine produced from raisins. Yugoslavia.

Proshek. *See* **Prosek.**

Prost, Château. (5) Barsac. 500 dozen bottles of red bordeaux. France.

Prost-Jean-Lève, Château. (5) Barsac. *Cru bourgeois.* 2,500 dozen bottles of white bordeaux. France.

Prouzet, Château du. (5) Graves de Bordeaux; Illats. An unclassified *cru.* 500 dozen bottles of red bordeaux; 2,000 white. France.

Provence. (14) Ancient Roman colony and former French province, the best vineyards of which are those of the Côtes de Provence, between the foothills of the Alps and the Mediterranean. Four districts are limited by the *Appellation d'Origine* laws: La Palette, Bellet, Bandol, Cassis. France.

Provencio, El. (29) South-central Spain. Ordinary to fair table wines. Spain.

Provera, Château. (3) Médoc; St-Christoly, north of St Seurin-de-Cadourne. *Cru bourgeois.* 1,000 dozen bottles of red bordeaux. France.

Providence, Château La. (5) Pomerol. 1,500 dozen bottles of red bordeaux. France.

Provilaro. (28) Calabria; Cosenza area approx. thirty-five miles north-west of Cantanzaro. Fair white table wine. Italy.

Pruliers, Les. (8) Côte de Nuits; Nuits-St-Georges vineyard. *Premier cru.* 17·5 acres. Red burgundy. France.

Ptuj. (33) North-eastern Slovenia; Drava valley, north-west Yugoslavia. Ancient wine centre. Yugoslavia.

Pucelles, Les. (8) Puligny-Montrachet. *Premier cru.* White burgundy. France.

Puch-Cabanac, Château. (5) Graves de Bordeaux; Cabanac-et-Villagrains, south of Cadaujac. An unclassified *cru.* 300 dozen bottles of red bordeaux; 200 white. France.

Puebla, La. (29) Majorca; Balearic Islands, off the coast east of Valencia. Ordinary table wines. Spain.

Puebla de Almoradiel. (29) West New Castile; Toledo, approx. forty miles south-west of Madrid. Ordinary to fair table wines. Spain.

Puebla de Hijar, La. (29) Aragon; Teruel. Ordinary table wines. Spain.

Puebla del Duc. (29) Valencia. Ordinary to fair white table wine. Spain.

Puente Canedos, (29) South Galicia; Ribera, Orense area. Ordinary table wines. Spain.

Puente Genil. (29) North-central Andalusia; Córdoba area north-east of Seville. Fair to fine white table wine. Spain.

Puente la Reina. (29) Navarre. Ordinary to fair white table wine. Spain.

Puerto de Santa Maria. (29) Cadiz. An important centre for the production of sherry. Spain.

Puerto Real. (29) Cadiz. Fair to fine white wines. Spain.

Puisieulx. (17) Marne *département*; Verzy canton, south-east of Sillery. Rated *grand cru*—100% growth. 33 acres. France.

Puisseguin. (5) Secondary red bordeaux producing district, adjoining St-Emilion, with the *AC Puisseguin-St-Emilion*. Ordinary to fair red bordeaux. France.

Pujois, Domaine de. (5) Premières Côtes de Bordeaux; Rions, north of Podensac. 1,000 dozen bottles of red bordeaux; 5,000 white. France.

Pülchen. (22) Saar; Filzen vineyard. Fair white table wine. West Germany.

Puligny-Montrachet. (8) Côte de Beaune, next to Chassagne-Montrachet. Mostly fine to very fine white burgundy considered by some to be the very best French dry wines. France.

Pünderich. (2) Lower Moselle; west of Zell. Ordinary, fair and some fine white table wines. West Germany.

Pusterla Bianca. (26) Lombardy; Brescia area. A rather bland, dry white table wine. Italy.

Puy, Château du. (5) St-Emilion; Parsac. 2,500 dozen bottles of red bordeaux. France.

Puy-Benet-Laffitte. (4) Blayais; Mazion, north-east of Blaye. 1,600 dozen bottles of red bordeaux; 500 white. France.

Puy-Blanquet, Château. (5) St-Emilion; St Etienne-de-Lisse. An unclassified *cru*. 15,000 dozen bottles of red bordeaux. France.

Puyfromage, Château. (5) St-Emilionnais; St-Cibard. An unclassified *cru*. 15,000 dozen bottles of red bordeaux; 1,500 white. France.

Puymouton, Château. (5) St-Emilion; St Christophe-des-Bardes, south-west of Parsac. An unclassified *cru*. 2,000 dozen bottles of red bordeaux. France.

Puynormand, Château. (5) St-Emilion; Parsac. An unclassified *cru*. 3,000 dozen bottles of red bordeaux. France.

Puy-Rigault. (16) Touraine; Savigny-en-Véron

vineyard, below Chinon. Fair red table wine. France.

Py, Le. (11) Beaujolais; Morgon vineyard. One of the top-grade beaujolais. France.

Quagliano. (26) Piedmont; Castiglione vineyard, Cuneo province. Ordinary sweet red table wine. Italy.

Quartiers de Nuits. (8) Côtes de Nuits; Flagey-Echézeaux vineyard. *Premier cru*. Red burgundy. France.

Quatourze. (13) Aude *département;* Narbonne area, approx. thirty-five miles north of Rivesaltes. *V.D.O.S.* red table wines, white and rosé table wines. France.

Quatre Moulins, Les. (16) Anjou; Chalonne-sur-Loire vineyard below Angers. Fair white table wine. France.

Quatre Vents, Les. (11) Beaujolais; Fleurie vineyard. Red beaujolais. France.

Quarts de Chaume. (16) Anjou. The best vineyard of the village of Chaume, near Rochecorbon, where the Layon flows into the Loire, south of Angers. Very fine white table and dessert wines made from Chenin Blanc grapes. France.

Quelle. (23) Palatinate; Ruppertsberg vineyard. Fair to fine white table wine. West Germany.

Quelltaler. (37) South Australia; Watervale, near Clare. One of State's most historic wine names, designating white wines—particularly a very old-established line of hock—marketed for eighty years by H. Buring & Sobels Ltd. and since 1969 by Quelltaler Wines Ltd following a takeover by a Melbourne merchant house. Famous too for Gran-fiesta flor sherry. Australia.

Quentin, Château. (5) St-Emilion; St Christophe-des-Bardes, south-west of Parsac. An unclassified *cru*. 10,000 dozen bottles of red bordeaux. France.

Quercy, Château. (5) St-Emilion; Vignonet. An unclassified *cru*. 2,000 dozen bottles of red bordeaux. France.

Quero. (29) West New Castile; Toledo, approx. forty miles south-west of Madrid. Ordinary table wines. Spain.

Quesetara. (35) Central Mexico. Large wine-producing area. Mexico.

Quétards, Les. (6) Auxerre area. *Premier cru*. Red burgundy. France.

Queue du Renard. (16) Anjou; Coteaux du Layon, Faye d'Anjou vineyard, south of Angers. Fine white table wine. France.

Queyrats, Château des. (5) Graves; St Pierre-de-Mons. An unclassified *cru*. 5,000 dozen bottles of white bordeaux. France.

Quince. (16) Anjou; Coteaux de l'Aubance, between Angers and Saumur. Fair white and rosé table wines. France.

Quincié. (11) Beaujolais. Ordinary to fair red beaujolais. France.

Quincy. (15) Cher *département;* near Bourges. Fair white table wine, low alcoholic content. France.

Quinquenets, Les. (16) Touraine; Chinon vineyard. Fair red table wine. France.

Quintana de la Orden. (29) West New Castile; Toledo, approx. forty miles south-west of Madrid. Ordinary table wines. Spain.

Quintanas del Rey. (29) East New Castile; Cuenca. Fair red table wine. Spain.

Quintas, Quinta. (30) *Região demarcada do Douro* (q.v.). Estate and vineyard in Pacos de Ferreira, twenty-five miles north-east of Oporto. Portugal.

Quintigny. (18) Jura; near l'Etoile, south-west of Château Chalon. Fair white table wine. France.

☙

Raba, Château. (5) St-Emilion; St Etiènne-de-Lisse. An unclassified *cru*. 2,000 dozen bottles of red bordeaux. France.

Rabaud-Promis, Château. (5) Sauternes; Bommes. *Premier cru classé*. 7,500 dozen bottles of fine white bordeaux. France.

Rablay-sur-Layon. (16) Anjou; Coteaux du Layon, south of Angers. Fair to fine and some very fine white table wine. France.

Rablot. (9) Chalonnais; Rully vineyard. Fine white burgundy. France.

Raboso. (26) Veneto; vineyards on Piave River plain, north-east of Venice. Ordinary red table wine made from Raboso black grapes. Italy.

Raboso Veronese. (26) Veneto; Verona area. Ordinary red table wine, from black Raboso grapes. There are also sweet, semi-sparkling versions. Italy.

Radein. (22) Moselle; Müden vineyard, north-east of Valwig. Ordinary to fair white table wine. West Germany.

Radich's. (38) North Island; Awani Winery and vineyard, approx. 160 miles north-west of Auckland. New Zealand.

Rafette, Château La. (5) Entre-deux-Mers; St-Loubes, north-east of Bordeaux. 1,000 dozen bottles of red bordeaux; 200 white. France.

Ragalna (Bianco, Rosso). (28) Sicily; Catania. Among the better of the modest red and white

table wines produced on the slopes of Mount Etna. Italy.

Ragunières, Les. (16) Touraine; Benais vineyard, Bourgueil area. Fair red table wine. France.

Rahoul, Château. (5) Graves de Bordeaux; Portets. An unclassified *cru*. 2,000 dozen bottles of red bordeaux; 1,500 white. France.

Ralingen. (22) Moselle; north-west of Trier. Ordinary to fair white table wine. West Germany.

Ramage-La Batisse, Château. (4) St-Sauveur. *Cru bourgeois supérieur*. 10,000 dozen bottles of red bordeaux. France.

Ramallosa. (29) West-central Galicia; Pontevedra. Rough, sharp, dark red table wine. North-west Spain.

Ramandolo. (26) Veneto; Udine province. Fair golden dessert wine. Italy.

Rambla, La. (29) North-central Andalusia; Córdoba area north-east of Seville. Fair white table wine. Spain.

Rame, Château La. (5) Côtes de Bordeaux; Ste Croix-du-Mont. 500 dozen bottles of red bordeaux; 2,000 white. France.

Rame, Domaine de la. (5) Premières Côtes de Bordeaux; Verdelais, north of Langon. 800 dozen bottles of red bordeaux; 2,000 white. France.

Ramie. (26) Piedmont; Pomaretto, Novara province. Ordinary light red table wine. Italy.

Rammersweier. (25) Baden; south-east of Strasbourg. Ordinary to fair red and white table wines. West Germany.

Ramondon, Château de. (5) Entre-deux-Mers; Capian, north-west of Loupiac. 7,000 dozen bottles of red bordeaux; 8,000 white. France.

Ramsthal. (25) Franconia; approx. twenty-five miles north-east of Würzburg. Fair to fine white table wine. West Germany.

Randazzo. (28) Sicily; vineyards on the foothills of Mount Etna, south of Catania. Ordinary red and white table wines. Italy.

Randersacker. (25) Franconia; just south-east of Würzburg. Ordinary red and fine white table wines. West Germany.

Ranina Radgona. (33) North-western Yugoslavia; Radgona, near Austrian border. 'Tiger Milk'. Table wine from Ranina Bouvier grape. Late-gathered grapes give a mild full sweet white wine. Yugoslavia.

Raposeira, Quinta. (30) *Região demarcada do Douro* (q.v.). Estate and vineyard in Cambres south-west of Régua. Also quality Portuguese sparkling wine. Portugal.

Raspail, Château. (12) Côtes du Rhône; Gigondas vineyard. Fair to fine red table wine. France.

Raspide, Cru. (5) Barsac. 600 dozen bottles of bordeaux. France.

Rasteau. (16) Côtes du Rhône *V.D.N.* Fair to fine dessert wines. France.

Rateau, Château. (3) Fronsadais; Guîtres canton, north of Libourne. 500 dozen bottles of red bordeaux; 4,000 white. France.

Rathausberg. (22) Moselle; Bruttig vineyard. Fair white table wine. West Germany.

Ratsch. (33) Steiermark (Styria); south-east and central Austria. Fair to fine white table wine. Austria.

Rauchloch. (24) Rhinegau; Hochheim vineyard. Fair to fine white table wine is produced. West Germany.

Rauenberg. (21) Baden; south of Heidelberg. Ordinary to fair red and white table wines. West Germany.

Rauenthal. (24) Rhinegau. Fair to fine and some very fine white table wines. West Germany.

Raul. (22) Moselle; Oberemmel vineyard. Fine white table wine. West Germany.

Raumbach. (24) Nahe; south-west of Bad Münster. Fair to fine white wine. West Germany.

Rausan-Ségla, Château. (4) Haut-Médoc; Margaux. *Deuxième cru classé.* 7,000 dozen bottles of red bordeaux. France.

Rausch. (22) Saar; Saarburg vineyard. Fair white table wine. West Germany.

Raux, Château du. (4) Cussac. *Cru bourgeois supérieur.* 2,000 dozen bottles of red bordeaux. France.

Rauzan-Gassies, Château. (4) Haut-Médoc; Margaux. *Deuxième cru classé.* 6,000 dozen bottles of red bordeaux. France.

Rauze-Sybil, Château. (5) Premières Côtes de Bordeaux; Cenac, east of Villenave d'Ornon. 5,000 dozen bottles of red bordeaux; 5,000 white. France.

Ravello (Bianco, Rosso and Rosato). (28) Campania; Sorrentino peninsula, south-east of Naples. Ordinary to fair light white, red and rosé table wines. The rosé tends to be sweetest, although there is a sweet, *frizzante* white. Italy.

Ravensburg. (25) Franconia; Thüngersheim vineyard, north-west of Würzburg. Fair white table wine. West Germany.

Ravinet, Les. (10) Mâconnais; St-Amour vineyard. Red burgundy. France.

Ravion, Domaine de. (4) Blayais; St Christophe-de-Blaye, east of Blaye. 300 dozen bottles of red bordeaux; 3,000 white. France.

Raviottes, Aux. (8) Côte de Nuits; Vosne-Romanée vineyard. *Troisième cru.* Red burgundy. France.

Ray, Martin Inc. (36) California; Saratoga.

Inoperative during 1970–71. Sold to Mt Eden Vineyards, Inc. who intend to continue producing quality wines. U.S.A.

Rayas, Château. (12) Côtes du Rhône; Châteauneuf-du-Pape vineyard. Fair to fine red table wine. France.

Raymond-Lafon, Château. (5) Sauternes. *Cru bourgeois.* 1,400 dozen bottles of white bordeaux. France.

Raynaud, Domaine de. (4) Bourgeais; Bourg. 2,000 dozen bottles of red bordeaux. France.

Rayne-Vigneau, Château. (5) Sauternes; Bommes. *Premier cru classé.* 10,000 dozen bottles of white bordeaux. France.

Réas, Clos des. (8) Côte de Nuits; Vosne-Romanée vineyard. *Premier cru.* Red burgundy. France.

Rebeymont, Château. (4) Bourgeais; Bourg. 7,000 dozen bottles of red bordeaux. France.

Rebouquet, Domaine de. (4) Blayais; Berson, south-east of Blaye. 3,000 dozen bottles of red bordeaux; 1,200 white. France.

Rebuillide, Château. (5) Entre-deux-Mers; Guillac, south of St Sulpice-de-Falyrens. 500 dozen bottles of red bordeaux; 8,000 white. France.

Recas. (33) Village in west Rumania. Fair to fine red table wine made from Pinot Noir grapes.

Rech. (21) Ahr; west of Linz. Ordinary red and white table wines. West Germany.

Rechtenbach. (23) Palatinate; south-west of Landau. Ordinary to fair red and white table wines. West Germany.

Rechweg. (24) Rhinehessia; Ockenheim vineyard, south-east of Bingen. Fair white table wine. West Germany.

Recioto. (26) Veneto; Verona area. Ordinary to fair full, heavy, red table wines made in two qualities, dry and sweet. Italy.

Recioto Amarone. (26) Ordinary to fair red table wine, said to be the best of its kind. Italy.

Recioto Bianco. (26) Veneto; Verona area. Ordinary to fair sweet white table wine (13°–14°) of Garganega white grapes. Italy.

Recioto Soave. (26) Veneto; Soave area, east of Verona. Ordinary to fair rather sweet white table wine, mostly made from Garganega white grapes. Italy.

Recougne, Château. (3) Fronsadais. 18,000 dozen bottles of red bordeaux; 4,500 white. France.

Redbank. (37) South Australia; Coonawarra. Winery established in 1969 by Redman family, which had relinquished their former Rouge-Homme property. Prizewinning dry reds. Australia.

Redon, Château. (5) Entre-deux-Mers; St Germain-de-Puch, west of St Sulpice-de-Falyrens. 5,000 dozen bottles of red bordeaux. France.

Reduda, Quinta. (30) *Região demarcada do Douro* (q.v.). Estate and vineyard in Folgosa east of Régua. Portugal.

Reetz. (21) Middle Rhine; Manubach vineyard, north-west of Bingen. Fair white table wine. West Germany.

Refène, La. (8) Côte de Beaune; Pommard vineyard. *Premier cru.* Red burgundy. France.

Refine, Cru. (5) Entre-deux-Mers; Daignac, south-west of St Sulpice-de-Falyrens. 300 dozen bottles of red bordeaux; 4,000 white. France.

Refosco. (26) Veneto; Friuli area, north and north-west of Udine. Red table wine of Refosco grapes; it is made in two grades, one lighter and the other heavier, darker and better than the first. Italy.

Regado, El. (29) South-central Aragon; Teruel. Ordinary table wines. Spain.

Regaule. (18) Jura; Arbois area. Ordinary to fair white and rosé table wines. France.

Regent, Château. (5) Côtes de St-Emilion. An unclassified *cru.* 2,000 dozen bottles of red bordeaux. France.

Região Demarcada do Douro. (30) This officially classified area of Portugal embraces the river Douro and many of its tributaries east of Régua to the Spanish frontier. It is here that the best Portuguese wines are produced.

Regnié. (11) Beaujolais. Ordinary to fair red beaujolais. France.

Reguengo, Quinta. (30) Pocinho. *Região demarcada do Douro* (q.v.). Estate and vineyard in Vila Nova de Foscoa in the Régua area. Used to belong to the Portuguese Royal Family. Portugal.

Rehborn. (23) Palatinate; south-west of Bad Münster. Fair to fine white table wine. West Germany.

Rehgasse. (24) Rhinehessia; Nierstein vineyard. Fari white table wine. West Germany.

Rehlingen. (22) Moselle; west of Saarburg. Ordinary to fair white table wine. West Germany.

Reichenau. (25) On an island in Lake Constance (Bodensee); west of Konstanz. Ordinary to fair red and white table wines. West Germany.

Reichenbach. (21) Baden; south of Darmstadt. Ordinary to fair red and white table wines. West Germany.

Reignac, Château de. (5) Entre-deux-Mers; St-Loubes, north-east of Bordeaux; 2,000 white. France.

Reignots, Aux. (8) Vosne-Romanée. *Premier cru.* Red burgundy. France.

Reil. (22) Middle Moselle; east of Zell. Ordinary, fair and fine white table wines. Best vineyards: Heisserstein, Görlay. West Germany.

Reisekahr. (24) Rhinehessia; Oppenheim vineyard. Fair to fine white table wine. West Germany.

Reiterpfad. (23) Palatinate; Middle Haardt, Ruppertsberg and Königsbach vineyards. Fine white table wine. West Germany.

Religieuses, Clos des. (5) St-Emilion; Puisseguin. An unclassified *cru.* 2,000 dozen bottles of red bordeaux. France.

Rembachel. (23) Palatinate; Wachenheim vineyard. Fair to fine white table wine. West Germany.

Rembacher Steig. (24) Rhinehessia; Nierstein vineyard. Fair to fine white table wine. West Germany.

Remera Aloque. (29) Guadalajara; north-east of Madrid. Ordinary red table wine. Spain.

Remerschen. (32) Moselle; near Wintrange. Ordinary to fair white table wine. Luxembourg.

Remich. (32) Fair white table wine is produced here. Luxembourg.

Remparts, Château des. (5) Premières Côtes de Bordeaux; Rions, north of Podensac. 600 dozen bottles of red bordeaux; 3,000 white. France.

Remparts-Guillemot, Château. (5) St-Emilion; St Christophe-des-Bardes, south-west of Parsac. An unclassified *cru.* 3,000 dozen bottles of red bordeaux. France.

Renaison. (15) Allier *département;* Roanne area, approx. forty-five miles south-east of St-Pourçain. Ordinary red table wines. France.

Renard, Clos. (16) Touraine; Montlouis vineyard, opposite Vouvray, just north-east of Tours. Fair white table wine. France.

Renard, Clos du. (31) Vaud canton; Dézaley vineyard. Fair to fine white table wine. Switzerland.

Renardes, Les. (8) Côte de Beaune; Aloxe-Corton vineyard. *Premier cru. AC Corton-Renardes.* Red burgundy. France.

Renard-Mondésir, Château. (3) Fronsadais. 8,000 dozen bottles of red bordeaux. France.

René, Domaine de. (5) Pomerol. 1,000 dozen bottles of red bordeaux. France.

Renmark. (37) South Australia; north-east of Berri. This State's first irrigation settlement was founded here in 1887 by Canadian-born brothers, W. B. and George Chaffey. There are now 8,000 acres of vines and orchards.

Renmark Growers' Distillery. (37) South Australia; Renmark, north-east of Berri. Founded 1916, was first co-operative winery and distillery in the State. There are over 500 grower-shareholders. Brandy, dessert and table wine. Australia.

Rennauds, Clos des. (31) Vaud canton; Yvorne vineyard. Fair white table wine. Switzerland.

Renon, Château. (5) Premières Côtes de Bordeaux; Tabanac, north-east of Portets. 2,000 dozen bottles of red bordeaux; 4,000 white. France.

Rennpfad. (23) Palatinate; Deidesheim vineyards. Fair to fine white table wine. 'Paradiesgarten' is the generic name for all Deidesheim wine. West Germany.

Repos-de-Saint-Martin. (16) Touraine; Chinon vineyard. Fair red table wine. France.

Repperndorf. (25) Franconia; south-east of Würzburg. Fair white table wine. West Germany.

Requena. (29) Uriel-Requena; approx. forty miles west of Valencia. Light red dry wine and dark, red, sweet dessert wine. Spain.

Respide, Château de. (5) St Pierre-de-Mons; Langon area. 5,000 dozen bottles of red bordeaux; 10,000 white. France.

Resses, Les. (10) Mâconnais; Fuissé vineyard. Fine white burgundy entitled to the *AC Pouilly-Fuissé*. France.

Restigné. (16) Touraine; Bourgueil area. Fair red table wine. France.

Retorta, Quinta. (30) *Região demarcada do Douro* (q.v.). Estate and vineyard in Ervedosa do Douro east of Régua. Portugal.

Retsina. A peculiarly Greek table wine with a resin flavour which is not usually appreciated when first tasted, but one that many grow to like in time. Greece.

Rettberg. (24) Rhinehessia; Laubenheim and Bodenheim vineyards. Fair white table wine. West Germany.

Rettigheim. (21) Baden; Bergstrasse; south of Heidelberg. Fair white table wine. West Germany.

Retzbach. (25) Franconia; north-west of Würzburg. Fair to fine white table wine. West Germany.

Retzgrube. (22) Moselle; Trier area. Ordinary to fair white table wine. West Germany.

Retzstadt. (25) Franconia; north of Würzburg. Fair to fine white table wine. West Germany.

Reuilly. (15) Quincy area, near the Cher in the Upper Loire valley. Fair white table wine, hard to find as the vineyards are being abandoned gradually. France.

Reus. (29) Tarragona. Ordinary to fair table and dessert wines. Spain.

Reusch. (25) Franconia; approx. nineteen miles south-east of Würzburg. Fair white table wine. West Germany.

Reuschberg. (25) Franconia; Hörstein vineyard. Fine white table wine. West Germany.

Reuscherberg. (24) Rhinegau; Hallgarten vineyard. Fine white table wine. West Germany.

Reutlingen. (25) Württemberg; approx. twenty miles south of Stuttgart. Ordinary to fair red and white table wines. West Germany.

Reve d'Or, Château. (5) Pomerol. 2,500 dozen bottles of red bordeaux. France.

Reverdi, Château. (4) Haut-Médoc; Listrac. *Cru bourgeois.* 1,500 dozen bottles of red bordeaux. France.

Reversées, Les. (8) Côte de Beaune; Beaune vineyard. *Premier cru.* Red burgundy. France.

Rey, Domaine du. (4) Fronsadais; Côtes de Fronsac. 3,000 dozen bottles of red bordeaux. France.

Reynauds, Domaine des. (5) Entre-deux-Mers; St Genes-de-Lomarde, east of Cadaujac. 500 dozen bottles of red bordeaux; 2,000 white. France.

Reynella. (37) South Australia. One of the State's earliest vineyards (1838); its founder, John Reynell, chose the site south of Adelaide two years after the founding of the original colony of South Australia. Taken over in 1970 by New South Wales interests.

Reysson, Château. (4) Haut-Médoc; Vertheuil. *Cru bourgeois.* 10,000 dozen bottles of red bordeaux. France.

Rheinberg. (24) Rhinehessia; Osthofen, between Worms and Alsheim, and Bingen vineyards. Fair white table wine. West Germany.

Rheinbreitbach. (21) Middle Rhine; north-west of Linz. Ordinary to fair red and white table wines. West Germany.

Rheinbrohl. (21) Middle Rhine; south-east of Linz. Fair red and white wines. West Germany.

Rheinfelden. (31) Aargau canton. 37·5 acres. Ordinary red table wine. Switzerland.

Rheingarten. (24) Rhinegau; Oestrich and Mittelheim vineyards. Fair to fine white table wine. West Germany.

Rheinhahl. (24) Rhinehessia; Nackenheim vineyard. Fair white table wine. West Germany.

Rheinhartshausen, Schloss. (24) Rhinegau. The castle and its vineyards are between Erbach and Oestrich. Fine white table wine. West Germany.

Rheinhell. (24) Rhinegau; Erbach vineyard. Fine white table wine. West Germany.

Rheinhohle. (24) Rhinehessia; Ober-Ingelheim vineyard, east of Bingen. Fair to fine white table wine. West Germany.

Rheinpfad. (24) Rhinehessia; Ludwigshöhe vineyard, between Alsheim and Dienheim. Fair white table wine. West Germany.

Rheinpflicht. (24) Rhinegau; Winkel vineyard. Fine white table wine. West Germany.

Rheintal. (24) Rhinehessia; Nackenheim vineyard. Fair to fine white table wine. West Germany.

Rhinegau. (24) The smallest of the main vinelands of the Rhineland. Its vineyards, between the Taunus hills and the Rhine, at a sharp bend of the river, face almost due south; they produce some of the greatest hocks, the finest white table wines in the world. West Germany.

Rhinehessia. The second largest of the main vinelands of the Rhineland. Its vineyards, on the left bank of the Rhine, produce ordinary to fair red and white table wines, as well as some fine and very fine white table wines. West Germany.

Rhodes. (34) North-east of Crete. The vineyards of this island have been producing wines for the past 5,000 years. Greece.

Rhône, Côtes du. (12) There are vineyards for practically the whole of the length of the Rhône river, from its high Alpine birthplace in Switzerland to the Mediterranean west of Marseilles. The wines known as Côtes du Rhône are those from the hillside vineyards of the valley of the Rhône from Ampuis, below Lyons, as far south as Avignon on the left bank and Tavel on the right bank. The Rhône *département* includes Lyons and the well-known Beaujolais country. France.

Riats, Les. (10) Mâconnais; Solutré vineyard. Fine white burgundy, entitled to the *AC Pouilly-Fuissé*. France.

Ribadavia. (29) South Galicia; Orense province. Ordinary to fair white table wine. Spain.

Ribatejo. (30) Red, white and rosé table wines from the south. Portugal.

Ribeira, Quinta. (30) *Região demarcada do Douro* (q.v.). Estate and vineyard in Sindim in the Régua area. Portugal.

Ribero or **Ribeiro.** (29) South Galicia; Orense province. Fair light, dry white table wine. Spain.

Ribeyre. (15) Haute Loire *département;* Brioude area, approx. seventy miles south of St-Pourçain. Ordinary red table wine. France.

Ribolla Gialla. (26) Udine province. Fair very light, golden, sweetish table or dessert wine. Italy.

Ribollito di Marsala. (28) Sicily; Marsala area, south-west of Trapani. Dark red, strong, ordinary table wine. Italy.

Ricadet, Domaine de. (4) Blayais; Cartelègue, north-east of Blaye. 300 dozen bottles of red bordeaux; 1,500 white. France.

Ricardell. (29) Gerona; north-east of Barcelona. Ordinary to fair sweet, red table or dessert wine. Spain.

Ricards, Château les. (4) Blayais; Cars, east of Blaye. 4,000 dozen bottles of red bordeaux; 1,000 white. France.

Ricaud, Château. (4) Blayais; Plassac, south-east of Blaye. 5,000 dozen bottles of red bordeaux. France.

Ricaud, Château de. (5) Entre-deux-Mers; Loupiac. 1,000 dozen bottles of red bordeaux; 12,500 white. France.

Ricaud, Château de. (5) Premières Côtes de Bordeaux; Villenave de Rions, north of Cérons. 700 dozen bottles of red bordeaux; 4,000 white. France.

Richardière, La. (16) Touraine; Brain-sur-l'Authion vineyard, north-west of Bourgueil. Fair white table wine. France.

Richebourg, Les. (8) Côte de Nuits; Vosne-Romanée vineyard. *Grand cru.* Red burgundy. France.

Richemone, La. (8) Côte de Nuits; Nuits-St-Georges vineyard. *Premier cru.* Red burgundy. France.

Ricla. (29) Aragón; Zaragoza. Ordinary to fair table wines. Spain.

Ricqmont, Domaine de. (5) Premières Côtes de Bordeaux; Cénac, east of Villenave d'Ornon. 500 dozen bottles of red and white bordeaux. France.

Rider, Château. (4) Bourgeais; Bourg. 5,000 dozen bottles of red bordeaux. France.

Riedlingen. (25) Baden; approx. twenty-two miles south-west of Freiburg. Ordinary to fair white table wine. West Germany.

Riesling Renano. (26) Veneto; Ronchi del Legionari vineyards, south-west of Gorizia. Fine white wine of Rhine Riesling grapes. Italy.

Riet. (25) Württemberg; north-west of Stuttgart. Ordinary to fair red and white table wines. West Germany.

Rieussec, Château. (5) Sauternes; Fargues. *Premier cru classé.* 10,000 dozen bottles of white bordeaux. France.

Rigaud, Château. (5) St-Emilion; Puisseguin. An unclassified *cru.* 3,000 dozen bottles of red bordeaux. France.

Rilly-la-Montagne. (17) Marne *département;* Verzy canton, south of Rheims. Rated *premier cru*—94% growth. 703 acres. France.

Rimaudière, La. (16) Anjou; Coteaux du Layon, Champ-sur-Layon vineyard, south of Angers. Fair to fine white table wine. France.

Rimauresq, Château de. (14) Côtes de Provence; Pignans vineyard, approx. twenty miles north-east of Toulons. Fair white and red table wines. France.

Rincon de Soto. (29) Logroño province; La Rioja area of the upper Ebro valley. Fair to fine red table wine. Spain.

Rinforzato. (26) Liguria; Monterosso al Mar vineyard, north-west of La Spezia. Ordinary to fair table and dessert white wines. Italy.

Ring. (24) Palatinate; Gleisweiler vineyard north-west of Landau. Fair white table wine. West Germany.

Ringelbach. (25) Baden; south-west of Baden-Baden. Ordinary to fair red and white table wines. West Germany.

Ringerzell. (24) Rhinehessia; Ockenheim vineyard, south-east of Bingen. Fair white table wine. West Germany.

Ringuat, Domaine de. (11) Beaujolais. Fair red beaujolais. France.

Rio Grande do Sul. (35) The southernmost state of Brazil, the vineyards of which produce approximately 75% of the total wine yield of Brazil.

Rioja, La. (29) A district of the upper Ebro valley where the little river Oja joins the Ebro. It is partly in the province of Navarre, Burgos (W.S.W. of Navarre) and Alara (W. of Navarre). It comprises the whole of Logroño to the southwest of Navarre province. The vineyards here produce the finest red table wines of Spain.

Riol. (22) Moselle; south-west of Trittenheim. Ordinary to fair white table wine. West Germany.

Rions. (5) Town and vineyards on the right bank of the Garonne, above Bordeaux, entitled to the *AC Premières Côtes de Bordeaux*. Fair red and white bordeaux. France.

Riotte, La. (8) Côte de Nuits; Morey-St-Denis vineyard. *Deuxième cru*. Red burgundy. France.

Riottes, Les. (8) Côte de Beaune; Pommard vineyard. *Deuxième cru*. Red burgundy. France.

Ripaille, Château de la. (16) Anjou; Coteaux de Saumur, Brézé vineyard, just south of Saumur. Fair to fine white table wine. France.

Ripeau, Château. (5) Côtes de St-Emilion. *Grand cru classé*. 5,000 dozen bottles of red bordeaux. France.

Rippchen. (22) Moselle; Könen vineyard, north-west of Trittenheim. Fair to fine white table wine. West Germany.

Riquewihr. (19) Haut-Rhin *département*. Fair to fine and some very fine white Alsace wine. France.

Risch. (22) Moselle; Thörnich vineyard, north-west of Trittenheim. Fair to fine white table wine West Germany.

Rischon-le-Zion. (34) The chief wine centre of Israel.

Rittergarten. (23) Palatinate; Bad Dürkheim vineyard. Fine white table wine is produced. West Germany.

Rittergut-Bangert. (23) Palatinate; Bad Kreuz-nach vineyard. Fine white table wine. West Germany.

Ritterpfad. (22) Saar; Wawern vineyard, south-west of Wiltingen. Fair to fine white table wine. West Germany.

Rivenich. (22) Moselle; north of Klüsserath. Ordinary to fair white table wine. West Germany.

Rivera. (27) Apulia; Castel del Monte vineyard, approx. seventeen miles east of L'Aquila. Fair red, white and rosé table wines made and marketed by the *Cooperativa Sociale* of the Castel del Monte growers. Italy.

Rivesaltes. (13) Roussillon town and vineyards on the foothills of the Pyrénées Orientales by the Mediterranean and near the Franco-Spanish frontier. The vineyards produce tawny dessert wine with the *AC Muscat de Rivesaltes;* and a fair tawny dessert wine with the *AC Rivesaltes*. France.

Riviera Berici. (26) Veneto; south of Vicenza. Another name for the Colli Berici (q.v.) vineyards and wines. Italy.

Rivière. (16) Touraine; Côte de Chinon vineyard. Fair red table wine. France.

Rivière, La. (3) Fronsadais; Fronsac village. Ordinary to fair red bordeaux. France.

Rivière, Château La. (3) Fronsac. 20,000 dozen bottles of red bordeaux. France.

Roaillan. (5) Village and vineyards near Langon. Ordinary to fair red and white bordeaux. France.

Robardelle. (8) Côte de Beaune; Volnay vineyard. *Premier cru*. Red burgundy. France.

Robertson. (39) Western Cape Province. Township and vineyards. South Africa.

Robinvale. (37) North-west Victoria. Irrigated wine-growing area.

Robledillo de Gata. (29) North Estremadura; Cáceres, approx. fifty miles west of Trujillo. Fair white table wine. Spain.

Robolo. (34) The island of Corfu; off the western coast of Greece. Ordinary red table wine. Greece.

Robres. (29) Aragon; Huesca. Ordinary table wines. Spain.

Roc, Château Le. (4) Bourgeais; Bourg-sur-Gironde. 2,500 dozen bottles of red bordeaux. France.

Roc, Château Le. (3) Médoc; St Christoly-de-Médoc, north of St Seurin-de-Cadourne. *Cru bourgeois*. 1,000 dozen bottles of red bordeaux. France.

Rochambeau. (16) Anjou, Coteaux de l'Aubance, Moulaines-sur-Aubance vineyard, between Angers and Saumur. Fair white table wine. France.

Rochaux, Les. (11) Beaujolais; Fleurie vineyard. *Beaujolais cru*. Red burgundy. France.

Roche, Clos de la. (16) Anjou; a vineyard in the *commune* of Rablay-sur-Layon, below Angers. Fine white table wine. France.

Roche, Clos de la. (8) Côte de Nuits; Morey-St-Denis vineyard. *Grand cru*. Red burgundy. France.

Roche, Domaine de la. (5) Graves de Bordeaux; Martillac. An unclassified *cru*. 1,200 dozen bottles of red bordeaux; 800 white. France.

Roche, La. (9) Chalonnais; St-Martin-sous-Montaigu vineyard. Fair red burgundy. France.

Roche, Le. (10) Mâconnais; Vergisson vineyard. *Premier cru*. White burgundy entitled to the *AC Pouilly-Fuissé*. France.

Roche-aux-Moines, La. (16) Anjou; Coteaux de la Loire, Savennières vineyard, below Angers. Fine white table wine. France.

Rochebelle, Château. (5) St-Emilion; St Laurent-des-Combes, west of St Etienne-de-Lisse. An unclassified *cru*. 1,000 dozen bottles of red bordeaux. France.

Rochebougre, Clos de. (16) Anjou, Coteaux de la Loire, Brain-sur-l'Authion, north-west of Bourgueil. Fair white table wine. France.

Roche-Claimault, La. (16) Touraine; Côte de Chinon vineyard. Fair red table wine. France.

Rochecorbon. (16) Touraine; Vouvray area just east of Tours. Fair to fine white table wine. France.

Roche-de-Mure, La. (16) Anjou; Coteaux de l'Aubance, Müre-Erigne vineyard, between Angers and Saumur. Fair white table wine. France.

Rochefort-sur-Loire. (16) Anjou; Coteaux du Layon, south of Angers. Fair to fine white table wine. France.

Rochegres. (11) Beaujolais; Chénas vineyard. *Premier cru. AC Moulin-à-vent*. One of the top-grade *Beaujolais crus*. Red burgundy. France.

Roche-Honneur. (16) Touraine; Beaumont-en-Véron, below Chinon. Fair red table wine. France.

Rochelle, La. (16) Touraine; Chinon vineyard. Fair red table wine. France.

Rochelle, La. (11) Beaujolais; Chénas vineyard. Fine red beaujolais. France.

Roche-Mercier, La. (16) Anjou; Coteaux de la Loire, St Georges-sur-Loire vineyard, below Angers. Fair to fine white table wine. France.

Rochepin. (16) Anjou; Coteaux de la Loire, Savennières vineyard, below Angers. Fair to fine white table wine. France.

Rocher, Château du. (5) St-Emilion; St Etienne-de-Lisse. An unclassified *cru*. 3,000 dozen bottles of red bordeaux. France.

Rocher, Clos du. (31) Vaud canton; Yvorne vineyard. Fair to fine white table wine. Switzerland.

Rocher, Cru du. (5) Entre-deux-Mers; Loupiac. 1,000 dozen bottles of red bordeaux; 2,000 white. France.

Pocher-Beauregard. (5) Pomerol. 1,000 dozen bottles of red bordeaux. France.

Rocher-Corbin, Château. (5) St-Emilion; Montagne. An unclassified *cru*. 4,000 dozen bottles of red bordeaux. France.

Rochère, La. (16) Touraine; St-Martin-le-Beau vineyard, Montlouis, opposite Vouvray, north-east of Tours. Fair to fine white table wine. France.

Rochers, Château des. (5) Sauternes; Preignac. *Cru bourgeois*. 1,500 dozen bottles of white bordeaux. France.

Roches, Clos des. (16) Touraine; Vouvray vineyard, just north-east of Tours. Fair to fine white table wine. France.

Roches, Les. (16) Anjou, Coteaux de Saumur, Parnay vineyard, Fair to fine white table wine. France.

Rochette-Saint-Jean. (16) Touraine; Chinon vineyard. Fair red table wine. France.

Roches-Saint-Paul. (16) Touraine; Ligré vineyard, above Chinon. Fair red table wine. France.

Rochette, La. (11) Beaujolais; Chénas vineyard. *Premier cru. AC Moulin-à-vent*. Red burgundy. France.

Rochusberg. (24) Rhinehessia; Bingen vineyard. Fair white table wine. West Germany.

Rochusweg. (24) Rhinehessia; Bingen vineyard. Fair white table wine. West Germany.

Rociano del Condado. (29) Huelva. Ordinary to fair table wines. Spain.

Rocs-Marchand, Château. (5) St-Emilion; Montagne. An unclassified *cru*. 5,000 dozen bottles of red bordeaux. France.

Rödelsee. (25) Franconia; south-east of Würzburg. Fair to fine white table wine. West Germany.

Rodensteiner. (24) Rhinehessia; Dalsheim vineyard, north-west of Worms. Fair white table wine. West Germany.

Rodillana. (29) West Old Castile; Valladolid, approx. seventy miles north of Avila. Ordinary to fair red, white and *clarete* table wines. Spain.

Rodo, Quinta. *Região demarcada do Douro* (q.v.). Estate and vineyard in Godim in the Régua area. Portugal.

Roeda, Quinta. (30) *Região demarcada do Douro* (q.v.). Estate and vineyard in Pinhao north-east of Régua. Considered one of the finest vineyards of the river Douro. Veiga Cabral wrote in 1865 'If the wine district were a golden ring, Roeda would be the diamond in that ring'. Portugal.

Roetschelt. (32) Bech-Kleinmacher; south-east

of Luxembourg city. Fair white table wine. Luxembourg.

Rognet-Corton, Clos. (8) Côte de Beaune; Ladoix-Serrigny vineyard. *Premier cru. AC Corton.* White burgundy. France.

Rohr. (24) Rhinehessia; Nierstein vineyard. Fine white table wine. West Germany.

Rohrendorf-St Laurent. (33) Lower Austria. Fair red and white table wine. Austria.

Rohrgasse. (24) Rhinehessia; Oppenheim vineyard. Fair to fine white table wine. West Germany.

Roi, Château de. (5) Côtes de St-Emilion. An unclassified *cru.* 2,500 dozen bottles of red bordeaux. France.

Roi, Clos du. (8) Côte de Beaune; Aloxe-Corton vineyard. *Premier cru.* Red burgundy. France.

Roi, Clos du. (8) Côte de Nuits; Chenôvc vineyards. *Deuxième cru* and *troisième cru.* Now taken into the suburbs of Dijon-Chenôve (1971). France.

Roi, Domaine de. (5) Côtes de St-Emilion. An unclassified *cru.* 2,000 dozen bottles of red bordeaux. France.

Roi-de-Fombrauge, Château. (5) St-Emilion; St Christophe-des-Bardes, west of St Etienne-de-Lisse. An unclassified *cru.* 1,800 dozen bottles of red bordeaux. France.

Roilette, La. (11) Beaujolais; Fleurie vineyard. Fine red beaujolais. France.

Roland, Domaine. (5) Graves de Bordeaux; Langon. An unclassified *cru.* 500 dozen bottles of red bordeaux; 1,500 white. France.

Rolandsberg. (25) Palatinate; Königsbach vineyard. Fine white table wine. West Germany.

Rolland, Château. (4) Haut-Médoc; Pauillac. *Cru bourgeois.* 3,500 dozen bottles of red bordeaux. France.

Roma Wine Company. (36) California; Fresno. Table, dessert and sparkling wines; also brandy and vermouth. U.S.A.

Romagnano (Romanesco). (27) Lazio; Amagni vineyard, approx. twenty miles north-east of Velletri. Fair white table wine. Italy.

Romalo. (37) South Australia; Magill, Adelaide suburb. State's largest sparkling wine cellars, founded 1919.

Romana, La. (29) Alicante; approx. forty miles south of Valencia. Ordinary to fair table wines. Spain.

Romanèche-Thorins. (10) Mâconnais village; at the southern end where it joins Beaujolais. Ordinary to fair red and white wines; some fine table wines. France.

Romanée, La. (8) Côte de Nuits; Vosne-Romanée vineyard. *Grand cru.* Red burgundy. France.

Romanée-Conti, La. (8) Côte de Nuits; Vosne-Romanée vineyard. *Grand cru.* Red burgundy. France.

Romanée-Saint-Vivant. (8) Côte de Nuits; Vosne-Romanée vineyard. *Grand cru.* Red burgundy. France.

Romaneira, Quinta. (30) *Região demarcada do Douro* (q.v.). Estate and vineyard in Cotas in the Régua area. Portugal.

Romarigo, Quinta. (30) *Região demarcada do Douro* (q.v.). Estate and vineyard in São João de Lobrigos in the Régua area. Portugal.

Romefort, Château. (4) Haut-Médoc; Cussac. *Cru bourgeois.* 2,000 dozen bottles of red bordeaux. France.

Romeira, Quinta. (30) *Região demarcada do Douro* (q.v.). Estate and vineyard in São João de the Régua area. Portugal.

Romer, Château. (5) Fargues. *Deuxième cru classé.* 1,500 dozen bottles of white bordeaux. France.

Römerberg. (24) Rhinehessia; Alsheim vineyard. Fair white table wine. West Germany.

Römerberg. (24) Nahe; Windesheim vineyard; north-west of Bad Kreuznach. Fair white table wine. West Germany.

Römerpfad. (22) Moselle; Mehring vineyard, south-west of Klüsserath. Ordinary to fair white table wine. West Germany.

Römerstein. (24) Rhinehessia; Mettenheim vineyard, south of Alsheim. Fair white table wine. West Germany.

Rommelshausen. (25) Württemberg; just east of Stuttgart. Ordinary to fair red and white table wines. West Germany.

Roncao, Quinta. (30) *Região demarcada do Douro* (q.v.). Estate and vineyard in Casal de Loivos and Vilarinho de Cotas in the Régua area. Portugal.

Roncière, La. (8) Côte de Nuits; Nuits-St-Georges vineyard. *Premier cru.* Red burgundy. France.

Roncières. (6) Chablis vineyard. *Premier cru.* White burgundy. France.

Ronciglione. (27) Lazio; Colli Cimini, south-east of Viterbo. Fair, dry or semi-sweet white table wine. Italy.

Rondillon-Haut-Loupiac, Château de. (5) Entre-deux-Mers; Loupiac. 1,000 dozen bottles of red bordeaux; 4,000 white. France.

Ropa. (34) The island of Corfu; off the western coast of Greece. Ordinary red table wine. Greece.

Roques, Château de. (5) St-Emilion; Puisseguin. An unclassified *cru.* 10,000 dozen bottles of red bordeaux. France.

Roques, Domain de. (5) Premières Côtes de

Bordeaux; Ste-Eulalie, north-east of Bordeaux. 2,000 dozen bottles of red bordeaux. France.

Roquette, Domaine de la. (12) Côtes du Rhone; Châteauneuf-du-Pape vineyard. Fair to fine red table wine. France.

Roquevielle, Château de. (5) St-Emilionnais; St Philippe-d'Aiguil, east of Parsac. An unclassified *cru*. 6,000 dozen bottles of red bordeaux. France.

Roqueys, Château. (5) Premières Côtes de Bordeaux; Carignan, east of Bègles. 1,200 dozen bottles of red bordeaux. France.

Roriz, Quinta. (30) *Região demarcada do Douro* (q.v.). Estate and vineyard in *Ervedosa do Douro* east of Régua. Portugal.

Rosal. (29) West-central Galicia; Pontevedra. Light and crisp white table wines. Spain.

Roschbach. (23) Palatinate; between Landau and Edenkoben. Ordinary to fair and some fine red and white table wines. West Germany.

Rose, Cru La. (5) Côtes de St-Emilion. An unclassified *cru*. 2,000 dozen bottles of red bordeaux. France.

Rose, Cru La. (5) Côtes de St-Emilion. An unclassified *cru*. 600 dozen bottles of red bordeaux. France.

Rosenberg. The name given to many Rhineland and Moselle vineyard sites. West Germany.

Rosenberg. (32) Moselle; Grevenmacher vineyard. Fair white table wine. Luxembourg.

Rosenberg. (24) Nahe; Windesheim vineyard, north-west of Bad Kreuznach. Fair white table wine. West Germany.

Rosenbrücke. (24) Rhinehessia; Freimersheim vineyard, south-west of Alsheim. Fair white table wine. West Germany.

Rosenbuckel. (23) Palatinate; Freinsheim vineyard. Fair white table wine. West Germany.

Roseneck. (24) Rhinegau; Rüdesheim vineyard. Fair to fine white table wine. West Germany.

Rosengärtchen. (22) Moselle; Neumagen vineyard. Fair white table wine. West Germany.

Rosenheck. (24) Nahe; Winzenheim vineyard, just north of Bad Kreuznach. Fair white table wine. West Germany.

Rosenhecke. (29) Nahe; Niederhausen vineyard, west of Bad Münster. Fair to fine white table wine. West Germany.

Rosenkranz. (22) Moselle; Ürzig vineyard. Fair white table wine. West Germany.

Rose-Pourret, Château La. (5) Côtes de St-Emilion. An unclassified *cru*. 3,500 dozen bottles of red bordeaux. France.

Rose-Rol, Château La. (5) Côtes de St-Emilion. An unclassified *cru*. 3,500 dozen bottles of red bordeaux. France.

Roseworthy. (37) South Australia; State Agricultural College includes Australia's only school of winemaking, where new $300,000 model winery was opened late 1971. Students have come from Cyprus, India and New Zealand to study here.

Rossberg. (25) Franconia; Würzburg vineyard. Fine white table wine. West Germany.

Rossel. (24) Nahe; Niederhausen vineyard, west of Bad Münster. Fine white table wine. West Germany.

Rossese di Val di Nervia. (26) Liguria; Bordighera, approx. twenty miles south-west of Imperia. Ruby-red table wine of Rossese grapes of ordinary to fair quality. Italy.

Rossese Rosato. (26) Liguria; Calice Ligure, south-west of Savona. Popular rosé table wine of ordinary quality. Italy.

Rossissimi del Reggiano. (27) Emilia-Romagna. Ordinary dark red table wine mostly used for the making of cheap rosé table wines. Italy.

Rosso dei Colli Euganei. (26) Veneto; Padua area vineyards, approx. twenty miles south-east of Vincenza. Ordinary to fair red wine. Italy.

Rosso dei Colli Lanuvi. (27) Lazio; Genzano, north-west of Velletri, and Lanuvio vineyards. Ordinary red table wines. Italy.

Rosso del Bosco. (27) Emilia-Romagna; Val Comacchio, approx. thirty miles south-east of Ferrara, Ferrara province. Fair, dry, rather sharp, red table wine. Italy.

Rosso della Sila. (28) Calabria; Cosenza vineyard, approx. thirty-five miles north-west of Cantanzaro. Ordinary red table wine. Italy.

Rosso del Venda. (26) Veneto; Padua area, approx. twenty miles south-east of Vincenza. Ordinary to fair red table wine. Italy.

Rosso di Bellagio. (26) Lombardy; Como area. Fair to good red table wine. Italy.

Rosso di Caldaro. (26) Alto Adige; Bolzano area. Ordinary red table wine. Italy.

Rosso di Dorgali. (28) Sardinia; Nuoro province. Very strong, dry red table wine. Italy.

Rosso di Terlaner. (26) Alto Adige; Bolzano area. Ordinary red table wine. Italy.

Rosso Montu. (26) Veneto; Pavia area. Ordinary hard, white table wine. Italy.

Rosso Piceno. (27) The Marches; Ascoli Piceno vineyards, approx. thirty-five miles north-east of L'Aquila. Ordinary red table wine. Italy.

Rosso Rubino del Viverone. (26) Piedmont; Cavaglia vineyards, Vercelli province. Ordinary to fair full red table wine. (11°–12°). Italy.

Rosstal. (24) Rhinehessia; Osthofen vineyard, between Worms and Alsheim. Fair white table wine. West Germany.

Rosswag. (25) Württemberg; north-west of Stuttgart. Ordinary red and white table wines. West Germany.

Rosswiese. (24) Rhinehessia; Dienheim vineyard. Fair white table wine. West Germany.

Rosteisen. (24) Rhinehessia; Gau-Bischofsheim vineyard, west of Nackenheim. Fair to fine white table wine. West Germany.

Rota Tent. (29) Cadiz. Extremely dark red wine. Spain.

Rotenberg. (21) Baden; south of Heidelberg. Ordinary to fair red and white table wines. West Germany.

Rotenfels. (24) Nahe; Münster-bei-Bingerbrück vineyard. Fair white table wine. West Germany.

Rotenstein. (24) Rhinehessia; Dalsheim vineyard, north-west of Worms. Fair white table wine. West Germany.

Roterd. (22) Moselle; Dhron vineyard, between Neumagen and Wintrich. Fair to fine white table wine. West Germany.

Roterde. (24) Nahe; Norheim vineyard, just south-west of Bad Münster. Fair white table wine. West Germany.

Rothbury Estate. (37) New South Wales; Pokolbin, Hunter Valley, north-east of Sydney. Conducted by syndicate formed 1968 by eleven professional and business men. Plantings of Shiraz, Cabernet Sauvignon, Semillon, Chardonnay, Blanquette, Pinot Noir, Merlot, Rhine Riesling. Traminer. Australia.

Rothenberg. (23) Nahe; Altenbamberg vineyard, Alsenz Valley, south-west of Bad Kreuznach. Fair white table wine. West Germany.

Rothenberg. (24) Rhinegau; Geisenheim vineyard. Fine white table wine. West Germany.

Rothenberg. (24) Rhinegau; Rauenthal vineyard. Fair to fine white table wine. West Germany.

Rothenberg. (24) Rhinehessia; Gau-Algesheim vineyard, south of Mittelheim. Fair white table wine. West Germany.

Rothlay. (22) Moselle; Niederemmel vineyard, south of Piesport. Fair to fine white table wine. West Germany.

Rotkäppchen. (22) Moselle; Eller vineyard. Fair white table wine. West Germany.

Rotkirch. (22) Moselle; Erden vineyard. Fair to fine white table wine. West Germany.

Rotlay. (22) Moselle; Zeltingen vineyard. Fair to fine table wine. West Germany.

Rott. (25) Baden, Bergstrasse; Auerbach vineyard, south-east of Karlsruhe. Fair white table wine. West Germany.

Röttingen. (25) Franconia; approx. nineteen miles south of Würzburg. Fair to fine white table wine. West Germany.

Rottland. (24) Rhinegau; Geisenheim vineyard. Fine white table wine. West Germany.

Roualere, La. (16) Anjou; Dampierre-sur-Loire, a *commune* on the Saumur hillsides. Fair red table wine. France.

Rouchards, Les. (10) Mâconnais; Romanèche-Thorins vineyard. *Premier cru.* Red burgundy. France.

Roudier, Château. (5) St-Emilion; Montagne. An unclassified *cru.* 12,500 dozen bottles of red bordeaux. France.

Rouet, Château. (5) Fronsadais; St Germain-la-Riviere, north-west of Fronsac. An unclassified *cru.* 12,000 dozen bottles of red bordeaux. France.

Rouffach. (19) Haut-Rhin *département.* Medium to fair white Alsace table wine. France.

Rouge-Homme. (37) South Australia; at Coonawarra. Fine quality red table wine. Australia.

Rouges-du-Bas, Les. (8) Côte de Nuits; Flagey-Echézeaux vineyard. *Premier cru.* Red burgundy. France.

Rouges-du-Dessus, Les. (8) Côte de Nuits; Flagey-Echézeaux vineyard. *Deuxième cru.* Red burgundy. France.

Rouget, Château. (5) Pomerol. *Grand cru.* 8,000 dozen bottles of red bordeaux. France.

Roulecul. (16) Anjou; a vineyard of the *commune* of St Aubin-de-Luigné, below Angers. Fair white table wine. France.

Roulerie, La. (16) Anjou; St Aubin-de-Luigné, below Angers. Fair white table wine. France.

Rousseau-Deslandes. (8) Beaune vineyard. Hospices de Beaune *cuvée.* Red burgundy. France.

Rousseliere, La. (16) Anjou; Coteaux de la Loire, La Possonnière vineyard, below Angers. Fair white table wine. France.

Rousset, Château. (3) Bourgeais; Somonac, north of Bourg. 7,500 dozen bottles of red bordeaux. France.

Rousset, Château. (18) Jura; Salin area. Fair red and white table wines. France.

Roussette, Vin de. (12) Savoie and Upper Rhône valley; ordinary to fair white table wine made from the white Roussette grape. France.

Roussillon. (13) Former province between Languedoc and the Franco-Spanish frontier on the Mediterranean. Its best wines are its dessert sweet wines. A vast quantity of *vin ordinaire* is made in Roussillon and much fortified wine, as well as a great quantity of wine vinegar. France.

Roussillon des Aspres. (13) Pyrénées Orientales *département.* Ordinary to fair *V.D.Q.S.* table wine, the red 11·5° and the white 12°. France.

Roustit, Château. (5) Côtes de Bordeaux; Ste Croix-du-Mont. 1,000 dozen bottles of red bordeaux; 5,000 white. France.

Roustit, Domaine de. (5) Ste Croix-du-Mont. 800 dozen bottles of white bordeaux. France.

Roxheim. (24) Nahe; north-west of Bad Kreuznach. Fair to fine white table wine. West Germany.

Roy, Château du. (5) Sauternes area; Preignac. *Cru bourgeois.* 1,000 dozen bottles of white bordeaux. France.

Roy, Clos du. (5) Pomerol. 1,500 dozen bottles of red bordeaux. France.

Royal-Médoc. The name given to the second-best red bordeaux of Château Cantemerle. France.

Rozay, Château. (12) Côtes du Rhône; Condrieu vineyard. Fine white table wine. France.

Rozier, Château. (5) St-Emilion; St Laurent-des-Combes, west of St Etienne-de-Lisse. An unclassified *cru*. 600 dozen bottles of red bordeaux. France.

Rua de Valdeorras. (29) South Galicia; Orense province. Ordinary to fair table wines. Spain.

Ruberberg. (22) Moselle; Poltersdorf vineyard, south-west of Bruttig. Ordinary to fair white table wine. West Germany.

Rubino. (28) Calabria; Reggio di Calabria. Ordinary very strong red table wine. Italy.

Rubino del Piave. (26) Veneto; vineyards on Piave River plain, north-east of Venice. Ordinary red table wine. Italy.

Rubino di Canavisse. (26) Liguria; Savona province. Ordinary, sharply dry, red table wine. Italy.

Ruchots, Les. (8) Côte de Nuits; Morey-St-Denis vineyard. *Premier cru.* Red burgundy. France.

Ruchottes-Chambertin and **Clos des Ruchottes.** (8) Côte de Nuits; Gevrey-Chambertin vineyard. *Grand cru.* Red burgundy. France.

Ruchsel. (33) Bratislava (Pressburg); thirty-five miles south-east of Pressburg. Ordinary to fair red and white table wines. Czechoslovakia.

Rück. (25) Franconia; approx. twenty-five miles east of Darmstadt. Ordinary to fair white table wine. West Germany.

Rüdelstein. (23) Palatinate; Kallstadt vineyard. Fair to fine white table wine. West Germany.

Rüdesheim. (24) Rhinegau. Ordinary, fair, fine and some very fine white table wines. West Germany.

Rüdesheim-Eibingen. (24) Rhinegau; outside Rüdesheim. Ordinary to fair white table wine. West Germany.

Rüdesheim-Nahe. (24) Nahe; west of Bad Kreuznach. Fair to fine white table wine. Its Rüdesheimer Rosengarten wine must not be confused with a wine from the great Rhinegau town. West Germany.

Rue-aux-Porc. (8) Côte de Beaune; Pommard vineyard. *Deuxième cru.* Red burgundy. France.

Rueda. (29) West Old Castile; Valladolid, approx. seventy miles north of Avila. Ordinary white table wine and fair *clarete* wine. Spain.

Ruelle, En. (9) Chalonnais; St Martin-sous-Montaigu vineyard. Ordinary to fair red burgundy. France.

Rue-Neuve, La. (16) Touraine; Vernon-sur-Brenne vineyard, above Tours. Fair white table wine. France.

Rufina. (27) Tuscany; town not far from Florence. Fair to fine red chianti. Italy.

Rufina Bianco. Another name for *pomino bianco* (q.v.). Italy.

Rugiens-Bas, Les. (8) Côte de Beaune; Pommard vineyard. *Premier cru.* Red burgundy. France.

Rugiens-Hauts. (8) Côte de Beaune; Pommard vineyard. *Premier cru.* Red burgundy. France.

Rully. (9) Chalonnais. Ordinary, fair and some fine red and white burgundy. France.

Rümmelsheim. (22) Nahe; south-west of Bingen. Fair white table wine. West Germany.

Rust. (33) Burgenland; south-east Austria, close to the Hungarian frontier. Fair to fine white table wine. Austria.

Rust. (24) Rhinehessia; Alsheim vineyard. Fair white table wine. West Germany.

Rute. (29) North-central Andalusia; Córdoba area north-east of Seville. Fair white table wine. Spain.

Rutherford. (36) California; Napa Valley. Location of Beaulieu (q.v.) and Inglenook (q.v.) vineyards and wineries. Mostly quality wines. U.S.A.

Rutherglen. (37) Victoria; Murray River wine region in the north-east of Victoria. There are many dessert wines produced, notably luscious muscats, and dry reds.

Ruwer. (22) Small river which joins the upper Moselle near Trier. Its slatey vineyards on very steep slopes produce some fine and very fine white table wines. West Germany.

Ruzica. (33) Very popular Serbian rosé wine varying from light to deep red produced from the Prokupac grape. Yugoslavia.

Ryecroft Vineyard. (37) South Australia; McLaren Vale, approx. twenty-five miles south of Adelaide. 200 acres; fair to fine table wines. Sold by the Ingoldby family to the Reed paper group in 1970. Australia.

Saale. (25) Franconia; valley on one of the tributaries of the river Main. Ordinary to fair white table wines; also some fine white wines. West Germany.

Saaleck, Schloss. (25) Franconia. Fair white table wine. West Germany.

Saar. (22) A tributary of the Moselle. The vineyards on the steep hillsides from Saarburg to Konz, near Trier, where the Saar joins the Moselle, produce ordinary, fair, fine and some very fine white table wines. Made from Riesling grapes they are very variable in quality but in good vintage years the wine is very good indeed. Saar wines carry the label Mosel-Saar-Ruwer. West Germany.

Saarburg-mit-Beurig-und-Niederleuken. (22) Saar. Ordinary, fair and some fine white table wines in good years. West Germany.

Saarfels, Schloss. (22) Saar; Serrig vineyard. Fair to fine white table wine. West Germany.

Sable, Château le. (5) St-Emilion; St Laurent-des-Combes, west of St Etienne-de-Lisse. An unclassified *cru*. 2,000 dozen bottles of red bordeaux. France.

Sables-Saint-Emilion. (5) An *AC* given to the red wines from vineyards in a sandy stretch of land between Pomerol and Libourne. France.

Sablet-Pres l'Ouvère. (12) Côtes du Rhône; north-east of Orange. Ordinary to fair red table wine. France.

Sablière, Château La. (5) Côtes de St-Emilion. An unclassified *cru*. 2,500 dozen bottles of red bordeaux. France.

Sablonnerie, La. (16) Anjou; Coteaux du Layon, Rablay-sur-Layon, south of Angers. Fine white table wine. France.

Sablons, Les. (16) Touraine; Bourgueil vineyard. Fair red table wine. France.

Sabordela, Quinta. (30) *Região demarcada do Douro* (q.v.). Estate and vineyard near Pinhão north-east of Régua. Portugal.

Sacedon. (29) Guadalajara; approx. thirty miles north-east of Madrid. Ordinary to fair red table wine. Madrid.

Sackträger. (24) Rhinehessia; Oppenheim vineyard. Fair to fine white table wine. West Germany.

Sacramento. (36) A county and a city, capital of California. The Sacramento Valley is the northern portion of the Central Valley; and the San Joaquin Valley is the southern part. Lodi is in San Joaquin County and also in the San Joaquin Valley. People would not refer to Lodi as being in the Sacramento region even though it is only 30 miles from Sacramento. Sacramento is a very minor wine producer. U.S.A.

Sacrantino. (27) Umbria; Assisi, south-east of

Perugia. Red dessert wine made in two grades, either sweet or semi-sweet. Italy.

Sacy. (17) Marne *département;* Ville-en-Tardenois canton, south-west of Rheims. Rated *premier cru* —90% growth. 301 acres. France.

Sadova. (33) South-west region; Dragasani area. Fair, medium-sweet rosé wine. Rumania.

Sagarcea. (33) Fair, or fine, sweet red table wine of Pinot Noir grapes left on the vine to dry in the sun. Rumania.

Sagra. (29) West New Castile; Toledo, approx. forty miles south-west of Madrid. Ordinary to fair table wines. Spain.

Sagrado, Quinta. (30) *Região demarcada do Douro* (q.v.). Estate and vineyard in Gouvaes in the Régua area. Portugal.

Sagunto. (29) Valencia. Ordinary to fair sweet red table wine. Spain.

Sahler. (24) Rhinehessia; Gau-Bischofsheim vineyard, west of Nackenheim. Fair to fine white table wine. West Germany.

Saillandrie, La. (16) Anjou; Coteaux du Layon, Faye d'Anjou vineyard, south of Angers. Fine white table wine. France.

St Agnes. (37) Renmark; north-east of Berri. One of Australia's best known brandies, made by Angove's.

Saint-Aignan. (3) Entre-deux-Mers; La Réole, north-west of Langon. Ordinary to fair red bordeaux. France.

Saint-Amand, Château. (5) Sauternes; Preignac. *Cru bourgeois.* 4,000 dozen bottles of white bordeaux. France.

Saint-Amour. (10) Mâconnais-Beaujolais border. Fair red burgundy. France.

Saint-Andelain. (10) Pouilly-sur-Loire. Fair to fine white table wine. France.

Saint-André, Domaine. (12) Côtes du Rhône; Gigondas vineyard. Fair to fine red table wine. France.

Saint-Andre-Bellevue, Château. (5) Néac; east of Pomerol. 2,000 dozen bottles of red bordeaux. France.

Saint-André-Corbin, Château. (5) St-Emilion; St-Georges. An unclassified *cru*. 5,000 dozen bottles of red bordeaux. France.

Saint-Aubin. (31) Neuchâtel canton; Sauges vineyard. 60·7 acres. Fair to fine white table wine. Switzerland.

Saint-Aubin-Côte de Beaune. (8) Côte d'Or. *AC Côte de Beaune Villages.* Ordinary to fair red and white burgundy. France.

Saint-Aubin-de-Luigné. (16) Anjou; Coteaux du Layon, south of Angers. Fair and fine white table wines. France.

Saint-Augustine-la-Grave, Château. (5) Graves

de Bordeaux; Martillac. An unclassified *cru*. 2,000 dozen bottles of red bordeaux. France.

Saint-Avertin. (16) Touraine; just south-east of Tours. Ordinary to fair red table wine. France.

Saint-Blaise. (31) Neuchâtel canton. 101 acres. Fair to fine white table wine. Switzerland.

Saint-Bonnet, Château. (3) Haut-Médoc; St Christoly-de-Médoc, north-west of St Seurin-de-Cadourne. *Cru bourgeois*. 6,000 dozen bottles of red bordeaux. France.

Saint-Chinian. (13) Hérault *département;* north-west of Béziers. *V.D.Q.S.* 11°. Red table wine. France.

Saint-Christoly, Château. (3) Médoc; St Christoly-de-Médoc, north-west of St Seurin-de-Cadourne. *Cru bourgeois*. 2,000 dozen bottles of red bordeaux. France.

Saint-Christoly-de-Médoc. (3) Médoc; north-west of St Seurin-de-Cadourne. Ordinary to fair red bordeaux. France.

Saint-Christophe, Château. (5) St-Emilion; St Christophe-des-Bardes. An unclassified *cru*. 6,000 dozen bottles of red bordeaux. France.

Saint-Christophe-des-Bardes. (5) St-Emilion; west of St Etienne-de-Lisse. Ordinary to fair red bordeaux. France.

Saint-Come, Clos. (16) Touraine; Vouvray vineyard, just north-east of Tours. Fair to fine white table wine. France.

Saint Cyr-en-Bourg. (16) Anjou; Saumur area. Ordinary to fair red, white and rosé table wines. France.

Saint Cyr-sur-Mer. (14) Côtes de Provence; Bandol area. Ordinary to fair red, white and rosé table wines. France.

Saint-Denis, Clos. (8) Côte de Nuits; Morey-St-Denis vineyard. *Premier cru*. Red burgundy. France.

Saint-Didier. (12) Côtes du Rhône; Côtes du Ventoux, south-west of Ouveze. Fair to fine red table wine. France.

Sainte-Barbe. (16) Anjou; Coteaux de la Loire, Chalonne-sur-Loire. Fair white table wine. France.

Sainte-Cécile-les-Vignes. (12) Vaucluse *département;* Côtes du Rhône. Mostly rosé table wines. France.

Sainte-Croix-du-Mont. (5) Entre-deux-Mers. Ordinary red and fair to fine white bordeaux. France.

Sainte-Eulalie. (3) Entre-deux-Mers; north-east of Bordeaux. Ordinary to fair red and white bordeaux. France.

Sainte-Foy-Bordeaux. (3) Town and *commune* south of the Dordogne above Castillon. Ordinary red and white bordeaux. France.

Saint-Elie. (34) Thira (Santorini); south-east of

Greece. Ordinary to fair red table wine. Greece.

Saint-Emilion. (5) Ancient little town overlooking the right bank of the Dordogne river valley. Its vineyards are divided into *Côtes* and *Graves*, roughly the vineyards of the upper (Côtes) and lower (Graves) slopes of the hills upon which St-Emilion stands. The vineyards of St-Emilion, and those of the surrounding country, known as St-Emilionnais, produce a great quantity of red wines, mostly ordinary to fair, but much wine also of fine and exceptionally fine quality. France.

Saint-Emilion, Clos. (5) Côtes de St-Emilion. 2,000 dozen bottles of red bordeaux. France.

Sainte-Radegonde. (16) Touraine; Vouvray area, just north-east of Tours. Fair white table wine. France.

Sainte-Rosaline. (14) Côtes de Provence; Les Arcs vineyard, east of Toulon. Fair red and white table wines. France.

Saint-Estèphe, Château. (4) Haut-Médoc; St-Estèphe. *Cru bourgeois supérieur*. 3,000 dozen bottles of red bordeaux. France.

Saint-Etienne-de-Lisse. (5) Village and vineyards east of St-Emilion, with the *AC St-Emilion*. Ordinary to fair red bordeaux. France.

Saint-Etienne-les-Cuilleres. (11) Beaujolais. *AC Beaujolais Villages*. Ordinary to fair red burgundy. France.

Saint-Etienne-la-Varenne. (11) Beaujolais. *AC Beaujolais Villages*. Ordinary to fair red burgundy. France.

Saint-Ferréol. (18) Salins vineyard, Jura. Fair red table wine. France.

Saint-Gayan, Domaine. (12) Côtes du Rhône; Gigondas vineyard. Fair red table wine. France.

Saint-Genès. (3) St-Emilionnais; north of Castillon. Ordinary red and white bordeaux. France.

Saint-Genoux-de-Scisse. (10) Mâconnais. Ordinary to fair burgundy. Mostly *Mâcon Blanc*, some red. France.

Saint-Genoux-le-Scisse. (10) Mâconnais. Ordinary to fair red burgundy. France.

Saint-Georges. (5) St-Emilion. *AC St George-St-Emilion*. Ordinary to fair red bordeaux. France.

Saint-Georges, Les. (8) Côte de Nuits. Perhaps Nuits-St-Georges' best vineyard. *Premier cru*. Red burgundy. France.

Saint-Georges-Côte-Pavie, Château. (5) Côtes de St-Emilion. *Grand cru classé*. 2,500 dozen bottles of red bordeaux. France.

Saint-Georges-sur-Layon. (16) Anjou; Coteaux du Layon, south of Angers. Fair to fine white and rosé table wines. France.

Saint-Georges-sur-Loire. (16) Anjou; Coteaux de la Loire, below Angers. Fair white table wines. France.

Saint-Germain, Château. (3) Premières Côtes de Bordeaux; St Germain-de-Graves, north-east of Langon. 1,000 dozen bottles of red bordeaux; 1,500 white. France.

Saint-Germain d'Esteuil. (3) Médoc; west of St Seurin-de-Cadourne. Ordinary to fair red bordeaux. France.

Saint-Germain-la-Rivière. (3) Fronsadais; north-west of Fronsac. Ordinary to fair red bordeaux. France.

Saint Hippolyte. (5) A village and vineyards near St-Emilion with the *AC St-Emilion*. Ordinary to fair red bordeaux. France.

Saint-Hippolyte. (19) Haut-Rhin *département*. Medium to fair white Alsace table wine. France.

Saint-Jacques. (16) Touraine; Jasnières vineyard, north of Vouvray. Fair white table wine. France.

Saint-Jacques, Clos. (8) Côte de Nuits; Gevrey-Chambertin vineyard. *Premier cru*. Red burgundy. France.

Saint-Jean. (16) Touraine; Chinon vineyard. Fair red table wine. France.

Saint-Jean, Clos. (8) Côte de Beaune; Chassagne-Montrachet vineyard. *Premier cru*. Red burgundy. France.

Saint-Jean, Clos. (16) Anjou; vineyard of the Turquant *commune* on the Saumur hillsides. Fair red table wine. France.

Saint-Jean-des-Mauvrets. (16) Anjou; Coteaux de l'Aubance, between Angers and Saumur. Fair white table wine. France.

Saint-Joseph. (11) Beaujolais *commune*. *AC Beaujolais Villages*. Red burgundy. France.

Saint-Julien. (4) Haut-Médoc; south of Pauillac. Formerly known as St Julien-Beychevelle. Fair to fine, and some very fine red bordeaux. France.

Saint-Just-sur-Dive. (16) Anjou; Saumur area. Fair red, white and rosé table wines. France.

Saint-Lager. (11) Beaujolais. Ordinary to fair red burgundy. France.

Saint-Lambert-du-Lattay. (16) Anjou; Coteaux du Layon, south of Angers. Fair to fine white and rosé table wines. France.

Saint-Laurent. (4) Haut-Médoc; north of Listrac. Fair to fine and some very fine red bordeaux. France.

Saint-Laurent-des-Combes. (5) Village and vineyards near St-Emilion, west of St-Etienne-de-Lisse. Ordinary to fair red bordeaux, with the *AC St-Emilion*. France.

Saint-Louans. (16) Touraine; Chinon vineyard. Fair red table wine. France.

Saint-Louis, Domaine. (5) St-Emilion; St-Georges, north of St-Emilion. An unclassified *cru*. 1,600 dozen bottles of red bordeaux. France.

Saint-Louis-du-Bosc, Château. (4) Haut-Médoc; St-Julien, south of Pauillac. *Cru bourgeois*. 1,000 dozen bottles of red bordeaux. France.

Saint-Maixant. (5) Premières Côtes de Bordeaux; south-east of Ste Croix-du-Mont. Village and vineyard with the *AC Premières Côtes de Bordeaux*. France.

Saint-Marc, Clos. (8) Côte de Nuits; Premeaux vineyard. *Premier cru*. Red burgundy. France.

Saint-Martin. (14) Côtes de Provence; Taradeau vineyard. Fair red and white table wines. France.

Saint-Martin, Clos. (5) Côtes de St-Emilion. An unclassified *cru*. 2,000 dozen bottles of red bordeaux. France.

Saint-Martin, Domaine de. (14) Côtes de Provence; Taradeau vineyard, St-Martin. Fair red and white table wines. France.

St Martin-d'Ablois. (17) Marne *département*; Epernay canton, south-west of Epernay. Rated— 86% growth. 170 acres. France.

Saint-Martin-le-Beau. (16) Touraine; Montlouis area, opposite Vouvray. Fair white table wine. France.

Saint-Martin-sous-Montaigu. (9) Chalonnais; near Givry. Fair red burgundy. France.

Saint-Mathurin. (16) Touraine; Vouvray area, just north-east of Tours. Ordinary to fair white table wine. France.

Saint-Médard d'Eyrans. (5) Graves de Bordeaux; south-east of Cadaujac. Ordinary to fair red bordeaux. France.

Saint Médard-en-Jalle. (4) Haut-Médoc; near Le Pian-Médoc. Ordinary to fair red bordeaux. France.

Saint-Melanie-sur-Aubance. (16) Anjou; Coteaux de l'Aubance, between Angers and Saumur. Fair to fine white and rosé table wines. France.

Saint-Michel, Clos. (14) Côtes de Provence; Cassis vineyard. Fair red table wine. France.

Saint-Morillon. (5) Graves de Bordeaux; west of Podensac. Ordinary to fair red bordeaux. France.

Saint-Nicolas-de-Bourgueil. (16) Touraine; Bourgueil area. Best red table wine of Touraine. France.

Saint-Pardon. (5) West of Langon. Ordinary to fair bordeaux wines. France.

Saint-Patrice, Château. (12) Côtes du Rhône; Châteauneuf-du-Pape vineyard. Fine red table wine. France.

Saint-Paul, Château. (4) Haut-Médoc; St Seurin-de-Cadourne. *Cru bourgeois*. 3,000 dozen bottles of red bordeaux. France.

Saint-Paul, Le Clos. (10) Mâconnais; Givry vineyard. Red burgundy. France.

Saint-Péray. (12) Ardèche *département;* Côtes du Rhône, just west of Valence. Ordinary to fair still and sparkling white wines are produced. France.

Saint-Pey, Château de. (5) St-Émilion; St Pey d'Armens. An unclassified *cru.* 10,000 dozen bottles of red bordeaux. France.

Saint-Pey d'Armens. (5) South-east of Libourne. Ordinary to fair bordeaux entitled to the *AC´ St-Émilion.* France.

Saint-Pey-de-Langon. (5) The former name of St Pierre-de-Mons, Graves de Bordeaux area. France.

Saint-Pierre, Clos. (12) Côtes du Rhône; Châteauneuf-du-Pape, Domaine Pierre Quiot. Fair to fine red table wine. France.

Saint-Pierre, Clos. (10) Mâconnais; Givry vineyard. Red burgundy. France.

Saint-Pierre-de-Mons. (5) Graves de Bordeaux; Langon. Ordinary to fair white bordeaux. France.

Saint-Pierre-de-Pomerol, Château. (5) Pomerol. 1,500 dozen bottles of red bordeaux. France.

Saint-Pourçain. (15) Ordinary red wines and fair white and rosé table wines. France.

Saint-Préfert. (12) Côtes du Rhône, Châteauneuf-du-Pape vineyard. Fair red and white table wines. France.

Saint-Robert, Château. (5) Barsac. *Cru bourgeois.* 1,000 dozen bottles of white bordeaux. France.

Saint-Robert, Clos. (5) Graves de Bordeaux; Pujols-sur-Ciron, north of Bommes. An unclassified *cru.* 7,000 dozen bottles of white bordeaux. France.

Saint-Roch, Domaine du Château. (12) Côtes du Rhône; Lirac. Fair to fine red and rosé table wines. France.

Saint-Romain. (8) Côte de Beaune. *AC Côte de Beaune Villages.* Ordinary to fair red and white burgundy. France.

Saint-Satur. (15) Cher *département;* Sancerre area. Fair white table wine. France.

Saint-Saturnin-sur-Loire. (16) Anjou; Coteaux de l'Aubance between Angers and Saumur. Fair white table wines. France.

Saint-Sauveur. (12) Côtes du Rhône; Côte du Ventoux, south-west of Ouveze. Fair to fine red table wine. France.

Saint-Sauveur. (4) Haut-Médoc. Ordinary to fair red bordeaux. France.

Saint-Selve. (3) Graves de Bordeaux; south-east of Bordeaux. Ordinary to fair red and white bordeaux. France.

Saint-Seurin-de-Cadourne. (4) Haut-Médoc. Ordinary to fair red and white bordeaux. France.

Saint-Sigismund. (16) Coteaux de la Loire; St Georges-sur-Loire, below Angers. Ordinary to fair white table wine. France.

Saints-Pères, Clos des. (16) Anjou; vineyard of the *commune* of Parnay, on the Saumur hillsides. Fair white table wine. France.

Saint-Sulpice-de-Faleyrens. (5) St-Émilion. Fair and some fine red bordeaux, with the *AC St-Émilion.* France.

Saint-Symphorien d'Ancelles. (10) Mâconnais; south-west of Romanèche-Thorins. Ordinary to fair red burgundy. France.

Saint-Thibault. (15) Cher *département;* Sancerre area. Fair white table wine. France.

Saint-Valéry, Clos. (5) Côtes de St-Émilion. An unclassified *cru.* 1,000 dozen bottles of red bordeaux. France.

Saint-Venand. (10) Mâconnais. Ordinary to fair red and white burgundy. France.

Saint-Verand. (10) Mâconnais. *AC Verand.* Ordinary to fair white burgundy. France.

St-Vincent. Patron saint of French wine growers.

Saint-Vincent. (16) Anjou; Dampierre-sur-Loire, a *commune* on the Saumur hillsides. Fair white table wine. France.

Saint-Vincent. (31) Vaud canton; Morges vineyard. Fair to fine white table wine. Switzerland.

Saint-Vivien. (3) Médoc; north-west of St Seurin-de-Cadourne. Ordinary to fair red bordeaux. France.

Saint-Yzans. (3) Médoc; north-west of St Seurin-de-Cadourne. Ordinary to fair red bordeaux. France.

Saix. (16) Anjou; Côte du Saumur. Fair to fine white table wine. France.

Sake. (1) A light, rice wine which is best drunk young. It is traditionally served warm, but is equally enjoyable cold or used in a cocktail. Japan.

Salamanca. (29) Ordinary to fair red table wine. Spain.

Salamino. (27) Emilia-Romagna; Ravenna province, approx. forty-five miles south-east of Bologna. Ordinary to fair red table wine. Italy.

Salas. (29) Aragon. Ordinary table wines. Spain.

Salento (Salentino). (28) Apulia; the area encompassing the 'heel' of the 'boot' of Italy. Ordinary to fair, though mostly ordinary, red and rosé table wines. They run from dry to semi-sweet and from fairly good to downright nasty. Much is exported for blending. Italy.

Sales, Château de. (5) Pomerol. 18,000 dozen bottles of red bordeaux. France.

Salette, Château La. (5) Graves de Bordeaux; Cérons. An unclassified *cru.* 2,500 dozen bottles of white bordeaux. France.

Salina. (28) Island of Lipari, off Sicily. Fair white dessert wine, made from Malvasia grapes. Italy.

Salinas. (29) Alicante; approx. forty miles south of Valencia. Ordinary to fair table wines. Spain.

Salins. (18) Jura. Ordinary to fair red, white and rosé wines. France.

Salins d'Hyères. (14) Côtes de Provence; Hyères vineyards near Carqueiranne. Ordinary to fair red and white table wines. France.

Salles-de-Castillon. (5) St-Émilionnais. Ordinary to fair red bordeaux. France.

Salomon, Clos. (10) Mâconnais; Givry. *Premier cru*. Fine red burgundy. France.

Salpètrerie, La. (16) Touraine; Bourgueil vineyard. Ordinary to fair red table wine. France.

Salsadella. (29) Castellón de la Plana; approx. forty miles north-east of Valencia. Ordinary stout red table wine. Spain.

Salta. (35) North Argentina. One of the important wine-producing provinces.

Saltillo. (35) North-eastern Mexico. Township and vineyard. Mexico.

Salvatierra de los Barros. (29) Estremadura; Badajoz, between Seville and Trujillo. Rather coarse, very dark red table wine. Spain.

Salvatierra de Mino. (29) North-west Spain; Pontavedra; south-western Galicia. Ordinary white wine. Spain.

Salvert, La. (16) Anjou; Côteaux de la Loire, Montjean vineyard, below Angers. Ordinary to fair white table wine. France.

Sambiase Rosso. (28) Calabria; Cantanzaro vineyard. Ordinary very strong red table wine, much of which is exported for blending. Italy.

Samion, Château. (5) St-Georges-St-Emilion; north-east of St-Émilion. An unclassified *cru*. 5,000 dozen bottles of red bordeaux. France.

Samonac ou Macay, Château de. (4) Bourgeais; north of Bourg. 8,000 dozen bottles of red bordeaux. France.

Samos. (34) Island off the west coast of Turkey. Ordinary to fair and some fine white and golden dessert wine. Greece.

Samper de Calanda. (29) South-central Aragon; Teruel. Ordinary table wines. Spain.

Sampigny-les-Maranges. (8) Côte de Beaune; northern end. *AC Côte de Beaune Villages*. Red burgundy. France.

San Adrian. (29) Logroño province; La Rioja area of the upper Ebro valley. Ordinary to fair red table wine. Spain.

San Carlo. (28) Apulia; Bari vineyard. Ordinary white table wine much exported as neutral base for vermouth. Italy.

Sance. (10) Mâconnais. Ordinary to fair red burgundy. France.

Sancerre. (15) Cher *département;* on the Upper Loire, 2,500 acres. But known *communes* in the Sancerre district are Armigny, Bué, Chavignol and Verdigny. Ordinary red table wine; fair and some fine white table wines. France.

San Clemente. (29) East New Castile; Cuenca. Ordinary to fair red table wine. Spain.

San Colombano. (26) Lombardy; the only vineyard in the Milan area. Very ordinary red table wine; some still and dry, some semi-sweet and semi-sparkling. Italy.

San Cugat. (29) Barcelona. Ordinary, light white table wine. Spain.

Sandalford. (37) Western Australia (Swan valley) winery and vineyards. 300 acres. Table wines and table grapes. Australia.

Sandalyon. (28) Sardinia; vineyards on Campidano plain reaching north-west from Cagliari. Ordinary red table wine. Italy.

Sandgrube. (24) Rhinegau; Kiedrich vineyard, north of Erbach. Fair to fine white table wine. West Germany.

Sandhöhle. (24) Rhinehessia; Alsheim vineyard. Fair white table wine. West Germany.

Sandkaut. (24) Rhinehessia; Bodenheim and Gau-Bischofsheim vineyards, west of Nackenheim. Fair white table wine. West Germany.

Sandweine. (33) Burgenland; south-east Austria close to the Hungarian border. Wines from sandy soil vineyards. Austria.

San Felice. Another name for Chiaretto del Garda. (q.v.). Italy.

Sang. (22) Ruwer; Eitelsbach Berg vineyard. Fine white table wine. West Germany.

Sang-de-Boeuf. (16) Champigny-le-Sec vineyard, approx. thirty miles south of Chinon. Ordinary to fair red table wine. France.

Sängerei. (22) Moselle; Dhron vineyard, between Neumagen and Wintrich. Fair to fine white table wine. West Germany.

Sanginella. (28) Campania; Irno valley at Salerno. Fair white table wine. Italy.

Sangioneto. (27) Tuscany; Elba Island vineyards, west of Grosetto. Ordinary to fair red table wine. France.

San Giorgio. (28) Campania; Benevento vineyard, north of Avellino. Fair white table wine. Italy.

Sangiovese di Arborea. (28) Sardinia; Campidano Terralba area, approx. forty miles north-west of Gagliari. Fair red table wine made from the Sangiovese grape. It is similar to chianti (q.v.) but rather stronger and fuller. Italy.

Sangiovese di Forli. (27) Emilia-Romagna. Fine red wine with a great reputation and protection by the local association. Italy.

Sangiovese di San Marino. (27) San Marino Republic; between Ancona and Bologna. Ordinary to fair red table wine. Italy.

Sangiovese Marchigiano. (27) The Marches; Pesaro vineyard, approx. thirty-five miles north-west of Ancona. Ordinary red table wine. Italy.

Sangiovese Romagnolo. (27) Emilia-Romagna. Fine red wine with a great reputation and protection by the local association. Italy.

Sangiovese Sardo. (28) Sardinia; Campidano Terralba area, approx. forty miles north-west of Cagliari. Fair red table wine made from the Sangiovese grape. It is similar to chianti but rather stronger and fuller. Italy.

Sangiustino. (27) Umbria; Perugia. Ordinary to fair white table wine. Italy.

Sanguesa. (29) Navarre. Ordinary red table wine. Spain.

Sanguie di Guida. (26) Lombardy; Oltrepo Pavese area, south of Pavia across the Po. Ordinary semi-sweet, semi-sparkling red wine. Italy.

San Juan. (35) The second largest wine-producing province of the Argentine, next to Mendoza. Approximately 49% dessert wines; 40% white and rosé table wines; 11% red table wines. Argentina.

San Juan del Puerto. (29) Huelva province. Ordinary to fair table wines. Spain.

Sankt Alban. (24) Rhinehessia; Bodenheim vineyard. Fair white table wine. West Germany.

Sankt Georgen. (25) Baden; Freiburg-in-Breisgau. Fair white table wine. West Germany.

Sankt Goar. (21) Middle Rhine; south-east of Koblenz. Fair white table wine. West Germany.

Sankt Goarhausen. (21) Middle Rhine; south-east of Koblenz. Ordinary white table wine. West Germany.

Sankt Gottesthal. (24) Rhinegau; Oestrich vineyard. Fair to fine white table wine. West Germany.

Sankt Irminer. (22) Saar; Ockfen vineyard, north-east of Saarburg. Fair to fine white table wine. West Germany.

Sankt Johann. (24) Rhinehessia; north-east of Bad Kreuznach. Ordinary to fair white table wine. West Germany.

Sankt Jost. (21) Middle Rhine; Steig vineyard, north-west of Bingen. Fair white table wine. West Germany.

Sankt Katharinen. (24) Nahe. Fair to fine white table wine. West Germany.

Sankt Kiliansberg. (24) Rhinehessia; Nierstein vineyard. Fine white table wine. West Germany.

Sankt Magdalener. (26) *See* **Santa Maddalena.**

Sankt Margarethen. (33) Burgenland; south-east Austria close to the Hungarian border. Mostly fair to fine white table wine. Austria.

Sankt Martin. (23) Palatinate; north-east of Edenkoben. Ordinary to fair red and white table wines. West Germany.

Sankt Martin. (24) Nahe; Bad Kreuznach vineyard. Fine white table wine. West Germany.

Sankt Nikolaus. (24) Rhinegau; Oestrich vineyard. Fine white table wine. West Germany.

Sankt Nikolaus Hospital. (22) Moselle; charitable institution in Kues (or Cues) endowed with a number of vineyards producing white table wines of fair to fine quality. West Germany.

Sankt Nikolauslay. (22) Moselle; Graach. Fair to fine white table wine. West Germany.

San Benito. (36) County in west-central California. More vineyards are being developed in this county since the population explosion is taking the arable lands of the Bay Area Counties. Table and dessert wines. U.S.A.

San Joaquin. (36) California. The second-largest wine-producing county. Eighty per cent of its production is dessert wine. U.S.A.

Sandusky. (35) Ohio; Lake Erie vineyard. Ordinary to fair red and white table wines. U.S.A.

San Lorenzo Savall. (29) Barcelona. Ordinary to fair light, dry table wine. Spain.

San Lúcar la Jayor. (29) Seville. Ordinary to fair sweet white wine. Spain.

San Luis Obispo. (36) One of the minor wine-producing counties of California. U.S.A.

San Luis Potosí. (35) Northern Mexico. One of the major wine-producing areas. Mexico.

San Marcos. (29) Castellón de la Plana; approx. forty miles north-east of Valencia. Ordinary to fair rather sweet red table wine. Spain.

San Martin de Valdeiglesias. (29) Madrid. Ordinary to fair red and white table wines. Spain.

San Martin Vineyards Company. (36) California; San Martin, Santa Clara County. Table, dessert and sparkling wines; also brandy and vermouth. U.S.A.

San Marzano. (26) Piedmont; Asti province. Ordinary to fair slightly sparkling, red table wine rebottled after two to three years. Italy.

Sanmichele (Bianco, Rosso). (27) Lazio. Very good white and red table wines produced at one experimental viticultural station. Italy.

San Miguel. (30) Ordinary Portuguese red table wine. Portugal.

San Pietro Vernotico. (28) Apulia; Salento area, the area encompassing the 'heel' of ·the 'boot'. Ordinary red and white table wines. Italy.

San Roque. (29) Cadiz. Ordinary to fair white table wine. Spain.

San Sadurni de Nova. (29) Barcelona; Villafranca del Panadés. Fair to fine sparkling white and still white, rosé and red table wines. Spain.

San Salvador. (28) Sicily; Catania area. Ordinary to fair, dry, deep-red table wine, aged in wood three years before bottling. Italy.

San Severo. (28) Apulia. Ordinary, rather coarse, white wine much used for the making of vermouth. Italy.

San Sidero. (28) Calabria; Catanzaro. Ordinary very strong red table wine. Italy.

Sansonnet, Château. (5) Côtes de St-Emilion. *Grand cru classé.* 3,500 dozen bottles of red bordeaux. France.

Santa Barbra, Quinta. (30) *Região demarcada do Douro* (q.v.). Estate and vineyard in Casais do Douro in the Régua area. This Quinta is used by the Government as an official experimental centre. Portugal.

Santa Barbara, Quinta. (30) *Região demarcada do Douro* (q.v.). Estate and vineyard in Valdigem south-west of Régua. Portugal.

Santa Catarina. (35) South Brazil. One of the minor wine-producing states south of São Paulo.

Santa Clara. (36) California. An important wine-producing county. The vineyards are giving way to housing as San Jose grows. U.S.A.

Santa Comba, Quinta. (30) *Região demarcada do Douro* (q.v.). Estate and vineyard in São Miguel dos Lobrigos north-east of Régua. Portugal.

Santa Cruz. (36) California; one of the wine-producing counties. Mostly ordinary to fair table wines. U.S.A.

Santa Cruz de la Zarza. (29) West New Castile; Toledo, approx. forty miles south-west of Madrid. Ordinary to fair table wines. Spain.

Santa Eufemia, Quinta. (30) *Região demarcada do Douro* (q.v.). Estate and vineyard in Parada do Bispo south-east of Régua. Portugal.

Santa Julia, Quinta. (30) *Região demarcada do Douro* (q.v.). Estate and vineyard in Loureiro north-west of Régua. Portugal.

Santa Maddalena (Sankt Magdalener). (26) Alto Adige; Bolzano area. The finest red wine of the area. Italy.

Santa Maria, Quinta. (30) *Região demarcada do Douro* (q.v.). Estate and vineyard in Godim in the Régua area. Portugal.

Santa Maria, Quinta. (30) *Região demarcada do Douro* (q.v.). Estate and vineyard in São Miguel dos Lobrigos in the Régua area. Portugal.

Santa Maria la Palma. (28) Sardinia. Ordinary to fair red and white table wines. Italy.

Santany. (29) Majorca; Balearic Islands, off the coast east of Valencia. Ordinary rather sweet red and white table wines. Spain.

Santa Rita. (35) Ordinary to fair red and white table wines. Chile.

Santas Creus. (29) Tarragona. Ordinary table wines. Spain.

Santenay. (8) Côte de Beaune; town and *commune*. Ordinary, fair and some fine red burgundy. France.

Santenots, Les. (8) Côte de Beaune; Volnay vineyard. It produces *premier cru* red burgundy. France.

Santenots du Dessous. (8) Côte de Beaune; Meursault vineyard. *Deuxième cru.* Red burgundy. Most red Meursaults are sold as Volnays. France.

Santenots du Dessus. (8) Côte de Beaune; Meursault vineyard. *Premier cru.* Red burgundy. Most red Meursaults are sold as Volnays. France.

Santenots du Milieu. (8) Côte de Beaune; Meursault vineyard. *Premier cru.* This vineyard is so close to the Volnay vineyards that its wine is marketed as Volnay-Santenots. Red burgundy. France.

Santinho, Quinta. (30) *Região demarcada do Douro* (q.v.). Estate and vineyard in Godim in the Régua area. Portugal.

Santo Antonio, Quinta. (30) *Região demarcada do Douro* (q.v.). Estate and vineyard in Cambres south-west of Régua. Built in 1720. Portugal.

Santo Antonio, Quinta. (30) *Região demarcada do Douro* (q.v.). Estate and vineyard in Gouvaes in the Régua area. Portugal.

Santo Antonio, Quinta. (30) *See* Bateira.

Santo Antonio, Quinta. (30) *Região demarcada do Douro.* Estate and vineyard in Valdigem south-west of Régua. Portugal.

Santo Antonio, Quinta. (30) *Região demarcada do Douro* (q.v.). Estate and vineyard in Juncal de Cima in the Régua area. Portugal.

Santo Isidro or Dos Pocos, Quinta. (30) *Região demarcada do Douro.* Estate and vineyard in Valdigem south-west of Régua. Portugal.

Santo Stefano. (28) Apulia; Foggia plain vineyards. Ordinary red table wine. Italy.

Santo Tomas. (35) A popular and quite ordinary table wine. Mexico.

San Vincente de la Sonsierra. (29) Logroño province; La Rioja area of the upper Ebro valley. Ordinary to fair semi-sweet red table wine. Spain.

San Zeno. (26) Alto Adige; Aldeno vineyard Trento. Fair, robust, red table wine. Italy.

Sao Domingos, Quinta. (30) *Região demarcada do Douro* (q.v.). Estate and vineyard in Oliveira in the Régua area. One of the oldest *quintas* in the Douro Valley. Portugal.

São Goncalo, Quinta. (30) *Região demarcada do*

Douro (q.v.). Estate and vineyard in Poiares north-east of Régua. Portugal.

São Jeronimo, Quinta. *See* **Ribeira.**

São João da Foz, Quinta. (30) Red and white table wines produced in the Douro Valley. Portugal.

São João da Vilarica, Quinta. (30) *Região demarcada do Douro* (q.v.). Estate and vineyard in Horta da Vilarica in the Régua area. Portugal.

São Luis, Quinta. (30) *Região demarcada do Douro* (q.v.). Estate and vineyard in Adorigo east of Régua. Portugal.

São Paulo. (35) Important wine-producing state of Brazil.

São Pedro, Quinta. (30) *Região demarcada do Douro* (q.v.). Nostim. Estate and vineyard in Mouramorta in the Régua area. Portugal.

Saperavi. (34) Eastern Georgia; bordering on Turkey and the Black Sea. Ordinary to fair red table wine. U.S.S.R.

Saransot-Dupré, Château. (4) Haut-Médoc; Listrac. *Cru bourgeois supérieur.* 4,000 dozen bottles of red bordeaux. France.

Sarap. (34) Ordinary to fair red table wine. Turkey.

Sarica Niculitel. (33) Ordinary to fair red and white table wines. Rumania.

Sariñeno. (29) Aragon; Huesca area west of Zaragoza. Ordinary table wines. Spain.

Sarmsheim. (21) Nahe; Bad Kreuznach vineyard. Fair to fine white wine. West Germany.

Sarnadelo, Quinta. (30) *Região demarcada do Douro* (q.v.). Estate and vineyard in Cever in the Régua area. Portugal.

Sarpe, Château de. (5) St-Emilion; St Christophe-des-Bardes, south-west of Parsac. An unclassified *cru*. 2,500 dozen bottles of red bordeaux. France.

Sarpe, Clos de. (5) St-Emilion; St Christophe-des-Bardes, south-west of Parsac. An unclassified *cru*. 1,500 dozen bottles of red bordeaux. France.

Sarpe-Grand-Jacques, Château de. (5) St-Emilion; St Christophe-des-Bardes, south-west of Parsac. An unclassified *cru*. 2,500 dozen bottles of red bordeaux. France.

Sarticola (Bianco, Rosso). (26) Liguria; Val di Magra vineyards, La Spezia province. Fair, sweet, semi-sparkling wine, and a stout, dry, red table wine. Italy.

Sasbach. (25) Baden; north-west of Freiburg. Ordinary to fair red and white table wines. West Germany.

Sasbachwalden. (25) Baden; south-west of Baden-Baden. Ordinary to fair red and white table wines. West Germany.

Sassari. (28) Sardinia. Ordinary to fair red table wine. Italy.

Sassay. (16) Touraine; Ligré, vineyard north-west of Chinon. France.

Sassella. (26) Lombardy; Valtellina vineyard. Very good red wine, much improved by great bottle-age (up to six years). Italy.

Sastago. (29) Aragon; Zaragoza. Ordinary to fair table wines. Spain.

Satz. (23) Palatinate; Königsbach vineyard. Fair to fine white table wine. West Germany.

Saukopf. (24) Rhinehessia; Gau-Bickelheim vineyard, east of Bad Kreuznach. Fair white table wine. West Germany.

Saulce, La. (12) Hautes-Alpes *département;* south-east France, approx. thirty-five miles south-east of Chatillon-en-Diois. Ordinary to fair still and sparkling white wines. France.

Saumagen. (23) Palatinate; Kallstadt vineyard. Fair to fine white table wine. West Germany.

Sauman, Château. (4) Bourgeais; Villeneuve, north-west of Bourg. 4,000 dozen bottles of fair red bordeaux. France.

Sauman, Château. (4) Bourgeais; Villeneuve, north-west of Bourg. 2,500 dozen bottles of good red bordeaux. France.

Saumur. (16) Anjou. Fair to fine white and rosé table wines; also fair to fine white sparkling wine. France.

Saumur Rosé de Cabernet. (16) Saumur. Fair to fine rosé table wine. France.

Sausenheim. (23) Palatinate; just south of Grünstadt. Ordinary to fair red and white table wines. West Germany.

Saut-du-Loup. (16) Coteaux de Saumur; Montsoreau vineyard. Fair white table wine. France.

Savennières. (16) Coteaux de la Loire; below Angers. Fair to fine white table wine. France.

Savennières, Château de. (16) Anjou; Savennières, below Angers. White table wine, the finest of the Coteaux de la Loire wines. France.

Savigny-en-Véron. (16) Touraine; Côte de Chinon. Ordinary to fair red table wine. France.

Sazenay, En. (9) Chalonnais; Touché, south-west of Chagny. Fine red burgundy. France.

Scacciadiavoli. (27) Umbria; Assisi area, south-east of Perugia. Coarse, dark red table wine. Italy.

Scandiano Bianco. (27) Emilia-Romagna; Reggio nell Emilia. Very modest still, dry and sweet sparkling white wines. Italy.

Schafböhl. (23) Palatinate; Deidesheim vineyard. Fine white table wine. West Germany.

Schäferlay. (2) Moselle; Briedel vineyard, west of Zell. Fair white table wine. West Germany.

Schaffhausen. (31) Swiss canton. Ordinary red and white table wines. Switzerland.

Schalksberg. (25) Franconia; Würzburg vineyard. Fair to fine white table wine. West Germany.

Schallbach. (25) Baden; approx. twenty-five miles south-west of Freiburg. Fair white table wine. West Germany.

Schallenberg. (24) Rhinehessia; Gau Odernheim vineyard west of Alsheim. Fair to fine white table wine. West Germany.

Schallstadt-Wolfenweiler. (25) Baden; south-west of Freiburg. Ordinary to fair and some fine white table wine. West Germany.

Schank. (23) Palatinate; Bergzabern vineyard. Ordinary to fair white table wine. West Germany.

Schanz. (24) Rhinehessia; Ockenheim vineyard, south-east of Bingen. Fair white table wine. West Germany.

Scharlach. (25) Franconia; Thüngershcim vineyard, north-west of Würzburg. Ordinary to fair white table wine. West Germany.

Scharlachberg. (24) Nahe; Bingen/Rüdesheim vineyard. Fine white table wine. West Germany.

Scharzberg. (22) Saar; Wiltingen and Oberemmel vineyard. Fine white table wine. Also in great vintage years, Oberemmel vineyard, fine white table wine. West Germany.

Scharzhofberg. (22) Saar; Wiltingen's best vineyard. Very fine white table wine which is called simply Scharzhofberger. West Germany.

Schaumwein. German for sparkling wine, more usually called Sekt.

Schelingen. (25) Baden; north-west of Freiburg. Ordinary to fair red and white table wines. West Germany.

Schenkenböhl. (23) Palatinate; Bad Dürkheim and Wachenheim vineyards. Fair to fine white table wines. West Germany.

Scherzingen. (25) Baden; south-west of Freiburg. Ordinary to fair white table wines. West Germany.

Schild. (23) Palatinate; Gimmeldingen vineyard. Fair white table wine. West Germany.

Schillerwein. Very ordinary pink wine made usually from red and white grapes grown together in the same vineyard. *Schillern* means 'to shimmer' in German. West Germany.

Schimsheim. (24) Rhinehessia; south-east of Bad Kreuznach. Ordinary to fair red and white table wines. West Germany.

Schinznach. (31) Aargau canton. Ordinary to fair white table wine. Switzerland.

Schlangenberg. (24) Rhinehessia; Nierstein vineyard. Fair to fine white table wine. West Germany.

Schlangengraben. (22) Saar; Wiltingen vineyard. Fine white table wine. West Germany.

Schlangenwingert. (22) Moselle; Longuich vineyard, north-east of Trier. Fair white table wine. West Germany.

Schlatt. (25) Baden; approx. thirty miles south-west of Stuttgart. Ordinary to fair white table wine. West Germany.

Schlehdorn. (24) Rhinegau; Mittelheim vineyard. Fair to fine white table wine. West Germany.

Schleich. (22) Moselle; south-west of Klusserath. Ordinary to fair white table wine. West Germany.

Schliengen. (25) Baden; approx. twenty miles south-west of Freiburg. Ordinary to fair white table wine. West Germany.

Schlossgarten. (23) Palatinate; Bad Dürkheim vineyard. Fine white table wine. West Germany.

Schlossgarten. (24) Rhinegau; Geisenheim vineyard. Fine white table wine. West Germany.

Schlossgarten. (24) Rhinehessia; Freidelsheim vineyard. Fine white table wine. West Germany. white table wine. West Germany.

Schlüchtern. (25) Württemberg; west of Heilbronn. Ordinary fair red and white table wines. West Germany.

Schlück. (33) Lenz; Lorenz Moser's vineyard. Fair to fine white table wine. Austria.

Schmidhausen. (25) Württemberg; south-east of Heilbronn. Ordinary to fair red and white table wines. West Germany.

Schmidtskapelle. (24) Rhinehessia; Nackenheim vineyard. Fair to fine white table wine. West Germany.

Schmitt. (24) Rhinehessia; Nierstein. Fair to fine white table wine. West Germany.

Schmittweiler. (23) Palatinate; south-west of Bad Münster. Fair white table wine. West Germany.

Schnack. (24) Rhinehessia; Kempten vineyard, near Bingen. Fair white table wine. West Germany.

Schnait. (25) Württemberg; east of Stuttgart. Ordinary to fair red and white table wine. West Germany.

Schnapp. (24) Rhinehessia; Osthofen vineyard, between Worms and Alsheim. Fair white table wine. West Germany.

Schappenberg. (24) Rhinehessia; Nierstein vineyard. Fair to fine white table wine. West Germany.

Schnepfenflug. (23) Palatinate; Deidesheim vineyard. Fair to fine white table wine. West Germany.

Schoden. (22) Moselle; north-east of Saarburg. Ordinary to fair white table wine. West Germany.

Schoenenberg. (19) Haut-Rhin *département*; Riquewihr. Finest vineyard growing Riesling grapes. France.

Schönberg. (22) Moselle; Erden vineyard. Fair white table wine. West Germany.

Schöneberg. (24) Nahe; south-west of Bingen. Fair to fine white table wine. West Germany.

Schönhell. (24) Rhinegau; Hallgarten vineyard. Fine white table wine. West Germany.

Schonungen. (25) Franconia; approx. twenty-five miles north-east of Würzburg. Fair white table wine. West Germany.

Schorndorf. (25) Württemberg; east of Stuttgart. Ordinary to fair red and white table wines. West Germany.

Schornsheim. (24) Rhinehessia; west of Oppenheim. Fair white table wine. West Germany.

Schozach. (25) Württemberg; south of Heilbronn. Ordinary red and white table wines. West Germany.

Schramsberg Vineyards. (36) California; Calistoga. Napa Valley producer of bottle-fermented American champagnes. Noted in the *Silverado Squatters* by Robert Louis Stevenson. 50 acres. 10,000 dozen bottles. U.S.A.

Schriesheim. (21) Baden, Bergstrasse; north of Heidelberg. Fair white table wine. West Germany.

Schubertslay. (22) Moselle; Piesport vineyard. Fair to fine white table wine. West Germany.

Schuttern. (25) Baden; south-east of Strasbourg. Fair white table wine. West Germany.

Schützenhaus. (24) Rhinegau; Hattenheim vineyard, west of Erbach. Fine white table wine. West Germany.

Schützenhohl. (24) Nahe; Bretzenheim vineyard, north-east of Bad Kreuznach. Fair to fine white table wine. West Germany.

Schützingen. (25) Württemberg; south-west of Heilbronn. Ordinary red and white table wines. West Germany.

Schwabenheim. (24) Rhinehessia; south of Erbach. Ordinary to fair red and white table wines. West Germany.

Schwabsburg. (24) Rhinehessia; south-west of Nierstein. Ordinary to fair white table wine. West Germany.

Schwaigern. (25) Württemberg; west of Heilbronn. Ordinary to fair red and white table wines. West Germany.

Schwanen. (22) Moselle; Bernkastel vineyard. Fair to fine white table wine. West Germany.

Schwanleite. (25) Franconia; Rödelsee, south-east of Würzburg. Fair to fine white table wine. West Germany.

Schwarze Katz. (22) Moselle; Zell vineyard. Popular fair white table wine. West Germany.

Schwarzenberg. (22) Moselle; Valwig and Senheim vineyards, south-east of Ellerz. Fair white table wine. West Germany.

Schwarzenstein. (24) Rhinegau; Johannisberg vineyard. Fair to fine white table wine. West Germany.

Schwarzes Kreutz. (24) Rhinehessia; Freinsheim vineyard, north-east of Bad Dürkheim. Fair to fine white table wine. West Germany.

Schwarzlay. (22) Moselle; Ürzig and Zeltingen vineyards. Fair white table wine. West Germany.

Schwätzerchen. (24) Rhinehessia; Bingen vineyard. Fair white table wine. West Germany.

Schwebsinger. (32) Moselle; just north of Wintrange. Ordinary to fair white table wines. Luxembourg.

Schwegenheim. (23) Palatinate; south-east of Neustadt. Ordinary to fair red and white table wines. West Germany.

Schweich. (22) Moselle; north-east of Trier. Ordinary to fair white table wine. West Germany.

Schweigen. (23) Palatinate; south-west of Landau. Ordinary to fair red and white table wines. West Germany.

Schweigern. (25) Franconia; approx. twenty-five miles north-east of Mosbach. Fair white table wine. West Germany.

Schweinfurt. (25) Franconia; approx. twenty-two miles north-east of Würzburg. Fair white table wine. West Germany.

Sciacchetra (Bianco). (26) Liguria; Monterosso vineyards, Savona province. A very rare fine sweet white dessert wine. This wine is known as *cinqueterre bianco* elsewhere. Italy.

Sciez. (31) Haute Savoie *département*; north-east of Geneva. Ordinary to fair white table wine. France.

Scoglitti. (28) Sicily; Vittoria, approx. forty miles west of Syracuse. Coarse, dark red table wine used mainly for mixing. Italy.

Seaview. (37) South Australia; McLaren Vale, approx. twenty-five miles south of Adelaide. Vineyard and winery. First grade table and dessert wines. Largest Cabernet Sauvignon vineyard in Australia; also grows Sauvignon Blanc et al. Australia.

Sebastiani, Samuel. (36) California; East Sonoma County. Table, dessert and sparkling wines; also vermouth. The reds are generally lighter than those of the Napa Valley. U.S.A.

Seca, La. (29) West Old Castile; Valladolid, approx. seventy miles north of Avila. Fair white and *clarete* table wines; ordinary red table wine. Spain.

Sechet. (6) Chablis; Yonne *département*. *Premier cru*. White burgundy. France.

Seckergrund. (24) Rhinehessia; Laubenheim vineyard. Fair to fine white table wine. West Germany.

Secobe. (29) Castellón de la Plana; approx. forty miles north-east of Valencia. Ordinary to fair strong, dark red table wine. Spain.

Secuita, La. (29) Tarragona. Ordinary table wines. Spain.

Seefelden. (25) Baden; south-west of Freiburg. Fair white table wine. West Germany.

Seelgass. (24) Rhinegau; Erbach vineyard. Fair to fine white table wine. West Germany.

Seewein. A name sometimes given, in Germany, to wines of the Lake Constance (Bodensee) region. West Germany.

Segarcea. (33) Ordinary to fair sweet red table wine. Rumania.

Segarcea Cabernet. (33) Fair to fine red table wine. Rumania.

Segnitz. (25) Franconia; south-east of Würzburg. Fair to fine white wines are produced. West Germany.

Segries, Domaine de. (12) Côtes du Rhône; Lirac. Fair rosé table wine. France.

Sehndorf. (22) Moselle; south-west of Saarburg. Fair white table wine. West Germany.

Seidenburg. (24) Rhinehessia; Nieder-Saulheim vineyard, west of Nierstein. Fair white table wine. West Germany.

Seinsheim. (25) Franconia; approx. sixteen miles south-east of Würzburg. Fair white table wine. West Germany.

Seizo, Quinta. (30) *Região demarcada do Douro* (q.v.). Estate and vineyard in São Pedro in the Régua area. Portugal.

Seizo e Martelo, Quinta. (30) *Região demarcada do Douro* (q.v.). Estate and vineyard in Valenca do Douro east of Régua. Portugal.

Sekt. The German name for sparkling wines, excluding champagne. West Germany.

Sele. (28) Campania; Eboli area, south-east of Salerno. Very ordinary red table wine from the Sele Valley vineyards. Italy.

Selle, Château de. (14) Côtes de Provence; Taradeau. Fair to fine white and rosé table wines. France.

Seloncourt, En. (8) Côte de Nuits; Chenove. The most northerly *commune* on the Côte de Nuits. *Deuxième cru.* Red burgundy. France.

Selva, La. (29) Tarragona. Ordinary to fair white dessert wine. Spain.

Selzen. (24) Rhinehessia; west of Nierstein. Fair white table wines. West Germany.

Semellerie, La. (16) Anjou; Cravant-les-Coteaux vineyard below Angers. Fair red table wine. France.

Semidano. (28) Sardinia; Campidano plain, reaching north-west from Cagliari. Ordinary to fair dry white table wine. Italy.

Seminargarten. (23) Palatinate; Haardt vineyard. Fair to fine white table wine. West Germany.

Senchen. (24) Rhinehessia; Aspishcim vineyard, south of Geisenheim. Fair white wine. West Germany.

Sendel. (24) Nahe; Münster-Sarmsheim vineyard at Bingen. Fair to fine white table wine. West Germany.

Senechal. (16) Touraine; Benais vineyard, Bourgueil district. Fair red table wine. France.

Sénéjac, Château. (4) Haut-Médoc; Le Pian. *Cru bourgeois supérieur.* 6,000 dozen bottles of red bordeaux. France.

Senheim. (22) Moselle; Krampen, south-east of Eller. Fair to fine white table wine. West Germany.

Senhora da Ribeira, Quinta. (30) *Região demarcada do Douro* (q.v.) Estate and vineyard in Seizo de Ansiaes in the Régua area. Portugal.

Sens, Clos de. (16) Touraine; Rochecorbon vineyard, north-east of Tours, Volnay vineyard. Fair to fine white table wine. France.

Sentiers, Les. (8) Côte de Nuits; Chambolle-Musigny vineyard. *Premier cru.* Red burgundy. France.

Seppeltsfield. (37) South Australia; near Tanunda, Barossa Valley, approx. thirty-five miles north-east of Adelaide. The original, and still the chief winery of B. Seppelt and Sons Pty Ltd, founded 1851. Seppelts are among Australia's biggest wine exporters.

Sequeiros, Quinta. (30) *Região demarcada do Douro* (q.v.). Estate and vineyard in Loureiro north-west of Régua. Portugal.

Serbia. (33) East-central Yugoslavia; one of the six republics. Very important wine-producing area. Yugoslavia.

Serpe, Quinta. (30) *Região demarcada do Douro* (q.v.). Estate and vineyard in São João de Lobrigos in the Régua area. Portugal.

Serpentières, Aux. (8) Côte de Beaune; Savigny-les-Beaune. *Premier cru.* Red burgundy. France.

Serprina. (26) Veneto; approx. seventeen miles south of Vicenza. Ordinary to fair white sparkling wine. Italy.

Serquin, Château. (3) Bourgeais; Gauriac, north-west of Bourg. 6,000 dozen bottles of red bordeaux. France.

Serre, Château La. (5) Côtes de St-Emilion. *Grand cru classé.* 3,500 dozen bottles of red bordeaux. France.

Serrig. (22) Saar. Ordinary, fair and fine white table wines. Most of its yearly harvest is used for making sparkling wines (*Sekt*). West Germany.

Serzikaras. (34) Near Syrian frontier, Gaziantepi. Ordinary red table wine. Lebanon.

Sétubal. (30) Table-wine-producing area south of

Lisbon on the River Tagus. Red and sweet white wines. Famous district for moscatel wines. Portugal.

Seuil, Château du. (5) Graves de Bordeaux; Cérons. An unclassified *cru*. 1,500 dozen bottles of white bordeaux. France.

Sevenhill Monastery. (37) South Australia; Clare Valley. Wines were planted 'here from 1853 onwards by Jesuit priests who came from Austria. Altar wines are supplied to Roman Catholic churches throughout Australia and in a number of export markets. Limited production also for commercial sale. Australia.

Seyssel. (12) Town and vineyards on both sides of the Rhône valley, about half-way between Geneva and Lyons. Still and sparkling white wines of ordinary and fair quality. France.

Siaurac, Château. (5) Néac; east of Pomerol. 10,000 dozen bottles of red bordeaux. France.

Sibio, Quinta. (30) *Região demarcada do Douro*. Estate and vineyard in Cotas in the Régua area. Portugal.

Sickershausen. (25) Franconia; south-east of Würzburg. Fair to fine white table wine. West Germany.

Sicots, Les. (16) Touraine; Montlouis vineyard. Fair white table wine. France.

Siculiana. (28) Sicily; Agrigento area, approx. sixty miles south-east of Palermo. Ordinary red table wine used for blending on the mainland. Italy.

Siebeldingen. (23) Palatinate; north-west of Landau. Fair to fine white table wine. West Germany.

Siebenmorgen. (24) Rhinegau; Rauenthal vineyard. Fine white table wine. West Germany.

Siegelsberg. (24) Rhinegau; Erbach vineyard. Fine white table wine. West Germany.

Sierre. (32) Valais canton. Fair to fine white table wine. Switzerland.

Sievering. (33) Vienna district; ordinary to fair white table wine. Austria.

Siglingen. (25) Württemberg. Ordinary to fair red and white table wines. West Germany.

Sigolsheim. (19) Haut-Rhin *département*. Fair white Alsace wine. France.

Silberbach. (23) Palatinate; Wachenheim vineyard. Fine white table wine. West Germany.

Silberberg. (24) Rhinehessia; Bodenheim vineyard. West Germany.

Silberberg. (22) Saar; Krettnach vineyard, north-east of Wiltingen. Ordinary to fair white table wine. West Germany.

Sillery. (17) Marne *département*; Verzy canton. Rated *grand cru*—100% growth. 197 acres. France.

Silva, Quinta. (30) *Região demarcada do Douro* (q.v.). Estate and vineyard in Custoias in the Régua area. Portugal.

Silveira, Quinta. (30) *Região demarcada do Douro* (q.v.). Estate and vineyard in Adeganha in the Régua area. Portugal.

Silzbrunnen. (24) Rhinehessia; Dienheim vineyard. Fair white table wine. West Germany.

Simancas. (29) West Old Castile; Valladolid, approx. seventy miles north of Avila. Ordinary red, fair white and fine *clarete* wines. Spain.

Simard, Château. (5) Côtes de St-Emilion. 10,000 dozen bottles of red bordeaux. France.

Simburesti. (33) Fair to fine red table wine. Rumania.

Simi Wineries. (36) California; Healdsburg, Sonoma County. Table, dessert and sparkling wines and vermouth. U.S.A.

Simonsberg. (22) Moselle; Wintrich vineyard. Fair white table wine. West Germany.

Sinzheim. (25) Baden; west of Baden-Baden. Fair red and white table wines. West Germany.

Sion. (31) Valais canton; upper Rhône valley. Fair to fine white and red table wines, including red Dôle wines and a good quality Mont d'Or. Switzerland.

Siran, Château. (4) Haut-Médoc; Labarde. *Cru bourgeois supérieur*. 10,000 dozen bottles of red bordeaux. France.

Sisante. (29) Huesca; area north of Zaragoza. Ordinary to fair red table wine. Spain.

Siserpe. (8) Côte de Beaune; Beaune vineyard. *Troisième cru*. Red burgundy. France.

Sisies, Les. (8) Côte de Beaune; Beaune vineyard. *Premier cru*. Red burgundy. France.

Sitges. (29) Lower Panadés; between Tarragona and Barcelona. Fair to fine white dessert wines. Spain.

Sitia. (34) Crete. Fair to fine dessert wine. Greece.

Sitters. (23) Palatinate; south-west of Bad Kreuznach. Fair white table wine. West Germany.

Sizzano. (26) Piedmont; Novara province. Fair red table wine similar to, but less fine than Gattinara (q.v.). Italy.

Slovakia. (33) Vineyards; over 35,000 acres. The major wine-producing region of Czechoslovakia is situated in the easternmost part of the country. With over 30,000 acres, Slovakia produces two-thirds to three-quarters of the country's 18,000,000 dozen bottles.

Slovenia. (33) Most northerly of the six republics. Most important wine-growing area producing the highest quality wines. Best known wine in Great Britain is the Riesling grown in the district of Lutomer (q.v.). Yugoslavia.

Smederevka. (33) Most common white grape variety in Yugoslavia, largely consumed as table grapes. Also used in production of table wine. Yugoslavia.

Smith-Haute-Lafitte, Château. (5) Graves de Bordeaux; Martillac. *Cru classé de Graves (en rouge).* 20,000 dozen bottles of red bordeaux; 5,000 white. France.

Soalheira, Quinta. (30) *Região demarcada do Douro* (q.v.). Estate and vineyard in São João da Pesqueira nineteen miles east of Régua. Portugal.

Soave. (26) Veneto; mostly in the Verona and Vicenza area. One of the most popular and one of the best white table wines of Italy; it is made from the white Soave grape. Italy.

Sobernheim. (24) Nahe; south-west of Bad Münster. Fair to fine white table wine. West Germany.

Sobradais, Quinta. (30) *Região demarcada do Douro* (q.v.). Estate and vineyard in Castedo north-east of Régua. Now linked with Quintas Fazendeira and Dona Margarida. Portugal.

Sociando-Mallet, Château. (4) Haut-Médoc; St Seurin-de-Cadourne. *Cru bourgeois.* 3,500 dozen bottles of red bordeaux. France.

Sohlbrunnen. (24) Rhinehessia; Dienheim vineyard. Fair to fine white table wine. West Germany.

Söhnchen. (24) Rhinegau; Oestrich vineyard. Fine white table wine. West Germany.

Solana. (29) New Castile; Ciudad Real, in the Valdepeñas area. Ordinary to fair red and white table wines. Spain.

Solana de los Barros. (29) New Castile; Ciudad Real, in the Valdepeñas area. Ordinary to fair white table wine. Spain.

Sölden. (25) Baden; south-west of Freiburg. Fair white table wine. West Germany.

Solcil de Sierre. (31) Valais canton; Sierre, upper Rhône valley. Fine white dessert wine (vin de paille). Switzerland.

Solichiara. (28) Sicily; Vineyards on the lower slopes of Mount Etna, south of Catania. Ordinary to fair red table wine. Italy.

Solichiata. (28) Sicily; Catania area. The name of an ordinary red table wine from the Mount Etna area. Italy.

Solitude, Domaine de la. (12) Côtes du Rhône; Châteauneuf-du-Pape vineyard. Fair red and white table wines. France.

Solitude, Domaine La. (5) Graves de Bordeaux; Martillac. An unclassified *cru.* 1,500 dozen bottles of red bordeaux; 500 white. France.

Solon, Clos. (8) Côte de Nuits; Morey-St-Denis vineyard. *Premier cru.* Red burgundy. France.

Solopaca (Bianca, Rosso and **Rosato).** (28) Campania; Benevento area, north of Avellino. Ordinary to fair white, red and rosé wines. Italy.

Solutré. (10) Mâconnais. *AC Pouilly-Fuissé.* Fair to fine white burgundy. France.

Somlauer. *See* **Somló.**

Somló. (33) West-central Hungary. Approx. 1,000 acres. One of the best-known table wine districts. Fair to fine table wines. Hungary.

Somlói Furmint Somló. (33) West-central Hungary; Somló area. Fair to fine white wine. Hungary.

Sommerau. (22) Moselle; south of Waldrach. Fair white table wine. West Germany.

Sommerhäuschen. (24) Rhinehessia; Alsheim vineyard. Fair white table wine. West Germany.

Sommerhausen. (25) Franconia; south-east of Würzburg. Fair white table wine. West Germany.

Sommerheil. (24) Rhinegau; Hochheim vineyard. Fair to fine white table wine. West Germany.

Sommerloch. (25) Nahe; north-west of Bad Kreuznach. Fair to fine white table wine. West Germany.

Sommerseite. (23) Palatinate; Herxheim vineyard. Fair white table wine. West Germany.

Sommerwinn. (24) Rhinehessia; Nackenheim vineyard. Fair white table wine. West Germany.

Sondrio. (26) Piedmont; Valtelline vineyards. Fair red table wine. Italy.

Sonnay, Coteau. (16) Touraine; Cravant-les-Coteaux vineyard, below Angers. Fair red table wine. France.

Sonnenberg. (22) Moselle; Treis vineyard, north-east of Valwig. Ordinary to fair white table wine. West Germany.

Sonnenberg. (24) Rhinegau; Eltville vineyard. Fair to fine white table wine. West Germany.

Sonnenberg. (24) Rhinehessia; Alsheim vineyard. West Germany.

Sonnenberg. (22) Ruwer; Eitelsbach vineyard. Fine white table wine. West Germany.

Sonnenberg. (22) Saar; Kanzem and Niedermennig vineyards, north-east of Wiltingen. Fair white table wine. West Germany.

Sonnenhalder. (31) Valais canton; Sierre vineyard. Fair to fine white wine. Switzerland.

Sonnenheil. (24) Rhinehessia; Framersheim vineyard, west of Alsheim. Fair white table wine. West Germany.

Sonnenküste. (33) Fair to fine white table wine. Bulgaria.

Sonnenlay. (22) Moselle; Mülheim and Wolf vineyards, between Bernkastel and Brauneberg. Fair white table wine. West Germany.

Sonnseite. (22) Moselle; Wintrich vineyard, north-west of Traben-Trarbach. Fair to fine white table wine. West Germany.

Sonnenstuhl. (25) Franconia; Randersacker vineyard, just south-east of Würzburg. Fine white table wine. West Germany.

Sonnenuhr. (22) Moselle. Wehlen's finest vineyard and often the finest white Moselle white wine of the vintage. West Germany.

Sonnenuhr. (22) Moselle; Zeltingen vineyard. Fair to fine white table wine. West Germany.

Sonnteilen. (22) Moselle; Bremm vineyard, Trittenheim. Fair white table wines. West Germany.

Sonoma. (36) County in California. Important wine-producing area for mostly table wines. U.S.A.

Sonora. (35) Northern Mexico. One of the wine-producing areas. Mexico.

Soproni. (33) Sopron vineyards; approx. thirty miles from Budapest. Popular, ordinary to fair red and white table wines. Hungary.

Sorbes, Clos. (8) Côte de Nuits; Morey-St-Denis vineyard. *Premier cru*. Red burgundy. France.

Sorbes, Les. (8) Côte de Nuits; Morey-St-Denis vineyard. *Premier cru*. Red burgundy. France.

Sörgenloch. (25) Rhinehessia; west of Nierstein. Ordinary to fair white table wine. West Germany.

Sorgues. (12) Côtes du Rhône; Côte Brulée. *AC Châteauneuf-du-Pape*. Fair to fine red table wine. France.

Sorni (Bianco, Rosso). (26) Alto Adige; San Michele dell'Adige vineyard, Trentino. Fair rather delicate white and a lightish red wine. Italy.

Sorriso d'Ischia. (28) Campania; island of Ischia, Bay of Naples. Unimportant sweetish table wine. Italy.

Sorriso d'Italia. (28) Lazio. Ordinary to fair very pale-red, almost rosé wine also known as Cecubo. Italy.

Sorso. (28) Sardinia; Sassari. Ordinary red table wine, also known as Rosso di Sorso. There is also a golden apéritif or dessert wine known as Dorato di Sorso. Italy.

Soucherie, La. (16) Anjou; Beaumont-sur-Layon vineyard, below Angers. Fair to fine white table wine. France.

Soulac. (3) Médoc. The most northerly *commune* at the mouth of the Gironde in the Atlantic. Average production is about 10,000 dozen bottles of red bordeaux. France.

Soulaines-sur-Aubance. (16) Anjou; below Angers. Coteaux de l'Aubance vineyard beyond the Drakenstein mountain. Fair white table wine. France.

Soulate, Château La. (3) Pomerol. 1,000 dozen bottles of red bordeaux. France.

Soultz. (19) Haut-Rhin *département*. Medium white Alsace wine. France.

Soultzmatt. (19) Haut-Rhin *département*. Ordinary to fair white Alsace wine. France.

Sous-Blagny. (8) Côte de Beaune; Meursault vineyard. *Premier cru. AC Meursault*. Fine white burgundy. France.

Sous-Les-Bois. (16) Touraine; Jasnières vineyard, Vouvray area north-east of Tours. Fair to fine white table wine. France.

Sous-Les-Puits. (8) Côte de Beaune; Puligny-Montrachet vineyard. *Deuxième cru*. White burgundy. France.

Soussans. (4) Haut-Médoc; north-west of Margaux. Ordinary, fair and some fine red bordeaux. France.

Soutard, Château. (5) Côtes de St-Emilion. *Grand cru classé*. 6,000 dozen bottles of red bordeaux. France.

Soutard-Cadet, Château. (5) Côtes de St-Emilion. An unclassified *cru*. 1,000 dozen bottles of red bordeaux. France.

South Africa. (39) Vineyards were planted in South Africa in the mid-17th century. The vineyards of South Africa of any importance are those of the Cape; around Cape Town itself, in the coastal belt, and inland in the Little Karoo. South Africa.

Souverain Cellars. (36) California; St Helena. Winery operation recently sold by founder, J. Leland Stewart. Table and quality wines; fine wines in the past. U.S.A.

Soyots, Les. (6) Chablis vineyard. *Deuxième cru*. White burgundy. France.

Spiegelberg. (24) Rhinehessia; Nierstein vineyard. Fair to fine white table wine. West Germany.

Spielberg. (25) Württemberg; south-east of Karlsruhe. Ordinary to fair red and white table wines. West Germany.

Spielweid. (23) Palatinate, Upper Haardt; Maikammer vineyards (between Neustadt and Edenkoben) and Diedesfeld vineyard (between Kirrweiler and Neustadt). Fair to fine white table wines. West Germany.

Spiess. (23) Palatinate; Ruppertsberg vineyard. Fair to fine white table wine is produced. West Germany.

Spitze. (22) Moselle; Brauneberg vineyard. Fine white table wine. West Germany.

Spitzenberg. (24) Rhinehessia; Nackenheim vineyard. Fair to fine white table wine. West Germany.

Split. (33) Dalmatia; central Adriatic coast. Cultural and economic centre. In its surroundings white and red wines and Opoli (Dalmatian rosé wines) are produced. Yugoslavia.

Sponsheim. (24) Nahe; south-east of Bingen. Fine white table wine. West Germany.

Sporen. (19) Haut-Rhin *département*; Riquewihr

vineyard. One of the finest white Alsace wines. France.

Sprendlingen. (24) Rhinehessia; east of Bad Kreuznach. Fair to fine white table wine. West Germany.

Spries, Les. (6) Irancy vineyard; north of Chablis. Ordinary to fair red burgundy made from Pinot and César grapes. France.

Springton. (37) South Australia; near Eden Valley, approx. thirty miles north-east of Adelaide, sharing that district's suitability for dry whites, and also notable for dry reds. Australia.

Spumante. Italian for sparkling.

Spumante dell'Oltrepo. (26) Lombardy; Santa Maria della Versa vineyards, approx. twenty miles south-west of Piacenza. Fair white sparkling wine from Pinot Noir grapes. Italy.

Spumante di Cingoli. (27) The Marches; Ascoli Piceno vineyards, approx. fifty miles south of Ancona. Ordinary white sparkling wine. Italy.

Spumante di Marino. (28) Lazio; Colli Lanuvio vineyards, south-east of Rome. Ordinary to fair red and rosé sparkling wines. Italy.

Spumante Dolce di Casatico. (27) Tuscany; Lucca. Ordinary to fair white sparkling wine. Italy.

Squinzano. (28) Apulia; Lecca area. Ordinary purple-red wine, mostly used for blending. Italy.

Staaden. (22) Moselle; Pünderich vineyards, west of Zell. Fair white table wine. West Germany.

Stabel. (24) Rhinegau; Hattenheim vineyard. Fair to fine white table wine. West Germany.

Stablay. (22) Moselle; Graach vineyard. Fair to fine white table wine. West Germany.

Stadecken. (24) Rhinehessia; south-west of Budenheim. Ordinary to fair red and white table wines. West Germany.

Stadtbredimus. (32) Moselle. Fair white table wine. Luxembourg.

Stammheim. (25) Franconia; approx. seventeen miles north-east of Frankfurt. Fair white table wine. West Germany.

Stanislaus. (36) California; wine-producing county. Mostly sweet wines. U.S.A.

Stanley Wines. (37) South Australia; Clare. Founded 1893 by four townsmen; controlled from 1912 by Knappstein family until sold in 1971 to American-owned H. J. Heinz Co. Australia Ltd., food processors. Superb dry white wines and rosé; good reds. Top white wine brand is Leasingham. Company has 600 acres of vines. Australia.

Staudernheim. (24) Rhinehessia; south-west of Bad Münster. Fair white table wine. West Germany.

Staufen. (25) Baden; south-west of Freiburg. Fair white table wine. West Germany.

Steeg. (22) Moselle; Kiedrich vineyard, north of Erbach. Fair white table wine. West Germany.

Stefanesti. (33) Approx. seventy miles north-west of Bucharest. Fair to fine red and white table wines. Rumania.

Steffensberg. (22) Moselle; Enkirch and Kröv vineyards. Fair white table wine. West Germany.

Steiermark (Styria). (33) Wine-producing areas of Austria in the south-east, close to the Yugoslav frontier. Graz is the centre. Fair white and rosé table wines. Austria.

Steig. (24) Rhinehessia; Güntersblum vineyard (between Alsheim and Dienheim) and Laubenheim vineyard; also Oppenheim vineyard. Fair to fine white table wines. West Germany.

Steinacker. (23) Palatinate, Middle Haardt; Kallstadt. Fine white table wine. West Germany.

Steinacker. (24) Rhinegau; Geisenheim and Johannisberg vineyards. Fair to fine white table wines. West Germany.

Stein-am-Kocher. (25) Baden; south-east of Mosbach. Fair white table wine. West Germany.

Steinberg. (29) Nahe; Niederhausen vineyard, west of Bad Münster. Fair to fine white table wine. West Germany.

Steinberg. (24) Palatinate; Herzheim vineyard, west of Erbach. Fine white table wine. West Germany.

Steinberg. (24) Rhinegau; Hattenheim's finest vineyard. One of the great Hocks of good vintages. West Germany.

Stein-Bockenheim. (24) Rhinehessia; south-east of Bad Münster. Fair white table wine. West Germany.

Steinchen. (24) Nahe; Langenlonsheim vineyard, south of Bingen. Fair white table wine. West Germany.

Steinchen. (24) Rhinegau; Winkel vineyard. Fair white table wine. West Germany.

Steinert. (29) Rhinehessia; Gau-Algesheim vineyard, south of Mittelheim. Fair white table wine. West Germany.

Steingebiss. (23) Palatinate; Kirrweiler vineyard. Fair white table wine. West Germany.

Steinhaufen. (24) Rhinegau; Rauenthal vineyard. Fine white table wine. West Germany.

Steinheim. (25) Franconia; Steinmantel vineyard, Würzburg area. Fine white table wine always bottled in Bocksbeutel. West Germany.

Steinheim an der Murr. (25) Württemberg; south-east of Heilbronn. Ordinary to fair red and white table wines. West Germany.

Steininger. (22) Ruwer; Kasel vineyard. Fair to fine white table wine. West Germany.

Steinkaul. (22) Moselle; Wehlen vineyard. Fine white table wine. West Germany.

Steinkopf. (21) Hesse; Heppenheim vineyard, Bergstrasse approx. sixteen miles south of Darmstadt. Fair white table wine. West Germany.

Steinmächer. (24) Rhinegau; Eltville vineyard. Fair to fine white table wine. West Germany.

Steinmauer. (22) Moselle; Zeltingen vineyard. Fair white table wine. West Germany.

Steinmorgen. (24) Rhinegau; Erbach vineyard. Fine white table wine. West Germany.

Steinweg. (24) Rhinehessia; Gau-Bickelheim vineyard east of Bad Kreuznach. Fair to fine white table wine. West Germany.

Steinwein. The name given in Germany to some of the fine white wines of Franconia. *See* Würzburg. West Germany.

Stellenbosch. (39) Cape Province. One of the earliest and still one of the important centres of the wine trade. South Africa.

Stelzenberg. (21) Middle Rhine; Oberdiebach vineyard, north-west of Bingen. Fair white table wine. West Germany.

Stephanslay. (22) Middle Moselle; Zeltingen vineyard. Fair to fine white table wine. West Germany.

Sternenfels. (25) Württemberg; approx. seventeen miles south-west of Heilbronn. Ordinary to fair red and white table wines. West Germany.

Stetten. (25) Franconia; north-west of Würzburg. Fair white table wine. West Germany.

Stetten. (25) Württemberg; approx. thirty-five miles west of Konstanz. Ordinary to fair red and white table wines. West Germany.

Steyer. (24) Nahe; Niederhausen vineyard, west of Bad Münster. Fair to fine white table wine. West Germany.

Stiehlweg. (29) Rhinegau; Hochheim vineyard. Fair to fine white table wine. West Germany.

Stiel. (29) Rhinehessia; Nackenheim vineyard. Fair white table wine. West Germany.

Stift. (23) Palatinate; Forst vineyard. Fair to fine white table wine. West Germany.

Stirn. (24) Rhinehessia; Nackenheim vineyard. Fair to fine white table wine. West Germany.

Stirn. (22) Ruwer; Eitelsbach vineyard. Fine white table wine. West Germany.

Stolzenberg. (22) Moselle; Detzem vineyard. Fair white table wine. West Germany.

Stolzenberg. (29) Rhinehessia; Gau-Algeshcim vineyard, south of Mittelheim. Fair to fine white table wine. West Germany.

Stonyfell. (37) One of the older (1858) wineries and vineyards in the Adelaide area. Situated in the foothills above the suburb of Burnside. All types of wines. Australia.

Stony Hill Vineyard. (36) California; St Helena, Napa County. Wines are of good quality, usually sold privately at the winery. U.S.A.

Strasse. (23) Middle Haardt, Palatinate; Forst and Deidesheim vineyards. Fine white table wines. West Germany.

Stravecchio Melini. (27) Tuscany. The finest red chianti marketed by the firm of Melini. Any *stravecchio* wine is 'very old', although this is sometimes an exaggeration. Italy.

Streichling. (25) Baden, Bergstrasse; Bensheim vineyard, north-east of Mannheim. Fair white table wine. West Germany.

Streng. (22) Rhinehessia; Nierstein vineyard. Fair to fine white table wine. West Germany.

Stromberg. (25) Nahe; south-west of Bingen. Fair to fine white table wine. West Germany.

Strümpfelbach. (25) Württemberg; east of Stuttgart. Ordinary to fair red and white table wines. West Germany.

Stumpfenort. (24) Rhinegau; Rüdesheim vineyard. Fair to fine white table wine. West Germany.

Stuttgart. (25) Württemberg. Ordinary to fair red and white table wines. West Germany.

Suau, Château. (5) Barsac. *Deuxième cru classé.* 1,500 dozen bottles of white bordeaux. France.

Subirats. (29) Barcelona; Panadés area between Tarragona and Barcelona. Ordinary to fair red and white table wines. Spain.

Suchots, Les. (8) Côte de Nuits; Vosne-Romanée vineyards. *Premier cru.* Red burgundy. France.

Suduiraut, Château. (5) Sauternes; Preignac. *Premier cru classé.* 10,000 dozen bottles of white bordeaux. France.

Sulz. (25) Baden; approx. thirty-three miles south-east of Baden-Baden. Fair white table wine. West Germany.

Sulzbach. (21) Württemberg; approx. twenty-two miles east of Darmstadt. Ordinary to fair red and white table wines. West Germany.

Sulzburg. (25) Baden; south-west of Freiburg. Fair white table wine. West Germany.

Sulzfeld. (25) Baden; approx. sixteen miles west of Heilbronn. Ordinary to fair red and white table wines. West Germany.

Sulzfeld. (25) Franconia; approx. thirty-six miles north-east of Würzburg. Fair white table wine. West Germany.

Sulzheim. (24) Rhinehessia; east of Bad Kreuznach. Ordinary to fair red and white table wines. West Germany.

Sulztal. (25) Franconia; approx. twenty-five miles north-east of Würzburg. Ordinary to fair red and white table wines. West Germany.

Sumleul-Silvaniei. (33) North-west Rumania; town in Transylvania. Fair to fine white dessert wine. Rumania.

Sumoll. (29) Barcelona. Ordinary, dark red table wine. Spain.

Surget, Château. (3) Néac; east of Pomerol. 1,800 dozen bottles of red bordeaux. France.

Sur-La-Curé. (31) Vaud canton; St Symphorin vineyard. Fair to fine white table wine. Switzerland.

Sur-Le-Moulin. (6) Chablis; Fleys vineyard. Fair white burgundy. France.

Sur-Les-Grèves. (8) Côte de Beaune; Beaune vineyard. *Premier cru*. Red burgundy. France.

Surmain, Domaine de. (10) Mâconnais; Mercurey vineyard. Red burgundy. France.

Survoisine, La. (9) Chalonnais; Givry vineyard. Fair red table wine. France.

Sury-en-Vaux. (15) Upper Loire valley, Sancerre area. Fair to fine white table wine. France.

Süssbuckel. (23) Middle Haardt, Palatinate; Wachenheim vineyard. Fair to fine white table wine. West Germany.

Sutter County. (36) North-central California; Sacramento Valley. Ordinary table and dessert wines. U.S.A.

Sutter Home Winery. (36) California; St Helena. An old winery, family owned and operated. Table wines and vermouth; good Zinfandel. U.S.A.

Sylvain-Moulin-à-Vent, Château. (5) Graves de Bordeaux; Cérons. An unclassified *cru*. 4,000 dozen bottles of white bordeaux. France.

Styria. *See* **Steiermark.**

Syrberg. (32) Moselle; Mertert vineyard, north-east of Grevenmacher. Ordinary to fair white table wine. Luxembourg.

Syria. (34) There are about 180,000 acres of vineyards, mostly in the hills of the Damascus-Aleppo-Homs regions. Mostly quite plain table wines.

Szerkszard. (33) Tolna; approx. sixty miles south-west of Budapest. Ordinary to fair red and white table wines. Hungary.

Szilvanyi Zold. (33) Ordinary to fair white table wine of Green Sylvaner grapes. Hungary.

🍇

Tâche, La. (8) Côte de Nuits; Vosne-Romanée vineyard. *Grand cru*. Red burgundy. France.

Tafalla. (29) Navarre. Ordinary to fair red table wine. Spain.

Tafelstein. (24) Rhinehessia; Dienheim vineyard. Fair white table wine. West Germany.

Tahbilk, Château. (37) Victoria; Tahbilk, on the Goulburn River, approx. seventy-six miles north of Melbourne. Dating from 1860 it is owned by the Purbrick family. Quality table wines. Australia.

Tailhas, Château. (5) Pomerol. 4,500 dozen bottles of red bordeaux. France.

Taillan, Château du. (4) Haut-Médoc; Le Taillan. *Cru bourgeois*. 5,000 dozen bottles of red bordeaux. France.

Taillan, Le. (4) Haut-Médoc; *commune* and vineyards. Ordinary to fair bordeaux wines are produced. France.

Taillefer, Château. (5) St-Emilion; Vignonet, south-west of St Pey d'Armens. An unclassified *cru*. 1,500 dozen bottles of red bordeaux. France.

Tainerée, Clos de la. (16) Touraine; Rochecorbon vineyard, north-east of Tours, Vouvray area. Fair to fine white table wine. France.

Talais. (4) Médoc; village and vineyards. 14,000 dozen bottles of red bordeaux; 500 white. France.

Talavera. (29) West New Castile; Toledo, approx. forty miles south-west of Madrid. Ordinary to fair red and white table wines. Spain.

Talbot, Château. (4) Haut-Médoc; St-Julien. *Quatrième cru classé*. 30,000 dozen bottles of red bordeaux. France.

Talence. (5) Graves de Bordeaux. Ordinary to fair and some fine red and white bordeaux. France.

Talheim. (24) Rhinehessia. Ordinary to fair red and white table wines. West Germany.

Talmettes, Les. (8) Côte de Beaune; Savigny-les-Beaune vineyard. *Premier cru*. Red burgundy. France.

Tamianca. (33) Fair to fine fortified dessert wine. Bulgaria.

Tamm. (25) Württemberg; north of Stuttgart. Ordinary to fair red and white table wines. West Germany.

Tanque, Quinta. *See* **Devesa.**

Tanunda. (37) South Australia; one of the three main wine centres of the Barossa Valley thirty-five miles north-east of Adelaide. Australia.

Tanunda, Château. (37) Tanunda area; south of Adelaide. A well known Australian brandy made by Seppelto. Australia.

Taormina. (28) Sicily; Taormina-Mount Etna vineyards, north of Catania. Very good fragrant white table wine. Italy.

Tapada, Quinta. (30) *Região demarcada do Douro* (q.v.). Estate and vineyard in Celeiros north-east of Régua. Portugal.

Taracon. (29) West New Castile; Toledo, approx. forty miles south-west of Madrid. Ordinary table wines. Spain.

Taradeau. (14) Côtes de Provence; Argens valley. Fair red, white and rosé table wines. France.

Tarantino. (28) Apulia; Taranto area. Very pedestrian, coarse, purple-red table wine used for blending at best. Italy.

Taranto. (28) Apulia. Ordinary to fair red and white table wines. Italy.

Tarazona de Aragon. (29) Aragon; Zaragoza. Ordinary to fair table wines. Spain.

Tarforst. (22) Moselle; west of Waldrach. Ordinary to fair white table wine. West Germany.

Tarija. (35) Township and vineyards on some of the eastern slopes of the Andes. Bolivia.

Tarragona. (29) Catalonia. Ordinary to fair table and dessert wines. Spain.

Tart, Le Clos de. (8) Morey-St-Denis vineyard; Clos de Nuits. Fine red burgundy. France.

Tasta, Château. (3) St-Aigan, north-west of Fronsac, Fronsadais. 5,000 dozen bottles of red bordeaux. France.

Tastes, Château de. (5) Ste Croix-du-Mont, Côtes de Bordeaux. 5,000 dozen bottles white bordeaux. France.

Tatachilla. (37) South Australia; former McLaren Vale vineyard, approx. twenty-five miles south of Adelaide, now defunct. Australia.

Taubenberg. (22) Moselle; Niederemmel vineyard. Fair white table wine. West Germany.

Taubenberg. (29) Rhinegau; Eltville vineyard. Fine white table wine. West Germany.

Taubenberg. (22) Ruwer; Kasel vineyard. Fine white table wine. West Germany.

Taubenbrunnen. (24) Palatinate; Zell vineyard. Fair to fine white table wine. West Germany.

Taubengarten. (22) Moselle; Piesport vineyard. Fine white table wine. West Germany.

Taubennest. (24) Rhinehessia; Nierstein. Fair to fine white table wine. West Germany.

Tauberbischofsheim. (25) Franconia; approx. seventeen miles south-west of Würzburg. Fair white table wine. West Germany.

Tauberrettersheim. (25) Franconia; approx. twenty miles south of Würzburg. Ordinary to fair white table wine. West Germany.

Tauberzell. (25) Franconia; approx. twenty-five miles south-east of Würzburg. Fair to fine white table wine. West Germany.

Taurasi. (28) Campania; Avellino. Fair sweetish red table wine. Italy.

Tauxières. (17) Marne *dèpartement ;* Ay canton, north-west of Bouzy. Rated *premier cru*—94% growth. 499 acres. France.

Tavannes, Les. (8) Côte de Beaune; Pommard vineyard. *Premier cru.* Red burgundy. France.

Tavannes, Clos de (8) Côte de Beaune; Santenay vineyard. Red burgundy. France.

Tavel. (13) Gard *département ;* Côtes du Rhône. The best rosé table wine of France. France.

Tawern. (22) Moselle; west of Filzen. Ordinary to fair white table wine. West Germany.

Tayac, Château. (3) Bourgeais; Bayon, north-west of Bourg. 7,000 dozen bottles of red bordeaux. France.

Tegea. (34) Kythera; island off southern coast of Greece. Ordinary to fair rosé table wine. Greece.

Tegnac, Château. (4) Haut-Médoc; St-Julien. *Cru bourgeois.* 1,500 dozen bottles of red bordeaux. France.

Tehigo. (29) Madrid. Ordinary, sharp dark red table wine. Spain.

Teichwiese. (29) Palatinate; Gimmeldingen vineyard. Fair white table wine. West Germany.

Teide. (40) Santa Cruz de Tenerife; Canary Islands off the north-west coast of Africa. Fair white dessert wine. Spain.

Télégraphe, Domaine du. (12) Côtes du Rhone; Châteauneuf-du-Pape vineyard. Fair to fine red table wine. France.

Temilobos, Quinta. (30) *Região demarcada do Douro* (q.v.). Estate and vineyard in Vacalar in the Régua area. Portugal.

Temmels. (22) Moselle; north-west of Saarburg. Ordinary to fair white table wine. West Germany.

Tempier, La. (14) Côtes de Provence; Domaine Le Castelet. *AC Bandol.* Fair red and rosé table wines. France.

Templiers, Clos des. (5) Pomerol. 2,000 dozen bottles of red bordeaux. France.

Tempranillo. (29) Alva, Alella, Barcelona, Orense, Pontevedra, Tarragona, Valladolid and Zamora areas. 'Black' (very dark red), coarse table wine. Spain.

Tenerife. (40) Santa Cruz de Tenerife vineyards; Canary Islands off the north-west coast of Africa. Ordinary table wines and some fair to fine dessert wines. Spain.

Tent. *See* **Rota Tent.**

Tercios, Los. (29) Cadiz and Jerez. Fair to fine Sherry wine. Spain.

Terlaner. *See* **Terlano.**

Terlano. (26) Alto Adige; Bolzano region. Fair to fine white table wine and ordinary red wine, to be drunk young. Italy.

Termeno. (26) Alto Adige; Caldaro area, south-west of Bolzano. Ordinary to fair dry, lightish red table wine to be drunk young. Italy.

Teroldego. (26) Trentino; Noce river valley vineyards, north-west of Trento. Fair to fine red table wines said to be the finest wine of the area. Italy.

Teroldigo. *See* **Teroldego.**

Terrano (Terrano del Carso). (26) Friuli-Venezia-Giulia; vineyards close to the Italo-Yugoslavian border, Gorizia-Trieste area. Ordinary to fair light red table wine drunk young and cool and very low on alcohol (9°–9·5°). Italy.

Terrasa. (29) Barcelona. Ordinary to fair white table wine. Spain.

Terrasse, Domaine de la. (3) Bourgeais; Villeneuve, south-east of Blaye. 2,500 dozen bottles of red bordeaux. France.

Terrasson, Domaine de. (5) Premières Côtes de Bordeaux; Langoiran, north-east of Portets. 1,000 dozen bottles of red bordeaux; 1,700 white. France.

Terre-Ferme, Domaine de. (12) Côtes du Rhône; Châteauneuf-du-Pape vineyard. Fair to fine red table wine. France.

Terrefort, Château. (5) Sauternes. *Cru bourgeois.* 800 dozen bottles of white bordeaux. France.

Terrefort-Quancard, Château de. (3) Fronsadais. 30,000 dozen bottles of red bordeaux; 3,000 white. France.

Terres-Rouges, Les. (16) Anjou; St Cyr-en-Bourg vineyard, just south of Saumur. Fair red table wine. France.

Tertre, Château du. (4) Haut-Médoc; Arsac. *Cinquième cru classé.* 10,000 dozen bottles of red bordeaux. France.

Tertre, Château Le. (5) St-Emilion; St Laurent-des-Combes, west of St Etienne-de-Lisse. An unclassified *cru*. 1,500 dozen bottles of red bordeaux. France.

Tertre-Daugay, Château. (5) Côtes de St-Emilion. *Grand cru classé.* 3,000 dozen bottles of red bordeaux. France.

Tessalah, Monts du. (40) South of Oran. Ordinary to fair red, white and rosé table wines of *V.D.Q.S.* standard. Algeria.

Testu, Clos. (16) Touraine; Chinon vineyard. Fair red table wine. France.

Teufelskeller. (25) Franconia; Randersacker vineyard, just south-east of Würzburg. Fine white table wine. West Germany.

Teufelskopf. (24) Rhinehessia; Ludwigshöhe vineyard, between Alsheim and Dienheim. Fair white table wine. West Germany.

Teufelsloch. (24) Rhinehessia; Nackenheim vineyard. Fair to fine white table wine. West Germany.

Teurons, Les. *See* **Theurons.**

Teya. (29) Barcelona. Ordinary to fair table wines. Spain.

Teyssier, Château. (5) St-Emilion; Puisseguin. An unclassified *cru*. 12,500 dozen bottles of red bordeaux. France.

Teysson, Château. (5) Néac, east of Pomerol. 5,000 dozen bottles of red bordeaux. France.

Thal. (24) Palatinate; Deidesheim vineyard. Fine white table wine. West Germany.

Thal. (24) Rhinehessia; Heddesheim vineyard, north-west of Bad Kreuznach. Fair white table wine. West Germany.

Thalabert, Domaine de. (12) Côtes du Rhône; Tain L'Hermitage vineyard. Fair to fine red table wine. France.

Thann. (19) Haut-Rhin *département;* south-west of Soultz. Ordinary white Alsace table wine. France.

Thau, Château de. (3) Bourgeois; north-west of Bourg. 5,500 dozen bottles of red bordeaux. France.

Thauvenay. (15) Upper Loire Valley; Sancerre area. Fair white table wine. France.

Theilheim. (25) Franconia; south-east of Würzburg. Fine white table wine. West Germany.

Theurons, Clos des. (9) Chalonnais; Couchés vineyard, south-west of Chagny. *Premier cru.* Red burgundy. France.

Theurons. (8) Côte de Beaune; Beaune vineyard. *Premier cru* and *deuxième cru.* Red burgundy. France.

Thibaudières, Les. (16) Touraine; Cravant-les-Coteaux vineyard, south-east of Chinon. Fair red table wine. France.

Thibaud-Maillet, Château. (5) Pomerol. 1,500 dozen bottles of red bordeaux. France.

Thiergarten. (22) Moselle; Trier vineyard. Ordinary to fair white table wine is produced. West Germany.

Thierlay. (22) Moselle; Neumagen vineyard. Fair white table wine. West Germany.

Thierrières, Clos des. (16) Touraine; Vernon-sur-Brenne vineyard, north-east of Tours. Fair white table wine. France.

Thira (Santorini). (33) Island south-east of Greek mainland. Ordinary to fair red and white table wines. Also some fair to fine sweet wine known as *vino santo.* Greece.

Thirin, Château. (11) Beaujolais; Brouilly vineyard. Red beaujolais. France.

Thomasberg. (22) Moselle; Urzig vineyard. Fair to fine white table wine. West Germany.

Thonon. (31) Haute-Savoie *département;* on the south shore of Lake Geneva. Fair white table wine. France.

Thorey, Les & Clos de. (8) Côte de Nuits; Nuits-St-Georges vineyard. *Premier cru.* Red burgundy. France.

Thorins. (10 & 11) Township and vineyards partly in Mâconnais, known as Romanèche-Thorins; partly in Beaujolais (Chenas *commune*), known as Les Thorins. Fair to fine red table wine. France.

Thörnich. (22) Moselle; south-west of Klüsserath. Fair white table wine. West Germany.

Thou, Château du. (15) Upper Loire valley; Sancerre area. Fair white table wine. France.

Thouarce. (16) Anjou; Coteaux du Layon vineyard, south of Angers. Fair to fine white and rosé table wines. France.

Thouil, Château de. (3) Villegouge, north-west of Fronsac, Fronsadais. 1,000 dozen bottles of white bordeaux. France.

Thüngen. (25) Franconia; north-west of Würzburg. Fine white table wine. West Germany.

Thüngersheim. (25) Franconia; north-west of Würzburg. Ordinary to fair red and white table wines. West Germany.

Thunots, Clos des. (9) Chalonnais; Couchés vineyard, south-west of Chagny. *Premier cru.* Red burgundy. France.

Thurgau. (3) Swiss canton. Vineyards produce some ordinary red table wine, and some fair white table wine. Switzerland.

Tiana. (29) Barcelona. Fair white table wine. Spain.

Tich, Domaine du. (5) Ste Croix-du-Mont, Côtes de Bordeaux. 1,000 dozen bottles white bordeaux. France.

Tiebas. (29) Navarre. Ordinary red and *clarete* table wines. Spain.

Tiefenbach. (21) Baden; approx. seventeen miles south-east of Heidelberg. Ordinary to fair red and white table wines. West Germany.

Tiefenthal. (24) Saar; west of Saarburg. Fair white table wine. West Germany.

Tiélandry. (8) Côte de Beaune; Beaune vineyard. *Premier cru.* Red burgundy. France.

Tiengen. (25) Baden; approx. thirty-three miles south-east of Freiburg. Fair white table wine. West Germany.

Tiergarten. (24) Palatinate; Deidesheim vineyard. Fair to fine white table wine. West Germany.

Tiferno. (27) Umbria; Upper Tiber valley vineyards. Modest red table wine, often *frizzante* and to be drunk young. Italy.

Tiffray, Château. (5) St-Emilion; Lussac. An unclassified *cru.* 2,500 dozen bottles of red bordeaux; 1,000 white. France.

Tigre. (16) Anjou; Coteaux du Layon below Angers. Fair to fine white and rosé table wines. France.

Tillac, Château du. (5) Entre-deux-Mers; Ambares, north-east of Bordeaux. 2,000 dozen bottles of red bordeaux. France.

Tillède, Château. (5) Graves de Vayres; south-west of Libourne. 5,500 dozen bottles of white bordeaux. France.

Tilleuls, Domaine des. (5) Premières Côtes de Bordeaux; Ornet, north of Ste Croix-du-Mont.

500 dozen bottles of red bordeaux; 2,000 white. France.

Timberlay, Château. (3) St André-de-Cubzac, Cubzaguais, south-east of Bourg. 50,000 dozen bottles of red bordeaux; 6,000 white. France.

Tina. (29) East New Castile; Cuenca. 'Black' (very dark red) ordinary table wine. Spain.

Tinoco, Quinta. (30) *Região demarcada do Douro* (q.v.). Estate and vineyard in Oliveira in the Régua area. Portugal.

Tintara. (37) South Australia; vineyard and winery at McLaren Vale, approx. twenty-five miles south of Adelaide, dating from early 1850s and acquired in 1873 by Hardy family which still controls it. Dry reds, port and a famous brandy. Australia.

Tintella de Rota. *See* **Rota Tent.**

Tintorro. (29) Any 'black' (very dark red) ordinary table wine. Spain.

Tirgo. (29) Logroño province; La Rioja area of the upper Ebro valley. Ordinary to fair red table wine. Spain.

Tirley. (22) Moselle; Graach vineyard. Fair white table wine. West Germany.

Tirnave. (33) North-west Rumania; vineyards on the Tirnave river hillsides. This area is in the middle of Transylvania, where there are two Tirnave rivers, both tributaries of the Muves river, which itself continues further into Hungary. Ordinary to fair red and white table wines; also fair to fine golden dessert wine. Rumania.

Tivisa. (29) Tarragóna. Ordinary to fair table wines. Spain.

Tlemcen, Côtes de. (40) Area south-west of Oran. Fair red and white table wines, accorded under French rule the *V.D.Q.S.* appellation provided their alcoholic strength reach 13°. Algeria.

Tobarra. (29) Alicante; approx. forty miles south of Valencia. Ordinary, strong, semi-sweet red table wine. Spain.

Toboso, El. (29) West New Castile; Toledo. Ordinary to fair table wines. Spain.

Tocai del Friuli. (26) Friuli Venezia-Giulia; Gorzia-Trieste area. Ordinary to fair golden-tawny dessert wine of Tocai (Pinot Gris) grapes. Italy.

Tocai di Lison. *See* **Tocai di Friuli,** Italy.

Tocai Rosato. (26) Emilia-Romagna; Parma area. Ordinary to fair rosé table wine. Italy.

Tocornal. (35) Ordinary to fair red table wine of Chile.

Tokaj (Tokay). (33) Carpathians; town and vineyards, north-east Hungary, approx. 110 miles from Budapest. The optimum wine production of the vineyards of the area (25 villages around

Tokaj) is well over 1,000,000 dozen bottles; table and dessert wines from ordinary to fine to great. The wine is made from Furmint grapes. Hungary.

Tokaji Aszu. (33) Tokaj (Tokay) vineyards; approx. 110 miles north-east of Budapest. The finest of all Tokay white dessert wine. Hungary.

Tokaji Essence (Essencia). (33) Tokaj (Tokay) vineyards; approx. 110 miles north-east of Budapest. The finest white dessert wine of Hungary.

Tokaji Szamorodni. (33) Tokaj (Tokay) vineyards; approx. 110 miles north-east of Budapest. Ordinary to fair white dessert wine. Hungary.

Tollana. (37) South Australia; wine brand of Tolley, Scott & Tolley Ltd of Adelaide, Nuriootpa and Waikerie. Recent figures say they have 1,000 acres of vineyards. Wine is made at Nuriootpa and is recent new venture; company previously made only brandy. Australia.

Tolley. (37) South Australia; name associated with two wine-making concerns, now separate though originally stemming from same family. *See* **T.s.T., Tollanda, Pedare.** Australia.

Tomelloso. (29) New Castile; Ciudad Real, in the Valdepeñas area. Ordinary to fair table wines. Spain.

Tonnelle, Château La. (3) Blaye. 2,100 dozen bottles of red bordeaux; 1,700 white. France.

Tonnerre, Le. (9) Chalonnais; Mercurey vineyard. Red burgundy. France.

Torbato Extra. (28) Sardinia; Alghero vineyard, Sassari. Fair medium sweet white dessert or apéritif wine. Italy.

Torbato Passito. (28) Sardinia; Sassari province. Fair very sweet white dessert wine similar in style to sherry. Italy.

Torbato Secco. (28) Sardinia; Alghero vineyards, Sassari province. Ordinary to fair dry apéritif wine. Italy.

Tordesillas. (29) West New Castile; Valladolid, approx. seventy miles north-east of Avila. Ordinary red, and fair white and *clarete* wines. Spain.

Torey. (8) Côte de Nuits; Nuits-St-Georges vineyard. *Premier cru.* Red burgundy. France.

Torrão, Quinta. (30) *Região demarcada do Douro* (q.v.). Estate and vineyard in Valdigem south-west of Régua. Portugal.

Torre del Campo. (29) Jaén province, north-east of Seville. Ordinary to fair red and *clarete* table wines. Spain.

Torre Dembarra. (29) Tarragona. Ordinary table wines. Spain.

Torre de'Passeri. Another name for Abruzzo Rosso (q.v.). Italy.

Torre Donjimano. (29) Jaén province, north-west of Seville. Ordinary table wines. Spain.

Torre Ercolana. (28) Lazio; Frosinone area, approx. thirty miles east of Velletri. Ordinary rather full red table wine. Italy.

Torre Giulia. (28) Puglia; Carignola vineyards, Foggia area. Ordinary to fair white table wine. Italy.

Torrelaguna. (29) Madrid. Ordinary, sharp red table wine. Spain.

Torremegia. (29) Badajoz, between Trujillo and Seville. Ordinary to fair white table wine. Spain.

Torrente. (29) Valencia. Ordinary, dark red, rather sweet table wine. Spain.

Torre Quarto (Bianco, Rosso). (28) Apulia; San Severo vineyards, approx. eighteen miles north-east of Foggia. Ordinary to fair red and white table wines. Italy.

Torretta di San Pietro. (26) Val d'Aosta. Rarely found rich red dessert wine. Italy.

Torrevecchia. (28) Sardinia; Marceddi al Faro di Capo, Frosca, coastal area approx. fifty miles north-west of Cagliari. Ordinary to fair, sometimes frothy and *frizzante*, red table wine. Italy.

Torrijos. (29) West New Castile; Toledo, approx. forty miles south-west of Madrid. Ordinary table wines. Spain.

Torrinha, Quinta. *See* **Carraschal.**

Torroja. (29) Tarragona; Priorato. Ordinary to fair table wines. Spain.

Torrox. (29) Malaga. Ordinary table wines. Spain.

Tortillière, Clos de la. (16) Touraine; Bourgueil. Fair to fine red table wine. France.

Tostado. (29) Southern Galicia; Orense province. Ordinary to fair golden dessert wine is produced. Spain.

Tostallido. (29) Southern Galicia; Orense province. Ordinary to fair golden dessert wine. Spain.

Totana. (29) Murcia. Dark red and rather sweet table wine which becomes light and dry with age. Spain.

Toto. (29) Castile; Zamora, north of Toto. Ordinary dark red wine and fair white and *clarete* table wines. Spain.

Touché, La. (16) Anjou; Coteaux du Layon, Rablay-sur-Layon vineyard, below Angers. Fine white table wine. France.

Touchés. (9) Chalonnais; Bourgneuf Val d'Or vineyard. Ordinary to fair red burgundy. France.

Toulifaut, Château. (5) Pomerol. 1,200 dozen bottles of red bordeaux. France.

Toulifaut, Clos. (5) Pomerol. 1,000 dozen bottles of red bordeaux. France.

Toumalin, Château de. (3) Fronsac, Fronsadais. 2,500 dozen bottles of red bordeaux. France.

Toumalin, Clos. (3) Côtes de Fronsac; Fronsadais. 5,500 dozen bottles of red bordeaux. France.

Toumil, Quinta. (30) *Região demarcada do Douro* (q.v.). Estate and vineyard in São João de Lobrigos in the Régua area. Portugal.

Toumion, Château et Château Cabanes. (5) St Pierre-de-Mons, Langon area. 1,400 dozen bottles of red bordeaux; 1,500 white. France.

Touraine. (16) The *département* of Indre-et-Loire corresponds to the greater part of what was until 1790 the province of Touraine. Its chief city is Tours, the capital of Touraine from Gallo-Roman times, and the vineyards produce a great deal of very nice wines, both white and red, still and sparkling. France.

Touraine-Amboise. (16) The *Appellation Contrôlée* of red and white table wines from the Amboise area vineyards. France.

Touraine-Azay-le-Rideau. (16) *Appellation Contrôlée* of red and white table wines from the Azay-le-Rideau vineyard, between Chinon and Tours. France.

Tourais, Quinta. (30) *Região demarcada do Douro* (q.v.). Estate and vineyard in Cambres south-west of Régua. Portugal.

Tour-Baladoz, Château la. (5) St-Emilion; St Laurent-des-Combes, west of St Etienne-de-Lisse. An unclassified *cru*. 1,500 dozen bottles of red bordeaux. France.

Tour-Beau-Site, Château la. (3) Fronsac. 5,000 dozen bottles of red bordeaux. France.

Tour-Bicheau, Château la. (5) Graves de Bordeaux; Portets. An unclassified *cru*. 2,000 dozen bottles of red bordeaux; 1,500 white. France.

Tour-Blanche, Château la. (5) Sauternes; Bommes. *Premier cru classé.* 9,000 dozen bottles of white bordeaux. France.

Tour-Canon, Château la. (3) Fronsac. 2,000 dozen bottles of red bordeaux. France.

Tour-Carnet, Château la. (4) Haut-Médoc; St-Laurent. *Quatrième cru classé.* 8,000 dozen bottles of red bordeaux. France.

Tour-Clanet, Château la. (3) St André-de-Cubzac, south-east of Bourg, Cubzaguais. 5,000 dozen bottles of red bordeaux; 1,500 white. France.

Tour-de-Boyrien, Château la. (5) Roaillon, south-west of Langon. 2,000 dozen bottles of white bordeaux. France.

Tour-de-By, Château la. (3) Médoc; Bégadan, north-west of St Seurin-de-Cadourne. *Cru bourgeois.* 17,000 dozen bottles of red bordeaux. France.

Tour-de-Grenet, Château la. (5) St-Emilion; Lussac. An unclassified *cru*. 9,000 dozen bottles of red bordeaux; 3,000 white. France.

Tour-de-l'Espérance, Château la. (3) Galgon, north of Fronsac, Fronsadais. 1,500 dozen bottles of white bordeaux. France.

Tour-de-Marbuzet, Château la. (4) Haut-Médoc; St-Estèphe. *Cru bourgeois.* 3,000 dozen bottles of red bordeaux. France.

Tour-de-Mons, Château La. (4) Haut-Médoc; Soussans. *Cru bourgeois supérieur.* 10,000 dozen bottles of red bordeaux. France.

Tour-des-Combes, Château La. (5) St Emilion; St Laurent-des-Combes, west of St Etienne-de-Lisse. An unclassified *cru*. 4,000 dozen bottles of red bordeaux. France.

Tour-de-Ségur, Château La. (5) St-Emilion; Lussac. An unclassified *cru*. 6,000 dozen bottles of red bordeaux; 1,000 white. France.

Tour-des-Termes, Château La. (4) Haut-Médoc; St-Estèphe. *Cru bourgeois.* 10,000 dozen bottles of red bordeaux. France.

Tour-du-Bief, Château La. (11) Beaujolais; Chénas vineyard. Red beaujolais. France.

Tour-du-Guetteur, Château La. (5) Côtes de St-Emilion. An unclassified *cru*. 300 dozen bottles of red bordeaux. France.

Tour-du-Marbuzet, Château la. (4) Haut-Médoc; St Seurin-de-Cadourne. *Cru bourgeois.* 2,000 dozen bottles of red bordeaux. France.

Tour-du-Pin-Figeac, Château La. (5) Graves de St-Emilion. *Grand cru classé.* 5,000 dozen bottles of red bordeaux. France.

Tour-du-Roc, Château La. (4) Haut-Médoc; Arcins, north of Bordeaux. *Cru bourgeois.* 3,000 dozen bottles of red bordeaux. France.

Tourelle, La. (14) Côtes de Provence; Sanary-sur-Mer, west of Toulon. *AC Bandol.* Fair red and rosé table wines. France.

Tourenne, Château. (5) St Germain-la-Rivière, north-west of Fronsac, Fronsadais. 2,000 dozen bottles of red bordeaux. France.

Tour-Figeac, Château La. (5) Graves de St-Emilion. *Grand cru classé.* 8,000 dozen bottles of red bordeaux. France.

Tour-Gayet, Château La. (3) Blayais; St-Androny, north of Blaye. 3,000 dozen bottles of red bordeaux; 1,600 white. France.

Tour-Gueyraud, Château La. (5) Premières Côtes de Bordeaux; Ste-Eulalie, north-east of Bordeaux. 4,000 dozen bottles of red bordeaux; 1,000 white. France.

Tour Haut Brion, Château La. (5) Graves de Bordeaux; Talence. *Cru classé de Graves en rouge.* 1,800 dozen bottles of red bordeaux. France.

Tour-Haut-Caussan, Château La. (3) Médoc; Blaignan, north-east of Pauillac. *Cru bourgeois*. 2,500 dozen bottles of red bordeaux. France.

Tour L'Aspic, Cru La. (4) Haut-Médoc; Pauillac. *Cru bourgeois*. 500 dozen bottles of red bordeaux. France.

Tour-Marcillanet, Château La. (4) Haut-Médoc; St-Laurent. *Cru bourgeois*. 2,000 dozen bottles of red bordeaux. France.

Tour-Martillac, Château La. (5) Graves de Bordeaux; Martillac. An unclassified *cru*. 4,000 dozen bottles of red bordeaux; 1,500 white. France.

Tour-Montagne, Château La. (5) St-Emilion; Montagne. An unclassified *cru*. 3,000 dozen bottles of red bordeaux. France.

Tournefeuille, Château. (5) Néac by Pomerol. 6,000 dozen bottles of red bordeaux. France.

Tournon. (12) Côtes du Rhône. Town on the right bank of the Rhône, opposite Tain L'Ermitage. There are no Tournon vineyards, but most of the ordinary to fair table wines from the Ardèche *département* vineyards are known as *Vins de Tournon*. France.

Tournus. (10) The most northerly part of the Mâconnais, where it meets the Chalonnais. Ordinary to fair and some fine red burgundy. 1971 very small production. France.

Tour-Pibran, Château La. (4) Haut-Médoc; Pauillac. *Cru bourgeois supérieur*. 2,500 dozen bottles of red bordeaux. France.

Tour-Pourret, Château La. (5) Côtes de St-Emilion. An unclassified *cru*. 2,000 dozen bottles of red bordeaux. France.

Tour-Puyblanquet, Château La. (5) St-Emilion; St Etienne-de-Lisse. An unclassified *cru*. 2,000 dozen bottles of red bordeaux. France.

Tours, Château des. (5) St-Emilion; Montagne. An unclassified *cru*. 30,000 dozen bottles of red bordeaux. France.

Tour-Saint-Bonnet, Château La. (3) Médoc; St Christoly-de-Médoc, north of St Seurin de Cadourne. *Cru bourgeois*. 22,000 dozen bottles of red bordeaux. France.

Tour-Saint-Christophe, Château La. (5) St-Emilion; St Christophe-des-Bardes, south-west of Parsac. An unclassified *cru*. 800 dozen bottles of red bordeaux. France.

Tour-Saint-Emilion, Château La. (5) Côtes de St-Emilion. An unclassified *cru*. 1,000 dozen bottles of red bordeaux. France.

Tour-Saint-Georges, Château La. (5) St-Emilion; St-Georges, north-west of Parsac. An unclassified *cru*. 6,000 dozen bottles of red bordeaux. France.

Tour-Saint-Joseph, Château La. (4) Haut-Médoc; Cissac. *Cru bourgeois*. 5,000 dozen bottles of red bordeaux. France.

Tour-Saint-Pierre, Château La. (5) Côtes de St-Emilion. An unclassified *cru*. 4,000 dozen bottles of red bordeaux. France.

Tours-sur-Marne (red). (17) Marne *département*; Ay canton, south-west of Ambonnay. Rated *grand cru*—100% growth. 124 acres. France.

Tourteau, Château. (5) St-Emilion; St-Georges, north-west of Parsac. An unclassified *cru*. 3,500 dozen bottles of red bordeaux. France.

Tourteau-Chollet, Château. (5) Graves de Bordeaux; Arbanats, north-west of Podensac. 2,000 dozen bottles of red bordeaux; 2,500 white. France.

Tour-Vachon, Château La. (5) Côtes de St-Emilion. An unclassified *cru*. 2,000 dozen bottles of red bordeaux. France.

Toussaints, Les. (8) Côte de Beaune; Beaune vineyard. *Premier cru*. Red burgundy. France.

Touzinat-Bragard, Domaine de. (5) St-Emilion; St Christophe-des-Bardes, south-west of Parsac. An unclassified *cru*. 1,500 dozen bottles of red bordeaux. France.

Tracy. (15) Nièvre *département*; Pouilly-sur-Loire area. Fair white table wine. France.

Tracy, Château de. (15) Tracy. Fair to fine white wine with the *AC Pouilly-Fumé*. France.

Traenheim. (19) Bas-Rhin *département*. Ordinary to medium white Alsace table wine. France.

Traiguera. (29) Castellón de la Plana; approx. forty miles north-east of Valencia. Ordinary to fair red rather sweet table wine. Spain.

Traisen. (24) Nahe; west of Bad Münster. Fair white table wine. West Germany.

Trakia. (33) One of the lighter red table wines of Bulgaria.

Traminer Aromatico. (26) Alto Adige; Bolzano province. Fair white table wine which improves with age. Italy.

Tramini. (33) West-central Hungary; Somló. Fair red table wine. Hungary.

Tramont, Château. (4) Haut-Médoc; Arcins, north of Bordeaux. *Cru bourgeois*. 10,000 dozen bottles of red bordeaux. France.

Tramonti. (28) Campania; Amalfi vineyards, south-west of Salerno. Ordinary to fair sweetish, local red table wine. Italy.

Trani. (28) Apulia. Very ordinary rough red table wine. Italy.

Tranqueira, Quinta. (30) *Região demarcada do Douro* (q.v.). Estate and vineyard in Sarzedinho east of Régua. One of the finest properties in the Douro Valley. Portugal.

Trapaud, Château. (5) St-Emilion; St Etienne-de-Lisse. An unclassified *cru*. 6,500 dozen bottles of red bordeaux. France.

Trapeau, Domaine de. (5) St-Emilion; St Sulpice-de-Faleyrens. An unclassified *cru*. 3,000 dozen bottles of red bordeaux. France.

Trasfigurato di Seminara. (28) Calabria; Seminara, approx. twenty miles north-east of Reggio. Ordinary red table wine, said to be smoked in jars. Italy.

Traubengarten. (22) Moselle; Niederemmel vineyard, south of Piesport. Fair white table wine. West Germany.

Trebbiano di Arboreao. (28) Sardinia. Fair white table wine. Italy.

Trebbiano Sardo (Di Arborea). (28) Sardinia; Campidano plains stretching north-west from Cagliari. Fair, light white table wine. Italy.

Trebbiano Spoletino. (27) Umbria. The name of a rather distinct species of white Trebbiano grapes; also the name of a fair white wine made from them; it is not unlike Orvieto (q.v.) *secco*. Italy.

Trebujena. (29) Cadiz and Jerez. Fair to fine sherry. Spain.

Trehon, Château Le. (3) Médoc; Bégadan, north-west of St Seurin-de-Cadourne. *Cru bourgeois*. 5,000 dozen bottles of red bordeaux. France.

Treille et Canton de Milloc, Cru La. (5) Entre-deux-Mers; St-Gemme. 1,500 dozen bottles of red bordeaux; 1,000 white. France.

Treilles, Clos des. (16) Anjou; Côtes du Saumur, Sizay vineyard. Fair white table wine. France.

Treis. (22) Lower Moselle; west of Valwig, near Kochem. Fair white table wine. West Germany.

Treizadura. (29) Southern Galicia; Orense province. Fair white table wine. Spain.

Treppchen. (22) Moselle; Erden vineyard. Fair to fine white table wine. West Germany.

Treppchen. (22) Ruwer; Mertesdorf vineyard, north-east of Trier. Fine white table wine. West Germany.

Treuenfels. (25) Nahe; Altenbamberg vineyard, Alsenz valley, south of Bad Münster. Fair to fine white table wine. West Germany.

Treux, Les. (8) Côte de Nuits; Flagey-Echézeaux vineyard. *Premier cru*. Red burgundy. France.

Treves. *See* **Trier.**

Trevoes, Quinta. (30) *Região demarcada do Douro* (q.v.). Estate and vineyard in Castanheiro do Norte in the Régua area. Portugal.

Treytorrens. (31) Vaud canton; Dézaley vineyard. Fair to fine white table wine is produced. France.

Trianon, Château. (5) Côtes de St-Emilion. An unclassified *cru*. 2,000 dozen bottles of red bordeaux. France.

Tribourg, Au. (8) Côte de Nuits; Nuits-St-Georges. *Troisième cru*. Red burgundy. France.

Trier. (22) Moselle. 321 acres. Ordinary to fair white table wines. West Germany.

Trignon, Domaine de. (12) Côtes du Rhône; Gigondas area. Fair red table wine. France.

Trigueros. (29) Huelva. Ordinary table wines. Spain.

Trift. (25) Nahe; Waldhilbersheim vineyard. Fair white table wine. West Germany.

Trift. (24) Palatinate; Kallstadt vineyard. Fair white table wine. West Germany.

Trillon, Château. (5) Sauternes. *Cru bourgeois*. 1,200 dozen bottles of white bordeaux. France.

Trimoulet, Château. (5) Côtes de St-Emilion. *Grand cru classé*. 6,000 dozen bottles of red bordeaux. France.

Trinquevèdel, Domaine de. (12) Côtes du Rhône; Tavel vineyard. Fair to fine rosé table wine. France.

Trintignat, Domaine. (12) Côtes du Rhône; Châteauneuf-du-Pape vineyard. Fair to fine red table wine. France.

Trintin, Château. (5) Pomerol. 1,000 dozen bottles of red bordeaux. France.

Trittenheim. (22) Middle Moselle. Fair to fine white table wine. West Germany.

Trnovo. (33) Important wine centre of northern Bulgaria.

Troême. (6) Chablis vineyard. *Premier cru*. White burgundy. France.

Troia. (28) Apulia; vineyards of a village named Troia, south-west of Foggia. Ordinary red table wine from red Troia grapes. Italy.

Tronquey-Lalande, Château. (4) Haut-Médoc; St-Estèphe. *Cru bourgeois supérieur*. 7,500 dozen bottles of red bordeaux. France.

Tropchaud, Château. (5) Pomerol. 500 dozen bottles of red bordeaux. France.

Tropchaud, Clos. (5) Pomerol. 1,200 dozen bottles of red bordeaux. France.

Troplong-Mondot, Château. (5) Côtes de St-Emilion. *Grand cru classé*. 12,500 dozen bottles of red bordeaux. France.

Trottevieille, Château. (5) Côtes de St-Emilion. *Premier grand cru classé*. 5,000 dozen bottles of red bordeaux. France.

Trotzenberg. (21) Ahr valley; Marienthal vineyard. Ordinary to fair red table wine. West Germany.

Trujillo. (29) Northern Estremadura; Cáceres province. Ordinary to fair *clarete* table wine. Spain.

Truquet, Château. (5) Côtes de St-Emilion. An unclassified *cru*. 2,000 dozen bottles of red bordeaux. France.

Tsinandali. (34) Western Georgia; bordering on Turkey and the Black Sea. Ordinary to fair white table wine. U.S.S.R.

T.S.T. (37) South Australia; one of Australia's most widely known brandies, made by Tolley, Scott & Tolley Ltd., of Adelaide, Nuriootpa and Waikerie (owned by the Distillers Co. Ltd., of U.K.). T.S.T. enjoys a substantial export market. Australia.

Tua, Quinta. (30) *Região demarcada do Douro* (q.v.). Estate and vineyard in Castanheiro do Norte in the Régua area. Portugal.

Tübingen. (25) Württemberg; approx. eighteen miles south west of Stuttgart. Ordinary to fair red and white table wines are produced. West Germany.

Tudela. (29) Navarre. Ordinary red table wine. Spain.

Tudelilla. (29) Logroño province; La Rioja area of the upper Ebro valley. Ordinary to fair red table wine. Spain.

Tuilerie, Domaine de la. (3) Entre-deux-Mers; Cassaul, north-east of Langon. 6,500 dozen bottles of white bordeaux. France.

Tuilière, Viné de la. (31) Geneva canton; Dardagny vineyard. Fair white table wine. Switzerland.

Tulare County. (36) California. Chiefly noted for its sweet, fortified dessert wines, which is true for most of the Central Valley. U.S.A.

Tulcea. (33) Town in south-east Rumania. Fair to fine white table wine. Rumania.

Tulloch's. (37) New South Wales; Pokolbin, Hunter River Valley, north-east of Sydney. Chiefly noted for quality red table wine. Now owned by the Reed paper group. Australia.

Tunisia. (40) Approximately 20,000,000 dozen red, white and rosé table wines. Also some Muscat dessert wines.

Tuquet, Château Le. (3) Graves de Bordeaux; Beautiran, south-east of Bordeaux. 7,500 dozen bottles of white bordeaux. France.

Turckheim. (19) Haut-Rhin *département*. Ordinary to fair and some fine white Alsace table wine. France.

Turis. (29) Valencia. Ordinary to fair white table wine which is made in two grades, dry and sweet. Spain.

Turmberg. (24) Rhinegau; Kiedrich vineyard. Fair to fine white table wine. West Germany.

Turpeau, Château. (4) Graves de Bordeaux; Isle-St-Georges, south-east of Bordeaux. 1,500 dozen bottles of red bordeaux. France.

Turquant. (16) Anjou; Coteaux de Saumur. Ordinary to fair red, white and rosé table wines. France.

Turque, La. (12) Côtes du Rhône; Ampuis vineyard. Fine red table wine. France.

Tuscany. (27) The birthplace of many Italian wines, none better nor better-known than chianti. Italy.

Tutschfelden. (25) Baden; north of Freiburg. Fair to fine white table wine. West Germany.

Tuy. (29) West-central Galicia; Pontevedra. Coarse, harsh, red table wine. Spain.

Twann. (31) Bern canton; northern shore of the Lake of Bienne. Fair white table wines. Switzerland.

Tyrrell's. (37) New South Wales; Hunter River Valley, north-east of Sydney. Ashman's winery and vineyards; noted for their table wines. Australia.

☙

Ubeda. (29) Jaén province, north-east of Seville. Ordinary red table wine. Spain.

Überlingen. (25) Lake Constance (Bodensee); north of Konstanz. Ordinary to fair red and white table wines. West Germany.

Ubrique. (29) Cadiz. Ordinary to fair white table wine. Spain.

Ubstadt. (21) Baden; approx. sixteen miles south of Heidelberg. Ordinary to fair white table wine. West Germany.

Uchaux. (12) Vaucluse *département*; near Orange. Fair red table wine. France.

Udenheim. (24) Rhinehessia; west of Dienheim. Fair white table wine. West Germany.

Uffhofen. (24) Rhinehessia; south-west of Bad Kreuznach. Ordinary to fair white table wine. West Germany.

Ugolino Bianco. (27) Tuscany; Livorno coastal vineyards. Fair white table wine. Italy.

Uhlen. (22) Lower Moselle; Kobern and Winningen vineyards. Fair white table wine. West Germany.

Ullastrell. (29) Barcelona. Ordinary to fair white table wine. Spain.

Ülversheim. (24) Rhinehessia; north-west of Alsheim. Ordinary to fair white table wine. West Germany.

Umbrete. (29) Seville. Ordinary to fair white wine. Spain.

Umbria. (27) Region north of Rome and south of Florence. Many locally drunk table wines are produced. The wines of Orvieto (q.v.) alone are worthy of note. Italy.

Undenheim. (25) Rhinehessia; west of Nierstein. Fair to fine white table wine. West Germany.

Underragua. (35) One of the best table wines of Chile.

Ungeiheim. (25) Palatinate; Forst vineyard. Fair to fine white table wine. West Germany.

Ungsberg. (22) Moselle; Trarbach vineyard. Fair to fine white table wine. West Germany.

Ungstein. (23) Middle Haardt, Palatinate; north of Bad Dürkheim. Fair to fine white table wine. West Germany.

Unkel. (21) Middle Rhine; north-west of Linz. Ordinary to fair red and white table wines. West Germany.

Unterberg. (22) Saar; Kanzem vineyard. Fair to fine white table wine. West Germany.

Unterdürrbach. (25) Franconia; just north-west of Würzburg. Ordinary to fair red and white table wines. West Germany.

Untereisenheim. (25) Franconia; north-east of Würzburg. Fair to fine white table wine. West Germany.

Unterglottertal. (25) Baden; north-east of Freiburg. Ordinary to fair red and white table wines. West Germany.

Untergriesheim. (25) Württemberg; north of Heilbronn. Ordinary to fair red and white table wines. West Germany.

Untergrombach. (25) Baden; north-east of Karlsruhe. Fair white table wine. West Germany.

Unterjesingen. (25) Württemberg; approx. nineteen miles south-west of Stuttgart. Ordinary to fair red and white table wines. West Germany.

Unterleinach. (25) Franconia; north-west of Würzburg. Fair to fine white wine. West Germany.

Unteröwisheim. (25) Baden; north-east of Karlsruhe. Ordinary to fair red and white table wine. West Germany.

Unterriexingen. (25) Württemberg; north-west of Stuttgart. Ordinary to fair red and white table wines. West Germany.

Untersteinbach. (25) Württemberg; west of Konstanz. Ordinary to fair red and white table wines. West Germany.

Urbelt. (22) Saar; Filzen vineyard. Fair white table wine. West Germany.

Urglück. (22) Moselle; Ürzig vineyard. Fair to fine white table wine. West Germany.

Urlay. (22) Moselle; Ürzig vineyard. Fair white table wine. West Germany.

Uruguay. (35) There are between 19,000,000 and 20,000,000 dozen bottles of red, white and rosé table wines produced in this small country; also some sparkling and fortified wines.

Urunuela. (29) Logroño province; La Rioja area

of the upper Ebro valley. Ordinary to fair red table wine. Spain.

Ürzig. (22) Moselle; west of Kinheim. Fair to fine white table wine. West Germany.

Utiel. (29) West-central Valencia; Utiel-Requena. Fair light red table wine. Spain.

Uza, Clos d'. (5) St Pierre-de-Mons, Langon area. 1,000 dozen bottles of red bordeaux; 8,000 white. France.

☙

Vachon, Château. (5) Côtes de St-Emilion. An unclassified *cru*. 700 dozen bottles of red bordeaux. France.

Vachon, Clos. (5) Côtes de St-Emilion. An unclassified *cru*. 1,000 dozen bottles of red bordeaux. France.

Vaduzer. (31) Liechtenstein; a tiny principality between Switzerland and Austria, due east of the St Gallen canton in Switzerland. Ordinary to fair table wines named after the capital Vaduz. Liechtenstein.

Vaillons. (6) Chablis. *Premier cru*. Fine white burgundy. France.

Vaillons, Les. *See* **Roncieres**.

Vaisinèrie, Château. (5) St-Emilion; Puisseguin. An unclassified *cru*. 1,000 dozen bottles of red bordeaux. France.

Valais. (31) One of the chief wine-producing cantons of Switzerland. The Valais covers the Upper Rhône valley, and there are vineyards from Visp, past Sion and Martigny to where the Rhône runs into Lake Geneva. The best-known wine is Fendant, a dry white table wine. Switzerland.

Valandons. (8) Côte de Nuits; Chenove. *Troisième cru*. 1971 fully urbanized, no vineyards remain. Red burgundy. France.

Valbom, Quinta. (30) *Região demarcada do Douro* (q.v.). Estate and vineyard in Poiares north-east of Régua. Portugal.

Val d'Alpone. (26) Veneto; Colli Veronesi, Verona area. Fair red table wine. Italy.

Val d'Anapo (Bianco, Rosso). (28) Sicily; Syracuse hinterland vineyards. Fair, very clear, dry and light red and exceptionally dry white table wines, among the island's pleasantest wines. Italy.

Val d'Aosta. (26) The Alpine vineyards on the Italian side of the Italo–Swiss frontier, in the Val d'Aosta region high up in the Dora Ribares Valley, running down to the great Lombardy plain. The vines flourish as high as 2,500 feet above sea level. Italy.

Valdarados, Quinta. *See* **São Domingos.**

Valdefinca. (29) Central León; Zamora. Ordinary red and some fine *clarete* table wines. Spain.

Valdemora. (29) Madrid. Ordinary red table wine. Spain.

Valdengo. (26) Piedmont; Vercelli province. Ordinary to fair red table wine. Italy.

Valdeorras. (29) South Galicia; Orense. Ordinary to fair red and white table wines. Spain.

Valdeorras Tostado. (29) South Galicia; Orense. Ordinary to fair golden dessert wine. Spain.

Valdepeñas. (29) New Castile; Ciudad Real. Ordinary to fair red and rosé table wines. Spain.

Val di Chiana (Valchiana). (27) Tuscany; Arezzo, approx. thirty miles north-east of Siena. Ordinary white table wine. Italy.

Val d'Illasi. (26) Veneto; Colli Veronesi, Verona area. Fair red table wine. Italy.

Val di Lupo (Bianco, Rosso, Rosato). (28) Sicily. Fair, delicate and soft red, white and rosé table wines. Italy.

Val di Nievole. (27) Tuscany; Mentecatini vineyards, north-east of Lucca. Ordinary red and white table wines. Italy.

Valea Calugareasca. (33) In the cleft of Carpathian foothills; approx. fifty miles from Bucharest. The name means the valley of the moon. Fair cabernet red table wine, and fine white muscat dessert wine. Rumania.

Vale de Figueira, Quinta. (30) *Região demarcada do Douro* (q.v.). Estate and vineyard in Covas do Douro in the Régua area. Fine Port wine. Portugal.

Vale de Mendiz, Quinta. (30) *Região demarcada do Douro* (q.v.). Estate in Vale de Mendiz north-east of Régua. Portugal.

Vale do Fojo, Quinta. *See* **Boavista.**

Valencia. (29) Ordinary to fair red, white and rosé table wines and sweet dessert wines. Spain.

Valencia. (37) Western Australia; winery and vineyards at Caversham, in the Swan valley. Table and dessert wines. Owned by the Emu Wine Co., of London. Australia.

Valentin, Clos. (5) Côtes de St-Emilion. An unclassified *cru*. 2,000 dozen bottles of red bordeaux. France.

Valgella. (26) Lombardy; Toglio, from the Valtelline area. Ordinary to fair red table wine. Italy.

Valladolid. (29) Castile north of the Valdepeñas area. Ordinary to fair table wines. Spain.

Valledormo. (28) Sicily; Palermo area. Ordinary to fair red and white table wines. Italy.

Vallelunga. (28) Sicily. Ordinary to fair red and white table wines. Italy.

Vallerots, Les. (8) Côte de Nuits; Nuits-St-Georges vineyard. *Deuxième cru.* Little planted. Red burgundy. France.

Vallier, Château du. (5) Premières Côtes de Bordeaux; Langoiran, north-east of Portets. 600 dozen bottles of red bordeaux; 5,000 white. France.

Vallombrosa. (31) Ticino (Tessin) canton; Castelrotto. Fair white table wine. Switzerland.

Valls. (29) Tarrogona. Ordinary to fair white table wine. Spain.

Val Mezzane (Rosso). (26) Veneto; Colli Veronesi, Verona area. Fair red table wine. Italy.

Valmojado. (29) West New Castile; Toledo, approx. forty miles south-west of Madrid. Ordinary table wines. Spain.

Valmur. (6) Chablis. *Grand cru.* Fine white burgundy. France.

Valois, Château de. (5) Pomerol. 1,000 dozen bottles of red bordeaux. France.

Valoria La Buena. (29) Castile; Valladolid, approx. seventy miles north of Avila. Ordinary to fair red table wine. Spain.

Valoux, Château. (5) Graves de Bordeaux; Cadaujac. An unclassified *cru*. 1,800 dozen bottles of red bordeaux. France.

Valozières, Les. (8) Côte de Beaune; Aloxe-Corton vineyard. *Deuxième cru.* Red burgundy. France.

Valpantena. (26) Veneto; Val Pantena vineyards, of the valley running north from Verona. Fair red table wine similar to, but drier than Bardolino (q.v.) and Valpolicella (q.v.). Italy.

Valpolicella. (26) Veneto; north-western section of Verona province. The most popular and one of the best red table wines. Italy.

Valrose, Château. (4) Blayais; St-Anorony; north-east of Blaye. 12,500 dozen bottles of red bordeaux; 8,000 white. France.

Val San Martino. (26) Lombardy; Colli dei Frati, Bergamo area. Ordinary to fair red table wine. Italy.

Valtellina Rosso. (26) Lombardy; Sondrio area and hilly town of the Valtelline area. General name for the undistinguished, ordinary to fair red wines produced in this area. Italy.

Valtenesi. (26) Lombardy; lakeside vineyard of Lake Garda, Brescia. Ordinary to fair red table wine. Italy.

Valtidone Bianco. (26) Emilia-Romagna; hillside vineyards south-west of Piacenza, overlooking the Trebbia valley. Ordinary white table wine. Italy.

Valtramigno. (26) Veneto; Colli Veronesi, in the Verona area. Ordinary to fair red table wine. Italy.

Valva, Vini di. Another name for *Sele wines* (q.v.). Italy.

Valwig. (22) Lower Moselle. Fair to fine white table wines. West Germany.

Varanda, Quinta. (30) *Região demarcada do Douro* (q.v.). Estate and vineyard in Cambres south-west of Régua. Portugal.

Varenne. (16) Anjou; Coteaux de la Loire, Saviennières vineyard. Fair to fine white table wine. France.

Varennes, Les. (14) Anjou; Parnay vineyard in the Saumur area. Fair red table wine. France.

Vargelas, Quinta. (30) *Região demarcada do Douro* (q.v.). Estate and vineyard in Vale de Figueira twenty-two miles south-east of Régua. Portugal.

Varnhalt. (25) Baden; south-west of Baden-Baden. Ordinary to fair white table wine. West Germany.

Varogne. (12) Côtes du Rhône; Tain l-ermitage vineyard. Fair red table wine. France.

Varrains. (16) Anjou; Coteaux de Saumur vineyard. Fair red and rosé table wines. France.

Vascongadas. *See* **Basque.**

Vau Breton, Le. (16) Touraine; Ligré vineyard, north-west of Chinon. Fair red table wine. France.

Vauchretien. (16) Anjou; Coteaux de l'Aubance vineyard, between Angers and Saumur. Fair white and rosé table wines. France.

Vaucoupin. (6) Chablis; Chichée vineyard. *Premier cru Chablis.* Fair to fine white burgundy. France.

Vaucrains, Les. (8) Côte de Nuits; Nuits-St-Georges vineyard. *Premier cru.* One of finest Nuits *cuvées.* Red burgundy. France.

Vaud. (31) One of the two more important wine-producing cantons of Switzerland. The vineyards stretching along the north shore of Lake Geneva on either side of Lausanne, produce ordinary to fair white wines from Fendant grapes. Switzerland.

Vaudemanges. (17) Marne *département;* Verzy canton, north-east of Ambonnay. Rated *premier cru*—90% growth. 79 acres. France.

Vaudieu, Château de. (12) Côtes du Rhône; Châteauneuf-du-Pape. Fine red table wine. France.

Vaudon. (6) Chablis; Chichée vineyard. *Deuxième cru Chablis.* Fair white burgundy. France.

Vaufoynard, Clos de. (16) Touraine; Rochecorbon vineyard, north-east of Tours. Fair to fine white table wine. France.

Vaufuget, Clos. (16) Touraine; Vouvray vineyard, just north-east of Tours. Fair white table wine. France.

Vaugiros. (6) Chablis; Chichée vineyard. *Premier cru Chablis.* Fine white burgundy. France.

Vaumareus, Clos du Château de. (31) Neuchâtel.

vineyard. Fair red and white table wines. Switzerland.

Vaumorillons. (6) Chablis; Tonnerre region. Ordinary to fair white burgundy. France.

Vaureitres, Les. (16) Touraine; Coteaux de la Loire, La Poissonnière vineyard, south-west of Angers. Fair white table wine. France.

Vaux. (11) Beaujolais. Ordinary to fair red burgundy. France.

Vaux, Clos de. (16) Touraine; Vernon-sur-Brenne vineyard, north-east of Tours. Fair white table wine. France.

Vazes, Quinta. (30) *Região demarcada do Douro* (q.v.). Estate and vineyard in Cever in the Régua area. Portugal.

V.D.N *See* **Vins Doux Naturels.**

V.D.Q.S. *See* **Vins Délimités De Qualité Supérieure.**

Veaugues. (15) Upper Loire valley; Sancerre area. Ordinary to fair white table wine. France.

Vecchienna (Bianco, Rosso). (27) Tuscany; Grosseto area. Ordinary to fair sweet white and sweetish red table wines. Italy.

Vedial, Quinta. (30) *Região demarcada do Douro* (q.v.). Estate and vineyard in Gouvaes in the Régua area. Portugal.

Vega, La. (29) Granada; between Málaga and Baza. Ordinary to fair red table wine. Spain.

Vega Sicilia. (29) Castile; Valladolid, approx. seventy miles north of Avila. One of the best of all Spanish red table wines. Spain.

Veitshöchheim. (25) Franconia; north-west of Würzburg. Ordinary to fair red and white table wines. West Germany.

Veldenz. (22) Middle Moselle; east of Wintrich. Ordinary, fair and some fine white table wine. West Germany.

Velez. (29) Granada; between Málaga and Baza. Ordinary to fair red table wine. Spain.

Velez Málaga. (29) Málaga. Ordinary to fair table wines. Spain.

Velletri. (28) Lazio. Ordinary to fair red table wine. Italy.

Veltiner. (26) Alto Adige; Bolzano province. Fair to fine white table wine of Veltiner white grapes. Italy.

Vendersheim. (24) Rhinehessia; north-east of Bad Kreuznach. Ordinary to fair red and white tables wines. West Germany.

Vendrell. (29) Lower Panadés; between Tarragona and Valencia. Ordinary to fair wines. Spain.

Venelle, Château de la. (3) Côtes de Fronsac. 3,000 dozen bottles of red bordeaux. France.

Veneto. (26) The Italian region north-east of Venice. Its vineyards produce mostly fair white and red table wines. Italy.

Venialto. (29) Castile; Zamora north of Toro. Coarse, strong red table wine, and fair to fine claret wine. Spain.

Venningen. (25) Palatinate; east of Edenkoben. Ordinary to fair red and white table wines. West Germany.

Venta del Moro. (29) West-central Valencia; Uriel-Requena. Ordinary to fair table wines. Spain.

Ventoseio, Quinta. (30) *Região demarcada do Douro* (q.v.). Estate and vineyard in Ervedosa do Douro east of Régua. Portugal.

Ventoux, Côtes du. (12) Côtes du Rhône; Carpentras area, south-east of Orange. Ordinary, fair and some fine red table wine. France.

Verbicaro, Rosso di. (28) Calabria; Cosenza area, approx. thirty-five miles north-west of Cantanzaro. Ordinary dry red table wine. Italy.

Vercots, Les. (8) Côte de Beaune; Aloxe-Corton vineyard. *Deuxième cru.* Red burgundy. France.

Verdea (Verdeca). (28) Apulia; Bari area. Ordinary to fair white table wine, sometimes *frizzante.* Italy.

Verdelho. (30) Fine medium-sweet fortified wine made in Madeira an island 400 miles south-west of Lisbon named after its own grape variety. Improves in bottle. Portugal.

Verdet, Clos. (5) Sables de St-Emilion. An unclassified *cru.* 1,500 dozen bottles of red bordeaux. France.

Verdicchio dei Castelli di Jesi. (27) The Marches; Esino River valley west of Ancona. Good, sound white table wine generally considered as the best white table wine of The Marches. Italy.

Verdier-Renardière, Château. (5) Entre-deux-Mers; St Sulpice-de-Pommiers, north-east of Langon. 2,500 dozen bottles of white bordeaux. France.

Verdignan et Plantey-de-la-Croix, Château. (4) Haut-Médoc; St Seurin-de-Cadourne. *Cru bourgeois.* 8,000 dozen bottles of red bordeaux. France.

Verdiso. (26) Veneto; Treviso area. Ordinary golden table wine of Verdiso white grapes to be drunk young. Italy.

Verduc, Clos. (5) Premières Côtes de Bordeaux; St-Maixant, south-east of Ste Croix-du-Mont. 800 dozen bottles of red bordeaux; 1,500 white. France.

Verdus, Château. (4) Haut-Médoc; St Seurin-de-Cadourne. *Cru bourgeois.* 3,000 dozen bottles of red bordeaux. France.

Verduzzo di Ramandolo. (26) Veneto; Udine province. Fair, full, golden, semi-sweet and sweet dessert wines. Italy.

Vergelesses, Les. (8) Côte de Beaune; Savigny-les-Beaune. *Premier cru.* Red burgundy. France.

Vergelesses, Ile des. (8) Côte de Beaune; Pernand Vergelesses vineyard, Pernand. *Premier cru.* Fine red burgundy. France.

Vergennes, Les. (8) Côte de Beaune; Ladoix-Serrigny vineyard. *Premier cru. AC Corton.* Red burgundy. France.

Verger, Clos de. (8) Côte de Beaune; Pommard vineyard. *Premier cru.* Red burgundy. France.

Vergisson. (10) Mâconnais. Ordinary to fair red and white burgundy. France.

Verillats, Les. (11) Beaujolais; Chénas vineyard. Fine red beaujolais. France.

Vermentino (Vermentino di Gallura). (28) Sardinia; Sassari vineyard. Fair amber table wine so dry that it makes a good sherry-like apéritif. Italy.

Vermentino (Vermentino di Pietra Ligure). (26) Liguria; Savona and Imperia areas. Fair white table wine, some is slightly sparkling. Italy.

Vernaccia di Aldeno. (26) Trentino; Trento in the Alto Adige area. Ordinary, delicate white table wine often *frizzante.* Italy.

Vernaccia di Cannara. (26) Umbria; Perugia area. Fair sweet, deep-red dessert wine. Italy.

Vernaccia di Corniglia. (26) Liguria; Cinqueterre, area north-west of La Spezia. Another name for the *Sciacchetra* (q.v.). Italy.

Vernaccia di San Gimignano. (27) Tuscany. Fair to fine important white table wine is produced. Italy.

Vernaccia di Serrapetrona. (27) The Marches. Ordinary sweet red sparkling dessert wine. Italy.

Vernaille. (10) Mâconnais; Solutré vineyard. Fine white burgundy. France.

Verneries, Clos des. (16) Touraine; Vouvray vineyard, just north-east of Tours. Fair to fine white table wine. France.

Vernice. (26) Liguria. Ordinary to fair white table wine; it is made in two styles, dry and sweet. Italy.

Vernous, Château. (4) Haut-Médoc; Lesparre. *Cru bourgeois.* 1,500 dozen bottles of red bordeaux. France.

Vernou-sur-Brenne. (16) Touraine; Vouvray area, just north-east of Tours. Fair to fine white table wine. France.

Veronnière, La. (16) Anjou; Coteaux de l'Aubance, Soulaines-sur-Aubance vineyard, between Angers and Saumur. Fair white table wine. France.

Versberg. (22) Moselle; Enkirch vineyard. Fair white table wine. West Germany.

Vertheuil. (4) Haut-Médoc. Ordinary to fair red bordeaux. France.

Vertus. (17) Marne *département*; Chalon canton. Rated *premier cru*—93% growth. 1,073 acres. France.

Verzé. (10) Mâconnais. Ordinary to fair red burgundy. France.

Verzenay. (17) Marne *département*; Verzy canton. Rated *grand cru* for black—100% growth; white 86%. 930 acres. France.

Verzy. (17) Marne *département*. Rated *premier cru* for black—99% growth; white 86%. 923 acres. France.

Vespaiolo. (26) Veneto. Fair, light, white, sparkling dessert wine. Italy.

Vesuvio (Bianco, Rosso). (28) Campania. Ordinary white and red table wine. Italy.

Vesuvio, Quinta. (30) *Região demarcada do Douro* (q.v.). Estate and vineyard in Numao e Seixas in the Régua area. Large property of 1,000 acres. Portugal.

Veyres, Château. (5) Sauternes; Preignac. *Cru bourgeois*. 2,500 dozen bottles of white bordeaux. France.

Veyrin, Château. (4) Haut-Médoc; Listrac. *Cru bourgeois*. 2,000 dozen bottles of red bordeaux. France.

Veyrolles. (14) Côtes de Provence; Bandol area. Fair red and rosé wines. France.

Viana, Quinta. (30) *Região demarcada do Douro* (q.v.). Nos Quatro Caminhos. Estate and vineyard in Godim in the Régua area. Portugal.

Viaud, Château de. (5) Lalande-de-Pomerol; north of Pomerol. 4,500 dozen bottles of red bordeaux. France.

Viaud, Domaine de. (5) Lalande-de-Pomerol; north of Pomerol. 4,000 dozen bottles of red bordeaux. France.

Victoria, Château. (4) Haut-Médoc; Vertheuil. *Cru bourgeois*. 6,000 dozen bottles of red bordeaux. France.

Videlot, Château de. (5) Sables de St-Emilion. An unclassified *cru*. 500 dozen bottles of red bordeaux. France.

Vieille-Curé, Château La. (3) Saillans, north of Fronsac. 10,000 dozen bottles of red bordeaux. France.

Vieille-Eglise. (11) Beaujolais; Juliénas vineyard. Red burgundy. France.

Vieille-Voie, La. (6) Chablis vineyard. *Deuxième cru*. White burgundy. France.

Vien Tosc Rosso. (26) Emilia-Romagna; Reggio Emilia province. Ordinary very light red table wines. Italy.

Vieux-Castel, Château du. (3) Néac by Pomerol. 2,400 dozen bottles of red bordeaux. France.

Vieux-Cep. (5) Côtes de St-Emilion. An unclassified *cru*. 1,000 dozen bottles of red bordeaux. France.

Vieux-Château-Certan, Château. (5) Pomerol. *Grand cru*. 5,000 dozen bottles of red bordeaux. France.

Vieux-Château-Chauvin. (5) Graves de St-Emilion. 2,000 dozen bottles of red bordeaux. France.

Vieux-Château Cloquet. (5) Pomerol. 800 dozen bottles of red bordeaux. France.

Vieux-Château-Peymouton. (5) St-Emilion; St Christophe-des-Bardes, south-west of Parsac. An unclassified *cru*. 2,000 dozen bottles of red bordeaux. France.

Vieux-Cru Perruchot. (5) Pomerol. 1,200 dozen bottles of red bordeaux. France.

Vieux-Maillet, Château. (5) Pomerol. 1,500 dozen bottles of red bordeaux. France.

Vieux-Moulin, Cru du. (12) Côtes du Rhône; Tavel vineyard. Fair to fine rosé table wine. France.

Vieux-Moulin, Le. (12) Côtes du Rhône; Châteauneuf-du-Pape vineyard. Fair to fine red table wine. France.

Vieux-Moulin-du-Cadet, Château. (5) Côtes de St-Emilion. An unclassified *cru*. 1,000 dozen bottles of red bordeaux. France.

Vieux-Moulin-Haut-Loupiac, Château du. (5) Premières Côtes de Bordeaux; Loupiac. 1,500 dozen bottles of red bordeaux; 3,500 white. France.

Vieux-Pourret, Château. (5) Côtes de St-Emilion. An unclassified *cru*. 1,500 dozen bottles of red bordeaux. France.

Vieux-Sarpe, Château. (5) St-Emilion; St Christophe-des-Bardes, south-west of Parsac. An unclassified *cru*. 2,500 dozen bottles of red bordeaux. France.

Vieux-Télégraphe. (12) Côtes du Rhône; Châteauneuf-du-Pape vineyard. Fair to fine red table wine. France.

Vignanello Bianco and **Rosso.** (28) Lazio; Colli Cimini, south-east of Viterbo. Ordinary to fair white and red table wines. Italy.

Vigneau, Clos du. (16) Touraine; Vouvray vineyard, just north-east of Tours. Fine white table wine. France.

Vigneau, Le. (16) Touraine; Bourgueil vineyard. Fair to fine red table wine. France.

Vigne-au-Saint, La. (8) Côte de Beaune; Aloxe-Corton vineyard. *Premier cru*. Red burgundy. France.

Vigne Blanche, La. (18) Jura; L'Etoile vineyard, south-west of Château Chalon. Fair white table wine. France.

Vigne-des-Champs, La. (9) Chalonnais; Touchés vineyard, south-west of Chagny. Red burgundy. France.

Vigne-du-Diable. (31) Neuchâtel canton; Cortaillot vineyard. Fair red table wine. Switzerland.

Vigne-du-Maillange. (9) Chalonnais; Couches vineyard, south-west of Chagny. Red burgundy. France.

Vignerondes, Les. (8) Côte de Nuits; Nuits-St-Georges vineyard. *Deuxième cru*. Red burgundy. France.

Vignes Blanches. (9) Chalonnais; Mercurey vineyard. Fine red burgundy. France.

Vignes Blanches, Les. (8) Côte de Nuits; Flagey-Echézeaux vineyard. *Premier cru*. Red burgundy. France.

Vignes Blanches, Les. (10) Mâconnais; Fuissé vineyard. Fine white burgundy entitled to the *AC Pouilly-Fuissé*. France.

Vignolles. (16) Anjou; Coteaux de Saumur, Montsoreau vineyard, south-east of Saumur. Fair to fine white table wine. France.

Vignon, Château du. (5) St-Emilion; Lussac. An unclassified *cru*. 2,000 dozen bottles of red bordeaux. France.

Vignonet. (5) St-Emilion *commune*. Fair red bordeaux. France.

Vignots, Les. (8) Côte de Beaune; Pommard vineyard. *Deuxième cru*. Red burgundy. France.

Viktoriaberg. (24) Rhinegau; Hochheim vineyard. Fine white table wine. West Germany.

Vilajuich. (29) Gerona; approx. twenty-five miles north-east of Barcelona. Ordinary to fair red and white table wines; also some fair white dessert wine. Spain.

Vila Maior, Quinta. (30) *Região demarcada do Douro* (q.v.). Estate and vineyard in São João de Lobrigos in the Régua area. Portugal.

Vilar, Quinta. (30) *Região demarcada do Douro* (q.v.). Estate and vineyard in Fontelo south-east of Régua. Portugal.

Vilarinho, Quinta. (30) *Região demarcada do Douro* (q.v.). Estate and vineyard in Vacalar in the Régua area. Four houses on the property. Portugal.

Vilarrodona. (29) Tarragona. Ordinary to fair table wines. Spain.

Vilaseca de Solcima. (29) Tarragona. Ordinary to fair white dessert wine. Spain.

Vilellas, La. (29) Tarragona. Ordinary to fair table wines. Spain.

Villacarillo. (29) Jaén province, north-east of Seville. Ordinary to fair red table wine. Spain.

Villa de Don Fabrique. (29) West New Castile; Toledo, approx. forty miles south-west of Madrid. Ordinary table wines. Spain.

Villa del Arzobispo. (29) Valencia. Ordinary to fair light, dry, white table wine. Spain.

Villaescusa. (29) Central León; Zamora. Ordinary, dark red table wine, and some fair to fine *clarete* wine. Spain.

Villa Felipe. (29) Aragon; Zaragoza. Ordinary table wines. Spain.

Villafranca. (29) Central Navarre; Peralta. Ordinary to fair table wines. Spain.

Villa Franca. (29) León. Ordinary, dry, sharp, red table wine. Spain.

Villafranca del Biezo. (29) South-western León; Valdeorras. Ordinary table wines. Spain.

Villafranca de los Barros. (29) Badajoz; between Seville and Trujillo. Fair white table wine. Spain.

Villafranca del Panadés. (29) Barcelona. A major centre of fair to fine table wines. Spain.

Village de Pommard. (8) Côte de Beaune; Pommard vineyard *Premier cru*. Red burgundy. France.

Village de Volnay. (8) Côte de Beaune; Volnay vineyard. Red burgundy. France.

Villagonzalo. (29) Badajoz; between Seville and Trujillo. Ordinary to fair white table wine. Spain.

Villagrande (Bianco, Rosso). (28) Sicily; Mount Etna foothills south of Catania. Ordinary red and white table wines. Italy.

Villalazan. (29) Central León; Zamora. Ordinary dark red table wine, and some fair to fine *clarete* wine. Spain.

Villalba del Alcor. (29) Huelva. Ordinary table wines. Spain.

Villalpando. (29) Central León; Zamora. Ordinary red and fair *clarete* table wines. Spain.

Villamare. (14) Côtes de Provence; Cassis. Fair red and rosé table wines. France.

Villamayor de Santiago. (29) East New Castile; Cuenca. Ordinary to fair red table wine. Spain.

Villamayor Moscatel. (29) Zaragoza. Ordinary to fair golden dessert wine. Spain.

Villamayro. (29) Old Castile; Salamanca south of Toro. Ordinary to fair light, dry, red table wine. Spain.

Villanueva de la Jara. (29) East New Castile; Cuenca. Ordinary red table wine. Spain.

Villanueva de la Serena. (29) Badajoz; between Seville and Trujillo. Ordinary to fair white table wine. Spain.

Villanyi Pécser. (33) Near Yugoslav border; Pécs area, approx. 100 miles south-west of Budapest. Strong red table wine. Hungary.

Villapando. (29) East New Castile; Cuenca. Ordinary red table wine. Spain.

Villarasa. (29) Huelva. Ordinary table wines. Spain.

Villarino. (29) Old Castile; Salamanca south of Toro. Ordinary to fair red table wine. Spain.

Villarobledo. (29) Albacete; approx. twenty-three

miles south-east of La Roda. Ordinary to fair red table wine. Spain.

Villarreal. (29) Valencia; Castellón de la Plana province. Ordinary to fair red table wine. Spain.

Villarya de la Sierra. (29) Aragon. Ordinary to fair table wines. Spain.

Villaviciosa de Córdoba. (29) Córdoba; Montilla-Morilles area, north-east of Seville. Fair to fine white table wine. Spain.

Villedieu, La. (13) Tarn-et-Garonne *département*. *V.D.Q.S.* red and white table wines. France.

Villedommange. (17) Marne *département*; Ville-en-Tardenois canton, south-west of Rheims. Rated *premier cru*—90% growth. 400 acres. France.

Villegeorge, Château. (4) Haut-Médoc; Avensan. *Cru exceptionnel.* 5,000 dozen bottles of red bordeaux. France.

Villemaurine, Château. (5) Côtes de St-Emilion. *Grand cru classé.* 7,000 dozen bottles of red bordeaux. France.

Villena. (29) Alicante; approx. forty miles south of Valencia. Ordinary table wines. Spain.

Ville-Morgon. (11) Beaujolais. Ordinary to fair and some fine red beaujolais. France.

Villenave-de-Rions. (5) Premières Côtes de Bordeaux; east of Portets. Ordinary to fair red and white bordeaux. France.

Villanueva. (29) Lower Panadés; between Tarragona and Barcelona. Ordinary table wines. Spain.

Villeneuve-sur-Yonne. (6) Joigny area; north of Auxerre. Fair white burgundy. 1971 now little wine produced. France.

Villers-Marmery. (17) Marne *département*; Verzy canton, south-east of Verzy. Rated *premier cru*—90% growth. 511 acres. France.

Villié-Morgon. (11) Town in Beaujolais. Ordinary to fair and some fine red burgundy sold as *AC Morgon.* France.

Villingen. (31) Aargau canton. Ordinary table wines, mostly red. Switzerland.

Vinaudières, Les. (16) Touraine; Restigné vineyards, Bourgueil area. Fair red table wine. France.

Vin Cotto. Literally, 'cooked wine'. Italian dessert wine made from must reduced over a slow heat to a fifth of its original volume; brought back to its original volume with must, it is then aged for two years, producing a sweet rich wine of about 20°. Italy.

Vin de Béarn. (2) Hautes Pyrénées and Gers *départements* of south-west France, north of Spanish border. *V.D.Q.S.* white and rosé table wines. France.

Vin de Costera. Another name for Reciotto del Trentino (q.v.). Italy.

Vin de Paille. Sweet, white dessert wine of over-ripe grapes which have been left on straw mats, after picking, when they lose some of their water content by evaporation, before being pressed. France.

Vin di Lusso. Italian for dessert wine. Italy.

Vindoux. (16) Touraine; Ligré vineyard, Chinon area. Fair red table wine. France.

Vinebre. (29) Tarragona. Ordinary table wines. Spain.

Vin Gris. (19) The inexpensive and ordinary very pale rosé—wines made from black grapes, in eastern France, especially Alsace. France.

Vinho Verde. (30) Literally 'green wine', although green here in the sense of 'youth'. Naturally petillant wines from a demarcated area north of the Douro Valley—in the Minho. Subdivided into six subregions. Red, white or rosé table wines. Portugal.

Vini Liquorosi. Italian for sweet dessert wines.

Vinillo Belmontino. *See* **Belmonte.**

Vin Jaune. (18) Deep-golden dessert wine of very ripe white grapes mostly from the Jura vineyards. France.

Vino Corriente. (29) Spanish for plain or 'ordinaire' table wines. Spain.

Vino Cotto. *See* **Vin Cotto.**

Vino da Frutta. Italian for dessert wine. Italy.

Vino da Pasto. Italian for table wine. Italy.

Vino da Pesce. Italian for a white light and dry wine best served with fish. Italy.

Vino de Anada. (29) Spanish for 'vintage wine' meaning wine classified by year rather than type or vineyard. Spain.

Vino de Color. (29) Spanish for a *Vino cotto* (q.v.), dark gold or tawny, not for drinking but for adding to sherries when it is considered desirable to make them darker and sweeter. Spain.

Vino del Ano. (29) Spanish for 'wine of the year' meaning not over twelve months old. Spain.

Vino della Serra. (26) Val d'Aosta; Ivrea area, approx. thirty miles north-east of Turin. Ordinary to fair red and white table wines. Italy.

Vino de Pasto. (29) The name given to a light and fairly dry sherry considered suitable to be served as a luncheon or table wine. Spain.

Vino de Quarte. (29) Valencia. Ordinary to fair rosé table wine. Spain.

Vino Dulce. (29) Concentrated grape-juice or must, laced with brandy, used to sweeten and fortify dessert wines. Spain.

Vino Frizzante. The semi-sparkling poor relation of the *vino spumante.* Italy.

Vino Maestro. A particularly sweet wine high in alcoholic strength, which is kept in reserve and used to 'improve' other wines. Italy.

Vino Nobile. Italian for a wine of outstanding quality. Italy.

Vin Ordinaire. The French name of all plain or 'ordinary' table wines. France.

Vino Santo. *See* Vin Santo.

Vino Tierno. Another name for *vino maestro* (q.v.). Italy.

Vin Santo. Sweet white dessert wine made of semi-dried, white grapes in many parts of Italy: there are many different grades of sweetness and of quality, some of the best comes from Urbino approx. forty-five miles north-west of Ancona and Ripatransone approx. forty miles south-east of Ancona. Italy.

Vins Delimités de Qualité Supérieure. Official certificate given to some very fine wine. France.

Vins Doux Naturels. (13) Languedoc and Roussillon. Sweet, unfortified, dessert wines, golden to tawny. France.

Vino Santo. (34) Island of Thira (Santorini); south-east of Greek mainland. Fair to fine white dessert wine. Greece.

Vinzelles. (10) Mâconnais. *AC Pouilly Vinzelles.* Ordinary to fair red and white burgundy.

Violette, Château La. (5) Pomerol. 2,000 dozen bottles of red bordeaux. France.

Vira. (29) Logroño province; La Rioja area of the Upper Ebro valley. Ordinary to fair white table wine. Spain.

Vire. (10) Mâconnais. Ordinary to fair red burgundy. France.

Virelade. (5) Graves de Bordeaux. Ordinary to fair table wines. France.

Virelade, Château de. (5) Graves de Bordeaux; Virelade, north-west of Podensac. An unclassified *cru*. 2,000 dozen bottles of red bordeaux; 1,000 white. France.

Virginia. (35) American State with only few vineyards which, however, yield table wines of very fair quality. U.S.A.

Vispthal. (31) Valais canton; Alpine vineyards at the head of Rhône valley, the highest in Europe. Ordinary to fair white wine is produced. Switzerland.

Vitulano (Bianco, Rosso). (28) Campania; Benevento vineyards, north of Avellino. Ordinary red table wine much used for mixing. Italy.

Vivier, Le. (11) Beaujolais; hamlet close by Fleurie vineyard. *AC Fleurie* and some *Beaujolais Villages.* Fair red burgundy. France.

Vogelsgarten. (24) Rhinehessia; Guntersblum area, between Alsheim and Dienheim. Fair white table wine. West Germany.

Vögisheim. (25) Baden; south-west of Freiburg. Ordinary to fair and some fine white table wine. West Germany.

Voiteur. (18) Jura; Arbois area. Fair *vin jaune* and ordinary white table wine. France.

Volkach. (25) Franconia; north-east of Würzburg. Fair to fine white table wine. West Germany.

Vollmersweiler. (23) Palatinate; south of Landau. Fair white table wine. West Germany.

Vollrads, Schloss. (24) Rhinegau; Winkel's finest estate and vineyard. Very fine white table wine. West Germany.

Volnay. (8) Côte de Beaune vineyard. Fair to fine red burgundy. France.

Volxheim. (29) Rhinehessia; east of Bad Münster. Fair to fine and some very fine white table wine. West Germany.

Vorbachzimmern. (25) Württemberg; approx. twenty-five miles south of Würzburg. Ordinary to fair red and white table wines. West Germany.

Vosgros. (6) Chablis area, Chichée vineyard. *Premier cru Chablis.* White burgundy. France.

Voslau. (33) Lower Austria; ordinary fair, and some fine red and white table wine. Also some red sparkling wine. Austria.

Vosne-Romanée. (8) Côte de Nuits. Perhaps the most famous *commune* in all Burgundy. Fair fine and very fine to great red burgundies come from seven or eight vineyards all labelled with the vineyard name alone—others bear the *commune* name. France.

Vougeot. (8) Côte de Nuits. A small *commune* on the Côte d'Or with the largest and most famous of all Burgundy vineyards, Clos de Vougeot (q.v.). France.

Vougeot, Clos de. (8) Vougeot. *Grand cru.* Owned by 65 different individual *vignerons* which accounts for the fact that perfectly genuine Clos de Vougeot wines are never identical in standard of quality. Fine red burgundy and a little white wine of good quality Clos Blanc de Vougeot (q.v.). France.

Vraye-Croix-de-Gay, Château. (5) Pomerol. 1,500 dozen bottles of red bordeaux. France.

Vully. (31) Neuchâtel canton. Fair white table wine. Switzerland.

🍇

Waadt. *See* Vaud.

Wachau. (33) Lower Austria; Danube valley. Fair to fine white table wine. Its best wines are those of Krems and Durstein. Austria.

Wachenheim. (23) Palatinate, Middle Haardt. Ordinary and fair red wine; fair, fine and some very fine white table wines. West Germany.

Wachenheim. (24) Rhinehessia; west of Worms. Ordinary to fair red and white table wines. West Germany.

Q

Wackernheim. (24) Rhinehessia; south-east of Erbach. Ordinary to fair red and white table wines. West Germany.

Wagenkehr. (24) Rhinegau; Rauenthal vineyard. Fair to fine white table wine. West Germany.

Wagenstadt. (25) Baden; north-west of Freiburg. Ordinary to fair red and white table wines. West Germany.

Wahlheim. (24) Rhinehessia; south-west of Alsheim. Fair to fine white table wine. West Germany.

Waikerie. (37) South Australia; fourth largest irrigation settlement in State and site of co-operative winery and distillery (formed in 1919) and of a branch of Hardy's Wines. Several other companies, based elsewhere, have vineyards downstream from Waikerie. Australia.

Waldberg. (23) Palatinate; Deidesheim vineyard. Fine white table wine. West Germany.

Waldböckelheim. (25) Nahe; west of Bad Münster. Fair to fine white table wine. West Germany.

Waldhilbersheim. (25) Nahe; north-west of Bad Kreuznach. Ordinary to fair white table wine. West Germany.

Waldlaubersheim. (25) Nahe; south-west of Bingen. Fair white table wine. West Germany.

Waldrach. (22) Ruwer. Fair to fine white table wine. Best vineyard: Doktor. West Germany.

Waldulm. (25) Baden; south-west of Baden-Baden. Fair red and white table wines. West Germany.

Walhöhle. (23) Palatinate; Forst vineyard. Fair to fine white table wine. West Germany.

Walkenberg. (24) Rhinegau; Niederwalluf vineyard. Fair to fine white table wine. West Germany.

Wallburg. (25) Baden; approx. twenty-two miles south-east of Strasbourg. Fair white table wine. West Germany.

Wallertheim. (24) Rhinehessia; east of Bad Kreuznach. Fair white table wine is produced. West Germany.

Wallhausen. (24) Nahe; north-west of Bad Kreuznach. Ordinary fair and some fine white table wines. West Germany.

Wallis. *See* **Valais.**

Walluf. (29) Rhinegau. Fair to fine white table wine. Two small towns, Nieder and Ober-Walluf, were amalgamated to form Walluf. West Germany.

Walporzheim. (21) Ahr valley; west of Linz. Fair to fine red table wine. West Germany.

Walsheim. (23) Palatinate; north of Landau. Ordinary to fair, and some fine red and white table wines. West Germany.

Walterberg. (22) Moselle; Kasel vineyard. Fair to fine white table wine. West Germany.

Waltershofen. (25) Baden; north-west of Freiburg. Fair white table wine. West Germany.

Wandkaut. (24) Rhinegau; Hochheim vineyard. Fair to fine white table wine. West Germany.

Wangen. (19) Bas-Rhin *département*; north-west of Molsheim. Ordinary to fair white Alsace table wine. France.

Warmark. (34) Ordinary to fair red and white table wines. Turkey.

Warna. (33) Ordinary to fair red and white table wines of Bulgaria.

Warte. (24) Rhinehessia; Nierstein vineyard. Fair white table wine. West Germany.

Wasenweiler. (25) Baden; north-west of Freiburg. Fair red and white table wines. West Germany.

Washington. (35) State north of California, with not many vineyards but they all grow the European (*vinifere*) grape and yield fair wines. U.S.A.

Wasserbillig. (22) Moselle; north-west of Kanzem, on the German-Luxembourg frontier. Ordinary white table wine. West Germany.

Wasserrose. (24) Rhinegau; Kiedrich vineyard. Fair to fine white table wines. West Germany.

Wawern. (22) Saar; west of Wiltingen. Fair to fine and some very fine white table wines. West Germany.

Weg. (24) Rhinegau; Oestrich and Hallgarten vineyards. Fine white table wine. West Germany.

Wehlen. (22) Middle Moselle. Fair, fine and some very fine white table wines. West Germany.

Wehling. (24) Rhinehessia; Gau-Bischofsheim vineyard, west of Nackenheim. Fair to fine white table wine. West Germany.

Wehweg. (24) Rhinehessia; Guntersblum vineyard, between Alsheim and Dienheim. Fair to fine white table wine. West Germany.

Weibel Champagne Vineyards. (36) California; Mission San José, Alameda County. Mostly American champagne, but also table wines and vermouth. U.S.A.

Weid. (24) Rhinegau; Hochheim vineyard. Fair to fine white table wine. West Germany.

Weierbach. (22) Moselle; Trittenheim vineyard. Fair white table wine. West Germany.

Weierberg. (29) Rhinegau; Kiedrich vineyard. Fair to fine white table wine. West Germany.

Weigenheim. (25) Franconia; approx. twenty miles south-east of Würzburg. Fair to fine white table wine. West Germany.

Weiher. (24) Rhinegau; Hochheim and Johannisberg vineyards. Fair to fine white table wine. West Germany.

Weikersheim. (25) Württemberg; approx. twenty miles south of Würzburg. Ordinary to fair red and white table wines. West Germany.

Weil-am-Rhein. (21) Baden; north-east of Basel. Fair red and white table wines. West Germany.

Weilberg. (23) Palatinate; Üngstein vineyard, north of Bad Dürkheim. Fair to fine white table wine. West Germany.

Weiler. (21) Lake Constance (Bodensee); north-west of Konstanz. Ordinary to fair red and white table wines. West Germany.

Weiler-an-der-Zaber. (25) Württemberg; south-west of Heilbronn. Ordinary red and white table wines. West Germany.

Weiler-bei-Bingerbrück. (24) Nahe; just south-west of Bingerbrück. Fair to fine white table wine. West Germany.

Weiler-bei-Monzingen. (24) Nahe; west of Bad Münster. Fine white table wine. West Germany.

Weilheim-an-der-Teck (25) Württemberg; approx. twenty miles south-east of Stuttgart. Fair white table wine. West Germany.

Weinbach. (23) Palatinate; Deidesheim vineyard. Fine white table wine. West Germany.

Weinborn. (23) Palatinate; Wachenheim vineyard. Fair to fine white table wine. West Germany.

Weingarten. (23) Palatinate; north-east of Landau. Fair to fine white table wine. West Germany.

Weingrübe. (22) Moselle; Reil vineyard, east of Zell. Fair white table wine. West Germany.

Weinheim. (21) Bergstrasse; north of Heidelberg. Fair to fine white table wine. West Germany.

Weinheim. (24) Rhinehessia; west of Alsheim. Fair to fine white table wine. West Germany.

Weinkammer. (22) Moselle; Enkirch vineyard. Fair to fine white table wine. West Germany.

Weinolsheim. (24) Rhinehessia; south-west of Dienheim. Fair to fine table wine. West Germany.

Weinsberg. (25) Württemberg; east of Heilbronn. Ordinary to fair red and white table wines. West Germany.

Weisenheim-am-Berg. (23) Palatinate; south-west of Dackenheim. Ordinary, fair and some fine red and white table wines. West Germany.

Weisenheim-am-Sand. (23) Palatinate; east of Dackenheim. Ordinary, fair and some fine red and white table wines. West Germany.

Weissach. (25) Württemberg; north-west of Stuttgart. Ordinary to fair white table wine. West Germany.

Weissenberg. (22) Moselle; Kobern and Briedel vineyards, between Zeller and Enkirch. Fair white table wine. West Germany.

Weissenauer. (23) Palatinate; Königsbach vineyard. Fine white table wine. West Germany.

Weissenstein. (22) Moselle; Kues vineyard. Fair white table wine. West Germany.

Weissert. (24) Rhinegau; Hochheim vineyard. Fair to fine white table wine. West Germany.

Weissmauer. (23) Palatinate; Königsbach vineyard. Fine white table wine. West Germany.

Welgesheim. (24) Rhinehessia; north-east of Bad Kreuznach. Fair red and white table wines. West Germany.

Wellenstein. (32) Moselle; south of Remich. Fair white table wines. Luxembourg.

Wellington. (39) Western Cape Province. One of the wine- and grape-producing centres. South Africa.

Wellmich. (21) Middle Rhine; south-east of Bingen. Ordinary to fair white table wine. West Germany.

Welschberg. (24) Nahe; Waldböckelheim vineyard, west of Bad Münster. Fair to fine white table wine. West Germany.

Wente Bros. (36) California; Livermore. Quality red and white table wines. Noted for the excellence of its white wines especially, Rhine and Burgundy types. U.S.A.

Werbach. (25) Baden; south-west of Würzburg. Fair white table wine. West Germany.

Westerberg. (24) Nahe; Heddesheim vineyard, north-west of Bad Kreuznach. Fair white table wine. West Germany.

Westerberg. (24) Rhinehessia; Niedersaulheim vineyard, west of Nierstein. Fair white table wine. West Germany.

Western Vineyard. (38) Auckland area; foothill vineyards of the Waitekere range, Henderson valley. New Zealand.

Westhalten. (19) Haut-Rhin *département*. Ordinary to fine white Alsace table wine. France.

Westhofen. (24) Rhinehessia; north-west of Worms. Ordinary to fair and some fine red and white table wines. West Germany.

Westrum. (24) Rhinehessia; Bodenheim vineyard. Fair white table wine. West Germany.

Wettelbrunnen. (25) Baden; south-west of Freiburg. Fair white table wine. West Germany.

Wetterkreuzberg. (23) Palatinate; Maikammer vineyard, between Neustadt and Edenkoben. Fair white table wine. West Germany.

Wettingen. (31) Aargau canton. Fair white table wine. Switzerland.

Wettolsheim. (19) Haut-Rhin *département*; south-east of Turckheim. Ordinary to fair white Alsace table wine. France.

Weyersborn. (24) Rhinehessia; Nackenheim vineyard. Fair white table wine. West Germany.

Weyher. (23) Palatinate; north-west of Landau. Ordinary to fair red and white table wines. West Germany.

Wicker. (24) Rhinegau; east of Hochheim. Fair white table wine. West Germany.

Widdern. (25) Württemberg; south-east of

Mosbach. Ordinary to fair red and white table wines. West Germany.

Wiesbaden. (24) Rhinegau. Fair white table wine. West Germany.

Wiesbaden-Dotzheim. (24) Rhinegau; at Wiesbaden. Ordinary white table wine. West Germany.

Wiesbaden-Schierstein. (24) Rhinegau. Fair white table wine. West Germany.

Wiesberg. (24) Nahe; Rüdesheim vineyard. Fair white table wine. West Germany.

Wiesberg. (24) Rhinegau; Rauenthal vineyard. Fair to fine white table wine. West Germany.

Wiesberg. (24) Rhinehessia; Gau-Bickelheim vineyard, east of Bad Kreuznach. Fair white table wine. West Germany.

Wiesenbronn. (25) Franconia; south-east of Würzburg. Fair white table wine. West Germany.

Wieshell. (24) Rhinegau; Rauenthal vineyard. Fine white table wine. West Germany.

Wiesloch. (21) Baden, Bergstrasse; south of Heidelberg. Ordinary to fair red and white table wines. West Germany.

Wies-Oppenheim. (24) Rhinehessia; south-west of Worms. Fair to fine white table wine. West Germany.

Willsbach. (25) Württemberg; east of Heilbronn. Ordinary to fair red and white table wines. West Germany.

Willsborn. (24) Rhinegau; Hattenheim vineyard, west of Erbach. Fair to fine white table wine. West Germany.

Wilm. (25) Franconia; Sommerach vineyard, north-east of Würzburg. Fair white table wine. West Germany.

Wiltingen. (22) Saar. Ordinary, fair and fine white table wines. West Germany.

Wincheringen. (22) Moselle; west of Saarburg. Ordinary to fair white table wine. West Germany.

Windesheim. (24) Nahe; south-west of Bingen. Ordinary to fair white table wine. West Germany.

Wingert. (24) Rhinegau; Rüdesheim vineyard. Fair to fine white table wine. West Germany.

Winkel. (24) Rhinegau. Fair to fine white table wine. West Germany.

Winnenden. (25) Württemberg; north-east of Stuttgart. Ordinary to fair red and white table wines. West Germany.

Winningen. (22) Lower Moselle. Ordinary to fair, and some fine white table wines. West Germany.

Winterborn. (23) Palatinate; south of Bad Kreuznach. Fair white table wine. West Germany.

Winterhausen. (25) Franconia; south-east of Würzburg. Fair white table wine. West Germany.

Wintersheck. (22) Saar; Serrig vineyard. Fair white table wine. West Germany.

Wintersheim. (24) Rhinehessia; west of Alsheim. Fair white table wine. West Germany.

Wintersweiler. (21) Baden; north of Basel. Fair white table wine. West Germany.

Wintrange. (32) Moselle. Ordinary to fair, and some fine white table wine. Luxembourg.

Wintrich. (22) Middle Moselle. Ordinary fair and fine white table wines. West Germany.

Wintzenheim. (19) Haut-Rhin *département*. Fair to fine white Alsace table wine. France.

Winzenheim. (24) Nahe; north of Bad Kreuznach. Fair to fine white table wines. West Germany.

Wipfeld. (25) Franconia; north-east of Würzburg. Fair white table wine. West Germany.

Wirmsthal. (25) Franconia; approx. sixty miles west of Frankfurt. Fair white table wine. West Germany.

Wisberg. (24) Nahe; Roxheim vineyard, north-west of Bad Kreuznach. Fair white table wine. West Germany.

Wisselbrunnen. (24) Rhinegau; Hattenheim vineyard, between Erbach and Mittelheim. Fine white table wine. West Germany.

Wissemburg. (19) Bas-Rhin *département*; north-east of Soultz. Ordinary white Alsace table wine. France.

Wittlich. (22) Middle Moselle; west of Ürzig. Ordinary fair and some fine white table wines. West Germany.

Wolf. (22) Middle Moselle; north-east of Traben-Trarbach. Fair white table wine. West Germany.

Wolfenweiler. (25) Baden; south-west of Freiburg. Fair white table wine. West Germany.

Wölflein. (25) Franconia; Thüngersheim vineyard, north-west of Würzburg. Fair white table wine. West Germany.

Wolfsberg. (22) Saar; Kanzem vineyard. Fair to fine white table wine. West Germany.

Wolfsdarm. (23) Palatinate; Wachenheim vineyard. Fair to fine white table wine. West Germany.

Wolfsheim. (24) Rhinehessia; north-east of Bad Kreuznach. Fair to fine white table wine. West Germany.

Wolfshöhle. (21) Middle Rhine; Bacharach vineyard, north-west of Bingen. Fair white table wine. West Germany.

Wolfstein. (23) Palatinate; approx. eighteen miles south-west of Bad Münster. Fair white table wine. West Germany.

Wollbach. (21) Baden; north-east of Basel. Fair white table wine. West Germany.

Wollmesheim. (23) Palatinate; south-west of Landau. Fair to fine white table wine. West Germany.

Wöllstein. (24) Rhinehessia; east of Bad Münster.

Fair red and white table wines. West Germany.

Wolm. (24) Rhinehessia; Bechtheim vineyard (south-west of Alsheim) and Osthofen vineyard (between Worms and Alsheim). Fair white table wines. West Germany.

Wolxheim. (19) Bas-Rhin *département*; north-east of Molsheim. Ordinary to fair white Alsace table wine. France.

Wonsheim. (24) Rhinehessia; south-west of Bad Münster. Fair white table wine. West Germany.

Woodley. (37) South Australia; Glen Osmond, foothills suburb of Adelaide. Vineyard planted 1865 is extinct, but winery with its famous old silver-mine tunnel storage continues under control of Melbourne interests. Australia.

Worcester. (39) Western Cape Province. One of the important wine centres. South Africa.

Wormeldange. (32) Moselle. Ordinary, fair and some fine table wines. Luxembourg.

Worms. (24) Rhinehessia. Ordinary white table wine. The home of Liebfraumilch wines. West Germany.

Worms-Horchheim. (24) Rhinehessia; outside Worms. Ordinary to fair red and white table wines. West Germany.

Worms-Leiselheim. (24) Rhinehessia. Ordinary to fair white table wine. West Germany.

Worms-Weinsheim. (24) Rhinehessia. Ordinary red table wine. West Germany.

Wörrstadt. (24) Rhinehessia; west of Dienheim. Ordinary to fair red and white table wines. West Germany.

Wöschbach. (25) Baden; east of Karlsruhe. Fair white table wine. West Germany.

Wülfen. (24) Rhinegau; Rauenthal vineyard. Fine white table wine. West Germany.

Würzberger-Helenenberg. (22) Saar; Serrig vineyard. Fair to fine white table wine. West Germany.

Würzberger-Marienberg. (22) Saar, Serrig vineyard. Fair to fine white table wine. West Germany.

Würzburg. (25) Franconia. The principal town in Franconia; the home of Steinwein. Fair, fine and some very fine white table wines. West Germany.

Wust. (24) Rhinegau; Rüdesheim vineyard. Fair white table wine. West Germany.

Wybong. (37) New South Wales; a 700-acre estate acquired by Penfolds in Upper Hunter Valley north-east of Sydney in 1960 and renamed Dalwood Estate. The company's big new winery there came into production in 1967. Australia.

Wynberg. (39) Cape Peninsula. Town where the first vineyard was planted in the 17th century in South Africa.

Wynn's Wines. (37) Victoria; South Australia, and New South Wales. Head office is in Melbourne; vineyards and wineries at Coonawarra, Modbury, Magill (South Australia) and Yenda (New South Wales). Company headed by Wynn family. Australia.

Xarello. (29) Barcelona. A white grape used for table wines. Spain.

Yakima Valley. (36) Washington State, north of California. The home of the best vineyards of the State. U.S.A.

Yakut Damilasi. (34) One of the better red table wines. Turkey.

Yaldara. (37) South Australia; Lyndoch Barossa Valley, approx. thirty-five miles north-east of Adelaide. Winery, founded 1957, it has made tremendous progress and has a château of art treasures gathered by proprietor Hermann Thumm. Australia.

Yalumba. (37) South Australia; Angaston, Barossa Valley, approx. thirty-five miles north-east of Adelaide. Founded in 1847 by Samuel Smith, English brewer; fourth and fifth generation of his descendants now conduct large winery producing all types of wines. Australia.

Yamanashi. (1) One of the chief wine-producing areas of Japan.

Yepes. (29) West New Castile; Toledo, approx. forty miles south-west of Madrid. Ordinary table wines. Spain.

Yesa. (29) Navarre. Ordinary red wine. Spain.

Yeste. (29) Albacete; approx. twenty-three miles south-east of La Roda. Ordinary, rather sweet, red table wine. Spain.

Yon, Château de. (5) St-Emilion; St Christophe-des-Bardes, south-west of Parsac. An unclassified *cru*. 3,000 dozen bottles of red bordeaux. France.

York Winery. (36) California; Templeton. Quality red and white table wines. U.S.A.

Yquem, Château d' (formerly Château Yquem). (5) Sauternes. *Premier grand cru classé*. The most famous and the best sweet white wine of Bordeaux. 10,000 dozen bottles. France.

Yverdon. (31) Neuchâtel canton. Fair to fine white table wine. Switzerland.

Yvonne, Clos. (16) Touraine; Côte de Montlouis, St Martin-le-Beau vineyard, east of Tours. Fair white table wine. France.

Yvrac. (5) Premières Côtes de Bordeaux; north-east of Bordeaux. Ordinary to fair red and white bordeaux. France.

☙

Zaberfeld. (25) Württemberg; south-west of Heilbronn. Ordinary to fair red and white table wines. West Germany.

Zaccar, Côtes du. (40) Ordinary to fair Algerian red and white table wines accorded the *V.D.Q.S.* appellation under French rule, when their alcoholic strength reached 12°. Algeria.

Zafra. (29) Badajoz; between Seville and Trujillo. Ordinary to fair white table wine. Spain.

Zagarese. (28) Apulia; Bari-Brindisi-Lecce area. Ordinary strong sweet dessert wine, like Málaga or Marsala. Italy.

Zagarolo (Bianco, Rosso). (28) Lazio; Palestrina, approx. twenty miles south-east of Rome. Fair, usually semi-sweet white dessert wine and ordinary red table wine. Italy.

Zahnacker. (19) Haut-Rhin *département*; Ribeauvillé vineyard. Fair to fine white Alsace table wine. France.

Zaisersweiher. (25) Württemberg; approx. eighteen miles south-west of Heilbronn. Ordinary to fair red and white table wines. West Germany.

Zancara. (29) New Castile; Ciudad Real, in the Valdepeñas area. Ordinary table wines. Spain.

Zederberg. (22) Moselle; Trier vineyard. Ordinary to fair white table wine. West Germany.

Zehnmorgen. (23) Palatinate; Diedesfeld vineyard, between Kirrweiler and Neustadt. Fair white table wine. West Germany.

Zehn-Morgen. (24) Rhinehessia; Nierstein vineyard. Fine white table wine. West Germany.

Zell. (25) Franconia. Fair white table wine. West Germany.

Zell. (22) Moselle. Fair white wine. West Germany.

Zell. (23) Palatinate; north-west of Worms. Ordinary to fair red and white table wines. West Germany.

Zellenberg. (19) Haut-Rhin *département*; just north-east of Riquewihr. Fair to fine white Alsace table wine. France.

Zellenberg. (22) Moselle; Mehring vineyard, south-west of Klüsserath. Fair white table wine. West Germany.

Zell-Weierbach. (25) Baden; approx. twenty-two miles south-west of Baden-Baden. Ordinary fair, and some fine white and red table wines. West Germany.

Zeltingen. (22) Moselle. Fair to fine white table wine. West Germany.

Zeppwingert. (22) Moselle; Enkirch vineyard. Fair to fine white table wine. West Germany.

Zeutern. (21) Baden; south of Heidelberg. Fair white table wine. West Germany.

Ziegler. (23) Palatinate; Forst vineyard. Fine white table wine. West Germany.

Zikhron. (34) One of the more important wine centres of Israel.

Zilavka. (33) West central Yugoslavia; Mostar, Hercegovina. Full, fine dry white table wine. One of the most famous wines from Yugoslavia. Yugoslavia.

Zinfandel. (36) California. The origin of this grape has never been determined. The vine has not been found in Europe even though it is certain that Agorton Hararzthy obtained cuttings in Europe. It is the distinctive grape of California, producing a fruity but very sound red table wine, which at its best is far greater than ordinary. U.S.A.

Zinkovich's Sunny Vineyard. (38) North Island; Kerikeri, Northland, approx. 120 miles north-west of Auckland. New Zealand.

Ziserser. (31) Ordinary, inexpensive, and popular rosé table wine. Switzerland.

Zoll-Haus. (24) Rhinegau; Rüdesheim vineyard. Fair white table wine. West Germany.

Zon, Quinta. (30) *Região demarcada do Douro* (q.v.). Estate and vineyard in Freixo de Espada a Cinta in the Régua area. Has been in the same family since 1684. Portugal.

Zornheim. (24) Rhinehessia; west of Nierstein. Fair white table wine. West Germany.

Zotzenheim. (24) Rhinehessia; north-east of Bad Kreuznach. Fair white table wine. West Germany.

Zucco. (28) Sicily; Palermo area. Fair white dessert wine made from Muscat grapes. Italy.

Zuckerberg. (24) Rhinehessia; Oppenheim vineyard. Fine white table wine is produced. West Germany.

Zuckernberg. (22) Saar; Konz vineyard, north of Filzen. Fair white table wine. West Germany.

Zunsweier. (25) Baden; approx. twenty-five miles south-west of Baden-Baden. Fair white table wine. West Germany.

Zupa. (33) Central Serbia; east-central Yugoslavia. Ordinary red and rosé wines. Yugoslavia.

Zurich. (31) Swiss canton. 1,700 acres of vineyards. Ordinary red and white table wines. Switzerland.

Zursach. (31) Aargau canton. Ordinary red table wine. Switzerland.

Zwingenberg. (21) Baden, Bergstrasse, Hesse: approx. seventeen miles north-east of Mannheim. Ordinary to fair red and white table wines. West Germany.

Zwölfmorgen. (24) Rhinehessia; Dienheim vineyard. Fair white table wine. West Germany.

SELECT BIBLIOGRAPHY

Although at present there is no other single volume which contains as much information about the wines and vineyards of the world as this compilation, it is still necessary to direct the reader to other works of reference in order to complete the picture of modern viticulture. Therefore, the following lists of books are included; the first to provide a general background of the wine arts, the second to enable the reader to gain a firm knowledge of the viticulture of one particular country or region.

Gold, Alec, ed. *Wines & Spirits of the World*, 1968.

Hyams, Edward. *Dionysus—A Social History of the Wine Vine*, 1965.

Johnson, Hugh. *Wine*, 1966.

Johnson, Hugh. The *World Atlas of Wine*, 1971.

Lichine, Alexis. *Encyclopedia of Wines & Spirits*, 1967.

Bradford, Sarah. *The Englishman's Wine*, 1969.

Cocks & Féret. *Bordeaux Et Ses Vins*, Bordeaux, Féret et Fils, 1969.

Forbes, Patrick. *Champagne*, 1967.

Gunyon, R. E. H. *The Wines of Central & South-Eastern Europe*, 1971.

Jeffs, Julian. *Sherry*, 1971.

Penning-Rowsell, Edmund. *The Wines of Bordeaux*, 1971.

Ray, Cyril. *The Wines of Italy*, 1966.

Simon, André. *The Noble Grapes & Great Wines of France*.

Simon, André & Hallgarten, S. F. *The Great Wines of Germany*, 1963.

Yoxall, H. W. *The Wines of Burgundy*, London, 1968.

MAPS OF THE VINELANDS OF THE WORLD

The lists accompanying each map group all the
vineyards described in the text for that area under
the names of the nearest town or other point of
reference that is marked on the map.

List of Maps

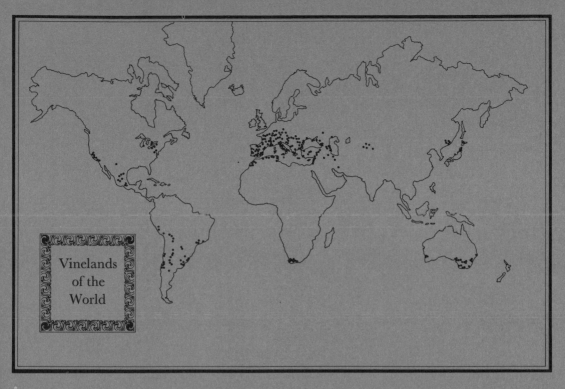

Map 1 — Vinelands of the World

Map 2 — Vinelands of France

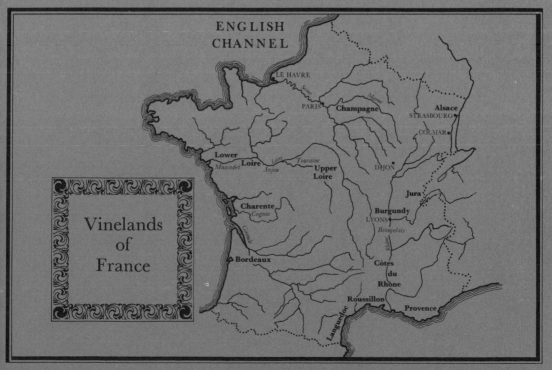

**ENGLISH
CHANNEL**

LE HAVRE

Seine

PARIS

Marne

Champagne

Alsace

STRASBOURG

COLMAR

**Lower
Loire**

Muscadet

Loire

Touraine

Anjou

**Upper
Loire**

DIJON

Jura

Charente

Cognac

Burgundy

LYONS

Beaujolais

Gironde

Bordeaux

Rhône

**Côtes
du
Rhône**

Roussillon

Provence

Languedoc

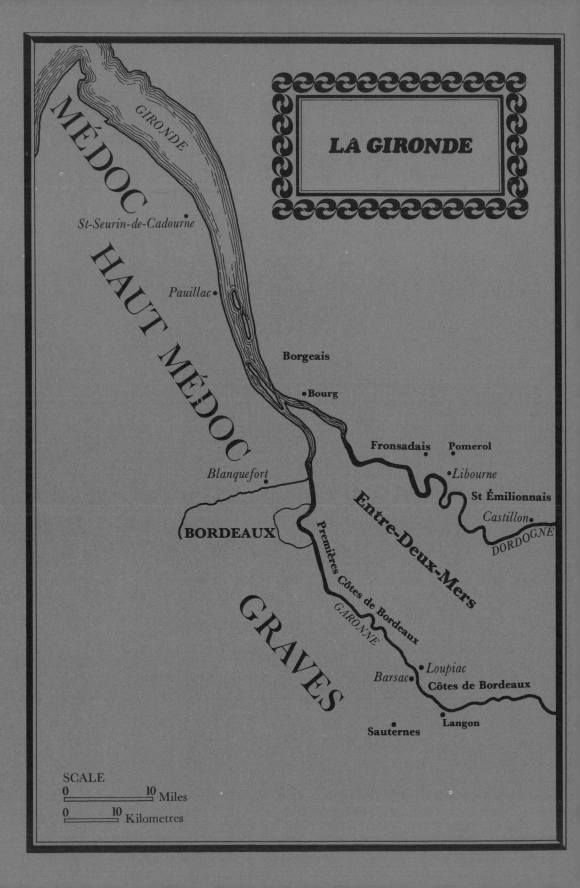

LÁ GIRONDE

GIRONDE

MÉDOC

HAUT MÉDOC

St-Seurin-de-Cadourne

Pauillac

Borgeais

Bourg

Fronsadais   Pomerol

Libourne

Blanquefort   St Émilionnais

Castillon

BORDEAUX   Entre-Deux-Mers   DORDOGNE

Premières Côtes de Bordeaux

GARONNE

GRAVES   Loupiac

Barsac   Côtes de Bordeaux

Langon

Sauternes

SCALE
0   10 Miles
0   10 Kilometres

Map 3   La Gironde

Barsac
Hallet, Château

Blanquefort
Lacanau, Domaine de
Malbec, Château
Montjon-Le-Gravier,
    Château

Blaye
Barbe, Château
Barre
Beney
Bouilh, Château du
Charron, Château
Gazin-Montaigu, Château
Pérenne, Château
Terrasse, Domaine de la
Tonnelle, Château La
Tour-Gayet, Château La

Bordeaux
Auriol, Cru
Cadillac
Gironde
Laroche, Domaine de
Picot-La-Plateyre,
    Domaine de
Saint-Eulalie
Saint-Selve
Tuquet, Château Le
Turpeau, Château

Borgeais
Barde, Château La
Blissa, Château de
Conilh-Haute-Libarde,
    Château
Croix-Miliorit, Château
    de la
Croute-Camponac,
    Château
Croute-Charlus, Château
Grand-Jour, Château

Bourg
Augiers, Château des
Beaulieu, Château
Bel-Air, Château
Berthou, Château
Cantenac, Clos de
Clotte-Blanche,
    Domaine de

Colbert, Château
Eyquem, Château
Falfas, Château
Grolet, Château La
Guerry, Château
Rousset, Château
Serquin, Château
Tayac, Château
Thau, Château de
Timberlay, Château
Tour-Clanet, Château La

Castillon
Cadet, Château
Cantemerle, Château
Castegens, Château
Chapelle-Monrepos,
    Château de la
Mondésir, Château
Sainte-Foy-Bordeaux
Saint-Genes

Frondsadais
Arnauton, Château
Asques
Barabaque, Château
Bellegarde, Château
Belloy, Château
Bodet, Château
Bouildé, Château
Bourdieu-la-Valade,
    Château
Bourdieu-Panet, Cru
Canon, Château
Canon-Lange, Château
Capet-Begaud, Château
Cartes, Château de
Catheyre, Domaine de
Chapelle-Lariveau,
    Château La
Cleyrac, Château
Comte, Château
Côtes-Canon-Fronsac
Croix, Château La
Croix-Gandineau,
    Château La
Dalem, Cru
Dauphine, Château La
Fontaine, Château La
Gaby, Château
Grave, Château La
Junayme, Château
Lagüe, Château

Larchevesque, Château
Malgarni-et-Coutreau,
    Château de
Marche-Canon,
    Château La
Mayne-Vieil, Château
Moulin-Pey-Labrie,
    Domaine du
Panet, Château
Pavillon-Haut-Gros-
    Bonnet, Château du
Pey-la-Brie, Château
Pichelèvre, Château
Pierres, Domaine des
Plainpoint, Château
Recougne, Château
Renard-Mondésir,
    Château
Rey, Domaine du
Rivière, La
Rivière, Château La
Rouet, Château
Saint-Germain-La Rivière
Tasta, Château
Terrefort-Quancard,
    Château de
Thouil, Château de
Toumalin, Château de
Toumalin, Clos
Tour-Beau-Site,
    Château La
Tour-Canon, Château La
Tour-de-l'Espérance,
    Château La
Tourenne, Château
Venelle, Château de la
Vieille-Cure, Château La

Gironde
Soulac

Langon
Cabanne
Saint-Aignan, Château
Saint-Germain, Château
Tuilerie, Domaine de la

Libourne
Rateau, Château

Loupiac
Arnaud-Jouan, Château
Moyne, Château Le

Lussac
Lucas, Château

Pauillac
Anseillan, Château
Couronne, Château La
Tour-Haut-Caussan,
    Château La

Pomerol
Bourg, Château du
Chatain
Chatain, Château
Croix, Château La
Cruzelles, Château des
Soulate, Château La
Surget, Château

**Première Côtes de
    Bordeaux**
Croix, Château La

St Seurin-de-Cadourne
Bégadan
Bel-Air-Mareil, Cru
Château-Bégadan-Médoc
Hermitage, Château L'
Lagune, Domaine de la
Landon, Château
Lartigue, Château
Lassalle, Cru
Laujac, Château
Livran, Château
Loudenne, Château
Monthil, Cru
Ordonnac-et-Potensac
Panigon, Château
Patache-d'Aux, Château
Potensac, Château de
Privera, Château
Roc, Château Le
Saint-Bonnet, Château
Saint-Christoly, Château
Saint-Christoly-de-Médoc
Saint-Germain d'Esteuil
Saint-Vivien
Saint-Yzans
Tour-de-By, Château La
Tour-Saint-Bonnet,
    Château La
Trehon, Château Le

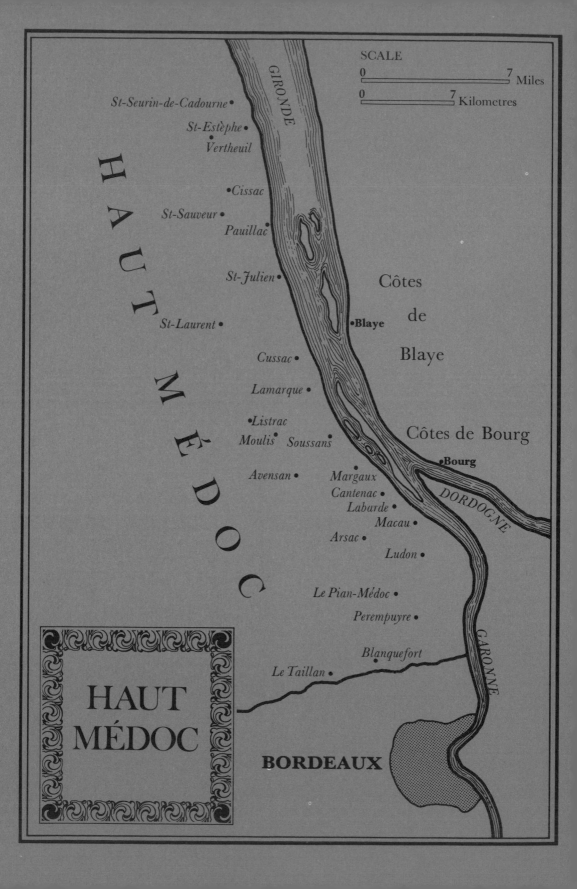

SCALE

0 ———————————— 7 Miles

0 ———————————— 7 Kilometres

GIRONDE

St-Seurin-de-Cadourne •

St-Estèphe •

Vertheuil •

• Cissac

St-Sauveur •

Pauillac •

St-Julien •

Côtes

de

St-Laurent •

• Blaye

Blaye

Cussac •

Lamarque •

• Listrac

Côtes de Bourg

Moulis • Soussans

• Bourg

Avensan • Margaux •

Cantenac •

DORDOGNE

Labarde •

Macau •

Arsac •

Ludon •

Le Pian-Médoc •

Perempuyre •

GARONNE

Blanquefort •

Le Taillan •

HAUT MÉDOC

BORDEAUX

H A U T   M É D O C

Map 4 – Haut Médoc

Arsac
Barreyre, Château
Coteau, Cru Le
Tertre, Château du

Avensan
Citran, Château
Meyre-Estèbe, Château
Villegeorge, Château

Blanquefort
Blanc, Château
Dillon, Château
Grand-Clapaud-Olivier,
    Château
Muscadet, Château

Blaye
Alberts, Château des
Bellevue-Gazin
Boisset, Château
Bourdieu, Château
Cabanne, Château La
Cayeaux, Château
Chay, Château Le
Cone-Neveu, Château Le
Cone-Sebillon,
    Château Le
Cone-Taillasson-
    Sabourin, Château Le
Croix-de-Merlet,
    Domaine de la
Crusquet-de-Lagarcie,
    Château
Cure, Château La
Des Moines, Château
Dupeyrat, Château
Escadre, Château L'
Garosse, Domaine de la
Gauvin, Château
Geneau, Château de
Gigault, Château
Girouette, Domaine de la
Gontier, Château
Grand-Porto, Domaine de
Grange-Marivins-de-
    Lupe, Château La
Hargue, Château La
Labrousse, Château La
Lamothe, Château
Lauberterie, Cru
Loumède, Domaine de
Magdeleine-Bouhou,
    Château La
Mayence, Château
Mayne-Boyer, Château
Mayne-Gazin,
    Château Le
Meneau, Château
Monconseil-Gazin,
    Château
Morillon, Château
Paillerie, Château La
Perreyre, Château
Petite-Roque, Cru La
Petits-Arnauds,
    Château des
Peybonhomme-Les-
    Tours, Château
Peyrebrune, Château

Peyredoulle, Château
Pinet, Château
Pinet-La-Roquette,
    Château
Piney, Clos du
Pomard, Clos
Prieuré, Château Le
Puy-Benet-Laffitte
Ravion, Domaine de
Rebouquet, Domaine de
Ricadet, Domaine de
Ricards, Château Les
Ricaud, Château
Valrose, Château

Bordeaux
Arcins
Arcins, Château d'
Arnauld, Château d'
Cap-de-Haut, Château
Grand-Arnaud
Tour-du-Roc, Château La
Tramont, Château

Bourg
Grolet, Château La
Haut-Libarde, Château de
Lagrange, Château
Lamothe, Château
Launay, Château
Laurensanne, Château
Marsillac, Château
Mendoce, Château
Mille-Secousses, Château
Monge, Château de la
Monge, Cru de la
Nodeau, Domaine de
Norion-Lalibarde,
    Château
Peychaud, Château
Peyrolan, Château
Piat, Clos du
Plantonne, Domaine de la
Poyanne, Cru de
Raynaud, Domaine de
Rébeymont, Château
Rider, Château
Roc, Château Le
Samonac ou Macay,
    Château de
Sauman, Château

Cantenac
Brane-Cantenac, Château
Cantenac-Brown, Château
Issan, Château d'
Kirwan, Château
Martinens, Château
Montbrun, Château
Palmer, Château
Pontac-Lynch, Château
Prieuré-Lichine, Château

Cissac
Breuil, Château du
Cissac, Château
Hanteillan, Château
Larrivaux, Château
Tour-Saint-Joseph,
    Château La

Côtes de Blaye
Bellevue, Château

Cussac
Beaumont, Château
Chesnaye-Sainte-Gemme,
    Château La
Fort-Médoc
Lamothe-de-Bergeron,
    Château
Lanessan, Château
Raux, Château du
Romefort, Château

Labarde
Dauzac, Château
Giscours, Château
Siran, Château

Lamarque
Cadillon, Cru
Castillon, Château du
Felletin, Château
Lamarque, Château de
Malescasse, Château

Le Pian Médoc
Malleret, Château
Saint Médard-en-Jalle
Sénéjac, Château

Le Taillan
Dame-Blanche,
    Château La
Fontanet, Château

Listrac
Bellegrave, Château
Fonréaud, Château
Fourcas-Dupré, Château
Fourcas-Hosten, Château
Lafon, Château
Lalande, Château
Lestage, Château
Moulin-de-Laborde,
    Domaine du
Moulin-du-Bourg,
    Domaine de
Pierre-Bibian, Château
Reverdi, Château
Saint-Laurent
Saransot-Dupré, Château
Veyrin, Château

Ludon
Aiche, Château d'
Barthez, Château
Bizeaudun, Cru de
Egmont, Château d'
Lafite-Canteloup,
    Château
Lagune, Château La
Lemaine-Lafont-Rochet,
    Château
Ludon-Pomies-Agassac,
    Château
Nexon-Lemoyne, Château

Macau
Beychevelle, Domaine de

Cantemerle, Château
Fellonneau-Labrie,
    Château
Montagnes, Château

Margaux
Angludet, Château
Boyd-Cantenac, Château
Desmirail, Château
Durfort-Vivens, Château
Ferrière, Château
Gurgue, Château La
Ile Margaux
Labégorce, Château
Lamouroux, Château
Lascombes, Château
Malescat-Saint-Exupéry,
    Château
Margaux, Château
Marquis d'Alesme-
    Becker, Château
Marquis-de-Terme,
    Château
Monbrison, Château
Pavillon Blanc du
    Château Margaux
Rausan-Ségla, Château
Rauzan-Gassies, Château

Moulis
Anthonic, Château
Chasse-Spleen, Château
Closerie-Grand-Poujeaux,
    Château La
Duplessis-Hauchecorne,
    Château
Dutruch-Grand-
    Poujeaux, Château
Ermitage, Château L'
Lestage-Darquier-Grand-
    Poujeaux, Château
Morère, Château La
Moulin-à-Vent, Château
Moulis, Château
Pomys, Château

Pauillac
Batailley, Château
Bellegrave, Château
Carruades, Grand Cru des
Clerc-Milon-Mondon,
    Château
Croizet-Bages, Château
Duhard-Milon, Château
Fonbadet, Château
Grand-Duroc-Milon,
    Château
Grand-Puy-Ducasse,
    Château
Grand-Puy-Lacoste,
    Château
Haut-Batailley, Château
Lafite (Lafite-
    Rothschild), Château
Latour, Château
Mongrand, Château
Mouton-Rothschild,
    Château
Pedesclaux, Château
Pibran, Château

Map 4 – Haut Médoc (continued)

Pichon-Longueville
(Baron), Château de
Pichon-Longueville-
Comtesse de Lalande,
Château
Pontet-Canet, Château
Rolland, Château
Saint-Julien
Saint-Louis-du-Bosc,
Château
Saint-Pierre-Bontemps,
Saint-Pierre-Sevaistre
and Bontemps-Dubarry
Tour L'Aspic, Cru La
Tour-Pibran, Château La

St-Estèphe
Beauséjour, Château
Beau-Site, Château
Beau-Site-Haut-Vignoble,
Château
Boscq, Château Le
Calon-Ségur, Château
Canteloup, Château
Capbern, Château
Clauzet, Château
Cos d'Estournel, Château
Cos Labory, Château
Crock, Château Le
Fonpetite, Château
Grand-Village-Capbern,
Château

Haye, Château La
Houissant, Château
Laffite-Carcasset, Château
MacCarthy, Château
Marbuzet, Château de
Meyney, Château
Montrose, Château
Morin, Château
Pey, Château de
Phelan-Ségur, Château
Picard, Château
Plantier-Rose, Château
Pomeys, Château
Saint-Estèphe, Château
Tour-de-Marbuzet,
Château La
Tour-des-Termes,
Château La
Tronquey-Lalande,
Château

St-Julien
Beychevelle, Château
Branaire-Ducru, Château
Chartrons
Ducru-Beaucaillou,
Château
Glana, Château du
Gloria, Château
Grand-Saint-Julien,
Château
Lagrange, Château

Langoa, Château
Léoville-Barton, Château
Léoville-Las-Cases,
Château
Léoville-Poyferré,
Château
Médoc, Château
Moulin-de-la-Rose,
Château
Tegnac, Château

St-Laurent
Camensac, Château
Corconac, Château
Cruscaut, Château
Fleur-Saint-Laurent,
Château La
Haut-Camensac
Larcis-Ducasse, Château
Tour-Carnet, Château La
Tour-Marcillanet,
Château La

St-Sauveur
Ecarts, Domaine des
Fonpiqueyre, Château
Fontesteau, Château
Liversan, Château
Peyrabon, Château
Ramage-la-Bâtisse,
Château

St Seurin-de-Cadourne
Bel-Orme-Tronquoy-de-
Lalande, Château
Bonneau-Livran, Château
Bries-Caillou, Château
Cardonne, Château La
Castera, Château du
Maurac, Château
Pontoise-Cabarrus-
Brochon, Château
Saint-Paul, Château
Sociando-Mallet, Château
Tour-du-Haut-Carmail,
Château La
Verdignan et Plantey-de-
la-Croix, Château
Verdus, Château

Soussons
Bel-Air Marquis d'Aligre,
Château
Bouqueyran, Château
Labégorce-Zédé, Château
Paveil-de-Luze, Château
Tour-de-Mons,
Château La

Vertheuil
Bourdieu, Château Le
Picourneau, Château
Reysson, Château
Victoria, Château

Map 5 – Garonne and Dordogne

Barsac
Beaulac, Château
Broustet, Château
Cantegril, Château
Carles, Château de
Climens, Château
Coutet, Château
Doisy-Daene, Château
Doisy-Védrines, Château
Dudon, Château
Fargues
Fontebride, Château
Liot, Château
Massereau-Lapachère,
Château
Mathalen, Château
Mayne-Bert, Château
Mercier, Château
Mont-Joie, Château
Myrat, Château
Nairac, Château
Pachère, Clos de la
Petit-Mayne, Château
Piada, Château
Pichon, Château
Pinesse, Cru de la
Princes, Clos des
Prost, Château

Prost-Jean-Lève, Château
Raspide, Cru
Saint-Robert, Château
Suau, Château

Beautiran
Beau-Chêne, Château de

Bègles
Hilde, Château de
Maille, Château
Roqueys, Château

Bommes
Aubépin, Château l'
Augey, Château d'
Bergeron, Château
Haut-Peyraguey, Château
Hère, Château Le
Lafaurie-Peyraguey,
Château
Lange, Château
Mauras, Château
Rabaud-Promis, Château
Rayne-Vigneau, Château
Saint-Robert, Clos
Tour-Blanche,
Château La

Bordeaux
Ambarès
Caneja
Cestas, Château
Pin, Château du
Rafette, Château La
Reignac, Château de
Rions
Roque, Domaine de
Tillac, Château du
Tour-Gueyraud,
Château La
Yvrac

Cadaujac
Bouscaut, Château
Castagnon, Domaine de
Lamothe-Bouscaut, Cru
Maran, Château
Pontrique, Château La
Pringuey
Puch-Cabanac, Château
Reynauds, Domaine des
Saint-Médard d'Eyrans
Valoux, Château

Cérons
Avocat, Cru de l'

Avocat, Clos de l'
Balestey, Château
Barthet, Château
Beaulieu, Château
Bourgelat, Clos
Cérons et de Calvimont,
Château
Emigré, Château de l'
Grand Enclos du Château
de Cérons
Haut-Mayne, Château
Larrouquey, Château
Moulin-à-Vent,
Château du
Moulins-à-Vent,
Château des
Peyrat, Château du
Pineau, Cru
Ricaud, Château de
Salette, Château La
Seuil, Château du
Sylvain-Moulin-à-Vent,
Château

Côtes de Bordeaux
Laborie, Château
Lafue, Château
Lamarque, Château

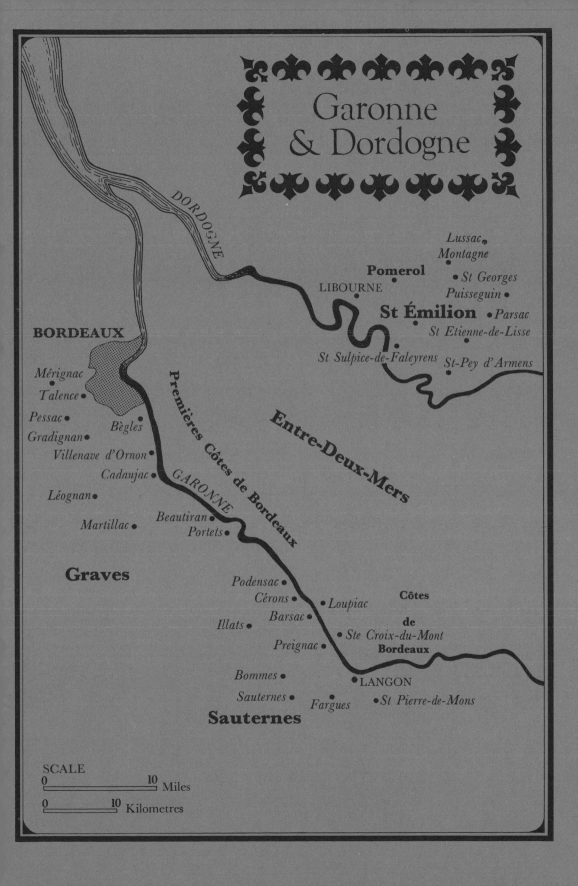

Garonne & Dordogne

DORDOGNE

Lussac
Montagne
Pomerol • St Georges
LIBOURNE Puisseguin •
St Émilion • Parsac
St Etienne-de-Lisse
St Sulpice-de-Faleyrens St-Pey d'Armens

BORDEAUX

Mérignac
Talence •
Pessac •
Gradignan • Bègles •
Villenave d'Ornon •
Cadaujac •
Léognan •
Martillac • Beautiran •
Portets •

Graves

Premières Côtes de Bordeaux

Entre-Deux-Mers

GARONNE

Podensac •
Cérons • • Loupiac **Côtes**
Barsac • **de**
Illats • • Ste Croix-du-Mont
Preignac • **Bordeaux**
Bommes •
Sauternes • Fargues LANGON
• St Pierre-de-Mons

Sauternes

SCALE
0 ———— 10 Miles
0 ———— 10 Kilometres

Map 5 – Garonne and Dordogne (continued)

Lamoureyre, Cru
Laurette, Château
Limbourg, Château
Loubens, Château
Louloumet, Clos
Tastes, Château de
Tich, Domaine du

Entre Deux Mers
Badailh, Domaine de
Brondeau, Château de
Ecluse, Domaine de l'
Grand-Peyrot,
    Château du
Jean, Clos
Laubu, Domaine de
Prieuse, Clos de la
Sainte-Croix-du-Mont
Treille et Canton de
    Milloc, Cru La

Fargues
Batsalles, Clos
Fargues, Château de
Partarieu, Château
Peillon-Claverie, Château
Rieussec, Château
Romer, Château
Tour-de-Boyrein,
    Château La

Gradignan
Poumey, Château

Graves de Bordeaux
Armajan, Clos d'
Graves, Vin de
Isle-Saint-Georges

Illats
Archambeau, Château
Bourdac, Château du
Haura, Château
Prouzet, Château du

Langon
Auros, Château d'
Baby, Château de
Cantalot, Clos
Castaing, Clos
Chanteloiseau, Château
Jaubertes, Château des
Jonka, Château
Lamothe, Domaine de
Langalerie, Château
Liloy, Domaine de
Menauchon, Domaine de
Parenchère, Château de
Pelletans, Château Les
Peyron, Château
Pireau, Domaine de
Rame, Domaine de la
Respide, Château de
Roaillan
Roland, Domaine
Saint-Pardon
Saint-Pierre-de-Mons
Toumilon et Château
    Cabanes, Château

Tour-de-Boyrien,
    Château La
Uza, Clos d'
Verdier-Renardière,
    Château

Léognan
Carbonnieux, Château
Château-Neuf
Chevalier, Domaine de
Desert, Château Le
Fieuzal, Château
France, Château de
Gazin, Château
Grandmaison,
    Domaine de
Hannetot, Château Le
Haut-Bailly, Château
Larrivet-Haut-Brion,
    Château
Louvière, Château La
Malartic-Lagravière,
    Château
Olivier, Château d'
Pape, Château Le

Libourne
Pomerol
Sables-Saint-Emilion
Saint-Pey d'Armens
Tillède, Château

Loupiac
Barbe-Morin, Château
Barberousse, Cru de
Bourdieu, Château
Caillavet, Château de
Fayau, Château
Grand-Moueys,
    Château du
Juge, Château du
Lagrange, Domaine de
Loupiac-Gaudiet,
    Château
Mazarin, Château
Montallier, Château de
Moulin-Neuf, Cru du
Noble, Domaine du
Pageot-Couloumet,
    Château
Passonne, Château de la
Peyrat, Château du
Pontac, Château
Prieur, Clos du
Ramondon, Château de
Rocher, Cru du
Rondillon-Haut-Loupiac,
    Château de
Vieux-Moulin-Haut-
    Loupiac, Château du

Lussac
Barbe-Blanche, Château
Bellevue, Château
Bois-Tiffray, Domaine de
Cassoret, Château
Courlat, Domaine du
Lussac, Château de
Lyonnat, Château du
Perrière, Château La

Tiffray, Château
Tour-de-Grenet,
    Château La
Tour-de-Ségur,
    Château La
Vignon, Château du

Martillac
Espérance, Château de l'
Ferran, Château
Fougères, Château des
Garde, Château La
Haut-Nouchet, Château
Labrède, Château de
Lespaut, Château
Malleprat, Château
Roche, Domaine de la
Saint-Augustine-La-
    Grave, Château
Smith-Haute-Lafitte,
    Château
Solitude, Domaine La
Tour-Martillac,
    Château La

Montagne
Bastienne, Château La
Beauséjour, Château
Corbin, Château
Coucy, Château
Croix-de-Mission,
    Domaine
Fontmurée, Château
Haut-Plaisance, Château
Jura-Plaisance, Château
Labatut, Domaine
Maison Blanche, Château
Maisonneuve, Château
Montaiguillon, Château
Moulin-Blanc, Château
Papeterie, Château La
Paradis, Château
Plaisance, Château
Rocher-Corbin, Château
Rocs-Marchand, Château
Roudier, Château
Tour-Montagne,
    Château La
Tours, Château des

Parsac
Badette, Château
Barde-Haut, Château
Baziliques, Château Les
Boutisse, Château de
Cauze, Château Le
Coudert, Château
Coudert-Pelletan,
    Château
Fombrauge, Château
Franc-Laporte, Château
Gaubert, Château
Haut-Langlade, Château
Haut-Lavallade, Château
Haut-Sarpe, Château
Langlade, Château
Lapelleterie, Château
Lavalade, Château
Malangin, Château
Marin, Château

Mazeran, Château
Monlabert, Château
Musset, Château
Pavillon-Figeac
Pelletan, Château
Piron, Château
Puy, Château du
Puymouton, Château
Puynormand, Château
Quentin, Château
Remparts-Guillemot,
    Château
Roqueville, Château de
Sarpe, Château de
Sarpe, Clos de
Sarpe-Grand-Jacques,
    Château de
Tour-Saint-Christophe,
    Château La
Tour-Saint-Georges,
    Château La
Tourteau, Château
Touzinat-Bragard,
    Domaine de
Vieux-Château-
    Peymouton
Vieux-Sarpe, Château
Yon, Château de

Pessac
Carmes-Haut-Brion,
    Château Les
Haut-Brion, Château
Pape-Clement, Château

Podensac
Arbanats
Arbanats, Château d'
Bedat, Château
Bichon, Cru
Bourdieu, Château Le
Bourg, Château du
Chaulet, Domaine de
Clinet, Château
Courreau, Château du
Espérance, Château de l'
Espinglet, Château de l'
Filh, Domaine de
Fougères, Château des
Giron, Domaine du
Grava, Château du
Hautes-Graves,
    Domaine des
Haux, Château de
Jourdan, Château
La Brède, Château
Madère, Château
Mauves, Château de
Mony, Château
Paillet, Château de
Panet, Château
Peneau, Château
Pin, Château du
Pin, Domaine du
Pujois, Domaine de
Remparts, Château des
Saint-Morillon
Tourteau-Chollet,
    Château
Virelade, Château de

Map 5 – Garonne and Dordogne (continued)

Pomerol

Annereaux, Château des
Beauregard, Château
Beauregard, Clos
Bel-Air, Château
Bel-Air, Château de
Bordes, Clos des
Bourgneuf-Vayron,
  Château
Bourseau, Château
Cabanne, Château La
Caillou, Château Le
Canon-Chaigneau,
  Château
Cantereau, Château
Carillon, Château Le
Certan, Château
Certan-de-May, Château
Certan-Giraud, Château
Certan-Marzelle, Château
Chaigneau, Château
Chaumes, Château Les
Chêne-Liège, Château
Chevrol Bel-Air, Château
Clinet, Château
Clocher, Clos du
Commanderie,
  Château de
Commanderie,
  Château La
Commandeur, Clos de
Conseillante, Château La
Croix, Château La
Croix-de-Gay,
  Château La
Croix-Saint-Georges
Eglise, Château d'
Eglise, Clos L'
Eglise-Clinet, Château L'
Enclos, Château L'
Evangile, Château L'
Faurie, Château
Ferrand, Château
Feytit, Château
Fleur, Château La
Fleur-du-Gazin,
  Château La
Fleur-Petrus, Château La
Fougeailles, Château
Franc-Maillet, Château
Gachet, Château
Garraud, Château
Gay, Château La
Gazin, Château
Gombaude-Guillot,
  Château
Grandes Versaines,
  Domaine de la
Grand-Ormeau, Château
Grand-Ormeau, Cru
Grand-Ormeau,
  Domaine du
Hautes-Rouzes,
  Château des
Haut-Maillet, Château
Haut-Pignon, Château de
Haut-Tropchaud,
  Domaine de
Laborde, Château
Lafleur, Château

Lagrange, Château
Latour-Pomerol, Château
Mazeyres, Clos
Moncets, Château
Moulin-à-Vent, Château
Moulin-Blanc, Château
Moulinet, Château
Musset, Château
Néac
Nenin, Château
Nouvelle-Eglise,
  Château de la
Patache, Château La
Perron, Château
Petit-Bois, Domaine du
Petit-Village, Château
Plince, Château
Pointe, Château La
Providence, Château La
René, Domaine de
Rêve d'Or, Château
Rocher-Beauregard,
  Château
Rouget, Château
Roy, Clos du
Saint-André-Bellevue,
  Château
Saint-Pierre-de-Pomerol,
  Château
Sales, Château de
Siaurac, Château
Templiers, Clos des
Teysson, Château
Thibaud-Maillet, Château
Toulifaut, Château
Toulifaut, Clos
Tournefeuille, Château
Trintin, Château
Tropchaud, Château
Tropchaud, Clos
Valois, Château de
Viaud, Château de
Viaud, Domaine de
Vieux-Castel, Château du
Vieux-Château-Certan,
  Château
Vieux-Château Cloquet
Vieux-Cru Perruchot
Vieux-Maillet, Château
Violette, Château La
Vraye-Croix-de-Gay,
  Château

Portets

Barakan, Domaine de
Biac, Château du
Cabannieux, Château
Crabitey, Château
Faubernet, Château
Ferrande, Château
Lagueloup, Château
Langoiran
Latour-Maudan, Château
Madrac, Château
Millet, Château
Peyruche, Château La
Poitevin, Château
Pommarède, Château de
Pommarede-de-Haut,
  Château

Rahoul, Château
Renon, Château
Terrasson, Domaine de
Tour-Bicheau,
  Château La
Vallier, Château du

Preignac

Arche-Pugneau,
  Domaine d'
Armajan-les-Ormes,
  Château d'
Commet-Magey, Château
Gilette, Château
Grandes-Vignes, Clos des
Haut-Bergeron, Château
Justices, Château Les
Laribotte, Château
Malle, Château de
Pape, Château du
Peyraguey-Le-Rousset,
  Château
Pick, Château du
Pleytegeat, Château
Rochers, Château des
Roy, Château du
Saint-Amand, Château
Suduiraut, Château
Veyres, Château

Premières Côtes de Bordeaux

Peyrat, Château du
Pic, Château de
Pierre-Jean, Clos de

Puisseguin

Basque, Château Le
Beauséjour, Château
Bel-Air, Château
Chêne-Vieux, Château
Croix-de-Justice, Château
Durand-Moureau,
  Château
Eglise, Clos de l'
Guibeau, Château
Guibeau-La-Fourvielle,
  Château
Laurets, Château des
Religieuses, Clos des
Rigaud, Château
Roques, Château de
Teyssier, Château
Vaisinerie, Château

Ste Croix de Mont

Carrières, Cru des
Chant-l'Oiseau Château
Labatut, Château
Mailles, Château des
Mont, Château du
Morange et La Gravière,
  Domaine de
Mouleyre, Château La
Pavillon, Château du
Pin, Cru du
Prioulette, Château La
Rame, Château La
Roustit, Château
Roustit, Domaine de

Saint-Maixant
Tilleuls, Domaine des
Verduc, Clos

St-Emilion

Angelus, Château de l'
Arrosée, Château l'
Ausone, Château
Badon, Clos
Baleau, Château
Balestard-La Tonnelle,
  Château
Bardes, Château Les
Belair, Château
Bellevue, Château
Bergat, Château
Berliquet, Château
Bragard, Château
Brun, Château
Cadet-Bon, Château
Cadet-Peychez, Château
Cadet-Piola, Château
Canon, Château
Canon-La Gaffelière,
  Château
Cantenac, Château
Cap-de-Mourlin, Château
Capelle, Château La
Capet-Guillier, Château
Cardinal-Villemaurine,
  Château
Carte et le Châtelet,
  Château La
Cassevert, Château
Chapelle-de-la-Trinité,
  Château
Chapelle-Madelaine,
  Château
Châtelet, Domaine du
Chauvin, Château
Cheval Blanc, Château
Cheval Noir, Château
Clotte, Château La
Clotte-Grande-Côte,
  Château La
Cluzière, Château La
Corbin, Château
Corbin-Fortin, Cru
Corbin-Michotte,
  Château
Cormey-Figeac, Château
Côtes de Rol-Valentin
Couspaude, Château La
Coutet, Château
Couvent, Château Le
Couvent des Jacobins
Croix-Chantecaille,
  Château La
Croque-Michotte,
  Château
Cruzeau, Château
Curé-Bon-La Madelaine,
  Château
Dominique, Château La
Doumayne, Château
Figeac, Château
Fleur, Château La
Fleur-Pourret,
  Château La
Fonplégade, Château

Map 5 – Garonne and Dordogne (continued)

Fonrayade, Château
Fonroque, Château
Fougeyrat, Château
Fourtet, Clos
Franc-Mayne, Château
Franc-Mazerat, Château
Franc-Patarabet, Château
Franc-Pourret, Château
Gaffelière, Château La
Garderose, Château
Gaudet-Saint-Julien,
    Château
Grace-Dieu, Cru
Grand-Barrail-
    Lamarzelle-Figeac,
    Château
Grandes-Murailles,
    Château
Grand-Faurie,
    Château Le
Grand-Faurie,
    Domaine du
Grand-Gonteil, Château
Grand-Mayne, Château
Grand-Mirande, Château
Grand-Pontet, Château
Graves-de-Saint Emilion
Graves-Geyrosse
Haut-Cadet, Château
Haut-Grand-Faurie,
    Château
Haut-La-Grace-Dieu,
    Château
Haut-La Rose, Château
Haut-Patarabet, Château
Haut-Pontet, Château
Haut-Pourret, Château
Haut-Simard, Château
Haut-Trimoulet, Château
Jacobins, Clos des
Jean-Faure, Château
Laniote, Château
Larcis-Sirey, Château
Larmande, Château
Larmande, Domaine de
Laroze, Château
Lassegue, Château
Lousteauneuf-Doumayne,
    Domaine de
Lussac
Madelaine, Clos de
Magdelaine, Château
Magdeleine, Clos de la
Magnan, Château
Magnan-La Gaffelière,
    Château
Malineau, Château
Martinet, Château
Matras, Château
Maurens, Château
Mauvezin, Château
Merle-Saint-Emilion,
    Domaine de
Mondésir, Cru
Moulin-Saint-Georges-
    Côte-Pavie, Château
Pailhas, Château
Patiras, Château
Pavie, Château

Pavie-Decesse, Château
Pavie-Macquin, Château
Pavillon-du-Cadet,
    Château
Petit-Clos-Figeac
Petit-Faurie-de-Soutard,
    Château
Petit-Gravet, Château
Petit-Val, Domaine de
Peyreau, Château
Pipeau, Cru
Pontet, Château du
Poteau, Domaine du
Puisseguin
Puyfromage, Château
Quercy, Château
Regent, Château
Ripeau, Château
Roi, Château de
Roi, Domaine de
Roi-de-Fombrauge,
    Château
Rose, Cru La
Rose-Pourret, Château La
Rose-Rol, Château La
Sablière, Château La
Saint-Christophe,
    Château
Saint-Emilion, Clos
Saint-Etienne-de-Lisse
Saint-Georges-Côte-
    Pavie, Château
Saint Hippolyte
Saint-Louis, Domaine
Saint-Martin, Clos
Saint-Sulpice-de-
    Faleyrens
Saint-Valéry, Clos
Sables-de-Castillon
Samion, Château
Sansonnet, Château
Serre, Château La
Simard, Château
Soutard, Château
Soutard-Cadet, Château
Tertre-Daugau, Château
Tour-du-Guetteur,
    Château La
Tour-du-Pin-Figeac,
    Château La
Tour-Figeac, Château La
Tour-Pourret, Château La
Tour-Saint-Emilion,
    Château La
Tour-Saint-Pierre,
    Château La
Tour-Vachon, Château La
Trianon, Château
Trimoulet, Château
Troplong-Mondot,
    Château
Trottevieille, Château
Truquet, Château
Vachon, Château
Vachon, Clos
Valentin, Clos
Verdet, Clos
Videlot, Château de
Vieux-Cep, Château
Vieux-Château Chauvin

Vieux-Moulin-du-Cadet,
    Château
Vieux-Pourret, Château
Vignonet
Villemaurine, Château

St Etienne-de-Lisse
Barde, Château La
Barde, Clos La
Beard, Château
Bellefont-Belcier, Château
Bouygue, Château La
Calvaire
Canterane, Château
Chapelle, Domaine de la
Godeau, Château
Guinot, Château
Haut-Rocher, Château
Lapeyre, Château
Lisse, Château de
Mangot, Château
Mondotte-Belille,
    Château
Petit-Mangot, Château
Peyrelongue, Cru
Peyrou-Grand-Champ,
    Cru
Pressac, Château de
Puy-Blanquet, Château
Raba, Château
Rochebelle, Château
Rocher, Château du
Rozier, Château
Sable, Château Le
Saint-Christophe-des-
    Bardes
Saint-Laurent-des-
    Combes
Tertre, Château Le
Tour-Baladoz,
    Château La
Tour-des-Combes,
    Château La
Tour-Puyblanquet,
    Château La
Trapaud, Château

St-Georges
Guillou, Château
Haut-Saint-Georges,
    Château
Saint-André-Corbin,
    Château

St-Pey d'Armens
Basque, Château du
Belles-Graves, Château
Dartus, Château
Destieu, Château
Fourche, Domaine de la
Fourney, Château
Haute-Rouchonne,
    Château La
Joly, Château
Moulin-Bellegrave,
    Château
Paradis, Château du
Peyroutas, Château
Platin, Château
Saint-Pey, Château de

St Pierre-de-Mons
Belfontaine, Château
Espagne, Cru d'
Lubat, Château de
Moulin-à-Vent, Clos du
Queyrats, Château des
Saint-Pey-de-Langon

St Suplice-de-Faleyrens
Balestard, Domaine de
Baleyrac, Château de
Bernachot, Château
Castelot, Château Le
Chapelle-Lescours,
    Château La
Grand-Pey-Lescours,
    Château
Grezolle, Domaine de la
Gros-Caillou, Château
Lande-de-Gravet,
    Château
Lescours, Château
Monbousquet, Château
Rebuillide, Château
Redon, Château
Refine, Cru
Trapeau, Domaine de

Sauternes
Arche, Château d'
Arche-Lafaurie,
    Château d'
Arche-Vimeney,
    Château d'
Barbier, Château
Brassens-Guiteronde,
    Château
Filhot, Château
Guiraud, Château
Guiteronde, Château
Haut-Bommes, Château
Lafon, Château
Lamothe-Bergey, Château
Preignac
Raymond-Lafon, Château
Terrefort, Château
Trillon, Château
Yquem, Château d'

Talence
Laville-Haut-Brion,
    Château
Mission Haut Brion,
    Château La
Tour-Haut-Brion,
    Château La

Villenave d'Ornon
Baret, Château
Barreyre, Domaine de
Cantebau-Couhins,
    Château
Couhins, Château
Montignac
Pontac-Monplaisir,
    Château
Rauze-Sybil, Château
Ricqmont, Domaine de

Map 6 – Chablis

Auxerre
Aube
Auxerrois
Avallon
Boivins, Les
Coulange-la-Vineux
Cravant
Jussy
Migraines, Les
Quetards, Les
Villeneuve-sur-Yonne

Beine
Côte de Troesme

Chablis
Basse Bourgogne
Beaury
Beri
Beugnons
Blanchots

Bougros
Butteaux, Les
Champlain
Chapelle-Vaupelleigne
Charlevaux, Les
Chatains
Cheilly-sur-Serein
Chichée
Clos, Les
Epinettes, Les
Fleys
Fontenay
Forêts (Forest)
Grand Chablis
Grenouilles
Ligny-le-Château
Ligorelles
Lys, Les
Melinots, Les
Milly
Mont-de-Milieu

Pargues
Prehy
Preuses, Les
Roncières or Vaillons, Les
Sechet
Soyots, Les
Troesme
Vaillons
Valmur
Vieille-Voie, La

Chichée
Vaucoupin
Vaudon
Vaugiros
Vosgros

Fleys
Côtes Neuves, Les
Fourneaux, Les
Sur-le-Moulin

Fyé
Chapelots, Les
Montée de Tonnerre

Milly
Champs Mitans
Charlevaux
Côte de Lechet

Poinchy
Baroy
Carreau
Côte de Fontenay
Fourchaume

Tonnerre
Damnenaine
Epineuil
Junay
Pres-Hauts, Les
Vaumorillons

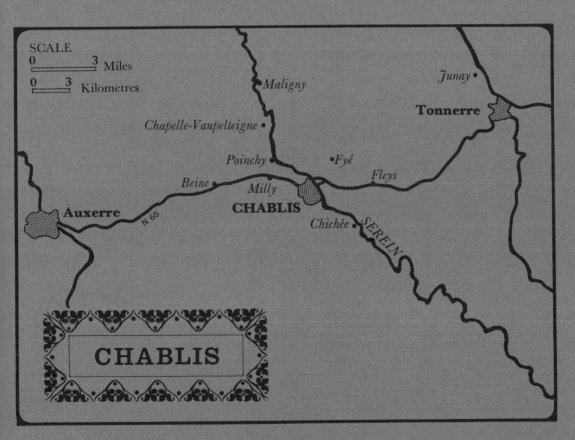

261

Map 7 – Côte d'Or

Côte de Beaune
Albert Grivault
Argillères, Les
Arrière Côtes de Beaune
Henri Gelicat
Hospices de Beaune

Côtes de Nuits
Arrière Côtes de Nuits
Jacquines, Les

Dijon
Couchey
Marsannay-la-Côte

Meursault
Jean Humblot
Jennelotte, La

Nuits-St-Georges
Allots, Aux
Argillats, Aux
Argillats, Les
Argillières, Clos des
Arlot, Clos
Hospices de Nuits

Santenay
Beauregard
Beaurepaire
Cheilly-Les-Maranges
Comme, La

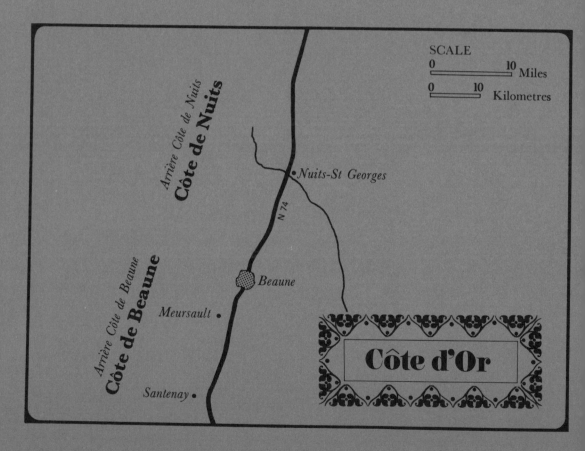

Map 8 – Burgundy

Aloxe-Corton
Boulotte, La
Bressandes, Les
Brunettes, Les
Caillettes, Les
Chaillots, Les
Charlemagne, En
Charlotte Dumay
Chaumes, Les
Chaumes-de-Vairosse
Citernes, Les
Combes, Les
Corton, Le
Corton-Charlemagne
Crais, Les
Cras-Poussuets, Les
Genevrières, Les
Greves, Les
Guerets, Les
Ladoise-Serrigny
Languettes, Les
Leurrées (Leurey), Au
Maréchaudes, Les
Meise, Les
Meise-Lallement, Les
Paulands, Les
Perrières, Les
Peste, Dr
Planchots, Les
Pougets, Les
Renardes, Les
Roi, Clos du
Valozières, Les
Vercats, Les
Vigne-au-Saint, La

Auxey-Duresses
Bas-des-Duresses
Duresses, Les
Grandes-Champs, Les
Grandes Vignes, Les

Beaune
Aigrots, Les
Avaux, Clos des
Avaux, Les
Bahezre de Lanlay, De
Bas-des-Teurons
Baudot
Betault
Blanches-Fleurs, Les
Blondeau
Boillot
Bons Feuvres
Boucherottes, Les
Bressandes, Les
Brunet
Cent Vignes, Les
Champs-Pimont, Les
Chassagne-Montrachet
Chaume-Gaufriot
Chilènes, Les
Chourcheux, Les
Coucherais, Aux
Cras (Crais), Les
Dames Hospitalières
Ecu, A L'
Enfant-Jesus, L'
Epenottes, Les
Estienne

Fèves, Les
Genet, En
Grèves, Les
Louis Max, Domaine
Marconnets, Les
Montagne-Saint-Désire
Montée Rouge
Montremenats, Les
Mouches, Clos des
Mousse, Clos de la
Nicolas Rolin
Orme, L'
Perrières, Les
Pertuisote, Les
Pommard
Prevales, Les
Reversées, Les
Roi, Clos du
Rousseau-Deslandes
Siserpe
Sisies, Les
Sur-Les-Brèves
Theurons (Teurons), Les
Tielandry
Toussaints, Les

Brochon
Champs Perrier

Chombolle Musigny
Amoureuses, Les
Argillères, Les
Athies, Les
Babillières, Les
Barottes, Les
Bas-Doix
Baudes, Les
Beaux-Bruns, Aux
Bonnes Mares
Borniques
Bussières, Les
Chabiots, Les
Chardannes, Les
Charmes, Les
Clos Saint-Jacques
Combattes, Aux
Combe d'Orveau
Cras, Les
Creux-Baissants
Croix, Aux
Danguerins, Les
Derrière-la-Grange
Derrière-le-Four
Drazey, Les
Echanges, Aux
Echeshaux, Les
Fouchères, Les
Fousselottes, Les
Fremières, Les
Fuées, Les
Gamaires, Les
Grands-Murs, Les
Gruenchers, Les
Hauts-Doix, Les
Herbues, Les
Lavrottes, Les
Maladière, La
Mal-Carrées, Les
Monbies, Les
Musigny

Nazoires, Les
Noirots, Les
Orme, Clos de L'
Plantes, Les
Sentiers, Les

Chassagne-Montrachet
Boudriotte, La
Champs-Gain
Chaumées, Les
Chevenottes, Les
Clos Devant
Clos Saint-Jean
Crets, Les
Maltroie, La
Mazèves, Les
Montrachet, Le
Morgeot, Abbaye de
Pitois, Clos
Puligny-Montrachet

Côte-de-Beaune
Aloxe-Corton
Auxey-Duresses
Bâtard-Montrachet
Beaune
Bienvenue-Bâtard-
  Montrachet
Billardet
Chorey-les-Beaune
Côte de Beaune Villages
Dezize-les-maranges
Meursault
Monthelie
Pernand-Vergelesses
Saint-Aubin-Côte de
  Beaune
Saint-Romain
Sampigny-Les-Maranges
Santenay
Volnay

Côte-de-Nuits
Chambrolle-Musigny
Clenove
Corgoloin
Fixin
Flagey-Echézeaux
Gevrey-Chambertin
Morey-Saint-Denis
Roi, Clos du
Seloncourt, En
Valandons
Vosne-Romanée
Vougeot

Fixin
Chapitre, Clos du
Cheusots, Aux
Entre-Deux-Velles
Hervelets, Les
Meix-Bas
Napoléon, Clos
Perrière, Clos de la

Flagey-Echézeaux
Beaux-Monts-Bas, Les
Chalandins, Les
Champs Traversins
Cruots, Les

Echézeaux-du-Dessus,
  Les
Grands-Echézeaux, Les
Loachausses
Maizières-Basses
Maizières-Hautes, Les
Orveaux, En
Poullaillières, Les
Quartiers de Nuits
Rouges-du-Bas, Les
Rouges-du-Dessus, Les
Treux, Les
Vignes Blanches, Les

Gevey Chambertin
Beze, Clos de
Brochon
Carougeot (Carre-
  Rougeot)
Cazetiers, Les
Chambertin, Le
Champaux, La
Champeaux
Chapelle-Chambertin
Charmes-Chambertin,
  Les
Combe-Aux-Moines, La
Combe-du-Dessus
Combottes, Les
Crebillon
Créole
Creot, Le
Croix-Violette, La

Ladoix-Serrigny
Rognet-Corton, Clos
Velouté, La
Vergennes, Les

Meursault
Bouchères, Les
Charmes-Dessous, Les
Charmes-Dessus, Les
Charrons, Les
Chevelière, La
Corbins, Les
Criots, Les
Cromin, Le
Dos d'Ane, En
Dos d'Ane, Sous le
Genevrières, Les
Goureau
Goutte d'Or
Loppin
Perrières, Aux
Petèves, Les
Pièce-Sous-Bois, La
Porusot Dessus, Le
Santenots du Dessous
Santenots du Dessus
Santenots du Milieu
Sous-Blagny

Monthélie
Champs Fulliots, Les
Gauthey, Le Clos
Lebelin

Morey-St Denis
Baulet, Clos

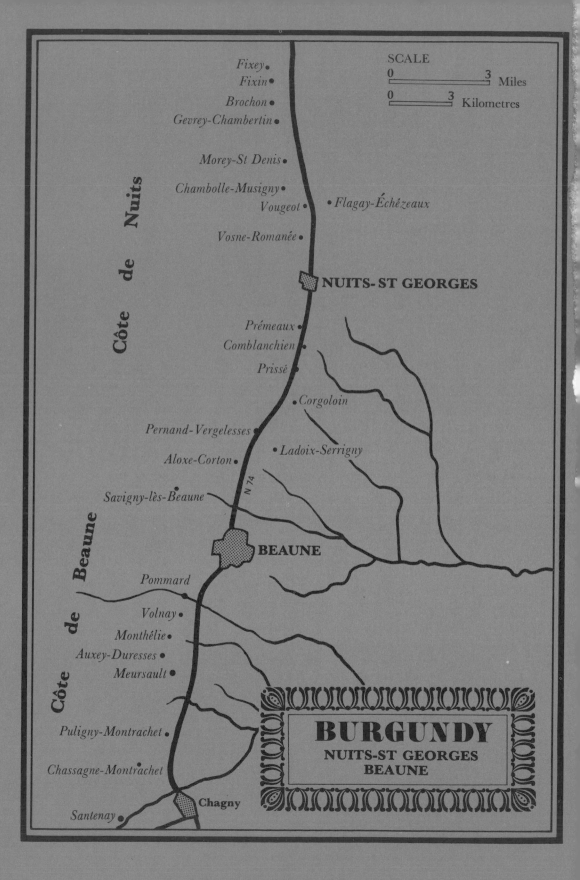

SCALE

0 ———————— 3 Miles

0 ———————— 3 Kilometres

Fixey

Fixin

Brochon

Gevrey-Chambertin

Morey-St Denis

Chambolle-Musigny

Vougeot

Flagay-Échézeaux

Vosne-Romanée

Côte   de   Nuits

NUITS-ST GEORGES

Prémeaux

Comblanchien

Prissé

Corgoloin

Pernand-Vergelesses

Ladoix-Serrigny

Aloxe-Corton

Savigny-lès-Beaune

N 74

BEAUNE

Côte   de   Beaune

Pommard

Volnay

Monthélie

Auxey-Duresses

Meursault

Côte   de   Beaune

Puligny-Montrachet

Chassagne-Montrachet

Chagny

Santenay

BURGUNDY
NUITS-ST GEORGES
BEAUNE

Map 8 – Burgundy (continued)

Blanchards, Les
Brussière, Clos de la
Calouère
Chabiots, Les
Chaffots, Les
Charmes, Aux
Charrières, Les
Chesaux, Aux
Clos de Tart, Le
Côte Rôtie
Faconnières, Les
Fremières, Les
Froichots, Les
Lambrays, Clos des
Maison-Brulée
Meix-Rentier, Le
Millandes
Mochamps
Monts-Luisants, Les
Morey
Ormes, Clos des
Riotte, La
Roche, Clos de la
Ruchots, Les
Saint-Denis, Clos
Salon, Clos
Sorbes, Clos
Sorbes, Les

Nuits-St-George
Barrières, Aux
Bas-de-Combe
Belle-Croix
Boudots, Aux
Bousselots, Aux
Brulées, Les
Cailles, Les
Chaboeufs, Les
Chaignots, Les
Chailots, Les
Chaines-Carteau, Les
Champs-Perdrix
Charmais, Les
Château Gris
Cras, Aux
Damades, Aux
Fleurières, Aux
Hauts-Pruliers, Les
Lavières, Aux
Maladière, La
Murgers, Aux
Perrière, La
Perrière-Noblet, En La
Plateaux, Les
Poirets (Porrets), Les
Poulettes, Les
Prémeaux

Procès, Les
Pruliers, Les
Richemonne, La
Roncière, La
Saint-Georges, Les
Thorey, Les
Thorey, Clos de
Torey
Tribourg, Au
Vallerots, Les
Vauerains, Les
Vignerondes, Les

Pernand Vergelesses
Basses-Vergelesses
Caradeux
Charlemagne, En
Corton, Le
Corton-Charlemagne
Corvées, Clos des
Côte de Beaune
Creux-de-la- Net
Vergelesses, Ile des

Pommard
Arvelets
Bas-des-Saussilles
Bertins
Blanc, Clos
Boeufs, Les
Chanière, La
Chanlins Bas, Les
Chaponnières, Les
Charmots
Combe-Dessus
Combotte, La
Commaraine, Clos de la
Cras, Les
Dames de la Charité
Derrière-Saint-Jean
Epeneaux, Clos des
Epenots, Les
Fremiers, Les
Jarollières, Les
Lavières, Les
Micat or Micaut, Clos
Perrières, Les
Petits-Epenots, Les
Petits-Noizons, Les
Pezerolles
Platière
Poutures, Les
Refene, La
Riottes, Les
Rue-aux-Parc
Rugiens-Bas, Les
Rugiens-Hauts

Tavannes, Les
Verger, Clos de
Vignots, Les
Village de Pommard

Prémeaux
Clos Arlot
Charbonnières, Les
Corvées-Paget, Les
Didiers, Les
Forêts, Clos des
Grandes Vignes, Les
Grandes Vignes, Clos des
Maréchale, Clos de la
Nuits-Saint-Georges
Perdrix, Les
Saint-Marc, Clos

Puligny-Montrachet
Blagny, Hameau de
Cailleret, Le
Champ-Canet
Chevalier-Montrachet
Clavoidlon
Combettes, Les
Falatières, Les
Grands-Champs
Pucelles, Les
Sous-Les-Puits

Santenay
Gravières, Les
Maladière, La
Tavannes, Clos de

Savigny-les-Beaune
Arthur Girard
Champagne, La
Charnières, Les
Cyrot
Du Bay-Peste
Forneret
Fouquerand
Godeaux, Les Petits
Grands-Picatins
Gravains, Aux
Guettes, Aux
Jarrons, Les
Lavières, Les
Narbantons, Les
Petits-Picattins, Les
Peuillets, Les
Pimentiers, Les
Serpentières, Aux
Talmettes, Les
Vergelesses, Les

Volnay
Angles, Les
Aussy, Les
Barre, La
Bousse d'Or
Brouillards, Les
Caillerets-Dessus, Les
Carelles-Dessus
Carelle-sous-la-Chapelle
Champans, Les
Chanlin
Chênes, Clos des
Chevret, En
Ducs, Clos des
Famines, Les
Fremiet, Les
Gauvain
General Muteau
Gigotte, La
Grands-Champs
Grands-Poisots
Jehan de Massol
Lurets, Les
Mitans, Les
Ormeau, En l'
Pitures-Dessus, Les
Pointes d'Angle
Robardelle
Santenots, Les
Village de Volnay

Vosne-Romanée
Barreaux, Les
Basses-Maizières, Les
Beaux-Monts, Les
Bossières
Brulées, Aux
Gaudichots, Les
Grande Rue
Hauts-Beaux-Monts, Les
Hauts-Maizières, Les
Malconsorts, Aux
Ormes, Aux
Petits-Monts, Aux
Raviottes, Aux
Reas, Clos des
Reignots, Aux
Richebourg, Les
Romanée, La
Romanée-Conti, La
Romanée-Saint-Vivant
Suchots, Les
Tache, La

Vougeot
Blanc de Vougeot, Clos
Vougeot, Clos

Map 9 – Chalonnais

Bourgneuf Val d'Or
Grandes Vignes, Les
Malliauge, Vigne de la
Miglan
Touches

Chagny
Folie, Domaine de la
Font, Le
Sanzenay, En
Theurons, Clos des
Thunots, Clos des
Vigne-des-Champs, La
Vigne-du-Maillange

Givry
Barande, La
Bois-Chevaux
Cellier-Aux-Moines, Le
Chanevarie
Marolles, Les
Saint-Martin-sous-
  Montaigu
Survoisine, La

Mercurey
Barraults, Les
Bourgneuf-Val-d'Or
Bussière du Haut
Byots, Les
Champs-Martins, Les
Côte Chalonnaise
Cret, Le
Evêque, Le Clos l'
Grands-Voyens

Nauges, Les
Nogues, Les
Petits-Voyens, Les
Tonnère, Le
Vignes Blanches

Rully
Chaume, La
Chêne
Folie Domaine de la
Fosse, La
Gresigny
Margottey
Marisson
Mont Palais
Mont-Palais
Mouènes, Les
Moulènes, Les
Moulin-à-Vent
Pillot
Préau
Rablot

St-Mard-de-Vaux
Brelot, Clos

**St-Martin-sous-
  Montaigu**
Chassière, La
Fourneaux, Les
Hates, Les
Libertins, Les
Paradis, Clos
Roche, La
Ruelle, En

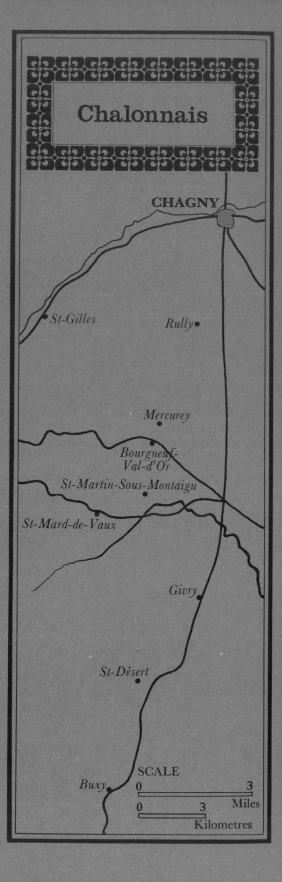

Map 10 – Mâconnais

Fuissé
Brulées, Les
Chardonnets, Les
Clos, Le
Long Poil
Menestrières, Les
Pelous, Les
Pouilly
Pouilly, Vers
Pouilly-Fuissé
Resses, Les
Verze
Vignes Blanches, Les

Loché
Pouilly Loché

Mâcon
Aze
Berzé-La Ville
Bulants, Les
Burgy
Charnay-Les-Mâcon
Clessé
Long Poil
Pouilly-Vinzelles
Prissé
Ravinet, Les
Romanèche-Thorins
Saint-Genoux-le-Scisse
Saint-Paul, Le Clos
Saint-Pierre, Clos
Saint-Symphorien
  d'Ancelles
Saint-Venand
Salomon, Clos
Sance
Surmain, Domaine de
Thorins
Tournus
Verze
Vire

Pouilly
Boutières, Les
Clos, Au
Davaye
Loché
Peloux, Au
Pouilly, Château
Pouilly, Château de
Pouilly Fumé
Pouilly-Vinzelles

Romanèche-Thorins
Breunes, Les
Carquelin, Le
Maison-Neuve
Montagny
Panclers, Les
Rouchauds, Les
Saint-Symphorien
  d'Ancelles
Thorins

St-Amour
Brosses, Les
Capitans, Les
Chaintre
Champ Grillé
Guillons, Les

Solutré
Bertelots
Frairie
Gerbeaux, Les
Loché
Mont Garain
Mure, La
Riats, Les
Vernaille

Vergisson
Pouilly-Fuissé
Prissé
Roche, La

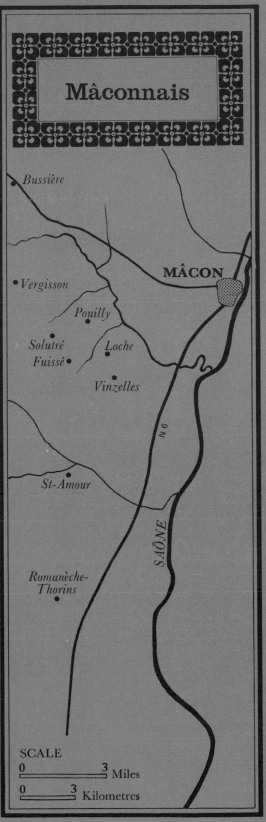

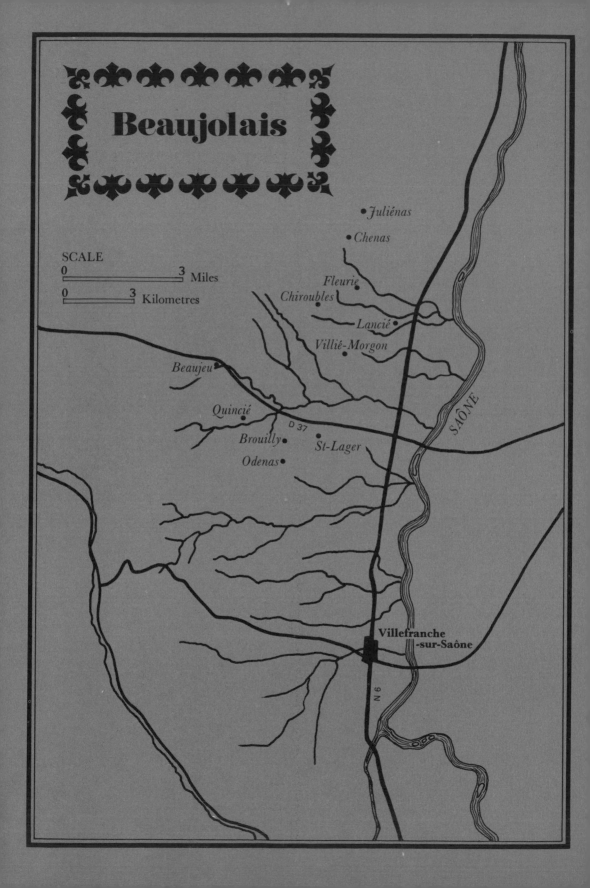

Beaujolais

SCALE

0 —————————— 3 Miles

0 —————————— 3 Kilometres

• *Juliénas*

• *Chenas*

Fleurie •
Chiroubles
• *Lancié*
Villié-Morgon •

Beaujeu •

Quincié •

D 37

Brouilly •   • *St-Lager*

Odenas •

SAÔNE

Villefranche
-sur-Saône

N 6

Map 11 – Beaujolais

Beaujeu
Arbuissonas
Brouilly
Brouilly, Côte de
Chénas
Chiroubles
Fleurie
Hospices de Beaujeu
Jacques, Château des
Juliénas
Lancié
Lantigne
Loyse, Château de
Moulin, Le
Moulin-à-Vent
Odenas
Pizay, Château de
Quincie
Regnie
Ringuat, Domaine de
Saint-Etienne-La-
  Varenne
Saint-Etienne-Les-
  Cuillères
Saint-Joseph

Saint-Lager
Vaux
Ville-Morgon

Brouilly
Brouilly, Côte de
Bussières, Les
Chaix
Garanche
Odenas
Pave, Le
Pierreux, Le
Thirin, Château

Chénas
Brureaux, Les
Caves, Les
Jacques, Château des
Michelon, Le
Moulin-à-Vent
Rochegres
Rochelle, La
Rochette, La
Thorins
Tour-du-Bief, Château La

Verillats, Les

Chiroubles
Bel-Air
Moulin, Le

Fleurie
Biaume, Le
Chapelle-Du-Bois
Garant, Au
Garants, Les
Moriers, Les
Point-du-Jour
Poncier, Le
Quatre Vents, Les
Rochaux, Les
Roilette, La
Vivier, Le

Juliénas
Bessay
Bucherats
Capitans, Les
Chanoriers, Aux
Guillons, Les

Mouilles, Les
Vieille-Eglise

Lancié
Gaillard, Château
Moulin-Lanciat
Moulin-Meziat

St-Lager
Cercié

Saône
Bourgogne Aligoté

Villefranche-Sur-
  Saône
Lachassagne

Villié-Morgon
Douby
Morgon
Pis (Py), Le
Pizay, Château de

Map 12 – Côtes du Rhône

Ampuis
Clapeyranne, La
Côte Blonde, La
Côte Brune
Côte Rôtie
Grande Plantée
Grande Vigne
Grosse Roche, La
Payette, La

Ardèche
Cornas
Montfleury

Avignon
Beaumes du Ventoux

Châteauneuf-du-Pape
Cabannes, Les
Cabrières, Domaine de
Condorcet
Courthézon
Enclos, Domaine de l'
Fond-du-Pape, Château
  de la
Gardine, Château La
Grand-Goulet,
  Château du
Le Baucou
Mas Saint-Louis
Maucoil, Château
Montolivet, Le
Mont-Redon
Nallys

Nerthe, Château de la
Rayées, Château
Roquette, Domaine de la
Saint-Patrice, Château
Saint-Pierre, Clos
Saint-Préfert
Solitude, Domaine de la
Télégraphe, Domaine du
Terre-Ferme, Domaine de
Trintignat, Domaine
Vaudieu, Château de
Vieux-Moulin, Le
Vieux-Télégraphe

Chatillon-en-Diois
Saulce, La

Condrieu
Grillet, Château
Rozay, Château

Cornas
Chambon
Mure, La
Pied-la-Vigne

Crozes-Hermitage
Conflans, Domaine de

Drôme
Clairette de Die
Piegon

Gigondas
Bosquets, Les

Longue Toque,
  Domaine de
Maine, Domaine du
Malijoy, Domaine du
Pallières, Les
Péage, Clos du
Raspail, Château
Saint-André, Domaine
Saint-Gayan, Domaine
Trignon, Domaine de

Isère
Murinais

Lirac
Moulin, Domaine du
Saint-Roch, Domaine du
  Château
Segries, Domaine de

Orange
Patriciens, Clos des
Sablet-Pres L'Ouvère
Uchaux

Ouvèze
Côtes du Ventoux
Saint-Didier
Saint-Sauveur

St-Péray
Moulin, Le

Seyssuel
Bon-Blanc

Tain-L'Hermitage
Beaumes, Les
Bessards, Les
Bessarots, Les
Chante-Alouette
Chapelle
Crozes-Hermitage
Diognières, Les
Ermite, L'
Greffieux, Les
Hermitage
Meal, Le
Murets, Les
Pierelle, La
Thalabert, Domaine de
Varogne

Tavel
Clary, Château de
Forcaière, Domaine de la
Genestière, Domaine de la
Manissy, Domaine de
Montezargues,
  Domaine de
Trinquevedel,
  Domaine de
Vieux-Moulin, Cru du

Vaucluse
Cairannes
Côtes du Luberon
Pertuis
Sainte-Cécile-les-Vignes

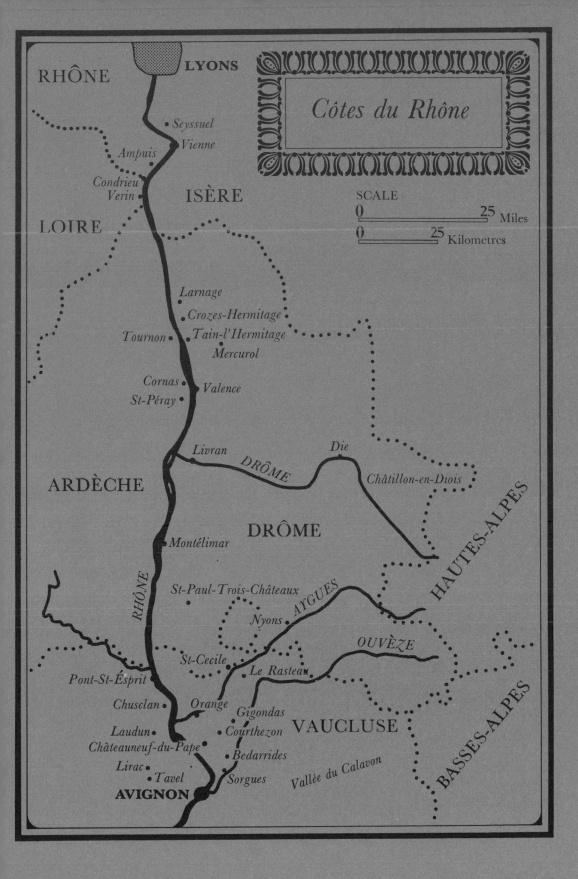

RHÔNE

LYONS

Seyssuel

Vienne

Ampuis

Condrieu
Verin

ISÈRE

LOIRE

Côtes du Rhône

SCALE

0 — 25 Miles

0 — 25 Kilometres

Larnage

Crozes-Hermitage

Tournon *Tain-l'Hermitage*

Mercurol

Cornas *Valence*
St-Péray

Livran *Die*

DRÔME *Châtillon-en-Diois*

ARDÈCHE

DRÔME

Montélimar

RHÔNE

St-Paul-Trois-Châteaux AYGUES

Nyons

OUVÈZE

St-Cecile

Le Rastean

HAUTES-ALPES

Pont-St-Ésprit

Chusclan *Orange*

Gigondas VAUCLUSE

Laudun *Courthezon*

Châteauneuf-du-Pape *Bedarrides*

Lirac *Tavel* *Sorgues* *Vallée du Calavon*

AVIGNON

BASSES-ALPES

Map 13 – Languedoc and Roussillon

Aude
Blanquette de Limoux
Clape, La
Corbières, Les
Corbières Supérieures
Limoux
Muscat de Saint Jean de
  Minervois

Banyuls
Côtes d'Agly

Béziers
Craillac
Craillac Premières Côtes
Montbartier
Montpeyroux
Saint-Chinian

Frontignan
Muscat de Frontignan

Gard
Lirac
Marausan, Château de
Midi, Vins du

Hérault
Cabrières *V.D.Q.S.*
Mejanelle, Coteaux de
Picpoul de Pinet

Lunel
Arles
Muscat de Lunel

Marseilles
Bregançon
Coteaux d'Aix
Coteaux de la Trevaresse
Coteaux de Sainte
  Victoire

Montpellier
Coteaux de Saint Christol
Coteaux de Verargues

Pyrénées-Orientales
Corbières du Roussillon
Corbières Supérieures du
  Roussillon
Roussillon des Aspres

Rivesaltes
Côte d'Agly
Côtes du Haut-Roussillon
Quatourze

Tarn
Cahors
Villedieu, La

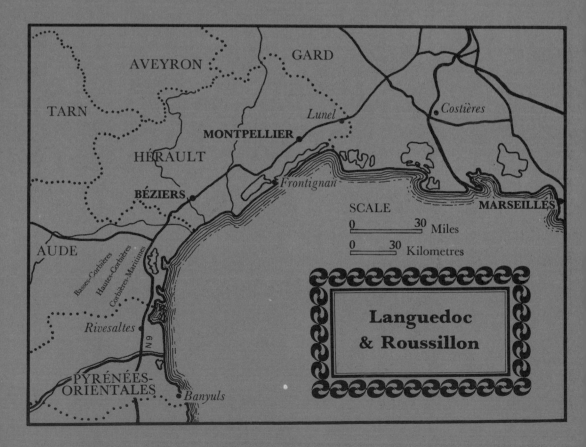

Map 14 – Provence

Bandol
Beausset, Le
Bourrasque, La
Braquetty, Les
Cadière, La
Castellet, Le
Moulin-de-la-Roque
Ollioules
Pey-Neuf, Domaine Le
Pradeaux, Château
Saint Cyr-Sur-Mey
Tempier
Veyrolles

Carqueiranne
Salins d'Hyères

Cassis
Grand Pin, Le
Mas Calen
Mas Canai
Paternel, Domaine du
Saint-Michel, Clos
Villamare

Grimaud
Galoupet, Domaine du

Taradeau
Castel Roubine
Saint-Martin
Saint-Martin, Domaine de

Selle, Château de

Toulon
Arcs, Les
Grande, La
Lafran-Veyrolles
Mauvanne, Domaine de
Moulières, Domaine des
Rimauresq, Château de
Tourelle, La

Var
Côte de Maures
Côtes de Provence

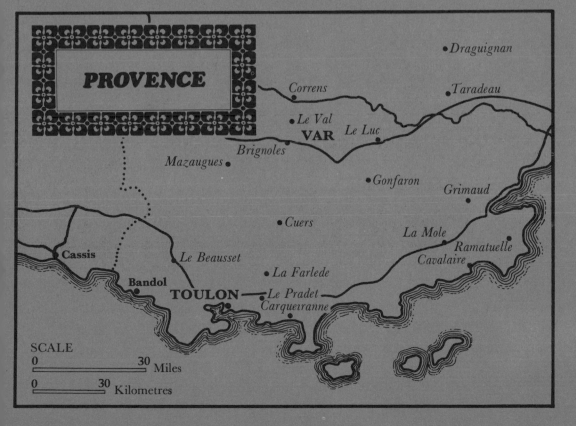

Map 15 – Upper Loire; Orléans

Bourges
Cler
Menetu-Salon

Moulins
Montlucon

Orléans
Côtes de Gien
Meung-Sur-Loire

Pouilly-Sur-Loire
Bernadats, Les
Blanc-Fumé
Chaumes, Les

Chaumiennes, Les
Chênes, Les
Cornets, Les
Côte de Nues
Lausserie
Prée, La
Tracy
Tracy, Château de

Quincy
Reuilly

Sancerre
Amigny
Bannay

Blanc-Fumé
Bue
Chambraste
Chasseignes, Les
Chavignol
Comtesse, Clos de la
Comtesses, Cru des
Crezanoy
Cul de Beaujeu
Fricambault
Grande Côte, La
Grandes Côtes de
   Chavignol
Monts-Damnes, Les
Moussière, Domaine de la
Nozet, Château du

Paradis, Le
Pave, La
Saint-Satur
Saint-Thibault
Sury-en-Vaux
Thauvenay
Thou, Château du
Veaugues

St-Pourçain
Aubière
Chantelle
Chanturgne
Corent
Renaise
Ribeyre

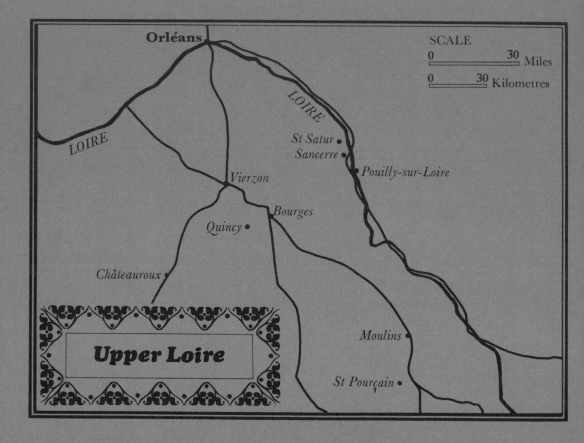

SCALE

0 — 30 Miles

0 — 30 Kilometres

Orléans

LOIRE

LOIRE

St Satur
Sancerre
Pouilly-sur-Loire

Vierzon

Bourges

Quincy

Châteauroux

Moulins

St Pourçain

Upper Loire

Map 16 – Lower Loire; Anjou

Map 16 – Lower Loire; Anjou (continued)

Bonnes Blanches, Les
Bonnezeaux
Bournais, Les
Bretonnières, Les
Brézé
Brézé, Château de
Brissac
Brondes, Clos des
Brosses, Les
Butte-de-Saumoussay
Cabernet Rosé de Saumur
Celliers, Les
Chacé
Cham-Chardon
Champ-Fougres
Champigny-le-Sec
Champ Picard
Chapelle
Château, Clos du
Chatelières, Les
Cristal, Clos
Coteau des Nouelles
Croix, Clos de la
Dampierre-Sur-Loire
Denée
Division, La
Dizay
Epinay, L'
Favettes, Les
Ferronnières, Les
Folie, Clos de la
Fouquet, Château
Gaillard, Château

Havarduère, La
Hermitage, L'
Jarretière, La
Juigné-Sur-Loire
La Corde
La Motte, Clos de
Loué-Sur-Loire
Maillaud
Martigneau
Martinière, La
Mattins, Les
Meigne
Menais, Les
Montjean
Montreuil-Bellay
Montsoreau
Morains
Mottouse, La
Müre-Erigne
Murs, Clos des
Notre Dame d'Alençon
Oratoriens, Les
Parnay
Parnay, Château de
Pavignolles, Les
Pavillon, Le
Pères, Clos des
Petite-Fontenelle, La
Pierre Blanche
Prince
Quincé
Ripaille, Château de la
Rochambeau

Roche-de-Mure, La
Roches, Les
Roualère, La
Saint Cyr-en-Bourg
Saint-Jean, Clos
Saint-Jean-des-Mauvrets
Saint-Just-Sur-Dive
Saint-Mélanie-sur-
  Aubance
Saint-Saturnin-sur-Loire
Saints-Pères, Clos des
Saint-Vincent
Saix
Saumur Rosé de Cabernet
Saut-du-Loup
Terres-Rouges, Les
Treilles
Turquant
Varrains
Véronnière, La
Vignolles

Tours
Amuseries, Clos des
Auberdière, L'
Azay-le-Rideau
Barguines, Les
Batonnières, Clos des
Baudoin, Clos
Bel-Air, Clos
Bellevue, Clos de
Bibaudières, Les
Boisrideau

Bois-Turmaux
Bouchet, Clos du
Boulay, Le
Bourg, Clos du
Bourgeot, Le
Bourgueil
Brunettes, Les
Cange
Chambray
Chatterie, La
Cinq Mars
Cosson, Les
Cosson, Clos de
Côte de Bourgueil
Côte de Montlouis
Côte de Vouvray
Dubois, Clos
Du Breuil, Château
Epenay, L'
Fougeray, Clos du
Fourneau-Saint-Jacques
Fourneaux, Les
Gaillardière, La
Gaimont, Le
Gaucherie, La
Girrardières, Les
Grand-Champs
Gue de Amant, Le
Halletière, Clos de la
Haut-Renondeau,
  Château
Hauts-Champs, Les
Lacassière, Clos de la

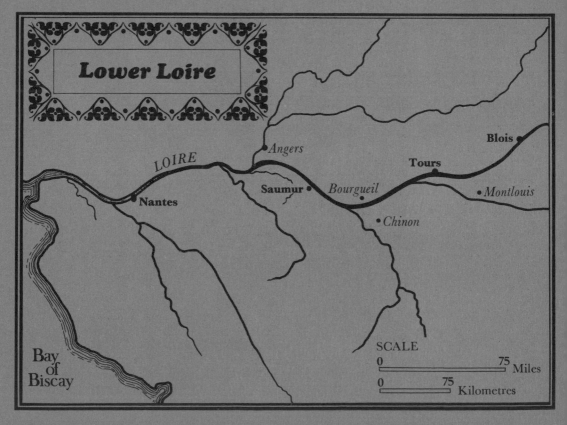

Map 16 – Lower Loire; Anjou (continued)

Liards, Les
Madères, Les
Marigny
Martin, Clos
Mesiand
Mollières
Moncontour, Château de
Moncontour, Clos
Mont, Clos Le
Montlouis
Mosny

Nobles, Cru des
Nouis, Clos de
Olivier, Clos l'
Paradis, Clos Le
Pentes, Clos des
Petit-Mont, Le
Petit Vouvray, Le
Platerie, Clos de la
Pomet
Portail, Le
Pouvray, Clos du

Renard, Clos
Rochecorbon
Rochère, La
Roches, Clos des
Rue-Neuve, La
Saint-Avertin
Saint-Come, Clos
Sainte-Radegonde
Saint-Mathurin
Sens, Clos de
Sous-Les-Bois

Tainère, Clos de la
Thierrières, Clos des
Touraine-Azay-le
  Rideau
Vaufuget, Clos
Vaufoynard, Clos de
Vaux, Clos de
Verneries, Clos des
Vernou-sur-Brenne
Vigneau, Clos du
Yvonne, Clos

Map 17 – Champagne

Ambonnay
Tours-sur-Marne
Vaudemanges

Avize
Graves
Le Mesnil-sur-Oger
Oger

Ay
Ay-Champagne
Champillon
Dizy
Hautvilliers
Mareuil-sur-Ay
Mutigny

Bouzy
Tauxières

Chouilly
Oiry

Cramant
Cuis

Épernay
Bisseuil
Chavot-Courcourt
Chouilly
Mardeuil
St Martin-d'Ablois

Ludes
Chamery

Pierry
Cuis
Monthelon
Moussy

Rheims
Beaumont-sur-Verle
Coulommes-la-Montagne
Ecueil
Mesneux, Les
Rilly-la-Montagne
Sacy
Villedommange

Sillery
Puisieulx

Trépail
Louvois

Vertus
Bergères-les-Vertus

Verzy
Ludes
Mailly Champagne
Verzenay
Villers-Marmery

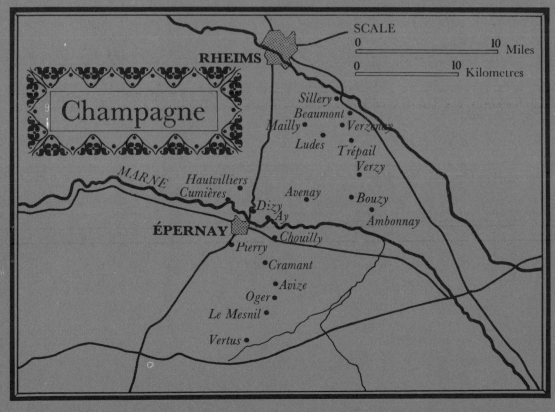

Map 18 – Jura

Ain
Bugey
Cerdon

Arbois
Etoile, L'

Marnoy
Monthallier
Nouvelles
Pinte, La
Régaule
Voiteur

Château Chalon
Montgenets, Les
Montmorins, Les
Quintigny
Vigne Blanche, La

Salins-Les-Bains
Chameaux, Les
Poligny
Rousset, Château
Saint-Ferréol

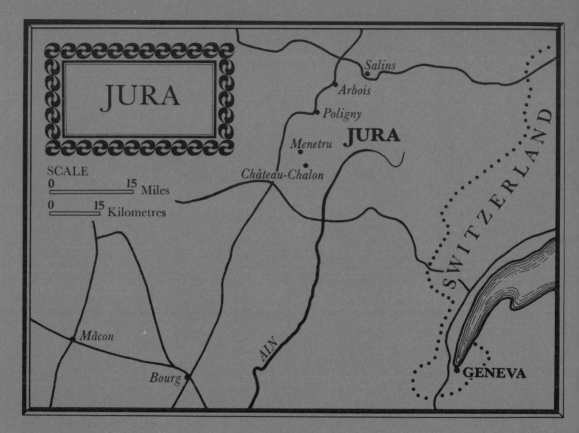

Map 19 – Alsace

Ammerschwihr
Katzenthal

Barr
Gertwiller
Mintzheim

Molsheim
Marlenheim
Traenheim

Wangen
Wissemburg
Wolxheim

Pfaffenheim
Gueberschwihr
Hattstatt

Ribeauville
Hunawihr

Riquewihr
Beblenheim
Mittelwihr
Zellenberg

Soultz
Thann

Turckheim
Ingersheim

Kafferkopf
Kanzelberg
Niedermorschwihr
Schoenenberg
Sporen
Wettolsheim
Wintzenheim
Zahnacker

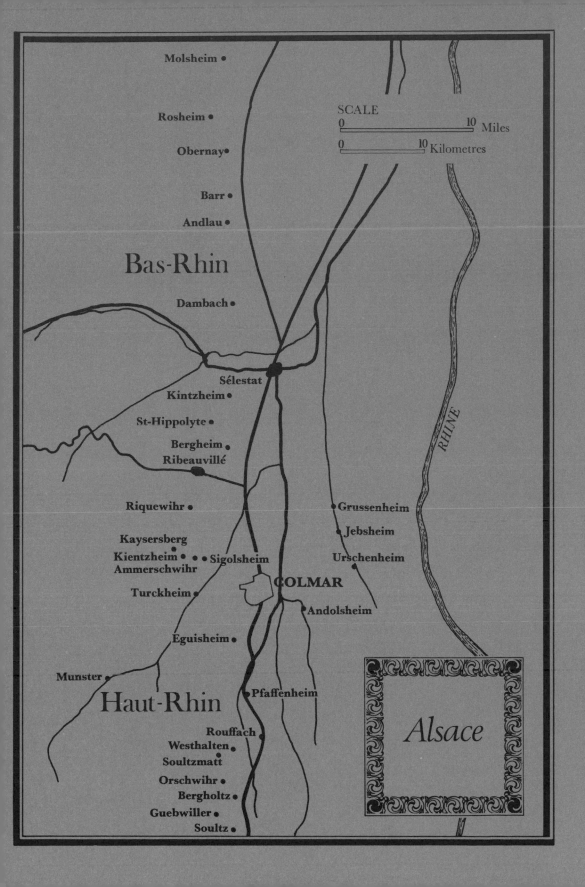

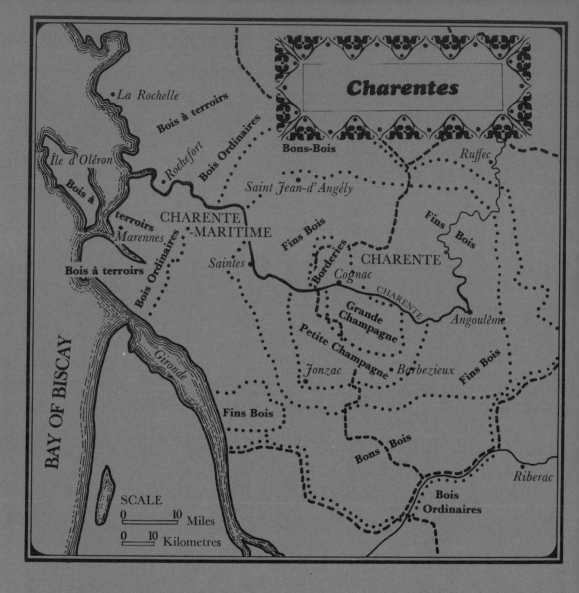

Map 20 – Charentes

Grande Champagne

Bois à Terroirs
Aigrefeuille

Map 21 – The Rhine Vinelands

Basel
Weil-am-Rhein
Winterweiler
Wollbach

Bingen
Bornich
Breitscheid
Burgen-St-Goar
Dellhofen
Flur
Fürstenberg
Hahn
Hub
Kaub
Kloster Fürstensthal
Lauerbaum

Manubach
Mühlberg
Niederheimbach
Oberdiebach-mit-
   Winzberg-und-
   Rheindiebach
Patersberg
Perscheid
Posten
Reetz
Sankt Jost
Stelzenberg
Wellmich
Wolfshöhle

Bonn
Drachenfels

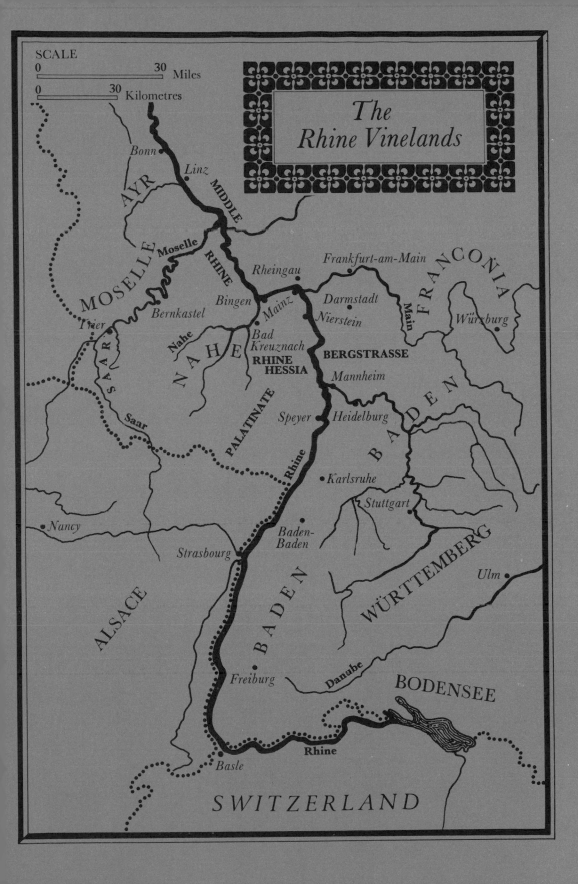

SCALE

0 — 30 Miles

0 — 30 Kilometres

The
Rhine Vinelands

Bonn

Linz

AYR

MIDDLE

Moselle

MOSELLE

RHINE

Rheingau

Frankfurt-am-Main

FRANCONIA

Bingen

Mainz

Darmstadt

Bernkastel

Nierstein

Würzburg

Trier

Nahe

Bad
Kreuznach

BERGSTRASSE

SAAR

NAHE

RHINE
HESSIA

Main

Mannheim

Saar

Speyer

Heidelburg

PALATINATE

BADEN

Rhine

Nancy

Karlsruhe

Stuttgart

Baden-
Baden

WÜRTTEMBERG

Strasbourg

Ulm

ALSACE

BADEN

Freiburg

Danube

BODENSEE

Rhine

Basle

SWITZERLAND

Map 21 – The Rhine Vinelands (continued)

Darmstadt
Gross-Umstadt
Grosswallstadt
Kleinwallstadt
Klingenberg-am-Main
Laudenbach
Reichenbach
Steinkopf
Sulzbach

Heidelberg
Eschelbach
Gross-Sachsen
Langenbrücken
Leiman
Lützelsachen
Malsch
Malschenberg
Michelfeld
Östringen
Rauenberg

Rettigheim
Rotenberg
Schriesheim
Tiefenbach
Übstadt
Weinheim
Wiesloch
Zeutern

Koblenz
Boppard
Braubach
Brey
Damscheid
Dörscheid
Ehrenbreitstein
Eisenberg
Fachbach
Hamm
Hammerstein
Hirzenach

Kamp
Kestert
Langscheid
Leutesdorf
Nassau
Niederberg
Nochen
Oberlahnstein
Sankt Goar
Sankt Goarhausen

Konstanz
Horn
Weiler

Linz
Ahrbleichert
Altenahr
Bodendorf
Dattenberg
Dernau

Erpel
Haardtberg
Honnef, Bad
Honningen
Karweiler
Kasbach
Kreuzberg
Mayschoss
Rech
Rheinbreitbach
Rheinbrohl
Unkel
Walporzheim

Mannheim
Zwingenberg

Stuttgart
Beutelsbach

Map 22 – Moselle, Saar, Ruwer

Bernkastel
Altenwald
Amorpfad
Badstube
Bernkasteler Doktor
Bitsch
Bratenhöfchen
Burgen-Bernkastel
Doktor
Doktor und Graben
Elisenberg
Falkenburg
Graben
Held
Himmelseiten
Johannisberg
Kloster
Königsstuhl
Maring
Matheisbildchen
Pfalzgraben
Schwanen
Sonnenlay

Brauneberg
Andel
Burgerslay
Carlsberg
Filzen
Hasenläufer
Himmelseiten
Johannisberg
Juffer
Kammer
Kloster
Mandelgarten
Mülheim
Nonnenlay
Obersberg
Osann

Sonnenlay
Spitze

Bruttig
Beilstein-Untermosel
Bienengarten
Brandenberg
Ellenz-Poltersdorf
Ernst
Fankel
Hahn
Kuckucksberg
Mesenich
Poltersdorf
Rathausberg
Rubertsberg

Detzem
Blattenberg
Engass
Königsberg
Leiwen
Maximiner-Klosterlay
Ohligberg
Stolzenberg

Eitelsbach
Burgberg
Orthsberg
Sang
Sonnenberg
Stirn

Eller
Aldegund
Alf
Baumberg
Beilstein-Untermosel
Bienengarten
Bienenlay

Bremm
Bullay
Ediger
Feuerberg
Hasensprung
Herl
Hotlay
Kalmond
Kapplay
Kirchenrain
Kirchenrech
Klosterkammer
Osterlämmchen
Palmenberg
Petersberg
Rotkäppchen
Senheim

Enkirch
Briedel
Burg
Engelsburg
Herzchel
Hinterberg
Kirche
Krov
Layen
Naktarsch
Paradies
Steffensberg
Versberg
Weinkammer
Weissenberg
Zeppwingert

Erden
Busslei
Forsterlay
Herzlay
Hotlei

Hupperath
Kammer
Kaufmannsberg
Kranklay
Lösnich
Prälat
Rotkirch
Schönberg
Treppchen

Filzen
Konen
Konz
Nonnenberg
Oberbillig
Paulinshofberg
Pülchen
Rippchen
Tawern
Zuckernberg

Graach
Abstsberg
Bergweiler
Bistum
Domprobst
Frohnwelt
Goldgrube
Goldwingert
Himmelreich
Josephshofer
Kirchlay
Munzlay
Petrus
Sankt Nikolauslay
Stablay
Tirley

Kanzem
Horeker

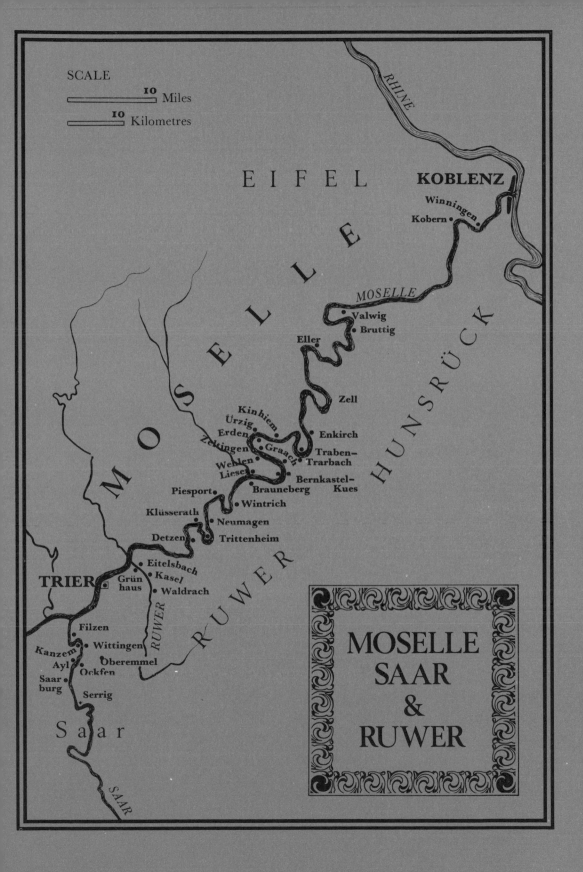

Map 22 – Moselle, Saar, Ruwer (continued)

Kelterberg
Langsur
Pinnerkreuzberg
Unterberg
Wasserbillig
Wolfsberg

Kasel
Dominikanberg
Hitzlay
Katharinenberg
Kaulgen
Kehrnagel
Kohlenberg
Lorenzberg
Maximiner-Staadter
Niesgen
Paulinsberg
Steininger
Taubenberg
Walterberg

Kinheim
Eulenberg
Eulenlay
Grauberg
Hahnen
Halsbach
Häschen
Heislay
Hubertushofberg
Hubertuslay
Kahlenberg
Kröv
Loewenberg
Löwenberg
Petrusberg
Urzig

Klüsserath
Bekond
Blattenberg
Bruderschaft
Engass
Ensch
Goldkupp
Heidenkupp
Honigsack
Huxlay
Königsberg
Kuckuckslay
Longen
Mehring
Michelsberg
Polich
Rivenich
Römerpfad
Schleich
Thörnich
Zellenberg

Kobern
Bienenberg
Brodenbach
Burgberg
Burgen
Dieblich
Elslay
Fahrberg
Hatzenport

Kattenes
Kollig
Lehmen
Löf
Moselkern
Muden
Niederfell
Oberfell
Pfarrberg
Uhlen
Weissenberg

Koblenz
Alken

Kues
Kalbrech
Sankt Nikolaus Hospital
Weissenstein

Neumagen
Dhron
Engelsgrube
Hengelberg
Hofberg
Kandel
Lasenberg
Laudamus Berg
Layen
Leiwen
Ohligberg
Pichter
Rosengärtchen
Roterd
Sängerei
Thierlay

Oberemmel
Agritiusberg
Eltzerberg
Hutte
Junkerberg
Lauterberg
Raul
Schwarzberg

Ockfen
Bockstein
Geisberg
Sankt Irminer

Piesport
Bildchen
Goldtröpfchen
Grafenberg
Grauberg
Guntherslay
Hinterslay
Hohlweid
Michelsberg
Rothlay
Schubertslay
Taubenberg
Taubengarten
Traubengarten

Saarburg
Antoniusbrunne
Flakenstein
Fellerich

Fels
Fuchs
Gippel
Heppenstein
Hubertusberg
Irsch-Saarburg
König Johannberg
Kreuzberg
Kreuzweiler
Krutweiler
Leyenkaut
Mühlenberg
Nennig
Onsdorf
Palzem
Rausch
Rehlingen
Sankt Irminer
Schoden
Sehndorf
Temmels
Tiefenthal
Wincheringen

Serrig
Hindenburglay
Perl
Schloss Saarfels
Wintersheck
Würzberger-Helenenberg
Würzberger-Marienberg

Traben-Trarbach
Halsberg
Hühnerberg
Krauterhaus
Krov
Lösnich
Sonnseite
Ungsberg
Wolf

Trier
Augenscheiner
Dom-Avelbach
Dom-Herrenberg
Fastrau
Fell
Franzenheim
Geisberg
Goldgrübchen
Grewenich
Hockweiler
Irsch-Trier
Johannisberg
Karthäuserhofberg
Kenn
Laurentiusberg
Longuich
Longuich-Kirsch
Marienholz
Maximiner-Grünhäuser
Maximiner-Herrenberg
Mertesdorf-Grünhaus
Metzdorf
Pichter
Pluwig
Probstberg
Ralingen
Retzgrube

Saar
Schlangenwingert
Schweich
Thiergarten
Treppchen
Zederberg

Trittenheim
Altärchen
Apotheke
Fahrfels
Falkenberg
Laurentiuslay
Riol
Risch
Sonnteilen
Weierbach

Ürzig
Altar
Kranklay
Kreuzwingert
Kunk
Maxberg
Michelslay
Michelsripp
Rosenkranz
Schwarzlay
Thomasberg
Urglück
Urlay
Wittlich

Valwig
Bienenberg
Brodenbach
Burgberg
Burgen
Elslay
Greismund
Grosslay
Hüttenberg
Kapellenberg
Klotten
Kochem
Langenberg
Neef
Pommern
Prälat
Radein
Schwarzenberg
Sonnenberg
Treis

Waldrach
Camp
Ehrenberg
Jesuitengarten
Krone
Marienlay, Schloss
Meisenberg
Ohligswingert
Sommerau
Tarforst

Wehlen
Bergweiler
Feinter
Klosterlay
Münzlay
Nonnenberg

Map 22 – Moselle, Saar, Ruwer (continued)

Sonnenuhr
Steinkaul

Wiltingen
Brauenfels
Braune Kupp
Braunfels
Braunhals
Dohr
Domschwarzhofberger
Elzosberg
Euchriusberg
Gottesfuss
Johannislay
Kommlingen
Krettnach
Kupp
Niedermennig
Nittel
Pellingen
Ritterpfad
Schwarzberg
Schwarzhofberg
Schlangengraben
Silberberg
Sonnenberg

Wawern

Winningen
Dieblich
Hamm
Uhlen

Wintrich
Bitsch
Dhron
Elisenberg
Geierskopf
Geierslay
Grosser Herrgott
Hengelberg
Hofberg
Kandel
Kesten
Kirschley
Minheim
Ohligsberg
Pichter
Roterd
Sängerei
Simonsberg
Velden

Zell
Aldegund
Alf
Baumberg
Bremm
Briedel
Bullay
Burg
Burglay
Engelsburg
Fahr
Farlay
Funkelshölle
Goldlay
Heissenstein
Hotlay
Kamp
Kirche
Klosterkammer
Königslay
Marienberg
Mauserberg
Mergerei-
  Ketterschauberg
Merl
Mönchlay

Mulay-Hofberg
Mullayhofberg
Nussberg
Palmenberg
Petersberg
Punderich
Reil
Schäferlay
Schwarze Katz
Staaden
Taubenbrunnen
Weingrube

Zeltingen
Bergweiler
Bickert
Engelsberg
Herzlay
Kirchenpfad
Kirchlay
Platten
Rotlay
Schwarzlay
Sonnenuhr
Steinmauer
Stephanslay

Map 23 – Palatinate

Bad Dürkheim
Annaberg
Fasanengarten
Feuerberg
Fuchsmantel
Gaiersbühl
Hochbenn
Hochmess
Kreuzmorgen
Lambsheim
Letten
Mandelgarten
Michelsberg
Nonnengarten
Osterberg
Proppenstein
Rittergarten
Schenkelbohl
Schlossgarten
Ungstein
Weilberg

Bad Kreuznach
Oberweiler-im-Tal
Rittergut-Bangert
Rothenberg
Sitters
Sommerloch
Waldhilbersheim
Winterborn

Bergzabern
Billigheim
Dörrenbach
Schank

Burrweiler
Albersweiler
Arzheim

Dackenheim
Berweg
Bissersheim
Bobenheim
Weisenheim-am-Berg
Weisenheim-am-Sand

Deidesheim
Brühl
Buschweg
Dopp
Gehen
Gehren
Grainhubel
Herrgottsacker
Hofstück
Hohenmorgen
Kapellengarten
Katharinenbild
Kieselberg
Kranzler
Langenbohl
Langenmorgen
Langenstück
Leinhöhle
Martenweg
Mauer
Maushöhle
Mühle
Nonnenstück
Rennpfad

Schafböhl
Schnepfenflug
Strasse
Thal
Tiergarten
Waldberg
Weinbach

Edenkoben
Altenweg
Bildhausel
Bobingen
Feuer
Galgenhöhe
Grain
Grossfischlingen
Heilig
Heiligenberg
Hundertmorgen
Maikammer-Alsterweiler
Mühle
Petersbrunnen
Pfeiffer
Roschbach
Sankt Martin
Spielweid
Venningen
Wetterkreuzberg

Forst
Abtsberg
Alser
Altenburg
Elster
Fleckinger

Freundstück
Granish
Jesuitengarten
Kirchenstück
Kranich
Langenacker
Langenbohl
Langenmorgen
Langkammer
Linsenstein
Mirrhe
Musenhang
Pechstein
Pfeiffer
Stift
Strasse
Walhöhle
Ziegler

Freinsheim
Gottesacker
Oschelskopf
Rosenbuckel
Schwarzes Kreutz

Gimmeldingen
Bienengarten
Hofstück
Kieselberg
Meerspinne
Schild
Teichwiese

Grünstadt
Albsheim

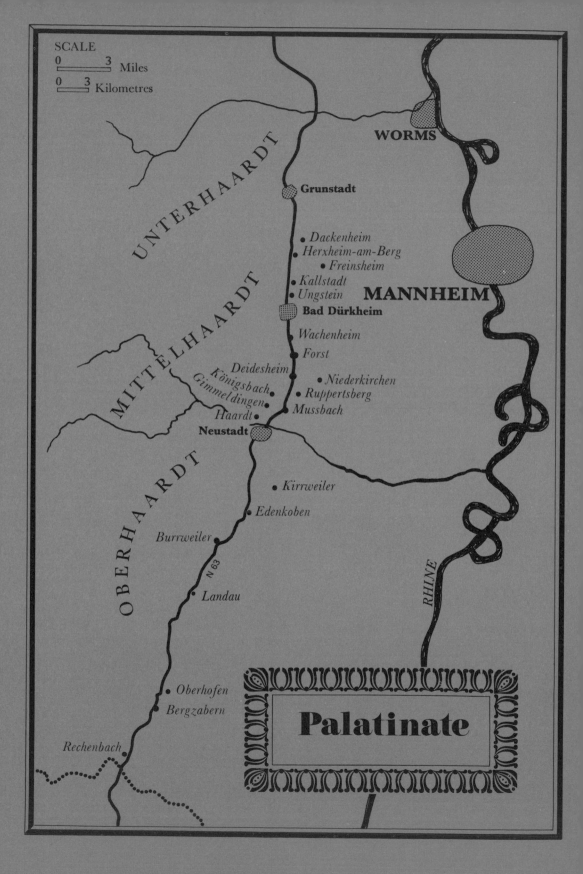

SCALE

0   3 Miles

0   3 Kilometres

WORMS

UNTERHAARDT

Grunstadt

Dackenheim
Herxheim-am-Berg
Freinsheim
Kallstadt
Ungstein

MANNHEIM

Bad Dürkheim

Wachenheim

Forst

MITTELHAARDT

Deidesheim
Königsbach
Gimmeldingen

Niederkirchen

Ruppertsberg

Mussbach

Haardt

Neustadt

Kirrweiler

Edenkoben

OBERHAARDT

Burrweiler

N 63

Landau

RHINE

Oberhofen
Bergzabern

Rechenbach

Palatinate

Map 23 – Palatinate (continued)

Alsenz
Battenberg
Berweg
Bischheim
Bissersheim
Bolanden
Breitheck
Colgenstein-Heidesheim
Dackenheim
Dirmstein
Einselthum
Eppelsheim
Grossbockenheim
Grosskarlbach
Harxheim
Hessheim
Heuchelheim Frankenthal
Hohl
Hollenberg
Ilbesheim
Kindenheim
Kirchheim-an-der-Eck
Kirchheim-an-der-
   Weinstrasse
Kirchheimbolanden
Kleinbockenheim
Kleinkarlbach
Laumersheim
Lauterecken
Leistadt
Mertesheim
Neuliningen
Obrigheim
Orlenberg
Sausenheim

Herxheim-am-Berg
Aspen
Bürgergarten
Herrengarten
Herzog
Himmelreich
Hofstück
Kalkgrube
Kansel
Kirchgarten
Kirchptad
Kirchtal
Mahlstein
Seminargarten
Sommerseite
Steinberg

Kallstadt
Annaberg
Benn
Erpolzheim
Hasenlauf

Horn
Hubbaum
Hühneracker
Kalkofen
Kreidekeller
Kreuzmorgen
Michelsberg
Nill
Osterberg
Rudelstein
Saumagen
Steinacker
Trift

Kirrweiler
Amstgarten
Diedesfeld
Goldmorgen
Hohweg
Johanniskirchel
Lercherberg
Spielweid
Steingebiss
Zehnmorgen

Königsbach
Bender
Falbert
Idig
Muchenhaus
Mühlweg
Reiterpfad
Rolandsberg
Satz
Weissmauer
Weissenauer

Landau
Appenhofen
Bellheim
Bornheim
Dammheim
Dierbach
Dudenhofen
Essingen
Frankweiler
Freckenfeld
Freisbach
Gleisweiler
Gocklingen
Godramstein
Gommersheim
Grafenhausen
Heiligenstein
Heuchelheim
Impflingen
Kapsweyer
Klingen

Klingenmünster
Knittelsheim
Leinsweiler
Mechtersheim
Mühlacker
Niederhochstadt
Niederhorbach
Nonnenhorn
Nussdorf
Oberhochstadt
Offenbach-an-der-Queich
Pleisweiler-Oberhofen
Rechtenbach
Ring
Roschbach
Schweigen
Siebeldingen
Vollmersweiler
Walsheim
Weingarten
Weyher
Wollmesheim

Mussbach
Bischofsweg
Glockenzeit
Pabst

Neustadt
Altenweg
Bildhausel
Bohl
Braungarten
Dackenheim
Diedesfeld
Duttweiler
Ellerstadt
Fautenbohl
Feuer
Goldmorgen
Grain
Guckingsland
Heiligenberg
Horst
Hundertmorgen
Johanniskirchel
Kalkberg
Kies
Kirchenberg
Lachen-Speyerdorf
Letten
Maikammer-Alsterweiler
Oberhausen
Petersbrunnen
Schwegenheim
Spielweid
Wetterkreuzberg
Zehnmorgen

Oberhofen
Albersweiler
Arzheim

Rechenbach
Dörrenbach

Ruppertsberg
Achtmorgen
Diedel
Gaisbohl
Goldschmidt
Helbig
Hofstuck
Höheburg
Kaft
Lindenbusch
Mandelacker
Mandelberg
Mühlweg
Nussbien
Quelle
Reiterpfad
Spiess

Ungstein
Diemart

Wachenheim
Altenburg
Bächel
Bohlig
Dankental
Friedelsheim
Fuchsmantel
Gerümpel
Goldbachel
Hell Holz
Höhe
Königswingert
Langenbachel
Luginsland
Mandelgarten
Odinstal
Rembachel
Schenkenbohl
Silberbach
Süssbuckel
Weinborn
Wolfsdarm

Worms
Gerolsheim
Grossniedesheim
Kleinniedesheim
Niefernheim
Zell

Map 24 – Rhinegau, Rhinehessia, Nahe

Alsheim
Alzey
Authenthal
Bechtheim
Bechtolsheim
Bende
Bergkloster
Biebelnheim
Brechtal
Dintesheim
Dorn-Dürkheim
Eimsheim
Esselborn
Feuerberg
Fischerpfad
Framersheim
Frettenheim
Friedrichsberg
Fuchsloch
Gau Heppenheim
Gau-Odernheim
Geyerscheid
Gimbsheim
Guntersblum
Hahl
Hand
Hangen-Weisheim
Hasenbiss
Hellborn
Hessensprung
Hessloch
Himmelthal
Kälbchen
Karstweg
Kellerstein
Kelterweg
Kettenheim
Kirchspiel
Klausenberg
Kloppberg
Lende
Liebfrauenberg
Liebfrauental
Löwenberg
Ludwigshöhe
Mauchenheim
Mausbrunnen
Mettenheim
Monzernheim
Nenenberg
Nieder-Wiesen
Offenheim
Ohligstück
Osthofen
Peterberg
Pilgerborn
Planig
Platte
Rheinberg
Rheinpfad
Römerberg
Römerstein
Rosenbrücke
Rosstal
Rust
Sandhöhle
Schallenberg
Schnapp
Sommerhäuschen
Sonnenberg

Sonnenheil
Steig
Teufelskopf
Uelversheim
Vogelsgarten
Wahlheim
Wehweg
Weinheim
Wintersheim
Wolm

Bad Kreuznach
Bechenheim
Bels
Bermersheim
Biebelsheim
Birkenberg
Bockenau
Bornheim
Boseberg
Braunweiler
Brückes
Burgsponheim
Colln
Dalberg
Dautenheim
Delichen
Desloch
Eckenroth
Ensheim
Frohngewann
Galenberg
Gau Nickelheim
Gau Nider-Weinheim
Gensingen
Gutenberg
Hackenheim
Hahnenkampf
Hargesheim
Heddesheim
Heiligenwann
Hergenfeld
Hinkelstein
Hinterberg
Hollenpfad
Horrweiler
Hüttenberg
Ippenheim
Jeckenbach
Jugenheim
Kahlenberg
Kapelle
Kauzenberg, Schloss
Kehrenberg
Krotenpfuhl
Layenweg
Mandel
Manik
Metzler
Mühlenberg
Mühlpieth
Nikolausberg
Pfaffen-Schwabenheim
Pfarrwingert
Römerberg
Rosenberg
Rosenheck
Roxheim
Rüdesheim-Nahe
Sankt Johann

Sankt Martin
Sarmsheim
Saukopf
Schimsheim
Schützenhohl
Sprendlingen
Steinweg
Sulzheim
Thal
Uffhofen
Vendersheim
Wallertheim
Wallhausen
Welgesheim
Westerberg
Wiesberg
Winzenheim
Wisberg
Wolfsheim
Zotzenheim

Bad Münster
Alsenz-Nahe
Altenbamberg
Bockelheim, Schloss
  Armsheim
Boos
Dautenpflanzer
Delichen
Dielkirchen
Duchroth
Ebernburg
Eckelsheim
Erbes-Büdesheim
Erzgrube
Feilbingert
Fels
Felsenberg
Felseneck
Frei-Laubersheim
Frohnholz
Gau Grehweiler
Gerbach
Gotzenfels
Gumbsheim
Heimberg
Hermannsberg
Hermannshöhle
Hinterfels
Hochstatten
Huffelsheim
Kafels
Kalkofen
Kapellenberg
Kerz
Kirschheck
Kirschroth
Kitzingen
Klamm
Königsberg
Königsfels
Krebsweiler
Kupfergrube
Langenberg
Lettweiler
Lohnweiler
Mannweiler
Martinstein
Meddersheim

Meisenheim
Merxheim
Monzingen
Mühl
Mühlberg
Mühlenberg
Nack
Nerzweiler
Neu-Bamberg
Niedereisenbach
Niederhausen-Schloss
  Bockelheim
Niedermoschel
Norheim
Oberstreit
Odernheim
Offenbach-am-Glan
Pfingstweider
Raumbach
Rehborn
Rosenhecke
Rossel
Roterde
Schmittweiler
Sobernheim
Staudernhaum
Steinberg
Stein-Bockenheim
Steyer
Volxheim
Traisen
Traienfels
Waldbäckelheim
Weiler-bei-Monzingen
Welschberg
Wolfstein
Wollstein
Wonsheim

Bingen
Affenberg
Albig
Anberg
Bacharach
Bienengarten
Bingen-Büdesheim
Bingen-Kempten
Bischofshub
Borngraben
Braunen
Bretzenheim
Büdesheim
Burgberg
Burggarten
Dietersheim
Dorsheim
Dromersheim
Eisel
Fullkopf
Gaulsheim Bingen
Gehaneweg
Geig
Gensingen
Goldloch
Grolsheim
Hasenlauf
Hinterberg
Hintere
Hinterhäuser
Hockenmühle

SCALE

0 — 10 Miles

0 — 10 Kilometres

R H I N E G A U

Kloster Eberbach

Rauenthal
Kiedrich
Martinsthal

WIESBADEN

Lorch

Hallgarten

Oberwalluf

Schloss Vollrads

Erbach

Oestrich

Eltville · Niederwalluf

Johannisberg

Geisenberg

Winkel

Rudesheim

Mittelheim

RHINE

Budenheim

Hochheim

MAINZ ·

MAIN

Bingerbruck ·   BINGEN

N A H E

NAHE

R·HINE-

Laubenheim

Bodenheim ·

Nackenheim ·

Nierstein ·

Oppenheim ·

Bad Kreuznach

Dienheim ·

Bad Münster

HESSE

Alsheim ·

Rhinegau
Rhinehesse
&
Nahe

RHINE

WORMS

Map 24 – Rhinegau, Rhinehessia, Nahe (continued)

Honigberg
Hütte
Ingelheim
Kilb
Kolbern
Laberstahl
Langenlonsheim
Lies
Münster-Sarmsheim
Nieder-Hilbersheim
Ober-Ingelheim
Oberwesel
Ohligberg
Pfarrgarten
Pittermännchen
Platte
Rechweg
Rheinhöhle
Ringerzell
Rochusberg
Rochusweg
Rummelsheim
Schanz
Scharlachberg
Schnack
Schöneberg
Schwätzerchen
Sendel
Sponsheim
Steinchen
Windesheim

Bingerbrück
Genheim
Pittersberg
Rotenfels
Weiler-bei-Bingerbrück

Bodenheim
Bock
Braunloch
Burgweg
Dachsberg
Ebersberg
Galgenheim
Hoch
Kahlenberg
Klein-Winternheim
Leidhecke
Leimen
Leistenberg
Rettberg
Sankt Alban
Silberberg
Westrum

Budenheim
Kieselberg
Stadecken

Dienheim
Authenthal
Dolgesheim
Ebenbreit
Falkenberg
Friesenheim
Gabsheim
Geierscheid
Goldgrube
Gumben

Guntersblum
Hand
Himmelthal
Kandelweg
Kelterweg
Krotenbrunnen
Langenweg
Langweg
Leckerberg
Lüdwigshöhe
Pflanzer
Rheinpfad
Rosswiese
Silzbrunnen
Sohlbrunnen
Steig
Tafelstein
Teufelskopf
Udenheim
Vogelsgarten
Wehweg
Weinolsheim
Wörrstadt
Zwölfmorgen

Eltville
Bunken
Freienborn
Grimmen
Hanach
Kalbpflicht
Klümbchen
Langenstück
Mönchhanach
Sonnenberg
Steinmächer
Taubenberg

Erbach
Bachhell
Bruhl
Bubenheim
Deitelsberg
Dillmetz
Engelsmannsberg
Engelstadt
Gemark
Gross-Winternheim
Hassel
Hattenheim
Heidesheim
Heiligenstock
Hohenrain
Honigberg
Honigsberg
Kilb
Kissling
Kränzchen
Mannberg
Marcobrunnen
Michelmark
Nussbrunnen
Partenheim
Pflanzer
Rheinhartshausen,
  Schloss
Rheinhell
Sandgrube
Schützenhaus
Schwabenheim

Seelgass
Siegelsberg
Stabel
Steeg
Steinberg
Steinmorgen
Wackernheim
Willsborn
Wisselbrunnen

Geisenheim
Altbaum
Aspisheim
Backenacker
Decker
Fuchsberg
Hoher Dekker
Kapellengarten
Katzenloch
Klauserweg
Kosakenberg
Laberstahl
Leyer
Lickerstein
Mäuerchen
Morschberg
Ockfen
Rothenberg
Rottland
Schlossgarten
Senchen
Steinacker

Hallgarten
Biegels
Boxberg
Deez
Deutelsberg
Egersburg
Frühenberg
Geyersberg
Hendelberg
Hindelberg
Hintersaune
Hitz
Jungfer
Kirchenacker
Kreuzberg
Mehrhölzchen
Neufeld
Reuscherberg
Schönhell
Weg

Hochheim
Bettelmann
Daubhaus
Domdechaney
Flörsheim
Gehitz
Hinter der Kirche
Kirchenstück
Kohlkaut
Massenheim
Pfanloch
Rauchloch
Sommerheil
Stiehlweg
Viktoriaberg
Wandkaut

Weid
Weiher
Weissert
Wicker

Johannisberg
Erntebringer
Hansenberg
Kerzenstück
Klauser Berg
Mittelholle
Schwarzenstein
Steinacker
Weiher

Kiedrich
Brück
Grafels
Langenberg
Turmberg
Wasserrose
Weierberg

Laubenheim
Edelmann
Häuschen
Hechtsheim
Heyl
Hitz
Kalkofen
Klosterneck
Mainz-Weisenau
Rettberg
Seckergrund
Steig

Lorch
Assmannshausen
Aulhausen
Backhaus
Bischofshub
Bodenthal
Honigberg
Kapelle
Krone
Lach
Lorchhausen
Pfaffenwees

Mainz
Brühl
Mainz-Kostheim
Mainz-Weisenau

Martinsthal
Geisberg
Langenberg
Oberrödchen

Mittelheim
Appenheim
Deitelsberg
Dillmetz
Edelmann
Engelmannsberg
Gau-Algesheim
Hasensprung
Heppel
Honigberg

Map 24 – Rhinegau, Rhinehessia, Nahe (continued)

Kandelberg
Magdalenenacker
Michelsberg
Oberberg
Rheingarten
Rothenberg
Schlehdorn
Steinert
Stolzenberg
Wisselbrunnen

Nackenheim
Dieterkapp
Ebersheim
Engelsberg
Fenchelberg
Fritzenhölle
Gau Bischofsheim
Glockenberg
Hahlkreuz
Hartenberg
Harxheim
Herrnberg
Hinterhaus
Kahlenberg
Kellerberg
Kircheck
Kreuzwingert
Kuppel
Langen Tag
Lieth
Lörzweiler
Nieder-Olm
Ober-Olm
Orlenberg
Pfaffenweg
Rheinharl
Rosteisen
Sahler
Sandkaut
Schmidtskapelle
Sommerwein
Spitzenberg
Stirn
Teufelsloch
Wehling
Weyersborn

Niederwalluf
Dreimorgen
Elsheim
Essenheim
Gottesacker
Marchauns
Oberberg
Walkenberg

Nierstein
Auflangen
Bildstock
Domtal
Findling
Flachenthal
Fockenberg
Galgenheim
Gemarkgasse
Glock
Glockenstrang
Guldenmorgen
Hauben

Heiligenbaum
Hinkelstein
Hintersaal
Hipping
Kehr
Kirschplatt
Mersch
Mommenheim
Mönchberg
Moosberg
Nieder-Saulheim
Ober-Saulheim
Oelberg
Olberg
Orbel
Paterberg
Pettental
Pfuhlweg
Rehgasse
Rembacher Steig
Rohr
Sankt Kiliansberg
Schlangenberg
Schmitt
Schnappenberg
Schwabsburg
Seidenburg
Selzen
Sörgenloch
Spiegelberg
Streng
Taubennest
Undenheim
Warte
Westerberg
Zehn-Morgen
Zornheim

Oestrich
Deez
Doosberg
Eisenberg
Eiserberg
Eiserweg
Gottestal
Kellerberg
Kerbersberg
Kranklay
Lenchen
Magdalenengarten
Mühlberg
Pfaffenpfad
Rheingarten
Rheinhartshausen,
    Schloss
Sankt Gottesthal
Sankt Nikolaus
Söhnchen
Weg

Oppenheim
Altdorr
Dabhaus
Dalheim
Daubhaus
Dexheim
Dittelsheim
Doktor
Domtal
Edenbreit

Falkenberg
Gaiersberg
Gansberg
Garten
Geyerscheid
Gottesgarten
Halmheim
Hayerweg
Herrenweiler
Hockbruck
Ibersheim
Kette
Köngernheim
Krotenberg
Krotenbrunnen
Kugel
Mönchberg
Ostertal
Reisekahr
Rohrgasse
Sackträger
Schornsheim
Steig
Zuckerberg

Rauenthal
Baiken
Burggraben
Burggrafen
Ehr
Eisweg
Gehren
Hilbitz
Hühnerberg
Kesselring
Langenstück
Laurentiusberg
Maasborn
Nonnenberg
Pfalzgraben
Rothenberg
Siebenmorgen
Steinhaufen
Wagenkehr
Wiesberg
Wieshell
Wülfen

Rüdesheim
Assmannshausen
Aulhausen
Backhaus
Badenheim
Bienengarten
Birgweg
Bischofsberg
Bronnen
Brunnen
Bubenstück
Decker
Dickerstein
Engerweg
Flecht
Häuserweg
Hellpfad
Hinterhaus
Kiesel
Klosterkiesel
Mühl
Mühlstein

Pares
Platz
Roseneck
Rüdesheim-Eibingen
Scharlachberg
Stumpfenort
Wiesberg
Wingert
Wust
Zoll-Haus

Wiesbaden
Wiesbaden-Dotzheim

Winkel
Anspach
Bienengarten
Dachsberg
Daubhaus
Eckeberg
Ensing
Erntebringer
Gutenberg
Hasensprung
Honigberg
Jesuitengarten
Kreuzberg
Lett
Oberberg
Plankener
Rheinpflicht
Steinchen
Vollrads, Schloss

Worms
Abenheim
Albisheim
Bermersheim-Worms
Brünnchen
Brunnenhäuschen
Dalsheim
Geiersberg
Gotteshilfe
Gundheim
Hackgraben
Hafenberg
Hasenbiss
Heppenheim
Hohen-Sulzen
Kohm
Kruck
Liebfrauenstift
Mittlere-Reitel
Molsheim
Morstadt
Ober-Flörsheim
Offstein
Osthofen
Pfeddersheim
Rheinberg
Rodensteiner
Rosstal
Rotenstein
Schnapp
Wachenheim
Westhofen
Wies-Oppenheim
Wolm
Worms-Horchheim

Map 25 – Franconia, Baden, Württemberg

Baden-Baden
Affenthaler
Bochingen
Bühlertal
Durbach
Eisental
Gaisbach
Hügelsheim
Kappelrodeck
Lauf
Lautenbach
Neusatz
Neuweier
Oberachern
Oberkirch
Obersasbach
Oberweiler
Ringeibach
Sasbachwalden
Sinzheim
Sulz
Varnhalt
Waldulm
Zell-Weierbach
Zunsweier

Bingen
Stromberg
Waldlaubersheim

Darmstadt
Grossheubach
Kleingartach
Ruck

Forst
Ungeiheim

Frankfurt-am-Main
Abtsberg
Almus
Feuerthal
Hammelburg
Nordheim
Stammheim
Wirmsthal

Freiburg
Achkarren
Bad Bellingen
Badenweiler
Bad Krozingen
Ballrechten
Bamlach
Bickensohl
Bischoffingen
Blansingen
Bollschweil
Bombach
Breisach
Britzingen
Burkheim
Eberniger
Ebringen
Efringen-Kirchen
Ehrenstetten
Eichstetten
Eimeldingen
Esslingen
Feldberg
Gottenheim

Grenzach
Grundelfingen
Haltingen
Hecklingen
Heimbach
Herten
Hertingen
Heuweiler
Hollbacker
Ihringen
Istein
Jechtingen
Kenzingen
Kiechlinsbergen
Kirchhofen
Kleinkems
Köndringen
Königschaffhausen
Lahr
Laufen
Leiselheim
Liel
Malterdingen
Markgrafler
Mauchen
Merdingen
Merzhausen
Mundingen
Neuershausen
Niederrimsingen
Nordweil
Obereggenen
Oberrotweil
Pfaffenweiler
Riedlingen
Sankt Georgen
Sasbach
Schallbach
Schallstadt-Wolfenweiler
Schelingen
Scherzingen
Schliengen
Seefelden
Sölden
Staufen
Sulzburg
Tiengen
Tutschfelden
Unterglottertal
Vögisheim
Wagenstadt
Waltershofen
Wasenweiler
Wettelbrunn
Wolfenweiler

Heilbronn
Abstatt
Bachenau
Beilstein-Württemberg
Besigheim
Bonnigheim
Brackenheim
Dahnfeld
Dürrenzimmern
Eibensbach
Ellhofen
Frauenzimmern
Geddelsbach

Gellmersbach
Gemmrigheim
Gräntschen
Gronau
Grossbottwar
Grossgartach
Guglingen
Gundelsheim
Haberschlacht
Hafnerhaslach
Heinsheim
Hessigheim
Hohenhaslach
Hohenstein
Horkheim
Kleinbottwar
Klingenberg
Kunzelsau
Landshausen
Lauffen
Lehrensteinsfeld
Leonbronn
Löwenstein mit Rettzach
    und Rittelhof
Mundelsheim
Neckarmühlbach
Neckarsulm
Neiperg
Nordhausen
Obergriesheim
Oberstenfeld-mit-
    Weingutlichtenberg
Ochsenbach
Oedheim
Pfaffenhofen
Schluchtern
Schmidhausen
Schozach
Schützingen
Schwaigern
Steinheim an der Murr
Sternenfels
Sulzfeld
Untergriesheim
Weiler-an-der-Zaber
Weinsberg
Willsbach
Zaberfeld
Zaisersweiher

Karlsruhe
Bruchsal
Dietlingen
Eisingen
Ellmendingen
Enzberg
Erlenbach
Ersingen
Freudenstein
Grafenhausen
Heidelsheim
Illingen
Knittlingen
Maulbronn
Mühlacker
Niebelsbach
Oberderdingen
Obergrombach
Ölbronn
Otisheim

Rott
Spielberg
Untergrombach
Unteröwisheim
Wöschbach

Konstanz
Bohlingen
Gaienhofen
Hagnau
Kippenhausen
Kressbronn
Markdorf
Meersburg
Ohningen
Reichenau
Stetten
Überlingen
Untersteinbach

Mannheim
Auerbach
Dirmstein
Dossenheim
Hambach
Laudenbach
Streichling

Mosbach
Bachenau
Bieringen
Diebach
Dörzbach
Eberstadt
Ernsbach
Grosslangheim
Grossostheim
Herbolzheim
Hollerbach
Ingelfingen
Jagsthausen
Klepsau
Laibach
Miltenberg
Möckmühl
Neckarzimmern
Olnhausen
Schweigern
Stein-am-Kocher
Stiel
Widdern

Strasbourg
Diersburg
Fessenbach
Friesenheim
Heiligenzell
Hugsweiler
Kippenheim
Kippenheimweiler
Mahlberg
Meissenheim
Nesselried
Niederschopfheim
Oberschopfheim
Offenburg
Ohlsbach
Rammersweier
Schüttern
Wallburg

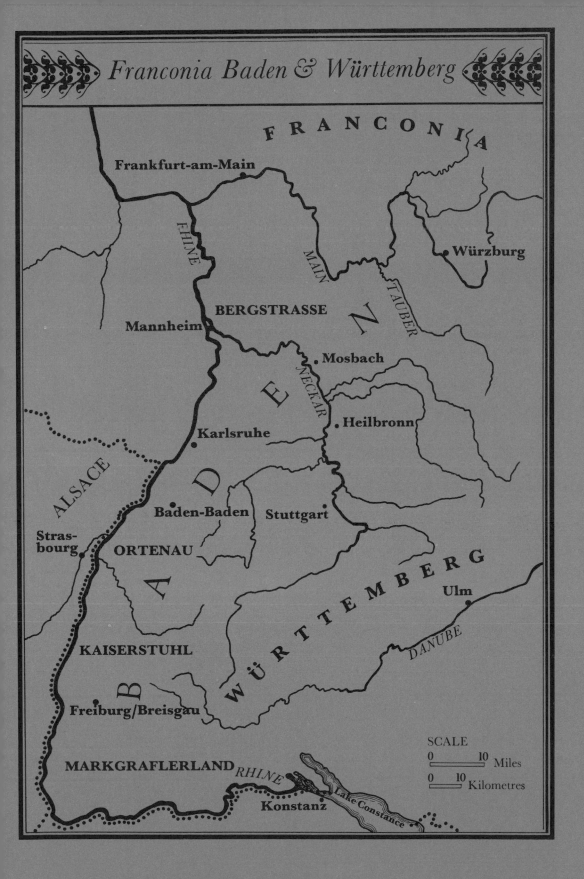

Franconia Baden & Württemberg

FRANCONIA

Frankfurt-am-Main

Würzburg

RHINE

MAIN

TAUBER

BERGSTRASSE

Mannheim

Mosbach

NECKAR

B A D E N

Heilbronn

Karlsruhe

ALSACE

Baden-Baden

Stuttgart

Stras-
bourg

ORTENAU

WÜRTTEMBERG

Ulm

KAISERSTUHL

DANUBE

Freiburg/Breisgau

MARKGRAFLERLAND

RHINE

Konstanz

Lake Constance

SCALE

0   10 Miles

0   10 Kilometres

Map 25 – Franconia, Baden, Württemberg (continued)

Stuttgart
Asperg
Auenstein
Bad Mergentheim
Benningen
Bietingheim
Dettingen
Diefenbach
Endersbach
Fellbach
Gerlingen
Grossheppach
Gundelbach
Hanweiler
Hertmannsweiler
Hopfigheim
Horrheim
Kappishäusern
Kenzenheim
Kirchberg-an-der-Murr
Kleinheppach
Kore-Steinreinach
Lippoldsweiler
Löchgau
Ludwigsberg
Markgroningen
Murr
Neckarweihingen
Neuffen
Oberstetten
Poppenweiler
Reutlingen
Riet
Rommelshausen
Rossweg
Schlatt
Schnait
Schorndorf
Strümpfelbach
Tamm
Tubingen
Unterjesingen
Unterriexingen
Weilheim-an-der-Teck
Weissach

Winnenden

Ulm
Bermatingen

Würzburg
Abtsleite
Almus
Astheim
Äusserer-Neuberg
Beckstein
Bettenberg
Buchbrunn
Bullenheim
Burgweg
Castell
Dettelbach
Deubach
Dittwar
Eibelstadt
Engelsberg
Erlabrunn
Erlenbach
Eschendorf
Eulengrube
Eussenheim
Federberg
Frickenhausen
Fuchstadt
Fürstenberg
Gerlachsheim
Gerolzhofen
Gossmannsdorf
Guntersleben
Hengstberg
Hergolshausen
Himmelstadt
Hohburg
Hoheim
Hohenfeld
Homburg
Humprechtsau
Huttenheim
Iffigheim
Impfingen

Ingolstadt
Iphofen
Ippesheim
Julius-Echter-Berg
Juliusspital
Kalb
Kallmuth
Karlstadt
Katzenkopf
Kleinochsenfurt
Königshofen
Krassölzheim
Krautostheim
Kreuzwertheim
Kronzberg
Lammerberg
Lauda
Leisten
Lengfurt
Leutershausen
Löffelstelzen
Lump
Machtilshausen
Mainberg
Mainstockheim
Marbach
Markelsheim
Marktbreit
Marksteft
Marsberg
Mühlbach
Neuses
Neusetz
Niederrimbach
Niederstetten
Obereisenheim
Oberlauda
Oberleinach
Obernbreit
Oberschupf
Oberschwarzach
Obervolkach
Ochsenfurt
Pfaffensteig
Pfulben

Ramsthal
Randersacker
Ravensburg
Repperndorf
Retzbach
Retzstadt
Reusch
Rodelsee
Rossberg
Rottingen
Schalksberg
Scharlach
Schönungen
Schwanleite
Schweinfurt
Segnitz
Seinsheim
Sickershausen
Sommerhausen
Sonnenstuhl
Steinheim
Stetten
Sulzfeld
Sulzthal
Tauberbischofsheim
Tauberrettersheim
Tauberzell
Teufelskeller
Theilheim
Thüngen
Thüngersheim
Unterdürrbach
Untereisenheim
Unterleinach
Veitshochheim
Volkach
Vorbachzimmern
Weigenheim
Weikersheim
Werbach
Wiesenbronn
Wilm
Winterhausen
Wipfeld
Wölflein

Map 26 – Vinelands of North Italy

Alessándria
Barbera d'Alessándria
Castel la Volta
Castello di Sommariva
Castel Tagliolo
Cortese dell'Alto
  Monfenato
Gavi
Langhe, Le

Asti
Alba
Barbera d'Asti
Barolo
Boca d'Asti
Brachetto d'Asti

Cortese d'Asti
Dolcetto d'Alba
Dolcetto delle Langhe
Montforte d'Alba
Morra, La
San Marzano

Bergamo
Colli dei Frati
Franciacorta
Giuramento
Pontida
Val San Martino

Bologna
Alfoma
Montuni

Salamino
Sangiovese di San Marino

Bolzano
Caldaro Appiano
Caldaro, Lago di
Castel Rametz
Castel Schwanburg
Colline Bolzano
Colline di Merano
Girlaner Hugel
Goyener Riesling
Grucina
Kalterer
Kuchelberger
Lagarina Rosato

Lagrein
Leitacher
Leitwein
Meranese di Collina
Missianer
Rosso di Terlaner
Santa Maddalena
Terlano
Termeno
Traminer Aromatico
Veltiner

Brescia
Cellatica
Chiaretto del Lago
  d'Iselo

Chiaretto di Cellatica
Gussago
Pusterla
Valtenesi

Como, Lake
Bellagio
Grinatino
Montevecchio

Cuneo
Alba
Barbaresco
Barberati
Barolo
Castel la Volte
Fontanafredda
Nebbiolo d'Alba
Nebbiolo di Canale
Nebbiolo di Castellinaldo
Pellaverga
Quagliano

Forli
Albana di Romagna
Cagnina

Garda, Lake
Bardolino
Breganze
Chiaretto del Garda
Colline Rocciose
Fara–Vicentino
Garda Trentino
Isera
Lambrusco

Lugana
Passito de Arco

Genoa
Bianco della Riviera
Coronata
Cortese di Liguria
Portofino

Gorizia
Bianco Brusco de Teolo
Bianco dei Colli Euganei
Bianco del Collio
Borgogna
Malvasia de Collio
Malvasia di Ronchi
Riesling Renano
Tocai del Friuli

Imperia
Busetto
Chiaretto di Liguria
Dolceacqua
Dolcetto Ligure
Limassina
Massara
Mattaosso
Moscadello
Piemarore
Rossese di Val di Nervia
Vermentino

Milan
San Colombano

Modena
Castelfranco

Novara
Barengo
Camarino
Ghemme
Grigionasco
Ramie
Sizzano

Parma
Barbera di Langhirano
Fogarina
Fortanella
Friularo
Malvasia di Malatico
Tocai Rosato

Pavia
Barbacarlo
Broni
Buttafuoco
Canneto
Casteggio
Clastidio
Clastidium
Croatlina
Gran Moscato
Lacrima Vitis
Monferrato
Monteceresino
Montelio
Montenapoleone
Oltrepo Pavese
Pezzalunga
Pinot dell'Oltrepo
Prosecco dell'Oltrepo
Rosso Montu
Sanguie di Guida

Piacenza
Gutturnio
Spumante dell'Oltrepo
Valtidone Bianco

Reggio-Emilia
Lancellotta
Vientoso

Savona
Barbarossa
Busetto
Campochiesa
Dolcetto delle Langhe
Massarda
Mattaosso
Rossese Rosato
Rubino di Canavisse
Sciacchetra
Vermentino

Spezia, La
Arcola
Bianco Cinqueterre
Bianco della Riviera
Chiaretto del Faro
Cinqueterre
Malvasia di Pietro Ligure
Marinasco
Morasca Cinqueterre
Polcevera
Pollera
Portofino
Rinforzato
Sarticola
Vernaccia di Corniglia

Map 26 – Vinelands of North Italy (continued)

Trento
Casteller Gran Rubino
Castelli Mezzocorona
Lambrusco
Marzemino
San Zeno
Sorni
Teroldego
Vernaccia di Aldeno

Treviso
Cartizze Colli di
   Asola-Maser
Colli di Congeliano
Colli di Valdobbiadene
Prosecco Spumante
Verdiso

Trieste
Monfalcone
Prosecco Triestino
Terrano
Tocai del Friuli

Turin
L'Aglie
Caluso
Campiglione
Carema
Cari
Cesnola

Chiomonte
Freisa di Chieri

Udine
Bianco Misto di Caneva
Malvasia Bianca/Friuliana
Piccolit
Ramandolo
Refosco
Ribolla Gialla
Verduzzo di Ramandolo

Val d'Aosta
Arvier
Blanc de Morgex
Chambave
Donnaz
Enfer
Malvasia di Nus
Montouvert
Passito della Val d'Aosta
Torretta di San Pietro
Vino della Serra

Valtellina
Forzato di Valtellina
Grigioni
Grumello
Inferno
Nebbiolo di Retorbido
Perla Villa
Sassela

Sondrio
Valgella
Valtellina Rosso

Venice
Colli Friulani
Colline Trevigiane
Marzemino Trevigiano
Raboso
Rubino del Piave

Vercelli
Chiaretto del Cavaglia
Chiaretto del Viverone
Gattinara
Lessona
Masserano
Mesolone
Mottalciata
Passito di Moncrivello
Rosso Rubino del
   Viverone
Valdengo

Verona
Bardolino
Botticino
Breganze
Chiaretto del Garda
Colline Rocciose
Colli Veronesi
Colognola

Fara-Vicentino
Isera
Lugana
Passito di Arco
Raboso Veronese
Recioto
Soave
Val d'Alpone
Val d'Illasi
Val Mezzane
Valpantena
Valpolicella
Valtramigno

Vicenza
Arcugnano
Arzignano
Barbarano
Brendola
Colli Berici
Colli Euganei
Colli Vicentini Centrale
Costoza
Durello
Gambellara
Malvasia di Nanto
Montelungo
Orgiano
Rosso del Venda
Serprina
Soave

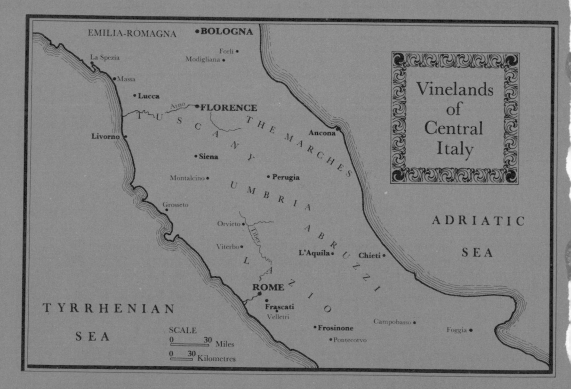

296

Map 27 – Vinelands of Central Italy

Ancona
Bianchillo Pesarese
Colli Piceni
Conero Rosso
Loro Piceno
Montesanto
Moscato Spumante di
  San Marino
Sangiovese di San Marino
Sangiovese Marchigiano
Spumante di Cingoli
Verdicchio dei Castelli
  di Jesi

Aquila, L'
Cerasuolo
Montepulciano
Peligno Bianco
Riviera
Rosso Piceno

Chieti
Città di Sant'Angelo

Florence
Capezzano Bianco
Carmignano Bianco
Chianti Montalbano
  Pistoiese
Chianti Classico
Colline Sanminiatesi
Cortona
Montalbano
Nipozzano
Pomino
Rufina

Foggia
Santo Stefano
Torre Giulia
Torre Quarto
Troia

Frascati
Colli Lanuvi

Frosione
Agnani
Barbera di Anagni
Olivella

Grosseto
Aleatico di Portoferraio
Ansonia
Maremma
Monteregio
Procanico
Sangioneto
Vecchienna

Livorno
Ugolino Bianco

Lucca
Colline Lucchesi
Colline Val di Nievole
Montecarlo
Spumante Dolce di
  Casatico
Val di Nievole

Perugia
Alte Valle del Tevere
Bastia
Bianco Piceno
Colline del Trasimeno

Colli Perugino
Corrona
Montecastelli
Panicale
Sacrantino
Sanguistino
Scacciadiavoli
Vernaccia di Cannara

Rome
Aprilia
Bianco dei Colli Albani
Bianco di Velletri
Canaiolo
Cannellino
Cantalupe in Sabina
Capena
Castelbracciano
Castelli Romani
Castel San Giorgio
Cerveteri
Cervicione
Cesanese del Castelli
  Romani
Colli Albani
Colonna
Cori
Fiorano Bianco
Fiorano Rosso
Fontesegale
Frascati
Grottaferrata
Maccarese
Marino
Mentana
Montecompatri
Morlupo
Nettuno Bianco

Ottonese
Pastoso
Spumante di Marino
Zagarolo

Siena
Arbia
Bianco di Santa
  Margherita
Brolio
Brunello di Montalcino
Chianti
Chianto Classico
Colli Salveti
Gaiole
Lacrima d'Aretusa
Montepulciano
Moscadello di
  Montalcino
Moscadello Lucuoroso
Val di Chiana

Velletri
Aleatico di Genzano
Bianco dei Colli Lanuri
Romagnano (Romanesco)
Rosso dei Colli Lanuvi

Viterbo
Aleatico di Gradoli
Aleatico di Viterbo
Bianco di Ronciglione
Castelbracciano
Colli Cimini
Colli Etruschi
Est! Est!! Est!!!
Montefiascone
Ronciglione
Vignanello

Map 28 – Vinelands of Southern Italy

Apulia
Casarino
Castel Asquaro
Castellabate
Copertina
Lacrima di Gallipoli
Mesagne
San Pietro Vernotico

Avellino
Barletta
Colli del Sannio
Fiano
Greco di Tufo
Malvasia di Vulture
Pannarano
Partento
San Giorgio
Solopaca
Taurasi
Vitulano

Bari
Bianco di Locorotondo

Castel del Monte
Castellana
Cerasuolo delle Murge
Colatamburo
Conversano
Lacrima di Corato
Locorotondo
Martina Franca
Primativo di Gioia
San Carlo
Verdea
Zagarese

Brindisi
Malvasia di Brindisi
Nero del Brindisino
Ostuni Bianco
Ottavianella
Zagarese

Cantanzaro
Balbino
Greco Rosso di
  Pontegrande

Limbadi Rosso
Magliocco
Nicastro Bianco
Provilaro
Rosso della Sila
Sambiase Rosso
San Sidero
Verbicaro

Catania (Sicily)
Adrano
Biancavilla Rosso
Ciclopi
Leonforte
Mascale
Ombra
Ragalna
Randazzo
San Salvador
Solichiata
Taormina
Villagrande

Foggia
Santo Stefano

Torre Giulia
Torre Quarto

Lecce
Barbera Leccese
Borraccio
Capo di Leuca
Doppo Secco
Melisano
Parasani
Squinzano
Zagarese

Messina, Sicily
Capo
Faro
Furnari (Bazia)
Malvasia di Milazzo
Mamertino
Marsala
Milazzo

Naples
Aglianico del Vulture

297

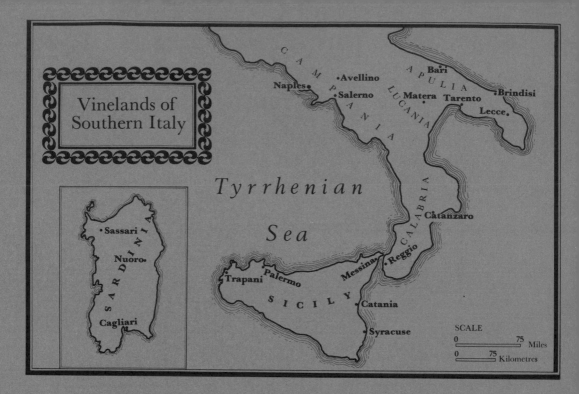

Map 28 – Vinelands of Southern Italy (continued)

Aglianichello
Aleatico di Terracina
Aleatico Secco
Asprino
Barano
Buonopane
Capri Bianco
Casamicciola
Cecubo
Colli Sorrentini
Falerno
Falernum
Fontana Serrara
Gragnano
Ischia Bianco
Monte Giove
Lacco Ameno
Lacrima Christi
Lettere
Pellagrello
Procida
Ravello
Sorriso d'Ischia

Palermo, Sicily
Akracas Bianco
Bianchi Carta
Corvo di Casteldaccia
Corvo di Colomba
  Platina
Marsala
Monreale
Passito di Misilmiri
Siciliana
Valledormo

Reggio (di Calabria)
Arghilla Rosato
Attafi Mantonaco
Attafi Greco
Attafi Rosso
Cirò
Donna Camilla
Greco di Gerace
Ieracare
Paci
Palizzi
Pellaro
Rubino
Trasfigurato di Seminara

Salerno
Alburno
Alto Cilento
Basso–Cilesto
Basso Sele
Furore Divina Costiera
Giovi Rosso
Gran Furor Divina
  Costiera
Irno
Sanginella
Sele
Tramonti

Taranto
Bianco di Martina Franca
Grottaglie
Manduria
Pollino
Primativo di Manduria

Sardinia
Anghelu Ruju
Barbera Sarda
Campidano di Cagliari
Cannonau
Capo Ferrato
Castelsardo
Dorato di Sorso
Dorgali
Fior di Romagnia
Gallura
Girò
Ipiani
Lagosta
Malvasia di Bosa
Malvasia di Cagliari
Mandrolisai
Marmilla
Mogoro
Monica di Sardegna
Nasco
Ninfeo
Nuoro
Nuraghe Majore
Nuragus
Nurra
Ogliastra
Oliena
Orbaia
Parteollese
Rosso di Dorgali
Sandalyon
Sangiovese di Arborea
Sangiovese Sardo
Santa Maria la Palma
Sassari

Semidano
Torbato
Torrevecchia
Trebbiano di Arborea
Trebbiano Sardo
Vermentino

Sicily
Aragona-Canicatti
Bianco Castellamare
Frappato di Vittoria
Lipari
Malvasia di Lipari
Mila, Bianco di
Partinico Bianco
Piana di Catania
Porto Casteldaccia
Salina
Val di Lupo
Vallelunga

Syracuse, Sicily
Albanello di Siracusa
Ambrato di Comiso
Cerasuolo di Vittoria
Francofonte
Maccarella
Pachino Rosso
Scoglitti
Val d'Anapo

Trapani, Sicily
Alcamo
Ribollito di Masala

298

Map 29 – Vinelands of Spain

Alella
Masnou
Mongat
Tempranillo

Andalusia
Dona Mercia
Mentilla
Mosiles
Posadas
Priego de Córdoba

Aragon
Albarracin
Aleariya
Balea
Belchite
Burbaguena
Calanda
Castellote
Cretas
Hijon
Jatiel
Olmos, Los
Puebla de Hijar, La
Regado
Robres
Salas
Samper de Calanda
Villarija de la Sierra

Asturias
Albarín
Candano
Carrasquín
Negrín

Avila
Ardenas de San Pedro
Calieyas
Cebreros
Cigales
Curiel
Medina del Campo
Mombeltran
Nava del Rey
Olivares de Duero
Peñafiel
Poyaldes
Rodillana
Rueda
Seca, La
Simancas
Tordesillas
Valaria la Buena
Vega Sicilia

Barcelona
Abrera
Aguamurcia
Albinana
Alella
Argenton
Avino
Cabrera
Cadaques
Caldas de Mombuy
Castelvi de la Marca
Castillo de Peralada
Espalla
Fontrubi
Iguanada
Llacuna, La
Llansa

Lledoner
Martorell
Masquefa
Mediona
Moja
Monjos
Montmell
Olesa de Bonesvallo
Pachs del Panadés
Pánades
Peralada
Pierola
Pontons
Ricardell
San Cugats
San Lorenyo Savall
San Sadurni de Nova
Subirats
Surnoll
Tempranillo
Terrasa
Teya
Tiana
Vilajuica
Vilastrell
Villafranca del Panadés
Villanueva
Xarelo

Baza
Albunal
Guadise
Vega, La
Veley

Bilbao
Alba

Castro Urdiales 'Chacoli'
Guitara
Herradilla
Lebana Tostadillo
Limpias
Martino
Pamplona
Parduca

Cádiz
Algodonales
Areos de la Frontera
Chiclana
Chipiona
Conil de la Frontera
Garrido Fino
Olvera
Perruño Fino
Puerto de Santa Maria
Puerto Real
Rota Tent
San Roque
Teraos, Los
Trebujena
Ubrique

Catalonia
Macabeo

Estremadura
Acebo
Aldea Nueva del Camino
Arroya de la Luy
Gatal

Galicia
Albarina

299

Map 29 – Vinelands of Spain (continued)

Amande
Berdellos
Caino
Caldetas
Cambados
Carballino
Castrelo del Mino
Fefinanes
Leiro
Meira
Menicia
Monterre
Orense
Piesal
Puente Canedos
Ramallosa
Ribadavia
Ribero a Ribeiro
Rua de Valdeonas
Salvatierra de Mino
Tostallido
Treiyadura
Tudelilla
Tuy
Urunuela
Valdeorras
Valdeorras Tostado
Viva

Guadalquivir
Almonte

Huelva
Bolullos del Condado
Bonares
Hinayos
Miebla
Palma del Condado
Palos de la Frontera
Rociano de Condado
San Juan del Puerto
Trigueros
Villalba del Alcor
Villarasa

Jerez de la Frontera
Albariya
Amontillado
Amoroso
Balbaina
Carraseal
Macharnudo
Madrolanes
Manyarilla
Pajarete
Tereios
Trebujena

La Rioja
Aldea Nueva de Ebro
Alfano
Baños de Ebro
Bienas
Calagrano
Calaharra
Cardouen
Cenicoo
Ceruera del Rio Albama
Cripa
Cuycurrita

El Ciego
Fuenmayor
Haro
Huereanos
Laguardia
Leya
Logroño
Majera
Marques de Murietta
Marques de Riseal
Mayuelo
Murillo del Rio Lera
Navarrete
Ollauri
Paceta
Rineón de Sato
San Adrian
San Vincente de la
   Sonsierra
Tirgo
Tudelilla

La Roda
Abanilla
Albacete
Almansa
Alpera
Hellin
Villarabledo
Yeste

León
Aranda de Duero
Arejanda
Baneya, La
Benavente
Cacabelos
Caniyo
Cantalapieba
Cantalpino
Carrales
Cepeda
Fermaselle
Fuentesauco
Madridanos
Miranda
Negro Rancio
Pelayos
Perena
Valdefinca
Villaeseusa
Villa Franca
Villafranca del Bieyo
Villalayan
Villalpando

Madrid
Alajeiros
Alameda de la Sangre
Anovar de Tajo
Canillas Moscatel
Chapineria
Chinchon
Colmenar de Oreja
Consueda
Epinola
Esealona
Esquinias
Fuencarral
Getafe

Guadalajara 'Pardillo'
Huerta
Lillo
Madridejos
Mentrida
Mora
Nablejos
Ocana
Orgay
Pardillo
Pastrana
Puebla de Alinoradiel
Quero
Quintaña de la Orden
Remoa Aloque
Sacedon
Sagra
San Martin de
   Valdeiglesias
Santa Cruy de la Zarya
Talavera
Taracón
Tehigo
Torrelaguna
Torrijos
Valdemora
Valmojado
Villa de don Fabrique
Yepes

Málaga
Albunal
Alcala de la Real
Algarroba
Algerinejo
Alora
Andujar
Antequera
Archidona
Areñas
Campillos
Colmenar
Competa
Cuevas de San Marco
Fatepona
Gaucin
Guadise
Lagrima
Lairen
Mohuyar
Nerja
Torrox
Vega, La
Veley
Veley, Málaga

Murcia
Bonete
Bullas
Caravaca
Casas Ibaney
Caudete
Cieya
Fortuna
Jumilla
Madriqueras
Moratell
Mula
Totana

Navarre
Artajona
Baños de Fitero
Campanas, Las
Caseante
Chacoli
Cintryenigo
Cordella
Estella
Eycola
Fitaro
Graciano
Lumbien
Mendagarria
Monteguada
Olite
Peralta
Pitillas
Puente la Reina
Sanguesa
Tafalla
Tilbas
Tudela
Villafranca
Yesa

New Castille
Alameda de la Sangre
Anovar de Tajo
Casas de Benito
Casas de Haro
Horeajo de Santiago
Illaña
Iniesta
Mesas, Las
Minglanilla
Mota de Cuervo
Motilla del Palancar
Pedroneras, Las
Quintañas del Rey
San Clemente
Tina
Toboso
Villamayor de Santiago
Villanueva de la Jara
Villapando

Seville
Aguilar de la Frontera
Alanjo
Albuquerque
Almendraljo
Baena
Baeya
Bouba
Cabeyas, Las
Castillo de Locubin
Castro del Rio
Cavidena
Cayella de la Sierra
Constantina
Córdoba
Feya
Espartina
Estepa
Fregenal de la Sierra
Fuente del Maestro
Fuenteobejuna
Guadalcayar

Map 29 – Vinelands of Spain (continued)

Guarena
Jáen Blanco
Jáen Doradillo
Jáen Tinto
Lapera
Lucena
Manyanilla
Merida
Monterubio de la Serena
Montijo
Negra de Almanralejo
Olivares
Palma del Rio
Pilas
Puente Genil
Rambla, La
Rute
Salvatierra de los Barros
San Lucar la Jayor
Torre del Campo
Torre Donjumano
Torremegiee
Ubreda
Umbrete
Villacarillo
Villafranca de los Barros
Villagonyalo
Villanueva de la Serena
Villaviciosa de Córdoba
Zafra

Tarragona
Aguamurcia
Albinana
Becas
Bisbal del Panadés
Cabrera
Capsanas
Cartuya de Seala Dei
Castel del Romy
Castelvi de la Marca
Clariana
Cornudella
Creiseell
Damos
Falsct
Fontrubi
Gandesa
Garnacha Blanca
Garnacha Tinta
Gratallops
Llacuna, La
Lloa
Masquefa
Moja
Monjos
Monlerio
Montblanch
Montmell
Morera, La
Olesa de Bonesvallo
Pachs del Panadés
Panadés
Picapoll
Pinell de Bray
Pira
Pobleda
Pontons
Porrera

Priarato
Reus
Santas Creus
Secuita, La
Selva, La
Sitges
Suleirats
Tempranillo
Torre Dembarre
Torroja
Valls
Venebell
Vilarrodona
Vilaseca de Salcima
Villellas, La
Villanueve
Vinebre

Toro
Toto
Verualto
Villamayro
Villarino

Trujillo
Alanjo
Albuquerque
Almendralijo
Baños de Montemayor
Barba
Broyas
Cabeyuela del Valle
Canamaro
Cayetana
Cechavin
Cilleres
Fregenal de la Sierre
Fuente del Maestro
Garganta de la Olla
Guarena
Hayos
Hervas
Jarandilla
Merida
Miajaelas
Montanchey
Monterubio de la Serena
Montijo
Negra de Almandralijo
Planta Nova
Robledillo de Gata
Salvatierra de los Barros
Torremegia
Villafranca de los Barros
Villagongyalo
Villanueva de la Serena
Zafra

Valdepeñas
Alagro
Aleayar de San Juan
Argamansilla de Alba
Belmonte (Vinillo
   Belmontino)
Cencibel
Cico Casas
Daniel
La Seca
Manyanares
Membrilla

Salana
Salana de los Barros
Tomelloso
Valladolid
Zaneara

Valencia
Alaro
Alba Filar
Albaide
Alberique
Aleala de Chivert
Aleyar
Alicante
Ana
Ayelo de Malferit
Dalcarics
Barriol
Batista
Benejama
Benicarlo
Benicasim
Beniganim
Benisa
Benisalem
Biar
Bobal
Barriol
Buñol
Camporrables
El Carao
Carlon
Cartuja de Porta Celi
Casinos
Castalla
Caudete de Las Fuentes
Chiva
Collet
Cuarte
Ducnas
Elche
Elda
Felanit
Fontillon
Fuenterrables
Hondon de los Freules
Inea
Jana, La
Jativa
Levante
Lluchmayor
Mahon
Manto Negro
Monovar
Nules
Onteniente
Orihuela de Segura
Orapesa
Paleda de Naves
Pedralba
Peniscala
Pinoso
Planta de Pedralba
Pollens
Ponsal
Puebla, La
Puebla del Due
Requena
Romaña, La
Saqunto

Salinas
Salsodella
San Marcos
Santany
Secobe
Tobarra
Torrente
Traiguera
Turis
Utiel
Valencia
Vendrell
Ventra de Moro
Villa de Aryobispo
Villarreal
Villena
Vino de Quatre

Zaragoza
Aguado
Alfamen
Ayerbe
Baguera
Barbastro
Belmonte de Calatayud
Benabarba
Berlango de Duero
Borja
Calatayud
Carinena
Cinco Villas, Las
Cosuenda
Daroca
Encinacorra
Epila
Fareet
Fuentes del Ebro
Fuentes del Jiloca
Laluney
Loarre
Lumpiaque
Maella
Mallen
Morata del Jalon
Paniya
Paracuellos de Jiloca
Ponyano
Riela
Sarineno
Sastago
Sistante
Tarayona de Aragon
Villa Felipe
Villamayor Moscatel

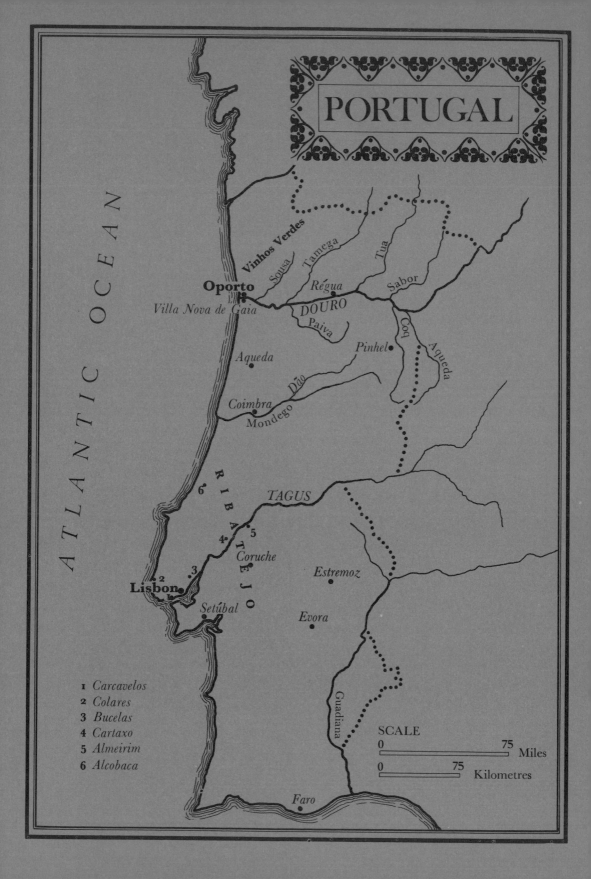

PORTUGAL

ATLANTIC OCEAN

Vinhos Verdes

Oporto

Villa Nova de Gaia

Sousa

Tamega

Régua

Tua

Sabor

DOURO

Paiva

Coq

Aqueda

Pinhel

Aqueda

Coimbra

Dão

Mondego

RIBATEJO

6

TAGUS

5

4

Coruche

3

2

Lisbon

Setúbal

Estremoz

Evora

Guadiana

1 *Carcavelos*
2 *Colares*
3 *Bucelas*
4 *Cartaxo*
5 *Almeirim*
6 *Alcobaca*

SCALE

0 — 75 Miles

0 — 75 Kilometres

Faro

Map 30 – Vinelands of Portugal

Douro River
Bairrada
Malvasia

Lisbon
Barracos
Bucelas
Carcavelos
Cartaxo
Colares
Monsanto, Quinta
Palmela
Periquita
Setubal
Verdelho

Oporto
Alto Douro
Castelo Borges, Quinta
Napoles, Quinta
Quintas, Quinta

Régua
Agua, Quinta
Alempassa, Quinta
Alto, Quinta
Assolveira, Quinta
Aveleira, Quinta
Avidagos, Quinta
Bairro, Quinta
Bandeirinha, Quinta
Barca, Quinta
Barreiro, Quinta
Barroquerio, Quinta
Bateira or Santo Antonio,
  Quinta
Beatas, Quinta
Bela Vista, Quinta
Bertelo, Quinta
Boavista, Quinta
Boavista or Vale do Fojo,
  Quinta
Bom Retiro, Quinta
Bonfim, Quinta
Borralheira, Quinta
Bouca, Quinta
Branca, Quinta
Brolas, Quinta
Cabanas, Quinta
Cabo, Quinta
Cabouco, Quinta

Cachao, Quinta
Campanha, Quinta
Carrascal or Torrinha,
  Quinta
Carvalhal, Quinta
Casa Nova, Quinta
Cascalheira, Quinta
Castelinho, Quinta
Castelo, Quinta
Cedovim, Quinta
Cerca de Santa Cruz
Cerdeirinha, Quinta
Chamind, Quinta
Cidro, Quinta
Cima, Quinta
Colmeal, Quinta
Cordeira, Quinta
Corta, Quinta
Corval, Quinta
Costa da Cima, Quinta
Covelo, Quinta
Currais, Quinta
Devesa or Tanque,
  Quinta
Eiravelha, Quinta
Enxodreiro, Quinta
Espirito Santo da
  Lameira, Quinta
Esteveira, Quinta
Faisca, Quinta
Ferradosa, Quinta
Fojo, Quinta
Fonte do Peso de Cima,
  Quinta
Foz, Quinta
Frada-Gorda, Quinta
Frades, Quinta
Granja, Quinta
Igreja, Quinta
Igreja, Quinta
Junco, Quinta
Lama do Lagur, Quinta
Lamego, Quinta
La Rosa, Quinta
Lobata, Quinta
Lobazim, Quinta
Lodeiro, Quinta
Loureiro, Quinta
Macedos, Quinta
Malvedos, Quinta
Mamalva, Quinta

Massas, Quinta
Mata de Baizo, Quinta
Mata do Porto de Bois,
  Quinta
Milagre, Quinta
Mina, Quinta
Monsul, Quinta
Monte-Bravo, Quinta
Montes, Quinta
Moura, Quinta
Murcas, Quinta
Murcas de Cima, Quinta
Nogueiras, Quinta
Nova do Rio Torto,
  Quinta
Noval, Quinta
Outeiro, Quinta
Paco, Quinta
Paradeita, Quinta
Pedra Caldeira, Quinta
Pedrecouto, Quinta
Penim, Quinta
Pescoca, Quinta
Peso, Quinta
Pilar or Piar, Quinta
Plombcira, Quinta
Pocinho, Quinta
Pocos de Cima, Quinta
Poldras, Quinta
Polidoro, Quinta
Porto de Bois, Quinta
Pousada, Quinta
Raposeira, Quinta
Reduda, Quinta
Região Demarcado do
  Douro
Reguengo, Quinta
Retorta, Quinta
Ribeira, Quinta
Ribeira or São Jeronimo,
  Quinta
Rodo, Quinta
Roeda, Quinta
Romancira, Quinta
Romarigo, Quinta
Romeira, Quinta
Roncao, Quinta
Rorriz, Quinta
Sabordela, Quinta
Sagrado, Quinta
Santa Barbra, Quinta

Santa Barbara, Quinta
Santa Comba, Quinta
Santa Eufemia, Quinta
Santa Julia, Quinta
Santa Maria, Quinta
Santinho, Quinta
Santo Antonio, Quinta
Santo Isidro or Dos
  Pocos, Quinta
São Domingos, Quinta
São Domingos or
  Valdarados, Quinta
São Goncalo, Quinta
São João da Vilarica,
  Quinta
São Luis, Quinta
São Pedro, Quinta
Sarnadelo, Quinta
Seizo, Quinta
Seizo e Martelo, Quinta
Senhora da Ribeira,
  Quinta
Sequeiros, Quinta
Sibio or Jordão, Quinta
Silva, Quinta
Silveira, Quinta
Soalheira, Quinta
Sobradais, Quinta
Tapada, Quinta
Temilobos, Quinta
Tinoco, Quinta
Torrão, Quinta
Toumil, Quinta
Tourais, Quinta
Tranqueira, Quinta
Trevoes, Quinta
Tua, Quinta
Valbom, Quinta
Vale de Figueira, Quinta
Vale de Mendiz, Quinta
Varanda, Quinta
Vargelas, Quinta
Vazes, Quinta
Vedial, Quinta
Ventoseio, Quinta
Vesuvio, Quinta
Viana or Louzada, Quinta
Vila Maior, Quinta
Vilar, Quinta
Vilarinho, Quinta
Zon, Quinta

Map 31 – Switzerland

Aargau Canton
Baden
Bugg
Laufenberg
Lenzburg
Rheinfelden
Schingnach
Villingen
Wettingen

Beine Canton
Biel
Erlach
Iwann

Geneva Canton
Berney
Côte, La
Germang, Cloude

Mandement, Cave du
Montalegré
Tuilière, Vin de la

Neuchâtel Canton
Auvernier
Auvernier, Château d'
Auvenier, Cru d'
Auvenier-Leuns, Cru d'

Beuvais
Bole
Boudry
Cèdres
Champréveyres, Cru de
Chypre, Les
Colombier
Corcelles-Dormondrèche
Cornaux

Map 31 – Switzerland (continued)

Cortaillod
Devins, Domaine des
Cressier
Fressens
Gorgien-chez-le-Bart
Grillette, La
Hauterive
Hôpital de Pourtalès
Landeron, Le
La Ville, Cru de
Marin-Epagier
Peseux
Saint-Aubin
Saint-Blaise
Vaumareus Clos du and,
   Château de
Vigne-du-Diable
Vully
Yverdon

Liechtenstein
Vaduzer

Schaffhausen Canton
Hallauer

St Gallen
Bucherdurger

Thurgau Canton
Karthäuser

Ticino Canton
Castelro
Nostrano
Vallombrosa

Valais Canton
Brule-Fer
Conthey
Dôle de Sion
Fendent de Sion
Glacier
Heidenwein
Hôpital de Sion
Mont, Château de

Mont Fleuri
Montibeux, Clos de
Musettes, Les
Sierre
Sion
Soleil de Sierre
Sonnenhalder
Vispthal

Vaud Canton
Abbayes, Clos des
Aigle
Arbalété, Clos de l'
Berf
Borne, Clos de la
Burignon
Chablais
Chardon d'Argent
Chardonne
Chantelard, Domaine du
Cloître, Clos du
Cully
Curé d'Attalens

Degaley
Gresses
Epinettes, Clos des
Faverger
Grand Brute
Grelotes, Clos des
Hospices Cantonnaux
Johannisberg de Degaley
Lavaux
Magnenaz, Clos de la
Marrens
Martigny
Moines, Clos des
Mont, Château de
Montagny, Schloss
Murailles, Clos des
Perroy, Château de
Philosophe
Renard, Clos du
Rennauds
Rocher, Clos du
Saint-Vincent
Sur-la-Cure

Map 32 – Luxembourg

Grevenmacher
Ahn
Bochsberg
Fels
Gollebour
Ongkaf
Palmberg
Rosenberg
Troerd
Syrberg

Luxembourg City
Bech-Kleinmacher
Foussach
Greiveldange
Herrenberg
Huette
Jongerberg
Kreitzberg
Roelschelt

Rimich
Hopertsbourg
Wellenstein

Stadtbredimus
Dreffert

Wintrange
Felsberg
Letschenberg

Remerschen
Schwebsinger
Hommelsberg

Wormeldange
Ahn
Elderberg
Nussbaum
Palmberg
Keopp

Map 33 – The Danube Valley

Austria
Anniger-Perle
Apetlon
Baden
Bisamberg
Burgenland
Donauland
Durnstdier
Eisenberg
Eppan
Gold
Grinzing
Gumpoldskirchen
Heiligen Stadt
Herrnbaumgarten
Hohenwarther Velliner
Kamptal
Kloch
Klosterneuberg
Krems

Lungenlois
Monchot
Neusiedl, Lake
Nieder-Österreich
Oggau
Poltersdorf
Ratsch
Rohrendorf-St Laurent
Rust
Sievering
Steiermark
Voslau
Wachau

Bulgaria
Bissen
Bulgarische Sonne
Dimiat
Gamza
Iskra

Maritza
Mauraud
Misket Karlova
Pamid
Perla
Plovdiv
Pomori
Sonnenküste
Tamiania
Trakia
Irnovo
Warner

Czechoslovakia
Bzenec
Ruchsel
Hrad
Melnick
Mutonich
Pezenok

Pressburg
Slovakia

Hungary
Adlersberg
Alford
Asztali
Badacsony
Balaton, Lake
Bikaver
Budai Zold
Bergersberg
Csopaki Furimint
Czopak
Debroi Harslevelu
Eger
Egri Kadarka
Ezerjo
Fünfkirchen
Furminti

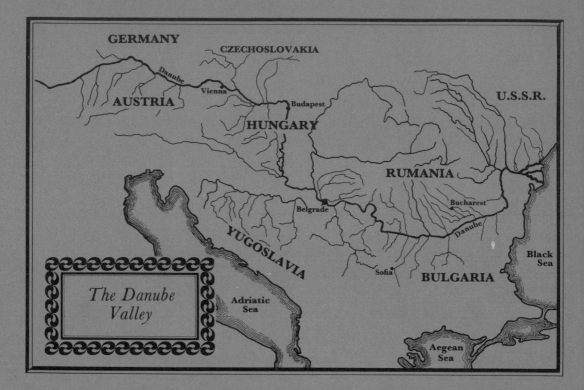

GERMANY
CZECHOSLOVAKIA
Danube
Vienna
AUSTRIA
Budapest
HUNGARY
U.S.S.R.
RUMANIA
Bucharest
Belgrade
YUGOSLAVIA
Danube
Black
Sea
Sofia
BULGARIA
Adriatic
Sea
Aegean
Sea

The Danube Valley

U.
Moldavia
Nikoleyev
Odessa
S.
Rostov
DON
S.
R.
Bessarabia
RUMANIA
Crimea
SEA OF
AZOV
Krasnador
YUGOSLAVIA
CAUCASUS
CASPIAN SEA
BULGARIA
BLACK SEA
GEORGIA
AZERBAIJAN
GREECE
Ankara
TURKEY
Tehran
Cyprus
IRAN
SYRIA
Lebanon
IRAQ
Israel

South Eastern Europe Near & Middle East

Map 33 – The Danube Valley (continued)

Gyöngyös
Juhfarku
Kararka-Silles
Kecskemet
Maslas
Mezesfehrer
Mór
Móri Ezerjo
Muskolaly
Pécs
Samló
Somlói Furmint Samlo
Soproni
Szilvanyi Zold
Szerkszard
Tokaj (Tokay)
Tramini
Villanyi Pecser

Rumania
Bacau
Bazau
Craiova
Cotnari
Creatna
Dealul-Buyor-Prut
Dealul-Mare
Dragasani
Halinga
Husi
Iassy
Lechinte
Minis
Murfatlar
Mustoasa
Nazarcea
Nicoresti

Odobesti
Pietroasa
Recas
Sadova
Sadarcea
Sarica Niculitel
Segarcea
Simburesti
Stefanesti
Sumleul-Silvanier
Tulcea
Tirnave
Valea Calugareasca

Yugoslavia
Biljanski Grici
Bizeljsko
Blatina

Bol
Croatia
Grk
Kosovo
Krajina
Lutomer
Macedonia
Maribor
Ptuj
Prokupac
Ranina Radgona
Ruzica
Slovenia
Serbia
Smederevka
Split
Zilavku
Zupa

Map 34 – South Eastern Europe; Near and Middle East

Cyprus
Agros
Commanderia
Kissamos
Kokkineli
Limassol
Paphos

Greece
Achea
Agios Georgios
Amorgiano
Antika
Archanes
Archova
Arvisio
Athiri
Attica
Boutza
Castel Danielis
Cephalonia
Chalkis
Chevalier
Chios
Como
Corfu
Demestica
Heraklion

Hymettus
Kalavryta
Kea
Kephesia
Kymi
Kytaera
Lemnos
Lesbos
Manteneia
Mavrodaphne
Megaspileon
Merta
Mykonos
Naxos
Nemea
Paros
Patras
Peloponnisos
Peza
Rhodes
Robolo
Ropa
Saint-Elie
Samos
Sitia
Tegea
Thira
Vino Santo

Iran
Khullar

Israel
Adom Atic
Carmel
Rischon-le-Zion
Zikhron

Lebanon
Serzrkaias

Syria
Chalybon

Turkey
Ankara
Beyaz
Boinova
Bursa
Buzbağ
Cubnik
Dikmen
Elazig
Feltu
Hasandede
Kalebag

Narince
Papazkarbib
Perapedra
Sarap
Warmork
Yakut Damilasi

Crimea Peninsula
Aidanil
Aloupka
Ay-Danic
Inkermann
Massandra

Georgia
Goojuani
Mukuzani
Napareuli
Saperavi
Tsinandali

Krasnodor
Abrau-Dursso

Moldavia
Aligote
Feliaska

Map 35 – North and South America

Argentina
Catamarca
Cordoba
Jujuy
Mendoza
Neuguen
Salta

Bolivia
Tarija

Brazil
Minas Gerais
Parana

Santa Catarina

Chile
Aconcagua Valley
Santa Rita
Tocornal
Underragua

Finger Lakes
Candaigua
Hammondspoort
Keuka, Lake
Pennyan

Mexico
Aguacateintes
Baja California
Barras
Chihuahua
Coahuila
Durango
Guanajuato
Jalisco
Michoacan
Saltillo
San Luis Potosi
Santo Thamar
Sonarer Zuesetara

Maryland (Md)
Boordy

New York State
High Tor

Ohio
Sandusky

Peru
Monguegua
Ocucaja
Petivilca

Michigan

New York

Ohio

Pennsylvania

N.J.

Md.

W.Virginia

Virginia

Mexico

PERU

BRAZIL

BOLIVIA

Paraguay

CHILE

Uruguay

ARGENTINA

N. AMERICA

NEW YORK STATE
Finger Lakes 1
Chautauqua L. 2

OHIO
Lake Erie 3

MICHIGAN
Benton Harbour 4

S. AMERICA

ARGENTINA
Buenos Aires 1
Mendoza 2
Neuquén 3
San Juan 4
Tucumán 5

BRAZIL
Alfredo Chaves 1
Rio de Janeiro 2
Rio Grande do Sul 3
São Paulo 4

CHILE
Santiago 1
Talcahuano 2
Valparaiso 3

PERU
Ica 1
Lima 2
Pisco 3

BOLIVIA
La Paz 1

URUGUAY
Montevideo 1

NORTH & SOUTH AMERICA

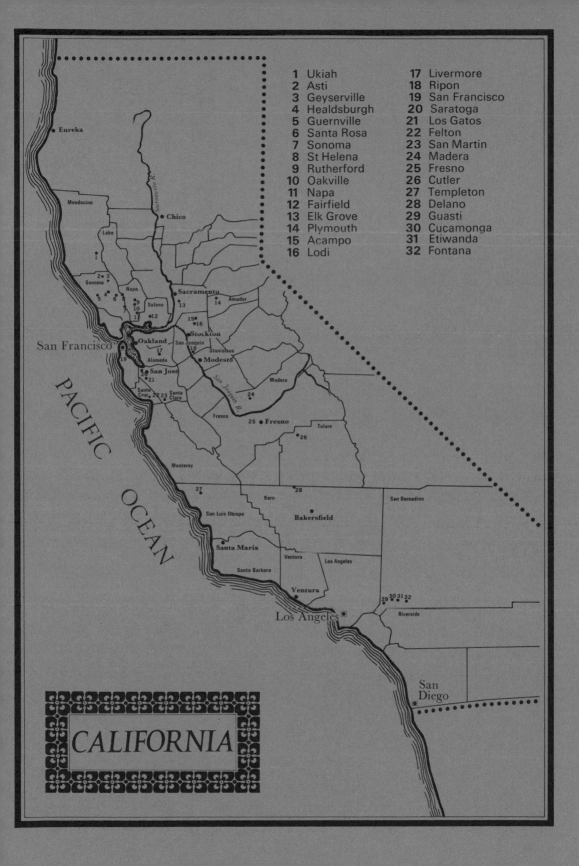

1	Ukiah	17	Livermore
2	Asti	18	Ripon
3	Geyserville	19	San Francisco
4	Healdsburgh	20	Saratoga
5	Guernville	21	Los Gatos
6	Santa Rosa	22	Felton
7	Sonoma	23	San Martin
8	St Helena	24	Madera
9	Rutherford	25	Fresno
10	Oakville	26	Cutler
11	Napa	27	Templeton
12	Fairfield	28	Delano
13	Elk Grove	29	Guasti
14	Plymouth	30	Cucamonga
15	Acampo	31	Etiwanda
16	Lodi	32	Fontana

PACIFIC OCEAN

CALIFORNIA

Map 36 – California

Asti
Italian-Swiss Colony

Elk Grove
Gibson Wine Co.

Fairfield
Cadenasso Winery

Fontana
Fontana Winery Inc.

Geyserville
Nervo Winery
Pedroncelli, John, Winery

Healdsburg
Simi Wineries

Livermore
Wente Bros

Madera
Allied Grape Growers
Ficklin Vineyard

Modesto
Gallo Winery (E. & J.)
Pirrone Wine Cellars

Napa Valley
Christian Brothers
Mayacamas Vineyards
Schramsberg Vineyards

Oakville
Mondari, Robert, Winery

Plymouth
D'Agostini Winery

Rutherford
Beaulieu
Inglenook Vineyards

St Helena
Christian Brothers
Freemarkabbey Winery
Heitz Wine Cellars
Kornell, Hanns,
  Champagne Cellars
Martini, Louis M.
Nichelini Vineyards
Souverain Cellars
Stony Hill Vineyard
Sutter Home Winery

San Francisco
Bargetto's
Contra Costa

San José
Mirassou Vineyards
Wibel Champagne
  Vineyards

Santa Clara
Bargetto's

Santa Rosa
Martini and Prate
  Wines Inc.

Saratoga
Ray, Martin Inc.

Sonoma County
Hanzell Vineyard
Korbel & Brothers Inc.
Sebastiani, Samuel

Templeton
York Winery

Ukiah
Parducci Wine
  Cellars Inc.

Map 37 – Australia

Adelaide
Amery
Angaston
Angle Vale
Angove
Arawatta

Auldana
Barossa Co-Operative
  Winery
Barossa Valley
Bilyara Vineyards
Bleasdale Vineyard

Clare-Watervale
D'Arenberg
Emu Wines
Ewell
Hamilton's Ewell
  Vineyard

Hardy's Tintara Winery
Henschke Winery
Hoffmann's
Kaiser Stuhl
Leonay, Château
Lyndoch

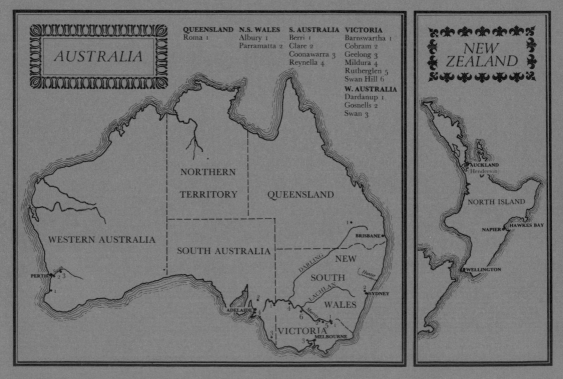

Map 37 – Australia (continued)

McLaren Vale
Magil
Modbury
Morphett Vale
Nuriootpa
Orlando
Pedare
Penfolde
Pewsey Vale
Pirramimma
Reynella
Romalo
Ryecroft Vineyard
Seaview
Seppeltsfield
Springton
Stonyfell
Tanunda
Tatachilla
Tintara
Tollana
T.S.T.
Woodley
Yaldara

Yalunba

Berri
Berri Co-operative
   Winery
Loxton
Renmark
St Agnes

Clare
Quelltaler
Sevenhill Monastery
Stanley Wines

Coonawarra
Keppoch
Redbank
Rouge-Homme
Wynn's Wines

Geelong
Chalambar
Great Western
Moyston

Melbourne
Lilydale
Michelton Vineyard
Tahbilk, Château

Murray, River
All Saints
Angove
Mildura Wines
Rutherglen

Perth
Houghton

Rutherglen
MiaMia
Milawa

Swan Hill
Griffith
Nildottle

Swan River Valley
Caversham

Sandalford
Valencia

Sydney
Ashman's Vineyards
Bellevue Winery
Ben Ean
Dalwood
Drayton's Bellevue
Elliot's Oakvale
Hungerford Hill
   Vineyards
Hunter River Valley
Lake's Folly
Lindeman's Ben Ean
McWilliams Mt Pleasant
   Winery
Minchenburg
Mount Danger
Mount Pleasant
Pokolbin
Tulloch's
Tyrell's
Wybong

Map 38 – New Zealand

Auckland
Luke Lunievich's Golden
   Vineyard
Markovich's
Nola's Dargaville
   Vineyard
Posinkovich's
Radich's
Western Vineyard
Zinkovich's Sunny
   Vineyard

Map 39 – South Africa

Cape Province
Caledon
Ceres
Constantia
Drakenstein
Huguenot
Malmesbury
Montagu
Robertson
Wellington
Worcester
Wynberg

Cape Town
Alphen
Bellingham

Paarl
Nederburg

Stellenbosch
French Hoek

Map 40 – North Africa

Morocco
Berkane

Algeria
Algiers
Haut-Dahara
Medea

Oran
Ain-Temouehent

Mascara
Mostaganem
Tessalah, Monts du
Hemcan, Côtes de

Tunisia
Cap Bon
Grombalia

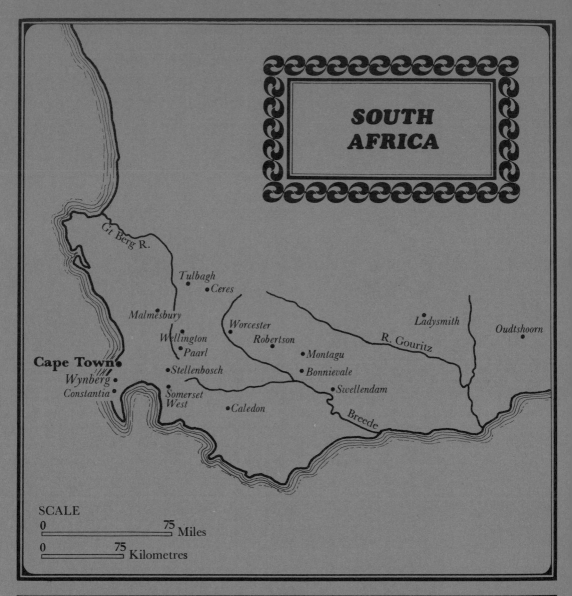

SOUTH AFRICA

Gt Berg R.

Tulbagh
● Ceres

Malmesbury

Worcester
Robertson

Wellington
● Paarl

Cape Town ●
Wynberg ●
Constantia

● Stellenbosch

Somerset
West

● Montagu
● Bonnievale

● Swellendam

Ladysmith

Oudtshoorn

R. Gouritz

● Caledon

Breede

SCALE

0 ————————— 75 Miles

0 ———— 75 Kilometres

NORTH AFRICA

Mediterranean Sea

SCALE

0 ————— 150 Miles

0 ——— 150 Kilometres

● Algiers

Médéa ●

Constantine

● Tunis ●

● Oran

● Mascara

Sousse ●

Sfax ●

● Rabat
● Meknes

Casablanca

MOROCCO

ALGERIA

TUNISIA

● Marrakesh